Rainbow Edition

Reading Mastery V
Presentation Book A

Siegfried Engelmann • Jean Osborn • Steve Osborn • Leslie Zoref

SRA

Macmillan/McGraw–Hill

Columbus, Ohio

SRA Macmillan/McGraw-Hill
250 Old Wilson Bridge Road
Suite 310
Worthington, Ohio 43085
Printed in the United States of America.
ISBN 0-02-686401-0
        5 6 7 8 9 0 UNG 99

Lesson 1

INTRODUCTION

1. You're going to start a new reading program. You'll work in three books—a skillbook, a textbook, and a workbook.
   - *Hold up a skillbook.* Each lesson starts with the words you will read in the skillbook. Later, in the lesson you'll answer questions in your skillbook. You'll write the answers on a piece of lined paper.
   - *Hold up a textbook.* Each day you'll read from your textbook.
   - *Hold up a workbook.* After you finish the questions in the skillbook, you'll answer questions in your workbook.

2. *Pass out the textbooks, workbooks, and skillbooks.* Open your workbook to page 1. *Check.*

3. Touch the row of boxes at the top of the page. *Check.* That is your point chart. You'll use those boxes to keep track of the points that you earn for each lesson.
   - Box **R** is for points you earn by reading a story. If the group reads without making too many mistakes, everybody earns points.
   - Box **IW** is for points you earn by doing the items in the skillbook and workbook. You will do these items independently.
   - Box **B** is a bonus box. If you do some things particularly well, you'll earn bonus points.
   - Box **T** is the total box. You add up all your points for a lesson to get your total. Today you can earn up to 12 points. Now close your workbook.

Lesson 1

PART A   **Word Lists**

1	2	3	4
North Dakota	airport	serve	**Vocabulary words**
Saint Bernard	haircut	preserve	1. game preserve
Kansas	pineapple	cell	2. poacher
Africa	grassland	cellar	3. cellar
flamingo		howl	4. marvelous
marvelous		Kenya	5. plain
inquire		poach	6. prepare
		poacher	7. mile
		howled	8. inquire

WORD PRACTICE AND VOCABULARY

Everybody, find lesson 1, part A in your skillbook. *Wait.*
First you'll read some words. Then you'll read a story. These words will be in the story. After you read all the words, we'll talk about what some of them mean.

To correct word-identification errors (**flamingo,** for example):
a. That word is **flamingo.**
   What word? *Signal.* **Flamingo.**
b. *Return to the first word in the column and present all the words in order.*

EXERCISE 1   Word practice

1. Everybody, touch column 1. *Check.*
   The words in column 1 are hard words that will be in your reading stories.
2. Touch under the first line. *Check.*
   Those words are **North Dakota.**
   What words? *Signal.* **North Dakota.**
3. Next line. *Pause.* Those words are **Saint Bernard.**
   What words? *Signal.* **Saint Bernard.**
4. Next word. *Pause.* That word is **Kansas.**
   What word? *Signal.* **Kansas.**
5. *Repeat step 4 for each remaining word in column 1.*
6. Your turn to read all those words.
   Touch under the first line in column 1. *Pause.*
   What words? *Signal.* **North Dakota.**
7. Next line. *Pause.* What words? *Signal.*
   Saint Bernard.
8. Next word. *Pause.* What word? *Signal.* **Kansas.**
9. *Repeat step 8 for each remaining word in column 1.*
10. *Repeat the words in column 1 until firm.*

EXERCISE 2   Word family

1. Everybody, touch column 2. *Check.*
   All those words are made up of two shorter words. Touch under the first word. *Pause.*
   What word? *Signal.* **Airport.**
2. Next word. *Pause.* What word? *Signal.*
   Haircut.
3. *Repeat step 2 for each remaining word in column 2.*
4. *Repeat the words in column 2 until firm.*

EXERCISE 3   Word practice

1. Everybody, touch under the first word in column 3. *Pause.* What word? *Signal.* **Serve.**
2. Next word. *Pause.* What word? *Signal.* **Preserve.**
3. *Repeat step 2 for each remaining word in column 3.*
4. *Repeat the words in column 3 until firm.*

EXERCISE 4   Vocabulary development

Task A

1. Everybody, touch column 4. *Check.*
   First you're going to read the words in column 4. Then we'll talk about what they mean.
2. Touch under the first line. *Pause.*
   What words? *Signal.* **Game preserve.**
3. Next word. *Pause.* What word? *Signal.*
   Poacher.
4. *Repeat step 3 for each remaining word in column 4.*
5. *Repeat the words in column 4 until firm.*

Task B

1. Now let's talk about what those words mean. The words in line 1 are **game preserve.** A **game preserve** is a large park where animals run wild. *Call on individual students.*
   Name some animals that you might see at a game preserve. *Responses:* Zebras, tigers, elephants, lions.
2. Everybody, what do we call a large park where animals run wild? *Signal.* **A game preserve.**

Task C

1. Word 2 is **poacher.** A **poacher** is a person who hunts on a game preserve. It is against the law to hunt on game preserves.
2. Everybody, what do we call a person who hunts on a game preserve? *Signal.* **A poacher.**

Task D

Word 3 is **cellar.** Another word for **basement** is **cellar.** Everybody, what's another word for **basement?** *Signal.* **Cellar.**

Task E

1. Word 4 is **marvelous.** Another word for **wonderful** is **marvelous.** Everybody, what's another word for **wonderful?** *Signal.*
   Marvelous.
2. Everybody, what's another way of saying **She had a wonderful time?** *Signal.*
   She had a marvelous time.
3. Everybody, what's another way of saying **The party was wonderful?** *Signal.*
   The party was marvelous.

Task F

Word 5 is **plain.** A **plain** is a flat place with few trees. Everybody, what's another word for a flat place with few trees? *Signal.* **A plain.**

Task G

1. Word 6 is **prepare.** When you **prepare** for something, you get ready for that thing. Everybody, what do you do when you get ready for something? *Signal.*
Prepare for that thing.
2. *Call on a student.* How would you prepare for a trip? *Accept reasonable response.*

Task H

Word 7 is **mile.** A **mile** is a distance that is 5,280 feet long. Everybody, what do we call a distance that is 5,280 feet? *Signal.* **A mile.**

Task I

1. Word 8 is **inquire.** When you ask about something you **inquire** about that thing. Everybody, what's another way of saying **She asked about the bus?** *Signal.*
She inquired about the bus.
2. Everybody, what's another way of saying **Will you ask about the time?** *Signal.*
Will you inquire about the time?

Lesson 1

Introduction to
The Secret Cave

1. Jill   Tom   Roger Saint Bernard   Mr. Williams Ranger

2. elephant   zebra   flamingo

3. Kansas   ATLANTIC OCEAN   AFRICA   Kenya

Lesson 1   Textbook   **1**

STORY READING

Note

1. *Unless otherwise directed, call on individual students to answer each question.*
2. *Questions that have only one correct answer are followed by the student's response. For example:* "What's the title of this story?"
The Secret Cave.
3. *Questions that have more than one correct answer are followed by Idea(s). For example:* "What do rangers do?" *Ideas:* Protect the forests, watch for forest fires, guard animals.

EXERCISE 5   Comprehension passage

1. Everybody, turn to lesson 1 in your textbook. *Check.*
I'll read the title, "Introduction to the Secret Cave." Look at item 1. *Check.*
   * Here are the characters that you're going to read about in the story that starts today.
   * What's the name of the first character? **Jill.**
   * What's the name of the second character? **Tom.**
   * The name of the next character is Roger. Roger is a Saint Bernard dog. What kind of dog is Roger? **A Saint Bernard.**
   * The last character is Mr. Williams. What kind of job does Mr. Williams have? **A ranger.**
   * What do rangers do?
   Ideas: Protect the forests; watch for forest fires; guard animals.
2. Everybody, look at item 2. *Check.*
Those pictures show some of the animals that you'll read about.
   * What's the first animal? **An elephant.**
   * What's the next animal? **A zebra.**
   * What's the last animal? **A flamingo.**
3. Everybody, look at item 3. *Check.*
   * That map shows where Jill and the others will go in this story.
   * Touch the place their trip starts. *Check.*
   * Their trip starts in the United States. Name the state it starts in. **Kansas.**
   * Then they go across the ocean to a large continent. What's the name of that continent? **Africa.**
   * What's the name of the country they go to? **Kenya.**

The Secret Cave
by Joyce Mann Ⓐ

PART 1

"Oh, no," Jill said to herself when her father began to talk about moving to a new place. Over the past five years, she had lived in five different places—Canada, Texas, Colorado, North Dakota, and Kansas. Every time it was the same. Just about the time Jill made friends and began to like the new place, her father would announce that he had a new job in another place. Then Jill and her brother would pack up and wave goodbye to their friends.Ⓑ

Jill looked at her father. He was smiling. "You'll love this new place," he said. ★2 ERRORS★

Jill's brother, Tom, said "I don't want to go, and I don't care where it is."

"Now, now, don't say that," her father said. "I know it's hard to leave, but this time prepare yourself for a real adventure."Ⓒ

Jill had lived through enough adventures to last her the rest of her life. She was unhappy. Why did her father have to be a ranger? Why did her father have to work as a troubleshooter for game preserves? Everybody who knew him said how smart he was, but why couldn't he just have one of those ordinary jobs and stay in one place?Ⓓ

Jill's father continued, "This time we're going nearly halfway around the world. We're going to Kenya, which is a country in Africa."Ⓔ

"Kenya?" Tom said, making a sour face. "Why would we want to go to Kenya?"

Jill's father looked very surprised. He said slowly, "I would think that you would be happy to go there."

Jill replied, "I'd rather stay here in Kansas."

"Me too," Tom said, "And so would Roger." Roger was their Saint Bernard dog.Ⓕ

"Yes," Jill said. "Can you picture poor Roger in Kenya? He almost died from the heat in Texas, with his long hair. What's he going to do in Kenya?"Ⓖ

Jill's father said, "Roger will be all right. And there is something you may like about Kenya."

"What's that?" Jill asked.

"Kenya has many wonderful animals that still live in the wild. You can see lions and zebras and even flamingos."

"Really?" Jill said. For a moment, Kenya didn't seem to be all that bad. But then Jill remembered something.

EXERCISE 6 Decoding

1. **Everybody, turn to page 2 in your textbook.** *Check.*
   - **You're going to read part of this story out loud. I'll call on different students to read. When you are not reading, you must follow along. When I call on you, have your place or you lose your turn to read.**

2. **There is a sign that says 2 errors on page 2 of the story. Touch that sign.** *Check.*
   - **If the group makes no more than 2 errors by the time we get to that sign, I'll read the first part of the story and ask questions.**
   - **If the group makes more than 2 errors, you'll have to read that part of the story again, until you read it with no more than 2 errors.**

3. *Call on individual students to read three to five sentences, starting with the title.*
   - *If the group makes no more than 2 errors before reaching the 2-error sign, say:*
     Good, now I'll read the first part of the story and ask questions. *Read the first part of the story aloud. Stop at each circled letter and present the task specified for that letter.*
   - *If the group makes more than two errors before reaching the 2-error sign, say:*
     a. **You made more than two errors on the first part of the story, so you'll have to read that part again. This time, be very careful when you read.**

   b. *When the group reads to the 2-error sign, with no more than 2 errors, say:*
      Good, now I'll read the first part of the story and ask questions. *Start with the title.*

4. *After you have read aloud to the 2-error sign, say:*
   Now, you'll read some more of the story. Everybody, touch the error sign after letter H. *Check. Call on a student.*
   What does the error sign say? 6 errors.
   You will earn 4 points for reading if you stay within that error limit. When you read, remember to stop when you get to a circled letter. I'll ask a question about what you just read.

5. *Call on individual students to read.*
   - *Present the tasks specified for each circled letter.*

---

*To correct word-identification errors (**troubleshooter**, for example):*
   a. **That word is troubleshooter.**
      What word? Troubleshooter.
   b. **Go back to the beginning of the sentence and read the whole sentence.**

EXERCISE 7 Comprehension tasks

Note: Unless otherwise directed, call on individual students to answer each question.

- **This story is divided into five parts. Today, we'll read Part One.**
- Ⓐ **What's the title of this story? The Secret Cave.**
- **Who is the author of this story? Joyce Mann.**
- Ⓑ **What does that mean: They would wave goodbye to their friends?** *Idea:* They'd have to leave their friends.
- **How did Jill feel about moving to new places?** *Idea:* She didn't like it.
- Ⓒ **What does her father think Jill should prepare herself for?** *Idea:* An adventure.
- Ⓓ **Listen to that part again. It tells a lot of information about Jill's father.**
- *Read from Ⓒ to Ⓓ.*
- **What job does Jill's father have?** *Ideas:* A ranger; a troubleshooter.
- **What do rangers do?** *Ideas:* Protect the forests; watch for forest fires; guard animals.
- **In what kind of place does Jill's father work?** *Idea:* A game preserve.
- **The story says that he is a troubleshooter. What's a troubleshooter?** *Idea:* Someone who solves hard problems.
- Ⓔ **Which country are they going to? Kenya.**
- **Which continent is Kenya in? Africa.**
- Ⓕ **What kind of dog is Roger? A St. Bernard.**
- Ⓖ **What gave Roger trouble in Texas?** *Idea:* The hot weather.
- **Why would he have trouble in Kenya?** *Idea:* Because it's hot there too.

"Wait a minute," she said. "Whenever you go to a new place there is some trouble. There must be trouble at this place."

"Well, not any serious trouble, just . . ." (H) ★6 ERRORS★

Tom said, "We've heard that before too. Remember when you said there wasn't any serious trouble in Texas? But when we got down there, there was a terrible problem with poachers. And when we went to North Dakota, you said there wasn't much trouble there, but there was trouble with . . ."

"All right," their father said. "There is some trouble. Poachers are hunting in the area. They are capturing flamingos, zebras, and elephants. If the poachers aren't stopped very soon, some of those animals will be completely wiped out—especially the flamingos."

"You mean, you're going to try to stop poachers again? That sounds like it could be very dangerous."

Jill's father put his arms around Jill and Tom. Softly he said, "Come on, everything's going to be all right. I'm sure of that and I really want to take this job. So, please come with me."

Jill no longer felt unhappy. She put her arms around her father's strong neck. "All right," she said as if she was still unhappy.

"All right," Tom said. Jill could tell that he wasn't unhappy either.

• • •

"Jill, wake up and look." Jill recognized her brother's voice, but for a moment, she didn't know where she was. Then she realized that she was on a plane, and that she had been on that plane for a long time. The trip from Kansas to Kenya took sixteen hours. Jill had stayed awake for a few hours, but then she had fallen asleep.

"Look," Tom was saying to her. "Jill, look out the window! We're over Kenya."

Jill sat up, stretched, rubbed her eyes, and looked out of the window. The land looked flat and green, with a few lakes and groves of trees. Jill's father, who was sitting next to her, explained, "The plain we're over is one of the most marvelous stretches of grassland in the world. And that's where we're going." Jill blinked and tried to act interested, but the plain didn't look very marvelous to her—just very green and very large. She said, "It was a lot like this in Kansas."

An hour later, they were on the ground. It felt very strange to walk, after sitting all that time. The air was hot and the land was flat. The sun was so bright that it hurt Jill's eyes. Roger had been locked up inside the plane during the trip and now he was very excited. He was panting, wagging his tail, sniffing everything, and barking.

Three tall people met Jill's family at the airport. The tallest man said, "We welcome the Williams family." These people worked at the game preserve. The people smiled and talked, as Jill stood there and felt as if the sun was melting her.

At last, the talking was over. Jill's family got into a jeep. Roger climbed into the back of the jeep. He howled and panted as the driver followed another jeep down a dusty road.

By the late afternoon, the Williams family was in their new house. It was a small, wooden building with three grass houses close by. The wooden house had a cellar, and Roger found that cellar very quickly, because it was cooler than the upstairs of the house.

After everybody unpacked, Jill's father prepared a dinner of meat, rice, and pineapple slices.

After dinner, Jill and Tom gave poor old Roger a haircut. Jill wasn't sure whether Roger was in worse shape before the haircut or afterwards. Before the haircut, he drooled and panted. After the haircut, he looked as if he had gone through a paper cutter. In places, he had patches of very short hair and in other places, he had no hair. It was the worst haircut that any dog ever had.

Jill couldn't help but laugh every time she looked at Roger, but the dog seemed a lot happier with short hair.

(H) I wonder what that trouble will be.
● Read the rest of the lesson to yourselves.
● Find out what the trouble is in the place they are going to. Find out how they get to Kenya. Find out who met them at the airport, and what happened to Roger at the end of this part. I'll ask questions about what you have read.
● You'll get to a line that has three dots. Those dots show that part of the story is missing.

After all students have finished reading:
● What was the trouble in Kenya? *Idea:* Poachers hunting in the area.
● What were the poachers doing? *Idea:* Capturing animals.
● Which animals were especially in danger of being wiped out if poachers continued to capture them? **Flamingos.**
● Were these poachers killing the animals or capturing them? **Capturing them.**
● What do you think they did with the animals that they captured? *Idea:* Sold them.
● How did Jill's family get to Kenya? *Idea:* They flew in an airplane.
● How long did the trip take? **16 hours.**
● Who met the Williams family at the airport? *Idea:* Some people.
● How did they get from the airport to their new house? *Idea:* In a jeep.
● What did Jill and Tom do with Roger after dinner? *Idea:* Gave him a haircut.
● Was it a good haircut? **No.**
● Why wasn't it a good haircut? *Idea:* Because after they were done, his hair was very short in places and there were bald spots.
● How did Roger feel about his haircut? *Idea:* He loved it.
● Why? *Idea:* Because it made him feel a lot cooler.

Story Items

1. Below is a list of events that happened in Part 1.
   - Write **beginning** if the event happened near the beginning.
   - Write **middle** if the event happened near the middle.
   - Write **end** if the event happened at the end.

   a. Tom woke Jill up to tell her something. *middle*

   b. Jill was unhappy because of the announcement her father made. *beginning*

   c. Jill had to laugh at Roger every time she looked at him. *end*

   d. Jill and Tom gave Roger a haircut. *end*

   e. Jill was in Kansas. *beginning*

   f. Jill was flying over Kenya. *middle*

Map Skills

2. Map 1 shows the four directions on all maps.
   North is always on the top of a map.
   South is always on the bottom of a map.
   East is on this side of a map: ⟶
   West is on this side of a map: ⟵
   - Fill in the boxes around map 1.

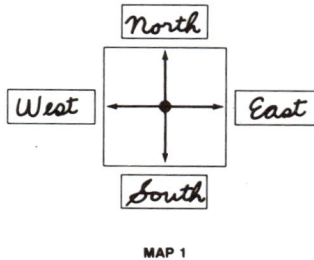

North *West* *East* *South*

MAP 1

3. Map 2 shows Jill and Tom's trip to Kenya.

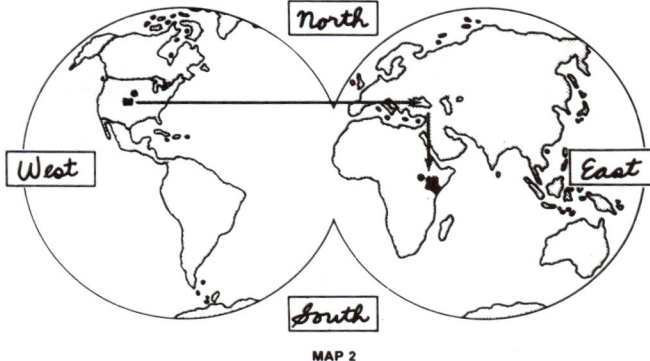

North *West* *East* *South*

MAP 2

   a. The arrows show the directions they went. In which direction did they go first? *east*

   b. In which direction did they go next? *South*

   c. Write the name of the place shown by each dot. *Kansas* *Kenya*

   d. Fill in the boxes around map 2.

EXERCISE 8   Awarding points

1. Now I will give you points for your reading. Everybody, take out your workbook.
2. Look at box **R** on page 1.
   - *If the group stayed within the error limit, have each student write 4 in box **R**.*
   - *If the group went over the error limit, direct the group to reread the lesson. Do not present the comprehension tasks again. If the group stays within the error limit on the second reading, give each student **one** point in box **R**.*

INDEPENDENT WORK

1. Now you're going to do your independent work in the skillbook and the workbook. I can't help you with this work, because your work shows me how much you are learning.
2. First you do all the items for lesson 1 in your skillbook. Then you do all the items for lesson 1 in your workbook.
3. Open your skillbook to lesson 1, part B. *Check.* Here are the rules:
   - Do not write in the book.
   - Write your answers on a piece of lined paper.
   - For each item write the number. If the item also has letters, write those letters.
4. Start now. When you're done with the skillbook, do the workbook items for lesson 1.

WORKCHECK

1. *After students finish their independent work, say:*
   - I'll read each item and give the correct answer. Mark the item with a **C** if it is correct and mark the item with an **X** if it is wrong.
   - Raise your hand if you have any questions about any item.
2. *Read the questions and answers for the skillbook and workbook.*
   - *Note: The answers preceded by the word Idea(s) indicate the general idea(s) that are to be conveyed by the student response. A good procedure for handling these items is to ask different students to read their answers. Indicate to the group whether each answer is correct.*

1. Look at the boxes at the top of page 1 in your workbook. *Check*.
2. You're going to write your points in the box that has **IW** above it.
   - If you made no errors on your independent work, give yourself 6 points.
   - If you made 1 or 2 errors, give yourself 4 points.
   - If you made 3, 4, or 5 errors, give yourself 2 points.
   - If you made more than 5 errors, you get no points.
3. If you made errors, fix the items you got wrong so that they are correct. Remember to fix your skillbook and workbook answers.
   - If you fix every item that you got wrong, I'll give you 2 bonus points. I'll also give 2 bonus points to students who didn't get any items wrong.
4. When you have corrected the items, hand in your work for lesson 1. I'll total your points.

ANSWER KEY FOR SKILLBOOK

PART B

1. **a.** A Saint Bernard
   b. 3
   c. *Ideas:* Troubleshooter for game preserves; ranger
2. **a.** Kansas
   b. Kenya
   c. Sixteen hours
3. **a.** No
   b. Yes
   c. *Ideas:* She didn't like it; unhappy
4. Poachers were capturing animals
5. **a.** *Any two:* Flamingos; elephants; zebras
   b. Capturing them
6. **a.** 3
   b. A jeep
7. **a.** *Idea:* Because of the heat
   b. Gave him a haircut
   c. Yes
   d. *Ideas:* His hair was short; he looked funny

Lesson 2

WORD PRACTICE AND VOCABULARY

To correct word-identification errors (*emeralds,* for example):
  a. That word is **emeralds.**
     What word? *Signal.* Emeralds.
  b. *Return to the first word in the column and present all the words in order.*

Lesson 2

PART A   Word Lists

1	2	3	4	5
glisten	incredible	Saint Bernard	**Vocabulary words**	**Vocabulary words**
evil	tunnel	flamingo	1. glisten	1. game preserve
emeralds	candle	cackle	2. brook	2. plain
diamonds	sparkle	herd	3. eager	3. prepare
	cackle	cackling	4. hideout	4. poacher
			5. diamonds	5. marvelous
			6. emeralds	6. inquire
				7. mile

EXERCISE 1   Word practice

1. Everybody, find lesson 2, part A in your skillbook. *Wait.* Touch column 1. *Check.* The words in column 1 are hard words that will be in your reading stories.
2. Touch under the first word. *Check.* The first word is **glisten.** What word? *Signal.* **Glisten.**
3. Next word. *Pause.* That word is **evil.** What word? *Signal.* **Evil.**
4. *Repeat step 3 for each remaining word in column 1.*
5. Your turn to read all those words. Touch under the first word in column 1. *Pause.* What word? *Signal.* **Glisten.**
6. Next word. *Pause.* What word? *Signal.* **Evil.**
7. *Repeat step 6 for each remaining word in column 1.*
8. *Repeat the words in column 1 until firm.*

EXERCISE 2   Word family

1. Everybody, touch column 2. *Check.* All those words end with the sound **lll.** Touch under the first word. *Pause.* What word? *Signal.* **Incredible.**
2. Next word. *Pause.* What word? *Signal.* **Tunnel.**
3. *Repeat step 2 for each remaining word in column 2.*
4. *Repeat the words in column 2 until firm.*

EXERCISE 3   Word practice

1. Everybody, touch under the first line in column 3. *Pause.* What words? *Signal.* **Saint Bernard.**
2. Next word. *Pause.* What word? *Signal.* **Flamingo.**
3. *Repeat step 2 for each remaining word in column 3.*
4. *Repeat the words in column 3 until firm.*

EXERCISE 4   Vocabulary development

Task A
1. Everybody, touch column 4. *Check.* First you're going to read the words in column 4. Then we'll talk about what they mean.
2. Touch under the first word. *Pause.* What word? *Signal.* **Glisten.**
3. Next word. *Pause.* What word? *Signal.* **Brook.**
4. *Repeat step 3 for each remaining word in column 4.*
5. *Repeat the words in column 4 until firm.*

Task B

1. Now let's talk about what those words mean. Word 1 is **glisten.** When something shines or sparkles it **glistens.** Everybody, what is something doing when it shines or sparkles? *Signal.* **Glistening.**
2. Everybody, what's another way of saying **The water sparkled?** *Signal.* **The water glistened.**

Task C

1. Word 2 is **brook.** Another word for a **little stream** is a **brook.**
2. Everybody, what's another word for a **little stream?** *Signal.* **A brook.**

Task D

1. Word 3 is **eager.** When you are **eager** for something to happen, you are really looking forward to that thing.
2. Everybody, how do you feel when you are really looking forward to something? *Signal.* **Eager.**

Task E

Word 4 is **hideout.** A **hideout** is a secret place that is hard to find. Crooks have **hideouts** so that police can't find them.

Task F

1. The last two words in this column are names for expensive jewels.
   Diamonds are clear. They look like glass, but they are very hard.
   Emeralds are green.
2. Everybody, tell me the name of the jewels that are clear. *Signal.* **Diamonds.**
   Everybody, tell me the name of the jewels that are green. *Signal.* **Emeralds.**
3. *Repeat step 2 until firm.*

EXERCISE 5   Vocabulary review

Task A

1. Everybody, touch column 5. *Check.*
   First you're going to read the words in column 5. Then we'll talk about what they mean.
2. Touch under the first line. *Pause.*
   What words? *Signal.* **Game preserve.**
3. Next word. *Pause.* What word? *Signal.* **Plain.**
4. *Repeat step 3 for each remaining word in column 5.*
5. *Repeat the words in column 5 until firm.*

Task B

1. You've learned the meaning for all these words. The words in line 1 are **game preserve.** *Call on a student.* What is a **game preserve?** *Idea:* A large park where animals run wild.
2. *Call on individual students.* Name some animals that you might see at a **game preserve.** *Responses:* Zebras, lions, elephants, tigers.

Task C

Word 2 is **plain.** *Call on a student.* What is a **plain?** *Idea:* A flat place with few trees.

Task D

1. Word 3 is **prepare.** *Call on a student.* What do you do when you **prepare** for something? *Idea:* Get ready for that thing.
2. *Call on a student.* How would you prepare for a trip? *Accept reasonable response.*

Task E

Word 4 is **poacher.** *Call on a student.* What is a **poacher?** *Idea:* A person who hunts on a game preserve.

Task F

1. Word 5 is **marvelous.** *Call on a student.* What does **marvelous** mean? *Idea:* Wonderful.
2. Everybody, what's another way of saying **The ride in the country was wonderful?** *Signal.* **The ride in the country was marvelous.**

Task G

1. Word 6 is **inquire.** *Call on a student.* What does **inquire** mean? *Idea:* Ask.
2. Everybody, what's another way of saying **She asked about the bus?** *Signal.* **She inquired about the bus.**

Task H

1. Word 7 is **mile.** Everybody, how long is a **mile?** *Signal.* **5,280 feet.**
2. Everybody, what do we call a distance that is 5,280 feet? *Signal.* **A mile.**

Lesson 2

The Secret Cave
PART 2 Ⓐ

The next morning was beautiful. There was no wind, and the grass glistened with silver drops of dew. Low clouds hid the tops of the faraway hills, and birds flew everywhere. The air was thick with their chirping and peeping and cackling. Ⓑ

Mr. Williams told Jill and Tom, "I'm going to a village that is about fifty miles from here. Maybe I can find out something about the poachers. I want both of you to stay close to the house. I'll be home by late afternoon." Ⓒ

"Okay," they said. "We'll stay close to the house." ★2 ERRORS★

But before noon, Jill, Tom, and Roger were over two miles from the house, walking next to a bubbling brook. They approached a strange grove of trees next to a great hill. Inside the grove was a marvelous tree. Its trunk seemed to be made up of many small trunks, all joined together. Tom said, "This tree is as thick as ten trees."

As Jill started to walk around the tree, she noticed that Roger had found a hole in the trunk. He walked right through the hole and into the tree. "Roger, get out of there," Jill called, but Roger remained inside the tree.

After calling several more times, Jill crawled through the hole. She was amazed to discover that the inside of the tree was hollow. There was a small room in the middle of the tree. Light came into this room through small holes in the tree trunk. Jill looked through one of these holes and saw Tom.

"Come inside," Jill called. "There's a little secret room inside the tree." Ⓓ

When Tom crawled into the tree and stood up, things were very crowded. Roger was panting and moving around. He bumped into Jill or Tom every time he moved.

As Jill turned around to examine the room, her gaze fell on a trapdoor in the middle of the floor. The door had a large metal handle. She hesitated a moment, then bent over and grabbed the handle. She tugged on the handle, and with a loud creak, the trapdoor opened. Jill felt her heart stop for a second. Below her were steps that led into a dark tunnel. Ⓔ
★6 ERRORS★

"What's that?" Tom said.

Before Jill could answer, Roger bounded over to Jill, licked her face twice, sniffed the air, and suddenly ran down the stairs.

"Come back, Roger," Jill called. But Roger was gone.

"What are we going to do now?" Tom asked.

Jill called Roger again and again, but Roger did not respond. Finally, she stopped and said, "We have to go after him."

Tom bent over next to Jill and stared down the dark stairway. After a moment he said, "Jill, there's a shelf down there with candles on it. I think there are matches there too. We could light the candles and take them with us and follow Roger."

Jill thought for a moment. Her heart was pounding wildly. "Okay," she said. She slowly walked down the stairs, running her hand along the smooth rocks that lined the tunnel. It was quite dark at the bottom of the stairs.

Tom lit two candles. He took one and handed the other to Jill. Slowly, Jill led the way down the tunnel. Tom walked behind her. Jill's eyes tried to look at everything at the same time.

The rocks that formed the walls of the tunnel made strange shadows that looked like evil faces. The candlelight seemed to dance with the faces. "Roger, where are you?" Jill called.

Now the tunnel got so small and low that Jill and Tom had to crawl. In some places, the walls of the tunnel glistened with tiny stones that looked like diamonds. These stones sparkled in the light of the candles. Jill could hear the distant sound of water dripping.

Jill and Tom went down the tunnel for what seemed like a long time. Suddenly, the tunnel widened and they entered a huge room with a high ceiling. "Wow," Jill said, holding her candle high. "We must be under the hill now."

"Yeah," Tom replied. "This room is huge."

They stood there silently, looking and listening. Suddenly, Jill was aware of a sound—it wasn't the sound of breathing and it wasn't the sound of dripping water. It was another sound, a strange, grinding sound.

"Roger, is that you? Come here . . . Come here." A moment later, a form appeared at the far side of the room. Jill jumped. Tom jumped. Then they both

---

EXERCISE 6 Decoding

1. Everybody, turn to page 5 in your textbook. *Wait. Call on a student.* What's the error limit for this lesson? **6 errors.**
You will earn 4 points if you stay within the error limit.

2. *Call on individual students to read three to five sentences, starting with the title.*
   - *When the group reads to the 2-error sign, making no more than 2 errors, you read the first part aloud, starting with the title. Present the specified comprehension tasks as you read.*
   - *If the group makes more than 2 errors:*
     a. *Direct the group to reread the first part until they can read it with no more than 2 errors.*
     b. *Then read the first part aloud and present the comprehension tasks.*

3. *After you have read the first part aloud, call on individual students to read. Present the comprehension tasks specified for each circled letter.*

---

*To correct word-identification errors (***poachers,*** for example):*
   a. That word is **poachers.** What word? **Poachers.**
   b. Go back to the beginning of the sentence and read the whole sentence.

EXERCISE 7 Comprehension tasks

Ⓐ Which African country are Jill and her family in? **Kenya.**
   - What job does Jill's father have? *Idea:* A ranger; a troubleshooter.
   - He came to Kenya because there was a problem. What problem was that? *Idea:* Poachers were hunting in the area.

Ⓑ Listen to that part again and get a picture of that early morning in Kenya.
   - *Read from* Ⓐ *to* Ⓑ.
   - What made the grass silver? *Idea:* The morning dew.
   - What color did the dew drops make the grass? *Idea:* Silver.
   - What was unusual about the hills? *Idea:* Clouds covered the tops of the hills.

Ⓒ Where is Mr. Williams going? **To a village.**
   - How far away is the village? **About fifty miles.**
   - When is he supposed to be back? **By late afternoon.**

laughed as they realized that it was Roger, carrying a large bone in his mouth.

"Where did you get that?" Jill inquired. Roger responded by wagging his tail and lying down in the middle of the large room. He began to chew on the bone.

"Now where did he get that bone?" Jill asked as she began to walk across the room.

Tom followed Jill as Roger continued to chew on the bone. When Jill approached the far side of the room, she stopped. There were other tunnels on this side of the room. "This is crazy," Jill said. "There are tunnels all over this cave."

"Yes," Tom said. "And Roger came out of one of them. And he got a bone somewhere in this cave." Tom bent down and peeked inside one tunnel and then another.

Jill said, "I'll bet I know what's going on here."

"What?" Tom asked.

"Poachers," Jill said. "The poachers use this cave. They must keep animals somewhere in this cave. They probably have hundreds of animals. Roger must have found some of the food they feed the animals."

Tom said, "Jill, stop making up stories. I'm scared already. You don't have to make things worse. We haven't seen any signs of poachers in this cave."

Jill asked, "Oh yeah? Where did the bone come from? And who made that secret room inside the tree trunk?"

Tom said, "How could the poachers take large animals through that tree? There is no way that the poachers could use that tree."

Jill smiled and replied, "Maybe there's another entrance. I don't know, but I'm telling Dad about this place because I think the poachers are somewhere right inside this cave."

"Well, you can tell him if you want, but I'm getting out of here right now," Tom said.

Tom walked back across the large room so fast that his candle went out. "Come on, Roger," Jill called. "Let's go."

Roger picked up his bone and followed Jill and Tom across the large room and back into the tunnel. Then all three of them followed the tunnel back to the tree.

The plain was very bright outside and the grass was very green—the color of emeralds.

Jill said, "I can't wait to tell Dad about this place."

(D) Everybody, look at the picture. *Check.*

- What's just behind the huge tree? *Idea:* A hill.
- Who is crawling through the hole in the tree? **Tom.**
- Who is peeping out of a small hole in the tree? **Jill.**

(E) What was the trapdoor hiding? *Ideas:* A tunnel; a cave; steps.
I wonder what they'll find.

- Read the rest of the lesson to yourselves. Find out what the cave looked like inside and what they found after they followed the tunnel.

After all students have finished reading:

- What did Jill and Tom use to give them light inside the cave? **Candles.**
- How many candles did each person have? **One.**
- After they followed the tunnel for a long time, what did they enter? *Idea:* A great big room.
- The story said that in parts of the tunnel there were small stones that glistened like diamonds. What color are diamonds? *Idea:* Clear.
- What sound did Jill hear as she stood inside the large room? *Idea:* A grinding sound.
- Who was making the sound? **Roger.**
- What was Roger chewing on? **A bone.**
- What did Jill find on the other side of the large room? *Idea:* Openings to other tunnels.
- Jill had an explanation for the bone that Roger had. What was Jill's explanation? *Idea:* It was part of the food the poachers fed the captured animals.
- Did Tom agree that poachers used the cave? **No.**
- Tom pointed out a problem that poachers would have if they tried to move large animals into the cave. What problem was that? *Idea:* Large animals could not fit through the tree.
- Who does Jill want to tell about the cave? *Ideas:* Mr. Williams; her father.

ANSWER KEY FOR WORKBOOK

Story Items

1. Below is a list of events that happened in Part 2.
   - Write **beginning** if the event happened near the beginning.
   - Write **middle** if the event happened near the middle.
   - Write **end** if the event happened at the end.

   a. Tom said, "I'm getting out of here right now." ___*end*___

   b. Roger, Jill, and Tom walked over two miles. ___*beginning*___

   c. Mr. Williams went to a village about 50 miles away. ___*beginning*___

   d. Tom lit two candles. ___*middle*___

   e. Tom and Jill left the tree to go home. ___*end*___

   f. Tom and Jill entered a huge room. ___*middle*___

Map Skills

2. The map below shows Jill and Tom's trip to Kenya.

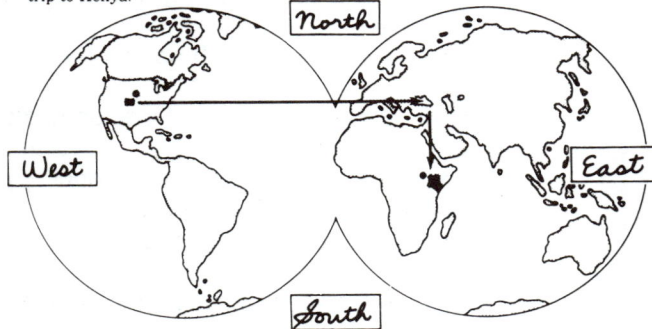

   a. The arrows show the directions they went. In which direction did they go first? ___*east*___

   b. In which direction did they go next? ___*south*___

   c. Write the name of the place shown by each dot. ___*Kansas*___ ___*Kenya*___

   d. Fill in the boxes around the map.

12   Lesson 2

EXERCISE 8   Awarding points

1. Now I will give you points for your reading. Everybody, take out your workbook.
2. Look at box **R** on page 2.
   - *If the group stayed within the error limit, have each student write 4 in box **R**.*
   - *If the group went over the error limit, direct the group to reread the lesson. Do not present the comprehension tasks again. If the group stays within the error limit on the second reading, give each student **one** point in box **R**.*

INDEPENDENT WORK

1. Now you're going to do your independent work in the skillbook and the workbook. I can't help you with this work, because your work shows me how much you are learning.
2. First you do all the items for lesson 2 in your skillbook. Then you do all the items for lesson 2 in your workbook.
3. Open your skillbook to lesson 2, part B. *Check.* Here are the rules:
   - Do not write in the book.
   - Write your answers on a piece of lined paper.
   - For each item write the number. If the item also has letters, write those letters.
4. Start now. When you're done with the skillbook, do the workbook items for lesson 2.

WORKCHECK

1. *After students finish their independent work, say:*
   - I'll read each item and give the correct answer. Mark the item with a **C** if it is correct and mark the item with an **X** if it is wrong.
   - Raise your hand if you have any questions about any item.
2. *Read the questions and answers for the skillbook and workbook.*
   - *Note: The answers preceded by the word Idea(s) indicate the general idea(s) that are to be conveyed by the student response. A good procedure for handling these items is to ask different students to read their answers. Indicate to the group whether each answer is correct.*

AWARD POINTS

1. Look at the boxes at the top of lesson 2 in your workbook. *Check.*
2. You're going to write your points in the box that has **IW** above it.
   - If you made no errors on your independent work, give yourself 6 points.
   - If you made 1 or 2 errors, give yourself 4 points.
   - If you made 3, 4, or 5 errors, give yourself 2 points.
   - If you made more than 5 errors, you get no points.
3. If you made errors, fix the items you got wrong so that they are correct. Remember to fix your skillbook and workbook answers.
   - If you fix every item that you got wrong, I'll give you 2 bonus points. I'll also give 2 bonus points to students who didn't get any items wrong.
4. When you have corrected the items, hand in your work for lesson 2. I'll total your points.

ANSWER KEY FOR SKILLBOOK

PART B

1. **a.** Morning
   b. *Idea:* To a village 50 miles away
   c. *Idea:* To find out about the poachers
   d. By late afternoon
   e. No
2. **a.** Jill
   b. A room
3. **a.** A trapdoor
   b. Jill
   c. *Ideas:* A tunnel; a cave; stairs
4. **a.** a hill
   b. diamonds
5. **a.** tunnels
   b. bone
6. **a.** Poachers
   b. food
7. *Idea:* The tree was too small to take large animals through

PART C

8. **a.** United States
   b. A Saint Bernard
   c. *Ideas:* He had a haircut; his hair was shorter
   d. *Ideas:* Ranger; troubleshooter
   e. *Ideas:* Poachers were capturing animals

Lesson 3

WORD PRACTICE AND VOCABULARY

*To correct word-identification errors (**sober**, for example):*

a. That word is **sober.**
What word? *Signal.* **Sober.**

b. *Return to the first word of the column and present all the words in order.*

Lesson 3

PART A	Word Lists		PART B

Vocabulary Sentences (PART B)

1	2	3
cupboard	pineapple	wood
sober	haircut	wooden
celebration	airport	terrible
Mombo	grassland	terribly
	hideout	

4	5
Vocabulary words	**Vocabulary words**
1. peg	1. cupboard
2. eager	2. sober
3. inquire	3. celebration
4. glisten	4. budge
5. mile	5. bounding
6. emeralds	
7. diamonds	

6
loudly
perfectly
slowly
politely
suddenly
anxiously

PART B — Vocabulary Sentences

1. This room contained a rusty-looking stove and a <u>cupboard</u> for the dishes.
   - cup • ceiling • cabinet
2. The sun and wind had taken the sparkle from her eyes and left them a <u>sober</u> gray.
   - serious • happy • red
3. They had a great <u>celebration</u>.
   - school • party • sleep
4. He tried to pull the post out of the ground, but the post would not <u>budge</u>.
   - glisten • disappear • move
5. The animals were <u>bounding</u> swiftly down the tunnel.
   - sitting • running • walking

EXERCISE 1   Word practice

1. Everybody, find lesson 3, part A in your skillbook. *Wait.* Touch column 1. *Check.*
   The words in column 1 are hard words that will be in your reading stories.
2. Touch under the first word. *Check.*
   The first word is **cupboard.**
   What word? *Signal* **Cupboard.**
3. Next word. *Pause.* That word is **sober.**
   What word? *Signal.* **Sober.**
4. *Repeat step 3 for each remaining word in column 1.*
5. Your turn to read all those words.
   Touch under the first word in column 1. *Pause.*
   What word? *Signal.* **Cupboard.**
6. Next word. *Pause.* What word? *Signal.* **Sober.**
7. *Repeat step 6 for each remaining word in column 1.*
8. *Repeat the words in column 1 until firm.*

EXERCISE 2   Word family

1. Everybody, touch column 2. *Check.*
   All those words are made up of two shorter words. Touch under the first word. *Pause.*
   What word? *Signal.* **Pineapple.**
2. Next word. *Pause.* What word? *Signal.* **Haircut.**
3. *Repeat step 2 for each remaining word in column 2.*
4. *Repeat the words in column 2 until firm.*

EXERCISE 3   Word practice

1. Everybody, touch under the first word in column 3. *Pause.* What word? *Signal.* **Wood.**
2. Next word. *Pause.* What word? *Signal.* **Wooden.**
3. *Repeat step 2 for each remaining word in column 3.*
4. *Repeat the words in column 3 until firm.*

EXERCISE 4   Vocabulary development

Task A

1. Everybody, touch column 4. *Check.*
   First you're going to read the words in column 4. Then we'll talk about what they mean.
2. Touch under the first word. *Pause.*
   What word? *Signal.* **Peg.**
3. Next word. *Pause.* What word? *Signal.* **Eager.**
4. *Repeat step 3 for each remaining word in column 4.*
5. *Repeat the words in column 4 until firm.*

Task B

Now let's talk about what those words mean.
Word 1 is **peg.** A piece of wood shaped like a crayon is called a **peg.** Everybody, what do we call a piece of wood shaped like a crayon? *Signal.* **A peg.**

Task C

Word 2 is **eager.** *Call on a student.*
What does **eager** mean? *Idea:* Really looking forward to something.

Task D

1. Word 3 is **inquire.** *Call on a student.*
   What does **inquire** mean? *Idea:* Ask.
2. Everybody, what's another way of saying **She asked about the bus?** *Signal.*
   She inquired about the bus.

Task E

1. Word 4 is **glisten.** *Call on a student.*
   What does **glisten** mean? *Idea:* Sparkle.
2. Everybody, what's another way of saying **The diamonds sparkled?** *Signal.*
   The diamonds glistened.

Task F

1. Word 5 is **mile.** Everybody, how long is a **mile?** *Signal.* **5,280 feet.**
2. Everybody, what do we call a distance that is 5,280 feet? *Signal.* **A mile.**

Task G

Word 6 is **emeralds.** Everybody, what color are **emeralds?** *Signal.* **Green.**

Task H

Word 7 is **diamonds.** Everybody, what color are **diamonds?** *Signal.* **Clear.**

EXERCISE 5   Vocabulary from context

Task A

1. Everybody, touch column 5. *Check.*
   The words in that column are words that you'll read in sentences.
2. Touch under the first word. *Pause.*
   What word? *Signal.* **Cupboard.**
3. Next word. *Pause.*
   What word? *Signal.* **Sober.**
4. *Repeat step 3 for each remaining word in column 5.*
5. *Repeat the words in column 5 until firm.*

Task B

1. Everybody, find part B.
   Those sentences contain words that you have just read. The words that we are interested in are underlined.
   Sentence 1. This room contained a rusty-looking stove and a cupboard for the dishes. The choices for **cupboard** are:
   * cup * ceiling * cabinet
   * Everybody, which is the best choice? *Signal.* **Cabinet.**
   * Everybody, read the sentence with the word **cabinet** instead of **cupboard.** *Signal.*
     This room contained a rusty-looking stove and a cabinet for the dishes.
2. Sentence 2. The sun and wind had taken the sparkle from her eyes and left them a sober gray. The choices for **sober** are:
   * serious * happy * red
   * Everybody, which is the best choice? *Signal.* **Serious.**
   * Everybody, read the sentence with the word **serious** instead of **sober.** *Signal.*
     The sun and wind had taken the sparkle from her eyes and left them a serious gray.
3. Sentence 3. They had a great celebration. The choices for **celebration** are:
   * school * party * sleep
   * Everybody, which is the best choice? *Signal.* **Party.**
   * Everybody, read the sentence with the word **party** instead of **celebration.** *Signal.*
     They had a great party.
4. Sentence 4. He tried to pull the post out of the ground, but the post would not budge. The choices for **budge** are:
   * glisten * disappear * move
   * Everybody, which is the best choice? *Signal.* **Move.**
   * Everybody, read the sentence with the word **move** instead of **budge.** *Signal.*
     He tried to pull the post out of the ground, but the post would not move.
5. Sentence 5. The animals were bounding swiftly down the tunnel. The choices for **bounding** are:
   * sitting * running * walking
   * Everybody, which is the best choice? *Signal.* **Running.**
   * Everybody, read the sentence with the word **running** instead of **bounding.** *Signal.*
     The animals were running swiftly down the tunnel.

EXERCISE 6   Words ending in **ly**

Task A

1. In a few days you're going to start reading a story that has a lot of words that end in **l-y.** First you're going to read the words in column 6. Then you're going to complete sentences using those words.
2. Put your finger under the first word in column 6. *Pause.*
   What word? *Signal.* **Loudly.**
3. Next word. *Pause.*
   What word? *Signal.* **Perfectly.**
4. *Repeat step 3 for each remaining word in column 6.*
5. *Repeat the words in column 6 until firm.*

Task B

1. Find part C. I'll do item 1.
   The picture was **perfect.**
   It was painted **perfectly.**
   * Your turn. The picture was **perfect.**
     It was painted *Pause. Signal.* **perfectly.**
2. Item 2. When he was hungry he would get **anxious.** So he waited for dinner *Pause. Signal.* **anxiously.**
3. Item 3. The young man was **polite.**
   So he acted *Pause. Signal.* **politely.**
4. Item 4. She had a **loud** voice.
   So she talked *Pause. Signal.* **loudly.**
5. Item 5. The noise was **sudden.**
   So we heard it *Pause. Signal.* **suddenly.**
6. Item 6. The car was very **slow.**
   So it went very *Pause. Signal.* **slowly.**
7. Later, you're going to write the answers on your paper.

Lesson 3

The Secret Cave

PART 3

Jill, Tom, and Roger walked across the emerald green fields back toward their house. After they had gone about a mile, they saw a large herd of zebras running very quickly across the plain. Roger picked up his ears and stared at Jill and Tom eagerly. For a moment, Jill thought that Roger would start to run after the zebras. But Roger just watched, and then continued to walk.

Mr. Williams was not at home when Tom and Jill arrived at the house. Jill was unhappy. She said, "We have important news and he isn't around. When is he coming back?"

★2 ERRORS★

"How do I know?" Tom said. "You know as much as I do. He was going to the village and coming back this afternoon."

As Tom continued to talk, Jill's mind returned to the cave. Was she right? Could that cave be the poacher's hideout? Where were the poachers? Were they in the village her father was visiting? Was her father in danger? "I wish Dad would come home," she said. She went to the kitchen and opened the cupboard door. She found some pineapple and began to eat it.

"Where's Roger?" Tom asked.

Jill looked around. "I don't know. Did he come inside with us?" Jill asked.

"I don't remember," Tom said.

Tom went outside and called for Roger again and again.

"I'll bet he went back to that cave," Jill said at last. "I'm going to look for him."

"Well, you're going alone," Tom said, "because I won't go near that cave again."

"All right. But I'll make a map that shows where I'm going. Give it to Dad when he comes back." Jill drew the map.(A)

Lesson 3   Textbook   **9**

Tom asked, "Are you really going back there?"

Jill told him that she was. Then Tom said, "Well, I've changed my mind. I'm going with you."

• • •

As they approached the strange grove of trees, Jill saw Roger. He was sitting in the shade under a tree and panting. When she called him, he walked slowly toward her dragging his tail. "Shame on you, Roger. You shouldn't go this far away from the house," she said.

Jill stopped in front of the large tree with the hollow trunk. She thought that she would take one more look inside the trunk of the tree. She didn't want to go into the cave again. But she wanted to see the inside of the tree once more. So she crawled through the hole, and stopped very suddenly. She noticed a large pair of feet right in front of her. She looked up and saw a large pair of legs. A very tall man was standing above her, with his arms folded.(B) ★7 ERRORS★

"Oh," she said. She didn't know what else to say. "I . . . I . . . ." Slowly she stood up. The man stared at her with a sober expression.

"Do you speak English?" Jill asked. Her voice trembled. The man did not move and did not respond.

Tom was coming through the hole on his hands and knees. Tom said, "What do you mean, do I speak English? Of course I speak English. I've . . . I've . . . ." Slowly he stood up and stared at the man. "Wow," he said slowly.

Jill said, "We didn't mean to come in here. Our dog . . ." Just then, Roger came through the hole. He looked at the man and let out a booming bark. The man smiled and barked back at the dog. Roger looked very puzzled.

Tom said to the man, "We don't know what you're doing here and we don't care if you poach. We're just on a trip and we're going back to our house right now. Goodbye. It was good to meet you, but we have to go back . . . ."

The man held up his hand and Tom stopped. The man stared at Tom. Then he spoke in a sober voice. "My name is Mombo. This is our tree. You should not be here."

"You're right," Tom said. "And we're going right now. And we'll never come back. And we don't know anything about what you do."

Mombo said, "We are not poachers. No poachers use this tree."

"You're right," Tom said. "We don't know anything about poachers."

Mombo said, "Poachers are bad."

"They really are," Tom said. "Very bad, but . . . ."

"Be quiet Tom," Jill said.

Mombo continued, "The people from the village use this tree. We have a special celebration here two times each year."

Jill thought for a moment. Then she said, "But our dog Roger found a bone inside the cave."

Mombo smiled, "So you have found the cave. The cave has many tunnels.

10   Lesson 3   Textbook

EXERCISE 7   Decoding

1. Everybody, turn to page 9 in your textbook. *Wait. Call on a student.* What's the error limit for this lesson? **7 errors.**
   You will earn 4 points if you stay within the error limit.

2. *Call on individual students to read three to five sentences, starting with the title.*
   ● *When the group reads to the 2-error sign, making no more than two errors, you read the first part aloud, starting with the title. Present the specified comprehension tasks as you read.*
   ● *If the group makes more than 2 errors:*
     a. *Direct the group to reread the first part until they can read it with no more than 2 errors.*
     b. *Then read the first part aloud and present the comprehension tasks.*

3. *After you have read the first part aloud, call on individual students to read. Present the comprehension tasks specified for each circled letter.*

To correct word-identification errors (pineapple, for example):
   a. That word is **pineapple**. What word? **Pineapple.**
   b. Go back to the beginning of the sentence and read the whole sentence.

EXERCISE 8   Comprehension tasks

Ⓐ Everybody, touch the house on the map. *Check.*
● In which direction does the arrow go to the large tree? **South.**
● How many miles is it from the house to the large tree? **Two miles.**
Ⓑ Where did Jill find Roger? *Idea:* Sitting under a tree.
● What did she decide to do before returning home with Roger? *Idea:* Look inside the tree one more time.
● When she went inside the trunk of the tree, she stopped suddenly. What did she see? *Idea:* A man.
● Read the rest of the lesson to yourselves.

After all students have finished reading:
● What was the name of the man inside the tree? **Mombo.**
● Was he a poacher? **No.**
● What did the people from the village do inside the cave? *Idea:* Held celebrations.
● When Tom came into the cave, he started to do some fast talking. Listen to that part of the chapter again. *Read the paragraphs beginning with, "Tom said to the man . . ." through "Be quiet Tom, . . ."*
Tom is really trying to talk his way out.

- What made Mombo and the others go farther into the cave? *Idea:* They were looking for Roger.
- Mombo led the others down the cave tunnel to the large room inside the cave. Then Mombo picked one of the tunnels on the other side of the room. How did he know which tunnel to pick? *Idea:* He saw pieces of Roger's hair.
- How do you think Jill feels going down that tunnel, farther and farther into the cave? *Idea:* Afraid.

EXERCISE 9   Awarding Points

1. Now I will give you points for your reading. Everybody, take out your workbook.
2. Look at box **R** on page 3.
   - *If the group stayed within the error limit, have each student write 4 in box **R**.*
   - *If the group went over the error limit, direct the group to reread the lesson. Do not present the comprehension tasks again. If the group stays within the error limit on the second reading, give each student **one** point in box **R**.*

Hundreds of tunnels. Hundreds of rooms. Why don't you show me where you went?" And Mombo slowly opened the trapdoor.

Suddenly, Roger picked up his ears, barked loudly, and dashed through the trapdoor and into the tunnel. Jill tried to grab him but she just missed the end of his tail as he ran into the dark tunnel.

Mombo said, "Something is strange in the cave. We will follow your dog and see what it is."

Mombo lit candles and then led the way down the tunnel to the large room. He went to the other side of the room, bent down, and looked inside each of the tunnels. At last he pointed to one of the tunnels and said, "Your dog went down this one. I can see pieces of his hair. Follow me."

Jill and Tom followed Mombo down the small, narrow tunnel, farther away from the tree, farther and farther under the great hill.

ANSWER KEY FOR WORKBOOK

Story Items

1. Below is a list of events that happened in Part 3.
   - Write **beginning** if the event happened near the beginning.
   - Write **middle** if the event happened near the middle.
   - Write **end** if the event happened at the end.

   a. Tom and Jill met Mombo in the tree. _middle_

   b. Roger ran down a tunnel. _end_

   c. Mombo looked inside each tunnel. _end_

   d. Mr. Williams was not at home. _beginning_

   e. Jill, Tom, and Roger saw some zebras. _beginning_

   f. Jill and Tom followed Mombo down the tunnel. _end_

Map Skills

2. **a.** Fill in the boxes on the map to tell the direction each arrow is pointing.
   b. Fill in the boxes around the map.

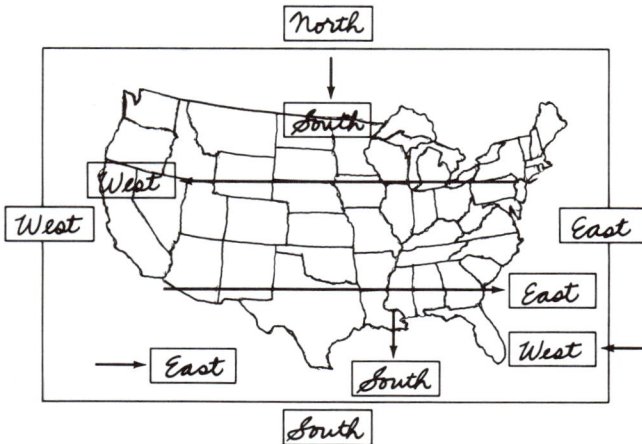

3. Some things on the map and in the boxes are wrong. Cross out the things that are wrong and write the correct information.

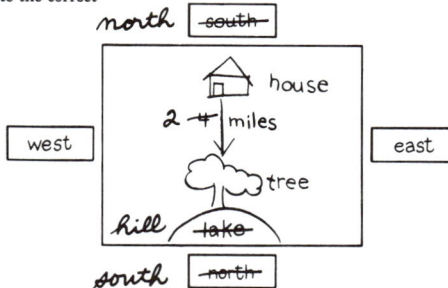

INDEPENDENT WORK

Do all the items in your skillbook and workbook for lesson 3.

WORKCHECK AND AWARDING POINTS

1. *Read the questions and answers for the skillbook and workbook.*
2. *Award points for independent work as follows:*

0 errors	6 points
1 or 2 errors	4 points
3, 4, or 5 errors	2 points
More than 5 errors	0 points

3. *Award bonus points for (a) correcting any missed items (2 points) or (b) getting all the items right (2 points).*

ANSWER KEY FOR SKILLBOOK

PART C

1. perfectly
2. anxiously
3. politely
4. loudly
5. suddenly
6. slowly

PART D

7. *Idea:* In another village
8. Jill
9. **a.** A map
   b. Two miles
   c. South
10. **a.** Roger
    b. Jill
    c. *Idea:* A pair of feet
    d. Tom
    e. Tom
    f. Mombo
    g. Twice a year
11. Roger barked and ran into the tunnel
12. hundreds
13. *Ideas:* By looking inside; by finding pieces of Roger's hair

PART E

14. **a.** poachers
    b. plain
    c. prepared
    d. wonderful

Lesson 4

Lesson 4

PART A **Word Lists**

1	2
sound	liver
shout	deliver
bound	terribly
loudly	wooden
found	

3	4
Vocabulary words	stiffly
1. CB radio	thoughtfully
2. flutter	gratefully
3. snarling	quietly
4. lanterns	
5. peg	
6. party	
7. sober	
8. bounding	
9. celebration	
10. budge	

PART B **Word Endings**

● Complete each item by adding the correct ending to the underlined word.
1. She felt <u>stiff</u>.
So she walked _____.
2. The little boy was <u>thoughtful</u>.
So he behaved _____.
3. They were <u>grateful</u>.
So they thanked him _____.
4. Deer are very <u>quiet</u>.
So the deer ran through the woods
_____.

WORD PRACTICE AND VOCABULARY

EXERCISE 1   Word family

1. Everybody, find lesson 4, part A in your skillbook. *Wait.* Touch column 1. *Check.*
All those words have the sound **ou** in them.
Touch under the first word. *Pause.*
What word? *Signal.* **Sound.**
2. Next word. *Pause.* What word? *Signal.* **Shout.**
3. *Repeat step 2 for each remaining word in column 1.*
4. *Repeat the words in column 1 until firm.*

EXERCISE 2   Word practice

1. Everybody, touch under the first word in column 2. *Pause.* What word? *Signal.* **Liver.**
2. Next word. *Pause.* What word? *Signal.* **Deliver.**
3. *Repeat step 2 for each remaining word in column 2.*
4. *Repeat the words in column 2 until firm.*

EXERCISE 3   Vocabulary development

Task A
1. Everybody, touch column 3. *Check.*
First you're going to read the words in column 3. Then we'll talk about what they mean.
2. Touch under the first line. *Pause.*
What words? *Signal.* **CB radio.**
3. Next word. *Pause.* What word? *Signal.* **Flutter.**
4. *Repeat step 3 for each remaining word in column 3.*
5. *Repeat the words in column 3 until firm.*

Task B
Now let's talk about what those words mean.
The words in line 1 are **CB radio.**
Call on a student. What is a **CB radio?**
Idea: A radio people use to talk to each other.

Task C
Word 2 is **flutter.** When a bird's wings **flutter,** they flap and move very fast. Everybody, what are wings doing when they flap very fast? *Signal.* **Fluttering.**

Task D
Word 3 is **snarling.** When you **snarl,** you show your teeth and growl. Everybody show me how you snarl. *Check.*

Task E
Word 4 is **lanterns.** Lamps that burn oil or candles are called **lanterns.** What are lamps that burn oil or candles? *Signal.* **Lanterns.**

Task F
Word 5 is **peg.** *Call on a student.* What is a **peg?** *Idea:* A piece of wood shaped like a crayon.

Task G
Word 6 is **party.** Another word for a **group of people** is a **party.** Everybody, what's another word for a **group of people?** *Signal.* **A party.**

Task H
Word 7 is **sober.** *Call on a student.* What does **sober** mean? *Idea:* Serious.

Task I
Word 8 is **bounding.** *Call on a student.* What is a dog doing when it is **bounding** down the steps. *Idea:* Running down the steps.

Task J
Word 9 is **celebration.** *Call on a student.* What is a **celebration?** *Idea:* A party.

Task K
Word 10 is **budge.** *Call on a student.* What does **budge** mean? *Idea:* Move.

EXERCISE 4   Words ending in **ly**

Task A
1. In a few days, you're going to start reading a novel that has a lot of words that end in **l-y.** First you're going to read the words in column 4. Then you're going to complete sentences using those words.
2. Put your finger under the first word in column 4. *Pause.* What word? *Signal.* **Stiffly.**
3. Next word. *Pause.*
What word? *Signal.* **Thoughtfully.**
4. *Repeat step 3 for each remaining word in column 4.*
5. *Repeat the words in column 4 until firm.*

Task B
1. Find part B. I'll do item 1.
She felt **stiff.** So she walked **stiffly.**
● Your turn. She felt **stiff.**
So she walked *Pause. Signal.* **stiffly.**
2. Item 2. The little boy was **thoughtful.**
So he behaved *Pause. Signal.* **thoughtfully.**
3. Item 3. They were **grateful.**
So they thanked him *Pause. Signal.* **gratefully.**
4. Item 4. Deer are very **quiet.**
So the deer ran through the woods *Pause. Signal.* **quietly.**
5. Later you're going to write the answers on your paper.

Lesson 4

The Secret Cave
PART 4Ⓐ

Jill and Tom were following Mombo down the tunnel, farther and farther into the cave. Once they saw a dim form bounding ahead of them. Jill said, "I think that was Roger."

Tom replied, "I hope that was Roger."

The tunnel curved to the right, curved to the left, and then went down so steeply that Jill almost slipped and fell.

"I can smell something," Tom said, as they followed the tunnel. "It smells like a circus."Ⓑ

Mombo stopped in front of Jill. He held his finger over his lips as a signal for the others to be quiet. ★2 ERRORS★

"Stay here," Mombo whispered. "I will go ahead and find out what is going on."

He came back a few minutes later and said very quietly, "I have found the poachers. They are in a large room ahead of us. They have many animals in the room. They have elephants, zebras, and flamingos. You follow me and please be quiet."

Mombo dropped to his hands and knees and crawled very slowly. Jill and Tom followed.

They were approaching the large room, but Jill still couldn't see inside it. Suddenly, a loud voice came from the large room ahead. "That dog is back again."

An instant later, Roger barked loudly. Another instant later, elephants began to make terrible noises, and men began to shout. "Get that dog out of here!" one voice shouted. "Grab him!"Ⓒ

A moment later, there was a terribly loud noise, followed by more screaming and shrieking and yelling. "Oh, no," Jill said aloud. She couldn't see anything, but she imagined what might have happened. She started to run forward, but Mombo grabbed her and held her.

"No," he said softly. "I could tell by the sound that they did not get your dog. He escaped."

"Oh, I'm glad," Jill whispered.Ⓓ
★6 ERRORS★

Slowly, the animals quieted again. As they did, Jill and the others crawled forward until they reached the room. It was so large that Jill could hardly believe what she saw. The room was as big as a circus tent. There were cages all around the rock walls—big cages, small cages,

Lesson 4 Textbook **13**

wooden cages, steel cages. In the middle of the room were huge piles of grass and food for the animals. There was a large hole in the ceiling and light from the outside was pouring into the room. On the far side of the room was a very large tunnel, big enough for an elephant to go through.

"I think that tunnel leads to the outside," Jill said. "It looks big enough for any animal to go through."

Mombo said, "You may be right. I do not know where the tunnel goes. I have never been in this part of the cave before."

Three men were standing in the huge room near the large tunnel. Mombo pointed to them and then quickly dashed into the room, moving very quickly and staying close to the floor. Jill and Tom followed. They ducked into a crack in the wall, waited a few seconds, and then went around some cages of flamingos. They ducked into another crack. The animals were quiet now, and Jill and Tom could hear the men talking.

One of them was saying, "No, we're not going to kidnap that troubleshooter. I don't like the idea."

Another man said, "But Al, we've got to do something, you know. We've got close to a million bucks worth of animals here. And if that troubleshooter finds us before we can get the animals out of here, we lose everything."

Al said, "Yeah, but maybe we can get them out of here the fast way, before that nosey troubleshooter finds us."

The third man said, "Yeah, let's get out of here the fast way."

As Jill listened from the dark crack, she felt something in her hair. She brushed it aside and it moved. It was alive, and it was some sort of animal. Jill realized that it was a bat hanging upside down. Just then Tom saw the bat. He was frightened and shouted, "Ooooo!"

"What was that?" Al said.

Quickly, the three men started to run toward where Jill and Tom were hiding. Just as quickly, Mombo sprang from his hiding place, and shouted, "Follow me." Then he started running back to the small tunnel.

Jill and Tom tried to follow Mombo, but they tripped over each other. Before they could get up, the men grabbed them. Meanwhile, the flamingos flapped their wings, the elephants trumpeted, and the other animals became excited.

A few moments later, the men put Jill and Tom inside one of the empty cages. Al stood in front of them, smiling. "I don't think we're going to have to worry about that troubleshooter bothering us," he said.

"What do you mean?" one of the other men asked.

"I think we've got his kids. And we're not going to let them go back and tell him we're here until we get the animals out."

"I get it," one of the other men said. "After a few hours, it won't make any difference if they tell, because we'll be gone, you know."

14 Lesson 4 Textbook

EXERCISE 5 Decoding

1. Everybody, turn to page 13 in your textbook. *Call on a student. Wait.* What's the error limit for this lesson? **6 errors.**
   You will get 4 points if you stay within the error limit.

2. *Call on individual students to read three to five sentences, starting with the title.*
   ● *When the group reads to the 2-error sign, making no more than two errors, you read the first part aloud, starting with the title. Present the specified comprehension tasks as you read.*
   ● *If the group makes more than 2 errors:*
      a. *Direct the group to reread the first part until they can read it with no more than 2 errors.*
      b. *Then read the first part aloud and present the comprehension tasks.*

3. *After you have read the first part aloud, call on individual students to read. Present the comprehension tasks specified for each circled letter.*

To correct word identification errors (poachers, for example):
a. That word is **poachers.**
   What word? Poachers.
b. Go back to the beginning of the sentence and read the whole sentence.

EXERCISE 6 Comprehension tasks

Ⓐ What were Jill and the others doing at the end of the last part? *Idea:* Going down a tunnel.
● How did Mombo know which tunnel to follow from the large room? *Idea:* He found some of Roger's hair in one tunnel.
Ⓑ What do you think is making that smell? *Idea:* A lot of animals.
Ⓒ Can Jill see what is happening? **No.** She **hears** things happening.
● Who was already in the large room? **Roger.**
● Had he been there before? **Yes.**
● How do you know? *Idea:* Because somebody in the room recognized him.
● What did the men want to do with Roger? *Ideas:* Grab him; get him out of there.
Ⓓ Do you think Roger is still in the room ahead? **No.**
● Read the rest of the lesson to yourselves.

Lesson 4 Textbook 15

The light coming into the cave told Jill that it was late in the afternoon. She and Tom were inside a cage. A large pole was propped against the outside of the door to the cage. The pole was jammed tightly against the bars of the cage. Jill had tried to push the door open but it wouldn't budge. She had tried to think of some way of knocking the pole out of the way, but the pole was very heavy and she could not move it.

"If we could get out of this cage, we could stop these poachers," she said.

"How?" Tom said.

"By opening all the animal cages and letting the animals out. Each cage is held shut with a heavy wooden peg. There are no locks on the cages. So, if we open the cages . . ."

16 Lesson 4 Textbook

After all students have finished reading:

- Describe the room that Jill and the others came to. Tell about the size of the room, the ceiling and some of the things that were in the room. *Call on individual students.*
  Ideas: It was a big room with a high ceiling; the ceiling had a hole in it that let light in; the room was full of cages with animals in them; a large tunnel came into the room.
- Jill and the others snuck inside the room and heard somebody talking. Who was talking?
  Ideas: Three men; Al.
- The men were worried about somebody. Who were they worried about? *Ideas:* Jill's father, Mr. Williams.
- Tom made a noise. Why did he do that?
  Idea: He was scared by a bat.
- What did Mombo do? *Idea:* Jumped up and ran back to the small tunnel.
- Where did the men put Jill and Tom?
  Idea: In a cage.
- What was holding the cage shut?
  Idea: A pole leaning against the door.
- Jill has a plan if she can get out of the cage. What's that plan. *Idea:* To let all the animals out of their cages.
- What's holding the animal cages closed?
  Idea: Wooden pegs.
- Everybody, look at the picture on page 16.
  Check.
- Everybody, touch one of the wooden pegs that is holding a cage shut. *Check.*
- Everybody, touch the thing that is holding Jill's cage shut. *Check.*
  That pole is propped against the door to the cage.
- Name the animals that you see in cages.
  Elephants, zebras, and flamingos.

EXERCISE 7 Awarding points

1. Now I will give you points for your reading. Everybody, take out your workbook.
2. Look at box **R** on page 5.
   - *If the group stayed within the error limit, have each student write 4 in box **R**.*
   - *If the group went over the error limit, direct the group to reread the lesson. Do not present the comprehension tasks again. If the group stays within the error limit on the second reading, give each student **one** point in box **R**.*

INDEPENDENT WORK

Do all the items in your skillbook and workbook for lesson 4.

Lesson 4 **21**

ANSWER KEY FOR WORKBOOK

Story Items

1. Below is a list of events that happened in Part 4.
   - Write **beginning** if the event happened near the beginning.
   - Write **middle** if the event happened near the middle.
   - Write **end** if the event happened at the end.

   a. Three poachers talked in the big room. _end_

   b. Tom said, "It smells like a circus." _beginning_

   c. Jill and Tom were in a cage. _end_

   d. Jill thought of a plan to get out of the cage. _end_

   e. Mombo ran across the room. _middle_

   f. Jill and Tom followed Mombo down the tunnel. _beginning_

Map Skills

2. a. Fill in the boxes on the map to tell the direction each arrow is pointing.
   b. Fill in the boxes around the map.

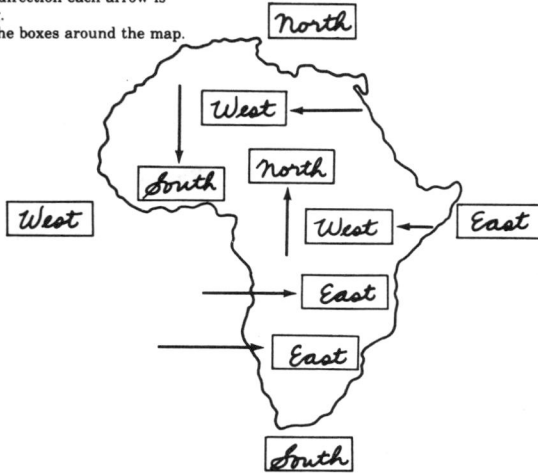

North / West / South / West / North / West / East / East / East / South

3. Some things on the map and in the boxes are wrong. Cross out the things that are wrong and write the correct information.

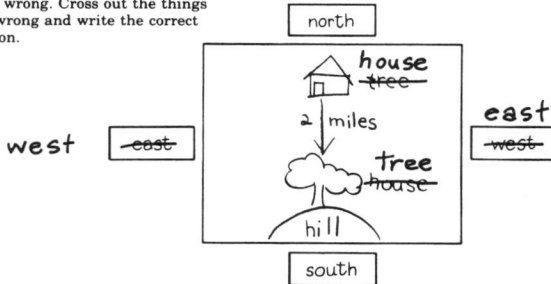

north / house ~~tree~~ / 2 miles / tree ~~house~~ / hill / west ~~east~~ / east ~~west~~ / south

22 Lesson 4

WORKCHECK AND AWARDING POINTS

1. *Read the questions and answers for the skillbook and workbook.*

2. *Award points for independent work as follows:*

0 errors	6 points
1 or 2 errors	4 points
3, 4, or 5 errors	2 points
More than 5 errors	0 points

3. *Award bonus points for (a) correcting any missed items (2 points) or (b) getting all the items right (2 points).*

ANSWER KEY FOR SKILLBOOK

PART B

1. stiffly
2. thoughtfully
3. gratefully
4. quietly

PART C

5. a. Mombo
   b. *Ideas:* By looking inside each tunnel opening; by finding pieces of Roger's hair
   c. smell
   d. *Idea:* Roger had entered the room
6. a. "Grab him!"
   b. circus tent
7. a. *Idea:* From a hole in the ceiling
   b. A big tunnel
   c. outside
8. *Ideas:* Cages; animals
9. a. Mr. Williams
   b. a million bucks
10. a. A bat
    b. *Idea:* He shouted and ran into the big tunnel
11. A few hours
12. *Idea:* Jill / Tom
13. *Idea:* A pole leaning against the door
14. Large wooden pegs
15. *Idea:* Let all the animals out of their cages

PART D

16. a. emeralds
    b. diamonds
    c. miles
    d. glistened
    e. inquired

Lesson 5

Lesson 5

PART A	Word Lists			PART B

PART B
Vocabulary Sentences

1	2	3	4
cyclone	cackle	whirl	sure
prairie	candle	whirlwinds	pressure
Dorothy	tunnel	electric	fun
Aunt	sparkle	surround	funnel
Toto	incredible	surroundings	anxious
horizon	startle	orphan	usual
	twinkle	rough	anxiously
		deliver	

5	6
Vocabulary words	**Vocabulary words**
1. in spite of	1. merrily
2. attic	2. mass
3. rust	3. cradle
4. horizon	4. wail
5. snarling	5. sober
6. lanterns	

1. The dog was happy and his eyes twinkled <u>merrily</u>.
   - sadly • happily • meanly
2. The sun had baked the plowed land into a gray <u>mass</u>.
   - house • ice floe
   - area with no shape
3. She felt as if she was being rocked gently, like a baby in a <u>cradle</u>.
   - truck • small bed • pillow
4. From the far north, they heard a low <u>wail</u> of the wind.
   - sea animal • howl • squeak
5. His expression was not <u>sober</u>.
   - eager • happy • serious

WORD PRACTICE AND VOCABULARY

EXERCISE 1 Word practice

1. Everybody, find lesson 5, part A in your skillbook. *Wait.* Touch column 1. *Check.* The words in column 1 are hard words that will be in your reading stories.
2. Touch under the first word. *Check.* The first word is **cyclone.** What word? *Signal.* **Cyclone.**
3. Next word. *Pause.* That word is **prairie.** What word? *Signal.* **Prairie.**
4. *Repeat step 3 for each remaining word in column 1.*
5. Now let's see if you remember all those words. Touch under the first word in column 1. *Pause.* What word? *Signal.* **Cyclone.**
6. Next word. *Pause.* What word? *Signal.* **Prairie.**
7. *Repeat step 6 for each remaining word in column 1.*
8. *Repeat the words in column 1 until firm.*

EXERCISE 2 Word family

1. Everybody, touch column 2. *Check.* All those words end with the sound lll. Touch under the first word. *Pause.* What word? *Signal.* **Cackle.**
2. Next word. *Pause.* What word? *Signal.* **Candle.**
3. *Repeat step 2 for each remaining word in column 2.*
4. *Repeat the words in column 2 until firm.*

EXERCISE 3 Word practice

1. Everybody, touch under the first word in column 3. *Pause.* What word? *Signal.* **Whirl.**
2. Next word. *Pause.* What word? *Signal.* **Whirlwinds.**
3. *Repeat step 2 for each remaining word in column 3.*
4. *Repeat the words in column 3 until firm.*
5. *Repeat steps 1–4 for column 4.*

EXERCISE 4 Vocabulary development

Task A

1. Everybody, touch column 5. *Check.* First you're going to read the words in column 5. Then we'll talk about what they mean.
2. Touch under the first line. *Pause.* What words? *Signal.* **In spite of.**
3. Next word. *Pause.* What word? *Signal.* **Attic.**
4. *Repeat step 3 for each remaining word in column 5.*
5. *Repeat the words in column 5 until firm.*

Task B

1. Now let's talk about what those words mean. The words in line 1 are **in spite of.** Here's another way of saying **Although there is danger: In spite of danger.** Everybody, what's another way of saying **Although there is danger?** *Signal.* **In spite of danger.**
2. Everybody, what's another way of saying **Although there is smoke?** *Signal.* **In spite of smoke.**
3. Everybody, what's another way of saying **Although there was trouble?** *Signal.* **In spite of trouble.**

Task C

Word 2 is **attic.** A storeroom near the top of a house is an **attic.**

Task D

Word 3 is **rust. Rust** is a red material that forms on iron and steel when they get wet.

Task E

Word 4 is **horizon.** The **horizon** is the line where the sky meets the land. Everybody, what do we call the line where the sky meets the land? *Signal.* **The horizon.**

Task F

Word 5 is **snarling.** *Call on a student.* Show me how you **snarl.**

Task G

Word 6 is **lanterns.** *Call on a student.* What are **lanterns?** *Idea:* Lamps that burn oil or candles.

EXERCISE 5 Vocabulary from context

Task A

1. Everybody, touch column 6. *Check.* The words in that column are words that you'll read in sentences.
2. Touch under the first word. *Pause.* What word? *Signal.* **Merrily.**
3. Next word. *Pause.* What word? *Signal.* **Mass.**
4. *Repeat step 3 for each remaining word in column 6.*
5. *Repeat the words in column 6 until firm.*

Lesson 5

PART A	Word Lists		
1	**2**	**3**	**4**
cyclone	cackle	whirl	sure
prairie	candle	whirlwinds	pressure
Dorothy	tunnel	electric	fun
Aunt	sparkle	surround	funnel
Toto	incredible	surroundings	anxious
horizon	startle	orphan	usual
	twinkle	rough	anxiously
		deliver	

5
Vocabulary words
1. in spite of
2. attic
3. rust
4. horizon
5. snarling
6. lanterns

6
Vocabulary words
1. merrily
2. mass
3. cradle
4. wail
5. sober

PART B
Vocabulary Sentences

1. The dog was happy and his eyes twinkled merrily.
   ● sadly   ——happily   ● meanly
2. The sun had baked the plowed land into a gray mass.
   ● house   ● ice floe
   ● area with no shape
3. She felt as if she was being rocked gently, like a baby in a cradle.
   ● truck   ● small bed   ● pillow
4. From the far north, they heard a low wail of the wind.
   ● sea animal   ● howl   ● squeak
5. His expression was not sober.
   ● eager   ● happy   ● serious

Lesson 5

The Secret Cave
PART 5 Ⓐ

It was almost night. The men lit four large lanterns. But the shadows of the cave were now very dark and the sounds of the animals were very strange. The three poachers were sitting on blankets, not far from Jill and Tom.

"This has been a bad day," one poacher said. "Everything went wrong all at once, you know."

"It's all right now," Al said. "At least we won't have to worry about the ranger snooping around." Ⓑ ★2 ERRORS★

Jill watched and waited. The men continued to talk. Slowly, however, they talked less and less. At last, one of them seemed to be sleeping. Then the others seemed to fall asleep. Things became very quiet. Suddenly, the flamingos started to make a fuss and Jill looked over near their cages. Something was moving from the tunnel into the large room. It looked something like a lion or something like . . . it was Roger, sneaking along the wall.

"Don't wake up," Jill said to herself as she glanced at the poachers. "Please don't wake up."

Roger snuck right past the sleeping men. Some of the animals were now becoming excited and making more noise. One of the men rolled over, but he didn't wake up. Jill held her breath and watched. As Roger approached the cage that held Jill and Tom, he began to wag his tail. When he reached the cage, he jumped up and started to pant.

Jill reached through the bars and petted Roger's head. "Good Roger," she said softly. Then she quickly moved to her right. "Come here," she said. Roger bounded toward her. He knocked against the pole that held the cage closed, but the pole didn't move.

Jill got Roger to stand up on his hind legs right next to the pole. Then she quickly moved over to the other side of the cage. "Here, Roger," she called. Ⓒ ★6 ERRORS★

Roger ran right into the pole and knocked it out of place. It banged to the floor of the cave and rolled a few feet before stopping. Jill held her breath again. The men were still sleeping. Jill pushed the door open and Roger bounded into the cage, wagging his tail and jumping all over Jill and Tom.

"You stay here, Roger," Jill said, as she and Tom slipped out of the cage. "Now, you stay."

She didn't want Roger around when

Lesson 5   Textbook   **17**

Task B
Everybody, find part B. *Wait.*
Those sentences contain words that you have just read. The words that we are interested in are underlined.
Sentence 1. The dog was happy and his eyes twinkled merrily. The choices for **merrily** are:
   ●sadly   ●happily   ●meanly
● Everybody, which is the best choice? *Signal.* **Happily.**
● Everybody, read the sentence with the word **happily** instead of **merrily.** *Signal.*
The dog was happy and his eyes twinkled happily.

2. Sentence 2. The sun had baked the plowed land into a gray mass. The choices for **mass** are:
   ●house   ●ice floe   ●area with no shape
● Everybody, which is the best choice? *Signal.*
Area with no shape.
● Everybody, read the sentence with the words **area with no shape** instead of **mass.** *Signal.*
The sun had baked the plowed land into a gray area with no shape.

3. Sentence 3. She felt as if she was being rocked gently, like a baby in a cradle. The choices for **cradle** are:
   ●truck   ●small bed   ●pillow
● Everybody, which is the best choice? *Signal.* **Small bed.**
● Everybody, read the sentence with the words **small bed** instead of **cradle.** *Signal.*
She felt as if she was being rocked gently, like a baby in a small bed.

4. Sentence 4. From the far north, they heard a low wail of the wind. The choices for **wail** are:
   ●sea animal   ●howl   ●squeak
● Everybody, which is the best choice? *Signal.* **Howl.**
● Everybody, read the sentence with the word **howl** instead of **wail.** *Signal.*
From the far north, they heard a low howl of the wind.

5. Sentence 5. His expression was not sober. The choices for **sober** are:
   ●eager   ●happy   ●serious
● Everybody, which is the best choice? *Signal.* **Serious.**
● Everybody, read the sentence with the word **serious** instead of **sober.** *Signal.*
His expression was not serious.

STORY READING

EXERCISE 6   Decoding

1. Everybody turn to page 17 in your textbook. *Wait. Call on a student.* What's the error limit for this lesson? **6 errors.**
2. *Call on individual students to read.*

zebras and elephants were running free inside the cave.

Quickly, she and Tom ran around to the cages that held the zebras and elephants. They pulled out the pegs that held the cages closed and opened each cage a crack. They planned to open all the cages and return to Roger's cage before any of the animals could get out of their cages. But that plan didn't work, thanks to Roger. When Jill and Tom were opening one of the last zebra cages, Roger started to bark, very loudly. His voice boomed through the cave. A moment later, elephants were screaming, zebras were kicking, and flamingos were fluttering around inside their cages.

One of the poachers woke up. "What are you doing?" he shouted to Jill and Tom. But before the poacher could do anything, one of the elephants pushed the door of its cage open. The elephant ran from the cage very quickly, looking frightened and dangerous. The poacher froze and said nothing. Now another elephant pushed a door open and ran out of its cage. Three zebras followed, running around the cave and kicking with their hind legs. The elephants held their trunks high, and their eyes looked frightened. The zebras began to run along the wall of the cave, away from the elephants. Then the elephants headed straight toward the large tunnel. One of the zebras followed them, running very fast, and keeping close to the wall of the cave. Now, two other elephants came from their cages and ran across the

18 Lesson 5 Textbook

middle of the room. And three more zebras . . . five more zebras . . . six more elephants. Two elephants started to fight. One rammed his head against another. The second elephant was pushed back into a zebra cage. The cage door opened and zebras were all over the place, trying to stay out of the way of the giant elephants.

Jill and Tom stood in one of the cracks of the cave wall. Bats inside the cave were starting to wake up and flutter around. Two of them brushed past Jill. Another was hanging right above her with his face in her face. But she didn't move. She just stared as all the animals ran toward the large tunnel.

Within less than a minute, all the animals had left the room, and run down the large tunnel. Only the flamingos were still in their cages.

The poachers were still in the cave. Al pointed to Jill. "You did this!" he shouted. "You did it and you're going to . . ."

"Go to jail," a familiar voice shouted. One second later, Mr. Williams, Mombo, and three other rangers stepped into the room.

"Dad, Dad!" Jill shouted and ran to her father. "Oh, am I glad to see you! Oh, Dad!" She threw her arms around her father's neck and squeezed him as hard as she could. Tom did the same thing.

During the next hour, Jill and Tom told their part of the story three or four times. Every time they told it, the story

---

sounded a little more exciting.

Then Mr. Williams told his part of the story. Mombo had come to the house just as Mr. Williams was returning. Mr. Williams used his CB radio and called the three other rangers. Mombo led the party to the large tree and through the tunnel. When they were close to the huge room that held the animals, they heard all the noise. The party entered the large room just as Al was yelling at Jill.

The next morning, Jill and Tom returned to the cave. They watched as Mr. Williams and the other rangers released the flamingos. The huge pink

birds climbed into the sky and then drifted into the distance.

After the last flamingo had disappeared, Mr. Williams put his arms around his children. He said, "Well, we finished up here a lot faster than I thought we would. But, we are in luck because I've just been offered a job back in Kansas. And . . ."

"Kansas!" Jill shouted. "Who wants to go to Kansas? We just got here and Kenya is beautiful. And . . ."

"But," Mr. Williams said, "you'll love Kansas, because . . ."

"Oh, no, not again . . ."

Lesson 5 Textbook **19**

---

3. *After the group reads to the 2-error sign without making more than 2 errors, reread the first part aloud and present the comprehension tasks.*

4. *After you have completed the first part, call on individual students to read. Present the comprehension tasks.*

EXERCISE 7 Comprehension tasks

Ⓐ Where are Jill and Tom?
   Idea: In a cage inside the cave.

● What does Jill want to do if she can get out of the cage? *Idea:* Let all the animals out of their cages.

Ⓑ How many poachers are in the cave? **Three.**

● What time of day is it? *Idea:* Almost night.

● Why do the poachers think that they won't have to worry about the ranger?
   Idea: Because Jill and Tom can't tell the ranger where they are.

Ⓒ Why is Jill calling Roger to go from one side of the door to the other? *Idea:* She is trying to get him to bump the pole and knock it down. If Roger hits that pole hard enough from the side, it will fall down.

● Read the rest of the lesson to yourselves. Try to get a picture of all the things that happen when the frightened animals get out of their cages.

After all students have finished reading:

● Jill's plan was to open the cages for all the animals and then return to the cage with Roger. Why didn't that plan work?
   Idea: Because Roger barked.

● Name some things that happened next.
   Call on individual students. Idea: Elephants and zebras got out of their cages; elephants started fighting; bats woke up and started flying around.

● Where did all the animals go?
   Idea: They ran out through the large tunnel.

● Where does that large tunnel lead?
   Idea: Outside.

● Which animals were left in their cages? **The flamingos.**

● After the animals left the room, what did Al start to do? *Idea:* Point to Jill and yell at her.

● Who entered the cave then? *Idea:* Mr. Williams, Mombo, and three other rangers.

● Who had Mr. Williams called? *Idea:* The other rangers.

● What's going to happen to all the poachers?
   Idea: They'll go to jail.

● Why did Jill and the others return to the cave the next morning? *Idea:* To release all the flamingos.

● Then what news did Mr. Williams have for them? *Idea:* That he had been offered a job in Kansas.

Award 4 points or have the students reread to the error limit sign.

ANSWER KEY FOR WORKBOOK

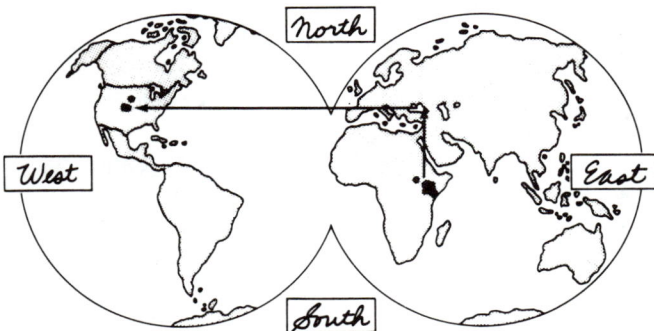

Special Project

1. The story, <u>The Secret Cave</u>, describes a great cave and tells about some of the rooms. The map shows what the cave would look like if you could see it from high above. The large shaded part is the hill.Ⓐ The room inside the tree is shown in the middle of the tree.Ⓑ

2. Finish the cave. **(student preference)**
   - Make a dotted line that shows the room where the poachers kept the animals.
   - Show the entrance the poachers used.
   - Show some of the tunnels and rooms that Jill and the others did not see.Ⓒ
   - Write labels on the rooms.Ⓓ

3. To find out more about caves, go to the library and read some books about caves.

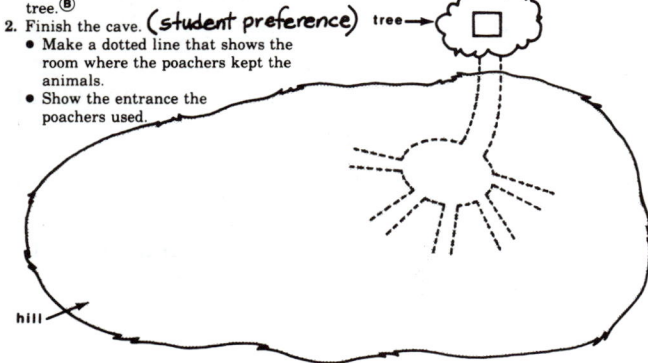

hill

tree →

Story Items

1. Below is a list of events that happened in Part 5. Tell when each event happened by writing **beginning, middle,** or **end** after the event.

   a. The poachers fell asleep.
   beginning

   b. Mr. Williams and Mombo walked into the cave. _end_

   c. The flamingos flew away.
   end

   d. Roger snuck past the sleeping men.
   beginning

   e. Jill and Tom opened the cages.
   middle

   f. The animals ran around the cave.
   middle

Map Skills

2. The map shows Africa and the United States.

   a. The arrows show the directions Jill and Tom will take to return to the United States. Which directions are those? _North and West_

   b. Write the name of the place shown by each dot.
   Kenya
   Kansas

   c. Fill in the boxes around the map.

North

West   _East_

South

SPECIAL PROJECT

1. *This special project can be scheduled during the reading period or during another part of the school day.*

2. We're going to do a project. For this project, we're going to work in pairs. *Assign pairs.*

3. Turn to page 6 in your workbook. *Check.*
   Call on individual students to read the project directions.

   Ⓐ Everybody, outline the entire hill with your finger. *Check.*

   Ⓑ Everybody, put your finger on that room. *Check.*

   Ⓒ Name some things that you're going to show.
   Idea: Tunnels, animals, rooms, cages.

   Ⓓ What are you going to write on the rooms? **Labels.**

   • Everybody, be sure to read through the story and find out about the tunnels and rooms in the cave. If you want, you can color the parts of the cave.

INDEPENDENT WORK

Do all the items in your skillbook and workbook for lesson 5. Start with part C in your skillbook.

WORKCHECK AND AWARDING POINTS

1. *Read the questions and answers for the skillbook and workbook.*

2. *Award points for independent work as follows:*

> *0 errors . . . . .6 points*
> *1 or 2 errors . . . . .4 points*
> *3, 4, or 5 errors . . . . .2 points*
> *More than 5 errors . . . . .0 points*

3. *Award bonus points for (a) correcting any missed items (2 points) or (b) getting all the items right (2 points).*

ANSWER KEY FOR SKILLBOOK

PART C

1. **a.** Three
   b. *Idea:* Fell asleep
2. Roger
3. **a.** *Idea:* Because she wanted him to knock the pole down
   b. Yes
   c. Roger
4. **a.** *Idea:* Opened the doors
   b. The flamingos
   c. Roger
   d. An elephant
5. *Idea:* Mr. Williams, Mombo, and three other men
6. Mr. Williams
7. flamingos
8. Kansas
9. *Idea:* She didn't want to

PART D

10. **a.** sober
    b. eager
    c. marvelous
    d. inquire
    e. game preserve

Lesson 6

Lesson 6

PART A   Word Lists

1	2	3	4
people	pressure	**Vocabulary words**	**Vocabulary words**
terrible	shriek	1. sober	1. in spite of
tinkle	whirlwinds	2. mass	2. attic
sprinkle	grownups	3. merrily	3. rust
	surroundings	4. wail	4. horizon
		5. cradle	5. mile

WORD PRACTICE AND VOCABULARY

EXERCISE 1   Word family

1. Everybody, find lesson 6, part A in your skillbook. *Wait.* Touch column 1. *Check.* All those words end with the sound **lll.** Touch under the first word. *Pause.* What word? *Signal.* **People.**
2. Next word. *Pause.* What word? *Signal.* **Terrible.**
3. *Repeat step 2 for each remaining word in column 1.*
4. *Repeat the words in column 1 until firm.*

EXERCISE 2   Word practice

1. Everybody, touch under the first word in column 2. *Pause.* What word? *Signal.* **Pressure.**
2. Next word. *Pause.* What word? *Signal.* **Shriek.**
3. *Repeat step 2 for each remaining word in column 2.*
4. *Repeat the words in column 2 until firm.*

EXERCISE 3   Vocabulary review

Task A
1. Everybody, touch column 3. *Check.* First you're going to read the words in column 3. Then we'll talk about what they mean.
2. Touch under the first word. *Pause.* What word? *Signal.* **Sober.**
3. Next word. *Pause.* What word? *Signal.* **Mass.**
4. *Repeat step 3 for each remaining word in column 3.*
5. *Repeat the words in column 3 until firm.*

Task B
You've learned the meaning for all these words. Word 1 is **sober.** *Call on a student.* What does **sober** mean? *Idea:* Serious.

Task C
Word 2 is **mass.** *Call on a student.* What is a **mass?** *Idea:* An area with no shape.

Task D
Word 3 is **merrily.** *Call on a student.* What does **merrily** mean? *Idea:* Happily.

Task E
Word 4 is **wail.** *Call on a student.* What does **wail** mean? *Idea:* Howl.

Task F
Word 5 is **cradle.** *Call on a student.* What is a **cradle?** *Idea:* A small bed.

EXERCISE 4   Vocabulary review

Task A
1. Everybody, touch column 4. *Check.* First you're going to read the words in column 4. Then we'll talk about what they mean.
2. Touch under the first line. *Pause.* What words? *Signal.* **In spite of.**
3. Next word. *Pause.* What word? *Signal.* **Attic.**
4. *Repeat step 3 for each remaining word in column 4.*
5. *Repeat the words in column 4 until firm.*

Task B
1. You've learned the meanings for all these words. The words in line 1 are **in spite of.** *Call on a student.* What's another way of saying **in spite of a problem?** *Idea:* Although there was a problem.
2. Everybody, what's another way of saying **In spite of trouble?** *Signal.* **Although there was trouble.**

Task C
Word 2 is **attic.** *Call on a student.* What's an **attic?** *Idea:* A storeroom near the top of a house.

Task D
Word 3 is **rust.** *Call on a student.* What is **rust?** *Idea:* Material that forms on iron and steel when they get wet.

Task E
Word 4 is **horizon.** *Call on a student.* What is the **horizon?** *Idea:* The line where the sky meets the land.

Task F
Word 5 is **mile.** Everybody, how many feet are in a **mile?** *Signal.* **5,280.**

EXERCISE 5   Adding l-y to words

1. Everybody, find part B.
2. You're going to add the letters **l-y** to those words. Some words already end in **y,** so you have to change the spelling of the words. The first row in part B shows how to change words that end in **y.**
3. That word is **happy.** Everybody, spell **happy.** *Signal.* **H-a-p-p-y.**
   Next to **happy** you can see how to spell that part when you add the letters **l-y.** H-a-p-p-i. Everybody, spell that part. *Signal.* **H-a-p-p-i.** Everybody, spell **happily.** *Signal.* **H-a-p-p-i-l-y.**
4. The next word is **angry.** How would you spell that part when you add the letters **l-y?** *Signal.* **A-n-g-r-i.**
   Everybody, spell **angrily.** *Signal.* **A-n-g-r-i-l-y.**
5. Later you'll write the words in part B. Remember to change words that already end in **y.**

Lesson 6

Life on the Prairie

Map 1 shows the main part of the United States as it looks today. There are forty-eight states in the main part. (A)

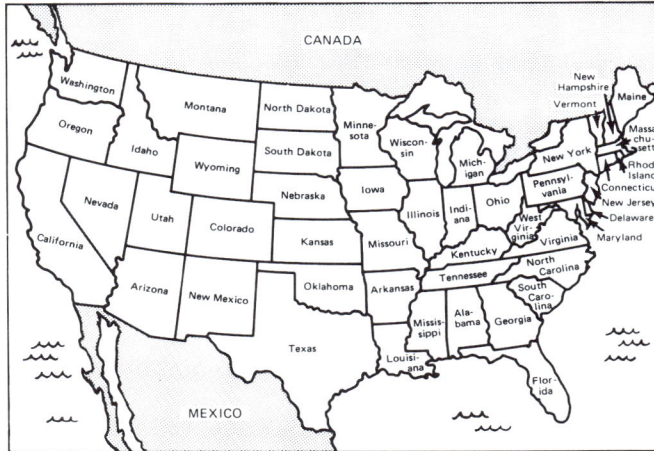

Map 2 shows the main part of the United States as it looked about one hundred years ago. The United States was still growing at that time, and it had only thirty-eight states. (B)

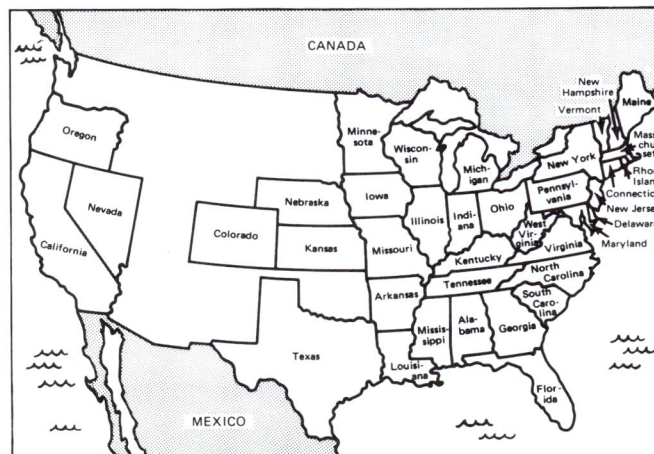

STORY READING

EXERCISE 6   Comprehension passage

1. Everybody, turn to page 20 in your textbook.
2. *Call on individual students to read three to five sentences.*
3. *Present the tasks specified for each circled letter.*
(A) How many states are there in the main part of the United States today? **Forty-eight.**
- Touch map 1. *Check.*
  The United States is made up of fifty states today, but two of them are not in the main part. What states are those?
  Hawaii and Alaska.
(B) Everybody, touch map 2.
- When did the United States look like map 2? **About one hundred years ago.**
- How many states were there then? **Thirty-eight.**
  You can see where there are no states.
- Compare map 1 with map 2 and name some states that are missing on map 2.
  Call on individual students.
- Remember, the United States was still growing one hundred years ago. Some parts of the United States were still very wild. Not many people lived in those wild parts.
  Call on a student to read from (B) to (C).

The famous novel that you will start reading today takes place in Kansas, about one hundred years ago.Ⓒ There were no electric lights. There were no cars. There were no washing machines, no radios, no telephones, and no televisions.Ⓓ

The state of Kansas was a great prairie.Ⓔ A prairie is a flat grassland with almost no trees.Ⓕ Many people came to Kansas to become farmers. But life was very hard for the early farmers in Kansas because the winters were cold and the summers were hot and dry.

In the summer, the hot sun would turn the green grass gray, and the land would dry up and crack.Ⓖ

During the late summer, there was very little water in Kansas because streams and ponds would dry up and the wind would blow great clouds of dust.Ⓗ

The Wizard of Oz
by L. Frank Baum

Ⓒ Everybody, touch the state of Kansas on map 2. *Check.* Turn back to page 22.
Call on a student to read from Ⓒ to Ⓓ.

Ⓓ Name some things that people didn't have one hundred years ago.
Call on individual students.

Ⓔ What was the state of Kansas?
A great prairie.

Ⓕ What is a prairie?
Idea: A flat grassland with no trees.

• If you lived on a prairie, would you have trouble building a wooden house? **Yes.**
Why? *Idea:* Because there are almost no trees.

Ⓖ Everybody, touch the picture. *Check.*

• The picture shows what the ground looks like when it dries up and cracks.

• Is that ground wet, or dry? **Dry.**

Ⓗ What would the wind blow in the late summer? **Great clouds of dust.**

• Where would the dust come from?
Idea: The dry land.

EXERCISE 7   Introduction to The Wizard of Oz

• Everybody, look at page 23 in your textbook.
Call on a student to read the title.

• What's the title of the novel that you're going to read? **The Wizard of Oz.**

• A long book that tells a story is called a novel. *The Wizard of Oz* is a novel. This novel was written in 1900. Many years after it was written, it came out as a movie called, "The Wizard of Oz." Raise your hand if you have seen that movie.

• There is also another movie that is based on this novel. Does anybody know the name of that movie? **The Wiz.**
The novel is a little different from the movies and I think you will like the novel even if you have seen the movies.

• *Call on a student to read the author's name.*

• That is the name of the man who wrote the novel. A person who writes novels is called an author.

• Who is the author of this novel?
L. Frank Baum.
Remember his name. Now turn the page.

CHAPTER 1
Kansas(A)

Dorothy lived in the middle of the great Kansas prairies, with Uncle Henry, who was a farmer, and Aunt Em, who was Uncle Henry's wife.(B) Their house was small, for the lumber to build it had to be carried by wagon many miles.(C) There were four walls, a floor and a roof, which made one room.(D) This room contained a rusty-looking cooking stove, a cupboard for the dishes, a table, four chairs and the beds. Uncle Henry and Aunt Em had a big bed in one corner and Dorothy a little bed in another corner.(E) ★2 ERRORS★ There was no attic at all, and no cellar—except a small hole, dug in the ground, called a cyclone cellar.(F) The family could go in the cellar in case one of those great whirlwinds arose, mighty enough to crush any building in its path.(G) The cellar was reached by a trapdoor in the middle of the floor. A ladder inside led down into a small, dark hole.(H)

When Dorothy stood in the doorway and looked outside, she could see nothing but the great, gray prairie on every side. No trees or houses could be seen on the flat country that reached the edge of the sky in all directions.(I)

The sun had baked the plowed land

EXERCISE 8   Decoding and comprehension

1. *Call on a student.* What's the error limit for this chapter? **6 errors.**
2. *Call on individual students to read.*
3. *After the group reads to the 2-error sign without making more than 2 errors, reread the first part aloud and present the comprehension tasks.*
4. *After you have completed the first part, call on individual students to read. Present the comprehension tasks.*

EXERCISE 9   Comprehension tasks

(A) That is the title of the first chapter of the novel. What's the title? **Kansas.**

● So what is the main thing this chapter is going to tell about? **Kansas.**

(B) Where did Dorothy live?
Idea: In the middle of the great Kansas prairies.

● Name the two people she lived with.
Uncle Henry and Aunt Em.

(C) Why was their house small?
Idea: Because the lumber to build it had to be carried by wagon many miles.

● What does lumber come from? *Idea:* Trees.

● Why didn't they just go outside and cut down trees for their house? *Idea:* Because there were no trees.

(D) How many rooms did the house have? **One.**
(E) Did they have much furniture? **No.**

● How many beds did they have? **Two.**

● Who slept in the big bed?
Uncle Henry and Aunt Em.

● Where did Dorothy sleep? *Idea:* In a little bed.

(F) What was the hole called? **A cyclone cellar.**

● What do you think they used the hole for?
Idea: To hide from cyclones.

(G) What is another name for that great whirlwind? **Cyclone.**

(H) Where was the trapdoor?
In the middle of the floor.

● How would you climb down into the cellar after you opened the trapdoor?
Idea: On a ladder.

(I) Were there any houses or trees? **No.**

● Everybody, look at the picture. The picture shows what you have just been reading about. The horizon is the line where the land meets the sky. Run your finger along the horizon. *Check.*

● Are there any houses or trees? **No.**

● What is the funny cloud on the left side of the picture? **A cyclone.**

● Who is standing in the doorway of the house? **Dorothy.**

● Who is standing in the field?
Uncle Henry and Aunt Em.

into a gray mass, with little cracks running through it. Not even the grass was green, for the sun had burned the tops of the grass blades until they were the same gray color as the land. Once, the house had been painted white, but the sun blistered the paint and the rains washed it away, and now the house was as dull and gray as everything else. Ⓙ

When Aunt Em came there to live, she was young and pretty. The sun and wind had changed her, too. They had taken the sparkle from her eyes and left them a sober gray. They had taken the red from her cheeks and lips, and they were gray also. She was thin and she never smiled, now. Ⓚ ★6 ERRORS★

Dorothy was an orphan, which was why she had come to live with her aunt and uncle.

At first, Aunt Em had been so startled by Dorothy's laughter that she would scream and press her hand upon her heart whenever Dorothy laughed.

Aunt Em was still amazed that Dorothy could find anything to laugh about.

Uncle Henry never laughed. He worked hard from morning till night and did not know what joy was. He was gray also, from his long beard to his rough boots. He looked stern and he rarely spoke.

It was Toto that made Dorothy laugh, and kept her from growing as gray as her surroundings. Toto was not gray. He was a little black dog, with long silky hair and small black eyes that twinkled merrily on either side of his funny, small nose. Toto played all day long, and Dorothy played with him, and loved him dearly.

Today, however, Dorothy and Toto were not playing. Uncle Henry sat on the doorstep and looked anxiously at the sky, which was even grayer than usual. Dorothy stood in the door with Toto in her arms, and looked at the sky too. Aunt Em was washing the dishes.

Ⓙ What color is the house now? Gray.
- Had the house always been gray? **No.**
- Name two things that made the house's color change. *Ideas:* The sun blistered the paint; the rain washed the paint away.
- What other things in the story are gray? *Call on individual students. Responses:* prairies; grass; land

Ⓚ What color were Aunt Em's eyes, cheeks, and lips now? **Gray.**
- Were they always that color? **No.**
- What made Aunt Em change? *Ideas:* The sun and wind; her hard life.
- Read the rest of the chapter to yourselves and be ready to answer some questions.

After all students have finished reading:
- What is an orphan? *Idea:* A child without any parents.
- How did Aunt Em feel when Dorothy laughed? *Idea:* Startled.
- Was Aunt Em used to hearing laughter? **No.**
- Everybody, show me a stern expression. *Check.* That's how Uncle Henry looked all the time.
- What kept Dorothy from growing as gray as her surrounding? **Toto.**
- What color was Toto? **Black.**
- What color was the sky? **Grayer than usual.**
- Uncle Henry was looking at the sky anxiously. What do you think he was worried about? *Idea:* A cyclone; a storm.

Award 4 points or have the students reread to the error limit sign.

EXERCISE 10   Writing assignment

1. Everybody, find lesson 6, part E in your skillbook. *Wait.*
2. Follow along as I read part E aloud: Write a paragraph that describes what Dorothy's house looks like. Be sure the paragraph answers the following questions:
   - What is the house made of?
   - What color is the house?
   - How many rooms does the house have?
   - What furniture does the house have?
3. *Call on several students to answer the first question.*
4. *Repeat step 3 with each remaining question.*
5. When you write your paragraph about Dorothy's house, make sure you answer all the questions. Remember, you have to write at least four sentences.

ANSWER KEY FOR WORKBOOK

Story Items

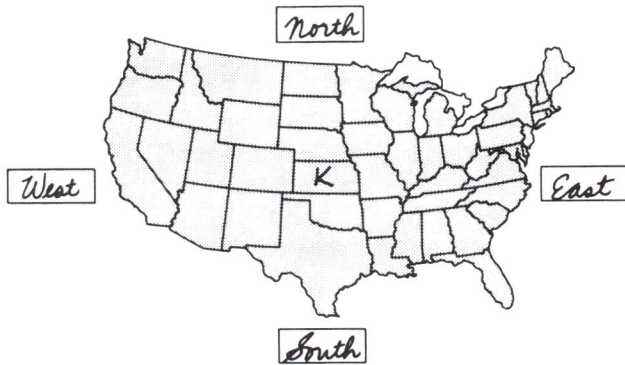

1. **a.** Fill in the boxes around the map.
   b. Put a **K** on the state where Dorothy lived.
   c. What is the name of that state?

   Kansas

2. Many of the things that Dorothy saw in Kansas were gray. Write **gray** next to the things that were gray. Write **not gray** next to the things that were not gray.

   a. The prairie _gray_

   b. Aunt Em _gray_

   c. Toto _not gray_

   d. The house _gray_

   e. The sky _gray_

   f. The grass _gray_

   g. Uncle Henry _gray_

3. Chapter 1 tells about four characters. Name those characters.

   a. _Dorothy_
   b. _Uncle Henry_
   c. _Aunt Em_
   d. _Toto_

4. Name the character that each sentence tells about.
   a. This character never laughed.

   Uncle Henry

   b. This character was thin and she never smiled. _Aunt Em_

   c. This character was an orphan.

   Dorothy

   d. This character laughed when she played with her dog.

   Dorothy

   e. This character had a long beard and rough boots.

   Uncle Henry

   f. This character had been changed by the sun and the wind.

   Aunt Em

INDEPENDENT WORK

Do all the items in your skillbook and workbook for lesson 6.

WORKCHECK AND AWARDING POINTS

1. *Read the questions and answers for the skillbook and workbook.*
2. *Award points for independent work as follows:*

0 errors	6 points
2 errors	4 points
3, 4, or 5 errors	2 points
5 or more errors	0 points

3. *Award bonus points as follows:*

Correcting missed item or getting all items right	2 points
Doing the writing assignment acceptably	2 points

ANSWER KEY FOR SKILLBOOK

PART B

1. angrily
2. easily
3. tightly
4. luckily
5. peacefully
6. entirely
7. merrily

PART C

8. **a.** The Wizard of Oz
   b. L. Frank Baum
   c. Kansas
   d. *Idea:* Kansas
9. *Idea:* Because the lumber to build it had to be carried many miles
10. *Idea:* Cyclone cellar
11. **a.** No
    b. *Idea:* Because the streams and ponds were dry
12. *Any four:* Electric lights; cars; washing machines; radios; telephones; televisions; etc.
13. **a.** Thirty-eight
    b. *Idea:* Because the weather was so dry

PART D

14. **a.** party
    b. move
    c. running
    d. prepared

Lesson 7

Lesson 7

PART A   Word Lists

1	2
accidents	bowed
dismally	danger
gorgeous	hollow
sorceress	
magician	
deaf	

3 Vocabulary words	4 Vocabulary words
1. for	1. deaf
2. prairie	2. ripples
3. cyclone	3. brilliant
4. orphan	4. bondage
5. rubies	5. dismally

PART B
Vocabulary Sentences

1. The wind shrieked so loudly that she nearly became <u>deaf</u>.
   - happy   • unable to hear
   - blind
2. The wind made waves and <u>ripples</u> in the grass.
   - small waves   • bricks
   - dandelions
3. The <u>brilliant</u> feathers of the birds were every color you could imagine.
   - gray   • bright and colorful
   - unhappy
4. We are grateful because you set us free from <u>bondage</u>.
   - slavery   • riches   • having fun
5. The lonely dog put his cold little nose into her face and whined <u>dismally</u>.
   - sadly   • eagerly   • rapidly

WORD PRACTICE AND VOCABULARY

EXERCISE 1   Word practice

1. Everybody, find lesson 7, part A in your skillbook. *Wait.* Touch column 1. *Check.*
   The words in column 1 are hard words that will be in your reading stories.
2. Touch under the first word. *Check.*
   The first word is **accidents.**
   What word? *Signal.* **Accidents.**
3. Next word. *Pause.* That word is **dismally.**
   What word? *Signal.* **Dismally.**
4. *Repeat step 3 for each remaining word in column 1.*
5. Now let's see if you remember all those words. Touch under the first word in column 1. *Pause.*
   What word? *Signal.* **Accidents.**
6. Next word. *Pause.* What word? *Signal.* **Dismally.**
7. *Repeat step 6 for each remaining word in column 1.*
8. *Repeat the words in column 1 until firm.*

EXERCISE 2   Word practice

1. Everybody, touch under the first word in column 2, but don't read it out loud. You can say that spelling as two different words.
2. One word rhymes with **showed.** Say that word. Get ready. *Signal.* **Bowed.**
   Something that is bent is bowed. The other word rhymes with **loud.** Say that word. Get ready. *Signal.* **Bowed.**
   When you bow, you bend politely from the waist.
3. *Repeat step 2 until firm.*
4. Both those words are spelled the same way: **b-o-w-e-d.**
5. Next word. *Pause.* What word? *Signal.* **Danger.**
6. *Repeat step 5 for **hollow**.*
7. *Repeat steps 2–5 until firm.*

EXERCISE 3   Vocabulary development

Task A

1. Everybody, touch column 3. *Check.*
   First you're going to read the words in column 3. Then we'll talk about what they mean.
2. Touch under the first word. *Pause.*
   What word? *Signal.* **For.**
3. Next word. *Pause.*
   What word? *Signal.* **Prairie.**
4. *Repeat step 3 for each remaining word in column 3.*
5. *Repeat the words in column 3 until firm.*

Task B

1. Now let's talk about what those words mean. Word 1 is **for.** Sometimes the word **for** is used the same way as the word **because.** Here's another way of saying **They stopped walking because they were tired: They stopped walking for they were tired.**
2. Everybody, what's another way of saying **They stopped walking because they were tired?** *Signal.* **They stopped walking for they were tired.**
3. Everybody, what's another way of saying **They laughed because they were happy?** *Signal.* **They laughed for they were happy.**
4. What's another way of saying **Dorothy ran because the storm was coming?** *Signal.* **Dorothy ran for the storm was coming.**
5. *Repeat steps 2–4 until firm.*

Task C

Word 2 is **prairie.** *Call on a student.*
What's a **prairie?** *Idea:* A grassland with few trees.

Task D

Word 3 is **cyclone.** *Call on a student.*
What's a **cyclone?** *Idea:* A strong wind that spins around and around.

Task E

Word 4 is **orphan.** *Call on a student.*
What's an **orphan?** *Idea:* Someone without any parents.

Task F

1. Word 5 is **rubies. Rubies** are expensive jewels that are red.
2. Everybody, tell me the name of the jewels that are red. *Signal.* **Rubies.**

EXERCISE 4   Vocabulary from context

Task A

1. Everybody, touch column 4. *Check.*
   The words in that column are words that you'll read in sentences.
2. Touch under the first word. *Pause.*
   What word? *Signal.* **Deaf.**
3. Next word. *Pause.* What word? *Signal.* **Ripples.**
4. *Repeat step 4 for each remaining word in column 4.*
5. *Repeat the words in column 4 until firm.*

Task B

1. Everybody, find part B.
   First we'll read each sentence and then we'll figure out what the underlined words could mean.
2. *Call on a student.* Read sentence 1 and the choices. *Wait.*
   Everybody, which is the best choice? *Signal.* **Unable to hear.**
3. *Repeat step 2 for sentences 2–5.*
   Answer key: Sentence 2. **Small waves.**
   Sentence 3. **Bright and colorful.**
   Sentence 4. **Slavery.**
   Sentence 5. **Sadly.**

EXERCISE 5   Adding **l-y** to words

1. Everybody, find part C.
2. Touch the first word in part C. *Pause.*
   The word is **hungry.** Everybody, how do you spell that part when you add the letters **l-y?**
   Signal. **H-u-n-g-r-i.** Everybody spell **hungrily.**
   Signal. **H-u-n-g-r-i-l-y.**
3. Everybody, touch the next word. *Pause.*
   That word is **angry.** Everybody, how do you spell that part when you add the letters **l-y?**
   Signal. **A-n-g-r-i.** Everybody, spell **angrily.**
   Signal. **A-n-g-r-i-l-y.**
4. Later you'll write the words in part C.

Lesson 7

Cyclones

The chapter that you will read today tells about a cyclone. Here are some facts about cyclones.

A cyclone is a strong wind that spins around and around.Ⓐ

One kind of cyclone looks like a giant funnel. This kind of cyclone is also called a tornado or a twister.Ⓑ The cyclone moves forward quickly, and destroys almost everything in its path.

The wind that forms the cyclone may spin as fast as three hundred miles an hour.Ⓒ

The middle of the cyclone is called the eye of the cyclone.Ⓓ Most eyes are narrow, but some are wider than a house. The air in the eye is very still, but it is surrounded by the spinning wind.Ⓔ The picture below shows the parts of a cyclone.Ⓕ

26   Lesson 7   Textbook

CHAPTER 2
The CycloneⒶ

Uncle Henry and Dorothy kept on looking at the sky. After a while, they heard a low wailing wind from the north. Uncle Henry and Dorothy could see where the long grass bent in waves before the coming storm.Ⓑ There now came a sharp whistling from the south. As they turned their eyes that way they saw ripples in the grass coming from that direction also.Ⓒ

Suddenly Uncle Henry stood up.

"There's a cyclone coming, Em," he called to his wife. "I'll go look after the animals." Then he ran towards the sheds where the cows and horses were kept.

★2 ERRORS★

Aunt Em dropped her work and came to the door. One glance told her of the danger close at hand.

"Quick, Dorothy!" she screamed. "Run for the cellar!"

Toto jumped out of Dorothy's arms and hid under the bed, and the girl went after him. Aunt Em was badly frightened. She threw open the trapdoor

in the floor and climbed down the ladder into the small, dark hole. Dorothy caught Toto at last, and started to follow her aunt. When she was halfway across the room there came a great shriek from the wind, and the house shook so hard that Dorothy lost her footing and sat down suddenly on the floor.

Then a strange thing happened.

The house whirled around two or three times and rose slowly through the air. Dorothy felt as if she were going up in a balloon.Ⓓ

The north and south winds met where the house stood, and made it the exact center of the cyclone. In the middle of a cyclone the air is generally still, but the great pressure of the wind on every side of the house raised it up higher and higher, until the house was at the very top of the cyclone. The house stayed at the top, and then it was carried miles and miles away as easily as you could carry a feather.Ⓔ

It became very dark, and the wind

Lesson 7   Textbook   **27**

EXERCISE 6   Comprehension passage

1. Everybody, turn to page 26 in your textbook.
2. *Call on individual students to read three to five sentences.*
3. *Present the tasks specified for each circled letter.*
Ⓐ What does the wind do? **Spins around and around.**
Ⓑ Tell me the other names for this kind of cyclone. **Tornado and twister.**
Ⓒ How fast can the spinning wind go? *Idea:* As fast as 300 miles an hour.
Ⓓ Where is the eye? **In the middle of the cyclone.**
Ⓔ What is the air like inside the eye? **Very still.**
● What is that air surrounded by? **The spinning wind.**
Ⓕ Everybody, look at the picture. Touch the part where the air is still. *Check.*
● What's that part called? **The eye.**
● Everybody, touch the part where the wind is spinning. *Check.* How fast can those winds move? *Idea:* As fast as 300 miles an hour.
● Everybody, touch the path that the cylcone made. *Check.* You can see that the cyclone has torn up a lot of things.
● Now move your finger in the direction the cyclone is moving. *Check.*
● What will happen to things in that direction? *Idea:* They will get torn up.

EXERCISE 7   Decoding

1. Everybody, look at page 27 in your textbook. *Wait. Call on a student.* What's the error limit for this chapter? **7 errors.**
2. *Call on individual students to read.*
3. *After the group reads to the 2-error sign without making more than 2 errors, reread the first part aloud and present the comprehension tasks.*
4. *After you have completed the first part, call on individual students to read. Present the comprehension tasks.*

EXERCISE 8   Comprehension tasks

Ⓐ What do you think this chapter is going to be about? *Idea:* A cyclone.
Ⓑ Which direction was the wind coming from? **The north.**
● What was making the long grass bend in waves? *Idea:* The wind.
Ⓒ One wind was coming from the north. Which direction was another wind coming from? **The south.**

36   Lesson 7

howled horribly, but Dorothy found she was riding quite easily. After the first few whirls around, and one other time when the house tipped badly, she felt as if she were being rocked gently, like a baby in a cradle.

Toto did not like it. He ran about the room, here and there, barking loudly. But Dorothy sat quite still on the floor and waited to see what would happen.

Once Toto got too near the open trapdoor, and fell in; and at first Dorothy thought she had lost him. But soon she saw one of his ears sticking up through the hole, for the strong pressure of the air was keeping him up. (F)

★7 ERRORS★

Dorothy crept to the hole, caught Toto, and dragged him into the room again. Then she closed the trapdoor so that no more accidents could happen.

Hour after hour passed away, and slowly Dorothy got over her fright. She still felt quite lonely, and the wind shrieked so loudly that she nearly became deaf. At first she had wondered if she would be smashed to pieces when the house fell again. But as the hours passed and nothing terrible happened, she stopped worrying and decided to wait calmly and see what would happen. At last she crawled over the swaying floor to her bed, and lay down upon it. Toto followed and lay down beside her.

In spite of the swaying of the house and the wailing of the wind, Dorothy soon closed her eyes and fell fast asleep.

(D) Listen to that part again and get ready to answer some questions. *Read from* (C) *to* (D).

- Why didn't Dorothy go into the cellar right away? *Idea:* Because she went after Toto.
- Did Dorothy make it to the cellar? **No.**
- Where was she when the cyclone hit the house? *Idea:* Halfway across the room.
- What does that mean: **She lost her footing?** *Idea:* She fell down.
- What did the house do first? *Idea:* It shook.
- What did the house do next? *Idea:* It whirled around and rose through the air.

(E) What is the air like in the middle of a cyclone? *Idea:* Still.

- To which part of the cyclone did the house move? *Idea:* To the very top.
- How far did the cyclone carry the house? *Idea:* Miles and miles.

(F) There was an open trapdoor in the middle of the room. What was below that trapdoor? *Idea:* The cyclone.

- When Toto fell through the trapdoor did he fall back to the ground? **No.**
- What kept him up? *Idea:* The strong pressure of the air.
- Read the rest of the chapter to yourselves and be ready to answer some questions.

After all students have finished reading:

- How long did the cyclone keep the house in the air? *Idea:* Hours.
- Dorothy was frightened for a while. How did she feel after that? *Idea:* Quite lonely.
- What made Dorothy almost become deaf? *Idea:* The shrieking wind.
- Why did Dorothy have to crawl across the room? *Idea:* Because the floor was swaying.
- The story says that the floor was swaying. Everybody, show me with your hand how the floor did that. *Check.*
- What did Dorothy do at the end of this chapter? *Idea:* Fell asleep.
- Dorothy fell asleep in spite of two things. What were those two things? *Idea:* The swaying of the house and the wailing of the wind.

Award 4 points or have the students reread to the error limit sign.

EXERCISE 9 Writing assignment

1. I'm going to read some of the best writing assignments from the last lesson.
   Read several good assignments aloud and explain what is good about them.
2. Now find lesson 7, part F in your skillbook. *Wait.*
3. Follow along as I read part F aloud: Write a paragraph about the brave things Dorothy did. Be sure the paragraph answers the following questions:
   - What did Dorothy do when Toto ran away?
   - How did Dorothy act while the house was spinning around?
   - What did Dorothy do when Toto fell through the hole?
4. *Call on several students to answer the first question.*
5. *Repeat step 4 with each remaining question.*
6. When you write your paragraph, make sure you answer all the questions. Remember, you have to write at least four sentences.

ANSWER KEY FOR WORKBOOK

Story Items

1. **a.** Draw an arrow on the map to show which way the cyclone is moving.
   b. Put a **C** on the spinning wind.
   c. How fast can that wind spin?
   300 miles an hour
   d. Put an **E** on the eye of the cyclone.
   e. What is the air like in the eye?
   Idea: still
   f. Put a **P** on the cyclone's path.

2. In Chapter 2, three events occurred before the cyclone hit the house.
   Put a **1** by the event that occurred **first.**
   Put a **2** by the event that occurred **next.**
   Put a **3** by the event that occurred **last.**
   _2_ Toto jumped out of Dorothy's arms.
   _1_ Uncle Henry ran to the shed.
   _3_ The wind shrieked and Dorothy sat on the floor.

3. What are two other names for cyclones?
   a. *tornado*
   b. *twister*
4. Chapter 2 tells about four characters. Name those characters.
   a. *Dorothy*
   b. *Uncle Henry*
   c. *Aunt Em*
   d. *Toto*

5. Name the character that each sentence tells about:
   a. This character closed her eyes and fell asleep.
   Dorothy
   b. This character went to look after the animals.
   Uncle Henry
   c. This character said, "Run for the cellar!"
   Aunt Em
   d. This character felt as if she were going up in a balloon.
   Dorothy

INDEPENDENT WORK

Do all the items in your skillbook and workbook for lesson 7.

WORKCHECK AND AWARDING POINTS

1. *Read the questions and answers for the skillbook and workbook.*
2. *Award points for independent work as follows:*

0 errors . . . . .6 points
2 errors . . . . .4 points
3, 4, or 5 errors . . . . .2 points
5 or more errors . . . . .0 points

3. *Award bonus points as follows:*

Correcting missed items or getting all items right . . . . .2 points
Doing the writing assignment acceptably . . . . .2 points

ANSWER KEY FOR SKILLBOOK

PART C

1. angrily
2. carefully
3. heartily
4. prettily
5. certainly
6. ordinarily
7. clearly

PART D

8. **a.** The Wizard of Oz
   b. L. Frank Baum
   c. The Cyclone
   d. *Idea:* A cyclone
9. Yes
10. a baby in a cradle
11. His ear
12. *Idea:* To prevent accidents
13. *Idea:* She would be smashed to pieces
14. wait calmly and see what would happen
15. **a.** To her bed
    b. *Idea:* Slept

PART E

16. **a.** lantern
    b. snarling
    c. budge
    d. mile

Lesson 8

Lesson 8

PART A   Word Lists

1	2	3
wizard	bowed	grownups
messenger	magician	polished
gracious	jolt	Munchkins
civilized	handkerchief	paused
leather	sunbonnet	magic
balanced		magical
calmly		

4
Vocabulary words
1. ripples
2. deaf
3. dismally
4. brilliant
5. bondage
6. inquired

5
Vocabulary words
1. cheering
2. balanced
3. for
4. rubies
5. emeralds
6. diamonds

6
Vocabulary words
1. messenger
2. civilized
3. gorgeous
4. brook
5. sprinkled
6. sorceress

PART B
Vocabulary Sentences

1. A <u>messenger</u> came to me and brought me the news.
   - thought
   - person who delivers messages
   - person who can't move
2. There are no witches in the great <u>civilized</u> countries.
   - well-mannered   • make-believe
   - unimportant
3. Everything was beautiful, especially the <u>gorgeous</u> flowers.
   - very pretty   • very loud
   - very ugly
4. The <u>brook</u> was filled with bubbling, sparkling water that rushed along.
   - small croak   • small stream
   - small puddle
5. Her white dress was <u>sprinkled</u> with bright little stars.
   - dotted   • blackened   • rough
6. She was such a powerful witch that people said she was the greatest <u>sorceress</u> in the land.
   - tree   • magician   • man

WORD PRACTICE AND VOCABULARY

EXERCISE 1   Word practice

1. Everybody, find lesson 8, part A in your skillbook. *Wait.* Touch column 1. *Check.* The words in column 1 are hard words that will be in your reading stories.
2. Touch under the first word. *Check.* The first word is **wizard.** What word? *Signal.* **Wizard.**
3. Next word. *Pause.* That word is **messenger.** What word? *Signal.* **Messenger.**
4. *Repeat step 3 for each remaining word in column 1.*
5. Now let's see if you remember all those words. Touch under the first word in column 1. *Pause.* What word? *Signal.* **Wizard.**
6. Next word. *Pause.* What word? *Signal.* **Messenger.**
7. *Repeat step 6 for each remaining word in column 1.*
8. *Repeat the words in column 1 until firm.*

EXERCISE 2   Word practice

1. Everybody, touch under the first word in column 2, but don't read it out loud. You can say that spelling as two different words.
2. One word rhymes with **showed.** Say that word. Get ready. *Signal.* **Bowed.** The other word rhymes with **loud.** Say that word. Get ready. *Signal.* **Bowed.**
3. *Repeat step 2 until firm.*
4. Both those words are spelled the same way: **b-o-w-e-d.**
5. Next word. *Pause.* What word? *Signal.* **Magician.**
6. *Repeat step 5 for each remaining word in column 2.*
7. *Repeat steps 2–5 until firm.*

EXERCISE 3   Word practice

1. Everybody, touch under the first word in column 3. What word? *Signal.* **Grownups.**
2. Next word. *Pause.* What word? *Signal.* **Polished.**
3. *Repeat step 2 for each remaining word in column 3.*
4. *Repeat the words in column 3 until firm.*

EXERCISE 4   Vocabulary review

Task A

1. Everybody, touch column 4. *Check.* First you're going to read the words in column 4. Then we'll talk about what they mean.
2. Touch under the first word. *Pause.* What word? *Signal.* **Ripples.**
3. Next word. *Pause.* What word? *Signal.* **Deaf.**
4. *Repeat step 3 for each remaining word in column 4.*
5. *Repeat the words in column 4 until firm.*

Task B

You've learned the meanings for all these words. Word 1 is **ripples.** *Call on a student.* What are **ripples?** *Idea:* Small waves.

Task C

Word 2 is **deaf.** *Call on a student.* What does **deaf** mean? *Idea:* Unable to hear.

Task D

Word 3 is **dismally.** *Call on a student.* What does **dismally** mean? *Idea:* Sadly.

Task E

Word 4 is **brilliant.** *Call on a student.* What does **brilliant** mean? *Idea:* Colorful and bright.

Task F

Word 5 is **bondage.** *Call on a student.* What does **bondage** mean? *Idea:* Slavery.

Task G

Word 6 is **inquired.** *Call on a student.* What does **inquired** mean? *Idea:* Asked.

Lesson 8

PART A Word Lists

1	2	3
wizard	bowed	grownups
messenger	magician	polished
gracious	jolt	Munchkins
civilized	handkerchief	paused
leather	sunbonnet	magic
balanced		magical
calmly		

4
Vocabulary words
1. ripples
2. deaf
3. dismally
4. brilliant
5. bondage
6. inquired

5
Vocabulary words
1. cheering
2. balanced
3. for
4. rubies
5. emeralds
6. diamonds

6
Vocabulary words
1. messenger
2. civilized
3. gorgeous
4. brook
5. sprinkled
6. sorceress

PART B
Vocabulary Sentences

1. A <u>messenger</u> came to me and brought me the news.
   - thought
   - person who delivers messages
   - person who can't move
2. There are no witches in the great <u>civilized</u> countries.
   - well-mannered
   - make-believe
   - unimportant
3. Everything was beautiful, especially the <u>gorgeous</u> flowers.
   - very pretty
   - very loud
   - very ugly
4. The <u>brook</u> was filled with bubbling, sparkling water that rushed along.
   - small croak
   - small stream
   - small puddle
5. Her white dress was <u>sprinkled</u> with bright little stars.
   - dotted
   - blackened
   - rough
6. She was such a powerful witch that people said she was the greatest <u>sorceress</u> in the land.
   - tree
   - magician
   - man

EXERCISE 5 Vocabulary development

Task A
1. Everybody touch column 5. *Check.*
   First you're going to read the words in column 5. Then we'll talk about what they mean.
2. Touch under the first word. *Pause.*
   What word? *Signal.* **Cheering.**
3. Next word. *Pause.* What word? *Signal.*
   Balanced.
4. *Repeat step 3 for each remaining word in column 5.*
5. *Repeat the words in column 5 until firm.*

Task B
Now let's talk about what those words mean.
Word 1 is **cheering.** When something is **cheering,** it makes you feel good.

Task C
Word 2 is **balanced.** When something is **balanced,** it won't tip over.

Task D
Word 3 is **for.** You already learned what **for** means. Everybody, what's another word that means **for?** *Signal.* **Because.**

Task E
1. Word 4 is **rubies,** word 5 is **emeralds,** and word 6 is **diamonds.**
2. Everybody, what color are rubies? *Signal.* **Red.**
   What color are **emeralds?** *Signal.* **Green.**
   What color are **diamonds?** *Signal.* **Clear.**

EXERCISE 6 Vocabulary from context

Task A
1. Everybody, touch column 6. *Check.*
   The words in that column are words that you'll read in sentences.
2. Touch under the first word. *Pause.*
   What word? *Signal.* **Messenger.**
3. Next word. *Pause.* What word? *Signal.* **Civilized.**
4. *Repeat step 3 for each remaining word in column 6.*
5. *Repeat the words in column 6 until firm.*

Task B
1. Everybody, find part B.
   First we'll read each sentence and then we'll figure out what the underlined words could mean.
2. *Call on a student.* Read sentence 1 and the choices. *Wait.*
   Everybody, which is the best choice? *Signal.*
   Person who delivers messages.
3. *Repeat step 2 for sentences 2–6.*
   Answer key: Sentence 2. **Well-mannered.**
   Sentence 3. **Very pretty.**
   Sentence 4. **Small stream.**
   Sentence 5. **Dotted.**
   Sentence 6. **Magician.**

EXERCISE 7 Adding l-y to words
1. Everybody, find part C.
2. Later, you'll add the letters **ly** to each word. But remember, you have to change the spelling of words if they end in a certain letter.
3. Everybody, what letter? *Signal.* **Y.**
   And what do you change the letter into?
   Signal. **I.**
4. *Repeat step 3 until firm.*

Lesson 8

CHAPTER 3
The Munchkins⒜

A sudden jolt awakened Dorothy. It was so sudden that it might have hurt her if she had not been lying on the soft bed.⒝ The jolt made her catch her breath and wonder what had happened. Toto put his cold little nose into her face and whined dismally. Dorothy sat up and noticed that the house was not moving; nor was it dark, for bright sunshine came in at the window, filling the little room.⒞ She sprang from her bed and with Toto at her heels ran and opened the door. ★2 ERRORS★

The girl looked around and gave a cry of amazement. Her eyes grew bigger and bigger at the wonderful sights she saw.⒟

The cyclone had set the house down in a country of marvelous beauty. There were lovely patches of green grass all around, with large trees bearing rich fruits. Gorgeous flowers were everywhere, and birds with brilliant feathers sang and fluttered in the trees and bushes. A small brook was close by, rushing and sparkling along between green banks. The sound of the brook was very cheering to the girl who had lived so long on the dry, gray prairies.⒠

While Dorothy stood looking eagerly at the beautiful sights, she noticed a group of strange people coming toward her. They were not as big as the grownups Dorothy was used to, but neither were they very small. In fact, they seemed about as tall as Dorothy, who was tall for her age, although they looked many years older.⒡

The group consisted of three men and one woman, and all were oddly dressed. They wore round hats that rose to a small point a foot above their heads. Little bells around the hat brims tinkled sweetly when the people moved. The hats of the men were blue. The woman's hat was white, and she wore a white gown that was sprinkled with little stars that glistened in the sun like diamonds. The men were dressed in blue, of the same shade as their hats, and wore well-polished boots with blue bands at the tops. The men, Dorothy thought, were about as old as Uncle Henry, for two of them had beards. But the woman looked much older: her face was covered with wrinkles, her hair was nearly white, and she walked rather stiffly.⒢

30   Lesson 8   Textbook

Lesson 8   Textbook   **31**

STORY READING

EXERCISE 8   Decoding

1. Everybody, turn to page 30 in your textbook. *Wait.Call on a student.* What's the error limit for this chapter?
2. *Call on individual students to read.*
3. *After the group reads to the 2-error sign without making more than 2 errors, reread the first part aloud and present the comprehension tasks.*
4. *After you have completed the first part, call on individual students to read. Present the comprehension tasks.*

EXERCISE 9   Comprehension tasks

Ⓐ What do you think this chapter is going to be about? *Idea:* The Munchkins.
● What was Dorothy doing at the end of the last chapter? **Sleeping.**
● Where was Dorothy's house? *Idea:* At the top of the cyclone.
Ⓑ What do you think made that jolt? *Idea:* The house landing.
Ⓒ Was the house moving any more? **No.**
● Why do you think the house stopped moving? *Idea:* Because it landed.
● Bright sunshine was coming in at the window. So could the house still be inside the cyclone? **No.**
● Why not? *Idea:* Because the sun wouldn't shine through the cyclone.
Ⓓ What do you think she saw? *Idea:* Student preference.
Ⓔ Listen to that part again and get ready to answer some questions. *Read from* Ⓓ *to* Ⓔ.
● What was the color of things in Kansas? **Gray.**
● Is that a happy color or a sad color? **A sad color.**
● What color did Dorothy see now? **Green.**
● Is that a happy color or a sad color? **A happy color.**
Ⓕ What were the strange people doing? *Idea:* Coming toward Dorothy.
● How big were these people? *Idea:* About as tall as Dorothy.
Ⓖ Everybody, look at the picture on the next page.
● Are those people dressed oddly? **Yes.**
● How many men are there? **Three.**
● How many women are there, other than Dorothy? **One.**
● What do the older people have around their hat brims? **Little bells.**
● What does the woman have on her dress? **Little stars.**

When these people came near the house where Dorothy was standing in the doorway, they paused and whispered among themselves. They acted as if they were afraid to come closer. But the old woman walked up to Dorothy, made a low bow and said, in a sweet voice, "You are welcome, most noble Sorceress, to the Land of the Munchkins. We are grateful to you for having killed the Wicked Witch of the East, and for setting our people free from bondage." (H)

Dorothy listened to this speech with wonder. What could the woman possibly mean by calling her a sorceress, and saying that she had killed the Wicked Witch of the East? Dorothy was a harmless little girl, who had been carried by a cyclone many miles from home; and she had never killed anything in all her life.

But the old woman seemed to expect an answer, so Dorothy said, "You are very kind, but there must be some mistake. I have not killed anything."

"Your house did, anyway," replied the old woman, with a laugh. "Look!" she continued, pointing to the corner of the house, "There are her two feet, still sticking out from under the house." (I)

Dorothy looked, and gave a little cry of fright. There, indeed, under the corner of the house, two feet were sticking out, wearing silver shoes with pointed toes.

"Oh, dear! oh, dear!" cried Dorothy, clasping her hands together.

"The house must have fallen on her. What shall we do?"

"There is nothing to be done, " said the woman, calmly.

"But who was she?" asked Dorothy.

"She was the Wicked Witch of the East, as I said," answered the woman. "She has held all the Munchkins in bondage for many years, making them slave for her night and day. Now they are all set free, and we are grateful to you." (J)

"Who are the Munchkins?" inquired Dorothy.

"They are the people who live in this Land of the East, where the Wicked Witch ruled."

"Are you a Munchkin?" asked Dorothy.

"No, but I am their friend, although I live in the Land of the North. When the Munchkins saw that the Witch of the East was dead, they sent a swift messenger to me, and I came at once. I am the Witch of the North." (K)

★11 ERRORS★

"Oh, gracious!" cried Dorothy; "are you a real witch?"

"Yes, indeed," answered the woman. "But I am a good witch, and the people love me. I am not as powerful as the Wicked Witch was; if I had been, I would have set the Munchkins free myself."

"But I thought all witches were wicked," said the girl, who was half-frightened at facing a real witch.

"Oh, no; that is not true. There

32   Lesson 8   Textbook

---

were only four witches in all the Land of Oz, and two of them, those who live in the North and the South, are good witches. I know this is true, for I am one of them myself, and cannot be mistaken. The witches who lived in the East and the West were, indeed, wicked witches. But now that you have killed one of them, there is only one wicked witch in all the Land of Oz—the one who lives in the West."

"But," said Dorothy, after a moment's thought, "Aunt Em had told me that the witches were all dead—years and years ago."

"Who is Aunt Em?" inquired the old woman.

"She is my aunt who lives in Kansas, where I came from."

The Witch of the North seemed to think for a time, with her head bowed and her eyes upon the ground. Then she looked up and said, "I do not know where Kansas is, for I have never heard of that country. But tell me, is it a civilized country?"

"Oh yes;" replied Dorothy.

"Then that explains it. In the civilized countries I believe there are no witches left; nor wizards, nor sorceresses, nor magicians. But, you see, the Land of Oz has never been civilized, for we are cut off from all the rest of the world. Therefore we still have witches and wizards."

"Who are the wizards?" asked Dorothy.

"Oz himself is the Great Wizard," answered the Witch, sinking her voice to a whisper. "He is more powerful than all the rest of us together. He lives in the Emerald City."

Lesson 8   Textbook   33

(H) Listen to what the woman said and get ready to answer some questions: "You are welcome, most noble Sorceress, to the Land of the Munchkins. We are grateful to you for having killed the Wicked Witch of the East, and for setting our people free from bondage."

- What does the woman think Dorothy is? **A noble Sorceress.**
- What is the name of the land that Dorothy is in? **The Land of the Munchkins.**
- The woman said that Dorothy killed somebody. Who was that? **The Wicked Witch of the East.**
- The woman also said that Dorothy did something for the people. What was that? *Idea:* Set them free from bondage.

(I) Whose feet was the woman talking about? **The Wicked Witch of the East's.**

(J) What had the Wicked Witch made the Munchkins do? *Idea:* Slave for her night and day.

- Who are the Munchkins grateful to? **Dorothy.**

(K) Who is the woman who is talking to Dorothy? **The Witch of the North.**

- Is the woman a Munchkin? **No.**
- Does the woman sound like a wicked witch, or a good witch? **A good witch.**
- Read the rest of the chapter to yourselves and be ready to answer some questions. Find out the two lands that had good witches and the two lands that had bad witches.

After all students have finished reading:

- Two witches in the Land of Oz were bad witches. Where did those witches live? *Idea:* In the East and the West.
- Two witches were good witches. Where did those witches live? *Idea:* In the North and the South.
- How many wicked witches are left in the Land of Oz? **One.**
- Which one is that? **The Wicked Witch of the West.**
- The Witch of the North said that there are no witches in civilized countries. Was the Land of Oz a civilized country? **No.**
- How do you know? *Idea:* Because it still had witches and wizards.
- Was Kansas civilized? **Yes.**
- So did Kansas have witches and wizards? **No.**
- Who is the most powerful wizard in the Land of Oz? **Oz.**
- Where does Oz live? **In the Emerald City.**

Award 4 points or have the students reread to the error limit sign.

EXERCISE 10   Writing assignment

1. I'm going to read some of the best writing assignments from the last lesson.
   Read several good assignments aloud and explain what is good about them.
2. Now find lesson 8, part F in your skillbook.
   Wait.
3. Follow along as I read part F aloud: Write a paragraph that compares Kansas with the Land of Oz. Be sure the paragraph answers the following questions:
   - What does Kansas look like?
   - What does the Land of Oz look like?
   - What kind of people live in Kansas?
   - What kind of people live in Oz?
4. *Call on several students to answer the first question.*
5. *Repeat step 4 with each remaining question.*
6. When you write your paragraph, make sure you answer all the questions. Remember, you have to write at least four sentences.

INDEPENDENT WORK

Do all the items in your skillbook and workbook for lesson 8.

WORKCHECK AND AWARDING POINTS

1. *Read the questions and answers for the skillbook and workbook.*
2. *Award points for independent work as follows:*

0 errors	6 points
2 errors	4 points
3, 4, or 5 errors	2 points
5 or more errors	0 points

3. *Award bonus points as follows:*

Correcting missed items or getting all items right	2 points
Doing the writing assignment acceptably	2 points

ANSWER KEY FOR WORKBOOK

Review Items

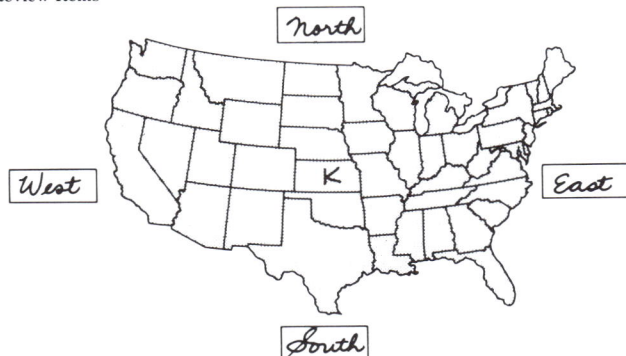

1. a. Fill in the boxes around the map.
   b. Put a K on the state where Dorothy lived.
   c. What is the name of that state?
      Kansas
2. What carried Dorothy's house to the Land of Oz? *a cyclone*
3. What are two other names for cyclones?
   a. *tornado*
   b. *twister*
4. Put an O next to the things that Dorothy saw in the Land of Oz. Put a K next to the things that Dorothy saw in Kansas.

a. gray grass		K
b. gorgeous flowers		O
c. birds with brilliant feathers		O
d. flat prairie		K
e. cracked land		K
f. large trees		O

5. Here are titles of chapters you have read:
   - Kansas
   - The Cyclone
   - The Munchkins

   Write the title of the chapter for each event.
   a. Dorothy looked at the prairie.
      Kansas
   b. A Munchkin greeted Dorothy.
      The Munchkins
   c. Dorothy was high in the air.
      The Cyclone
   d. The men near the house were dressed in blue.
      The Munchkins
   e. A great wind carried Dorothy.
      The Cyclone
   f. Aunt Em went into the cellar.
      The Cyclone

ANSWER KEY FOR SKILLBOOK

PART C

1. awfully
2. heavily
3. naturally
4. luckily
5. merrily
6. heartily
7. seriously
8. ordinarily

PART D

9. a. Munchkins
   b. Blue
   c. East
   d. a good witch
   e. North
   f. The Witch of the North
   g. White
   h. *Idea:* A noble Sorceress
10. a. East
    b. a bad witch
11. a. bondage
    b. Slave for her night and day
12. *Idea:* Dorothy killed the Witch of the East
13. she was not as powerful as the Witch of the East
14. a. No
    b. *Idea:* Because Kansas is a civilized country
    c. *Idea:* Because Oz is not a civilized country
15. a. Oz
    b. Emerald City

PART E

16. a. slavery
    b. orphan
    c. happily
    d. cyclone

Lesson 9

Lesson 9

PART A   Word Lists

1	2
desert	gracious
Quadlings	handkerchief
Gillikins	exactly
solemn	magical
delicious	Winkies
journey	sunbonnet
gingham	

3
Vocabulary words
1. gorgeous
2. messenger
3. civilized
4. sprinkled
5. brook

4
Vocabulary words
1. gingham
2. velvet
3. silk
4. leather

5
Vocabulary words
1. balanced
2. delicious
3. slate
4. pave
5. apparent

6
Vocabulary words
1. solemn
2. charm
3. sob
4. journey
5. injured
6. trot
7. brisk

PART B
Vocabulary Sentences

1. She looked very serious as she counted in a <u>solemn</u> voice.
   - clear   • serious   • happy
2. Her shoes had a secret <u>charm</u> that kept her out of danger.
   - shoelaces   • magic power   • hat band
3. Dorothy began to <u>sob</u> and large tears fell from her eyes.
   - cry   • smile   • listen
4. It was a long <u>journey</u> through the forest and past the fields.
   - turkey   • moment   • trip
5. She fell down and <u>injured</u> her knee.
   - hurt   • tickled   • listened to
6. The dog's legs were so short that he had to <u>trot</u> to keep up with his master.
   - sleep   • run slowly   • eat
7. She walked at such a <u>brisk</u> pace that she arrived at the city an hour before the others.
   - slow   • happy   • fast

WORD PRACTICE AND VOCABULARY

EXERCISE 1   Word practice

1. Everybody, find lesson 9, part A in your skillbook. *Wait.* Touch column 1. *Check.* The words in column 1 are hard words that will be in your reading stories.
2. Touch under the first word. *Check.* The first word is **desert.** What word? *Signal.* **Desert.**
3. Next word. *Pause.* That word is **Quadlings.** What word? *Signal.* **Quadlings.**
4. *Repeat step 3 for each remaining word in column 1.*
5. Now let's see if you remember all those words. Touch under the first word in column 1. *Pause.* What word? *Signal.* **Desert.**
6. Next word. *Pause.* What word? *Signal.* **Quadlings.**
7. *Repeat step 6 for each remaining word in column 1.*
8. *Repeat the words in column 1 until firm.*

EXERCISE 2   Word practice

1. Everybody, touch under the first word in column 2. *Pause.* What word? *Signal.* **Gracious.**
2. Next word. *Pause.* What word? *Signal.* **Handkerchief.**
3. *Repeat step 2 for each remaining word in column 2.*
4. *Repeat the words in column 2 until firm.*

EXERCISE 3   Vocabulary review

Task A

1. Everybody, touch column 3. *Check.* First you're going to read the words in column 3. Then we'll talk about what they mean.
2. Touch under the first word. *Pause.* What word? *Signal.* **Gorgeous.**
3. Next word. *Pause.* What word? *Signal.* **Messenger.**
4. *Repeat step 3 for each remaining word in column 3.*
5. *Repeat the words in column 3 until firm.*

Task B

You've learned the meanings for all these words. Word 1 is **gorgeous.** *Call on a student.* What does **gorgeous** mean? *Idea:* Very pretty.

Task C

Word 2 is **messenger.** *Call on a student.* What is a **messenger?** *Idea:* A person who delivers messages.

Task D

Word 3 is **civilized.** *Call on a student.* What does **civilized** mean? *Idea:* Well-mannered.

Task E

Word 4 is **sprinkled.** *Call on a student.*
What does **sprinkled** mean? *Idea:* Dotted.

Task F

Word 5 is **brook.** *Call on a student.*
What is a **brook?** *Idea:* A small stream.

EXERCISE 4 Vocabulary development

1. Everybody, touch under the first word in column 4. *Pause.*
   What word? *Signal.* **Gingham.**
   Next word. *Pause. Signal.* **Velvet.**
   Next word. *Pause. Signal.* **Silk.**
   Next word. *Pause. Signal.* **Leather.**
2. *Repeat step 1 until firm.*
3. Those words are names for different materials. **Gingham** is a kind of cotton. It is used for dresses and shirts. **Velvet** is a very soft material. It is used for fancy coats and hats. **Silk** is a very fine material. It is used for fancy shirts and dresses. **Leather** is a very tough material. It is used for boots and belts.
4. Tell me the name of the material that is a kind of cotton. *Signal.* **Gingham.**
 ● Tell me the name of the material that is very soft. *Signal.* **Velvet.**
 ● Tell me the name of the material that is very fine. *Signal.* **Silk.**
 ● Tell me the name of the material that is very tough. *Signal.* **Leather.**
5. *Repeat step 4 until firm.*
6. Remember those materials. You'll be reading about them.

EXERCISE 5 Vocabulary development

Task A

1. Everybody, touch column 5. *Check.*
   First you're going to read the words in column 5. Then we'll talk about what they mean.
2. Touch under the first word. *Pause.*
   What word? *Signal.* **Balanced.**
3. Next word. *Pause.* What word? *Signal.*
   Delicious.
4. *Repeat the words in column 5 until firm.*

Task B

Now let's talk about what those words mean.
Word 1 is **balanced.** *Call on a student.*
What does it mean when something is **balanced?** *Idea:* It won't tip over.

Task C

Word 2 is **delicious.** *Call on a student.*
When is something **delicious?**
Idea: When it tastes good.

Task D

Word 3 is **slate.** A **slate** is a little chalkboard.

Task E

Word 4 is **pave.** When you **pave** a road, you cover it with bricks or concrete.

Task F

1. Word 5 is **apparent.** When something is **apparent,** it is easy to see or understand. Here's another way of saying **Her problem was easy to see: Her problem was apparent.**
2. Everybody, what's another way of saying **The answer was easy to understand?** *Signal.*
   The answer was apparent.

EXERCISE 6 Vocabulary from context

Task A

1. Everybody, touch column 6. *Check.*
   The words in column 6 are words that you'll read in sentences. Then you'll learn what those words mean.
2. Touch under the first word. *Pause.*
   What word? *Signal.* **Solemn.**
3. Next word. *Pause.* What word? *Signal.* **Charm.**
4. *Repeat step 3 for each remaining word in column 6.*
5. *Repeat the words in column 6 until firm.*

Task B

1. Everybody, find part B. First we'll read each sentence and then we'll figure out what the underlined words could mean.
2. *Call on a student.* Read sentence 1 and the choices. *Wait.*
   Everybody, which is the best choice? *Signal.*
   Serious.
3. *Repeat step 2 for sentences 2–7.*
   Answer key: Sentence 2. **Magic power.**
     Sentence 3. **Cry.**
     Sentence 4. **Trip.**
     Sentence 5. **Hurt.**
     Sentence 6. **Run slowly.**
     Sentence 7. **Fast.**

Lesson 9

CHAPTER 4
The Yellow Brick Road Ⓐ

Dorothy was going to ask another question, but just then the Munchkins, who had been standing silently by, gave a loud shout and pointed to the corner of the house where the Wicked Witch had been lying.

"What is it?" asked the good witch. She looked, and began to laugh. The feet of the dead witch had disappeared entirely and nothing was left but the silver shoes.

"She was so old," explained the Witch of the North, "that she dried up quickly in the sun. That is the end of her. But the silver shoes are yours, and you shall have them to wear."

★2 ERRORS★

The Witch of the North reached down and picked up the shoes, and after shaking the dust out of them handed them to Dorothy. "The Witch of the East was proud of those silver shoes," said the old woman. They have some kind of magical charm, but I do not know what it is." Ⓑ

Dorothy carried the shoes into the house and placed them on the table. Then she came out again to the Munchkins and said, "I am anxious to get back to my aunt and uncle, for I am sure they will worry about me. Can you help me find my way?"

The Munchkins and the Witch first looked at one another, and then at Dorothy, and then shook their heads. Ⓒ

"I am afraid," said the old lady, "that there is a great desert that surrounds the whole Land of Oz, and no one can live to cross it."

The woman reached behind her back and pulled out a slate. All at once, a map of the Land of Oz appeared on the slate. Ⓓ

One Munchkin pointed to the Land of the East and said, "This is where we are now. You can see that the desert is not far from here."

The second Munchkin pointed to the Land of the South. "The South is where the Quadlings live, and they have the same desert, for I have been there and seen it."

"I am told," said the third Munchkin, "that the West also has the same desert. And that country, where the Winkies live, is ruled by the Wicked Witch of the West. She would make you her slave if you passed her way."

"The North is my home, and the Gillikins live there," said the old lady.

"This same great desert is also at its edge. I am sorry, my dear, but it appears that you will have to live with us, because you cannot cross the desert." Ⓔ

Dorothy began to sob at this, for she felt lonely among all these strange people. Her tears seemed to make the kindhearted Munchkins sad, for they immediately took out their handkerchiefs and also began to weep.

As for the old woman, she put the slate on the ground, took off her round hat, turned it upside down, and balanced the point on the end of her nose. Then she counted, "one, two, three" in a solemn voice.

All at once the map faded away, and big white letters appeared in its place. The letters said: LET DOROTHY GO TO THE EMERALD CITY. Ⓕ

The old woman read the words on the slate and asked, "Is your name Dorothy, my dear?"

"Yes," answered the child, looking up and drying her tears.

"Then you must go to the Emerald City. Perhaps Oz will help you."

"Where is this city?" asked Dorothy.

"It is exactly in the center of the country, and it is ruled by Oz, the Great Wizard I told you about." Ⓖ

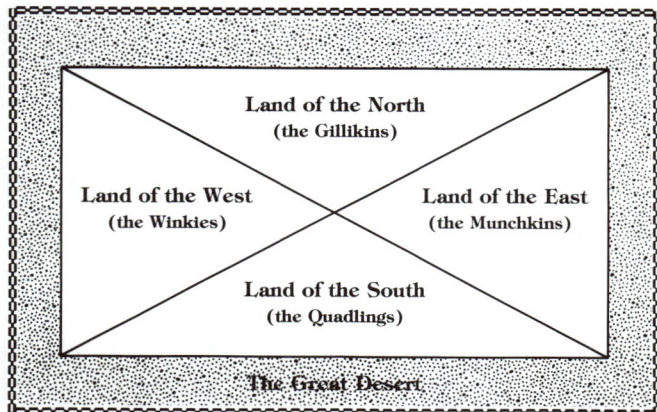

Land of the North
(the Gillikins)

Land of the West
(the Winkies)

Land of the East
(the Munchkins)

Land of the South
(the Quadlings)

The Great Desert

STORY READING

EXERCISE 7 Decoding

1. Everybody, turn to page 34 in your textbook. *Wait. Call on a student.* What's the error limit for this chapter? **11 errors.**
2. *Call on individual students to read.*
3. *After the group reads to the 2-error sign without making more than 2 errors, reread the first part aloud and present the comprehension tasks.*
4. *After you have completed the first part, call on individual students to read. Present the comprehension tasks.*

EXERCISE 8 Comprehension tasks

Ⓐ What was the name of the country that Dorothy was in? **The Land of Oz.**
- Which person was Dorothy talking to? **The Witch of the North.**
- Was that woman a good witch or a bad witch? **A good witch.**

Ⓑ What is a magical charm? *Ideas:* A special kind of power; a spell.
- Does the Witch of the North know what magical charm the shoes have? **No.**

Ⓒ What did Dorothy want to do? *Idea:* Go back to her aunt and uncle.
- Do the Munchkins act as if they can help Dorothy? **No.**

Ⓓ What is the weather like on a desert? *Idea:* Hot and dry.
- How did the map get on the slate? *Idea:* It appeared by magic.
  That doesn't sound like an ordinary slate to me.

Ⓔ Everybody, look at the map.
- What goes all the way around the land of Oz? **The Great Desert.**
- How many parts are inside the Land of Oz? **Four.**
- The parts are labeled. Look at the part that Dorothy is in. Everybody, what's the name of that part. **The Land of the East.**
  Which people live there? **The Munchkins.**
- What's the name of the western part? **The Land of the West.**
  Which people live there? **The Winkies.**
- What's the name of the northern part? **The Land of the North.**
  Which people live there? **The Gillikins.**
- What's the name of the southern part? **The Land of the South.**
  Which people live there? **The Quadlings.**

"Is Oz a good man?" inquired the girl, anxiously.

"He is a good wizard. Whether he is a man or not I cannnot tell, for I have never seen the wizard."

"How can I get there?" asked Dorothy.

"You must walk. It is a long journey, through a country that is sometimes pleasant and sometimes dark and terrible. However, I will use all the magic arts I know of to keep you from harm."

"Won't you go with me?" pleaded the girl, who had begun to think that the old woman was her only friend.

"No, I cannot do that," she replied. "But I will give you my kiss, and no one will dare injure a person who has been kissed by the Witch of the North."

She came close to Dorothy and kissed her gently on the forehead. Her lips left a round, shining mark on Dorothy's skin. Ⓗ

"The road to the Emerald City is paved with yellow brick," said the Witch. "So you cannot miss it. When you get to Oz do not be afraid. Just tell your story and ask the wizard to help you. Goodbye, my dear."

The three Munchkins bowed low to Dorothy and wished her a pleasant journey, after which they walked away through the trees. The Witch gave Dorothy a friendly little nod, whirled around on her left heel three times, and disappeared, much to the surprise of little Toto. Ⓘ ★11 ERRORS★

36 Lesson 9 Textbook

But Dorothy, who knew that the woman was a witch, had expected her to disappear in just that way, and was not surprised in the least.

When Dorothy was left alone she began to feel hungry. So she went into the house and cut herself some bread, which she spread with butter. She gave some of the bread to Toto. Then she took a pail from the shelf and carried the pail down to the little brook, where she filled it with clear, sparkling water. Toto ran over to the trees and began to bark at the birds sitting there. Dorothy went to get him, and saw such delicious fruit hanging from the branches that she gathered some of it. It was just what she wanted to complete her breakfast.

Then she went back to the house. She helped herself and Toto to a good drink of the cool, clear water, and she started to prepare for the journey to the Emerald City.

Dorothy had only one other dress, but that happened to be clean and was hanging on a peg beside her bed. It was gingham, with checks of white and blue; and although the blue was somewhat faded, it was still a pretty dress. The girl washed herself carefully, dressed herself in the clean gingham, and put her pink sunbonnet on her head. She took a little basket and filled it with bread from the cupboard, and laid a white cloth over the top. Then she looked down at her feet and noticed how old and worn her shoes were.

"They surely will never do for a

---

long journey, Toto," she said. And Toto looked up into her face with his little black eyes and wagged his tail to show that he knew what she meant.

At that moment Dorothy saw the Wicked Witch's silver shoes lying on the table.

"I wonder if they will fit me," she said to Toto. "They would be just the thing to take a long walk in, for they could not wear out."

She took off her old leather shoes and tried on the silver ones. They fit her just as well as if they had been made for her.

Finally she picked up her basket.

"Come along, Toto," she said. "We will go to the Emerald City and ask the

Great Oz how to get back to Kansas again."

She closed the door, locked it, and put the key carefully in the pocket of her dress. And so, with Toto trotting along behind her, she started on her journey.

There were several roads near by, but it did not take her long to find the one paved with yellow brick. Within a short time she was walking briskly toward the Emerald City, her silver shoes tinkling merrily on the hard, yellow roadbed. The sun shone brightly and the birds sang sweetly. Dorothy did not feel at all sad, even though she had been taken from her home and set down in a strange land.

Lesson 9 Textbook **37**

Ⓕ What did the slate say now?
Let Dorothy go to the Emerald City.

● What happened to the map? *Idea:* It faded away.

● The witch did five things to make the message appear on the slate. I'll read that part again. See if you can remember all five things. *Read the paragraph that begins with, "As for the little old woman, . . ."* Call on a student. Name those things in order.
Idea: Put the slate on the ground; took off her round hat; turned the hat upside down; balanced the point on the end of her nose; counted one, two, three in a solemn voice.

Ⓖ Where is the Emerald City? *Idea:* Exactly in the center of the country.

● Everybody, touch that place on the map. *Check.* Who rules that city? **Oz.**

Ⓗ Could people see the place where the witch kissed Dorothy? **Yes.**

● What kind of mark did the kiss leave? *Idea:* Round and shining.

Ⓘ What did the witch do before she disappeared?
Whirled around on her left heel three times.

● Would that surprise you to see somebody disappear like that? *Response:* Student preference.

● Read the rest of the chapter to yourselves and be ready to answer some questions.

After all students have finished reading:

● Dorothy dressed up to go someplace. Where was she going? **To the Emerald City.**

● Name the things she put on. *Idea:* A gingham dress, a pink sunbonnet, and the silver shoes.

● Which road did Dorothy take?
The yellow brick road.

● What sound did Dorothy's shoes make as she walked? *Idea:* They tinkled.

● Why did the shoes make that sound?
Idea: Because the shoes were metal and the road was hard brick.

● Did Dorothy feel sad when she started her journey? **No.**

Award 4 points or have the students reread to the error limit sign.

INDEPENDENT WORK

Do all the items in your skillbook and workbook for lesson 9.

Lesson 9 **47**

ANSWER KEY FOR WORKBOOK

Story Items

1. Some of the things in Chapter 4 are magical.
   Write **magical** next to the magical things.
   Write **not magical** next to the things that are not magical.
   a. The slate

   magical
   b. The pail

   not magical
   c. The gingham dress

   not magical
   d. The leather shoes

   not magical

e. The witch's kiss

magical
f. The silver shoes

magical

2. So far Dorothy knows only a few things about the Wizard of Oz.
   Put an **X** next to the things that she knows for sure about Oz.
   a. Oz is a great wizard.   X

   b. Oz is a man.   ____

   c. Oz wears green shoes.
   d. Oz is more powerful than
      all the witches.   X
   e. Oz lives in the Emerald
      City.   X

   f. Oz will definitely help her.   ____

Map Skills

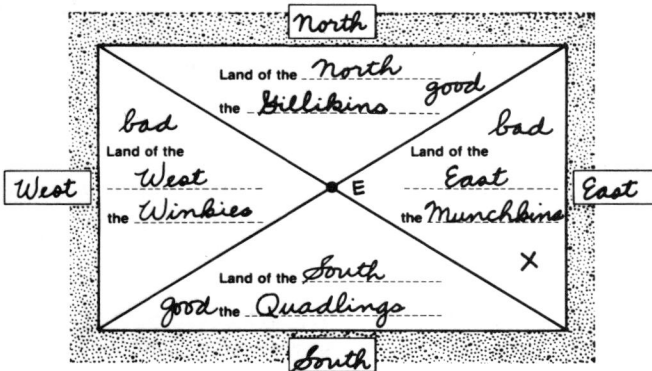

3. Write **North**, **East**, **South** and **West** in the boxes around the map.
4. Fill in the blanks.
   a. On the map, write the name of each land.
   b. Then write the name of the people who live in that land.
5. Write **bad** on the lands that had bad witches. Write **good** on the lands that had good witches.
6. Put an **X** on the land that Dorothy is in.
7. The big dot in the center of the map shows the city that Dorothy must walk to.
   a. Put an **E** next to the dot.
   b. Write the name of the city.

   Emerald City

WORKCHECK AND AWARDING POINTS

1. *Read the questions and answers for the skillbook and workbook.*
2. *Award points for independent work as follows:*

0 errors	*6 points*
2 errors	*4 points*
3, 4, or 5 errors	*2 points*
5 or more errors	*0 points*

3. *Award bonus points as follows:*

Correcting missed items or getting all items right	*2 points*
Doing the writing assignment acceptably	*2 points*

ANSWER KEY FOR SKILLBOOK

PART C

1. a. The Wizard of Oz
   b. L. Frank Baum
   c. The Yellow Brick Road
   d. *Idea:* The yellow brick road
2. a. Uncle Henry and Aunt Em
   b. The great desert
   c. No
3. East
4. a. North
   b. On her forehead
   c. *Idea:* A round, shining mark
5. a. The yellow brick road
   b. *Idea:* They tinkled
   c. No

PART D

6. a. Gillikins
   b. Winkies
   c. Munchkins
   d. Quadlings
7. a. Land of Oz
   b. Kansas
   c. Land of Oz
   d. Land of Oz
   e. Land of Oz
   f. Kansas
   g. Land of Oz
   h. Land of Oz
8. a. brilliant
   b. wail
   c. orphan
   d. prairie
   e. dismally

Lesson 10

Lesson 10

PART A	Word Lists		PART B

Vocabulary Sentences

1 curiosity Boq clumsiness	2 earnestly politely gratefully apparently	3 secret scarecrow embarrassed uncomfortable

1. Dorothy was so hungry that she ate a <u>hearty</u> supper.
   ● tiny   ● late   ● large
2. The dog looked so funny that she <u>amused</u> all of us.
   ● saddened   ● bit   ● entertained
3. Although he felt like crying, he <u>resolved</u> to keep the tears back.
   ● made his bed   ● made up his mind
   ● made a mistake
4. The mask that she wore <u>represented</u> the face of a gorilla.
   ● looked like   ● sounded like
   ● listened to
5. She wanted them to understand, so she told about her problem very <u>earnestly</u>.
   ● sincerely   ● happily   ● timidly
6. He was a big man and he spoke in a <u>husky</u> voice.
   ● small   ● high   ● deep or thick
7. He wasn't sure, but he <u>suspected</u> that she was a witch.
   ● thought   ● suspended   ● knew

4 Vocabulary words 1. brisk 2. injured 3. solemn 4. trot 5. journey	5 Vocabulary words 1. field of grain 2. apparent 3. crops 4. dome 5. fiddlers

6 Vocabulary words 1. leather 2. velvet 3. gingham 4. silk	7 Vocabulary words 1. hearty 2. amused 3. resolved 4. represented 5. earnestly 6. husky 7. suspected

WORD PRACTICE AND VOCABULARY

EXERCISE 1   Word practice

1. Everybody, find lesson 10, part A in your skillbook. *Wait.* Touch column 1. *Check.*
   The words in column 1 are hard words that will be in your reading stories.
2. Touch under the first word. *Check.*
   The first word is **curiosity.**
   What word? *Signal.* **Curiosity.**
3. Next word. *Pause.* That word is **Boq.** *(Rhymes with rock)*
   What word? *Signal.* **Boq.**
4. *Repeat step 3 for* **clumsiness.**
5. Now let's see if you remember all those words. Touch under the first word in column 1. *Pause.*
   What word? *Signal.* **Curiosity.**
6. Next word. *Pause.* What word? *Signal.* **Boq.**
7. *Repeat step 6 for* **clumsiness.**
8. *Repeat the words in column 1 until firm.*

EXERCISE 2   Word family

1. Everybody, touch column 2. *Check.*
   All those words end with the letters **l-y.**
2. Touch under the first word. *Pause.*
   What word? *Signal.* **Earnestly.**
3. Next word. *Pause.* What word? *Signal.* **Politely.**
4. *Repeat step 2 for each remaining word in column 2.*
5. *Repeat the words in column 2 until firm.*

EXERCISE 3   Word practice

1. Everybody, touch under the first word in column 3. *Pause.*
   What word? *Signal.* **Secret.**
2. Next word. *Pause.*
   What word? *Signal.* **Scarecrow.**
3. *Repeat step 2 for each remaining word in column 3.*
4. *Repeat the words in column 3 until firm.*

EXERCISE 4   Vocabulary review

Task A

1. Everybody, touch column 4. *Check.*
   First you're going to read the words in column 4. Then we'll talk about what they mean.
2. Touch under the first word. *Pause.*
   What word? *Signal.* **Brisk.**
3. Next word. *Pause.* What word? *Signal.* **Injured.**
4. *Repeat step 3 for each remaining word in column 4.*
5. *Repeat the words in column 4 until firm.*

Task B

You've learned the meanings for all these words. Word 1 is **brisk.** *Call on a student.*
What does **brisk** mean? *Idea:* Fast.

Task C

Word 2 is **injured.** *Call on a student.*
What does **injured** mean? *Idea:* Hurt.

Task D

Word 3 is **solemn.** *Call on a student.*
What does **solemn** mean? *Idea:* Serious.

Task E

Word 4 is **trot.** *Call on a student.*
What does **trot** mean? *Idea:* Run slowly.

Task F

Word 5 is **journey.** *Call on a student.*
What is a **journey?** *Idea:* A trip.

Lesson 10

PART A Word Lists

1	2	3
curiosity	earnestly	secret
Boq	politely	scarecrow
clumsiness	gratefully	embarrassed
	apparently	uncomfortable

4
Vocabulary words
1. brisk
2. injured
3. solemn
4. trot
5. journey

5
Vocabulary words
1. field of grain
2. apparent
3. crops
4. dome
5. fiddlers

6
Vocabulary words
1. leather
2. velvet
3. gingham
4. silk

7
Vocabulary words
1. hearty
2. amused
3. resolved
4. represented
5. earnestly
6. husky
7. suspected

PART B
Vocabulary Sentences

1. Dorothy was so hungry that she ate a <u>hearty</u> supper.
   - tiny • late • large
2. The dog looked so funny that she <u>amused</u> all of us.
   - saddened • bit • entertained
3. Although he felt like crying, he <u>resolved</u> to keep the tears back.
   - made his bed • made up his mind • made a mistake
4. The mask that she wore <u>represented</u> the face of a gorilla.
   - looked like • sounded like • listened to
5. She wanted them to understand, so she told about her problem very <u>earnestly</u>.
   - sincerely • happily • timidly
6. He was a big man and he spoke in a <u>husky</u> voice.
   - small • high • deep or thick
7. He wasn't sure, but he <u>suspected</u> that she was a witch.
   - thought • suspended • knew

EXERCISE 5 Vocabulary development

Task A
1. Everybody, touch column 5. *Check.*
   First you're going to read the words in column 5. Then we'll talk about what they mean.
2. Touch under the first line. *Pause.*
   What words? *Signal.* **Field of grain.**
3. Next word. *Pause.* What word? *Signal.*
   Apparent.
4. *Repeat step 3 for each remaining word in column 5.*
5. *Repeat the words in column 5 until firm.*

Task B
Now let's talk about what those words mean. The words in line 1 are **field of grain.** A **field of grain** is a field that is filled with plants like wheat and corn.

Task C
1. Word 2 is **apparent.** *Call on a student.*
   When is something **apparent?** *Idea:* When it is easy to see or understand.
2. Everybody, what's another way of saying **The next step was easy to understand?**
   Signal. **The next step was apparent.**

Task D
Word 3 is **crops. Crops** are vegetables and grains that are raised on a farm.
Call on individual students. Name some **crops.**
Responses: Rice, spinach, corn, onions, etc.

Task E
Word 4 is **dome.** A **dome** is a kind of roof. It looks like a round hat.

Task F
Word 5 is **fiddlers.** A **fiddler** is someone who plays the violin. **Fiddlers** call their violins fiddles.

EXERCISE 6 Vocabulary development

1. Everybody, touch under the first word in column 6. *Pause.*
   What word? *Signal.* **Leather.**
2. Next word. *Pause.*
   What word? *Signal.* **Velvet.**
3. *Repeat step 2 for each remaining word in column 6.*
4. Those words are names for different materials.
5. Tell me the name of the material that is very fine. *Pause.* Get ready. *Signal.* **Silk.**
   - Tell me the name of the material that is very soft. *Pause.* Get ready. *Signal.* **Velvet.**
   - Tell me the name of the material that is a kind of cotton. *Pause.* Get ready. *Signal.* **Gingham.**
   - Tell me the name of the material that is very tough. *Pause.* Get ready. *Signal.* **Leather.**
6. *Repeat step 5 until firm.*

EXERCISE 7 Vocabulary from context

Task A
1. Everybody, touch column 7. *Check.*
   The words in that column are words that you'll read in sentences.
2. Touch under the first word. *Pause.*
   What word? *Signal.* **Hearty.**
3. Next word. *Pause.* What word? *Signal.* **Amused.**
4. *Repeat step 3 for each remaining word in column 7.*
5. *Repeat the words in column 7 until firm.*

Task B
1. Everybody, find part B. First we'll read each sentence and then we'll figure out what the underlined words could mean.
2. *Call on a student.* Read sentence 1 and the choices. *Wait.*
   Everybody, which is the best choice? *Signal.* **Large.**
3. *Repeat step 2 for sentences 2–7.*
   Answer key: Sentence 2. **Entertained.**
   Sentence 3. **Made up his mind.**
   Sentence 4. **Looked like.**
   Sentence 5. **Sincerely.**
   Sentence 6. **Deep or thick.**
   Sentence 7. **Thought.**

Lesson 10

CHAPTER 5
The Scarecrow

Dorothy was surprised, as she walked along, to see how pretty the country was. There were neat fences at the sides of the road, painted a blue color, and beyond them were fields of grain and vegetables. Apparently, the Munchkins were good farmers and knew how to raise large crops. Once in a while she would pass a house, and the people would come out to look at her. They would bow low as she went by, for everyone knew she had destroyed the Wicked Witch and set them free from bondage. ★2 ERRORS★

The houses of the Munchkins were odd looking—each was round, with a big dome for a roof. All were painted blue, for in this country of the East, blue was the favorite color. Ⓐ

Towards evening, when Dorothy was tired from her long walk and began to wonder where she should pass the night, she came to a house that was larger than the rest. Many men and women were dancing on the green lawn in front of the house. Five little fiddlers played as loudly as possible and the people were laughing and singing, while a big table nearby was loaded with delicious fruits, nuts, pies, cakes, and many other good things to eat.

The people greeted Dorothy kindly, and invited her to dinner. They asked her to spend the night with them. The home belonged to one of the richest Munchkins in the land, and his friends were gathered with him to celebrate their

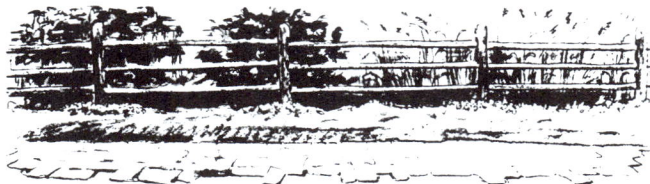

freedom from the bondage of the Wicked Witch.

Dorothy ate a hearty supper and was waited upon by the rich Munchkin himself, whose name was Boq. Then she sat down on a bench and watched the people dance.

When Boq saw her silver shoes he said, "You must be a great sorceress."

"Why?" asked the girl.

"Because you wear silver shoes and have killed the Wicked Witch. Besides, you have white in your dress, and only witches and sorceresses wear white." Ⓑ

"My dress is blue and white checked," said Dorothy, smoothing out the wrinkles in it.

"It is kind of you to wear that," said Boq. "Blue is the color of the Munchkins, and white is the witch color; so we know you are a friendly witch." Ⓒ

Dorothy did not know what to say to this, for all the people seemed to think that she was a witch. But she knew very well that she was only an ordinary little girl.

When Dorothy grew tired of watching the dancing, Boq led her into the house, where he gave her a room with a pretty bed in it. The sheets were made of blue cloth, and Dorothy slept soundly on them till morning, with Toto curled up on the blue rug beside her.

She ate a hearty breakfast, and watched a small Munchkin baby, who played with Toto and pulled his tail and laughed in a way that greatly amused Dorothy. Toto was a curiosity to all the

people, for they had never seen a dog before. Ⓓ

"How far is it to the Emerald City?" the girl asked.

"I do not know," answered Boq, solemnly. "I have never been there. It is better for people to keep away from Oz, unless they have business with him. But it is a long way to the Emerald City, and it will take many days. The country here is rich and pleasant, but you must pass through rough and dangerous places before you reach the end of your journey." Ⓔ

Boq's statement worried Dorothy a little, but she knew that only the Great Oz could help her get to Kansas again, so she bravely resolved not to turn back.

She said goodbye to her friends, and again started along the yellow brick road. When she had gone several miles she wanted to rest, and so she climbed to the top of the fence beside the road and sat down. There was a large cornfield beyond the fence, and not far away she saw a Scarecrow, placed high on a pole to keep the birds away from the ripe corn. Ⓕ

Dorothy leaned her chin upon her hand and gazed thoughtfully at the Scarecrow. Ⓖ The Scarecrow's head was a small sack stuffed with straw with eyes, nose, and mouth painted on it to represent a face. He had an old, pointed, blue Munchkin hat on his head, and he wore a faded, blue suit of clothes, which were also stuffed with straw. On his feet were some old boots with blue tops, just

STORY READING

EXERCISE 8   Decoding

1. Everybody, turn to page 38 in your textbook. *Wait. Call on a student.* What's the error limit for this chapter? **15 errors.**
2. *Call on individual students to read.*
3. *After the group reads to the 2-error sign without making more than 2 errors, reread the first part aloud and present the comprehension tasks.*
4. *After you have completed the first part, call on individual students to read. Present the comprehension tasks.*

EXERCISE 9   Comprehension tasks

Ⓐ What was the color of the fences? **Blue.**
● What was the color of the houses? **Blue.**
● What shape were the houses? **Round.**
● What did the people do when Dorothy walked by? *Idea:* Looked at her and bowed low.
● Why did the people do that? *Idea:* Because they knew that Dorothy had destroyed the Wicked Witch and set them free.
Ⓑ What was the name of the rich Munchkin? **Boq.**
● Boq thought that Dorothy was a sorceress for three reasons. Listen to that part of the story again and find out the three reasons. *Read from, "When Boq saw her silver shoes he said, . . ." to* Ⓑ.
● Name those three reasons. *Ideas:* She was wearing silver shoes; she had killed the Wicked Witch; she had white in her dress.
● Was white the only color in Dorothy's dress? **No.**
● What was the other color? **Blue.**
● Who else wore white? **The Witch of the North.**
Ⓒ Dorothy's dress had two colors. Which color showed that she was friendly to Munchkins? **Blue.**
● Which color showed that she was a witch? **White.**
● What kind of witch did Boq think Dorothy was? **A friendly witch.**
Ⓓ Why did the people think that Toto was a curiosity? *Idea:* Because they had never seen a dog before.
Ⓔ How long will it take Dorothy to reach the Emerald City? *Idea:* Many days.
● What must she pass through to get there? *Idea:* Rough and dangerous places.
Ⓕ What did Dorothy see inside the field? **A scarecrow.**
● What is the purpose of a scarecrow? *Idea:* To scare crows away from fields.
● What kind of crop grew in the field? **Corn.**
Ⓖ Everybody, show me how she did that? *Check.*

like those that Munchkin men wore. The Scarecrow was raised above the stalks of corn by a pole stuck up his back.(H)

When Dorothy was looking earnestly into the strange, painted face of the Scarecrow, she was surprised to see one of the eyes slowly wink at her.(I) She thought she was seeing things, at first, for none of the scarecrows in Kansas ever winked at her. Then the Scarecrow nodded his head to her in a friendly way. She climbed down from the fence and walked up to him, while Toto ran around the pole and barked.

"Good day," said the Scarecrow, in a rather husky voice.

"Did you speak?" asked the girl, in wonder.

"Certainly," answered the Scarecrow. "How do you do?"

"I'm pretty well, thank you," replied Dorothy, politely. "How do you do?"

"I'm not feeling well," said the Scarecrow, with a smile, "for it is very boring to be stuck up here night and day to scare away crows."

"Can't you get down?" asked Dorothy.

"No, for this pole is stuck up my back. If you will please take away the pole, I will be very grateful to you."

Dorothy reached up her arms and easily lifted the Scarecrow off the pole. Because he was stuffed with straw, the Scarecrow was quite light.(J)

"Thank you very much," said the Scarecrow, when he had been set down

on the ground. "I feel like a new man."

Dorothy thought it was odd to hear a stuffed man speak, and to see him bow and walk along beside her.(K)

★15 ERRORS★

"Who are you?" asked the Scarecrow when he had stretched himself and yawned. "And where are you going?"

"My name is Dorothy," said the girl, "and I am going to the Emerald City, to ask the Great Oz to send me back to Kansas."

"Where is the Emerald City?" he inquired. "And who is Oz?"

"Why, don't you know?" she answered, in surprise.

"No, indeed. I don't know anything. You see, I am stuffed with straw, so I have no brains at all," he said, sadly.

"Oh," said Dorothy, "I'm awfully sorry for you."

The Scarecrow asked, "Do you think that if I go to the Emerald City with you, Oz would give me some brains?"

"I do not know," she answered, "but you may come with me, if you like. If Oz will not give you any brains you will be no worse off than you are now."

"That is true," said the Scarecrow. "You see," he continued, "I don't mind my legs and arms and body being stuffed, because I cannot get hurt. If anyone steps on my toes or sticks a pin into me, it doesn't matter, for I can't feel it. But I do not want people to call me a

Lesson 10   Textbook   **41**

fool, and if my head stays stuffed with straw instead of with brains, how am I ever to know anything?"

"I understand how you feel," said the girl, who was truly sorry for him. "If you will come with me I'll ask Oz to do all he can for you."

"Thank you," he answered, gratefully.

They walked back to the road. Dorothy helped him over the fence, and they started along the yellow brick road for the Emerald City.

Toto did not like the Scarecrow, at first. He sniffed around the stuffed man as if he suspected there might be a nest of rats in the Scarecrow's straw, and he

often growled at the Scarecrow in an unfriendly way.

"Don't mind Toto," said Dorothy, to her new friend. "He never bites."

"Oh, I'm not afraid," replied the Scarecrow. "He can't hurt the straw. Do let me carry that basket for you. I won't mind it, for I can't get tired. I'll tell you a secret," he continued, as he walked along. "There is only one thing in the world that I am afraid of."

"What is that?" asked Dorothy. "The Munchkin farmer who made you?"

"No," answered the Scarecrow. "The only thing I fear is a lighted match."

42   Lesson 10   Textbook

(H) What was the color of the Scarecrow's clothes? **Blue.**

● Were those clothes old or new? **Old.**

● What kept the Scarecrow from falling over? *Idea:* The pole stuck up his back.

(I) Everybody, show me how the Scarecrow did that. *Check.*

(J) Why was it easy for Dorothy to lift the Scarecrow? *Idea:* Because he was light.

(K) Do you think it is odd to hear a scarecrow speak? *Response:* Student preference.

● Read the rest of the chapter to yourselves and be ready to answer some questions.

After all students have finished reading:

● Did the Scarecrow know about the Emerald City and the Wizard? **No.**
Why not? *Idea:* Because he didn't know anything.

● Why did the Scarecrow want to see the Wizard? *Idea:* To get some brains.

● Could the Scarecrow get hurt? **No.**

● Why not? *Idea:* Because he was stuffed with straw.

● Would the Scarecrow get tired on a long trip? **No.**

● How did Toto like the Scarecrow at first? *Idea:* Not very much.

● Was the Scarecrow afraid of Toto? **No.**
What was the only thing he was afraid of? *Idea:* A lighted match.

● Why do you think the Scarecrow was afraid of a lighted match? *Idea:* Because the match might burn his straw.

Award 4 points or have the students reread to the error limit sign.

ANSWER KEY FOR WORKBOOK

Story Items

1. Many events occurred in Chapter 5. Put those events in the right order by numbering them from **1** through **5**.

   3 The Scarecrow winked at Dorothy.
   1 Dorothy met Boq.
   5 Dorothy and the Scarecrow walked down the road.
   2 A baby played with Toto.
   4 Dorothy lifted the Scarecrow off the pole.

Map Skills

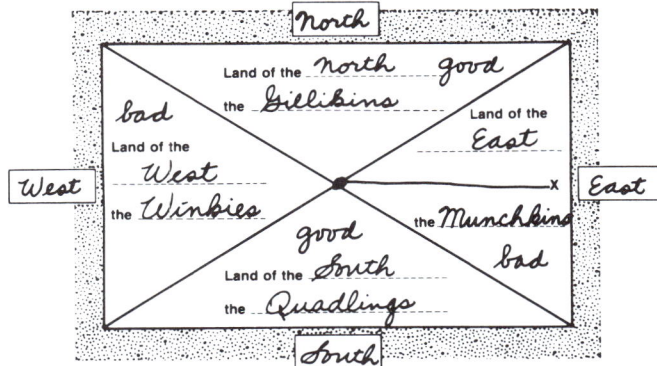

2. Write **North, East, South** and **West** in the boxes around the map.
3. Fill in the blanks.
   a. On the map, write the name of each land.
   b. Then write the name of the people who live in that land.
4. Write **bad** on the lands that had bad witches. Write **good** on the lands that had good witches.
5. a. On the map, make a dot to show the city that Dorothy is walking to.
   b. Write the name of that city.

   Emerald City

6. The **X** shows where Dorothy is now.
   a. Draw a straight line to show the road that Dorothy must take.
   b. What's the name of that road?

   Yellow Brick Road

   c. Write the direction Dorothy will go.

   West

Crossword Puzzle

To work the puzzle, read an item and figure out which word the item describes. Then write the word in the puzzle. Complete the entire puzzle.

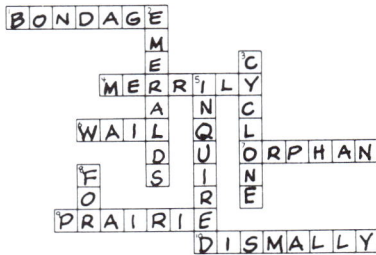

Across

1. Dorothy set the Munchkins free from _____.
4. Another word for **happily** is _____.
6. During a storm, you can hear the _____ of the wind.
7. A person without any parents is an _____.
9. A grassland with no trees.
10. Another word for **sadly** is _____.

Down

2. Expensive green jewels.
3. A strong wind that spins around and around.
5. Another word for **asked** is _____.
8. Another word for **because** is _____.

INDEPENDENT WORK

Do all the items in your skillbook and workbook for lesson 10.

WORKCHECK AND AWARDING POINTS

1. *Read the questions and answers for the skillbook and workbook.*
2. *Award points for independent work as follows:*

0 errors	6 points
2 errors	4 points
3, 4, or 5 errors	2 points
5 or more errors	0 points

3. *Award bonus points as follows:*

Correcting missed items or getting all items right	2 points
Doing the writing assignment acceptably	2 points

ANSWER KEY FOR SKILLBOOK

PART C

1. East
2. a. North
   b. *Idea:* A round, shining mark
3. a. Blue
   b. *Any two: fences, houses; clothes*
   c. Gray
4. she had destroyed the evil witch
5. celebrate their freedom from bondage
6. a. Blue and white
   b. White
   c. Blue
   d. *Idea:* A friendly witch
7. many
8. a. A scarecrow
   b. Straw
   c. Brains
   d. No
   e. *Idea:* Because he was stuffed with straw and could not feel it
   f. *Ideas:* fire; a lighted match
   g. *Idea:* Because it could burn his straw

Lesson 11

Lesson 11

PART A   Word Lists

1	2
shoulder	husky
inconvenient	hearty
one-legged	ordinary
fortunate	curiosity
	dreary

3

Vocabulary words
1. people of flesh and blood
2. spoil
3. husky
4. earnestly
5. suspected
6. hearty
7. represent
8. resolved

4

Vocabulary words
1. clumsiness
2. fortunate
3. dreary

PART B
Vocabulary Sentences

1. He kept falling down but he laughed at his own <u>clumsiness</u>.
   - gracefulness   • awkwardness
   - skill
2. After they were saved from the witch they all felt <u>fortunate</u> to be alive.
   - lucky   • sober   • disappointed
3. Our homes were gray and very <u>dreary</u> looking.
   - dull   • happy   • beautiful

PART C
Reading Checkout Rules

1. If I read the passage in less than one minute, I get points as follows:
   No errors—3 points.
   1 or 2 errors—1 point.
   More than 2 errors—no points.
2. If I take more than one minute to read the passage, I get no points. But I will reread the passage until I can read it in one minute with no more than 2 errors.
3. I will write the number of points I earn in the checkout box for today's lesson.

WORD PRACTICE AND VOCABULARY

EXERCISE 1   Word practice

1. Everybody, find lesson 11, part A in your skillbook. *Wait.* Touch column 1. *Check.*
   The words in column 1 are hard words that will be in your reading stories.
2. Touch under the first word. *Check.*
   The first word is **shoulder.**
   What word? *Signal.* **Shoulder.**
3. Next word. *Pause.* That word is **inconvenient.**
   What word? *Signal.* **Inconvenient.**
4. *Repeat step 3 for each remaining word in column 1.*
5. Now let's see if you remember all those words.
   Touch under the first word in column 1. *Pause.*
   What word? *Signal.* **Shoulder.**
6. Next word. *Pause.* What word? *Signal.*
   Inconvenient.
7. *Repeat step 6 for each remaining word in column 1.*
8. *Repeat the words in column 1 until firm.*

EXERCISE 2   Word family

1. Everybody, touch column 2. *Check.*
   All those words end with the same sound.
   Touch under the first word. *Pause.*
   What word? *Signal.* **Husky.**
2. Next word. *Pause.* What word? *Signal.* **Hearty.**
3. *Repeat step 2 for each remaining word in column 2.*
4. *Repeat the words in column 2 until firm.*

EXERCISE 3   Vocabulary development

Task A

1. Everybody, touch column 3. *Check.*
   First you're going to read the words in column 3. Then we'll talk about what they mean.
2. Touch under the first line. *Pause.*
   What words? *Signal.* **People of flesh and blood.**
3. Next word. *Pause.* What word? *Signal.* **Spoil.**
4. *Repeat step 3 for each remaining word in column 3.*
5. *Repeat the words in column 3 until firm.*

Task B

Now let's talk about what those words mean.
The words in line 1 are **people of flesh and blood.** Real people are sometimes called **people of flesh and blood.**

Task C

1. Word 2 is **spoil.** Another word for **ruin** is **spoil.** Here's another way of saying **They ruined the party: They spoiled the party.**
2. Everybody, what's another way of saying **Will that ruin the paint?** *Signal.*
   Will that spoil the paint?

Task D

You've learned the meanings for the rest of the words in column 3. Word 3 is **husky.**
Call on a student. What does **husky** mean?
Idea: Deep or thick.

Task E

Word 4 is **earnestly.** *Call on a student.*
What does **earnestly** mean? *Idea:* Sincerely.

Task F

Word 5 is **suspected.** *Call on a student.*
What does **suspected** mean? *Idea:* Thought.

Task G

Word 6 is **hearty.** *Call on a student.*
What does **hearty** mean? *Idea:* Large.

Task H

Word 7 is **represent.** *Call on a student.*
What does **represent** mean? *Idea:* Look like.

Task I

Word 8 is **resolved.** *Call on a student.* What does **resolved** mean? *Idea:* Made up your mind.

EXERCISE 4   Vocabulary from context

Task A

1. Everybody, touch column 4. *Check.*
   The words in that column are words that you'll read in sentences.
2. Touch under the first word. *Pause.*
   What word? *Signal.* **Clumsiness.**
3. Next word. *Pause.* What word? *Signal.* **Fortunate.**
4. *Repeat step 3 for **dreary**.*
5. *Repeat the words in column 4 until firm.*

Lesson 11

CHAPTER 6
The Road Gets Rough

After a few hours the road began to get rough, and the walking became so difficult that the Scarecrow often stumbled over the yellow bricks, which were now very uneven.(A) Sometimes, indeed, the bricks were broken or missing altogether, leaving holes that Toto jumped across and Dorothy walked around. But the Scarecrow, who had no brains, walked straight ahead, and so stepped into the holes and fell down on the yellow bricks. It never hurt him, however, and Dorothy would pick him up and set him on his feet again, while he joined her in laughing merrily at his own clumsiness. ★2 ERRORS★

The farms were not nearly so well cared for here as they were farther back. There were fewer houses and fewer fruit trees, and the farther the travelers went the more dismal and lonesome the country became.(B)

At noon Dorothy and the Scarecrow sat down by the roadside, near a little brook, and Dorothy opened her basket and took out some bread. She offered a piece to the Scarecrow, but he refused.

"I am never hungry," he said, "and it is a lucky thing that I am not. For my mouth is only painted, and if I were to cut a hole in it so I could eat, the straw I am stuffed with would come out, and that would spoil the shape of my head."(C)

Dorothy saw at once that this was true, so she only nodded and went on eating her bread.

When Dorothy had finished her dinner, the Scarecrow said, "Tell me something about yourself, and the country you came from." So she told him all about Kansas, and how gray everything was there, and how the cyclone had carried her to this strange Land of Oz. The Scarecrow listened carefully, and said, "I cannot understand why you want to leave this beautiful country and go back to the dry gray place you call Kansas."

"That is because you have no brains," answered the girl. "No matter how dreary and gray our homes are, we people of flesh and blood would rather live there than in any other country, no matter how beautiful it is. There is no place like home."(D)

The Scarecrow sighed.

"Of course I cannot understand it," he said. "If your heads were stuffed with straw, like mine, you would probably all live in the beautiful places, and then Kansas would have no people at all. It is fortunate for Kansas that you have brains."(E) ★7 ERRORS★

Task B

1. Everybody, find part B. First we'll read each sentence and then we'll figure out what the underlined words could mean.
2. *Call on a student.* Read sentence 1 and the choices. *Wait.*
   Everybody, which is the best choice? *Signal.*
   Awkwardness.
3. *Repeat step 2 for sentences 2 and 3.*
   Answer Key: Sentence 2. **Lucky.**
   Sentence 3. **Dull.**

STORY READING

EXERCISE 5   Decoding

1. Everybody, turn to page 43 in your textbook. *Wait. Call on a student.* What's the error limit for this chapter? **7 errors.**
2. *Call on individual students to read.*
3. *After the group reads to the 2-error sign without making more than 2 errors, reread the first part aloud and present the comprehension tasks.*
4. *After you have completed the first part, call on individual students to read. Present the comprehension tasks.*

EXERCISE 6   Comprehension tasks

(A) The chapter says that the bricks were uneven. What does that mean?
   Idea: That they were not flat.
(B) Name some ways that the country changed as Dorothy went farther down the road.
   Ideas: There were fewer houses; there were fewer fruit trees; it was more dismal; it was more lonesome.
(C) What would happen if the Scarecrow tried to cut a hole in his mouth?
   Idea: The straw would come out and his head would lose its shape.
(D) Which place is more beautiful, Kansas or the Land of Oz? **The Land of Oz.**
- Why doesn't Dorothy want to stay in the land of Oz? *Idea:* Because she wants to go home.
(E) Listen to what the Scarecrow said and get ready to answer some questions.
   Read from (D) *to* (E).
- Where would people who had no brains live?
   Idea: In the beautiful places.
- Would they live in Kansas if people had no brains? **No.**
- Why not? *Idea:* Kansas is not beautiful.
- Why does the Scarecrow think it is fortunate for Kansas that people have brains? *Idea:* Because otherwise people wouldn't live there.
- Does the Scarecrow sound smart? **Yes.**
   I wonder how he could be so smart if he doesn't have brains.

Award 4 points or have the students reread to the error limit sign.

ANSWER KEY FOR WORKBOOK

Review Items

1. Put a **1** next to the words that tell how the land looked when Dorothy began her journey.
Put a **2** next to the words that tell how the land looked in this chapter.

   a. Neat fences by the side of the road ___1___

   b. Only a few fruit trees ___2___

   c. Dismal and lonesome country ___2___

   d. Round blue houses ___1___

   e. Farms that were not well cared for ___2___

2. Many events have occurred in the story so far. Put these events in the right order by numbering them from 1 through 5.

   ___3___ The Witch of the North gave Dorothy some silver shoes.

   ___2___ Dorothy's house landed on top of the Witch of the East.

   ___5___ Dorothy met the Scarecrow.

   ___1___ Dorothy was living in Kansas.

   ___4___ Dorothy met Boq.

3. Put an **X** next to the things that Dorothy knows for sure about Oz.

   a. Oz is a great wizard. ___X___

   b. Oz is bald. _____

   c. Oz is more powerful than the witches. ___X___

   d. Oz lives in the Emerald City. ___X___

   e. Oz will definitely help her. _____

Map Skills

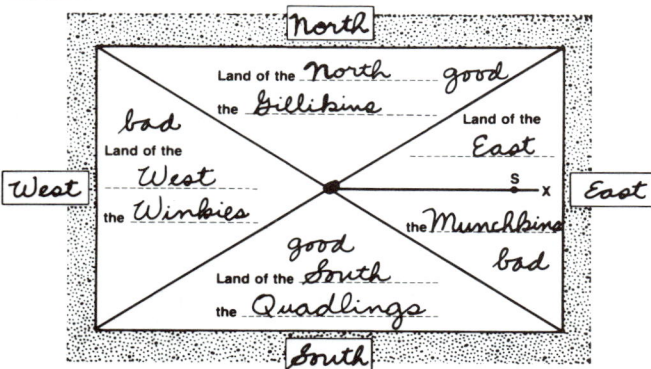

4. Write **North, East, South** and **West** in the boxes around the map.
5. Fill in the blanks.
   a. On the map, write the name of each land.
   b. Then write the name of the people who live in that land.
6. Write **bad** on the lands that had bad witches. Write **good** on the lands that had good witches.
7. **a.** Make a **dot** on the map to show the city that Dorothy is going to.
   b. What is the name of that city?

   Emerald City

   c. Write the direction Dorothy will go. _West_

8. The **X** shows where Dorothy started out. The **line** shows the road she is on. What's the name of that road?

   Yellow Brick Road

9. The **S** shows where Dorothy met somebody in a cornfield. Who was that?

   Scarecrow

CHECKOUT LESSONS

1. *Every tenth lesson, starting with lesson 11 is a reading checkout lesson. A checkout lesson is a lesson in which you check each student's reading rate and reading accuracy.*

2. *A checkout lesson follows the normal lesson plan, except that the Group Reading segment is shortened, allowing you time to give each student an individual reading checkout.*

3. *To conduct a checkout, call one student at a time to your desk, while the rest of the group works on independent activities.*

● *Ask the student to bring his or her textbook. Have the student read from the title to the 2-error sign of the preceding day's lesson. For example, today students read the first paragraph in lesson 10.*

● *Time each student and keep track of his or her errors.*

4. *If the student finishes the passage in one minute or less, award points as follows:*

0 errors	3 points
1 or 2 errors	1 point
More than 2 errors	0 points

● *After the checkout, remind the student to record his or her points in the box labeled CO on page 14 in the workbook.*

5. *If a student takes more than one minute to read the passage, the student does not earn any points, but have the student reread the passage until he or she is able to read it in no more than one minute with no more than two errors.*

6. *Have the students read the reading checkout rules on page 14 in their skillbook.*

INDEPENDENT WORK

Do all the items in your skillbook and workbook for lesson 11.

WORKCHECK AND AWARDING POINTS

1. *Read the questions and answers for the skillbook and workbook.*

2. *Award points for independent work as follows:*

> *0 errors . . . . .6 points*
> *2 errors . . . . .4 points*
> *3, 4, or 5 errors . . . . .2 points*
> *5 or more errors . . . . .0 points*

3. *Award bonus points as follows:*

> *Correcting missed items*
> *or getting all items right . . . . .2 points*
> *Doing the writing*
> *assignment acceptably . . . . .2 points*

4. *Remind the students to put the points they earned for their reading checkout, in the box labeled* **CO.**

ANSWER KEY FOR SKILLBOOK

PART D
1. The Road Gets Rough
2. **a.** No
   b. *Idea:* The straw would come out
3. **a.** The Witch's of the East
   b. The Witch of the North
   c. A round, shining mark
4. **a.** Straw
   b. Brains
   c. *Ideas:* Fire; a lighted match
   d. *Idea:* Because it could burn his straw

PART E
5. **a.** Kansas
   b. Uncle Henry and Aunt Em
   c. A cyclone
   d. Gray
6. **a.** Blue
   b. White
7. **a.** North
   b. East
   c. West
   d. South
8. **a.** Scarecrow
   b. Dorothy
   c. Scarecrow
   d. Dorothy
9. **a.** brilliant
   b. balanced
   c. very pretty
   d. move
   e. civilized
   f. magician

Lesson 12

WORD PRACTICE AND VOCABULARY

EXERCISE 1   Word practice

1. Everybody, find lesson 12, part A in your skillbook. *Wait.* Touch column 1. *Check.* The words in column 1 are hard words that will be in your reading stories.
2. Touch under the first word. *Check.* The first word is **comrade.** What word? *Signal.* **Comrade.**
3. Next word. *Pause.* That word is **passage.** What word? *Signal.* **Passage.**
4. *Repeat step 3 for each remaining word in column 1.* Now let's see if you remember all those words. Touch under the first word in column 1. *Pause.* What word? *Signal.* **Comrade.**
6. Next word. *Pause.* What word? *Signal.* **Passage.**
7. *Repeat step 6 for each remaining word in column 1.*
8. *Repeat the words in column 1 until firm.*

EXERCISE 2   Word practice

1. Everybody, touch under the first word in column 2. *Pause.* What word? *Signal.* **Fastened.**
2. Next word. *Pause.* What word? *Signal.* **Embarrass.**
3. *Repeat step 2 for each remaining word in column 2.*
4. *Repeat the words in column 2 until firm.*
5. *Repeat steps 1–4 for column 3.*

EXERCISE 3   Vocabulary review

Task A

1. Everybody, touch column 4. *Check.* First you're going to read the words in column 4. Then we'll talk about what they mean.
2. Touch under the first word. *Pause.* What word? *Signal.* **Fortunate.**
3. Next word. *Pause.* What word? *Signal.* **Clumsiness.**
4. *Repeat step 3 for* **dreary.**
5. *Repeat the words in column 4 until firm.*

Task B

You've learned the meanings for all these words. Word 1 is **fortunate.**
Call on a student. What does **fortunate** mean?
Idea: Lucky.

Task C

Word 2 is **clumsiness.** *Call on a student.* What does **clumsiness** mean?
Idea: Awkwardness.

Task D

Word 3 is **dreary.** *Call on a student.* What does **dreary** mean? *Idea:* Dull.

EXERCISE 4   Vocabulary development

Task A

1. Everybody, touch column 5. *Check.* First you're going to read the words in column 5. Then we'll talk about what they mean.
2. Touch under the first line. *Pause.* What words? *Signal.* **Ray of sunshine.**
3. Next word. *Pause.* What word? *Signal.* **Maiden.**
4. *Repeat step 3 for each remaining word in column 5.*
5. *Repeat the words in column 5 until firm.*

Task B

Now let's talk about what those words mean. The words in line 1 are **ray of sunshine.** A **ray of sunshine** is the kind of streak that sunshine makes when it comes through a window or a cloud.

Task C

Word 2 is **maiden.** A **maiden** is a young woman who isn't married. Everybody, what do we call a young woman who isn't married? *Signal.* **A maiden.**

Task D

1. Word 3 is **satisfaction.** When you're pleased over something you do, you feel **satisfaction** over doing that thing. Here's another way of saying **She felt pleased over winning the race: She felt satisfaction over winning the race.**

2. Everybody, what's another way of saying **She felt pleased over the dinner she cooked?** *Signal.* **She felt satisfaction over the dinner she cooked.**

Task E

Word 4 is **inconvenient.** If something is **inconvenient,** it is either annoying or it requires work that is not necessary. Everybody, what do we call something that is annoying or requires work that is not necessary? *Signal.* **Inconvenient.**

Task F

Word 5 is **deserted.** When you **desert** people, you leave them when they need you. Everybody, what do you do when you leave people when they need you? *Signal.* **You desert them.**

Task G

Word 6 is **companions.** The word **companions** comes from the word **company.** So **companions** are people who keep you **company.** Everybody, what do we call people who keep you **company?** *Signal.* **Companions.**

Task H

Word 7 is **mystery.** If you don't understand something that is very strange, that thing is a **mystery.** Everybody, what do you call something you don't understand? *Signal.* **A mystery.**

EXERCISE 5   Vocabulary from context

Task A

1. Everybody, touch column 6. *Check.* The words in that column are words that you'll read in sentences.

2. Touch under the first word. *Pause.* What word? *Signal.* **Declared.**

3. Next word. *Pause.* What word? *Signal.* **Motionless.**

4. *Repeat step 3 for* **comforted.**

5. *Repeat the words in column 6 until firm.*

Task B

1. Everybody, find part B. First we'll read each sentence and then we'll figure out what the underlined words could mean.

2. *Call on a student.* Read sentence 1 and the choices. *Wait.* Everybody, which is the best choice? *Signal.* **Said.**

3. *Repeat step 2 for sentences 2 and 3.*
Answer Key: Sentence 2. **Without movement.**
      Sentence 3. **More comfortable.**

EXERCISE 6   Introduction of glossary

1. Your textbook has a glossary. The glossary is a list of the new words that are introduced in this program. The words are listed in alphabetical order. For each word, the glossary gives information about what the word means.

2. Turn to the glossary at the end of your textbook. *Wait.* Get ready to find the meanings of some words.

3. The first word is **coronation.** What word? *Signal.* **Coronation.** What letter does coronation start with? *Signal.* **C.**

• In the glossary, find the words that start with **c** and look for the word **coronation.** Raise your hand when you have found the word. *Wait.*

4. *Call on a student.* Read what the glossary says about the word **coronation.** **A coronation is an important event in which the crown is officially placed on the head of a new king.**

5. The next word is **motley.** What word? *Signal.* **Motley.** Raise your hand when you have found that word.

6. *Call on a student.* Read what the glossary says about the word **motley.** **Something that is made up of many different types of things is called motley.**

7. Remember how to use the glossary. Later you will find the meanings of other words.

Lesson 12

CHAPTER 7
The Forest

Dorothy and the Scarecrow were still sitting by the roadside. Dorothy said, "Won't you tell me a story, while we are resting?"

The Scarecrow seemed a little embarrassed and began to tell the story of his life.Ⓐ

My life has been so short that I really don't know anything. I was only made the day before yesterday. What happened in the world before that time is all unknown to me.Ⓑ *Luckily, when the farmer made my head, one of the first things he did was to paint my ears, so that I heard what was going on. There was another Munchkin with him, and the first thing I heard was the farmer saying, "How do you like those ears?"*Ⓒ

"They aren't straight," answered the other Munchkin.

"Never mind," said the farmer. "They are ears just the same," which was true.

"Now I'll make the eyes," said the farmer. So he painted my right eye, and as soon as it was finished I found myself looking at him and at everything around me with a great deal of curiosity, for this was my first glimpse of the world.

"That's a rather pretty eye," remarked the Munchkin who was watching the farmer; "blue paint is just the color for eyes."

"I think I'll make the other a little bigger," said the farmer; and when the second eye was done I could see much better than before. Then the farmer made my nose and my mouth; but I did not speak.

I had fun watching them make my body and my arms and legs. And when they fastened on my head, at last, I felt very proud, for I thought I was just as good a man as anyone.

"This fellow will scare the crows," said the farmer. "He looks just like a man."

"Why, he is a man," said the other. The farmer carried me under his arm to the cornfield, and set me up on a tall stick. Then he and his friend walked away and left me alone.

I did not like to be deserted this way, so I tried to walk after them. But my feet would not touch the ground, and I was forced to stay on that pole. It was a lonely life, for I had nothing to think of, since I had just been made a little while before. Many crows and other birds flew into the cornfield, but as soon as they saw me they flew away again, thinking I was a Munchkin. This pleased me and made me

feel that I was quite an important person.

After a while, an old crow flew near me. After looking at me carefully, he landed upon my shoulder and said, "I wonder if that farmer thought he could fool me by putting you here. Any smart crow can see that you are only stuffed with straw." Then he hopped down at my feet and ate all the corn he wanted. When the other birds saw that I did not harm the old crow, they also came to eat the corn and in a short time there was a great flock of them around me.Ⓓ

I felt sad because it seemed that I was not such a good Scarecrow after all, but the old crow comforted me, saying: "If you only had brains in your head you would be as good a man as any of them, and a better man than some of them. Brains are the only things worth having in this world, whether you are a crow or a man."

After the crows had gone I thought about what the old crow had said. I decided I would try hard to get some brains.Ⓔ *Then Dorothy came along and pulled me off the stake, and from what she said, I am sure the great Oz will give me brains as soon as I get to the Emerald City.*Ⓕ

"I hope the Wizard will help you," said Dorothy, earnestly, "since you seem anxious to have brains."

"Oh, yes. I am anxious," returned the Scarecrow. "It is such an uncomfortable feeling to know that I am a fool."

"Well," said the girl, "let's go." And she handed the basket to the Scarecrow.

There were no fences at all by the roadside now, and there were no farms.Ⓖ Towards evening they came to a great forest, where the trees grew so big and close together that their branches met over the road. It was almost dark under the trees, for the branches shut out the daylight; but the travelers did not stop, and went on into the forest.Ⓗ

"If this road goes in, it must come out," said the Scarecrow. "And since the Emerald City is at the other end of the road, we must go wherever it leads us."Ⓘ

"Anyone would know that about the road," said Dorothy.

"Certainly; that is why I know it," answered the Scarecrow. "If I had needed brains to figure it out, I never could have said it."Ⓙ ★**13 ERRORS**★

After an hour or so the light faded away, and they found themselves stumbling along in the darkness. Dorothy could not see at all, but Toto could, for some dogs see very well in the dark; and the Scarecrow declared he could also see well.

So Dorothy took hold of the Scarecrow's arm, and managed to get along.

She said, "If you see any house, or any place where we can pass the night, you must tell me. It is very uncomfortable to walk in the dark."

Soon the Scarecrow stopped.

"I see a little cottage to the right of us," he said. "It is built of logs and branches. Shall we go there?"

STORY READING

EXERCISE 7   Decoding

1. Everybody, turn to page 45 in your textbook. *Wait. Call on a student.* What's the error limit for this chapter? **13 errors.**
2. *Call on individual students to read.*
3. *After the group reads to the 2-error sign without making more than 2 errors, reread the first part aloud and present the comprehension tasks.*
4. *After you have completed the first part, call on individual students to read. Present the comprehension tasks.*

EXERCISE 8   Comprehension tasks

Ⓐ Look at the different writing below. That writing is different because it's the story that the Scarecrow tells Dorothy. You can see that the story is quite long. Remember, the next part is the Scarecrow's story.

Ⓑ How long has the Scarecrow been alive? **Two days.**

● What does he know about what happened before then? *Idea:* Nothing.

Ⓒ Whose ears is the farmer talking about? **The Scarecrow's.**

● Could the Scarecrow see what was happening? **No.**

● Why not? *Idea:* Because he didn't have any eyes yet.

Ⓓ At first, did the crows stay away from the Scarecrow? **Yes.**

● What kind of person did they think the Scarecrow was? **A Munchkin.**

● Did the old crow think that the Scarecrow was a Munchkin? **No.**

● So what did the old crow start to do? *Idea:* Eat all the corn he wanted.

● What did the other crows do when they saw the old crow eating corn? *Idea:* They started eating corn too.

Ⓔ What did the crow say were the only things worth having? **Brains.**

● Did the Scarecrow agree with the crow? **Yes.**

● What did the Scarecrow decide to do? *Idea:* Get some brains.

Ⓕ Are we at the end of the Scarecrow's story? **Yes.**

● How do you know? *Idea:* Because the writing changed back to what it was before.

● Where were Dorothy and the Scarecrow when the Scarecrow told his story? *Idea:* Sitting by the roadside.

Ⓖ Dorothy handed the basket to the Scarecrow. How tired would he get when he carried it? *Idea:* Not tired at all.

● Name two things that are no longer by the roadside. **Fences and farms.**

Ⓗ Who were the travelers? **Dorothy, Toto, and the Scarecrow.**

"Yes, indeed," answered the girl. "I am all tired out."

So the Scarecrow led her through the trees until they reached the cottage, and Dorothy entered and found a bed of dried leaves in one corner. She lay down at once with Toto beside her. She soon fell into a sound sleep. The Scarecrow, who was never tired, stood up in another corner and waited until morning came.

When Dorothy awoke the sun was shining through the trees and Toto was outside, chasing birds. The Scarecrow was still standing in his corner, waiting for her.

"We must go and search for water," she said to him.

"Why do you want water?" he asked.

"To wash the road dust off my face, and to drink, so the dry bread will not stick in my throat."

"It must be inconvenient to be made of flesh," said the Scarecrow, thoughtfully. "You must sleep, and eat, and drink. However, you have brains, and it is worth a lot of trouble to be able to think properly."

They left the cottage and walked through the trees until they found a little spring of clear water, where Dorothy drank and bathed and ate her breakfast. She saw that there was not much bread left in the basket, and the girl was thankful that the Scarecrow did not have to eat anything, for there was barely enough for herself and Toto for the day.

When she had finished her meal, and was about to go back to the yellow brick road, she was startled to hear a deep groan nearby.

"What was that?" she asked.

"I don't know," replied the Scarecrow, "but we can go and see."

Just then another groan reached their ears, and the sound seemed to come from behind them. They turned and walked through the forest a few steps. Dorothy saw something shining in a ray of sunshine. She ran to the place and then stopped short, with a cry of surprise.

One of the big trees had been partly chopped through, and standing beside it, with an uplifted axe in his hands, was a man made entirely of tin. He stood perfectly motionless, as if he could not move at all.

Dorothy looked at him in amazement, and so did the Scarecrow, while Toto barked sharply and made a snap at the tin legs, which hurt his teeth.

"Did you groan?" asked Dorothy.

"Yes," answered the tin man, "I did." I've been groaning for more than a year, and no one has ever heard me before or come to help me."

(I) Did the Scarecrow say something that was pretty smart? **Yes.**

● Why do they have to follow the road wherever it goes? *Idea:* Because the Emerald City is at the other end.

(J) Does the Scarecrow think that he is smart? **No.**

● Dorothy didn't think the Scarecrow was smart. Do you agree with Dorothy? *Idea:* Student preference.

● Read the rest of the chapter to yourselves and be ready to answer some questions.

After all students have finished reading:

● The travelers walked through the forest before they came to a place to sleep. What time of day was it? *Idea:* Night.

● Who couldn't see in the dark? **Dorothy.**

● Who could see in the dark? **Toto and the Scarecrow.**

● Where did the travelers spend the night? *Idea:* In a cottage.

● What did the Scarecrow do while Dorothy slept? *Idea:* Stood up in a corner and waited for morning.

● In the morning, Dorothy went to get some water. Name two reasons why Dorothy wanted water. *Ideas:* To wash the road dust off her face; to drink, so the bread will not stick in her throat.

● Right after Dorothy finished her meal, she heard something. What did she hear? *Idea:* A tin man making a deep groan.

● What was the tin man next to? **A tree.**

● How long had the tin man been groaning? *Idea:* For more than a year.

Award 4 points or have the students reread to the error limit sign.

INDEPENDENT WORK

Do all the items in your skillbook and workbook for lesson 12.

ANSWER KEY FOR WORKBOOK

Story Items

1. Put the following story events in the right order by numbering them from 1 through 5.

   _5_ Dorothy saw a man with an axe.

   _1_ Dorothy's house killed the Witch of the East.

   _3_ Dorothy met the Scarecrow.

   _2_ Dorothy met the Witch of the North.

   _4_ Dorothy and the Scarecrow stayed in a cottage.

Map Skills

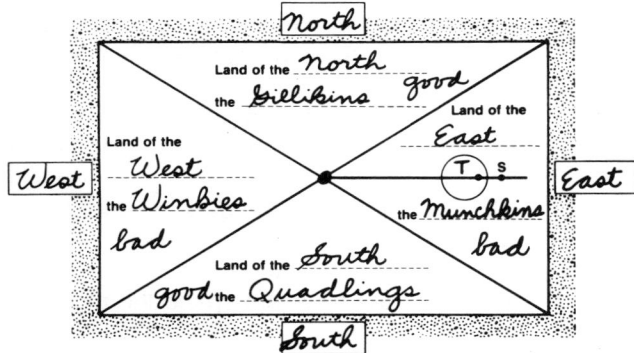

2. Write **North, East, South** and **West** in the boxes around the map.
3. Fill in the blanks.
   a. On the map, write the name of each land.
   b. Then write the name of the people who live in that land.
4. Write **bad** on the lands that had bad witches. Write **good** on the lands that had good witches.
5. The **circle** on the road shows the forest that the travelers came to.
   a. Make a **T** in the circle to show where the travelers are now.
   b. Who did they see in the forest?

   Tin Woodman

6. a. Make a big **dot** on the map to show the city where Dorothy is going.
   b. What is the name of that city?

   Emerald City

7. a. Name the direction the travelers are going. _West_
   b. The **line** shows the road that Dorothy is on. What is the name of that road?

   Yellow Brick Road

8. The **S** shows where Dorothy met someone. Who was that?

   Scarecrow

WORKCHECK AND AWARDING POINTS

1. *Read the questions and answers for the skillbook and workbook.*
2. *Award points for independent work as follows:*

0 errors	6 points
2 errors	4 points
3, 4, or 5 errors	2 points
5 or more errors	0 points

3. *Award bonus points as follows:*

Correcting missed items or getting all items right	2 points
Doing the writing assignment acceptably	2 points

ANSWER KEY FOR SKILLBOOK

PART C

1. The Forest
2. a. Two days
   b. Nothing
   c. *Idea:* A Munchkin farmer
3. a. *Idea:* Because he thought he was just as good a man as anyone
   b. *Idea:* A Munchkin
   c. *Idea:* A man stuffed with straw
   d. Brains
   e. Yes
4. a. *Ideas:* Evening; night
   b. Dorothy
   c. Toto and the Scarecrow
5. a. *Idea:* In a cottage
   b. *Idea:* Because he was never tired
6. a. A tin man
   b. For more than a year
7. a. Scarecrow
   b. farmer
   c. Scarecrow
   d. old crow
   e. farmer
   f. Scarecrow

PART D

8. a. The Scarecrow
   b. The Yellow Brick Road
   c. The Forest
   d. The Scarecrow
   e. The Yellow Brick Road
   f. The Forest
9. a. sprinkled
   b. injured
   c. apparent
   d. brisk
   e. delicious
   f. trip
   g. serious
   h. trot

Lesson 13

WORD PRACTICE AND VOCABULARY

EXERCISE 1 Word practice

1. Everybody, find lesson 13, part A in your skillbook. *Wait.* Touch column 1. *Check.* The words in column 1 are hard words that will be in your reading stories.
2. Touch under the first word. *Check.* The first word is **shiver.** What word? *Signal.* **Shiver.**
3. Next word. *Pause.* That word is **jagged.** What word? *Signal.* **Jagged.**
4. *Repeat step 3 for each remaining word in column 1.*
5. Now let's see if you remember all those words. Touch under the first word in column 1. *Pause.* What word? *Signal.* **Shiver.**
6. Next word. *Pause.* What word? *Signal.* **Jagged.**
7. *Repeat step 6 for each remaining word in column 1.*
8. *Repeat the words in column 1 until firm.*

EXERCISE 2 Word practice

1. Everybody, touch under the first word in column 2. *Pause.* What word? *Signal.* **Marriage.**
2. Next word. *Pause.* What word? *Signal.* **Cruel.**
3. *Repeat step 2 for each remaining word in column 2.*
4. *Repeat the words in column 2 until firm.*

EXERCISE 3 Vocabulary review

Task A

1. Everybody, touch column 3. *Check.* First you're going to read the words in column 3. Then we'll talk about what they mean.
2. Touch under the first word. *Pause.* What word? *Signal.* **Comforted.**
3. Next word. *Pause.* What word? *Signal.* **Motionless.**
4. *Repeat step 3 for each remaining word in column 3.*
5. *Repeat the words in column 3 until firm.*

Task B

You've learned the meanings for all these words. Word 1 is **comforted.** *Call on a student.* What does **comforted** mean? *Idea:* To make more comfortable.

Task C

Word 2 is **motionless.** *Call on a student.* What does **motionless** mean? *Idea:* Without movement.

Task D

Word 3 is **inconvenient.** *Call on a student.* What does **inconvenient** mean? *Ideas:* Annoying; requiring work that isn't necessary.

Task E

Word 4 is **declared.** *Call on a student.* What does **declared** mean? *Idea:* Said.

Task F

Word 5 is **deserted.** *Call on a student.* What do you do when you **desert** people? *Idea:* You leave them alone when they need you.

Task G

Word 6 is **maiden.** *Call on a student.* What is a **maiden**? *Idea:* A young, unmarried woman.

Task H

1. Word 7 is **satisfaction.** *Call on a student.* When you feel **satisfaction** over something you do, how do you feel? *Idea:* Pleased.
2. Everybody, what's another way of saying **She felt pleased over winning the race?** *Signal.* **She felt satisfaction over winning the race.**

EXERCISE 4 Vocabulary development

Task A

1. Everybody, touch column 4. *Check.* First you're going to read the words in column 4. Then we'll talk about what they mean.
2. Touch under the first word. *Pause.* What word? *Signal.* **Courage.**
3. Next word. *Pause.* What word? *Signal.* **Awkward.**
4. *Repeat step 3 for each remaining word in column 4.*
5. *Repeat the words in column 4 until firm.*

Task B

1. Now let's talk about what those words mean. Word 1 is **courage.** Here's another way of saying **She was brave: She had courage.**
2. Everybody, what's another way of saying **She was brave?** *Signal.* **She had courage.**
3. Everybody, what's another way of saying **He was not brave?** *Signal.* **He did not have courage.**

Lesson 13

PART A	Word Lists		PART B

PART A   Word Lists

1	2	3
shiver	marriage	**Vocabulary words**
jagged	cruel	1. comforted
sorrow	halves	2. motionless
courage	alas	3. inconvenient
guide		4. declared
approve		5. deserted
awkward		6. maiden
		7. satisfaction

4	5
Vocabulary words	**Vocabulary words**
1. courage	1. shouldered his axe
2. awkward	2. comrade
3. jagged	3. passage
4. moved	4. misfortune

PART B
Vocabulary Sentences

1. The woodman <u>shouldered his axe</u> and marched through the forest.
   - brought his axe to his shoulder
   - thought his axe was his shoulder
   - made his axe look like a shoulder
2. They met a <u>comrade</u> who joined them on their journey.
   - enemy   • tree   • friend
3. The woodman cleared a <u>passage</u> through the thick shrubs and bushes.
   - passenger   • idea   • path
4. The woman had the <u>misfortune</u> of cutting her leg with her axe.
   - good luck   • bad luck   • blade

Task C

1. Word 2 is **awkward**. Another word for **clumsy** is **awkward**.
2. Everybody, what's another way of saying **She was so clumsy that she kept falling down.** *Signal.* **She was so awkward that she kept falling down.**
3. Everybody, what's another way of saying **When she joined the baseball team, she was clumsy?** *Signal.* **When she joined the baseball team, she was awkward.**

Task D

1. Word 3 is **jagged**. Something that is sharp and uneven is **jagged**.
2. Everybody, what's another way of saying **The rocks were sharp and uneven.** *Signal.* **The rocks were jagged.**

Task E

1. Word 4 is **moved**. When you are **moved** by something that you see or hear, that thing makes you feel happy or sad. A sad story might **move** you. Everybody, how would it make you feel? *Signal.* **Sad.**
2. Looking at little kids having fun at the circus might **move** you. *Call on a student.* How would that make you feel? *Idea:* Happy.

EXERCISE 5   Vocabulary from context

Task A

1. Everybody, touch column 5. *Check.* The words in that column are words that you'll read in sentences.
2. Touch under the first line. *Pause.* What words? *Signal.* **Shouldered his axe.**
3. Next word. *Pause.* What word? *Signal.* **Comrade.**
4. *Repeat step 3 for each remaining word in column 5.*
5. *Repeat the words in column 5 until firm.*

Task B

1. Everybody, find part B. First we'll read each sentence and we'll figure out what the underlined words could mean.
2. *Call on a student.* Read sentence 1 and the choices. *Wait.* Everybody, which is the best choice? *Signal.* **Brought his axe to his shoulder.**
3. *Repeat step 2 for sentences 2–4.*
   Answer Key: Sentence 2. **Friend.**
   Sentence 3. **Path.**
   Sentence 4. **Bad luck.**

EXERCISE 6   Glossary practice

1. *Call on a student.* Where is the glossary located? *Idea:* In the back of the textbook. *Call on a student.* What do you find in the glossary? *Idea:* New words in the program.
2. Everybody, turn to the glossary, and get ready to look up some words. *Wait.*
3. The first word is **lumbering**. What word? *Signal.* **Lumbering.**
   - Raise your hand when you have found that word in the glossary. *Wait. Call on a student.* Read what the glossary says about the word **lumbering.** **When you walk with very heavy steps, you are lumbering.**
4. *Repeat step 3 for ruffian and lash.*
   *Answer Key: ruffian–*A rude and rough person is a ruffian.
   *lash–*Another word for whip is lash.

Lesson 13

CHAPTER 8
The Tin Woodman

Dorothy was startled to hear the tin man speak, and was moved by his sad voice.

"What can I do for you?" she inquired, softly.

"Get an oilcan and oil my joints," he answered. "They are rusted so badly that I cannot move them at all.Ⓐ The Tin Woodman continued, "If I am well oiled I will soon be all right again. You will find an oilcan on a shelf in my cottage."

Dorothy at once ran back to the cottage where she had spent the night and found the oilcan. Then she returned and asked anxiously, "Where are your joints?" ★2 ERRORS★

"Oil my neck, first," replied the Tin Woodman. So she oiled it. Because the neck was quite badly rusted, the Scarecrow took hold of the tin head and moved it gently from side to side until it moved freely, and then the man could turn it himself.

"Now oil the joints in my arms," he said. And Dorothy oiled them and the Scarecrow bent them carefully until they were quite free from rust and as good as new.

The Tin Woodman gave a sigh of satisfaction and lowered his axe, which he leaned against the tree.Ⓑ

"This is a great comfort," he said. "I have been holding that axe in the air ever since I rusted, and I'm glad to be able to put it down at last. Now, if you will oil the joints of my legs, I shall be all right once more."

So they oiled his legs until he could move them freely. The Tin Woodman thanked the travelers again and again for saving him, for he seemed a very polite man, and very grateful.

"I might have stood there always if you had not come along," he said. "You have certainly saved my life. How did you happen to be here?"

"We are on our way to the Emerald City, to see the great Oz," she answered. "We stopped at your cottage to pass the night."

"Why do you wish to see Oz?" he asked.

"I want him to send me back to Kansas, and the Scarecrow wants him to put a few brains into his head," she replied.

The Tin Woodman appeared to

think deeply for a moment. Then he said, "Do you suppose Oz could give me a heart?"Ⓒ

"Why, I guess so," Dorothy answered. "It would be as easy as giving the Scarecrow brains."

"True," the Tin Woodman replied. "So, if you will allow me to join your party, I will also go to the Emerald City and ask Oz to help me."

"Come along," said the Scarecrow. Then Dorothy said that she would be pleased to have the Tin Woodman join them. So the Tin Woodman shouldered his axe and they all walked through the forest until they came to the yellow brick road.

The Tin Woodman had asked Dorothy to put the oilcan in her basket. "For," he said, "if I should get caught in the rain, and rust again, I would need the oilcan badly."

It was a bit of good luck to have their new comrade join the party, for soon after they had begun their journey they came to a place where the trees and branches grew so thickly over the road that the travelers could not pass.Ⓓ But the Tin Woodman set to work with his axe and chopped so well that soon he cleared a passage for the entire party.

Dorothy was thinking so earnestly as they walked along that she did not notice when the Scarecrow stumbled into a hole and rolled over to the side of the road. Indeed, he had to call to her to help him up again.

"Why didn't you walk around the

hole?" asked the Tin Woodman.

"I don't know enough," replied the Scarecrow, cheerfully. "My head is stuffed with straw, you know, and that is why I am going to Oz to ask him for some brains."Ⓔ

"Oh, I see," said the Woodman. "But, after all, brains are not the best things in the world."

"Do you have any?" inquired the Scarecrow.

"No, my head is quite empty," answered the Woodman. "But I once had brains, and also a heart. Having tried them both, I would much rather have a heart."Ⓕ

"And why would you rather have a heart?" asked the Scarecrow.

"I will tell you my story, and then you will know."

So, while they were walking through the forest, the Tin Woodman told the following story:Ⓖ

I was born the son of a woodman who chopped down trees in the forest and sold the wood for a living.Ⓗ When I grew up I too became a woodchopper, and after my father died I took care of my old mother as long as she lived. Then I made up my mind that instead of living alone I would marry, so that I would not become lonely.

There was a Munchkin girl who was so beautiful that I soon grew to love her with all my heart. She promised to marry me as soon as I could earn enough money to build a better house for her; so I set to work harder than ever. But the girl lived with an old woman who did not want her to marry

STORY READING

EXERCISE 7   Decoding

1. *Everybody,* turn to page 49 in your textbook. *Wait. Call on a student.* What's the error limit for this chapter? **16 errors.**
2. *Call on individual students to read.*
3. *After the group reads to the 2-error sign without making more than 2 errors, reread the first part aloud and present the comprehension tasks.*
4. *After you have completed the first part, call on individual students to read. Present the comprehension tasks.*

EXERCISE 8   Comprehension tasks

Ⓐ The joints are where two bones come together. Show me some joints in your arm. *Check.*

• Show me some joints in your leg. *Check.*

• What does Dorothy have to do to help the Tin Woodman? *Idea:* Get an oilcan and oil all his joints.

• What does oil do when you put it on rusty things? *Idea:* Makes the rust go away.

Ⓑ Everybody, give me a sigh of satisfaction. *Check.*

Ⓒ What does the Tin Woodman want? **A heart.**

Ⓓ What is blocking the travelers way? *Ideas:* Trees and branches.

• Who could help them solve the problem of getting through the trees? **The Tin Woodman.**

• How could he do that? *Idea:* By cutting down the trees.

Ⓔ What reason did the Scarecrow give for not going around holes? *Idea:* He has no brains.

Ⓕ Did the Tin Woodman have brains? **No.**

• What did the Tin Woodman think was more important, a brain or a heart? **A heart.**

Ⓖ How can you tell that the next part is the Tin Woodman's story? *Idea:* Because the writing is different.

Ⓗ Who was born the son of a woodman? **The Tin Woodman.**

• What did his father do? *Idea:* Chopped down trees and sold the wood.

anyone, for the woman was so lazy that she wanted the girl to remain with her and do the cooking and the housework. Ⓘ *So the old woman went to the Wicked Witch of the East, and promised the witch two sheep and a cow if she would prevent the marriage.* Ⓙ *The Wicked Witch agreed to help and put a spell on my axe.* Ⓚ *One day, when I was chopping away very hard, the axe slipped and cut off my left leg.*

At first, this seemed a great misfortune, for I knew a one-legged man could not do very well as a woodchopper. So I went to a tinsmith and had him make me a new leg out of tin. Ⓛ *The leg worked very well, once I was used to it; but my action angered the Wicked Witch of the East, because I could still marry the pretty Munchkin girl.* Ⓜ ★ 16 ERRORS ★

When I began chopping again, my axe slipped and cut off my right leg. Again I went to the tinsmith, and again he made me a leg out of tin. After this the axe cut off my arms, one after the other, but I had them replaced with tin arms. The Wicked Witch then made the axe slip and cut off my head, and at first I thought that was the end of me. But the tinsmith happened to come along, and he made me a new head out of tin.

I thought I had tricked the Wicked Witch then, and I worked harder than ever. But I did not know how cruel my enemy could be. She thought of a new way to kill my love for the beautiful Munchkin maiden, and made my axe slip again, so that it cut right through my body, splitting me into two halves. Once more the tinsmith came to my

aid and made me a body of tin. He fastened my tin arms and legs and head to my tin body, by means of joints, so that I could move around as well as ever. But, alas! Now I had no heart, so that I lost all my love for the Munchkin girl, and did not care whether I married her or not. I suppose she is still living with the old woman, waiting for me to come after her.

My body shone so brightly in the sun that I felt very proud of it and it did not matter now if my axe slipped, for it could not cut me. There was only one danger—my joints would rust. But I kept an oilcan in my cottage and took care to oil myself whenever I needed it. However, one day I forgot to oil myself. I got caught in a rainstorm, and before I knew it, my joints had rusted, so that I was forced to stand in the woods until you came to help me. Standing there for a year was terribly hard, but while I stood there I had time to think that the greatest loss I had known was the loss of my heart.

When I was in love I was the happiest man on earth. But you cannot love if you do not have a heart, and so I am resolved to ask the Wizard of Oz to give me one. If the Wizard gives me a heart I will go back to the Munchkin maiden and marry her.

Both Dorothy and the Scarecrow had been greatly interested in the story of the Tin Woodman, and now they knew why he was so anxious to get a new heart.

"All the same," said the Scarecrow, "I will ask for brains instead of a heart, for a fool would not know what to do

---

Ⓘ Listen to that part again and get ready to answer some questions. *Read from* Ⓗ *to* Ⓘ.

- Who did the Tin Woodman want to marry? *Idea:* A Munchkin girl.
- What did he have to do before he could marry her? *Idea:* Earn enough money to build her a house.
- Who did the Munchkin girl live with? **An old woman.**
- Did the woman want the girl to marry? **No.**
- Why not? *Idea:* Because she was so lazy that she wanted the girl to do the cooking and housework.

Ⓙ What did the old woman want the Wicked Witch to do? *Idea:* Prevent the marriage.

Ⓚ What happens when you put a spell on something? *Idea:* You make it do magical things.

I wonder what that ax will do.

Ⓛ What job does a tinsmith have? *Idea:* Working with tin.

- What job would a goldsmith have? *Idea:* Working with gold.

Ⓜ How did the witch feel when the Tin Woodman got a new leg? *Idea:* Angry.

- When the witch put a spell on the ax, she wanted to prevent the Woodman from doing something. What was that? *Idea:* Marrying the Munchkin girl.
- Did her plan work? **No.**
- Why not? *Idea:* Because the Woodman got a new leg.
- Read the rest of the chapter to yourselves and be ready to answer some questions.

After all students have finished reading:

- Which leg did the Woodman cut off first? *Idea:* His left leg.
- Which leg did he cut off next? *Idea:* His right leg.
- What did the Woodman do to replace the right leg? *Idea:* Got a new one from the tinsmith.
- Which parts did the Woodman lose next? *Idea:* His arms.
- What happened to his arms? *Idea:* The ax cut them off.
- Which part did the Woodman lose next? **His head.**
- Who made a new head for the Woodman? **The tinsmith.**
- Which part did the Woodman lose next? **His body.**
- When the Woodman was made of tin, did he still love the Munchkin girl? **No.**
- Why not? *Idea:* Because he no longer had a heart.
- What kind of weather made the Woodman rusty? *Idea:* The rainstorm.
- The Woodman wanted the Wizard of Oz to give him something. What was that? **A heart.**

with a heart if he had one."

"I shall take the heart," answered the Tin Woodman. "Brains do not make you happy, and happiness is the best thing in the world."

Dorothy did not say anything, for she did not know which of her two friends was right, and she wondered if she would ever get back to Kansas and Aunt Em.

What worried her most was that the bread was nearly gone, and another meal for herself and Toto would empty the basket. To be sure, neither the Woodman nor the Scarecrow ever ate anything, but she was not made of tin or straw, and could not live unless she was fed.

- What will the Woodman do if the Wizard gives him a heart? *Idea:* Marry the Munchkin girl.
- Everybody, look at the last sentence in the Tin Woodman's story. *Check.*
- Read that sentence. *Wait.*
- After that sentence, the story picks up with Dorothy, the Woodman, and the Scarecrow walking along. I'll read that part. *Read the rest of the story.*
- The Woodman thought that happiness is the best thing in the world. What body part would give him happiness? **A heart.**
- The Scarecrow didn't think a heart would be of much use to him. Why not? *Idea:* Because a fool would not know what to do with a heart.

Award 4 points or have the students reread to the error limit sign.

INDEPENDENT WORK

Do all the items in your skillbook and workbook for lesson 13.

WORKCHECK AND AWARDING POINTS

1. *Read the questions and answers for the skillbook and workbook.*
2. *Award points for independent work as follows:*

0 errors	6 points
2 errors	4 points
3, 4, or 5 errors	2 points
5 or more errors	0 points

3. *Award bonus points as follows:*

Correcting missed items or getting all items right	2 points
Doing the writing assignment acceptably	2 points

ANSWER KEY FOR WORKBOOK

Review Items

1. Write which character said each sentence. Choose from **Dorothy,** the **Scarecrow,** or the **Tin Woodman.**
   a. This character said, "I might have stood there always if you had not come along."
   Tin Woodman
   b. This character said, "I want Oz to send me back to Kansas."
   Dorothy
   c. This character said, "My head is stuffed with straw."
   Scarecrow
   d. This character said, "There was a Munchkin girl who was so beautiful that I soon grew to love her."
   Tin Woodman
   e. This character said, "Happiness is the best thing in the world."
   Tin Woodman
   f. This character said, "A fool would not know what to do with a heart if he had one."
   Scarecrow

2. Write whether each phrase describes **Kansas,** the **Land of the Munchkins,** or the **forest.**
   a. Gray grass
   Kansas
   b. Branches growing over the road
   Forest
   c. Fences beside the road
   Land of the Munchkins
   d. Road well cared for
   Land of the Munchkins
   e. Round houses
   Land of the Munchkins
   f. Cracked land
   Kansas
   g. Thick trees everywhere
   Forest

3. Put an **X** next to the things that Dorothy knows for sure about Oz.
   a. Oz is more powerful than the witches. *X*
   b. Oz lives in the Emerald City. *X*
   c. Oz will send her back to Kansas. ___
   d. Oz will give the Scarecrow brains. ___
   e. Oz is a wizard. *X*
   f. Oz will give the Tin Woodman a heart. ___

Study Skills

4. Find the following words in your glossary. Copy what the glossary says about each word.
   a. lash *Another word for whip is lash.*
   b. burly *Another word for stout and strong is burly.*

ANSWER KEY FOR SKILLBOOK

PART C

1. The Tin Woodman
2. a. *Idea:* Because he was rusted
   b. An oilcan
   c. *Ideas:* In his joints; on his neck
   d. *Ideas:* Rain; water; tears
3. a. The Munchkin girl
   b. An old woman
   c. The Wicked Witch
4. a. The tinsmith
   b. Tin
   c. A heart
   d. No
5. a. *Idea:* A trip back to Kansas
   b. Brains
   c. A heart
   d. *Idea:* Marry the Munchkin girl

PART D

6. a. Quadlings
   b. Munchkins
   c. Winkies
   d. Gillikins
7. a. entertained
   b. gorgeous
   c. crops
   d. balanced
   e. made up her mind
   f. looked like
   g. solemn
   h. suspected

Lesson 14

Lesson 14

PART A   Word Lists

1	2	3	4	5 Vocabulary words	6 Vocabulary words
peculiar	hinges	here	guide	1. comrade	1. approve of
manage	places	hereafter	welcome	2. passage	2. sorrow
Kalidahs	fences	bearable	ashamed	3. misfortune	3. unbearable
fierce	cottages	unbearable	dangerous		4. astonished
relief	manages				5. remarkable
adventure					6. shiver
disease					7. coward
					8. strides

PART B   Vocabulary Sentences

1. Toto did not <u>approve of</u> the new comrade and <u>tried</u> to bite him.
   ● smell   ● look at   ● like
2. When his friends left, he felt great <u>sorrow</u> and started to cry.
   ● happiness   ● anger   ● sadness
3. When she couldn't stand being alone any more, she cried, "This is <u>unbearable</u>."
   ● something I don't mind
   ● something I can't stand
   ● something I like
4. When she saw the Scarecrow wink at her, she was <u>astonished</u>.
   ● not interested   ● surprised
   ● hopeful

5. The dog was <u>remarkable</u> because it had a coat of seven different colors.
   ● ordinary   ● boring   ● unusual
6. When she went outside without a coat on, she began to <u>shiver</u> from the cold.
   ● tremble and vibrate
   ● run and jump   ● sweat and pant
7. He was such a <u>coward</u> that he would pick on very little people, but he was afraid of everybody else.
   ● brave person   ● chicken
   ● nice person
8. The Lion's <u>strides</u> were so long that he took one step each time Dorothy took three steps.
   ● steps   ● windows   ● hooves

WORD PRACTICE AND VOCABULARY

EXERCISE 1   Word practice

1. Everybody, find lesson 14, part A in your skillbook. *Wait.* Touch column 1. *Check.*
   The words in column 1 are hard words that will be in your reading stories.
2. Touch under the first word. *Check.*
   The first word is **peculiar.**
   What word? *Signal.* **Peculiar.**
3. Next word. *Pause.* That word is **manage.**
   What word? *Signal.* **Manage.**
4. *Repeat step 3 for each remaining word in column 1.*
5. Now let's see if you remember all those words. Touch under the first word in column 1. *Pause.*
   What word? *Signal.* **Peculiar.**
6. Next word. *Pause.* What word? *Signal.* **Manage.**
7. *Repeat step 6 for each remaining word in column 1.*
8. *Repeat the words in column 1 until firm.*

EXERCISE 2   Word family

1. Everybody, touch column 2. *Check.*
   All those words end with the letters **c-e-s** or **g-e-s.** Touch under the first word. *Pause.*
   What word? *Signal.* **Hinges.**
2. Next word. *Pause.* What word? *Signal.* **Places.**
3. *Repeat step 2 for each remaining word in column 2.*
4. *Repeat the words in column 2 until firm.*

EXERCISE 3   Word practice

1. Everybody, touch under the first word in column 3. *Pause.* What word? *Signal.* **Here.**
2. Next word. *Pause.* What word? *Signal.* **Hereafter.**
3. *Repeat step 2 for each remaining word in column 3.*

4. *Repeat the words in column 3 until firm.*
5. *Repeat steps 1–4 for column 4.*

EXERCISE 4   Vocabulary review

Task A

1. Everybody, touch column 5. *Check.*
   First you're going to read the words in column 5. Then we'll talk about what they mean.
2. Touch under the first word. *Pause.*
   What word? *Signal.* **Comrade.**
3. Next word. *Pause.* What word? *Signal.* **Passage.**
4. *Repeat step 3 for* **misfortune.**
5. *Repeat the words in column 5 until firm.*

Task B

You've learned the meanings for all these words. Word 1 is **comrade.** *Call on a student.* What is a **comrade?** *Idea:* A friend.

Task C

Word 2 is **passage.** *Call on a student.* What is a **passage?** *Idea:* A path.

Task D

Word 3 is misfortune. *Call on a student.* What does **misfortune** mean?
Idea: Bad luck.

EXERCISE 5   Vocabulary from context

Task A

1. Everybody, touch column 6. *Check.*
   The words in that column are words that you'll read in sentences.
2. Touch under the first line. *Pause.*
   What words? *Signal.* **Approve of.**
3. Next word? *Pause.* What word? *Signal.* **Sorrow.**
4. *Repeat step 3 for each remaining word in column 6.*
5. *Repeat the words in column 6 until firm.*

Task B

1. Everybody, find part B. First we'll read each sentence and then we'll figure out what the underlined words could mean.
2. *Call on a student.* Read sentence 1 and the choices. *Wait.*
   Everybody. which is the best choice? *Signal.* **Like.**
3. *Repeat step 2 for sentences 2–8.*
   Answer Key: Sentence 2. **Sadness.**
   Sentence 3. **Something I can't stand.**
   Sentence 4. **Surprised.**
   Sentence 5. **Unusual.**
   Sentence 6. **Tremble and vibrate.**
   Sentence 7. **Chicken.**
   Sentence 8. **Steps.**

Lesson 14

CHAPTER 9
The Cowardly Lion

All this time Dorothy and her companions had been walking through the thick woods. The road was still paved with yellow brick, but the bricks were covered by dried branches and dead leaves from the trees, and it was difficult to walk.

There were very few birds in this part of the forest, for the birds of Oz love the open country where there is plenty of sunshine.Ⓐ Now and then the travelers would hear a deep growl from some wild animal hidden among the trees. These sounds made Dorothy's heart beat fast, for she did not know what made the sounds. But Toto knew, and he walked close to Dorothy's side, and did not even bark.Ⓑ ★2 ERRORS★

"How long will it be," Dorothy asked the Tin Woodman, "before we are out of the forest?"

"I cannot tell," answered the Tin Woodman, "for I have never been to the Emerald City. But my father went there once, when I was a boy, and he said it was a long journey through a dangerous country. But I am not afraid so long as I have my oilcan, and nothing can hurt the Scarecrow. As for you, you have the mark of the good Witch's kiss on your forehead, and that will protect you from harm."Ⓒ

"But Toto!" said Dorothy, anxiously. "What will protect him?"

"We must protect him ourselves, if he is in danger," replied the Tin Woodman.

Just as he spoke, a terrible roar came from the forest, and the next moment a great Lion bounded into the road. With one blow of his paw he sent the Scarecrow spinning over and over to the edge of the road, and then he struck at the Tin Woodman with his sharp claws. But, to the Lion's surprise, he could make no dent in the tin, although the Woodman fell over in the road and lay still.Ⓓ

Little Toto, now that he had an enemy to face, ran barking toward the Lion, and the great beast opened his mouth to bite the dog. But Dorothy, fearing Toto would be killed, rushed forward and slapped the Lion on his nose as hard as she could, while she cried out, "Don't you dare bite Toto! You ought to be ashamed of yourself, a big beast like you, to bite a poor little dog!"

"I didn't bite him," said the Lion, as he rubbed his nose with his paw

where Dorothy had hit it.Ⓔ

Dorothy said, "No, but you tried to. You are nothing but a big coward."Ⓕ

"I know that I am a coward," said the Lion, hanging his head in shame. "I've always known it. But how can I help it?"

"I don't know, I'm sure. To think of your striking a stuffed man, like the poor Scarecrow!"

"Is he stuffed?" asked the Lion, in surprise, as he watched her pick up the Scarecrow, set him on his feet, and pat him into shape again.

"Of course he's stuffed," replied Dorothy, who was still angry.

"So that's why he went over so easily," remarked the Lion. "It astonished me to see him whirl around like that. Is the other one stuffed, also?"

"No," said Dorothy. "He is made of tin." And she helped the Woodman up.

"That's why he nearly ruined my claws," said the Lion. "When they scratched against the tin it made a cold shiver run down my back. What is that little animal you are so fond of?"

"He is my dog," answered Dorothy.

STORY READING

EXERCISE 6   Decoding

1. Everybody, turn to page 54 in your textbook. *Wait. Call on a student.* What's the error limit for this chapter? **14 errors.**
2. *Call on individual students to read.*
3. *After the group reads to the 2-error sign without making more than 2 errors, reread the first part aloud and present the comprehension tasks.*
4. *After you have completed the first part, call on individual students to read. Present the comprehension tasks.*

EXERCISE 7   Comprehension tasks

Ⓐ What kind of place were the travelers walking through? *Idea:* Thick woods.
● Why weren't there many birds? *Idea:* Because birds love open country.
Ⓑ Who knew what was making those sounds? **Toto.**
● How do you think he could tell? *Idea:* By the sounds they made.
● How did Toto behave? *Idea:* He walked close to Dorothy and did not bark.
Ⓒ Did the Woodman think that the Scarecrow could be hurt by anything? **No.**
● Was the Woodman right? **No.**
● What could harm the Scarecrow? **Fire.**
Ⓓ Who did the Lion attack first? **The Scarecrow.**
● Who did the Lion attack next? **The Tin Woodman.**
● Did the Lion dent the Woodman? **No.**
Ⓔ What did Dorothy do to the Lion? *Idea:* Slapped him on the nose.
● Did it take a lot of courage to do that? **Yes.**
● What would an ordinary lion do if it got slapped on the nose? *Idea:* Fight back.
● What did this lion do? *Idea:* Rubbed its nose.
Ⓕ What's a coward? *Idea:* Someone who is afraid.

"Is he made of tin, or stuffed?" asked the Lion.

"Neither. He's just a dog," said the girl.

"Oh! He's a curious animal, and seems remarkably small, now that I look at him. No one would think of biting such a little thing except a coward like me," continued the Lion, sadly. Ⓖ

"What makes you a coward?" asked Dorothy, looking at the great beast in wonder, for he was as big as a small horse.

"It's a mystery," replied the Lion. "I suppose I was born that way. All the other animals in the forest naturally expect me to be brave, for the Lion is supposed to be the King of Beasts. I learned that if I roared very loudly every living thing was frightened and got out of my way." Ⓗ

The Lion continued, "Whenever I've met people, I've been awfully scared. But I just roared at them, and they have always run away as fast as they could go. If the elephants and the tigers and the bears had ever tried to fight me, I would have run myself—I'm such a coward. But just as soon as they hear me roar they all try to get away from me, and of course I let them go." Ⓘ

The Scarecrow said, "But that isn't right. The King of Beasts shouldn't be a coward."

"I know it," answered the Lion, wiping a tear from his eye with the tip of his tail. "It is my great sorrow and makes my life very unhappy. But

whenever there is danger my heart begins to beat fast."

"Perhaps you have heart disease," said the Tin Woodman.

"It may be," said the Lion.

"If you have," continued the Tin Woodman, "you ought to be glad, for it proves you have a heart. As for me, I have no heart, so I cannot have heart disease." Ⓙ ★14 ERRORS★

Thoughtfully, the Lion said, "Perhaps if I had no heart I would not be a coward."

"Do you have brains?" asked the Scarecrow.

"I suppose so. I've never looked to see," replied the Lion.

"I am going to the great Oz to ask him to give me some brains," remarked the Scarecrow, "for my head is stuffed with straw."

"And I am going to ask him to give me a heart," said the Tin Woodman.

"And I am going to ask him to send Toto and me back to Kansas," added Dorothy.

"Do you think Oz could give me courage?" asked the cowardly Lion.

"Just as easily as he could give me brains," said the Scarecrow.

"Or give me a heart," said the Tin Woodman.

"Or send me back to Kansas," said Dorothy.

"Then, if you don't mind, I'll go with you," said the Lion, "for my life is simply unbearable without a bit of courage."

56 Lesson 14 Textbook

"You will be very welcome," answered Dorothy, "for you will help to keep away the other wild beasts. It seems to me they must be more cowardly than you are if they let you scare them so easily."

"They really are," said the Lion. "But that doesn't make me any braver, and as long as I know that I am a coward I will be unhappy."

So once more the little party set off upon the journey, the Lion walking with proud strides at Dorothy's side. Toto did not approve of this new comrade at first. He could not forget how he had almost been crushed between the Lion's great jaws, but after a time he became more relaxed. Soon, Toto and the cowardly Lion became good friends.

The group traveled peacefully for the rest of that day. Once, the Tin Woodman stepped on a beetle that was crawling along the road, and killed the poor little thing. This made the Tin Woodman very unhappy, for he was always careful not to hurt any living creature; and as he walked along he wept several tears of sorrow. These tears ran slowly down his face and over the hinges of his jaw, and they rusted the hinges.

When Dorothy asked him a question the Tin Woodman could not open his mouth, for his jaws were tightly rusted together. He became greatly frightened at this and made many motions to Dorothy to help him, but she could not understand, nor could the Lion. But the Scarecrow took the oilcan from Dorothy's basket and oiled the Woodman's jaws, so that after a few moments he could talk as well as before.

"This will teach me a lesson," he said, "to look where I step. For if I should kill another bug or beetle I would surely cry again, and crying rusts my jaws so that I cannot speak."

After that the Tin Woodman walked very carefully, with his eyes on the road, and when he saw a tiny ant going by he would step over it, so as not to harm it. The Tin Woodman knew very well that he had no heart, and therefore he took great care never to be cruel or unkind to anything.

"You people with hearts," he said, "have something to guide you, and need never do wrong. But I have no heart, and so I must be very careful. When Oz gives me a heart, of course, I won't have to be so careful."

Lesson 14 Textbook 57

Ⓖ Would a coward try to pick a fight with a strong animal? **No.**

● Does the Lion know that he is a coward? **Yes.**

Ⓗ What is the lion supposed to be? **The King of Beasts.**

● What does that mean? *Idea:* That he is the most powerful animal.

● The Lion learned that if he did something, everybody got out of his way. What did he learn to do? *Idea:* Roar very loudly.

Ⓘ What would the Lion have done if a tiger or a bear had ever tried to fight him? *Idea:* He would have run away.

● But did those animals ever try to fight the Lion? **No.**

● What did he do that frightened them? *Idea:* Roared.

Ⓙ What disease did the Tin Woodman think the Lion might have? **Heart disease.**

● If the Lion has heart disease, that proves that he has something else. What is that? **A heart.**

● Read the rest of the chapter to yourselves and be ready to answer some questions.

After all students have finished reading:

● Which person wants a heart? **The Tin Woodman.**

● How did the Tin Woodman feel after he stepped on the beetle? *Idea:* Very unhappy. I wonder how he could feel so unhappy if he didn't have a heart.

● Which person wants brains? **The Scarecrow.**

● The Scarecrow figured out something that nobody else could figure out. What was that? *Idea:* What was wrong with the Tin Woodman. I wonder how he could be so smart if he doesn't have any brains.

Award 4 points or have the students reread to the error limit sign.

INDEPENDENT WORK

Do all the items in your skillbook and workbook for lesson 14.

Lesson 14 **71**

ANSWER KEY FOR WORKBOOK

Map Skills

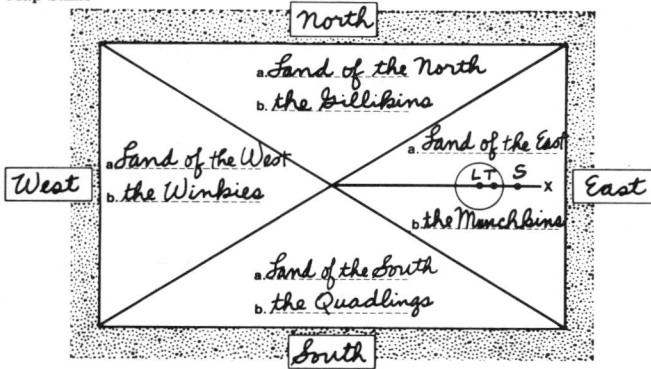

1. Write **North, East, South** and **West** in the boxes around the map.
2. Fill in the blanks.
   a. On the map, write the name of each land.
   b. Then write the name of the people who live in that land.
3. The **X** shows where Dorothy started out.
   a. Write the name of the Witch that Dorothy met there.

   Witch of the North

   b. The **line** shows the road that Dorothy is on. What is that road made out of? *Idea: brick*
4. There are **dots** on the line to show where Dorothy met her friends.
   a. Put an **S** on the dot where she met the Scarecrow.
   b. Put a **T** on the dot where she met the Tin Woodman.
   c. Put an **L** on the dot where she met the Lion.
5. The **circle** shows the place that Dorothy is now in. What kind of place does the circle show?

   Idea: forest
6. Write the direction the travelers are going. *West*
7. What is the name of the city at the end of the road?

   Emerald City

Study Skills

8. Find the following words in your glossary. Copy what the glossary says about each word.

   a. tussle *When you tussle with somebody, you wrestle with that person.*

   b. ruffian *A rude and rough person is a ruffian.*

WORKCHECK AND AWARDING POINTS

1. *Read the questions and answers for the skillbook and workbook.*
2. *Award points for independent work as follows:*

0 errors	6 points
2 errors	4 points
3, 4, or 5 errors	2 points
5 or more errors	0 points

3. *Award bonus points as follows:*

Correcting missed items or getting all items right	2 points
Doing the writing assignment acceptably	2 points

ANSWER KEY FOR SKILLBOOK

PART C

1. The Cowardly Lion
2. *Ideas:* A forest; thick woods
3. a. The Scarecrow
   b. The Tin Woodman
   c. Dorothy
4. coward
5. a. bravely
   b. Beasts
6. a. Roared
   b. *Idea:* The Lion would have run away
7. a. Courage
   b. Brains
   c. A heart
   d. *Idea:* A trip back to Kansas
8. a. *Idea:* Wept
   b. They rusted together
   c. The Scarecrow
   d. The oilcan

PART D

9. a. Tin Woodman
   b. Dorothy
   c. Lion
   d. Lion
   e. Tin Woodman
   f. Lion
   g. Dorothy
   h. Scarecrow
10. a. Tin Woodman, Scarecrow
    b. Dorothy, Toto, Lion
    c. Tin Woodman, Scarecrow
    d. Dorothy, Toto, Lion
11. a. delicious
    b. thought
    c. apparent
    d. represented
    e. hurt
    f. husky

Lesson 15

Lesson 15

PART A Word Lists

1	2	3
distances	adventure	faintest
edges	delight	shaggy
cottages	delightful	relief
fences	fierce	Kalidahs
places		

4
Vocabulary words
1. approve of
2. sorrow
3. unbearable
4. strides
5. astonished
6. remarkable
7. awkward
8. jagged

5
Vocabulary words
1. snug
2. crouch
3. gloomy

6
Vocabulary words
1. splendid
2. peculiar
3. dreadful

PART B
Vocabulary Sentences

1. Dorothy built a splendid fire that made large flames and gave off a lot of heat.
   • ugly • marvelous • small
2. They saw peculiar looking people who had three eyes and four arms.
   • ordinary • regular • strange
3. When she saw the horrible things the tigers did, she said, "Those beasts are dreadful."
   • horrible • great • silly

WORD PRACTICE AND VOCABULARY

EXERCISE 1 Word family

1. Everybody, find lesson 15, part A in your skillbook. *Wait.* Touch column 1. *Check.*
   All those words end with the letters **c-e-s** or **g-e-s.** Touch under the first word. *Pause.*
   What word? *Signal.* **Distances.**
2. Next word. *Pause.* What word? *Signal.* **Edges.**
3. *Repeat step 2 for each remaining word in column 1.*
4. *Repeat the words in column 1 until firm.*

EXERCISE 2 Word practice

1. Everybody, touch under the first word in column 2. *Pause.* What word? *Signal.*
   Adventure.
2. Next word. *Pause.* What word? *Signal.* **Delight.**
3. *Repeat step 2 for each remaining word in column 2.*
4. *Repeat the words in column 2 until firm.*
5. *Repeat steps 1–4 for column 3.*

EXERCISE 3 Vocabulary review

Task A

1. Everybody, touch column 4. *Check.*
   First you're going to read the words in column 4. Then we'll talk about what they mean.
2. Touch under the first line. *Pause.*
   What words? *Signal.* **Approve of.**
3. Next word. *Pause.* What word? *Signal.* **Sorrow.**
4. *Repeat step 3 for each remaining word in column 4.*
5. *Repeat the words in column 4 until firm.*

Task B

You've learned the meanings for all these words. The words in line 1 are **approve of.**
Call on a student. What do the words **approve of** mean? *Idea:* Like.

Task C

Word 2 is **sorrow.** *Call on a student.*
What is **sorrow?** *Idea:* Sadness.

Task D

Word 3 is **unbearable.** *Call on a student.*
What does **unbearable** mean? *Idea:* Something you can't stand.

Task E

Word 4 is **strides.** *Call on a student.*
What are **strides?** *Idea:* Long steps.

Task F

Word 5 is **astonished.** *Call on a student.*
What does **astonished** mean? *Idea:* Surprised.

Task G

Word 6 is **remarkable.** *Call on a student.*
What does **remarkable** mean? *Idea:* Unusual.

Task H

Word 7 is **awkward.** *Call on a student.*
What does **awkward** mean? *Idea:* Clumsy.

Task I

1. Word 8 is **jagged.** *Call on a student.*
   What does **jagged** mean? *Idea:* Sharp and uneven.
2. Everybody, what's another way of saying
   The edge of the chainsaw was sharp and uneven? *Signal.*
   The edge of the chainsaw was jagged.

EXERCISE 4 Vocabulary development

Task A

1. Everybody, touch column 5. *Check.*
   First you're going to read the words in column 5. Then we'll talk about what they mean.
2. Touch under the first word. *Pause.*
   What word? *Signal.* **Snug.**
3. Next word. *Pause.* What word? *Signal.* **Crouch.**
4. *Repeat step 3 for gloomy.*
5. *Repeat the words in column 5 until firm.*

Task B

1. Word 1 is **snug.** Something that is **snug** fits tightly.
2. Everybody, what would we call a tightly fitting glove? *Signal.* **A snug glove.**
3. Everybody, what would we call a tightly fitting pair of blue jeans? *Signal.*
   A snug pair of blue jeans.

Task C

1. Word 2 is **crouch.** When you **crouch,** you bend your legs and get ready to spring forward.
2. Everybody, what are you doing when you bend your legs and get ready to spring forward?
   Signal. **Crouching.**

Task D

Word 3 is **gloomy.** Something that looks **gloomy** looks dismal. Everybody, what's another word for **dismal?** *Signal.* **Gloomy.**

Lesson 15

PART A   Word Lists

1	2	3
distances	adventure	faintest
edges	delight	shaggy
cottages	delightful	relief
fences	fierce	Kalidahs
places		

4
Vocabulary words
1. approve of
2. sorrow
3. unbearable
4. strides
5. astonished
6. remarkable
7. awkward
8. jagged

5
Vocabulary words
1. snug
2. crouch
3. gloomy

6
Vocabulary words
1. splendid
2. peculiar
3. dreadful

PART B
Vocabulary Sentences

1. Dorothy built a <u>splendid</u> fire that made large flames and gave off a lot of heat.
   ● ugly   ● marvelous   ● small
2. They saw <u>peculiar</u> looking people who had three eyes and four arms.
   ● ordinary   ● regular   ● strange
3. When she saw the horrible things the tigers did, she said, "Those beasts are <u>dreadful</u>."
   ● horrible   ● great   ● silly

Lesson 15

CHAPTER 10
The Kalidahs

The travelers had to camp out that night under a large tree in the forest, for there were no houses near. The tree made a good shelter, and the Tin Woodman chopped a great pile of wood with his axe and Dorothy built a splendid fire that warmed her and made her feel less lonely. She and Toto ate the last of their bread, and now she did not know what they would do for breakfast. (A)

"If you wish," said the Lion, "I will go into the forest and kill a deer for you. You can roast it by the fire, since your tastes are so peculiar that you prefer cooked food, and then you will have a very good breakfast." ★2 ERRORS★

"Don't please don't," begged the Tin Woodman. "I would certainly weep if you killed a poor deer, and then my jaws would rust again." (B)

But the Lion went away into the forest and found his own supper, and no one ever knew what it was, for he didn't mention it. (C)

The Scarecrow found a tree full of nuts and filled Dorothy's basket with them, so that she would not be hungry for a long time. She thought this was very kind and thoughtful of the Scarecrow, but she laughed heartily at the awkward way in which the poor creature picked up the nuts. His padded hands were so clumsy and the nuts were so small that he dropped almost as many as he put in the basket. But the Scarecrow did not mind how long it took him to fill the basket. The nut tree was far away from the fire and the Scarecrow feared a spark from the fire might get into his straw and burn him up. (D) The Scarecrow only came near the fire to cover Dorothy with dry leaves when she lay down to sleep. These kept her very snug and warm and she slept soundly until morning.

When it was daylight the girl bathed her face in a little rippling brook and soon after, they all started toward the Emerald City.

This was to be an important day for the travelers. They had hardly been walking an hour when they saw a great ditch in front of them that crossed the road and divided the forest as far as they could see on either side. It was a very wide ditch, and when they crept up to the edge and looked into it they could see it was also very deep, and there were many big, jagged rocks at the bottom.

58   Lesson 15   Textbook

EXERCISE 5   Vocabulary from context

Task A

1. Everybody, touch column 6. *Check.*
   The words in that column are words that you'll read in sentences.
2. Touch under the first word. *Pause.*
   What word? *Signal.* **Splendid.**
3. Next word. *Pause.* What word? *Signal.* **Peculiar.**
4. *Repeat step 3 for* **dreadful.**
5. *Repeat the words in column 6 until firm.*

Task B

1. Everybody, find part B. First we'll read each sentence and then we'll figure out what the underlined words could mean.
2. *Call on a student.* Read sentence 1 and the choices. *Wait.*
   Everybody, which is the best choice? *Signal.* **Marvelous.**
3. *Repeat step 2 for sentences 2 and 3.*
   Answer Key: Sentence 2. **Strange.**
   Sentence 3. **Horrible.**

STORY READING

EXERCISE 6   Decoding

1. Everybody, turn to page 58 in your textbook. *Wait. Call on a student.* What's the error limit for this chapter? **14 errors.**
2. *Call on individual students to read.*
3. *After the group reads to the 2-error sign without making more than 2 errors, reread the first part aloud and present the comprehension tasks.*
4. *After you have completed the first part, call on individual students to read. Present the comprehension tasks.*

EXERCISE 7   Comprehension tasks

(A) Where were Dorothy and the others camping that night? *Idea:* Under a large tree.
● Who chopped wood for the fire? **The Tin Woodman.**
● How much food did Dorothy have after she and Toto ate the bread? *Idea:* None.
(B) The Tin Woodman said he would do something if the Lion killed a deer. What was that? **Weep.**
● Would the Woodman be able to feel so sorry for the deer if he didn't have a heart? *Idea:* Probably not.
(C) What kind of food would a lion have for supper? *Idea:* Meat.
● Would a lion cook its supper? **No.**
(D) Was the Scarecrow happy to be far away from the fire? **Yes.**
● Why? *Idea:* Because he was afraid it might burn him up.

The sides were so steep that nobody could climb down, and for a moment it seemed that their journey must end.

"What shall we do?" asked Dorothy, despairingly.

"I haven't the faintest idea," said the Tin Woodman. And the Lion shook his shaggy mane and looked thoughtful. Ⓔ

The Scarecrow said, "We cannot fly, that is certain. Neither can we climb down into this great ditch. Therefore, if we cannot jump over it, we must stop where we are."

"I think I could jump over it, said the cowardly Lion, after measuring the distance carefully in his mind.

"Then we are all right," answered

the Scarecrow, "for you can carry us all over on your back, one at a time." Ⓕ

"Well, I'll try it," said the Lion. "Who will go first?"

"I will," declared the Scarecrow. "For, if you found that you could not jump over the ditch, Dorothy would be killed, or the Tin Woodman badly dented on the rocks below. But if I am on your back it will not matter so much, for the fall would not hurt me at all." Ⓖ

"I am terribly afraid of falling myself," said the cowardly Lion, "but I suppose there is nothing to do but try it. So get on my back and we will make the attempt."

The Scarecrow sat on the Lion's back, and the big beast walked to the edge of the ditch and crouched down.

"Why don't you run and jump?" asked the Scarecrow.

"Because that isn't the way we lions do these things," he replied. Then he sprang forward through the air and landed safely on the other side. Ⓗ They were all greatly pleased to see how easily the Lion had jumped, and after the Scarecrow got down from his back the Lion sprang across the ditch again.

Dorothy thought she should go next, so she took Toto in one arm and climbed on the Lion's back, holding tightly to his mane with her free hand. Ⓘ The next moment it seemed as if she was flying through the air. And then, before she had time to think about it, she was safe on the other side. The Lion went back a third time and got the Tin Woodman.

Then they all sat down for a few moments to give the beast a chance to rest. Ⓙ The Lion's great leaps had made his breath short, and he panted like a big dog that has been running too long. Ⓚ

The forest was very thick on this side, and it looked dark and gloomy. After the Lion had rested, they started along the yellow brick road silently wondering if they would ever come to the end of the woods and reach the bright sunshine again. To add to their discomfort, they soon heard strange noises coming from the forest, and the Lion whispered to them that the Kalidahs lived in this part of the country. Ⓛ ★14 ERRORS★

"What are the Kalidahs?" asked Dorothy.

"They are monstrous beasts with bodies like bears and heads like tigers," replied the Lion. "Their claws are so long and sharp that they could tear me in two as easily as I could kill Toto. I'm terribly afraid of the Kalidahs."

"I'm not surprised that you are," replied Dorothy. "They must be dreadful beasts."

The Lion was about to reply when suddenly they came to another ditch across the road. This ditch was so broad and deep that the Lion knew at once that he could not leap across it.

So they sat down to consider what they should do, and after serious thought the Scarecrow said, "Here is a large tree, standing close to the ditch. If the Tin Woodman can chop it down, so that the

---

Ⓔ What was blocking their way?
Idea: A great ditch.

● Why didn't they climb down?
Idea: Because the sides were so steep.

● What was at the bottom of the ditch.
Idea: Big jagged rocks.

● Everybody, look at the picture. You can see the ditch blocking the road.

● Can you think of a way that they might get across the ditch? *Idea:* Student preference.

● Everybody, look at the picture again. The lion's mane is the long hair around the lion's neck. Touch the lion's mane. *Check.*

Ⓕ Who figured out how to get across the ditch? **The Scarecrow.**

● Would he be able to do that if he didn't have any brains? *Idea:* Probably not.

● What was the Scarecrow's plan?
Idea: To have the Lion jump over the ditch with them on his back, one at a time.

Ⓖ The Scarecrow had another smart idea. Why did he think that he should go across first?
Idea: Because he would not be hurt by the fall.

Ⓗ Did it take courage for the Lion to do that? **Yes.**

Ⓘ Dorothy held onto the Lion's mane with her free hand. What was Dorothy doing with her other hand? **Holding Toto.**

Ⓙ Who needed a chance to rest?
Ideas: The Lion; the beast.

Ⓚ Show me how the Lion did that? *Check.*

Ⓛ Who was making the strange noises? **The Kalidahs.**

● Read the rest of the chapter to yourselves and be ready to answer some questions.

After all students have finished reading:

● What did the Kalidahs' heads look like? **Tigers.**

● What did the Kalidahs' bodies look like? **Bears.**

● What was on their paws? *Idea:* Long sharp claws.

● As Dorothy and the others walked along they came to something that blocked their path.

● What was that? **Another ditch.**

● Who came up with a plan for getting across the ditch? **The Scarecrow.**

top falls on the other side, we can walk across it easily."

"That is a first-rate idea," said the Lion. "One would almost think you had brains in your head, instead of straw."

The Woodman set to work at once, and his axe was so sharp that he soon chopped most of the way through the tree. Then the Lion put his strong front legs against the tree and pushed with all his might. The big tree tipped and fell with a crash across the ditch, with its top branches on the other side.

They had just started to cross this tree bridge when a sharp growl made them all look up, and to their horror they saw two great beasts running toward them. These beasts had bodies like bears and heads like tigers.

"They are the Kalidahs!" said the cowardly Lion, beginning to tremble.

"Quick!" cried the Scarecrow, "Let's cross over."

So Dorothy went first, holding Toto in her arms. The Tin Woodman followed, and the Scarecrow came next. The Lion, although he was certainly afraid, turned to face the Kalidahs, and then he gave a roar that was so loud and terrible that Dorothy screamed and the Scarecrow fell over backwards. Even the Kalidahs stopped short and looked at him in surprise.

But, seeing they were bigger than the Lion, and remembering that there were two of them and only one of him, the Kalidahs again rushed forward. The Lion crossed over the tree and turned to see what they would do next. Without stopping an instant, the fierce beasts also began to cross the tree, and the Lion said to Dorothy, "We will lose, for they will surely tear us to pieces with their sharp claws. But stand close behind me, and I will fight them as long as I am alive."

"Wait a minute!" called the Scarecrow. He had been thinking what to do, and now he asked the Woodman to chop away the end of the tree that rested on their side of the ditch. The Tin Woodman began to use his axe at once, and just as the two Kalidahs were nearly across, the tree fell with a crash into the ditch, carrying the ugly, snarling beasts with it. Both fell on the sharp rocks at the bottom.

"Well," said the cowardly Lion, heaving a sigh of relief, "I see we are going to live a little while longer, and I am glad, for it must be a very uncomfortable thing not to be alive. Those creatures frightened me so badly that my heart is pounding."

"Ah," said the Tin Woodman, sadly, "If I only had a heart."

- What was the plan? *Idea:* To cut down a tree and use it as a bridge.
- Who pushed the tree over after it was cut? **The Lion.**
- How did the Lion do that? *Idea:* He pushed it with his legs.
- As the travelers started to cross the bridge they had made, they saw something. What did they see? **The Kalidahs.**
- What did the Lion do when the Kalidahs appeared? *Idea:* Turned around and roared.
- Did that take courage? **Yes.**
- Who came up with the plan that stopped the Kalidahs? **The Scarecrow.**
- What was that plan? *Idea:* To chop down the tree.
- Did the plan work? **Yes.**
- What happened to the Kalidahs when the end of the tree was cut away? *Idea:* They fell down on the sharp rocks.

Award 4 points or have the students reread to the error limit sign.

INDEPENDENT WORK

Do all the items in your skillbook and workbook for lesson 15.

WORKCHECK AND AWARDING POINTS

1. *Read the questions and answers for the skillbook and workbook.*
2. *Award points for independent work as follows:*

> *0 errors* . . . .*6 points*
> *2 errors* . . . .*4 points*
> *3, 4, or 5 errors* . . . .*2 points*
> *5 or more errors* . . . .*0 points*

3. *Award bonus points as follows:*

> *Correcting missed items*
> *or getting all items right* . . . .*2 points*
> *Doing the writing*
> *assignment acceptably* . . . .*2 points*

ANSWER KEY FOR WORKBOOK

Story Items

1. Put the following story events in the right order by numbering them from 1 through 5.

   2 The Lion jumped across a ditch.

   5 The Kalidahs fell to the bottom of the ditch.

   1 The travelers camped out under a large tree.

   3 The Lion pushed a tree across a ditch.

   4 The Kalidahs chased the travelers across a tree.

Crossword Puzzle

To work the puzzle, read an item and figure out which word the item describes. Then write the word in the puzzle. Complete the entire puzzle.

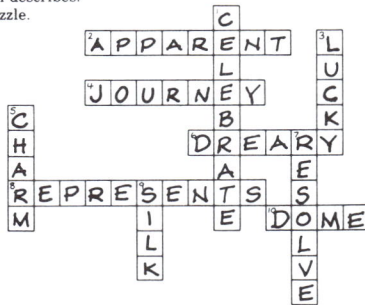

```
                C
   ²A P P A R E N T      ³L
                L         U
      ⁴J O U R N E Y      C
        ⁵C     B          K
         H     ⁶D R E A R Y
         A     A          E
        ⁸R E P R E ⁹S E N T S
         M     I     E   ¹⁰D O M E
               L     E      L
               K            V
                            E
```

Across

2. When something is easy to see or understand, it is _____.
4. Another word for **trip** is _____.
6. Another word for **dull** is _____.
8. That mask _____ the face of a witch.
10. A round roof that looks like a hat.

Down

1. Another word for **have fun** is _____.
3. Another word for **fortunate** is _____.
5. A magic power is a _____.
7. When you make up your mind to do something, you _____ to do it.
9. A very fine material that is used in fancy dresses and shirts.

Study Skills

2. Find the following words in your glossary. Copy what the glossary says about each word.

   a. gnaw *When you chew on something that is very hard, you gnaw on that thing.*

   b. lumbering *When you walk with very heavy steps, you are lumbering.*

ANSWER KEY FOR SKILLBOOK

PART C

1. The Kalidahs
2. None
3. *Idea:* By killing a deer
4. Cry *or* weep/rust
5. *Idea:* Because he was afraid that it might burn him
6. a. *Idea:* Because the sides were too steep
   b. The Scarecrow
   c. *Idea:* Jump across the ditch
   d. *Idea:* On the Lion's back
7. a. The Scarecrow
   b. The Tin Woodman
   c. The Lion
8. a. bear/tiger
   b. *Idea:* Long and sharp
9. a. Roared
   b. stopped for an instant and continued
10. a. The Scarecrow
    b. *Idea:* To cut away the end of the tree
    c. *Idea:* They fell to the bottom of the ditch on the sharp rocks

PART D

11. a. South
    b. West
    c. East
    d. North
12. a. Kansas
    b. Kansas
    c. Land of the Munchkins
    d. Forest
    e. Forest
13. a. The Kalidahs
    b. The Tin Woodman
    c. Kansas
    d. Kansas
    e. The Tin Woodman
14. a. amused
    b. looked like
    c. satisfaction
    d. companion
    e. mystery

Lesson 16

Lesson 16

PART A	Word Lists		PART B

PART A   Word Lists

1	2	3
beckon	downstream	adventure
scent	cornfield	fastened
curtsy	harmless	dismal
hurriedly	wildcat	dismally
	indeed	
	hereafter	

4	5
Vocabulary words	**Vocabulary words**
1. raft	1. delightful
2. meadow	2. refreshed
3. cozy	3. glare
4. cluster	
5. scarlet	
6. dazzle	
7. scarcely	

PART B
Vocabulary Sentences

1. They were pleased to see this <u>delightful</u> meadow before them.
   - ugly   • wonderful   • sad
2. The next morning, Dorothy said, "I feel great. The long sleep made me feel <u>refreshed</u>."
   - tired   • lonesome
   - full of energy
3. The <u>glare</u> of the lights almost blinded her.
   - sound   • feeling   • brightness

WORD PRACTICE AND VOCABULARY

EXERCISE 1   Word practice

1. Everybody, find lesson 16, part A in your skillbook. *Wait.* Touch column 1. *Check.*
   The words in column 1 are hard words that will be in your reading stories.
2. Touch under the first word. *Check.*
   The first word is **beckon.** What word? *Signal.* **Beckon.**
3. Next word. *Pause.* That word is **scent.** What word? *Signal.* **Scent.**
4. *Repeat step 3 for each remaining word in column 1.*
5. Now let's see if you remember all those words. Touch under the first word in column 1. *Pause.* What word? *Signal.* **Beckon.**
6. Next word. *Pause.* What word? *Signal.* **Scent.**
7. *Repeat step 6 for each remaining word in column 1.*
8. *Repeat the words in column 1 until firm.*

EXERCISE 2   Word family

1. Everybody, touch column 2. *Check.*
   All those words are made up of two shorter words. Touch under the first word. *Pause.* What word? *Signal.* **Downstream.**
2. Next word. *Pause.* What word? *Signal.* **Cornfield.**
3. *Repeat step 2 for each remaining word in column 2.*
4. *Repeat the words in column 2 until firm.*

EXERCISE 3   Word practice

1. Everybody, touch under the first word in column 3. *Pause.* What word? *Signal.* **Adventure.**
2. Next word. *Pause.* What word? *Signal.* **Fastened.**
3. *Repeat step 2 for each remaining word in column 3.*
4. *Repeat the words in column 3 until firm.*

EXERCISE 4   Vocabulary development

Task A

1. Everybody, touch column 4. *Check.*
   First you're going to read the words in column 4. Then we'll talk about what they mean.
2. Touch under the first word. *Pause.*
   What word? *Signal.* **Raft.**
3. Next word. *Pause.* What word? *Signal.* **Meadow.**
4. *Repeat step 3 for each remaining word in column 4.*
5. *Repeat the words in column 4 until firm.*

Task B

Now let's talk about what those words mean. Word 1 is **raft.** A **raft** is a flat boat with no sides. Everybody, what do we call a flat boat with no sides? *Signal.* **A raft.**

Task C

Word 2 is **meadow.** Another word for a **field** is a **meadow.** Everybody, what's another word for a **field?** *Signal.* **A meadow.**

Task D

Word 3 is **cozy.** A place that is **cozy** is very comfortable. Everybody, what do we call a place that is very comfortable? *Signal.* **Cozy.**

Task E

Word 4 is **cluster.** Here's another way of saying **a group of flowers: A cluster of flowers.** Everybody, what's another way of saying **A group of flowers?** *Signal.* **A cluster of flowers.**

Task F

Word 5 is **scarlet.** Something that is **scarlet** is bright red. Everybody, what's another word for bright red? *Signal.* **Scarlet.**

Task G

1. Word 6 is **dazzle.** Something that **dazzles** you is so brilliant that it shocks you. Here's another way of saying **The light was so brilliant that it shocked them: The light was so brilliant that it dazzled them.**
2. Everybody, what's another way of saying **The light was so brilliant that it shocked them?** *Signal.* **The light was so brilliant that it dazzled them.**
3. Everybody, what's another way of saying **The diamond was so bright that it shocked them?** *Signal.* **The diamond was so bright that it dazzled them.**

Task H

1. Word 7 is **scarcely.**
   If you can **scarcely** do something, you can hardly do it. Everybody, what's another way of saying **She could hardly read?** *Signal.* **She could scarcely read.**

2. Everybody, what's another way of saying **They could hardly climb the mountain?** *Signal.* **They could scarcely climb the mountain.**

EXERCISE 5   Vocabulary from context

Task A

1. Everybody, touch column 5. *Check.* The words in that column are words that you'll read in sentences.

2. Touch under the first word. *Pause.* What word? *Signal.* **Delightful.**

3. Next word. *Pause.* What word? *Signal.* **Refreshed.**

4. *Repeat step 3 for* **glare.**

5. *Repeat the words in column 5 until firm.*

Task B

1. Everybody, find part B. First we'll read each sentence and then we'll figure out what the underlined words could mean.

2. *Call on a student.* Read sentence 1 and the choices. *Wait.* Everybody, which is the best choice? *Signal.* **Wonderful.**

3. *Repeat step 2 for sentences 2 and 3.* Answer Key: Sentence 2. **Full of energy.** Sentence 3. **Brightness.**

Lesson 16

CHAPTER 11
The River

The adventure with the Kalidahs made the travelers more anxious than ever to get out of the forest, and they walked so fast that Dorothy became tired, and had to ride on the Lion's back. To their great joy the trees became thinner the farther they went, and in the afternoon they suddenly came upon a broad river, flowing swiftly just before them.Ⓐ On the other side of the water they could see the yellow brick road running through a beautiful country, with green meadows dotted with bright flowers, and with trees full of delicious fruits. They were greatly pleased to see this delightful country before them.

★2 ERRORS★

"How shall we cross the river?" asked Dorothy.

"That is easily done" replied the Scarecrow. "The Tin Woodman must build us a raft, so we can float to the other side."Ⓑ

So the Woodman took his axe and began to chop down small trees to make a raft, and while he was busy at this the Scarecrow found a tree full of fine fruit on the riverbank. This pleased Dorothy, who had eaten nothing but nuts all day, and she made a hearty meal of the ripe fruit.Ⓒ

It takes time to make a raft, even when one is as hard-working as the Woodman, and when night came the work was not done. So they found a cozy place under the tree where Dorothy, Toto, and the Lion slept well until morning. Dorothy dreamed of the Emerald City, and of the Wizard, who would soon send her back to her own home.Ⓓ

Dorothy and the Lion awakened the next morning refreshed and full of hope, and Dorothy had a breakfast of peaches and plums from the trees beside the river. Behind them was the dark forest they had passed safely through, but in front of them was a lovely, sunny country that seemed to beckon them on to the Emerald City.Ⓔ

To be sure, the broad river now cut them off from this beautiful land. But the raft was nearly done, and after the Tin Woodman had cut a few more logs and fastened them together with wooden pins, they were ready to start. Dorothy sat down in the middle of the raft and held Toto in her arms.Ⓕ When the cowardly Lion stepped upon the raft it tipped badly, for he was big and heavy; but the Scarecrow and the Tin Woodman

---

STORY READING

EXERCISE 6   Decoding

1. Everybody turn to page 62 in your textbook. *Wait. Call on a student.* What's the error limit for this chapter? **11 errors.**

2. *Call on individual students to read.*

3. *After the group reads to the 2-error sign without making more than 2 errors, reread the first part aloud and present the comprehension tasks.*

4. *After you have completed the first part, call on individual students to read. Present the comprehension tasks.*

EXERCISE 7   Comprehension tasks

Ⓐ What happened to the trees as the travelers went farther? *Idea:* The trees became thinner.

● What does **the trees became thinner** mean? *Idea:* There were fewer trees.

● What did the travelers come to in the afternoon? *Idea:* A river.

Ⓑ Was that a smart plan? **Yes.**

Ⓒ What had Dorothy been eating all day? **Nuts.**

● What was she eating now? **Fruit.**

● Who found that fruit? **The Scarecrow.**

Ⓓ Was the raft finished that night? **No.**

● What did Dorothy dream about? *Idea:* The Emerald City and the Wizard of Oz.

Ⓔ Everybody, show me how you would beckon somebody to come over to where you are? *Check.*

That's what the beautiful country seemed to do to Dorothy and the others. It beckoned them.

Ⓕ Everybody, hold your hand out flat, as if it's the raft. With your other hand, point to the place where Dorothy sat. *Check.*

stood upon the other end to balance it. **(G)**

The Scarecrow and the Tin Woodman had long poles in their hands to push the raft through the water. **(H)** They got along quite well at first, but when they reached the middle of the river the swift current swept the raft downstream, farther and farther away from the yellow brick road. The water soon grew so deep that the long poles could not touch the bottom. **(I)**

"This is bad," said the Tin Woodman, "for we are getting farther from the road to the Emerald City. If we lose our way, I couldn't get a heart."

"And then I would get no brains," said the Scarecrow.

"And I would get no courage," said the cowardly Lion.

"And I would never get back to Kansas," said Dorothy.

"We must certainly get to the Emerald City if we can," the Scarecrow said. And he pushed so hard on his long pole that it stuck fast in the mud at the bottom of the river. Before he could pull it out again, or let go, the raft was swept away and the poor Scarecrow was left clinging to the pole in the middle of the river. **(J)**

"Goodbye!" the Scarecrow called after them, and they were very sorry to leave him. Indeed, the Tin Woodman began to cry, but fortunately he remembered that he might rust, and so he dried his tears.

Meanwhile, the Scarecrow started to think. "I am now worse off than when I first met Dorothy," he thought. "Then, I was stuck on a pole in a cornfield, where I could try to scare the crows. But surely there is no use for a Scarecrow stuck on a pole in the middle of a river. I am afraid I will never have any brains, after all!" **(K)** ★11 ERRORS★

Lesson 16 Textbook **63**

(G) Who got on after Dorothy and Toto? **The cowardly Lion.**

- What happened to the raft when the Lion got on? *Idea:* It tipped.
- Why did the raft do that? *Idea:* Because the Lion was heavy.
- Everybody, hold your hand out flat and show what happened when the Lion got on one side. *Check.*
- Who got on the other side to balance the raft? **The Scarecrow and the Tin Woodman.**

(H) How were they going to move the raft through the river? *Idea:* With the poles.

- Everybody, look at the picture. You can see them using the poles. They are pushing the poles against the bottom of the river. When they push backward, the raft moves forward.

(I) Why didn't the poles work in the middle of the river? *Idea:* Because they could not touch the bottom.

- What was making the raft move downstream? *Idea:* The swift current.

(J) What happened to the end of the pole? *Idea:* It got stuck in the mud.

- Who was hanging onto the other end of the pole? **The Scarecrow.**
  The pole was standing still, stuck in the mud.
- What did the raft do? *Idea:* Kept going down the river.

- So where did that leave the Scarecrow? *Idea:* In the middle of the river.

(K) Why was there no use for the Scarecrow in the middle of the river? *Idea:* Because he could not scare birds anymore.

- So was the Scarecrow better off or worse off than he was before? **Worse off.**

Award 4 points or have the students reread to the error limit sign.

EXERCISE 8   Fact game

1. You're going to play a game that uses the facts you have learned. You will take turns. When it is your turn, you'll read a question out loud and then you'll answer it. If you answer all parts of the question correctly, you earn 1 point. During the game, you may earn more than 13 points. If you do, you get 5 bonus points.

2. Everybody, open your workbook to page 20. I will show you how to play the game. *Choose four students to sit at a table.* I'll be the monitor for now. First the monitor hands the dice to the person to the left. That person rolls the dice.
   Hand the dice to the student on your left. Tell the student: Roll the dice.

3. The person who rolls the dice tells the number of dots that are showing.
   Tell the student who rolled the dice: Count up the dots and tell us how many.

4. Now the person who rolled the dice reads the question for that number out loud. *Ask the student who rolled the dice:* What question are you going to read out loud? Read your question and then answer it.

5. The monitor uses the answer key at the back of the workbook. The monitor compares the player's answer with the correct answer. If the answer is correct, the monitor tells the player that the answer is correct. Then the monitor gives the player one point by putting a check mark on the player's scorecard. The first check mark goes in box 1. Every time a player answers a question correctly, the monitor puts a check mark in the next box on the player's card. If the player's answer is not correct, the monitor says the correct answer. The player does not get a point.
   If the student answered the item correctly, say: That's the right answer. *Then record one point on the student's scorecard.*
   If the student answered the item incorrectly, say: That's the wrong answer. The answer is _____.

FACT GAME

FACT GAME SCORECARD

1	2	3	4	5	6	7	8	9	10
11	12	13	14	15	16	17	18	19	20
21	22	23	24	25	26	27	28	29	30

Fact Game

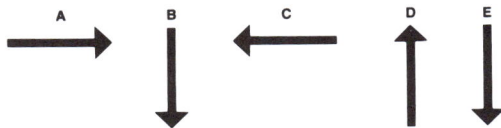

2. Tell which direction each arrow points. Start with arrow A.
3. **a.** Which country does the map below show?

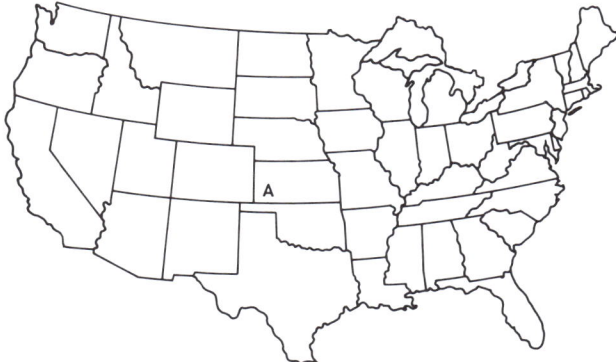

   b. Which state has an **A** on it?

4. **a.** What does the picture below show?

   b. What is the name of part **A**?
5. Tell whether Dorothy saw each thing in Kansas or the Land of Oz.
   a. Gray grass
   b. Round blue houses
   c. Beautiful flowers
   d. Flat prairie
6. **a.** What surrounded the Land of Oz?
   b. What city was in the middle of the Land of Oz?
7. Tell which group of people lived in each land.
   a. The Land of the North
   b. The Land of the South
   c. The Land of the West
   d. The Land of the East
8. Tell where each witch is from.
   a. This good witch gave Dorothy a kiss.
   b. This bad witch was still alive.
   c. This bad witch was killed by Dorothy's house.
   d. Dorothy had never seen this good witch.
9. **a.** What color was the road that Dorothy took?
   b. What color was Kansas?

   c. What color were the Munchkin houses?
   d. What color did good witches wear?
10. Tell which character wanted each thing.
   a. Brains
   b. Courage
   c. A trip back to Kansas
   d. A heart
11. Tell which character each statement describes.
   a. This character was part tiger and part bear.
   b. This character ruled over the Emerald City.
   c. This character could only bark.
12. Pretend you are in the Emerald City. Tell which direction you would go to find each thing.
   a. The Munchkins
   b. The witch who gave Dorothy a kiss
   c. The bad witch who was still alive
   d. The Kalidahs

6. The player passes the dice to the person to the left and that player rolls the dice. Remember, roll the dice, figure out the number of the question, read the question out loud, and answer it. The monitor gives the points and tells the correct answer. Do not argue with the monitor. If you argue, you lose your next turn.

7. If a group of players play the game quickly and smoothly, each player in that group will earn 5 bonus points. I'll tell each group whether the players in that group earned 5 bonus points.

8. *Divide the students into groups of four or five each. Identify a monitor for each group. Give each group a pair of dice.*
   Monitors, open your workbooks to page 121. That page gives the correct answers for this game. Don't show the answers to the other players.
   Everybody, you have 20 minutes to play the game. Keep taking turns until I tell you to stop.
   Permit the game to be played for 20 minutes. When 15 minutes have elapsed, remind the group that only 5 minutes remain.

9. *After the game has been played for 20 minutes, have all students who earned more than **13 points** stand up. Award 5 bonus points to these players and praise them for doing a very good job. (**Note:** Nearly all players should earn more than 13 points.)*

10. *Award points to monitors. Monitors receive the number of points earned by the highest performer in the monitor's group.*

● *For each game that ran smoothly, tell the monitor:* Your group did a good job. Give yourself and each of your players 5 bonus points.

● Everybody, write your game points in box FG on your point chart. Write your bonus points in the **bonus** box.

INDEPENDENT WORK

Do all the items in your skillbook for lesson 16.

WORKCHECK AND AWARDING POINTS

1. *Read the questions and answers for the skillbook and workbook.*
2. *Award points for independent work as follows:*

```
0 errors ..................... 6 points
2 errors ..................... 4 points
3, 4, or 5 errors ............ 2 points
5 or more errors ............. 0 points
```

3. *Award bonus points as follows:*

```
Correcting missed items
or getting all items right ......... 2 points
Doing the writing
assignment acceptably ........... 2 points
```

ANSWER KEY FOR SKILLBOOK

PART C

1. A river
2. a. The Scarecrow
   b. *Idea:* To build a raft
   c. The Tin Woodman
3. a. *Idea:* The bottom of the river
   b. Arrow A
   c. Arrow B
4. a. *Idea:* The current
   b. Because the water was too deep
   c. *Idea:* yellow brick road
5. a. *Idea:* It got stuck in the mud
   b. Yes
   c. *Idea:* Floating downstream
   d. *Idea:* Stuck on the pole
   e. No
   f. *Idea:* In the cornfield

PART D

6. a. When something grates, it grinds against a hard surface.
   b. Another work for a living room or a small sitting room is parlor.

PART E

7. a. suspected
   b. clumsiness
   c. fortunate
   d. dull
   e. inconvenient
   f. declared
   g. comforted
   h. deserted

ANSWER KEY FOR FACT GAME

2. A—East
   B—South
   C—West
   D—North
   E—South
3. a. The United States
   b. Kansas
4. a. A cyclone
   b. Eye
5. a. Kansas
   b. Land of Oz
   c. Land of Oz
   d. Kansas
6. a. The Great Desert
   b. The Emerald City
7. a. The Gillikins
   b. The Quadlings
   c. The Winkies
   d. The Munchkins
8. a. Land of the North
   b. Land of the West
   c. Land of the East
   d. Land of the South
9. a. Yellow
   b. Gray
   c. Blue
   d. White
10. a. The Scarecrow
    b. The Lion
    c. Dorothy
    d. Tin Woodman
11. a. Kalidah
    b. Oz
    c. Toto
12. a. East
    b. North
    c. West
    d. East

Lesson 17

Lesson 17

PART A   Word Lists

1	2	3	4
spicy	shallow	**Vocabulary words**	**Vocabulary words**
odor	blossoms	1. beckon	1. fond of
mistress	carpet	2. dazzle	2. scent, odor
	poison	3. scarlet	3. mistress
	poisonous	4. cluster	4. shrill
		5. scarcely	5. timid
		6. dreadful	6. permit
		7. refreshed	7. curtsy
		8. glare	8. spicy
		9. delightful	9. therefore

WORD PRACTICE AND VOCABULARY

EXERCISE 1   Word practice

1. Everybody, find lesson 17, part A in your skillbook. *Wait.* Touch column 1. *Check.* The words in column 1 are hard words that will be in your reading stories.
2. Touch under the first word. *Check.* The first word is **spicy.** What word? *Signal.* **Spicy.**
3. Next word. *Pause.* That word is **odor.** What word? *Signal.* **Odor.**
4. *Repeat step 3 for* **mistress.**
5. Now let's see if you remember all those words. Touch under the first word in column 1. *Pause.* What word? *Signal.* **Spicy.**
6. Next word. *Pause.* What word? Signal. **Odor.**
7. *Repeat step 6 for* **mistress.**
8. *Repeat the words in column 1 until firm.*

EXERCISE 2   Word practice

1. Everybody, touch under the first word in column 2. *Pause.* What word? *Signal.* **Shallow.**
2. Next word. *Pause.* What word? *Signal.* **Blossoms.**
3. *Repeat step 2 for each remaining word in column 2.*
4. *Repeat the words in column 2 until firm.*

EXERCISE 3   Vocabulary review

Task A

1. Everybody, touch column 3. *Check.* First you're going to read the words in column 3. Then we'll talk about what they mean.
2. Touch under the first word. *Pause.* What word? *Signal.* **Beckon.**
3. Next word. *Pause.* What word? *Signal.* **Dazzle.**
4. *Repeat step 3 for each remaining word in column 3.*
5. *Repeat the words in column 3 until firm.*

Task B

You've learned the meanings for all these words. Word 1 is **beckon.** Everybody, show me how you would **beckon** someone to come over to where you are. *Check.*

Task C

1. Word 2 is **dazzle.** *Call on a student.* What does **dazzle** mean? *Idea:* Shock.
2. Everybody, what's another way of saying **The jewel was so bright that it shocked them?** *Signal.* **The jewel was so bright that it dazzled them.**

Task D

Word 3 is **scarlet.** Everybody, tell me another name for the color **scarlet.** *Signal.* **Red.**

Task E

1. Word 4 is **cluster.** *Call on a student.* What does **cluster** mean? *Idea:* Group.
2. Everybody, what's another way of saying **A group of flowers?** *Signal.* **A cluster of flowers.**

Task F

1. Word 5 is **scarcely.** *Call on a student.* What does **scarcely** mean? *Ideas:* Hardly; barely.
2. Everybody, what's another way of saying **They could hardly jump over the creek?** *Signal.* **They could scarcely jump over the creek.**

Task G

Word 6 is **dreadful.** *Call on a student.* What does **dreadful** mean? *Idea:* Horrible.

Task H

Word 7 is **refreshed.** *Call on a student.* What does **refreshed** mean? *Idea:* Full of energy.

Task I

Word 8 is **glare.** *Call on a student.* When something **glares** how does it look? *Idea:* Bright.

Task J

Word 9 is **delightful.** *Call on a student.* What does **delightful** mean? *Idea:* Wonderful.

Lesson 17

PART A   Word Lists

1	2	3	4
spicy	shallow	**Vocabulary words**	**Vocabulary words**
odor	blossoms	1. beckon	1. fond of
mistress	carpet	2. dazzle	2. scent, odor
	poison	3. scarlet	3. mistress
	poisonous	4. cluster	4. shrill
		5. scarcely	5. timid
		6. dreadful	6. permit
		7. refreshed	7. curtsy
		8. glare	8. spicy
		9. delightful	9. therefore

EXERCISE 4   Vocabulary development

Task A

1. Everybody, touch column 4. *Check.*
   First you're going to read the words in column 4. Then we'll talk about what they mean.
2. Touch under the first line. *Pause.*
   What words? *Signal.* **Fond of.**
3. Next line. *Pause.* What words? *Signal.*
   Scent and odor.
4. Next word. *Pause.* What word? *Signal.* **Mistress.**
5. *Repeat step 4 for each remaining word in column 4.*
6. *Repeat the words in column 4 until firm.*

Task B

1. Now let's talk about what those words mean. The words in line 1 are **fond of**. When you're **fond of** something, you like that thing. Here's another way of saying **She liked ice cream: She was fond of ice cream.** Everybody, what's another way of saying **She liked ice cream?** *Signal.* **She was fond of ice cream.**
2. Everybody, what's another way of saying **She liked the lion?** *Signal.* **She was fond of the lion.**

Task C

1. The words in line 2 are **scent** and **odor**. Both those words mean **smell**. A pleasant smell is a pleasant **odor** or **scent.**
   Call on a student. What are two new ways of saying **a pleasant smell?** *Idea:* A pleasant odor, a pleasant scent.
2. *Call on a student.* What are two new ways of saying **a bad smell?** *Idea:* A bad odor, a bad scent.

Task D

Word 3 is **mistress.** A dog's **mistress** is the woman who owns the dog. Everybody, what do we call the woman who owns the dog? *Signal.* **The dog's mistress.**
Who is Toto's mistress? *Signal.* **Dorothy.**

Task E

Word 4 is **shrill.** A **shrill** sound is one that is high and sharp. Everybody, what do we call a sound that is high and sharp? *Signal.*
A shrill sound.

Task F

1. Word 5 is **timid.** Someone who is very shy is **timid.** Everybody, what's another way of saying **She was very shy?** *Signal.* **She was timid.**
2. Everybody, what's another way of saying **Her voice was very shy?** *Signal.*
   Her voice was timid.

Task G

1. Word 6 is **permit.** When you let somebody do something, you **permit** that person to do it. Here's another way of saying **He let me go outside: He permitted me to go outside.** Everybody, what's another way of saying **He let me go outside?** *Signal.*
   He permitted me to go outside.
2. Here's another way of saying **They don't let you sit on the curb: They don't permit you to sit on the curb.** Everybody, what's another way of saying **They don't let you sit on the curb?** *Signal.*
   They don't permit you to sit on the curb.

Task H

Word 7 is **curtsy.** A **curtsy** is a kind of bow that women make in front of important people. I'll show you how to curtsy. *Curtsy.* Everybody, what did I make? *Signal.* **A curtsy.**

Task I

Word 8 is **spicy.** Things that are **spicy** contain spices such as pepper or cinnamon.

Task J

Word 9 is **therefore.** Another word for **so** is **therefore.**

Lesson 17

CHAPTER 12
The Field of Flowers

The raft floated downstream, and the poor Scarecrow was left far behind. Then the Lion said, "Something must be done to save us. I think I can swim to the shore and pull the raft after me, if you will only hold on to the tip of my tail." Ⓐ

So the Lion sprang into the water and the Tin Woodman caught a hold of his tail. Then the Lion began to swim with all his might toward the shore. It was hard work, even though he was so big, but after a while he pulled them out of the current. When they reached the shallow water, Dorothy took the Tin Woodman's long pole and helped push the raft to the land. ★2 ERRORS★

They were all tired out when they finally reached the shore and stepped off on to the pretty green grass. But their troubles were not over. The current had carried them a long way past the yellow brick road that led to the Emerald City.

"What shall we do now?" asked the Tin Woodman, as the Lion lay down on the grass to let the sun dry him.

"We must get back to the road," said Dorothy.

"The best plan would be to walk along the riverbank until we come to the road again," remarked the Lion.

So, when they were rested, Dorothy picked up her basket and they started along the grassy bank, back to the road from which the river had carried them. It was a lovely country, with plenty of flowers and fruit trees and sunshine to cheer them, and if they had not felt so sorry for the poor Scarecrow they would have been very happy.

They walked along as fast as they could. Dorothy only stopped once to pick a beautiful flower. After a time, the Tin Woodman cried out, "Look!"

Then they all looked at the river and saw the Scarecrow hanging onto his pole in the middle of the water, looking very lonely and sad. Ⓑ

"What can we do to save him?" asked Dorothy.

The Lion and the Woodman both shook their heads, for they did not know. So they sat down upon the bank and gazed at the Scarecrow until a Stork flew by. Ⓒ

When the Stork saw them, it stopped to rest at the water's edge.

"Who are you and where are you going?" asked the Stork.

"I am Dorothy," answered the girl.

64   Lesson 17   Textbook

"These are my friends, the Tin Woodman and the cowardly Lion. We are going to the Emerald City."

"This isn't the road," said the Stork, as she twisted her long neck and looked sharply at the strange party.

"I know it," answered Dorothy. "But we have lost the Scarecrow, and are wondering how we will get him again."

"Where is he?" asked the Stork.

"Over there in the river," answered Dorothy.

"If he wasn't so big and heavy I would get him for you," remarked the Stork.

"He isn't a bit heavy," said Dorothy, eagerly. "He is stuffed with straw, and if you will bring him back to us we will thank you ever and ever so much."

"Well, I'll try," said the Stork. "But if I find he is too heavy to carry I shall have to drop him in the river again."

So the big bird flew into the air and over the water until she came to where the Scarecrow was hanging onto his pole. Then the Stork grabbed the Scarecrow with her great claws and carried him up into the air and back to the bank, where Dorothy and the Lion and the Tin Woodman and Toto were sitting. Ⓓ

When the Scarecrow found himself among his friends again he was so happy that he hugged them all, even the Lion

Lesson 17   Textbook   65

EXERCISE 5   Decoding

1. **Everybody, turn to page 64 in your textbook.** *Wait. Call on a student.* **What's the error limit for this chapter?** 12 errors.
2. *Call on individual students to read.*
3. *After the group reads to the 2-error sign without making more than 2 errors, reread the first part aloud and present the comprehension tasks.*
4. *After you have completed the first part, call on individual students to read. Present the comprehension tasks.*

EXERCISE 6   Comprehension tasks

Ⓐ **That sounds like a dangerous thing to do. Would it take courage for the Lion to jump in the river?** Yes.

Ⓑ **The current had taken the travelers far down the river. What were they doing to get back to the yellow brick road?**
Idea: Walking along the river.

- **Who did they see in the river?** *Signal.*
  The Scarecrow.

- **Everybody, look at the picture on the next page. You can see the Scarecrow in the river and the others on the shore.**

Ⓒ **You can see the stork in the picture. The stork is the large bird on the left.**

Ⓓ **How do you think the travelers felt when the Scarecrow came back?** *Idea:* Very happy.

and Toto. And as they walked along he sang, for he felt so happy.

"I was afraid I would have to stay in the river forever," he said, "but the kind Stork saved me, and if I ever get any brains I shall find the Stork again and return the favor."

"That's all right," said the Stork, who was flying along beside them. "I always like to help anyone in trouble. But I must go now, for my babies are waiting in the nest for me. I hope you will find the Emerald City and that Oz will help you."

"Thank you," replied Dorothy, and then the kind Stork flew into the air and was soon out of sight.

They walked along listening to the singing of the bright-colored birds and looking at the lovely flowers, which now became so thick that the ground was covered with them. There were big yellow and white and blue and purple blossoms, and also great clusters of scarlet flowers, which were so brilliant in color they almost dazzled Dorothy's eyes. Ⓔ ★12 ERRORS★

"Aren't they beautiful?" the girl asked, as she breathed in the spicy scent of the flowers.

"I suppose so," answered the Scarecrow. "When I have brains I will probably like them better."

"If I only had a heart I would love them," added the Tin Woodman.

"I always did like flowers," said the Lion. "They seem so helpless. But there are none in the forest as bright as these."

They now came upon more and more of the big scarlet flowers, and fewer and fewer of the other flowers; and soon they found themselves in the middle of a great meadow of scarlet flowers. Now, when there are many of these flowers together, their odor is so powerful that anyone who breathes them falls asleep, and if the sleeper is not carried away from the flowers he sleeps on and on forever. But Dorothy did not know this, nor could she get away from the bright scarlet flowers that were everywhere. Her eyes soon grew heavy, and she felt she must sit down to rest and to sleep.

But the Tin Woodman would not let her do this.

"We must hurry and get back to the yellow brick road before dark," he said, and the Scarecrow agreed with him. So they kept walking until Dorothy could stand no longer. Her eyes closed and she forgot where she was and she fell among the flowers, fast asleep.

"What shall we do?" asked the Tin Woodman.

"If we leave her here she will die," said the Lion. "The smell of the flowers is killing us all. I can scarely keep my eyes open and the dog is asleep already."

It was true—Toto had fallen down beside his mistress. But the Scarecrow and the Tin Woodman, since they weren't made of flesh, were not troubled by the odor of the flowers.

"Run fast," said the Scarecrow to the Lion, "and get out of this deadly flower bed as soon as you can. We will

bring the little girl with us, but if you should fall asleep you are too big to be carried."

So the Lion bounded forward as fast as he could go. In a moment he was out of sight.

"Let us make a chair with our hands, and carry her," said the Scarecrow. So they picked up Toto and put the dog in Dorothy's lap, and then they made a chair with their hands for the seat, and their arms for the chair's arms, and carried the sleeping girl between them through the flowers.

On and on they walked, and it seemed that the great carpet of deadly flowers that surrounded them would never end. They followed the bend of the river, and at last came upon their friend the Lion, lying fast asleep among the flowers. The flowers had been too strong

for the huge beast and he had given up at last. He had fallen only a short distance from the end of the field, where the sweet grass spread in beautiful green fields before them.

"We can do nothing for him," said the Tin Woodman, sadly. "He is much too heavy to lift. We must leave him here to sleep on forever, and perhaps he will dream that he has found courage at last."

"I'm sorry," said the Scarecrow. "The Lion was a very good comrade for one so cowardly. But let us go on."

They carried the sleeping girl to a pretty spot beside the river, far enough from the field so that she could not breathe any more of the deadly flowers, and here they laid her gently on the soft grass and waited for the fresh breeze to wake her up.

Ⓔ Tell me another name for the color scarlet. **Red.**

These flowers are poisonous. If Dorothy smells them too much, she'll go into a deep sleep.

- Read the rest of the chapter to yourselves and be ready to answer some questions.

After all students have finished reading:

- Who was the first traveler to become tired from the flowers? **Dorothy.**
- Who tried to keep Dorothy moving toward the yellow brick road?
  The Scarecrow and the Tin Woodman.
- What happened to Dorothy and Toto after a while? *Idea:* They fell asleep.
- Who else became sleepy from the smell of the flowers? **The Lion.**
- Who was not bothered by the smell of the flowers? **The Scarecrow and the Tin Woodman.**
- Why weren't they bothered by the smell?
  Idea: Because they were not made of flesh and blood.
- Did the Lion make it out of the field of flowers? **No.**
- How did the Scarecrow and the Tin Woodman carry Dorothy and Toto?
  Idea: They made a chair with their hands.
- Everybody, look at the picture. The picture shows Dorothy and Toto being carried. Who is lying in the flowers? **The Lion.**
- Where did the Scarecrow and the Tin Woodman take Dorothy and Toto after they left the field of flowers? *Idea:* To the river.
- What was the air like beside the river? **Fresh.**
- What will happen if Dorothy breathes this fresh air for a while? *Idea:* She will wake up.
- Who is still in the field of flowers? **The Lion.**

Award 4 points or have the students reread to the error limit sign.

INDEPENDENT WORK

Do all the items in your skillbook and workbook for lesson 17.

ANSWER KEY FOR WORKBOOK

Review Items

1. Write whether each thing would happen to you in the **forest**, the **river**, or the **field of flowers**.
   a. You smell something and fall asleep.
      field of flowers
   b. You float downstream.
      river
   c. You get chased by Kalidahs.
      forest
   d. You sleep forever.
      field of flowers
   e. You steer a raft.
      river
   f. You see flowers everywhere.
      field of flowers
   g. You have to cross deep ditches.
      forest

Crossword Puzzle

To work the puzzle, read an item and figure out which word the item describes. Then write the word in the puzzle. Complete the entire puzzle.

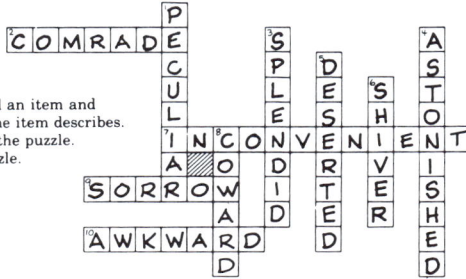

```
        P
²C O M R A D E      ³S      D      ⁴A
        C           P      E      S
        U           L      S   ⁶S T
        L           E      R    H O
⁷I N C O N V E N I E N T    I   N
        A           D      P   V I
    ⁸S O R R O W     I      E   E S
        A           D      R   H
    ⁹A W K W A R D          T   E
```

Across

2. A friend is a _____.
7. Another word for **annoying** is _____.
9. Another word for **sadness** is _____.
10. When you are clumsy, you are _____.

Down

1. Another word for **strange** is _____.
3. Another word for **marvelous** is _____.
4. When you are really surprised, you are _____.
5. When you are left alone, you feel _____.
6. When it is cold, your body begins to _____.
8. When you are not brave, you are a _____.

WORKCHECK AND AWARDING POINTS

1. *Read the questions and answers for the skillbook and workbook.*

2. *Award points for independent work as follows:*

0 errors	6 points
2 errors	4 points
3, 4, or 5 errors	2 points
5 or more errors	0 points

3. *Award bonus points as follows:*

Correcting missed items or getting all items right	2 points
Doing the writing assignment acceptably	2 points

ANSWER KEY FOR SKILLBOOK

PART B

1. a. The current
   b. The Lion
   c. *Idea:* Road
   d. Scarecrow
2. a. A stork
   b. *Idea:* Because he was so light
3. a. Scarlet
   b. *Idea:* You get sleepy
   c. *Idea:* You could sleep forever
4. a. *Idea:* Beside the river
   b. *Idea:* Fresh
   c. *Idea:* She will wake up
   d. No
   e. *Idea:* He will sleep forever
5. a. The Lion pulled the raft to shore
   b. The Lion fell asleep

PART C

6. a. When somebody is beaten with a whip or a switch, that person is flogged.
   b. Wood that has been badly burned is charred wood.

PART D

7. a. Dorothy
   b. The Scarecrow
   c. The Tin Woodman
   d. The Lion
8. a. without movement
   b. comforted
   c. misfortune
   d. dreary
   e. comrade
   f. passage
   g. inconvenient
   h. sorrow
   i. surprise
   j. remarkable

Lesson 18

WORD PRACTICE AND VOCABULARY

EXERCISE 1   Word practice

1. Everybody, find lesson 18, part A in your skillbook. *Wait.* Touch column 1. *Check.* The words in column 1 are hard words that will be in your reading stories.
2. Touch under the first word. *Check.* The first word is **majesty.** What word? *Signal.* **Majesty.**
3. Next word. *Pause.* That word is **limbs.** What word? *Signal.* **Limbs.**
4. *Repeat step 3 for each remaining word in column 1.*
5. Now let's see if you remember all those words. Touch under the first word in column 1. *Pause.* What word? *Signal.* **Majesty.**
6. Next word. *Pause.* What word? *Signal.* **Limbs.**
7. *Repeat step 6 for each remaining word in column 1.*
8. *Repeat the words in column 1 until firm.*

EXERCISE 2   Word practice

1. Everybody, touch under the first word in column 2. *Pause.* What word? *Signal.* **Beast.**
2. Next word. *Pause.* What word? *Signal.* **Poisonous.**
3. *Repeat step 2 for each remaining word in column 2.*
4. *Repeat the words in column 2 until firm.*

EXERCISE 3   Vocabulary review

Task A
1. Everybody, touch column 3. *Check.* First you're going to read the words in column 3. Then we'll talk about what they mean.
2. Touch under the first line. *Pause.* What words? *Signal.* **Fond of.**
3. Next line. *Pause.* What words? *Signal.* **Scampered off.**
4. Next word. *Pause.* What word? *Signal.* **Curtsy.**
5. *Repeat step 4 for each remaining word in column 3.*
6. *Repeat the words in column 3 until firm.*

Task B
1. You've learned the meanings for all these words. The words in line 1 are **fond of.** *Call on a student.* What do the words **fond of** mean? *Idea:* Like.
2. Everybody, what's another way of saying **He liked going to the circus?** *Signal.* **He was fond of going to the circus.**

Task C

The words of line 2 are **scampered off.**
Call on a student. What do the words **scampered off** mean? *Idea:* Ran away fast.

Task D

Word 3 is **curtsy.** *Call on a student.*
What is a **curtsy?** *Idea:* A bow that women do in front of important people.

Task E

1. Word 4 is **timid.** *Call on a student.*
   What does **timid** mean? *Idea:* Shy.
2. Everybody, what's another way of saying **The dog was very shy?** *Signal.*
   The dog was very timid.

Task F

Word 5 is **shrill.** *Call on a student.*
What is a **shrill** sound? *Idea:* A high, sharp sound.

Task G

Word 6 is **therefore.** *Call on a student.*
What's another word for **therefore?** So.

Task H

1. Word 7 is **permit.** *Call on a student.*
   What does **permit** mean? *Ideas:* Let; allow.
2. Everybody, what's another way of saying **My parents let me watch TV?** *Signal.*
   My parents permitted me to watch TV.

EXERCISE 4   Vocabulary development

Task A

1. Everybody, touch column 4. *Check.*
   First you're going to read the words in column 4. Then we'll talk about what they mean.
2. Touch under the first word. *Pause.*
   What word? *Signal.* **Stunned.**
3. Next word. *Pause.* What word? *Signal.* **Drawn.**
4. *Repeat step 3 for each remaining word in column 4.*
5. *Repeat the words in column 4 until firm.*

Task B

1. Now let's talk about what those words mean.
   Word 1 is **stunned.** Someone who is knocked out is **stunned.**
2. Everybody, what's another way of saying **The hammer knocked him out?** *Signal.*
   The hammer stunned him.
3. Everybody, what's another way of saying **The turtle was knocked out?** *Signal.*
   The turtle was stunned.

Task C

1. Word 2 is **drawn.** If something is pulled by a horse, it is **drawn** by a horse.
2. Everybody, what's another way of saying **The cart was pulled by a horse?** *Signal.*
   The cart was drawn by a horse.

Task D

1. Word 3 is **dwelled.** When you live in a place, you **dwell** in that place.
2. Everybody, what's another way of saying **She lived in the city?** *Signal.*
   She dwelled in the city.
3. Everybody, what's another way of saying **Oz lived in a palace?** *Signal.*
   Oz dwelled in a palace.

Task E

Word 4 is **presence.** When you're in somebody's **presence,** you're where that person can see you.

Task F

1. Word 5 is **glittered.** Another word for **glistened** or **sparkled** is **glittered.**
2. Everybody, what's another way of saying **The emeralds sparkled?** *Signal.*
   The emeralds glittered.
3. Everybody, what's another way of saying **The city glistened?** *Signal.* **The city glittered.**

Task G

Word 6 is **throne.** A **throne** is a fancy chair that only a queen, a king or a very important person can sit on.

Task H

1. Word 7 is **oats. Oats** are a kind of grain. **Oats** are used in making oatmeal.
2. Everybody, what grain is used to make oatmeal? *Signal.* **Oats.**

Lesson 18

CHAPTER 13
The Field Mice Ⓐ

"We cannot be far from the yellow brick road, now," remarked the Scarecrow, as he stood beside Dorothy. "We have come nearly as far as the river carried us away. Ⓑ

The Tin Woodman was about to say something when he heard a low growl, and turning his head he saw a strange beast come bounding over the grass toward them. It was, indeed, a great yellow wildcat. The Woodman thought it might be chasing something, for its ears were lying close to its head and its mouth was wide open, showing two rows of ugly teeth, while its red eyes glowed like balls of fire. Ⓒ ★2 ERRORS★

As the wildcat came nearer, the Tin Woodman saw that a little gray field mouse was running in front of the beast. Although the Woodman had no heart, he knew it was wrong for the wildcat to try to kill such a pretty, harmless creature. Ⓓ

So the Woodman raised his axe, and as the wildcat ran by he gave it a quick blow that stunned the beast, and it rolled over at his feet. Ⓔ

Now that it was freed from its enemy, the field mouse stopped. Coming slowly up to the Woodman it said, in a squeaky little voice, "Oh, thank you!

Thank you ever so much for saving my life."

"Don't speak of it, please," replied the Woodman. "I have no heart, you know, so I am careful to help all those who may need a friend, even if it happens to be only a mouse."

"Only a mouse!" cried the little animal. "Why, I am a Queen—the Queen of all the field mice!" Ⓕ

"Oh, indeed," said the Woodman, making a bow.

The Queen continued, "Therefore you have done a great deed, as well as a brave one, in saving my life."

At that moment several mice came running up as fast as their little legs could carry them, and when they saw their Queen they exclaimed, "Oh, Your Majesty, we thought you would be killed! How did you manage to escape the great wildcat?" They all bowed so low to the little Queen that they almost stood upon their heads. Ⓖ

"This funny tin man," she answered, "stunned the wildcat and saved my life. So hereafter you must all serve him, and obey his wishes."

"We will!" cried all the mice, in their shrill voices. And then they

68 Lesson 18 Textbook

---

scampered off in all directions, for Toto had awakened from his sleep. Ⓗ When Toto saw all these mice around him he gave one bark of delight and jumped right into the middle of the group. Toto had always loved to chase mice when he lived in Kansas, and he saw no harm in it.

But the Tin Woodman caught the dog in his arms and held him tightly while he called the mice, "Come back! come back! Toto will not hurt you."

When the Woodman said this, the Queen of the Mice stuck her head out from underneath a clump of grass and asked, in a timid voice, "Are you sure he will not bite us?"

"I will not let him," said the Woodman. "Do not be afraid."

One by one the mice came creeping back, and Toto did not bark again, although he tried to get out of the Woodman's arms. Finally one of the biggest mice spoke. "Is there anything we can do," it asked, "to repay you for saving the life of our Queen?" Ⓘ

"I can't think of anything you could do," answered the Woodman. Ⓙ

The Scarecrow, who had been trying to think, but could not because his head was stuffed with straw, said quickly, "Oh, yes. You can save our friend, the cowardly Lion, who is asleep in the field." Ⓚ

"A lion!" cried the little Queen. "Why, he would eat us all up."

"Oh, no," declared the Scarecrow. "This lion is a coward."

"Really?" asked the Queen.

"He says so himself," answered the Scarecrow, "and he would never hurt anyone who is our friend. If you will help us to save him I promise that he will treat you with kindness."

"Very well," said the Queen. "We will trust you. But what shall we do?"

The Scarecrow asked the Queen, "Are there many mice that are willing to obey you?"

"Oh, yes, there are thousands," she replied.

"Then ask them all to come here as soon as possible, and tell each one to bring a long piece of string." Ⓛ
★11 ERRORS★

The Queen turned to the mice that were with her and told them to go at once and get all her mice. As soon as they heard her orders they ran away in every direction as fast as possible.

"Now," said the Scarecrow to the Tin Woodman, "you must go to those trees by the riverside and make a cart that will carry the Lion."

So the Woodman went to the trees and began to work. He cut down the limbs of some trees, and then he chopped away all their twigs and leaves. He made a cart out of the limbs, and fastened it together with wooden pegs. Then he sliced four pieces from a big, round tree trunk and used the pieces for wheels. He worked so fast and well that by the time the mice began to arrive the cart was all ready for them.

They came from all directions, and

Lesson 18 Textbook **69**

STORY READING

EXERCISE 5   Decoding

1. Everybody, turn to page 68 in your textbook. *Wait. Call on a student.* What's the error limit for this chapter? **11 errors.**
2. *Call on individual students to read.*
3. *After the group reads to the 2-error sign without making more than 2 errors, reread the first part aloud and present the comprehension tasks.*
4. *After you have completed the first part, call on individual students to read. Present the comprehension tasks.*

EXERCISE 6   Comprehension tasks

Ⓐ Where is the Lion at the beginning of the chapter? *Idea:* In the field.

Ⓑ What was Dorothy doing when the Scarecrow spoke? *Idea:* Sleeping.

● The travelers went far down the river. What took their raft so far down the river? *Idea:* The strong current.

● Then the travelers walked back next to the river. They came to a place where they had a problem. What place was that? **The field of flowers.**

● What problem did they have? *Ideas:* Getting past the flowers; the flowers' odor was poisonous.

Ⓒ *Call on individual students.* Name two things about the wildcat that made the Tin Woodman think that the wildcat was chasing something. *Ideas:* Its ears were close to its head; its mouth was wide open; its eyes were glowing.

Ⓓ Do you think the Tin Woodman would know that if he didn't have a heart? **No.**

Ⓔ Did the Tin Woodman kill the wildcat? **No.**

● What happened if you stunned something? *Idea:* You knocked it out.

Ⓕ Was that mouse just an ordinary mouse? **No.**

● What was special about the mouse? *Idea:* She was the Queen.

Ⓖ When you talk to a king or queen, you call them, "Your Majesty." What do you call a king or a queen? **Your Majesty.**

Ⓗ What did they do when they scampered off? *Idea:* Ran away quickly.

Ⓘ Those mice will do anything that the Woodman wants them to do. Can you think of something the Woodman might want them to do? *Response:* Student preference.

Ⓙ Who do you think will come up with a good idea? **The Scarecrow.**

Ⓚ Did the Scarecrow come up with a good idea? **Yes.**
The chapter says that the Scarecrow couldn't think because his head was filled with straw. But the Scarecrow comes up with all the good ideas.

90   Lesson 18

there were thousands of them—big mice and little mice and middle-sized mice. And each one brought a piece of string in its mouth.

It was about this time that Dorothy woke from her long sleep and opened her eyes. She was greatly astonished to find herself lying upon the grass, with thousands of mice standing around and looking at her timidly. But the Scarecrow told her about everything, and turning to the Queen, he said, "Permit me to introduce you to Her Majesty, the Queen."

Dorothy nodded gravely and the Queen made a curtsy, after which she became quite friendly with Dorothy.

The Scarecrow and the Woodman now began to fasten the mice to the cart, using the strings they had brought. One end of each string was tied around the neck of each mouse and the other end to the cart. Of course the cart was a thousand times heavier than any of the mice; but when all the mice had been harnessed they were able to pull the cart quite easily. Even the Scarecrow and the Tin Woodman could sit on the cart, and they were drawn swiftly by their strange little horses to the place where the Lion lay asleep.

After a great deal of hard work, they managed to get the Lion up on the cart. Then the Queen hurriedly gave her mice the order to start, for she feared that if the mice stayed among the flowers too long they would also fall asleep.

At first the little creatures could hardly move the heavy cart. But the Woodman and the Scarecrow both pushed from behind, and they got along better. Soon they rolled the Lion out of the flower bed to the green fields, where he could breathe the sweet, fresh air again, instead of the poisonous odor of the flowers.

Dorothy came to meet them and thanked the little mice warmly for saving her companion from death. She had grown so fond of the big Lion that she was glad he had been rescued.

Then the mice were unharnessed from the cart and they scampered away through the grass to their homes. The Queen of the Mice was the last to leave. She handed Dorothy a little whistle and said, "If ever you need us again, come out into the field and blow this whistle. We shall hear you and come to help you. Goodbye!"

"Goodbye!" they all answered, and away the Queen ran. Dorothy held Toto tightly so that he would not run after the Queen and frighten her.

After this they sat down beside the Lion, waiting for him to wake up. The Scarecrow brought Dorothy some fruit from a tree nearby, which she ate for her dinner.

70 Lesson 18 Textbook

Lesson 18 Textbook 71

Ⓛ How many mice are willing to obey the Queen? **Thousands.**

● What does the Scarecrow want each mouse to bring? **A long piece of string.**

● What do you think the Scarecrow wants the mice to do with the string? *Response:* Student preference.

● Read the rest of the chapter to yourselves and be ready to answer some questions.

After all students have finished reading:

● What did the Scarecrow tell the Tin Woodman to make? **A cart.**

● What did Dorothy see when she woke up? **Mice.**

● What did the Scarecrow and the Tin Woodman do with the pieces of string? *Idea:* Harnessed the mice to the cart.

● The Woodman and the Scarecrow were drawn to a place. Who is at that place? **The Lion.**

● Why isn't Dorothy with them? *Idea:* Because she would fall asleep again.

● Why did the mice have to work fast after the Lion was on the cart? *Idea:* Because the flowers might make them fall asleep.

● Everybody, look at the picture. Touch the mice. *Check.*

● What are they harnessed to? **The cart.**

● Everybody, touch the material that harnesses them to the cart. *Check.*

● What is that material? **String.**

● Where did they take the Lion? *Idea:* To the green fields.

● What did the Queen give Dorothy to use if she ever needed help again? **A whistle.**

● Listen to this sentence from the chapter: "Even the Scarecrow and the Tin Woodman could sit on the cart, and they were drawn swiftly by their strange little horses to the place where the Lion lay asleep."

● The story says that the cart was drawn by little horses. Was the cart really pulled by strange little horses? **No.**

● What were the strange little horses? **Mice.**

● The story says that the Woodman cut down the limbs of some trees and then chopped away the twigs from these limbs. What are the limbs of the trees? *Idea:* Branches.

● What are the twigs on the limbs? *Idea:* Little sticks at the end of the branches.

Award 4 points or have the students reread to the error limit sign.

INDEPENDENT WORK

Do all the items in your skillbook and workbook for lesson 18.

ANSWER KEY FOR WORKBOOK

Map Skills

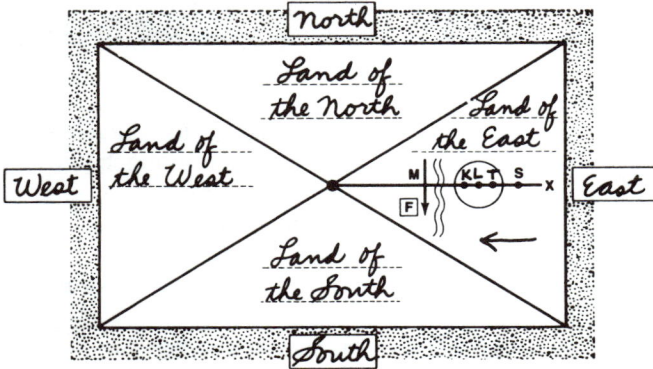

1. Write **North**, **South**, **East** and **West** in the boxes around the map.
2. On the map, write the name of each land.
3. The **X** shows where Dorothy started out. Which people lived near the **X**?

   Munchkins
4. The **dot** in the middle of the map shows where Dorothy is going. What is the name of that place?

   Emerald City
5. What place does the **circle** show?

   forest
6. What place does the **wavy line** show?

   river
7. The **arrow** next to the **wavy line** shows the way the travelers went on the river.
   a. Write the direction they floated when they went downstream.

   South

   b. Draw an **arrow** on the map to show the direction they were trying to go.
   c. Which direction does your arrow point? *West*
8. The **F** shows a place they came upon that made some of the travelers sleepy.
   a. What was the name of that place?

   Field of flowers

   b. Write the direction the travelers went to get back to the Yellow Brick Road.

   North
9. The **M** shows where the travelers met some animals. Which animals did they meet? *mice*
10. a. Write **T** on the dot where Dorothy met the Tin Woodman.
    b. Write **L** on the dot where Dorothy met the Lion.
    c. Write **K** on the dot where Dorothy met the Kalidahs.

WORKCHECK AND AWARDING POINTS

1. *Read the questions and answers for the skillbook and workbook.*
2. *Award points for independent work as follows:*

0 errors	*6 points*
2 errors	*4 points*
3, 4, or 5 errors	*2 points*
5 or more errors	*0 points*

3. *Award bonus points as follows:*

Correcting missed items or getting all items right	*2 points*
Doing the writing assignment acceptably	*2 points*

ANSWER KEY FOR SKILLBOOK

PART B

1. a. A wildcat
   b. The Tin Woodman
   c. Thousands
2. a. *Idea:* Because the Tin Woodman had saved the life of the Queen
   b. No
   c. The Scarecrow
3. a. *Idea:* Because they thought the Lion would eat them
   b. coward
4. a. The Tin Woodman saved the Queen
   b. The Queen promised to help the travelers again
5. a. The Tin Woodman
   b. *Idea:* A tree trunk
   c. *Idea:* Because of the flowers
   d. *Idea:* So they will not fall asleep
6. a. *Idea:* Blow the whistle
   b. *Idea:* Student preference

PART C

7. a. Dorothy
   b. Tin Woodman
   c. Lion
   d. Tin Woodman
   e. Lion
   f. Scarecrow
   g. Dorothy
   h. Scarecrow
8. a. shivered
   b. lucky
   c. coward
   d. steps
   e. marvelous
   f. refreshed

Lesson 19

WORD PRACTICE AND VOCABULARY

EXERCISE 1   Word practice

1. Everybody, find lesson 19, part A in your skillbook. *Wait.* Touch column 1. *Check.*
The words in column 1 are hard words that will be in your reading stories.
2. Touch under the first word. *Check.*
The first word is **generously.**
What word? *Signal.* **Generously.**
3. Next word. *Pause.* That word is **cereal.**
What word? *Signal.* **Cereal.**
4. *Repeat step 3 for each remaining word in column 1.*
5. Now let's see if you remember all those words. Touch under the first word in column 1. *Pause.* What word? *Signal.* **Generously.**
6. Next word. *Pause.* What word? *Signal.* **Cereal.**
7. *Repeat step 6 for each remaining word in column 1.*
8. *Repeat the words in column 1 until firm.*

EXERCISE 2   Word practice

1. Everybody, touch under the first word in column 2. *Pause.* What word? *Signal.* **Yawning.**
2. Next word. *Pause.* What word? *Signal.* **Shadows.**
3. *Repeat step 2 for each remaining word in column 2.*
4. *Repeat the words in column 2 until firm.*
5. *Repeat steps 1–4 for column 3.*

EXERCISE 3   Vocabulary review

Task A

1. Everybody, touch column 4. *Check.*
First you're going to read the words in column 4. Then we'll talk about what they mean.
2. Touch under the first word. *Pause.*
What word? *Signal.* **Presence.**
3. Next word. *Pause.* What word? *Signal.* **Glittered.**
4. *Repeat step 3 for* **dwelled.**
5. *Repeat the words in column 4 until firm.*

Task B

You've learned the meanings for all these words. Word 1 is **presence.** *Call on a student.* What does it mean when you're in somebody's **presence?** *Idea:* You're where that person can see you.

Task C

1. Word 2 is **glittered.** *Call on a student.* What does **glittered** mean? *Idea:* Sparkled.
2. Everybody, what's another way of saying **The diamonds sparkled?** *Signal.*
The diamonds glittered.

Task D

1. Word 3 is **dwelled.** *Call on a student.* What does **dwelled** mean? *Idea:* Lived.
2. Everybody, what's another way of saying **They lived on a farm?** *Signal.*
They dwelled on a farm.

EXERCISE 4   Vocabulary development

Task A

1. Everybody, touch column 5. *Check.*
First you're going to read the words in column 5. Then we'll talk about what they mean.
2. Touch under the first word. *Pause.*
What word? *Signal.* **Countless.**
3. Next word. *Pause.* What word? *Signal.* **Tint.**
4. *Repeat step 3 for each remaining word in column 5.*
5. *Repeat the words in column 5 until firm.*

Task B

1. Now let's talk about what those words mean. Word 1 is **countless.** If there are too many things to count, they are **countless** things. Too many stones to count are **countless** stones.
2. Everybody, what are too many jewels to count? *Signal.* **Countless jewels.**

Lesson 19

PART A — Word Lists

1	2	3	4	5
generously	yawning	silver	**Vocabulary words**	**Vocabulary words**
cereal	shadows	silvery	1. presence	1. countless
basin	starved	guard	2. glittered	2. tint
spectacles	palace	guarded	3. dwelled	3. guardian
apron	arched	guardian		4. marble
	honest	disturbed		5. studded
	scrambled			6. admit
	ceiling			7. basin
				8. prefer
				9. spectacles

Task C

1. Word 2 is **tint**. A very slight color is a **tint**. Something that is slightly green has a green **tint**.
2. Everybody, what does something that is slightly pink have? *Signal.* **A pink tint.**

Task D

1. Word 3 is **guardian**. The person who **guards** the castle is the **guardian** of the castle.
2. Everybody, what would you call the person who **guards** the gates? *Signal.* **The guardian of the gates.**
3. Everybody, what would you call the person who **guards** the throne room? *Signal.* **The guardian of the throne room.**

Task E

Word 4 is **marble**. **Marble** is a beautiful rock that has wavy colored patterns in it.

Task F

1. Word 5 is **studded**. When something has a lot of shiny things in it, we say it's **studded** with shiny things. Here's another way of saying **A night sky full of stars: A night sky studded with stars.**
2. Everybody, what's another way of saying **A throne full of jewels?** *Signal.* **A throne studded with jewels.**

Task G

1. Word 6 is **admit**. When you **admit** someone to a place, you let that person come in. Here's another way of saying **He will not let the dog in: He will not admit the dog.**
2. Everybody, what's another way of saying **He will not let the dog in?** *Signal.* **He will not admit the dog.**
3. Everybody, what's another way of saying **Oz will not let them in?** *Signal.* **Oz will not admit them.**

Task H

1. Word 7 is **basin**. Another word for **sink** is **basin.**
2. Everybody, what would you call **a small sink?** *Signal.* **A small basin.**
3. Everybody, what would you call **a laundry sink?** *Signal.* **A laundry basin.**

Task I

1. Word 8 is **prefer**. Something that you **prefer** is something that you would choose over other things. If you would choose vanilla over chocolate, you **prefer** vanilla.
2. Everybody, if you would choose a bicycle over roller skates, you *Pause. Signal.* **Prefer a bicycle.**

Task J

1. Word 9 is **spectacles**. Another word for **glasses that you wear** is **spectacles.**
2. Everybody, what's another word for **glasses that you wear?** *Signal.* **Spectacles.**

STORY READING

EXERCISE 5   Decoding

1. Everybody, turn to page 72 in your textbook. *Wait. Call on a student.* What's the error limit for this chapter? **11 errors.**
2. *Call on individual students to read.*
3. *After the group reads to the 2-error sign without making more than 2 errors, reread the first part aloud and present the comprehension tasks.*
4. *After you have completed the first part, call on individual students to read. Present the comprehension tasks.*

CHAPTER 14
The Land of Oz

It was some time before the cowardly Lion awakened, for he had slept among the flowers a long while, breathing in their deadly odor. When he did open his eyes and roll off the cart, he was very glad to find himself still alive.(A)

"I ran as fast as I could," he said, sitting down and yawning. "But the flowers were too strong for me. How did you get me out?"(B)

Then Dorothy and the others told the Lion of the field mice, and how the mice had generously saved him from death. The cowardly Lion laughed, and said, "I have always thought that I was very big and terrible. ★2 ERRORS★ Yet such little things as flowers came near to killing me, and such small animals as mice have saved my life. How strange it all is! But, comrades, what shall we do now?"

"We must journey on until we find the yellow brick road again," said Dorothy. "And then we can go on to the Emerald City."

So, when the Lion was fully refreshed, and felt like himself again, they all started upon the journey. They greatly enjoyed the walk through the soft, fresh grass. It was not long before they reached the yellow brick road and turned again toward the Emerald City where the Great Oz dwelled.

The road was smooth and well paved now, and the country was beautiful. The travelers were happy that the forest was far behind, and with it the many dangers they had met in its dark shadows.(C) Once more they could see fences built beside the road; but these were painted green, not blue.(D) They saw a small house, in which a farmer lived, and that was also painted green. They passed by several of these houses during the afternoon, and sometimes people came to the doors and looked at them as if they would like to ask questions. But no one came near them nor spoke to them, for they were afraid of the great Lion. The people were all dressed in lovely emerald green clothing and wore green hats that were shaped like those of the Munchkins.(E)

"This must be the Land of Oz," said Dorothy, "and we are surely getting near the Emerald City."

"Yes," answered the Scarecrow. "Everything is green here, while in the country of the Munchkins blue was the

favorite color. But the people do not seem to be as friendly as the Munchkins, and I'm afraid we shall be unable to find a place to spend the night."(F)

"I would like something to eat besides fruit," said the girl, "and I'm sure Toto is nearly starved. Let's stop at the next house and talk to the people."

So, when they came to a good-sized farm house, Dorothy walked boldly up to the door and knocked. A woman opened it just far enough to look out, and said, "What do you want, child, and why is that great lion with you?"

"We wish to pass the night with you, if you will allow us," answered Dorothy. "The Lion is my friend and comrade, and would not hurt you for the world."

"Is he tame?" asked the woman, opening the door a little wider.

"Oh, yes," said the girl, "and he is a great coward, too. He will be more afraid of you than you are of him."

"Well," said the woman, after thinking it over and taking another peek at the Lion, "if that is the case you may come in, and I will give you some dinner and a place to sleep."

So they all entered the house. Inside were the woman, two children and a man. The man had hurt his leg, and was lying on a couch in the corner. The people seemed greatly surprised to see so strange a party, and while the woman was busy setting the table the man asked, "Where are you all going?"

"To the Emerald City," said Dorothy, "to see the Great Oz."

"Oh, indeed! exclaimed the man. "Are you sure that Oz will see you?"

"Why not?" she replied.

"It is said that he never lets anyone come into his presence. I have been to the Emerald City many times, and it is a beautiful and wonderful place. But I have never been permitted to see the Great Oz, nor do I know of any living person who has seen him."(G)

★11 ERRORS★

"Does the Wizard never go out?" asked the Scarecrow.

"Never. He sits day after day in the great throne room of his palace, and even those who serve him do not see him face to face."

"What is he like?" asked Dorothy.

"That is hard to tell," said the man, thoughtfully. "You see, Oz is a Great Wizard, and can take on any form he wishes. Some say he looks like a bird, and some say he looks like an elephant, and some say he looks like a cat. To others he appears as a beautiful princess, or in any other form that pleases him. But no one knows who the real Oz is or when he is in his own form."

"That is very strange," said Dorothy. "But we must try to see him or we shall have made our journey for nothing."

"Why do you wish to see the terrible Oz?" asked the man.

"I want him to give me some brains," said the Scarecrow eagerly.

"Oh, Oz could do that easily

EXERCISE 6   Comprehension tasks

(A) Did the Lion wake up right away? **No.** Why not? *Idea:* Because he had slept in the flowers for a long while.

(B) What's the answer to the Lion's question? *Idea:* On a cart pulled by mice.

(C) What was wrong with the road in the forest? *Ideas:* It had holes; it was uneven; it was covered with branches.

● How does the road in the forest compare to the road they are on now? *Idea:* The road in the forest was much worse.

(D) Are the travelers still in the Land of the Munchkins? **No.**

● How do you know? *Idea:* Because the fences are green.

● What is the color of things where the Munchkins live? **Blue.**

● What color is an emerald? **Green.**

● So do you think they are near the Emerald City? **Yes.**

(E) What was the shape of the Munchkin's hats? *Ideas:* Round and pointed; like a cone.

● Why didn't the people come out and ask Dorothy and the others questions? *Idea:* Because they were afraid of the Lion.

(F) Who did the Scarecrow think were friendlier, the Munchkins or the people they were now seeing? **The Munchkins.**

● Why did the Scarecrow think that? *Idea:* Because the people did not speak to them. That's another thing the Scarecrow figured out.

(G) Had the man been to the Emerald City before? **Yes.**

● How often had he been there? *Idea:* Many times.

● Had the man ever seen Oz? **No.**

● Read the rest of the chapter to yourselves and be ready to answer some questions.

After all students have finished reading:

● Does it sound like it will be easy for Dorothy to see Oz? **No.**

● The man said that the Wizard could take on different forms. *Call on individual students.* Name some of the forms Oz could take. *Ideas:* A bird; an elephant; a cat; a beautiful princess.

● Did the man know what Oz looks like when he is in his own form? **No.**

● Did the man think that Oz could help the Scarecrow? **Yes.**

enough," declared the man. "He has more brains than he needs."

"And I want him to give me a heart," said the Tin Woodman.

"That will not trouble him," continued the man. "Oz has a large collection of hearts, of all sizes and shapes."

"And I want him to give me courage," said the cowardly Lion.

"Oz keeps a great pot of courage in his throne room," said the man. "He covers the pot with a golden plate, to keep it from running over. He will be glad to give you some."

"And I want him to send me back to Kansas," said Dorothy.

"Where is Kansas?" asked the man, with surprise.

"I don't know," replied Dorothy, sorrowfully. "But it is my home, and I'm sure it's somewhere."

"Oz can do anything, so I suppose he will find Kansas for you. But first you must get to see him, and that will be a hard task. The Great Wizard does not like to see anyone, and he usually has his own way. But what do you want?" he continued, speaking to Toto. But Toto only wagged his tail, for he could not speak.

The woman now called to them that dinner was ready, so they gathered around the table. Dorothy ate some delicious hot cereal and a dish of scrambled eggs and a plate of nice white bread, and enjoyed her meal. The Lion ate some of the hot cereal, but did not care for it, saying it was made from oats and oats were food for horses, not for lions. The Scarecrow and the Tin Woodman ate nothing at all. Toto ate a little of everything, and was glad to get a good dinner again.

The woman now gave Dorothy a bed to sleep in, and Toto lay down beside her, while the Lion guarded the door of her room so that Dorothy would not be disturbed. The Scarecrow and the Tin Woodman stood up in a corner and kept quiet all night, although of course they could not sleep.

The next morning, as soon as the sun was up, they started on their way, and soon saw a beautiful green glow in the sky just in front of them.

"That must be the Emerald City," said Dorothy.

As they walked on, the green glow became brighter and brighter, and it seemed that at last they were nearing the end of their travels. Yet it was afternoon before they came to the great wall that surrounded the city. The wall was high, and thick, and had a bright green color.

In front of them, at the end of the yellow brick road, was a big gate, all studded with emeralds that glittered so much in the sun that even the painted eyes of the Scarecrow were dazzled by their brightness.

There was a bell beside the gate, and Dorothy pushed the button and heard a silvery tinkling sound on the other side. Then the big gate swung slowly open. They all went through and

found themselves in a room with a high arched ceiling. The walls of the room glistened with countless emeralds.

In front of them stood a little man about the size of a Munchkin. He was clothed all in green, from his head to his feet, and even his skin had a greenish tint. At his side was a large green box.

- What did Oz have that could help the Woodman? *Idea:* A collection of hearts.
- Did the man think that Oz could help the Lion? **Yes.**
- What did Oz have that could help the Lion? *Idea:* A pot of courage.
- What did Dorothy eat that night? *Idea:* Cereal, eggs, bread.
- How did the Lion like the cereal? *Idea:* He didn't.
- Why did the Lion feel that way? *Idea:* Because oats are not for lions.
- What did the Woodman and the Scarecrow eat? **Nothing.**
- The next morning, the travelers started walking. What was the first thing they saw? *Idea:* A green glow.
- What did that glow turn out to be? *Idea:* The Emerald City.
- What surrounded the city? *Idea:* A wall.
- What was the gate covered with? *Idea:* Emeralds.
- Who did something to make the gate open? **Dorothy.**
- What did she do? *Idea:* Pushed a button.
- Who met them inside. *Idea:* A little green man.
- What was the man wearing? *Idea:* Green clothes.
- What was next to the man? *Idea:* A green box.
- Everybody, look at the picture on page 75. The picture shows the room with the high arched ceiling. What are all those shining things in the walls? *Idea:* Emeralds.
- Did you think that the man is the Wizard of Oz? *Response:* Student preference.
- The man with the broken leg said many things about the Wizard of Oz. Had that man ever seen Oz? **No.**
  Yes, the man said many things. I wonder how many of those things are true.
- The story said that at the end of the yellow brick road was a gate studded with emeralds that glittered so much in the sun that even the painted eyes of the Scarecrow were dazzled by their brightness. What does glittered mean? *Ideas:* Glistened; sparkled; bright.
- Everybody, look at the picture again. Touch the ceiling where it is arched. *Check.*

Award 4 points or have the students reread to the error limit sign.

INDEPENDENT WORK

Do all the items in your skillbook and workbook for lesson 19.

ANSWER KEY FOR WORKBOOK

Review Items

1. The travelers heard many things about Oz. Write **Oz** next to the things they have heard.
   a. "He is more powerful than all the witches." _____*Oz*_____
   b. "He always looks like a monster." _____
   c. "He sits in a throne room." _____*Oz*_____
   d. "He never lets anyone see him." _____*Oz*_____
   e. "He is afraid of the witches." _____*Oz*_____
   f. "Many people have seen him." _____
   g. "No one knows what his real form is." _____*Oz*_____
   h. "He can take any form he wants." _____*Oz*_____
   i. "He walks around the Emerald City." _____
   j. "He has a collection of hearts." _____*Oz*_____

2. Put the following story events in the right order by numbering them from 1 through 5.
   _2_ The stork rescued the Scarecrow.
   _4_ The travelers talked to a man with a bad leg.
   _1_ The Lion jumped across a wide ditch.
   _5_ The travelers entered the Emerald City.
   _3_ The Tin Woodman saved the Queen of the Mice.

3. Write whether each sentence describes the **Land of the Munchkins,** the land near the **Emerald City,** or **Kansas.**
   a. The grass was gray, and the wind howled.
   _____*Kansas*_____
   b. Some people had green hats.
   _____*Emerald City*_____
   c. There were round houses with blue domes.
   _____*Land of the Munchkins*_____
   d. There were blue fences by the side of the road.
   _____*Land of the Munchkins*_____
   e. Green fences lined the road.
   _____*Emerald City*_____
   f. People lived in green houses.
   _____*Emerald City*_____

WORKCHECK AND AWARDING POINTS

1. *Read the questions and answers for the skillbook and workbook.*
2. *Award points for independent work as follows:*

0 errors	*6 points*
2 errors	*4 points*
3, 4, or 5 errors	*2 points*
5 or more errors	*0 points*

3. *Award bonus points as follows:*

Correcting missed items or getting all items right	*2 points*
Doing the writing assignment acceptably	*2 points*

ANSWER KEY FOR SKILLBOOK

PART B

1. a. Blue
   b. Green
   c. Yellow
2. *Idea:* Because they were afraid of the Lion
3. a. Yes
   b. No
   c. No
4. a. *Any three:* Bird, elephant, cat, princess
   b. *Idea:* Nobody
5. a. *Idea:* Because Oz has more brains than he needs
   b. *Idea:* Because Oz has a large collection of hearts
   c. *Idea:* Because Oz has a pot of courage
6. a. Green
   b. The Emerald City
   c. wall
7. a. Emeralds
   b. *Idea:* A green man
   c. *Idea:* A green box

PART C

8. a. awkwardness
   b. dreadful
   c. deserted
   d. peculiar
   e. snug
   f. crouched
   g. gloomy
   h. cozy

Lesson 20

PART A   Word Lists

1	2	3	4
sunshine	cereal	uniform	**Vocabulary words**
wildcat	honest	furniture	1. guardian
woodman	ceiling	whistle	2. prefer
scarecrow	lemonade	fountain	3. basin
everything			4. studded
therefore			5. admit
			6. marble

WORD PRACTICE AND VOCABULARY

EXERCISE 1   Word family

1. Everybody, find lesson 20, part A in your skillbook. *Wait.* Touch column 1. *Check.*
All those words are made up of two shorter words. Touch under the first word. *Pause.* What word? *Signal.* **Sunshine.**
2. Next word. *Pause.* What word? *Signal.* **Wildcat.**
3. *Repeat step 2 for each remaining word in column 1.*
4. *Repeat the words in column 1 until firm.*

EXERCISE 2   Word practice

1. Everybody, touch under the first word in column 2. *Pause.* What word? *Signal.* **Cereal.**
2. Next word. *Pause.* What word? *Signal.* **Honest.**
3. *Repeat step 2 for each remaining word in column 2.*
4. *Repeat the words in column 2 until firm.*
5. *Repeat steps 1–4 for column 3.*

EXERCISE 3   Vocabulary review

Task A

1. Everybody, touch column 4. *Check.*
First you're going to read the words in column 4. Then we'll talk about what they mean.
2. Touch under the first word. *Pause.* What word? *Signal.* **Guardian.**
3. Next word. *Pause.* What word? *Signal.* **Prefer.**
4. *Repeat step 3 for each remaining word in column 4.*
5. *Repeat the words in column 4 until firm.*

Task B

You've learned the meanings for all these words. Word 1 is **guardian.** *Call on a student.* What is a **guardian?** *Idea:* A person who guards something.

Task C

Word 2 is **prefer.** *Call on a student.* What does **prefer** mean? *Idea:* To choose one thing over another thing.

Task D

Word 3 is **basin.** *Call on a student.* What is a **basin?** *Idea:* A sink.

Task E

1. Word 4 is **studded.** *Call on a student.* What does **studded** mean? *Idea:* Full of.
2. Everybody, what's another way of saying **A ring full of rubies?** *Signal.* **A ring studded with rubies.**

Task F

1. Word 5 is **admit.** *Call on a student.* What does **admit** mean? *Idea:* Let in.
2. Everybody, what's another way of saying **Oz would not let Dorothy in?** *Signal.* **Oz would not admit Dorothy.**

Task G

Word 6 is **marble.** *Call on a student.* What is **marble?** *Idea:* A beautiful rock with wavy colored patterns.

Lesson 20

CHAPTER 15
The Emerald City Ⓐ

When the little green man saw Dorothy and her companions, he asked, "What do you wish in the Emerald City?"

"We came here to see the Great Oz," said Dorothy.

The man was so surprised at this answer that he sat down to think it over. Ⓑ

"It has been many years since anyone asked me to see Oz," the green man said. "He is powerful and terrible, and if you come here for the foolish reason of bothering the wise thoughts of the great Wizard, he might be angry and destroy you all in an instant."

★2 ERRORS★

"But it is not a foolish reason," replied the Scarecrow. "It is important, and we have been told that Oz is a good Wizard."

"So he is," said the green man. "And he rules the Emerald City wisely and well. But to those who are not honest, or who approach him out of curiosity, he is most terrible, and few have ever asked to see his face. I am the Guardian of the Gates, and since you demand to see the great Oz I must take you to his palace. But first you must put on these spectacles." Ⓒ

"Why?" asked Dorothy.

"Because if you did not wear spectacles the brightness of the Emerald City would blind you. Even those who live in the City must wear spectacles night and day. The spectacles are all locked on, for Oz so ordered it when the city was first built, and I have the only key that will unlock them."

The green man opened the big green box, and Dorothy saw that it was filled with spectacles of every size and shape. All of them had green glass in them. Ⓓ The Guardian of the Gates found a pair that fit Dorothy and put them over her eyes. The spectacles had two golden bands fastened to them that passed around the back of Dorothy's head. The Guardian of the Gates locked the bands together with a little key that was at the end of a chain that he wore around his neck. Ⓔ

When the spectacles were on, Dorothy could not take them off, but of course she did not wish to be blinded by the glare of the Emerald City, so she said nothing.

Then the green man put spectacles on the Scarecrow and the Tin Woodman

76   Lesson 20   Textbook

Lesson 20   Textbook   77

STORY READING

EXERCISE 4   Decoding

1. Everybody, turn to page 76 in your textbook. *Wait. Call on a student.* What's the error limit for this chapter? **15 errors.**
2. *Call on individual students to read.*
3. *After the group reads to the 2-error sign without making more than 2 errors, reread the first part aloud and present the comprehension tasks.*
4. *After you have completed the first part, call on individual students to read. Present the comprehension tasks.*

EXERCISE 5   Comprehension tasks

Ⓐ Where were the travelers at the end of the last chapter. *Idea:* In the Emerald City.
● Who met them inside the gate? *Idea:* A little green man.
Ⓑ Was the man used to having people come to see Oz? **No.**
● How do you know? *Idea:* Because he was very surprised at what Dorothy said.
Ⓒ Is the man going to take the travelers to see Oz? **Yes.**
● But what must the travelers do first? *Idea:* Put on the spectacles.
● Why do you think the travelers would need glasses to see Oz? *Response:* Student preference.
Ⓓ If you wore green glasses, what color would everything look? *Idea:* Green.
I wonder why people would have to wear green glasses if they were in a city that was already green.
Ⓔ Everybody, look at the picture on the next page. You can see the Guardian of the Gates locking the spectacles on Dorothy.

and the Lion, and even on little Toto; and all were locked with the key.

Then the Guardian of the Gates put on his own glasses and told the travelers that he was ready to show them to the palace. Taking a big golden key from a peg on the wall, he opened another gate, and they all followed him through the gate and into the streets of the Emerald City.

Even with their eyes protected by the green spectacles, Dorothy and her friends were at first dazzled by the brightness of the wonderful city. The streets were lined with beautiful houses built of green marble and studded everywhere with sparkling emeralds.(F) The party walked on a sidewalk made of the same green marble. All the pieces of the marble were joined together by rows of emeralds that glittered in the brightness of the sun. The window panes were made of green glass. Even the sky above the city had a green tint, and the rays of the sun were green.

There were many men, women and children walking around. These people were all dressed in green clothes and had greenish skin. They looked at Dorothy and her strange companions with wondering eyes. The children all ran away and hid behind their mothers when they saw the Lion. No one spoke to the travelers.

The street had many shops, and Dorothy saw that everything in them was green. Green candy and green popcorn were for sale, as well as green shoes,

green hats and green clothes of all sorts. At one place, a man was selling green lemonade, and when the children bought it Dorothy could see that they paid for it with green pennies.

There seemed to be no horses. The men carried things around in little green carts, which they pushed in front of them. Everyone seemed happy and rich.

The Guardian of the Gates led them through the streets until they came to a big building, exactly in the middle of the city, which was the Palace of Oz, the Great Wizard. There was a soldier in front of the door, dressed in a green uniform and with a long green beard.(G)

"Here are some strangers," the Guardian of the Gates said to the soldier. "They demand to see the Great Oz."

"Step inside," answered the soldier, "and I will carry your message to him."

So they passed through the palace gates and were led to a big room with a green carpet and lovely green furniture studded with emeralds. The soldier made all of them wipe their feet upon a green mat before he let them enter this room. When they were inside he said, politely, "Please make yourselves comfortable while I go to the door of the throne room and tell Oz you are here."(H)

The party had to wait a long time before the soldier returned. When he finally came back, Dorothy asked, "Have you seen Oz?"

"Oh, no," replied the soldier. "I have never seen him. But I just spoke to him as he sat behind his screen, and gave

him your message.(I) Oz said he will see you if you want, but each one of you must enter his presence alone, and he will admit only one each day. Therefore, since you will have to remain in the palace for several days, I will have someone take you to rooms where you may rest in comfort after your journey."(J) ★15 ERRORS★

"Thank you," replied Dorothy. "That is very kind of Oz."

The soldier now blew on a green whistle, and at once a young girl, dressed in a pretty green silk gown, entered the room. She had lovely green hair and green eyes, and she bowed low before Dorothy as she said, "Follow me and I will show you your room."

So Dorothy said goodbye to all her friends except Toto. She took the dog in her arms and followed the green girl through seven hallways and up three flights of stairs until they came to a room at the front of the palace. It was the sweetest little room in the world, with a soft comfortable bed that had sheets of green silk and a green blanket. There was a tiny fountain in the middle of the room, which shot a spray of green perfume into the air, and the perfume fell back into a beautifully carved green marble basin. Beautiful green flowers stood in the windows, and there was a shelf with a row of little green books. When Dorothy had time to open these books she found them full of strange green pictures that made her laugh.

The closet had many green dresses,

made of silk and satin and velvet; and all of them fit Dorothy exactly.

"Make yourself at home," said the green girl. "And if you want anything ring the bell. Oz will send for you tomorrow morning."

She left Dorothy alone and went back to the others. She also led them to rooms, and each one of them stayed in a very pleasant part of the palace. Of course this politeness was wasted on the Scarecrow; for when he found himself alone in his room, he stood in one spot, right next to the door, to wait until morning. He had no need to lie down, and he could not close his eyes. So he stood up all night staring at a little spider which was weaving its web in a corner of the room. The spider didn't act as if it were in one of the most wonderful rooms in the world.

The Tin Woodman lay down on his bed, for he remembered what he did when he was made of flesh. But since he was unable to sleep, he spent the night moving his legs and arms up and down to make sure that they were in good working order. The Lion would have preferred a bed of dried leaves in the forest, and did not like being shut up in a room. But he had too much sense to let this worry him, so he sprang on the bed and rolled himself up like a cat and fell asleep in a minute.

The next morning, after breakfast, the green girl came to get Dorothy, and she helped Dorothy dress in a pretty green satin gown. Dorothy put on a

(F) What color were the houses? **Green.**

● What were the houses studded with? **Sparkling emeralds.**
I wonder what those houses would look like if they didn't have green glasses on.

(G) Were there any horses or other animals in the city? **No.**

● Were the people poor? **No.**

● What was exactly in the middle of the city? **The Palace of Oz.**

(H) Where is the soldier going? *Idea:* To the throne room.

(I) Had the soldier ever seen Oz? **No.**

● Where was Oz when the soldier gave him the message? *Idea:* Behind a screen.

(J) Did Oz agree to see Dorothy and the others? **Yes.**

● How many of them would Oz see at a time? *Idea:* Only one.

● How many people would Oz see each day? *Idea:* Only one.

● Where will the travelers stay while they are waiting to see Oz? *Idea:* In the palace.

● Read the rest of the chapter to yourselves and be ready to answer some questions.

After all students have finished reading:

● Who showed Dorothy to her room? *Idea:* The girl.

● What kind of bed did the room have? *Idea:* Comfortable.

● What was in the middle of the room? *Idea:* A fountain.

● What was in the closet? *Idea:* Green dresses.

● What did the Scarecrow do that night? *Idea:* Stood in one spot.

● What did the Woodman do that night? *Idea:* Lay down and moved his arms and legs up and down.

● What did the Lion do that night? *Idea:* Slept on the bed.

● Who was the first person to see Oz? **Dorothy.**

● Who helped Dorothy get ready to see Oz? *Idea:* The green girl.

green silk apron and tied a green ribbon around Toto's neck, and they started for the throne room of the Great Oz.

First they came to a great hall in which many ladies and gentlemen were standing around, all dressed in fancy clothes. These people had nothing to do but talk to each other, but they always came to wait outside the throne room every morning, although they were never permitted to see Oz. As Dorothy entered they looked at her curiously, and one of them whispered, "Are you really going to look upon the face of Oz the Terrible?"

"Of course," answered Dorothy, "if he will see me."

"Oh, he will see you," said the soldier who had taken her message to the Wizard, "although he does not like to have people ask to see him. Indeed, at first he was angry, and said I should send you back where you came from. Then he asked me what you looked like, and when I mentioned your silver shoes he was very much interested. At last I told him about the mark upon your forehead, and he decided he would admit you to his presence."

Just then a bell rang, and the green girl said to Dorothy, "That is the signal. You must go into the throne room alone."

- The soldier told Dorothy that at first Oz didn't want to see her. Then the soldier told Oz about two things that Dorothy had. *Call on individual students.* What two things did the soldier tell Oz about? *Idea:* The silver shoes and the witch's kiss.
- So what did Oz decide to do? *Idea:* See Dorothy.
- Who was going into the throne room at the end of the chapter? **Dorothy.**
- What would the Woodman be able to do if his arms and legs were in good working order? *Idea:* Move them around easily.
- Everybody, look at the picture on page 80. *Wait.* This picture shows an apron. An apron is like a bib that covers the front of a person. You can see Dorothy's apron in the picture. Touch it. *Check.*
- Why do people wear aprons? *Idea:* To keep their clothes clean.

Award 4 points or have the students reread to the error limit sign.

INDEPENDENT WORK

Do all the items in your skillbook and workbook for lesson 20.

WORKCHECK AND AWARDING POINTS

1. *Read the questions and answers for the skillbook and workbook.*
2. *Award points for independent work as follows:*

0 errors	*6 points*
2 errors	*4 points*
3, 4, or 5 errors	*2 points*
5 or more errors	*0 points*

3. *Award bonus points as follows:*

Correcting missed items or getting all items right	*2 points*
Doing the writing assignment acceptably	*2 points*

Map Skills

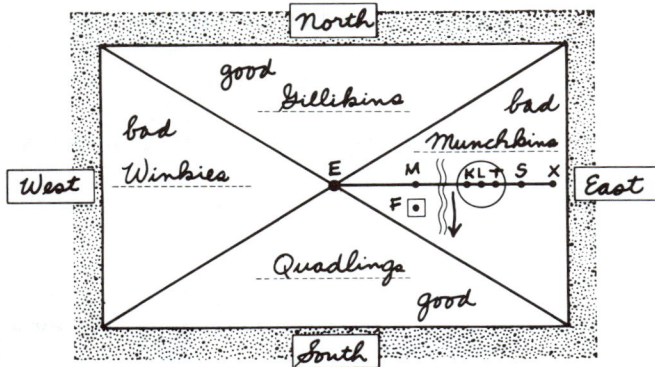

1. Write **North, East, South** and **West** in the boxes around the map.
2. Write the name of the people who live in each land.
3. Write **bad** on the lands that had bad witches. Write **good** on the lands that had good witches.
4. The map has **dots** to show where different things happened.
   a. Put an **S** on the dot where Dorothy met a man who needed brains.
   b. Put an **E** on the dot where a wizard lived.
   c. Put an **M** on the dot where the travelers met some small animals.
   d. There is an **L** on the dot where Dorothy met an animal who needed courage. What animal was that?
      Lion
   e. Put a **T** on the dot where Dorothy met a man who needed a heart.
   f. Put a **K** on the dot where the Kalidahs attacked the travelers.
   g. Put an **X** on the dot where Dorothy's house landed.
   h. Put an **F** on the dot where Dorothy smelled a strong odor.
5. a. What does the **wavy line** show?
      river
   b. Draw an **arrow** on the map to show the direction the travelers floated when they went on the river.
   c. Write the direction they floated when they went downstream.
      south
   d. Write the direction they went to get back to the Yellow Brick Road.
      north

ANSWER KEY FOR SKILLBOOK

PART B

1. a. *Idea:* See Oz
   b. surprised
2. *Idea:* Destroy them
3. a. Green
   b. Green
   c. *Idea:* Everybody
4. *Idea:* The brightness of the city
5. a. Marble
   b. Emerald
   c. No
   d. *Idea:* The Palace of Oz
6. a. One
   b. One
   c. *Idea:* In a room in the Palace
7. a. Dorothy, Toto, the Lion
   b. The Scarecrow, the Tin Woodman

PART C

8. a. Emerald City
   b. Field of Flowers
   c. River
   d. Emerald City
   e. Emerald City
   f. River
   g. Emerald City
   h. Emerald City
9. a. refreshed
   b. dazzled
   c. fortunate
   d. companion
   e. inconvenient
   f. peculiar
   g. hardly
   h. scarlet
   i. crouch
   j. deserted

Lesson 21

WORD PRACTICE AND VOCABULARY

EXERCISE 1   Word practice

1. Everybody, find lesson 21, part A in your skillbook. *Wait.* Touch column 1. *Check.*
   The words in column 1 are hard words that will be in your reading stories.
2. Touch under the first word. *Check.*
   The first word is **rhinoceros.**
   What word? *Signal.* **Rhinoceros.**
3. Next word. *Pause.* That word is **singe.**
   What word? *Signal.* **Singe.**
4. *Repeat step 3 for* **grindstone.**
5. Now let's see if you remember all those words. Touch under the first word in column 1. *Pause.* What word? *Signal.* **Rhinoceros.**
6. Next word. *Pause.* What word? *Signal.* **Singe.**
7. *Repeat step 6 for* **grindstone.**
8. *Repeat the words in column 1 until firm.*

EXERCISE 2   Word family

1. Everybody, touch column 2. *Check.*
   All those words end with the sound **us.**
   Touch under the first word. *Pause.*
   What word? *Signal.* **Enormous.**
2. Next word. *Pause.* What word? *Signal.*
   Tremendous.
3. *Repeat step 2 for each remaining word in column 2.*
4. *Repeat the words in column 2 until firm.*

EXERCISE 3   Word practice

1. Everybody, touch under the first word in column 3. *Pause.* What word? *Signal.* **Giant.**
2. Next word. *Pause.* What word? *Signal.*
   Disappointed.
3. *Repeat step 2 for each remaining word in column 3.*
4. *Repeat the words in column 3 until firm.*

EXERCISE 4   Vocabulary development

Task A

1. Everybody, touch column 4. *Check.*
   First you're going to read the words in column 4. Then we'll talk about what they mean.
2. Touch under the first word. *Pause.*
   What word? *Signal.* **Enormous.**
3. Next word. *Pause.* What word? *Signal.* **Meek.**
4. *Repeat step 3 for each remaining word in column 4.*
5. *Repeat the words in column 4 until firm.*

Task B

1. Now let's talk about what those words mean.
   Word 1 is **enormous.** Another word for **huge** is **enormous.** Everybody, what would you call **a huge lion?** *Signal.* **An enormous lion.**
2. Everybody, what would you call **a huge mountain?** *Signal.* **An enormous mountain.**

Task C

1. Word 2 is **meek.** Another word for **timid** is **meek.** Everybody, what's another way of saying **She spoke timidly?** *Signal.*
   She spoke meekly.
2. Everybody, what's another way of saying **Her expression was timid?** *Signal.*
   Her expression was meek.

Task D

Word 3 is **weep.** Another word for **cry** is **weep.**
Everybody, what's another way of saying **Cry very hard?** *Signal.* **Weep very hard.**

Task E

Word 4 is **willingly.** When you do something on purpose, you do it **willingly.**
Everybody, what's another way of saying **I never killed anything on purpose?** *Signal.*
I never killed anything willingly.

Task F

1. Word 5 is **tremendous.** Another word for **very great** is **tremendous.**
   Everybody, what's another way of saying **There was a very great storm?** *Signal.*
   There was a tremendous storm.
2. Everybody, what's another way of saying **She had very great powers?** *Signal.*
   She had tremendous powers.

Lesson 21

PART A Word Lists

1	2	3	4
rhinoceros	enormous	giant	**Vocabulary words**
singe	tremendous	disappointed	1. enormous
grindstone	anxious	dreadfully	2. meek
	gorgeous	expect	3. weep
			4. willingly
			5. tremendous
			6. grant
			7. terror
			8. request
			9. singed

PART B Reading Checkout Rules

1. If I read the passage in less than one minute, I get points as follows:
   No errors—3 points.
   1 or 2 errors—1 point.
   More than 2 errors—no points.
2. If I take more than one minute to read the passage, I get no points. But I will reread the passage until I can read it in one minute with no more than 2 errors.
3. I will write the number of points I earn in the checkout box for today's lesson.

Lesson 21

CHAPTER 16
The Wizard and Dorothy Ⓐ

Dorothy opened the door to the throne room and walked boldly through. She found herself in a wonderful place. It was a big, round room with a high arched roof, and the walls and ceiling and floor were covered with large emeralds set closely together. In the center of the roof was a great light, as bright as the sun, which made the emeralds sparkle in a wonderful way.

But what interested Dorothy most was the big throne of green marble that stood in the middle of the room. It was shaped like a chair and sparkled with gems, as did everything else. In the center of the chair was an enormous head, floating by itself, without a body, arms or legs. Ⓑ ★2 ERRORS★ There was no hair on the floating head, but it had eyes and a nose and a mouth, and was much bigger than the head of the biggest giant.

Task G

Word 6 is **grant.** When you give a person what the person wishes, you **grant** that person's wish. Everybody, what do you do when you give a person what the person wishes? *Signal.* **You grant that person's wish.**

Task H

1. Word 7 is **terror.** Another word for **great fear** is **terror.** Everybody, what's another way of saying **She felt great fear?** *Signal.* **She felt terror.**
2. Everybody, what's another way of saying **He almost passed out from great fear?** *Signal.* **He almost passed out from terror.**

Task I

1. Word 8 is **request.** When you ask for something, you **request** that thing. Here's another way of saying **She asked for a glass of milk: She requested a glass of milk.** Everybody, what's another way of saying **She asked for a glass of milk?** *Signal.* **She requested a glass of milk.**
2. Everybody, what's another way of saying **The Woodman asked for a heart?** *Signal.* **The Woodman requested a heart.**

Task J

Word 9 is **singed.** Something that is slightly burned is **singed.** Everybody, what's another way of saying **The fire slightly burned her hair?** *Signal.* **The fire singed her hair.**

STORY READING

EXERCISE 5 Decoding

1. Everybody, turn to page 81 in your textbook. *Wait. Call on a student.* What's the error limit for this chapter? **9 errors.**
2. *Call on individual students to read.*
3. *After the group reads to the 2-error sign without making more than 2 errors, reread the first part aloud and present the comprehension tasks.*
4. *After you have completed the first part, call on individual students to read. Present the comprehension tasks.*

EXERCISE 6 Comprehension tasks

Ⓐ What was Dorothy doing at the end of the last chapter? *Idea:* Going into the throne room.
Ⓑ Name some things that Dorothy saw in the throne room. *Ideas:* A high arched roof; large emeralds; a great light; a big throne; an enormous head.

As Dorothy gazed at the head in wonder and fear, the eyes turned slowly and looked at her sharply and steadily. ⓒ Then the mouth moved, and Dorothy heard a voice say, "I am Oz, the Great and Terrible. Who are you, and why did you want to see me?"

Oz's voice was not as awful as she had expected, so she took courage and answered, "I am Dorothy, the Small and Meek. I have come to you for help." ⓓ

The eyes looked at her thoughtfully for a full minute. Then Oz said, "Where did you get the silver shoes?" ⓔ

"I got them from the Wicked Witch of the East, when my house fell on her and killed her," she replied.

"Where did you get the mark on your forehead?" Oz continued. ⓕ

"That is where the good Witch of the North kissed me when she said goodbye and sent me to you," said the girl.

Again the eyes looked at her sharply, and they saw that she was telling the truth. Then Oz asked, "What do you want me to do?"

"Send me back to Kansas, where my Aunt Em and Uncle Henry are," she answered earnestly. "I don't like your country, although it is beautiful. And I am sure Aunt Em is dreadfully worried over my being away so long."

The eyes blinked three times. Then they turned up to the ceiling and down to the floor and rolled around so strangely that they seemed to see every part of the room. And at last they looked at Dorothy again.

"Why should I do this for you?" asked Oz.

"Because you are strong and I am weak; because you are a great Wizard and I am only a small child."

"But you were strong enough to kill the Wicked Witch of the East," said Oz.

"That just happened," answered Dorothy. "I could not help it."

"Well," said Oz, "I will give you my answer. You have no right to expect me to send you back to Kansas unless you do something for me. In this country people must pay for everything they get. If you want me to use my magic power to send you home again you must do something for me first. Help me and I will help you."

"What must I do?" asked the girl.

"Kill the Wicked Witch of the West," answered Oz. ⓖ ★9 ERRORS★

"But I cannot!" exclaimed Dorothy, greatly surprised.

"You killed the Witch of the East and you wear the silver shoes, which have a magic charm. There is now only one Wicked Witch left in all this land, and when you can tell me that she is dead I will send you back to Kansas—but not before."

The girl was so disappointed that she began to weep. The eyes blinked again and looked at her anxiously, as if the great Oz felt that she could help him if she wanted to.

"I never killed anything, willingly," she said. "And even if I wanted to, how

could I kill the Wicked Witch? If you, who are great and terrible, cannot kill her yourself, how do you expect me to do it?"

"I do not know," said Oz. "But that is my answer, and until the Wicked Witch dies you will not see your uncle and aunt again. Remember that the Witch is wicked—tremendously wicked—and must be killed. Now go, and do not ask to see me again until you have done your task."

ⓒ When you look at something steadily, you don't move your eyes around. You keep them steady. Everybody, look at me steadily. *Check.*

ⓓ Oz said that he was Great and Terrible. What did Dorothy say that she was? *Idea:* Small and Meek.

● What does **meek** mean? *Idea:* Timid.

ⓔ What's the answer to Oz's question? *Idea:* From the Witch of the East.

ⓕ What's the answer to Oz's question? *Idea:* From the Witch of the North.

ⓖ The head told Dorothy that in this country people must pay for something. What must they pay for? *Idea:* Everything they get.

● What does that mean: **They must pay for everything they get?** *Idea:* People have to do something in return for Oz using his power.

● What did Dorothy want Oz to do for her? *Idea:* Send her back to Kansas.

● What did Oz say that she would have to do first? *Idea:* Kill the Wicked Witch of the West.

● Read the rest of the chapter to yourselves and be ready to answer some questions.

After all students have finished reading.

● What did Oz tell Dorothy that she must do? *Idea:* Kill the Wicked Witch of the West.

● How did Dorothy respond when she found out what she had to do? *Idea:* She didn't want to do it.

● Did Oz know how to kill the Wicked Witch? **No.**

● Did Oz tell Dorothy how to kill the Witch? **No.** Dorothy has a difficult job ahead of her.

Award 4 points or have the students reread to the error limit sign.

EXERCISE 7   Individual reading checkout

1. *For the individual reading checkout, each student will read 100 words. The passage to be read is the shaded area on the reproduced textbook page for lesson 21 in this presentation book.*

2. Today is a reading checkout day. While you're doing your independent work, I'll call on each student to read part of yesterday's chapter.

3. Find part B on page 31 in your skillbook. *Wait.* The rules in part B tell how many points you can earn for reading quickly and carefully.

4. When I call on you, come up to my desk and bring your textbook with you. After you have read, I'll tell you how many points you can write in the checkout box that's at the top of your workbook page.

5. *If the student finishes the passage in one minute or less, award points as follows:*

0 errors	3 points
1 or 2 errors	1 point
More than 2 errors	0 points

6. *If a student takes more than one minute to read the passage, the student does not earn any points, but have the student reread the passage until he or she is able to read it in no more than one minute with no more than two errors.*

7. *Have the students read the reading checkout rules on page 31 in their skillbook.*

ANSWER KEY FOR WORKBOOK

Review Items

1. Write which character said each sentence. Choose between **Dorothy** and **Oz**.
   a. This character said, "Why did you want to see me?" ___*Oz*___
   b. This character said, "You must do something for me first. Help me and I will help you." ___*Oz*___
   c. This character said, "I never killed anything, willingly." ___*Dorothy*___
   d. This character said, "I am the Great and Terrible." ___*Oz*___
   e. This character said, "You were strong enough to kill the Wicked Witch of the East." ___*Oz*___
   f. This character said, "I am the Small and Meek." ___*Dorothy*___
   g. This character said, "I have come to you for help." ___*Dorothy*___
   h. This character said, "Where did you get the silver shoes?" ___*Oz*___

2. Each sentence describes a witch. Write whether that witch comes from the **East**, the **North**, or the **West**.
   a. Oz ordered Dorothy to kill her. ___*West*___
   b. She lived in the Land of the Gillikins. ___*North*___
   c. Dorothy had taken her silver shoes. ___*East*___
   d. She lived in the Land of the Winkies. ___*West*___
   e. She had given Dorothy a kiss on the forehead. ___*North*___
   f. Dorothy's house killed this witch. ___*East*___

3. Write whether each sentence describes the **Emerald City, Dorothy's room,** or the **throne room.**
   a. It had a closet with green dresses. ___*Dorothy's room*___
   b. It had a palace in the middle. ___*Emerald City*___
   c. This room had a floating head in it. ___*throne room*___
   d. It had a shelf of green books. ___*Dorothy's room*___
   e. There was a great light in the center of its roof. ___*throne room*___
   f. The sidewalks were made of marble. ___*Emerald City*___
   g. There were stores that sold green candy. ___*Emerald City*___
   h. It had a fountain in the middle. ___*Dorothy's room*___
   i. It had a throne in the middle. ___*throne room*___

INDEPENDENT WORK

Do all the items in your skillbook and workbook for lesson 21.

WORKCHECK AND AWARDING POINTS

1. *Read the questions and answers for the skillbook and workbook.*

2. *Award points for independent work as follows:*

0 errors	6 points
2 errors	4 points
3, 4, or 5 errors	2 points
5 or more errors	0 points

3. *Award bonus points as follows:*

Correcting missed items or getting all items right	2 points
Doing the writing assignment acceptably	2 points

4. *Remind the students to put the points they earned for their reading checkout, in the box labeled* **CO.**

ANSWER KEY FOR SKILLBOOK

PART C

1. a. The throne room
   b. Emeralds
2. a. Marble
   b. *Idea:* On the throne
   c. head
   d. her shoes; the mark
3. a. *Idea:* Send her back to Kansas
   b. *Idea:* Kill the Witch of the West
4. *Idea:* Nobody
5. a. Dorothy entered the throne room
   b. Oz told Dorothy to kill the Wicked Witch of the West

PART D

6. a. dreadful
   b. wonderful
   c. scarcely
   d. mystery
   e. cluster
   f. dismal
   g. refreshed
   h. smell
   i. timid

Lesson 22

Lesson 22

PART A   Word Lists

1	2	3	4	5
daisies	singe	**Vocabulary words**	**Vocabulary words**	**Vocabulary words**
telescope	single	1. tremendous	1. slightest	1. pack
castle	sorrowfully	2. meek	2. kingdom	2. flock
	rhinoceros	3. enormous	3. grindstone	3. swarm
	singed	4. terror	4. pure	
	cackle	5. singed	5. advance	
	cackling	6. request	6. scatter	
		7. grant		

WORD PRACTICE AND VOCABULARY

EXERCISE 1   Word practice

1. Everybody, find lesson 22, part A in your skillbook. *Wait.* Touch column 1. *Check.* The words in column 1 are hard words that will be in your reading stories.
2. Touch under the first word. *Check.* The first word is **daisies.** What word? *Signal.* **Daisies.**
3. Next word. *Pause.* That word is **telescope.** What word? *Signal.* **Telescope.**
4. *Repeat step 3 for* **castle.**
5. Now let's see if you remember all those words. Touch under the first word in column 1. *Pause.* What word? *Signal.* **Daisies.**
6. Next word. *Pause.* What word? *Signal.* **Telescope.**
7. *Repeat step 6 for* **castle.**
8. *Repeat the words in column 1 until firm.*

EXERCISE 2   Word practice

1. Everybody, touch under the first word in column 2. *Pause.* What word? *Signal.* **Singe.**
2. Next word. *Pause.* What word? *Signal.* **Single.**
3. *Repeat step 2 for each remaining word in column 2.*
4. *Repeat the words in column 2 until firm.*

EXERCISE 3   Vocabulary review

Task A

1. Everybody, touch column 3. *Check.* First you're going to read the words in column 3. Then we'll talk about what they mean.
2. Touch under the first word. *Pause.* What word? *Signal.* **Tremendous.**
3. Next word. *Pause.* What word? *Signal.* **Meek.**
4. *Repeat step 3 for each remaining word in column 3.*
5. *Repeat the words in column 3 until firm.*

Task B

1. You've learned the meanings for all these words. Word 1 is **tremendous.** *Call on a student.* What does **tremendous** mean? *Idea:* Very great.
2. Everybody, what's another way of saying **There was a very great storm?** *Signal.* **There was a tremendous storm.**

Task C

1. Word 2 is **meek.** *Call on a student.* What does **meek** mean? *Idea:* Timid.
2. Everybody, what's another way of saying **Her expression was timid?** *Signal.* **Her expression was meek.**

Task D

1. Word 3 is **enormous.** *Call on a student.* What does **enormous** mean? *Idea:* Huge.
2. Everybody, what's another way of saying **A huge mountain?** *Signal.*

Task E

1. Word 4 is **terror.** *Call on a student.* What is **terror?** *Idea:* Great fear.
2. Everybody, what's another way of saying **He almost passed out from great fear?** *Signal.* **He almost passed out from terror.**

Task F

1. Word 5 is **singed.** *Call on a student.* What does **singed** mean? *Idea:* Slightly burned.
2. Everybody, what's another way of saying **The fire slightly burned her hair?** *Signal.* **The fire singed her hair.**

Task G

1. Word 6 is **request.** *Call on a student.* What does **request** mean? *Idea:* Ask for.
2. Everybody, what's another way of saying **She asked for a piece of pie?** *Signal.* **She requested a piece of pie.**

Task H

Word 7 is **grant.** *Call on a student.* What does **grant** mean? *Idea:* What you do when you give a person what that person wishes.

Lesson 22

1	2	3	4	5
daisies	singe	**Vocabulary words**	**Vocabulary words**	**Vocabulary words**
telescope	single	1. tremendous	1. slightest	1. pack
castle	sorrowfully	2. meek	2. kingdom	2. flock
	rhinoceros	3. enormous	3. grindstone	3. swarm
	singed	4. terror	4. pure	
	cackle	5. singed	5. advance	
	cackling	6. request	6. scatter	
		7. grant		

EXERCISE 4   Vocabulary development

Task A

1. Everybody, touch column 4. *Check.*
   First you're going to read the words in column 4. Then we'll talk about what they mean.
2. Touch under the first word. *Pause.*
   What word? *Signal.* **Slightest.**
3. Next word. *Pause.* What word? *Signal.* **Kingdom.**
4. *Repeat step 3 for each remaining word in column 4.*
5. *Repeat the words in column 4 until firm.*

Task B

1. Now let's talk about what those words mean.
   Word 1 is **slightest.** Another word for **smallest** is **slightest.**
   Everybody, what's another way of saying **The smallest breeze?** *Signal.*
   The slightest breeze.
2. Everybody, what's another way of saying **The smallest whisper?** *Signal.*
   The slightest whisper.

Task C

Word 2 is **kingdom.** A **kingdom** is a place that is ruled by a king. *Call on a student.*
What's the name of the **kingdom** that is ruled by Oz? *Ideas:* The Land of Oz; Emerald City.

Task D

Word 3 is **grindstone.** A large stone that is used to sharpen knives and axes is called a **grindstone.** Everybody, what do we call a large stone that is used to sharpen knives and axes? *Signal.* **A grindstone.**

Task E

Word 4 is **pure.** If something is not mixed with anything else, that thing is **pure.** If the color white is not mixed with any other color, it is **pure** white. Everybody, what would we call a sound that is not mixed with any other sound? *Signal.* **A pure sound.**

Task F

1. Word 5 is **advance.** When you move forward, you **advance.**
   Everybody, what's another way of saying **They moved forward through the forest?**
   Signal. **They advanced through the forest.**
2. Everybody, what's another way of saying **They could not move forward very fast?**
   Signal. **They could not advance very fast.**

Task G

Word 6 is **scatter.** When you throw things here and there, you **scatter** the things.

EXERCISE 5   Vocabulary development

1. Everybody, touch under the first word in column 5. *Pause.*
   What word? *Signal.* **Pack.**
   Next word. *Pause. Signal.* **Flock.**
   Next word. *Pause. Signal.* **Swarm.**
2. *Repeat step 1 until firm.*
3. Those words tell about the names we give groups of different animals.
   We call a group of wolves or dogs a **pack.**
   We call a group of birds or sheep a **flock.**
   We call a group of bees a **swarm.**
4. What do we call a group of wolves? *Signal.* **A pack.**
   What do we call a group of sheep? *Signal.* **A flock.**
   What do we call a group of bees? *Signal.* **A swarm.**
5. *Repeat step 4 until firm.*
6. Remember those group names. You'll be reading about them.

Lesson 22

CHAPTER 17
The Wizard's Commands Ⓐ

Dorothy was very sad when she left the throne room. She went back to where the Lion and the Scarecrow and the Tin Woodman were waiting to hear what Oz had said to her.

"There is no hope for me," Dorothy said sadly. "Oz will not send me home until I have killed the Wicked Witch of the West, and I cannot do that."

Her friends were sorry, but could do nothing to help her. So she went to her own room and lay down on the bed and went to sleep.

The next morning the soldier with the green whiskers came to the Scarecrow and said, "Come with me, for Oz has sent for you." ★2 ERRORS★

So the Scarecrow followed him and went into the great throne room, where he saw a most lovely lady sitting on the emerald throne. Ⓑ

The lady was dressed in green silk and wore a crown of jewels upon her flowing green hair. Gorgeously colored wings were growing from her shoulders. The wings were so light that they fluttered if the slightest breath of air reached them. Ⓒ

The Scarecrow made a clumsy bow before this beautiful creature. She looked upon him sweetly, and said, "I am Oz, the Great and Terrible. Who are you, and why do you seek me?"

The Scarecrow, who had expected to see the great head Dorothy had told him about, was amazed that Oz was now a woman; but he answered her bravely.

"I am only a Scarecrow, stuffed with straw. Therefore, I have no brains, and I come to you hoping that you will put brains in my head instead of straw, so that I may become as much a man as any other in your kingdom."

"Why should I do this for you?" asked Oz.

"Because you are wise and powerful, and no one else can help me," answered the Scarecrow.

"In this country people must pay for everything they get," said Oz. Ⓓ "If you will kill the Wicked Witch of the West for me, I will give you a great many brains, and such good brains that you will be the wisest man in all the Land of Oz."

"I thought you asked Dorothy to kill the Witch," said the Scarecrow, in surprise.

"So I did. I don't care who kills her. But until she is dead I will not grant your wish. Now go, and do not ask to see me again until you have earned the brains you so greatly desire." Ⓔ

The Scarecrow went sorrowfully back to his friends and told them what Oz had said; and Dorothy was surprised to find that the great Wizard was not a head, as she had seen him, but a lovely lady.

"All the same," said the Scarecrow, "she needs a heart as much as the Tin Woodman."

On the next morning the soldier with whiskers came to the Tin Woodman and said, "Oz has sent for you. Follow me."

So the Tin Woodman followed the soldier and came to the great throne room. He did not know whether Oz would be a lovely lady or a head, but he hoped Oz would be the lovely lady. Ⓕ The Tin Woodman said to himself, "If it is the head, I am sure I will not be given a heart, since a head has no heart of its own and therefore cannot feel for me. But if it is the lovely lady I will beg hard for a heart, for all ladies are supposed to be kindhearted."

But when the Tin Woodman entered the great throne room he saw neither the head nor the lady, for Oz had taken the shape of a terrible beast. It was nearly as big as an elephant, and the green throne seemed barely strong enough to hold its weight.

STORY READING

EXERCISE 6   Decoding

1. Everybody, turn to page 84 in your textbook. *Wait. Call on a student.* What's the error limit for this chapter? **11 errors.**
2. *Call on individual students to read.*
3. *After the group reads to the 2-error sign without making more than 2 errors, reread the first part aloud and present the comprehension tasks.*
4. *After you have completed the first part, call on individual students to read. Present the comprehension tasks.*

EXERCISE 7   Comprehension tasks

Ⓐ What are commands? *Idea:* Orders.
* Oz already gave a command to Dorothy. What was that command? *Idea:* To kill the Wicked Witch of the West.
* Who else is Oz going to talk to? *Idea:* The other travelers.
* Oz told Dorothy that in this land people must pay for something. What must they pay for? *Idea:* Everything they get.
* Do you think that Oz is going to give the Tin Woodman and the others favors if they don't first do something for him? **No.**
* What do you think Oz will tell the others to do? *Response:* Student preference.
Ⓑ Is that what Dorothy saw on the throne? **No.**
* What did Dorothy see? *Idea:* A head.
* Everybody, look at the picture. You can see the lovely lady on the throne.
Ⓒ When something flutters, it moves back and forth. It vibrates. Everybody, hold your arm out as if it is a wing and show me how it would move when it flutters. *Check.*
Now show me how it would move when it flaps. *Check. The students' arms should move slower when they flap.*
Ⓓ Do you think Oz will promise the Scarecrow some brains? **Yes.**
* But what do you think the Scarecrow will have to do first? *Response:* Student preference.
Ⓔ What must the Scarecrow do to earn his brains? *Idea:* Kill the Wicked Witch.
Ⓕ Do you think that Oz will be a lady, a head, or something else? *Response:* Student preference.
* What is the Tin Woodman going to ask Oz for? **A heart.**
* But what do you think Oz will tell the Tin Woodman he must do before he gets a heart? *Idea:* Kill the Wicked Witch.

The beast had a head like a rhinoceros, except that its face had five eyes. There were five long arms growing out of its body and it also had five long, slim legs. Thick hair covered every part of it, and it was the most dreadful looking monster that the Tin Woodman had ever seen. It was fortunate that the Tin Woodman had no heart, for it would have beat loud and fast from terror. But since he had no heart, the Tin Woodman was not at all afraid, although he was very disappointed. ⓖ ★11 ERRORS★

"I am Oz, the Great and Terrible," said the beast, in a roaring voice. "Who are you, and why do you seek me?"

"I am a Woodman and made of tin. Therefore I have no heart, and cannot love. I want you to give me a heart so that I may be like other men."

"Why should I do this?" demanded the beast.

"Because I ask it and because you alone can grant my request," answered the Tin Woodman.

Oz gave a low growl at this, but said, "If you really want a heart, you must earn it."

"How?" asked the Tin Woodman.

"Help Dorothy kill the Wicked Witch of the West," replied the beast. "When the Witch is dead, come to me,

86   Lesson 22 Textbook

and I will then give you the biggest and kindest and most loving heart in all the Land of Oz."

So the Tin Woodman was forced to return sorrowfully to his friends and tell them of the terrible beast he had seen. They were all amazed by how many forms the great Wizard could take, and the Lion said, "If he is a beast when I go to see him, I will roar my loudest, and frighten him so much that he will grant all I ask. And if he is the lovely lady, I will pretend to spring at her, and make her do what I want. And if he is the great head, I will roll him all around the room until he promises to give us what we desire. So be happy, my friends, for everything will go well."

The next morning the soldier with the green whiskers led the Lion to the great throne room.

The Lion at once passed through the door, and glancing around saw to his surprise that a ball of fire was in front of the throne. The ball was so fierce and glowing that the Lion could scarcely bear to look at it. The Lion's first thought was that Oz had accidentally caught on fire and was burning up. But when the Lion tried to go nearer, the heat was so great that it singed his whiskers, and he crept back tremblingly to a spot near the door.

Then a low, quiet voice came from the ball of fire, and this is what it said, "I am Oz, the Great and Terrible. Who are you, and why do you seek me?"

The Lion answered, "I am a cowardly Lion, afraid of everything. I come to you to beg that you give me courage, so that I may become the King of Beasts."

"Why should I give you courage?" demanded Oz.

"Because of all the Wizards you are the greatest, and because you alone have the power to grant my request," answered the Lion.

The ball of fire burned fiercely for a time, and then the voice said, "Bring me proof that the Wicked Witch is dead, and then I will give you courage. But as long as the Witch lives you must remain a coward."

The Lion was angry at this speech, but could say nothing in reply, and while he stood silently gazing at the ball of fire it became so unbearably hot that he turned around and rushed from the room. He was glad to find his friends waiting for him, and told them about his terrible meeting with the Wizard.

"What shall we do now?" asked Dorothy, sadly.

"There is only one thing we can do," answered the Lion, "and that is to go to the Land of the West, seek out the Wicked Witch, and destroy her."

"But suppose we cannot?" said the girl.

"Then I will never have courage," declared the Lion.

"And I will never have brains," added the Scarecrow.

"And I will never have a heart," said the Tin Woodman.

Lesson 22 Textbook   87

ⓖ Everybody, look at the picture. You can see the form that Oz took when he talked to the Tin Woodman.

• Read the rest of the chapter to yourselves and be ready to answer some questions. Find out what the Lion said he would do if Oz was a beast, a lady, or a head.

After all students have finished reading:

• What did the beast tell the Tin Woodman he must do before he could get a heart? *Idea:* Kill the Wicked Witch.

• Did that make the Tin Woodman happy? **No.**

• The Lion bragged about the things that he would do when he met Oz. What did the Lion say he would do if Oz was a beast? *Idea:* Roar at the beast and frighten it.

• What did the Lion say he would do if Oz was a lady? *Idea:* Pretend to spring at her.

• What did the Lion say he would do if Oz was a head? *Idea:* Roll the head around the room.

• But did Oz take any of these forms when the Lion saw him? **No.**

• What was Oz when the Lion saw him? *Idea:* A ball of fire.

• What did the Lion ask for? **Courage.**

• What did the ball of fire tell the Lion he must do before he could get courage? *Idea:* Kill the Wicked Witch.

• Which land did the travelers have to go to, to find the Wicked Witch? **The Land of the West.**

• Oz asked for proof that the Wicked Witch was dead. What do you think Dorothy could bring back with her to prove that the witch is dead? *Response:* Student preference.

• Did the travelers think that they would be able to kill the Witch? **No.**

Award 4 points or have the students reread to the error limit sign.

INDEPENDENT WORK

Do all the items in your skillbook and workbook for lesson 22.

"And I will never see Aunt Em and Uncle Henry," said Dorothy.

Dorothy looked at her friends and said, "I suppose we must try it. But I am sure I do not want to kill anybody, even to see Aunt Em again."

"I will go with you," said the Lion. "But I'm too much of a coward to kill the Witch."

"I will go too," declared the Scarecrow. "But I won't be of much help to you because I am a fool without any brains."

"I haven't the heart to harm even a witch," remarked the Tin Woodman. "But if you go I certainly must go with you."

Therefore, they decided to start their journey to the Land of the West the next morning. The Tin Woodman sharpened his axe on a green grindstone and had all his joints properly oiled. The Scarecrow stuffed himself with fresh straw and Dorothy put new paint on his eyes so that he could see better. The green girl, who was very kind to them, filled Dorothy's basket with good things to eat, and fastened a little green bell around Toto's neck with a green ribbon.

Dorothy, Toto, and the Lion went to bed quite early and slept soundly until daylight.

They were awakened by the crowing of a green rooster that lived in the backyard of the Palace, and by the cackling of a green hen that had laid a green egg. They were ready to start on their journey to the west.

ANSWER KEY FOR WORKBOOK

Review Items

1. Below are some things that people told the travelers about Oz.
Write **true** next to the things that turned out to be true.
Write **false** next to the things that turned out to be false.
a. "He lives in the Emerald City." _true_
b. "He can take any form he wants." _true_
c. "He sits in the throne room." _true_
d. "He will destroy you." _false_
e. "He never lets anyone come into his presence." _false_

2. Write whether each thing could happen to you in the **forest**, the **field of flowers**, or the **Emerald City**.
a. You sleep forever. _field of flowers_
b. You walk by a palace. _Emerald City_
c. You see flowers everywhere. _field of flowers_
d. You jump over a wide ditch. _forest_
e. You walk on marble sidewalks. _Emerald City_
f. You smell something that makes you sleepy. _field of flowers_
g. You pay for candy with green money. _Emerald City_
h. You get chased by Kalidahs. _forest_
i. You have to wear glasses all day long. _Emerald City_

3. Put the following story events in the right order by numbering them from 1 through 4.
_3_ Oz takes the form of a ball of fire.
_1_ The Guardian of the Gates locked green spectacles on the travelers.
_4_ The travelers decided to kill the Wicked Witch of the West.
_2_ Oz took the form of a giant head.

WORKCHECK AND AWARDING POINTS

1. *Read the questions and answers for the skillbook and workbook.*
2. *Award points for independent work as follows:*

0 errors	6 points
2 errors	4 points
3, 4, or 5 errors	2 points
5 or more errors	0 points

3. *Award bonus points as follows:*

Correcting missed items or getting all items right	2 points
Doing the writing assignment acceptably	2 points

ANSWER KEY FOR SKILLBOOK

PART B

1. a. *Idea:* A giant head
   b. *Idea:* A lovely lady
   c. *Idea:* A beast
   d. *Idea:* A ball of fire
2. a. The Tin Woodman
   b. The Scarecrow
   c. Dorothy
   d. The Lion
   e. The Tin Woodman
3. a. Brains
   b. A heart
   c. Courage
4. a. Yes
   b. *Idea:* Kill the Witch of the West

PART C

5. a. The Lion
   b. The Scarecrow
   c. The Tin Woodman
6. a. *Idea:* The Land of the West
   b. The Winkies
   c. West
7. a. odor
   b. therefore
   c. permit
   d. shy
   e. stunned
   f. presence
   g. admit
   h. preferred
   i. tint
   j. glittered

Lesson 23

Lesson 23

PART A   **Word Lists**

1	2	3	4
seize	buttercups	**Vocabulary words**	**Vocabulary words**
threaten	disobey	1. advance	1. untilled
desperate	daisy	2. scatter	2. castle
rejoice	daisies	3. pure	3. strike
	hill	4. flock	4. heap
	hillier	5. swarm	5. rage
	fierce	6. pack	6. spear
			7. seize
			8. fate
			9. tempt
			10. fine

WORD PRACTICE AND VOCABULARY

EXERCISE 1   Word practice

1. Everybody, find lesson 23, part A in your skillbook. *Wait.* Touch column 1. *Check.*
The words in column 1 are hard words that will be in your reading stories.
2. Touch under the first word. *Check.*
The first word is **seize.**
What word? *Signal.* **Seize.**
3. Next word. *Pause.* That word is **threaten.**
What word? *Signal.* **Threaten.**
4. *Repeat step 3 for each remaining word in column 1.*
5. Now let's see if you remember all those words.
Touch under the first word in column 1. *Pause.*
What word? *Signal.* **Seize.**
6. Next word. *Pause.* What word? *Signal.*
Threaten.
7. *Repeat step 6 for each remaining word in column 1.*
8. *Repeat the words in column 1 until firm.*

EXERCISE 2   Word practice

1. Everybody, touch under the first word in column 2. *Pause.* What word? *Signal.*
Buttercups.
2. Next word. *Pause.* What word? *Signal.* **Disobey.**
3. *Repeat step 2 for each remaining word in column 2.*
4. *Repeat the words in column 2 until firm.*

EXERCISE 3   Vocabulary review

Task A
1. Everybody, touch column 3. *Check.*
First you're going to read the words in column 3. Then we'll talk about what they mean.
2. Touch under the first word. *Pause.*
What word? *Signal.* **Advance.**
3. Next word. *Pause.* What word? *Signal.* **Scatter.**
4. *Repeat step 3 for each remaining word in column 3.*
5. *Repeat the words in column 3 until firm.*

Task B
1. You've learned the meanings for all these words. Word 1 is **advance.**
Call on a student. What does **advance** mean?
Idea: Move forward.
2. Everybody, what's another way of saying **They moved forward through the forest?**
Signal. **They advanced through the forest.**
3. Everybody, what's another way of saying **They could not move forward very fast?**
Signal. **They could not advance very fast.**

Task C

1. Word 2 is **scatter.** *Call on a student.*
   What does **scatter** mean? *Idea:* To throw here and there.
2. Everybody, what's another way of saying **The wind threw the straw here and there?** *Signal.* **The wind scattered the straw.**

Task D

1. Word 3 is **pure.** *Call on a student.*
   What does **pure** mean? *Idea:* Not mixed with anything else.
2. Everybody, what would we call a sound that is not mixed with any other sound? *Signal.*
   A pure sound.

Task E

1. Word 4 is **flock,** word 5 is **swarm,** and word 6 is **pack.**
2. Everybody, what do we call a group of birds? *Signal.* **A flock.**
   Everybody, what do we call a group of bees? *Signal.* **A swarm.**
   Everybody, what do we call a group of wolves? *Signal.* **A pack.**
3. *Repeat step 2 until firm.*

EXERCISE 4   Vocabulary development

Task A

1. Everybody, touch column 4. *Check.*
   First you're going to read the words in column 4. Then we'll talk about what they mean.
2. Touch under the first word. *Pause.*
   What word? *Signal.* **Untilled.**
3. Next word. *Pause.* What word? *Signal.* **Castle.**
4. *Repeat step 3 for each remaining word in column 4.*
5. *Repeat the words in column 4 until firm.*

Task B

Now let's talk about what those words mean.
Word 1 is **untilled.** Another word for **plowed** is **tilled.** Everybody, what's another word for **unplowed?** *Signal.* **Untilled.**

Task C

Word 2 is **castle.** A **castle** is something like a palace.

Task D

Word 3 is **strike.** Another word for **hit** is **strike.**
Everybody, what's another way of saying **He will hit the punching bag?** *Signal.*
He will strike the punching bag.
Everybody, what's another way of saying **Don't hit the animals?** *Signal.*
Don't strike the animals.

Task E

Word 4 is **heap.** A **heap** is a **pile.** Everybody, what's a **heap?** *Signal.* **A pile.**

Task F

Word 5 is **rage.** Another word for **great anger** is **rage.** Everybody, what's another way of saying **She had a fit of great anger?**
Signal. **She had a fit of rage.**

Task G

Word 6 is **spear.** A **spear** is a weapon that is thrown at the enemy. A spear has a long shaft and a pointed tip.

Task H

1. Word 7 is **seize.** When you **seize** something, you grab it and hang onto it. Everybody, what's another way of saying **He grabbed the money that was on the table?** *Signal.*
   He seized the money that was on the table.
2. Everybody, what's another way of saying **They grabbed the dog?** *Signal.*
   They seized the dog.

Task I

Word 8 is **fate.** The things that happen to you are called your fate. If good things happen to you, you have a good fate. Everybody, what would you have if bad things happened to you?
Signal. **A bad fate.**

Task J

Word 9 is **tempt.** When you **tempt** people, you try to get them to do things by offering them something they really want. If you offer them gold, you tempt them with gold. Everybody, what do you do if you promise them a lot of money? *Signal.* **You tempt them with a lot of money.**

Task K

Word 10 is **fine.** The word **fine** sometimes means very small. Everybody, what's another way of saying **The grains of sand were very small?** *Signal.* **The grains of sand were fine.**

Lesson 23

CHAPTER 18
The Search for the Wicked Witch

The soldier with the green whiskers led Dorothy and her friends through the streets of the Emerald City until they reached the room where the Guardian of the Gates lived. The Guardian unlocked their spectacles and put them back in his green box, and then he politely opened the gate for the travelers.

"Which road leads to the Wicked Witch of the West?" asked Dorothy.

"There is no road," answered the Guardian of the Gates. "No one ever wishes to go that way." (A) ★2 ERRORS★

"How, then, can we find her?" inquired the girl.

"That will be easy," replied the man. "When she knows you are in the country of the Winkies she will find you, and make you all her slaves."

"Perhaps not," said the Scarecrow, "for we hope to destroy her."

"Oh, that is different," said the Guardian of the Gates. "No one has ever destroyed her before, so I naturally thought she would make slaves of you. But take care, for she is wicked and fierce, and may try to destroy you first. Keep going west, where the sun sets, and you cannot fail to find her."

They thanked him and said goodbye, and turned toward the west, walking over fields of soft grass dotted here and there with daisies and buttercups. (B) Dorothy still wore the pretty silk dress she had put on in the Palace; but now, to her surprise, she found that it was no longer green, but pure white. (C) The ribbon around Toto's neck had also lost its green color and was as white as Dorothy's dress.

The Emerald City was soon far behind them. As they advanced, the ground became rougher and hillier, for there were no farms or houses in this country of the West, and the ground was untilled. (D)

In the afternoon the sun shone hot in their faces, for there were no trees to offer them shade. The sun made Dorothy and Toto and the Lion very tired, and before night, they lay down on the grass and fell asleep, with the Tin Woodman and the Scarecrow keeping watch.

Now the Wicked Witch of the West had only one eye, but it was as powerful as a telescope, and could see everywhere. (E) So, as she sat in the door of her yellow castle, she happened to see Dorothy lying asleep, with her friends all around her. They were a long way away,

*Lesson 23   Textbook   **89***

but the Wicked Witch was angry to find them in her country; so she blew on a silver whistle that hung around her neck. (F)

All at once a pack of great wolves came running to the Witch from all directions. They had long legs and fierce eyes and sharp teeth. (G)

"Go to those people," said the Witch, "and tear them to pieces."

"Aren't you going to make them your slaves?" asked the leader of the wolves.

"No," she answered. "One is made of tin, and one of straw; one is a girl, and another a lion. None of them is fit to work, so you may tear them into small pieces."

"Very well," said the wolf, and he dashed away at full speed, followed by the other wolves.

"Luckily, the Scarecrow and the Tin Woodman were wide awake and heard the wolves coming.

"This is my fight," said the Tin Woodman. "Get behind me and I will meet them as they come."

The Tin Woodman turned his axe so that the flat side was facing out, for he did not want to strike the wolves with the blade. When the leader of the wolves came on, the Tin Woodman swung the axe and struck the wolf on the head. The sharp blow stunned the wolf, and it fell at the Tin Woodman's feet. There were forty wolves, and forty times a wolf was stunned; so that at last they all lay in a heap before the Tin Woodman. (H)

Then the Tin Woodman put down his axe and sat beside the Scarecrow, who said, "It was a good fight, friend."

Dorothy knew nothing of the fight, for she slept through it. When she woke up the next morning, the wolves had gone and the Tin Woodman and the Scarecrow were standing watch as they had been standing when she went to sleep. When the Tin Woodman told her what had happened, she thanked him for saving them and sat down to breakfast. Then they started their journey again. (I) ★11 ERRORS★

That morning the Wicked Witch came to the door of her yellow castle and looked out with her one powerful eye. The strangers were still traveling through her country. This made her angrier than before, and she blew her silver whistle twice.

All at once, a great flock of wild crows came flying toward her. They darkened the sky. And the Wicked Witch said to the King Crow, "Fly at once to the strangers. Peck out their eyes and tear them to pieces."

The wild crows flew in one great flock toward Dorothy and her companions. When the girl saw them coming she was afraid. But the Scarecrow said, "This is my battle. Lie down beside me and you will not be harmed."

So they all lay upon the ground except the Scarecrow, and he stood up and stretched out his arms. And when the crows saw him they were frightened,

90   *Lesson 23   Textbook*

STORY READING

EXERCISE 5   Decoding

1. Everybody, turn to page 89 in your textbook. *Wait. Call on a student.* What's the error limit for this chapter? **11 errors.**
2. *Call on individual students to read.*
3. *After the group reads to the 2-error sign without making more than 2 errors, reread the first part aloud and present the comprehension tasks.*
4. *After you have completed the first part, call on individual students to read. Present the comprehension tasks.*

EXERCISE 6   Comprehension tasks

(A) In which direction do the travelers have to go to reach the Wicked Witch? **West.**
- Which road will they follow? *Idea:* There is no road.

(B) Buttercups are flowers. What color are buttercups? **Yellow.**

(C) When Dorothy was in the Emerald City, what did everybody have to wear? *Idea:* Green glasses.
- Is she wearing those glasses now? **No.**
- What color was the dress without the glasses? **White.**
- Do you think that some of the other things in the Emerald City might not be green? *Response:* Student preference.

(D) What does **untilled** mean? *Idea:* Not plowed.

(E) What do you use a telescope for? *Idea:* To see things that are far away.

(F) How many eyes does the Witch have? **One.**
- The chapter tells that the Witch's eye was as powerful as a telescope. What does that mean? *Idea:* That she could see far.
- How did the Witch feel about Dorothy being in her country? *Idea:* Very angry.
- What did the Witch do after she spotted Dorothy and her friends? *Idea:* Blew on a silver whistle.

(G) What do you think the Witch is going to have the wolves do? *Response:* Student preference.

(H) Did the Tin Woodman hit the wolf with the sharp side of the axe? **No.**
- Which side did he hit the wolf with? *Idea:* The flat side.
- What did that do to the wolf? *Idea:* Stunned it.
- How many wolves were there? **Forty.**
- How many were stunned by the Woodman? **Forty.**

(I) Did Dorothy see the fight? **No.**
- Why not? *Idea:* Because she was asleep.
- How did Dorothy find out about the fight? *Idea:* The Tin Woodman told her.
- Read the rest of the chapter to yourselves and be ready to answer some questions.

114   Lesson 23

and did not dare to come any nearer. But the King Crow said, "It is only a stuffed man. I will peck his eyes out."

But just as the crow was about to attack the Scarecrow's face, the Scarecrow began spinning around and making a terrible noise. The crows, who had never seen a scarecrow behave like this, became so frightened that they flew far off into the sky, casting a great shadow over the bare hills below them. Then the Scarecrow called to his companions to rise, and they continued their journey.

When the Wicked Witch looked out again and saw that the travelers were still alive, she got into a terrible rage, and blew on her silver whistle three times.

All at once, there was a great buzzing in the air, and a swarm of black bees came flying toward her.

"Go to the strangers and sting them to death!" commanded the Witch, and the bees turned and flew rapidly until they came to where Dorothy and her friends were walking. But the Tin Woodman had seen them coming and the Scarecrow had decided what to do.

"Take out my straw and scatter it over Dorothy and Toto and the Lion," the Scarecrow said to the Tin Woodman," and the bees will not be able to sting them." Dorothy lay down next to the Lion and held Toto in her arms while the Tin Woodman covered them with straw.

The bees came and found no one but the Tin Woodman to sting, so they flew at him and broke off all their stingers against the tin, without hurting the Tin Woodman at all. And since bees cannot live in the Land of the West when their stingers are broken, they all died. They lay scattered thickly on the ground around the Tin Woodman, like little heaps of fine coal.

Then Dorothy and the Lion got up, and the girl helped the Tin Woodman put the straw back into the Scarecrow again, until he was as good as ever. So they started upon their journey once more.

The Wicked Witch was so angry when she saw her black bees in little heaps like fine coal that she stamped her foot and tore her hair and ground her teeth. And then she called a dozen of her slaves, who were the Winkies, and gave them sharp yellow spears, and told them to go to the strangers and destroy them.

The Winkies were not a brave people, but they had to do as they were told; so they marched away until they came near Dorothy. Then the Lion gave a great roar and sprang toward them, and the poor Winkies were so frightened that they ran back to the castle as fast as they could.

When the Winkies returned to the Wicked Witch she sent them back to their work. Then she sat down to think about what to do next. She could not understand how all her plans to destroy these strangers had failed. But she was a powerful Witch, as well as a wicked one, and she soon decided what to do next.

After all students have finished reading:

- How did the Witch feel when she saw that the travelers were still in her country the next morning? *Idea:* Very angry.
- Who came when the Witch blew her silver whistle twice. **The crows.**
- What did the Scarecrow do to get rid of the crows? *Idea:* He spun around and made a terrible noise.
- The story tells that the crows cast a great shadow over the bare hills. Why did the crows cast a shadow that was so big? *Idea:* Because there were so many of them.
- Who did the Witch call for after the crows failed to kill the travelers? **The black bees.**
- How many times did the Witch blow on her whistle to call the bees? **Three.**
- How were Dorothy, Toto, and the Lion protected from the bees? *Idea:* By the Scarecrow's straw.
- Who did the bees try to sting? **The Tin Woodman.**
- Did the stings hurt the Tin Woodman? **No.**
- Why did the bees die? *Idea:* Because their stingers were broken.
- Who did the Witch call after the bees failed? **The Winkies.**
- The Witch called a dozen Winkies. How many Winkies would that be? **Twelve.**
- Who took care of the Winkies? **The Lion.**
- How did the Lion do that? *Idea:* He roared and sprang at them.
- What did the Witch do to the Winkies when they returned to the castle? *Idea:* Sent them back to work.
- Did the Witch give up at the end of this chapter? **No.**
- At one part of the story, the Scarecrow called his companions to rise. What does somebody do when that person rises? *Idea:* Stands up.

Award 4 points or have the students reread to the error limit sign.

INDEPENDENT WORK

Do all the items in your skillbook and workbook for lesson 23.

ANSWER KEY FOR WORKBOOK

Map Skills

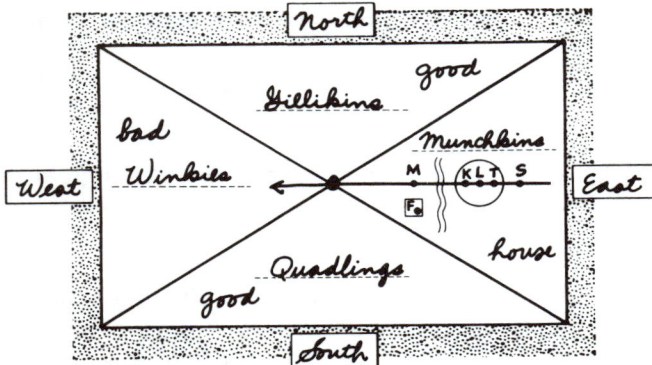

1. Write **North, East, South** and **West** in the boxes around the map.
2. On the map, write the name of the people who live in each land.
3. **a.** Write **good** on the lands that had **good** witches.
   b. Write **house** on the land where a house killed a **bad** witch.
   c. Write **bad** on the land that still had a **bad** witch.
4. **a.** Put a **dot** on the place where the travelers saw the Wizard.
   b. What's the name of that place?
   Emerald City
5. On the map, draw an **arrow** from the Emerald City to show which way the travelers went after they left the city.

6. **a.** What happened at the dot marked with an F? *Idea:* *Dorothy and the Lion fell asleep.*
   b. What happened at the dot marked with a K? *Idea:* *The travelers met the Kalidahs.*
7. **a.** Write **S** on the dot where Dorothy met the Scarecrow.
   b. Write **L** on the dot where Dorothy met the Lion.
   c. Write **T** on the dot where Dorothy met the Tin Woodman.
   d. Write **M** on the dot where the travelers met some small animals.

WORKCHECK AND AWARDING POINTS

1. *Read the questions and answers for the skillbook and workbook.*
2. *Award points for independent work as follows:*

0 errors	*6 points*
2 errors	*4 points*
3, 4, or 5 errors	*2 points*
5 or more errors	*0 points*

3. *Award bonus points as follows:*

Correcting missed items or getting all items right	*2 points*
Doing the writing assignment acceptably	*2 points*

ANSWER KEY FOR SKILLBOOK

PART B

1. **a.** No
   b. No
   c. Green
   d. White
   e. *Idea:* Student preference
2. **a.** One
   b. *Idea:* It was powerful
   c. *Idea:* Angry
   d. A silver whistle
3. **a.** The wolves
   b. *Ideas:* Kill the travelers; tear the travelers into small pieces
   c. The Tin Woodman
   d. *Idea:* His axe
4. **a.** The crows
   b. The Scarecrow
   c. made a strange noise
5. **a.** The bees
   b. The Scarecrow
   c. The Tin Woodman
   d. *Idea:* Because their stingers were broken

PART C

6. **a.** The Tin Woodman
   b. Dorothy
   c. The Lion
   d. The Tin Woodman
   e. Dorothy
   f. The Scarecrow
7. **a.** smell
   b. permit
   c. admitted

Lesson 24

Lesson 24

PART A   **Word Lists**

1	2	3	4
seize	chatter	**Vocabulary words**	**Vocabulary words**
threatened	invisible	1. fate	1. chattering
disobey	struggle	2. seize	2. battered
seized	strange	3. tempt	3. bundle
desperate	chattering		4. courtyard
desperately			5. desperately
			6. cunning
			7. rejoice

WORD PRACTICE AND VOCABULARY

EXERCISE 1   Word practice

1. Everybody, find lesson 24, part A in your skillbook. *Wait.* Touch under the first word in column 1. *Pause.* What word? *Signal.* **Seize.**
2. Next word. *Pause.* What word? *Signal.* **Threatened.**
3. *Repeat step 2 for each remaining word in column 1.*
4. *Repeat the words in column 1 until firm.*
5. *Repeat steps 1–4 for column 2.*

EXERCISE 2   Vocabulary review

Task A

1. Everybody, touch column 3. *Check.* First you're going to read the words in column 3. Then we'll talk about what they mean.
2. Touch under the first word. *Pause.* What word? *Signal.* **Fate.**
3. Next word. *Pause.* What word? *Signal.* **Seize.**
4. *Repeat step 3 for* **tempt.**
5. *Repeat the words in column 3 until firm.*

Task B

1. You've learned the meanings for all these words. Word 1 is **fate.** *Call on a student.* What is **fate?** *Idea:* Things that happen to you.
2. Everybody, what would you have if bad things happen to you? *Signal.* **A bad fate.**

Task C

1. Word 2 is **seize.** *Call on a student.* What does **seize** mean? *Idea:* Grab.
2. Everybody, what's another way of saying **They grabbed the baby?** *Signal.* **They seized the baby.**
3. Everybody, what's another way of saying **They grabbed the jewels that were on the table?** *Signal.* **They seized the jewels that were on the table.**

Task D

1. Word 3 is **tempt.** *Call on a student.* What does **tempt** mean? *Idea:* You get people to do things by offering them something they really want.
2. Everybody, what do you do if you offer them gold? *Signal.* **You tempt them with gold.**

EXERCISE 3   Vocabulary development

Task A

1. Everybody, touch column 4. *Check.* First you're going to read the words in column 4. Then we'll talk about what they mean.
2. Touch under the first word. *Pause.* What word? *Signal.* **Chattering.**
3. Next word. *Pause.* What word? *Signal.* **Battered.**
4. *Repeat step 3 for each remaining word in column 4.*
5. *Repeat the words in column 4 until firm.*

Task B

Now let's talk about what those words mean. Word 1 is **chattering.** A **chattering** sound is the kind of sound that monkeys make. Chi, chi, chi. Everybody, what kind of sound is that? *Signal.* **A chattering sound.**

Task C

1. Word 2 is **battered.** Something that is full of dents and beat up is **battered.** Everybody, what's another way of saying **The car was full of dents?** *Signal.* **The car was battered.**
2. Everybody, what's another way of saying **The Tin Woodman was full of dents?** *Signal.* **The Tin Woodman was battered.**

Task D

Word 3 is **bundle.** When you roll up clothes into a tight ball, you make a **bundle.** Everybody, what do you make when you roll up clothes into a tight ball? *Signal.* **A bundle.**

Task E

Word 4 is **courtyard.** The yard outside of a castle is called a **courtyard.** Everybody, what's the yard outside a castle called? *Signal.* **A courtyard.**

Task F

Word 5 is **desperately.** When you want something very, very much, you **desperately** want that thing. Here's another way of saying **She very much wanted Dorothy's shoes: She desperately wanted Dorothy's shoes.** Everybody, what's another way of saying **She very much wanted Dorothy's shoes?** *Signal.* **She desperately wanted Dorothy's shoes.**

Lesson 24

PART A Word Lists

1	2	3	4
seize	chatter	**Vocabulary words**	**Vocabulary words**
threatened	invisible	1. fate	1. chattering
disobey	struggle	2. seize	2. battered
seized	strange	3. tempt	3. bundle
desperate	chattering		4. courtyard
desperately			5. desperately
			6. cunning
			7. rejoice

Lesson 24

CHAPTER 19
The Witch's Castle

The Wicked Witch had a golden cap in her cupboard. The cap was studded with diamonds and rubies and it had a special power.Ⓐ Whoever owned the cap could call upon the Winged Monkeys, who would obey any order they were given. But no person could command these strange creatures more than three times.Ⓑ The Wicked Witch had already used the cap twice. The first time was when she had made the Winkies her slaves, and made herself the ruler of their country. The Winged Monkeys had helped her do this. The second time was when she had fought against the great Oz, and driven him out of the Land of the West. The Winged Monkeys had also helped her do this. Ⓒ

★2 ERRORS★

But now the Witch could use the golden cap only one more time, which was why she had tried all her other powers first. Her fierce wolves and her wild crows and her stinging bees had failed, and her slaves had been scared away by the cowardly Lion. So she knew that the cap was the only way left to destroy Dorothy and her friends.

So the Wicked Witch took the golden cap from her cupboard and placed it on her head. Then she stood on her left foot and said, slowly, "Ep-pe, pep-pe, bep-pe!"

Next she stood on her right foot and said. "Hil-lo, hol-lo, hel-lo!"

After that she stood on both feet and cried in a loud voice, "Ziz-zy, zuz-zy, zik!"

Now the charm began to work. The sky was darkened, and a low rumbling sound came through the air. The Witch heard the flapping of many wings, then a great chattering and laughing. When the sun came out of the dark sky, the Wicked Witch was surrounded by a crowd of monkeys.Ⓓ Each monkey had a pair of large and powerful wings on his shoulders.

Lesson 24 Textbook **93**

Task G

Word 6 is **cunning.** Someone who is dishonest, but tricky is **cunning.** Everybody, what's another way of saying **The witch was dishonest, but tricky?** *Signal.*
The witch was cunning.

Task H

Word 7 is **rejoice.** When you act very happy, you **rejoice.** Everybody, what's another way of saying **They acted very happy?** *Signal.*
They rejoiced.

STORY READING

EXERCISE 4 Decoding

1. Everybody, turn to page 93 in your textbook. *Wait. Call on a student.* What's the error limit for this chapter? **10 errors.**
2. *Call on individual students to read.*
3. *After the group reads to the 2-error sign without making more than 2 errors, reread the first part aloud and present the comprehension tasks.*
4. *After you have completed the first part, call on individual students to read. Present the comprehension tasks.*

EXERCISE 5 Comprehension tasks

Ⓐ What was the cap studded with?
Idea: Diamonds and rubies.
● What color are rubies? **Red.**
● What color are diamonds? **Clear.**
Ⓑ Who can you command if you own the cap?
The Winged Monkeys.
● How many times can a person command the Monkeys? **Three times.**
Ⓒ How many times had the Witch commanded the Winged Monkeys before? **Two times.**
● So how many more times could she command them? **One more time.**
● What did the Monkeys do for the Witch the first time she commanded them?
Idea: Helped her conquer the Winkies.
● What did the Monkeys do for the Witch the second time she commanded them?
Idea: Helped her fight Oz.
No wonder Oz wants the Witch killed.
Ⓓ The story tells that when the sun came out of the dark sky, the Wicked Witch was surrounded by a crowd of Monkeys.
● What made the sky dark in the first place?
Idea: The Monkeys.
● Everybody, look at the picture. You can see the Winged Monkeys flying towards the Witch.

One monkey, much bigger than the others, seemed to be the leader. He flew close to the Witch and said, "You have called us for the third and last time. What do you command?"

"Go to the strangers who are within my land and destroy them all except the lion," said the Wicked Witch. "Bring the beast to me, for I have a mind to harness him like a horse, and make him work." Ⓔ

"Your commands shall be obeyed," said the leader. And then, with a great deal of chattering and noise, the Winged Monkeys flew away to the place where Dorothy and her friends were walking.

Some of the Monkeys seized the Tin Woodman and carried him through the air until they were over a plain that was thickly covered with sharp rocks. Here they dropped the poor Tin Woodman, who fell a great distance to the rocks. Ⓕ The Tin Woodman became so battered and dented that he could neither move nor groan.

Other Monkeys caught the Scarecrow, and with their long fingers pulled all the straw out of his clothes and head. They made his hat and boots and clothes into a small bundle and threw the bundle into the top branches of a tall tree. Ⓖ

The remaining Monkeys threw pieces of thick rope around the Lion and wound the rope around his body and head and legs, until he was unable to bite or scratch or struggle in any way. Then they lifted him up and flew away with

him to the Witch's castle, where he was placed in a small yard with a high iron fence around it, so that he could not escape. Ⓗ

But they did not harm Dorothy at all. She stood, with Toto in her arms, watching the sad fate of her comrades and thinking it would soon be her turn. The leader of the Winged Monkeys flew up to her with his long, hairy arms stretched out and his ugly face grinning terribly. But when he saw the mark of the good Witch's kiss on Dorothy's forehead, he stopped short, and told the other Monkeys not to touch her. Ⓘ

★10 ERRORS★

"We dare not harm this girl," he said to them, "for the mark on her forehead shows that she is protected by the Power of Good, and that is greater than the Power of Evil. All we can do is carry her to the castle of the Wicked Witch and leave her there."

So, carefully and gently, they lifted Dorothy in their arms and carried her swiftly through the air until they came to the yellow castle, where they set her down on the front doorstep. Then the leader said to the Witch, "We have obeyed you as far as we were able. The Tin Woodman and the Scarecrow are destroyed, and the Lion is tied up in your yard. We dare not harm the girl, nor the dog she carries in her arms. Your power over us is now ended, and you will never see us again."

Then all the Winged Monkeys, with much laughing and chattering and noise,

flew into the air and were soon out of sight.

The Wicked Witch was both surprised and worried when she saw the mark on Dorothy's forehead, for she knew very well that she dare not hurt the girl in any way. She looked down at Dorothy's feet, and when she saw the silver shoes, she began to tremble with fear, for she knew what a powerful charm the shoes had. At first the Witch was tempted to run away from Dorothy; but she happened to look into the girl's eyes and realized that the girl did not know of the wonderful power of the silver shoes. So the Wicked Witch laughed to herself, and thought, "I can still make her my slave, for she does not know how to use her power."

Then she said to Dorothy, severely, "Come with me. And see that you obey me, for if you do not I will make an end of you, as I did of the Tin Woodman and the Scarecrow."

Dorothy followed her through many of the beautiful rooms in her castle until they came to the kitchen, where the Witch ordered her to clean the pots and kettles and sweep the floor and feed the fire with wood.

Dorothy went to work meekly, with her mind made up to work as hard as she could; for she was glad the Wicked Witch had decided not to kill her.

After Dorothy was hard at work the Witch decided to go into the courtyard and harness the cowardly Lion like a horse. The Witch wanted to make him

pull her chariot whenever she wanted to go somewhere. But as she opened the gate the Lion gave a loud roar and sprang at her so fiercely that the Witch was afraid, and ran out and shut the gate again.

"If I cannot harness you," said the Witch to the Lion, speaking through the bars of the gate, "I can starve you. You shall have nothing to eat until you do as I wish."

So after that she took no food to the Lion; but every day she came to the gate at noon and asked, "Are you ready to be harnessed like a horse?"

And the Lion would answer, "No. If you come in this yard I will bite you."

The reason the Lion did not give in to the Witch was that every night, while the Witch was asleep, Dorothy brought him food from the cupboard. After the Lion had eaten he would lie down on his bed of straw, and Dorothy would lie beside him and put her head on his soft, shaggy mane, while they talked about their troubles and tried to plan some way to escape. But they could find no way to get out of the castle, for it was constantly guarded by the yellow Winkies, who were the slaves of the Wicked Witch and too afraid of her to disobey her.

The girl had to work hard during the day, and often the Witch threatened to beat her with the old umbrella she always carried in her hand. But, in truth, she did not dare to strike Dorothy, because of the mark upon her forehead. The girl did not know this, and was full

---

Ⓔ How many of the travelers had the Witch wanted killed earlier? *Idea:* All of them.

• Which traveler does she want to save now? **The Lion.**

• Why does she want to save the Lion? *Idea:* Because she wants to harness him and make him work.

Ⓕ What did the Monkeys do to the Tin Woodman? *Idea:* Carried him in the air and dropped him on the sharp rocks.

• What do you think will happen to the Tin Woodman when he falls on those rocks? *Idea:* He will become dented.

Ⓖ What did the Monkeys do to the Scarecrow's straw? *Idea:* Pulled it out of his clothes and head.

• What did the Monkeys do with the Scarecrow's clothes? *Idea:* Threw them into the top branches of a tall tree.

Ⓗ What did the Monkeys do to the Lion? *Idea:* Tied him with rope and carried him to the Witch's castle.

Ⓘ The leader of the Monkeys saw something on Dorothy that made him stop. What did the leader see? *Idea:* The Witch's kiss.

• Read the rest of the chapter to yourselves and be ready to answer some questions.

After all students have finished reading:

• What did the leader of the Monkeys think was more powerful, the Power of Good, or the Power of Evil? **The Power of Good.**

• What did the Monkeys do with Dorothy? *Idea:* Took her to the Witch.

• Were the Monkeys rough with Dorothy? **No.**

• Why not? *Idea:* Because they did not dare to harm her.

• How did the Witch react when she saw the mark on Dorothy's forehead? *Idea:* She was surprised and worried.

• Did the Witch dare to hurt Dorothy? **No.**

• Did Dorothy have a lot of power? **Yes.**

• But did Dorothy know about her power? **No.**

• What did the Witch order Dorothy to do? *Idea:* Work in the kitchen.

• Did Dorothy do what the Witch ordered? **Yes.**

• What did the Witch want the Lion to pull? *Idea:* Her chariot.

• What is a chariot? *Idea:* A fancy cart.

• Did the Lion act like he was afraid of the Witch? **No.**

• What did the Lion do when the Witch opened the gate? *Idea:* Roared and sprang at her.

• So what did the Witch do to make the Lion obey her? *Idea:* Tried to starve him.

• Did the Lion get food? **Yes.**

• How did he get food? *Idea:* Dorothy brought it to him at night.

• What did the Witch threaten to do to Dorothy if she did not work hard? *Idea:* Beat her with the old umbrella.

• But could the Witch really beat Dorothy? **No.**

of fear for herself and Toto. Once the Witch hit Toto with her umbrella and the brave little dog flew at her and bit her leg, in return. The Witch did not bleed where she was bitten, for she was so wicked that the blood in her had dried up many years before.

Dorothy's life became very sad, for it now seemed harder than ever to get back to Kansas and Aunt Em.

Sometimes she would feel terrible despair. Toto would sit at her feet and look into her face, whining dismally to show how sorry he was for his mistress. Toto did not really care whether he was in Kansas or the Land of Oz, so long as Dorothy was with him. But he knew the girl was unhappy, and that made him unhappy too.

- **Why couldn't the Witch beat Dorothy?** *Idea:* Because she was protected by the Witch's kiss.
- **What came out of the Witch's leg when Toto bit her?** *Idea:* Nothing.
- **Why didn't anything come out?** *Idea:* Because all her blood had dried up.

Award 4 points or have the students reread to the error limit sign.

INDEPENDENT WORK

Do all the items in your skillbook and workbook for lesson 24.

WORKCHECK AND AWARDING POINTS

1. *Read the questions and answers for the skillbook and workbook.*
2. *Award points for independent work as follows:*

> *0 errors . . . . .6 points*
> *2 errors . . . . .4 points*
> *3, 4, or 5 errors . . . . .2 points*
> *5 or more errors . . . . .0 points*

3. *Award bonus points as follows:*

> *Correcting missed items or getting all items right . . . . .2 points*
> *Doing the writing assignment acceptably . . . . .2 points*

ANSWER KEY FOR WORKBOOK

Review Items

1. Write whether each sentence describes the **wolves**, the **crows**, the **bees**, the **Winkies**, or the **Winged Monkeys.**
   a. They dropped the Woodman on to some sharp rocks.
      Winged Monkeys
   b. They were scared away by a man made out of straw.
      crows
   c. They broke their stingers on a piece of metal.
      bees
   d. They carried Dorothy to the Witch.
      Winged Monkeys
   e. They were the first to attack the travelers.
      wolves
   f. They obeyed whoever owned the golden cap.
      Winged Monkeys
   g. They were stunned by an axe.
      wolves
   h. They were scared away by a loud roar.
      Winkies

2. Write whether each sentence describes the **Land of the Munchkins** or the **Land of the Winkies.**
   a. There were round blue houses.
      Land of the Munchkins
   b. The ground was untilled.
      Land of the Winkies
   c. The land was rough and hilly.
      Land of the Winkies
   d. There were blue fences beside the road.
      Land of the Munchkins
   e. There were no farms or houses.
      Land of the Winkies
   f. There was no road.
      Land of the Winkies

3. Put the following story events in the right order by numbering them from 1 through 4.
   1 The travelers walk toward the Emerald City.
   3 Monkeys attack the travelers.
   2 The travelers walk away from the Emerald City.
   4 Dorothy works in the Witch's kitchen.

ANSWER KEY FOR SKILLBOOK

PART B

1. **a.** golden cap
   b. Three
   c. Two
   d. Lion
   e. *Idea:* They had wings
2. **a.** *Idea:* Sharp rocks
   b. *Idea:* It was battered and dented
3. **a.** *Idea:* Pulled it out
   b. *Idea:* The Scarecrow's clothes
4. **a.** *Idea:* Because the Witch wanted him alive
   b. *Idea:* To the Witch's castle
5. **a.** *Idea:* Because he saw the mark on her forehead
   b. The Power of Good
6. **a.** *Ideas:* The Witch's kiss; the silver shoes
   b. Oz
   c. No

7. The kitchen
8. **a.** The Lion
   b. starve him
   c. *Idea:* Because Dorothy fed him
9. *Idea:* Because she was so wicked that her blood had dried up

PART C

10. **a.** Green
    b. Blue
    c. Yellow
11. **a.** shrill
    b. presence
    c. permit
    d. dwelled
    e. cry
    f. tremendous
    g. great fear
    h. asked for

Lesson 25

Lesson 25

PART A   Word Lists

1	2	3	4
anxious	holiday	**Vocabulary words**	**Vocabulary words**
gorgeous	despair	1. cunning	1. cruelty
enormous	desperate	2. rejoice	2. feast
tremendous	straightened	3. desperately	3. tenderly
	despairing		4. mend
	invisible		
	bathe		
	bathing		

WORD PRACTICE AND VOCABULARY

EXERCISE 1   Word family

1. Everybody, find lesson 25, part A in your skillbook. *Wait.* Touch column 1. *Check.* All these words end with the sound **us.** Touch under the first word. *Pause.* What word? *Signal.* **Anxious.**
2. Next word. *Pause.* What word? *Signal.* **Gorgeous.**
3. *Repeat step 2 for each remaining word in column 1.*
4. *Repeat the words in column 1 until firm.*

EXERCISE 2   Word practice

1. Everybody, touch under the first word in column 2. *Pause.* What word? *Signal.* **Holiday.**
2. Next word. *Pause.* What word? *Signal.* **Despair.**
3. *Repeat step 2 for each remaining word in column 2.*
4. *Repeat the words in column 2 until firm.*

EXERCISE 3   Vocabulary review

Task A
1. Everybody, touch column 3. *Check.* First you're going to read the words in column 3. Then we'll talk about what they mean.
2. Touch under the first word. *Pause.* What word? *Signal.* **Cunning.**
3. Next word. *Pause.* What word? *Signal.* **Rejoice.**
4. *Repeat step 3 for desperately.*
5. *Repeat the words in column 3 until firm.*

Task B
1. You've learned the meanings for all these words. Word 1 is **cunning.** *Call on a student.* What does **cunning** mean? *Idea:* Clever but sneaky.
2. Everybody, what's another way of saying **The witch was clever but sneaky?** *Signal.* **The witch was cunning.**

Task C
1. Word 2 is **rejoice.** *Call on a student.* What does **rejoice** mean? *Idea:* To act very happy.
2. Everybody, what's another way of saying **They acted very happy?** *Signal.* **They rejoiced.**

Task D
1. Word 3 is **desperately.** *Call on a student.* What does it mean when you **desperately** want something? *Idea:* You want that thing very much.
2. Everybody, what's another way of saying **She very much wanted Dorothy's shoes?** *Signal.* **She desperately wanted Dorothy's shoes.**

EXERCISE 4   Vocabulary development

Task A
1. Everybody, touch column 4. *Check.* First you're going to read the words in column 4. Then we'll talk about what they mean.
2. Touch under the first word. *Pause.* What word? *Signal.* **Cruelty.**
3. Next word. *Pause.* What word? *Signal.* **Feast.**
4. *Repeat step 3 for each remaining word in column 4.*
5. *Repeat the words in column 4 until firm.*

Task B
Now let's talk about what those words mean. Word 1 is **cruelty.** When a person acts **cruelly,** that person acts with **cruelty.** Here's another way of saying **The witch treated them cruelly: The witch treated them with cruelty.** Everybody, what's another way of saying **The witch treated them cruelly?** *Signal.* **The witch treated them with cruelty.**

Task C
Word 2 is **feast.** A **large meal** is called a **feast.** Everybody, what's another word for a **large meal?** *Signal.* **A feast.**

Task D
Word 3 is **tenderly.** When you act gently and lovingly, you act **tenderly.** If you pick up something gently, you pick it up **tenderly.** Everybody, what do you do if you hold something lovingly? *Signal.* **You hold it tenderly.**

Task E
1. Word 4 is **mend.** When you fix something that is torn or broken, you **mend** it. Everybody, what's another way of saying **Fix a fence?** *Signal.* **Mend a fence.**
2. Everybody, what's another way of saying **Fix the Scarecrow?** *Signal.* **Mend the Scarecrow.**

Lesson 25

CHAPTER 20
The Rescue Ⓐ

Now, the Wicked Witch desperately wanted to have Dorothy's silver shoes. Her bees and her crows and her wolves were gone, and she had used up all the power of the golden cap; but if she could only get hold of the silver shoes they would give her more power than all the other things she had lost. Ⓑ She watched Dorothy carefully, to see if she ever took off her shoes. Ⓒ But Dorothy was so proud of her pretty shoes that she never took them off except at night and when she took her bath. The Witch was too afraid of the dark to go in to Dorothy's room at night to take the shoes. Ⓓ ★2 ERRORS★ And the Witch's fear of water was greater than her fear of the dark, so she never came near when Dorothy was bathing. Ⓔ Indeed, the old Witch never touched water, nor ever let water touch her in any way.

The Witch was very cunning, and she finally thought of a trick that would give her what she wanted. She placed an iron bar in the middle of the kitchen floor, and then, using her magic arts, she made the iron invisible to human eyes. Ⓕ When Dorothy walked across the floor she stumbled over the invisible bar, and fell down. She was not hurt, but as she fell one of the silver shoes came off, and before she could reach it the Witch seized it and put it on her own skinny foot. Ⓖ

The wicked woman was greatly pleased with the success of her trick, for as long as she had one of the shoes she owned half the power of their charm, and Dorothy could not use the magic against her, even if she had known how to do so.

The girl, seeing that she had lost one of her pretty shoes, grew angry, and said to the Witch, "Give me back my shoe!"

"I will not," replied the Witch, "for it is now my shoe, and not yours."

"You are a wicked creature!" said Dorothy. "You have no right to take my shoe from me."

"I will keep it, just the same," said the Witch, laughing at her, "and some day I will get the other one from you, too."

This made Dorothy so angry that she picked up the bucket of water that stood near and threw it over the Witch, soaking her from head to foot.

Instantly, the wicked woman gave a loud cry of fear, and then, as Dorothy looked at her in wonder, the Witch began to shrink and fall away. Ⓗ

STORY READING

EXERCISE 5   Decoding

1. Everybody, turn to page 97 in your textbook. *Wait. Call on a student.* What's the error limit for this chapter? **10 errors.**
2. *Call on individual students to read.*
3. *After the group reads to the 2-error sign without making more than 2 errors, reread the first part aloud and present the comprehension tasks.*
4. *After you have completed the first part, call on individual students to read. Present the comprehension tasks.*

EXERCISE 6   Comprehension tasks

Ⓐ What happens when a rescue takes place? *Idea:* People are saved.
● Who do you think will be rescued in this chapter? *Idea:* The travelers.
● Who do you think will do the rescuing? *Response:* Student preference.
Ⓑ What does the Witch want to get a hold of? **The silver shoes.**
● How powerful are the silver shoes? *Idea:* More powerful than everything she had lost.
Ⓒ What do you think the Witch would do if Dorothy took the shoes off? *Idea:* Steal them.
● Why couldn't the Witch just take the shoes from Dorothy? *Idea:* Because of the Witch's kiss.
Ⓓ Why didn't the Witch go into Dorothy's room at night and take the shoes? *Idea:* Because she was afraid of the dark. That's strange.
Ⓔ What was the Witch more afraid of than the dark? **Water.** That's strange, too.
Ⓕ What did the Witch put in the middle of the kitchen floor? **An iron bar.**
● What did the Witch do to the iron bar? *Idea:* Made it invisible.
Ⓖ What happened when Dorothy tripped? *Idea:* One of the shoes came off.
● What did the Witch do with the shoe? *Idea:* Put it on her own foot.
Ⓗ What did Dorothy do when she got angry? *Idea:* Threw water on the Witch.
● What happened to the Witch when the water hit her? *Idea:* She began to shrink and fall away.
● What did the Witch do as she began to shrink? *Idea:* She got smaller and smaller.

"See what you have done!" she screamed. "In a minute I will melt away."

"I'm very sorry," said Dorothy, who was truly frightened to see the Witch actually melting away before her eyes.

"Didn't you know that water would be the end of me?" asked the Witch, in a wailing, despairing voice.

"Of course not," answered Dorothy. "How could I?"

"Well, in a few minutes I will be all melted, and you will have the castle to yourself. I have been wicked in my day, but I never thought a girl like you would ever be able to melt me and end my wicked deeds. Look out—here I go!"

With these words the Witch fell down in a brown, melted, shapeless mass, and began to spread over the kitchen floor. Seeing that the Witch had really melted away to nothing, Dorothy got another bucket of water and threw it over the mess. Then she swept it all out the door. She picked up the silver shoe, which was all that was left of the old woman, cleaned and dried it with a cloth, and put it on her foot again. Then free at last, she ran out to the courtyard to tell the Lion that the Wicked Witch had died, and that they were no longer prisoners in a strange land. ①

★10 ERRORS★

The cowardly Lion was very pleased to hear that the Wicked Witch had been melted by a bucket of water, and Dorothy at once unlocked the gate and set him free. They went into the castle together, where Dorothy called all the Winkies together and told them that they were no longer slaves.

There was great rejoicing among the yellow Winkies, for the Wicked Witch had made them work hard and had always treated them with great cruelty. The Winkies decided to make that day a holiday, and began feasting and dancing.

"If only our friends, the Scarecrow and the Tin Woodman, were with us," said the Lion, "I would be quite happy."

"Don't you think we could rescue them?" asked the girl, anxiously.

"We can try," answered the Lion.

So they called the yellow Winkies and asked them if they would help them rescue their friends, and the Winkies said that they would be delighted to do everything they could for Dorothy, who had set them free from bondage. So she chose the Winkies who looked as if they knew the most, and they all started away. They traveled that day and part of the next until they came to the rocky plain where the Tin Woodman lay, all battered and bent. His axe was near him, but the blade was rusted and the handle was broken.

The Winkies lifted him tenderly in their arms, and carried him back to the yellow castle. Dorothy shed many tears at the sad fate of her old friend, and the Lion looked sober and sorry. When they reached the castle Dorothy said to the Winkies, "Do you have any tinsmiths?"

"Oh, yes; we have some very good tinsmiths," they told her.

Lesson 25 Textbook   99

"Then bring them to me," she said. And when the tinsmiths came, bringing with them all their tools in baskets, Dorothy asked, "Can you straighten out those dents in the Tin Woodman, and bend him back into shape again, and put him back together?"

The tinsmiths looked the Tin Woodman over carefully and then answered that they thought they could mend him so he would be as good as ever. So they set to work in one of the big yellow rooms of the castle and worked for three days and four nights, hammering and twisting and bending and polishing and pounding at the legs and body and head of the Tin Woodman, until at last he was straightened out into his old form, and his joints worked as well as ever. To be sure, there were several patches on him, but the tinsmiths did a good job, and the Tin Woodman did not mind the patches at all.

When, at last, he walked into Dorothy's room and thanked her for rescuing him, he was so pleased that he wept tears of joy, and Dorothy had to wipe every tear carefully from his face with her apron, so his joints would not be rusted. At the same time her own tears fell thick and fast at the joy of meeting her old friend again, and these tears did not need to be wiped away. As for the Lion, he wiped his eyes so often with the tip of his tail that it became quite wet, and he had to go out into the courtyard and hold his tail in the sun until it dried.

"If we only had the Scarecrow with us again," said the Tin Woodman, when Dorothy had finished telling him everything that had happened, "I would be quite happy."

"We must try to find him," said the girl.

So she called the Winkies to help her, and they walked all that day and part of the next until they came to the tall tree where the Winged Monkeys had tossed the Scarecrow's clothes.

It was a very tall tree, and the trunk was so smooth that no one could climb it; but the Tin Woodman said at once, "I'll chop it down, and then we can get the Scarecrow's clothes."

Now, while the tinsmiths had been mending the Tin Woodman, another Winkie, who was a goldsmith, had made an axe handle of solid gold and fitted it on the Tin Woodman's axe, instead of the old broken handle. Other Winkies had polished the blade until all the rust was removed and it glistened like silver.

As soon as he had spoken, the Tin Woodman began to chop. In a short time the tree fell over with a crash, and the Scarecrow's clothes fell out of the branches and dropped to the ground.

Dorothy picked them up and had the Winkies carry them back to the castle, where they were stuffed with nice, clean straw—and behold, here was the Scarecrow, as good as ever, thanking them over and over again for saving him.

100   Lesson 25   Textbook

---

① Name some things that Dorothy did after the Witch became a brown mass. *Idea:* Threw a bucket of water over the mess; swept it all out the door; put on the silver shoe; ran to tell the Lion.

● Read the rest of the chapter to yourselves and be ready to answer some questions.

After all students have finished reading:

● How did the Winkies feel when Dorothy told them that they were no longer slaves? *Idea:* Very happy.

● Who did Dorothy and the Lion take with them to try to rescue the Woodman and the Scarecrow? *Idea:* The smartest Winkies.

● Who fixed the Tin Woodman? **The tinsmiths.**

● How long did it take the tinsmiths to fix him? **Three days and four nights.**

● When the Tin Woodman thanked Dorothy, what did he start to do? **Cry.** I wonder how he could do that without a heart.

● Where were the Scarecrow's clothes? *Idea:* In the tall tree.

● Why couldn't anybody climb up the tree to get the clothes? *Idea:* Because the trunk was smooth.

● Who solved the problem with the tree? **The Tin Woodman.**

● What did the Tin Woodman do? *Idea:* Chopped down the tree.

● How had the Tin Woodman's axe been changed? *Idea:* It had a new gold handle and the blade had been sharpened.

● Where did the Winkies carry the Scarecrow's clothes? *Idea:* Back to the castle.

● What did the Winkies do with the clothes back at the castle? *Idea:* Stuffed them with new straw. So the Scarecrow was as good as new again.

Award 4 points or have the students reread to the error limit sign.

INDEPENDENT WORK

Do all the items in your skillbook and workbook for lesson 25.

ANSWER KEY FOR WORKBOOK

Map Skills

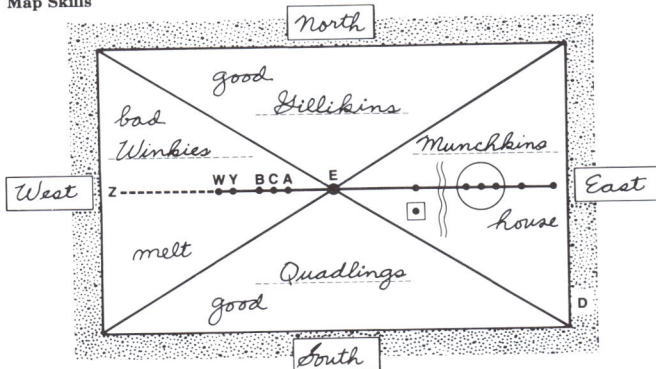

1. Write **North**, **East**, **South** and **West** in the boxes around the map.
2. On the map, write the name of the people who live in each land.
3. Write the place the letter **D** is on.

   The Desert

4. **a.** Write **good** on the lands that had **good** witches.
   b. Write **house** on the land where a house killed a **bad** witch.
   c. Write **bad** on the land that still had a **bad** witch.
   d. Write **melt** on the land where a Wicked Witch melted.
5. The map has **dots** and **letters** to show where different things happened.
   a. The **E** shows where the travelers started out to find the Witch. What's the name of that place?

   Emerald City

   b. Write the direction the travelers were going.

   West

   b. What is at **Z** on the map? **Circle the correct answer.**
   - (The Witch's Castle)
   - Emerald City
   - Land of the Munchkins
   - Kansas

The **A** shows where the travelers were attacked by the wolves.
   c. Which animals attacked them at **C**?

   Crows

   d. Which animals attacked them at **B**?

   Bees

   e. Which people attacked them at **Y**?

   Winkies

   f. Which animals attacked at **W**?

   Winged Monkeys

   g. Who lived at **Z**? *Idea*: *Wicked Witch of the West*

6. The **solid** line shows where Dorothy walked. That line goes from **E** to **W**. The **dotted** line shows where Dorothy did not walk. That line goes from **W** to **Z**.
   a. How did Dorothy get from **W** to **Z**? **Circle the correct answer.**
   - In a cart
   - On a boat
   - (In the air)

7. **a.** Where will the travelers go now that the Witch is dead? *Idea*:

   Emerald City

   b. Write the direction the travelers will go? *East*

   c. Draw an **arrow** on the map to the place they want to go next.

WORKCHECK AND AWARDING POINTS

1. *Read the questions and answers for the skillbook and workbook.*
2. *Award points for independent work as follows:*

0 errors	.6 points
2 errors	.4 points
3, 4, or 5 errors	.2 points
5 or more errors	.0 points

3. *Award bonus points as follows:*

Correcting missed items or getting all items right	.2 points
Doing the writing assignment acceptably	.2 points

ANSWER KEY FOR SKILLBOOK

PART B

1. *Idea:* Water and the dark
2. **a.** *Idea:* Because they would give her power
   b. *Idea:* Because she was afraid of the dark
   c. *Idea:* Because she was afraid of water
3. **a.** The Witch
   b. *Idea:* It was invisible
   c. Dorothy
   d. *Idea:* One of the silver shoes
4. **a.** Water
   b. *Idea:* She melted away
5. **a.** The Munchkins
   b. Yellow
6. **a.** *Idea:* It was battered and dented
   b. The tinsmiths
   c. A tinsmith
   d. In a tree
   e. *Idea:* He chopped down the tree
   f. *Idea:* Fresh straw
7. **a.** The Witch made an iron bar invisible
   b. Dorothy threw a bucket of water at the Witch
   c. Dorothy freed the Lion

PART C

8. **a.** scent
   b. preferred
   c. presence
   d. weep
   e. tremendous
   f. slightest
   g. pure
   h. advanced
   i. scatter
   j. requested

Lesson 26

Lesson 26

PART A   Word Lists

1	2	3
reunited	handsome	**Vocabulary words**
bracelet	costume	1. reunited
tongue	husband	2. bracelet
mischief	guest	3. inlaid
ache	prompt	4. grumble
	promptly	5. plead
		6. exclaim
		7. promptly

WORD PRACTICE AND VOCABULARY

EXERCISE 1   Word practice

1. Everybody, find lesson 26, part A in your skillbook. *Wait.* Touch column 1. *Check.*
The words in column 1 are hard words that will be in your reading stories.
2. Touch under the first word. *Check.*
The first word is **reunited.**
What word? *Signal.* **Reunited.**
3. Next word. *Pause.* That word is **bracelet.**
What word? *Signal.* **Bracelet.**
4. *Repeat step 3 for each remaining word in column 1.*
5. Now let's see if you remember all those words.
Touch under the first word in column 1. *Pause.*
What word? *Signal.* **Reunited.**
6. Next word. *Pause.* What word? *Signal.* **Bracelet.**
7. *Repeat step 6 for each remaining word in column 1.*
8. *Repeat the words in column 1 until firm.*

EXERCISE 2   Word practice

1. Everybody, touch under the first word in column 2. *Pause.* What word? *Signal.*
Handsome.
2. Next word. *Pause.* What word? *Signal.* **Costume.**
3. *Repeat step 2 for each remaining word in column 2.*
4. *Repeat the words in column 2 until firm.*

EXERCISE 3   Vocabulary development

Task A

1. Everybody, touch column 3. *Check.*
First you're going to read the words in column 3. Then we'll talk about what they mean.
2. Touch under the first word.
What word? *Signal.* **Reunited.**
3. Next word. *Pause.* What word? *Signal.* **Bracelet.**
4. *Repeat step 3 for each remaining word in column 3.*
5. *Repeat the words in column 3 until firm.*

Task B

1. Now let's talk about what those words mean. Word 1 is **reunited. United** means put together. When something is **reunited,** it is put together again. Here's another way of saying **A group of friends was put together again: A group of friends was reunited.**
2. Everybody, what's another way of saying **A group of friends was put together again?** *Signal.* **A group of friends was reunited.**

Task C

Word 2 is **bracelet.** *Call on a student.*
What's a **bracelet?** *Idea:* A piece of jewelry you wear on your wrist.

Task D

Word 3 is **inlaid.** When something is **inlaid** with jewels or gold, the jewels or gold are set in the thing. A crown that has jewels set in it is **inlaid** with jewels.
Call on a student. Tell me about a crown that has gold set in it. *Idea:* It is inlaid with gold.

Task E

Word 4 is **grumble.** When you **grumble,** you talk in a **grumpy** way. Everybody, let's hear you **grumble** to yourself. *Check.*

Task F

Word 5 is **plead.** When you beg somebody for something, you **plead** with that person. Here's another way of saying **He begged for another chance: He pleaded for another chance.**
Everybody, what's another way of saying **He begged for another chance?** *Signal.* **He pleaded for another chance.**

Task G

Word 6 is **exclaim.** When you say something very forcefully, you **exclaim.** Everybody, what do you do when you say something very forcefully? *Signal.* **You exclaim.**
Let's hear you **exclaim** this: What a nice day! *Check for strong, expressive voices.*

Task H

1. Word 7 is **promptly.** When you do something on time, you do it **promptly.**
Everybody, what's another way of saying **She was at school on time?** *Signal.* **She was at school promptly.**
2. Everybody, what's another way of saying **The movie started on time?** *Signal.* **The movie started promptly.**

Lesson 26

CHAPTER 21
The Journey Back

Now that they were reunited, Dorothy and her friends spent a few happy days at the Witch's castle, where they found everything they needed to make themselves comfortable. (A) But one day the girl thought of Aunt Em, and said, "We must go back to Oz, and claim his promise." (B)

"Yes," said the Tin Woodman, "I will get my heart at last."

"And I will get my brains," added the Scarecrow, joyfully.

"And I will get my courage," said the Lion, thoughtfully.

"And I will get back to Kansas," cried Dorothy, clapping her hands. "Oh, let's start for the Emerald City tomorrow!"

So, they decided to go see Oz.

★2 ERRORS★ The next day they called the Winkies together and said goodbye. The Winkies were sorry to see them go, and they had grown so fond of the Tin Woodman that they begged him to stay and rule over them and the yellow Land of the West. (C) They gave Toto and the Lion each a golden collar. To Dorothy they presented a beautiful gold bracelet, studded with diamonds. They gave a gold-headed walking stick to the

Scarecrow, to keep him from stumbling. And to the Tin Woodman they presented a silver oilcan that was inlaid with gold and studded with precious jewels. (D)

Each one of the travelers made the Winkies a grateful speech in return, and all shook hands until their arms ached.

Dorothy went to the Witch's cupboard to fill her basket with food for the journey, and there she saw the golden cap. She tried it on her own head and found that it fit her exactly. She did not know anything about the charm of the golden cap, but she saw that it was pretty, so she made up her mind to wear it and carry her sun bonnet in the basket. (E)

Then they all started for the Emerald City; and the Winkies gave them three cheers and many good wishes to carry with them.

Now, you will remember there was no road—not even a pathway—between the castle of the Wicked Witch and the Emerald City. When the four travelers had gone in search of the Witch she had seen them coming and sent the Winged Monkeys for them. But it was much harder to find their way back through the big fields of buttercups and bright

Lesson 26   Textbook   **101**

STORY READING

EXERCISE 4   Decoding

1. Everybody, turn to page 101 in your textbook. *Wait. Call on a student.* What's the error limit for this chapter? **9 errors.**
2. *Call on individual students to read.*
3. *After the group reads to the 2-error sign without making more than 2 errors, reread the first part aloud and present the comprehension tasks.*
4. *After you have completed the first part, call on individual students to read. Present the comprehension tasks.*

EXERCISE 5   Comprehension tasks

(A) What does that mean: **They were reunited?** *Idea:* They got back together.

(B) Name the promises the travelers want to claim from Oz. *Ideas:* A heart; brains; courage; a trip to Kansas.

● What did they have to do before Oz would grant them their wishes? *Idea:* Kill the Witch of the West.
They killed the Witch. So now they can claim their promise from Oz.

(C) What did the Winkies want the Tin Woodman to do? *Idea:* Stay and rule over them.

● Did the Tin Woodman have other plans? **Yes.**

● What were they? *Idea:* To marry the Munchkin maiden.

(D) Listen to that part again and get ready to answer some questions. *Read the paragraph that begins with, "So, they decided . . ." to* (D).

● What did they give to Toto and the Lion? *Idea:* Golden collars.

● What did they give to Dorothy? *Idea:* A beautiful bracelet.

● What did they give to the Scarecrow? *Idea:* A walking stick.

● What did they give to the Tin Woodman? *Idea:* A silver oilcan.

(E) What did she find? *Idea:* The golden cap.

● Is that a magic cap? **Yes.**

● Who used the cap to control the Winkies, the Winged Monkeys, and the others? **The Wicked Witch of the West.**

● Does Dorothy know that? **No.**

● Why did Dorothy decide to wear it? *Idea:* Because it was pretty.

daisies. They knew, of course, that they had to go straight east, toward the rising sun, and they started off in the right way. Ⓕ

But then at noon, when the sun was over their heads, they did not know which was east and which was west, and they soon became lost in the great fields. Ⓖ They kept on walking, however, and at night the moon came out and shone brightly. So they lay down among the sweet smelling flowers and slept soundly until morning—all but the Scarecrow and the Tin Woodman.

The next morning the sun was behind a cloud, but they started on, as if they were quite sure which way they were going. Ⓗ ★9 ERRORS★

"If we walk far enough," said Dorothy, "we will soon come to some place, I am sure."

But day by day passed away, and they still saw nothing before them but the yellow fields. The Scarecrow began to grumble a bit. "We have surely lost our way," he said. "And unless we find it again in time to reach the Emerald City I will never get my brains."

"And I won't get my heart," declared the Tin Woodman. "I can scarcely wait until I get to Oz, and you must admit that this is a very long journey."

"You see," said the cowardly Lion, with a whimper, "I don't have the courage to keep tramping for ever, without getting anywhere at all."

Then Dorothy became discouraged. She sat down on the grass and looked at her companions, and they sat down and looked at her, and Toto found that for the first time in his life he was too tired to chase a butterfly that flew past his head. So he put out his tongue and panted and looked at Dorothy as if to ask her what they should do next.

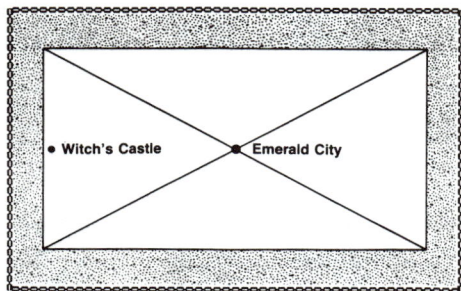

• Witch's Castle   • Emerald City

102   Lesson 26   Textbook

Ⓕ Everybody, look at the map. Touch the Emerald City. Move your finger to show the direction they went to reach the Wicked Witch. *Check.*

• Everybody, which direction did you move? *Signal.* **West.**

• Now move your finger to show the direction they had to go to return to the Emerald City. *Check.*

• Everybody, which direction is that? *Signal.* **East.**

Ⓖ In the morning, they knew which direction east was by looking at the sun. Where does the sun come up? **In the east.**

• So if you wanted to walk east in the morning, what would you walk toward? *Idea:* The rising sun.

But at noon, the sun is overhead. So now they couldn't tell which direction was east.

Ⓗ Do you think they'll go in the right direction? *Call on individual students. Responses:* Student preference.

• Read the rest of the story to yourselves and be ready to answer some questions.

After all students have finished reading:

• Did they find their way out of the fields? **No.**

• How did Dorothy feel at last? *Ideas:* Discouraged; tired.

• Even Toto was too tired to do something he would normally do. What was that? *Idea:* Chase a butterfly.

• Name some things they might do to find their way out of those fields. *Call on individual students. Responses:* Student preference.

• Everybody, look at the map again. *Check.* Where does the sun come up? **In the east.**

• So, if you wanted to walk east in the morning, what would you walk toward? *Idea:* The rising sun.

• If you wanted to walk west in the evening, what would you walk toward? *Idea:* The setting sun.

Award 4 points or have the students reread to the error limit sign.

FACT GAME

FACT GAME SCORECARD

1	2	3	4	5	6	7	8	9	10
11	12	13	14	15	16	17	18	19	20
21	22	23	24	25	26	27	28	29	30

Fact Game

2. **a.** What object does the picture show?
   b. What is the name of part **Z**?

3. Tell which direction each arrow points. Start with arrow **A**.

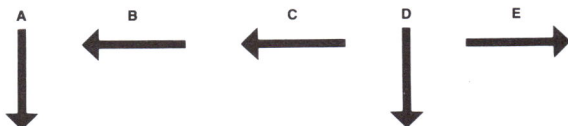

4. Tell which land each group of people lived in.
   a. Gillikins
   b. Quadlings
   c. Winkies
   d. Munchkins
5. Tell which color each thing is.
   a. Munchkin hats
   b. The Emerald City
   c. Kansas
   d. Winkies
6. Tell which character could have made each statement.
   a. "There is no place like home."
   b. "A match might burn my straw."
   c. "I will rust if I cry."
   d. "I am supposed to be the King of Beasts."
7. Tell which land each Witch is from.
   a. This Witch had only one eye.
   b. This Witch was killed by a house.
   c. This Witch commanded the Winged Monkeys.
   d. This Witch lived with the Gillikins.
8. Pretend you are in the Emerald City. Tell which direction you would go to find each thing.
   a. A forest with Kalidahs in it.
   b. A castle that was once ruled by an evil Witch.
   c. A house that had landed from the sky.
   d. A Witch that Dorothy had never seen.

9. a. Which city was in the middle of the Land of Oz?
   b. Who ruled that city?
   c. What was the Land of Oz surrounded by?
10. Tell which group each statement describes.
   a. This group slaved for the Wicked Witch of the West.
   b. This group pulled a cart to save the Lion.
   c. This group chased the travelers across a ditch.

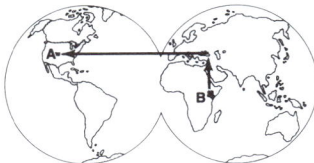

11. a. Tell the name of place **A**.
   b. Tell the name of place **B**.
   c. Which directions do you go to get from **B** to **A**?
12. Tell which event happened first.
   • Dorothy killed the Witch of the West.
   • Dorothy met Oz.
   • Dorothy met the Scarecrow.

EXERCISE 6   Fact game

1. Everybody, find lesson 26 in your workbook. *Wait.* You're going to play a game that uses the facts you have learned. Here are the rules: The player rolls the dice, figures out the number of the question, reads that question out loud, and answers it. The monitor tells the player if the answer is right or wrong. If it's wrong, the monitor tells the right answer. If it's right, the monitor gives the player one point. Don't argue with the monitor. The dice goes to the left and the next player has a turn.

2. If the game goes smoothly, all players in that game will earn 5 bonus points. I'll tell the groups whether they earn the bonus points. Each player who gets more than 13 points will earn another 5 bonus points. You'll play the game for 20 minutes.

3. *Divide students into groups of four or five. Assign monitors. Tell monitors the answers are on workbook page 121. Circulate as students play the game. Comment on groups that are playing well.*

4. *At the end of 20 minutes, have all students who earned more than* **13 points** *stand up. Award 5 bonus points to those players.*

• *Award points to monitors. Monitors receive the number of points earned by the highest performer in the group.*

• *Tell the monitor of each game that ran smoothly:* Your group did a good job. Give yourself and each of your players 5 bonus points.

• Everybody, write your game points in box FG on your point chart. Write your bonus points in the **bonus** box.

INDEPENDENT WORK

Do all the items in your skillbook for lesson 26.

WORKCHECK AND AWARDING POINTS

1. *Read the questions and answers for the skillbook and workbook.*
2. *Award points for independent work as follows:*

```
0 errors . . . . . . . . . . . . . . . . . . . . .6 points
2 errors . . . . . . . . . . . . . . . . . . . . .4 points
3, 4, or 5 errors . . . . . . . . . . . . . .2 points
5 or more errors . . . . . . . . . . . . . .0 points
```

3. *Award bonus points as follows:*

```
Correcting missed items
or getting all items right . . . . . . . .2 points
Doing the writing
assignment acceptably . . . . . . . . . .2 points
```

ANSWER KEY FOR FACT GAME

2. **a.** Cyclone
   b. Eye
3. A—South
   B—West
   C—West
   D—South
   E—East
4. **a.** Land of the North
   b. Land of the South
   c. Land of the West
   d. Land of the East
5. **a.** Blue
   b. Green
   c. Grey
   d. Yellow
6. **a.** Dorothy
   b. Scarecrow
   c. Tin Woodman
   d. Lion
7. **a.** Land of the West
   b. Land of the East
   c. Land of the West
   d. Land of the North
8. **a.** East
   b. West
   c. East
   d. South
9. **a.** Emerald City
   b. Oz
   c. The Great Desert
10. **a.** Winkies
    b. Field mice
    c. Kalidahs
11. **a.** Kansas
    b. Kenya
    c. North, West
12. Dorothy met the Scarecrow

ANSWER KEY FOR SKILLBOOK

PART B

1. *Idea:* To claim Oz's promise
2. **a.** The Tin Woodman
   b. The Scarecrow
   c. Dorothy
   d. Toto and the Lion
3. **a.** The Winged Monkeys
   b. No
   c. *Idea:* Because it was pretty
4. **a.** West
   b. East
   c. the rising sun
5. Noon
6. *Idea:* Because it was cloudy
7. **a.** Yellow
   b. West
   c. Daisies and buttercups
8. discouraged

PART C

9. **a.** Dorothy
   b. The Lion
   c. The Tin Woodman
   d. Dorothy
   e. The Scarecrow
   f. The Tin Woodman
   g. The Scarecrow
   h. The Lion
   i. The Scarecrow
   j. Dorothy
10. **a.** huge
    b. terror
    c. flock
    d. requested
    e. pack
    f. strike
    g. swarm
    h. great anger

Lesson 27

Lesson 27

PART A **Word Lists**

1	2	3
Gayla	promptly	**Vocabulary words**
Quel	fortunately	1. pattering
ventriloquist	solemnly	2. mischief
uneasily	presently	3. lining
bulged		4. spare
		5. bride
		6. capture

WORD PRACTICE AND VOCABULARY

EXERCISE 1   Word practice

1. Everybody, find lesson 27, part A in your skillbook. *Wait.* Touch column 1. *Check.* The words in column 1 are hard words that will be in your reading stories.
2. Touch under the first word. *Check.* The first word is **Gayla.** What word? *Signal.* **Gayla.**
3. Next word. *Pause.* That word is **Quel.** What word? *Signal.* **Quel.**
4. *Repeat step 3 for each remaining word in column 1.*
5. Now let's see if you remember all those words. Touch under the first word in column 1. *Pause.* What word? *Signal.* **Gayla.**
6. Next word. *Pause.* What word? *Signal.* **Quel.**
7. *Repeat step 6 for each remaining word in column 1.*
8. *Repeat the words in column 1 until firm.*

EXERCISE 2   Word family

1. Everybody, touch column 2. *Check.* All those words end with the letters **l-y.** Touch under the first word. *Pause.* What word? *Signal.* **Promptly.**
2. Next word. *Pause.* What word? *Signal.* **Fortunately.**
3. *Repeat step 2 for each remaining word in column 2.*
4. *Repeat the words in column 2 until firm.*

EXERCISE 3   Vocabulary development

Task A

1. Everybody, touch column 3. *Check.* First you're going to read the words in column 3. Then we'll talk about what they mean.
2. Touch under the first word. *Pause.* What word? *Signal.* **Pattering.**
3. Next word. *Pause.* What word? *Signal.* **Mischief.**
4. *Repeat step 3 for each remaining word in column 3.*
5. *Repeat the words in column 3 until firm.*

Task B

Now let's talk about what those words mean. Word 1 is **pattering.** A **pattering** sound is the sound of something that goes **pat, pat, pat.** Feet that go **pat, pat, pat** are called **pattering** feet. Everybody, what are feet that go **pat, pat, pat** called? *Signal.* **Pattering feet.**

Task C

Word 2 is **mischief. Naughty behavior** is **mischief.** Everybody, what's another way of saying **She was full of naughty behavior?** *Signal.* **She was full of mischief.**

Task D

Word 3 is **lining.** The **lining** of something is the material on the inside. Everybody, what do we call the material on the inside of something? *Signal.* **The lining.**

Task E

Word 4 is **spare.** When a king **spares** somebody's life, the king lets that person live.

Task F

Word 5 is **bride.** *Call on a student.* What's a **bride?** *Idea:* A woman who gets married in a wedding.

Task G

Word 6 is **capture.** When you catch a wild animal, you **capture** that animal. Everybody, what's another way of saying **She caught the thief?** *Signal.* **She captured the thief.**

Lesson 27

CHAPTER 22
The Winged Monkeys Ⓐ

Dorothy and her friends sat in the fields for a long time. Then Dorothy said, "Why don't we call the field mice? They could probably tell us the way to the Emerald City."

"Why, of course they could," cried the Scarecrow. "Why didn't we think of that before?"

Dorothy blew the little whistle she had always carried around her neck since the Queen of the Mice had given it to her. In a few minutes they heard the pattering of tiny feet, and many of the small gray mice came running up to her. ★2 ERRORS★ The Queen was among them and she asked, in her squeaky little voice, "What can I do for my friends?"

"We have lost our way," said Dorothy. "Can you tell us where the Emerald City is?"

"Certainly," answered the Queen. "It is a great way off, for it has been behind you all this time." Then she noticed Dorothy's golden cap, and said, "Why don't you use the charm of the cap, and call the Winged Monkeys? They will carry you to the Emerald City in less than an hour."

"I don't know how to use the charm," answered Dorothy, in surprise.

"How do I make it work?"

"The directions for using the charm are written inside the golden cap," replied the Queen of the Mice. "But if you are going to call the Winged Monkeys we must run away, for they are full of mischief and think it is great fun to chase us." Ⓑ

"Won't the Winged Monkeys hurt me?" asked the girl, anxiously.

"Oh, no; they must obey the wearer of the cap. Goodbye!" And the Queen scampered out of sight, with all the mice hurrying after her.

Dorothy looked inside the golden cap and saw some words written on the lining. These, she thought, must be the charm, so she read the directions carefully and put the cap on her head.

"Ep-pe, pep-pe, bep-pe!" she said, standing on her left foot.

"What did you say?" asked the Scarecrow, who did not know what she was doing.

"Hil-lo, hol-lo, hel-lo!" Dorothy went on, standing this time on her right foot.

"Hello!" replied the Tin Woodman, calmly. Ⓒ

"Ziz-zy, zuz-zy, zik!" said Dorothy,

who was now standing on both feet. Suddenly, they heard a great chattering and flapping of wings, as the band of Winged Monkeys flew up to them. The King bowed low before Dorothy, and asked, "What is your command?"

"We want to go to the Emerald City," said the girl, "and we have lost our way."

"We will carry you," replied the King, and no sooner had he spoken than two of the Monkeys caught Dorothy in their arms and flew away with her. Other Monkeys took the Scarecrow and the Tin Woodman and the Lion, and one little Monkey seized Toto and flew after the others, although the dog tried hard to bite him. Ⓓ

The Scarecrow and the Tin Woodman were rather frightened at first, for they remembered how badly the Winged Monkeys had treated them before. Ⓔ But the Scarecrow and the Tin Woodman saw that the Monkeys were not going to hurt them, so they rode through the air quite cheerfully, and had a fine time looking at the pretty gardens and woods far below. Ⓕ

STORY READING

EXERCISE 4   Decoding

1. Everybody, turn to page 103 in your textbook. *Wait. Call on a student.* What's the error limit for this chapter? **15 errors.**
2. *Call on individual students to read.*
3. *After the group reads to the 2-error sign without making more than 2 errors, reread the first part aloud and present the comprehension tasks.*
4. *After you have completed the first part, call on individual students to read. Present the comprehension tasks.*

EXERCISE 5   Comprehension tasks

Ⓐ What do you think the Winged Monkeys will do? *Call on individual students. Responses:* Student preference.
- Where did we leave Dorothy and the others? *Idea:* In the fields.
- How were they feeling? *Ideas:* Unhappy; discouraged.

Ⓑ The field mice have to leave before the Winged Monkeys come. What would the Winged Monkeys do if they saw the mice? *Idea:* Chase them.

Ⓒ Why did he say hello? *Idea:* Because Dorothy did.

Ⓓ Did Toto know that the Monkey was helping him get to the Emerald City? *Idea:* Probably not.

Ⓔ What had the Winged Monkeys done to the Tin Woodman? *Idea:* Dropped him on sharp rocks.
- What had the Monkeys done to the Scarecrow? *Ideas:* Thrown his clothes into a tree; pulled all the straw out of his clothes. I don't blame them for feeling frightened.

Ⓕ Think about how that would feel, to be flying along over the woods and gardens. I think that would be a lot of fun.

Dorothy was being carried by two of the biggest Monkeys, and one of them was the King Monkey. They had made a chair out of their hands and were careful not to hurt her.

"Why do you have to obey the charm of the golden cap?" Dorothy asked.

"That is a long story," answered the King, with a laugh. "But since we have a long journey before us I will pass the time by telling you about it, if you wish."

"I would be glad to hear it," she replied.

So the King Monkey told his story. (G)

Once we were a free people, living happily in the great forest, flying from tree to tree, eating nuts and fruit, and doing just as we pleased without obeying anybody. Perhaps some of us were too full of mischief at times, flying down to pull the tails of the animals that had no wings, chasing birds, and throwing nuts at the people who walked in the forest. But we were careless and happy and full of fun, and enjoyed every minute of the day. This was many years ago, long before Oz came out of the clouds to rule over this land. (H)

Now, at that time, a beautiful princess, who was also a powerful sorceress, lived in the Land of the North. (I) *All her magic was used to help the people, and she was never known to hurt anyone who was good. Her name was Gayla and she lived in a handsome palace built from great blocks of rubies. Everyone loved her, but she was* very sad because she could find no one to love in return, since all the men were much too stupid and ugly for someone so beautiful and wise. At last, however, she found a boy who was handsome and manly and wise beyond his years. Gayla made up her mind that when he grew to be a man she would make him her husband, so she took him to her ruby palace and used all her magic powers to make him as strong and good and lovely as any woman could wish. When he grew to manhood, Quel, as he was called, was said to be the best and wisest man in all the land, while his manly beauty was so great that Gayla loved him dearly and hurried to make everything ready for the wedding.

My grandfather was at that time the King of the Winged Monkeys, and the old fellow loved a good joke better than a good dinner. One day, just before the wedding, my grandfather was flying around with his band when he saw Quel walking beside the river. Quel was dressed in a rich costume of pink silk and purple velvet, and my grandfather decided to make some mischief. (J) ★15 ERRORS★

At grandfather's command, the band flew down and seized Quel, carried him in their arms until they were over the middle of the river, and then dropped him into the water.

"Swim out, my fine fellow," cried my grandfather, "and see if the water has spotted your clothes." Quel was much too wise not to swim, and he was not in the least spoiled by all his good fortune. He laughed when he came to the top of the water, and swam to shore. But when Gayla

Lesson 27   Textbook   **105**

came running out to him, she found his silks and velvet all ruined by the river.

The princess was very angry, and she knew, of course, who had done it. She had all the Winged Monkeys brought before her, and she had their wings tied. Then she said they should be treated as they had treated Quel. But my grandfather pleaded hard, for he knew the Monkeys would drown in the river with their wings tied, and Quel said a kind word for them also. So Gayla finally spared them. But she said that the Winged Monkeys must obey three commands given by the person who owned the golden cap. This cap had been made for a wedding present to Quel, and it cost more than anything in the kingdom. Of course, my grandfather and all the other Monkeys agreed to the plan, and that is how it happens that we must obey the owner of the golden cap.

Quel was the first owner of the golden cap and he was the first to command us. Since his bride could not bear the sight of us, he called us all together in the forest after he had married her. He ordered us always to keep far away from Gayla's kingdom. We were glad to do this, for we were all afraid of her.

And that was all we ever had to do until the golden cap fell into the hands of the Wicked Witch of the West, who made us capture the Winkies, and afterwards drive Oz himself out of the Land of the West. Now the golden cap is yours, and you have the right to command us two more times.

When the King Monkey finished his story, Dorothy looked down and saw the green, shining walls of the Emerald City below them. She was amazed to see how rapidly the Monkeys had flown, but she was glad the journey was over. The strange creatures set the travelers down carefully in front of the gate of the city. The King bowed low to Dorothy, and then he flew swiftly away, followed by all his band.

"That was a good ride," said the girl.

"Yes, and a quick way out of our troubles," replied the Lion. "How lucky it was that you took the wonderful cap!"

106   Lesson 27   Textbook

(G) Everybody, show me the story the King Monkey tells. Go all the way to the end of it. *Check.*

• Go back to the beginning of the King Monkey's story. Remember, the King Monkey is talking now.

(H) What kinds of things did the Monkeys like to do before they had to obey the golden cap? *Call on individual students. Responses:* Pull animals' tails; chase birds; throw nuts at people; etc.

No wonder the field mice were afraid of the Monkeys.

• How long ago did the Monkeys behave in this carefree way? *Idea:* Many years ago.

(I) If she was a sorceress, what could she do? *Idea:* Magic things.

(J) What do you think the grandfather could do to be mischievious? *Call on individual students. Responses:* Student preference.

• Read the rest of the chapter to yourselves and be ready to answer some questions.

After all students have finished reading:

• What had the Monkeys done to Quel? *Idea:* Thrown him in a river.

• So what did Gayla want to do to the Monkeys? *Idea:* Tie their wings and throw them in the river.

• Why did the grandfather plead for the Monkeys? *Idea:* He knew they would drown.

• Who else spoke up for the Monkeys? **Quel.**

• So, instead of drowning the Monkeys, what did Gayla decide to make the Monkeys do instead? *Idea:* They must obey three commands given by the person who owned the golden cap.

• Did the Monkeys agree to this plan? **Yes.**

• Who was the first person to own the cap? **Quel.**

• How many commands did he give the Monkeys? **One.**

• What was that command? *Idea:* Stay far away from Gayla's kingdom.

• Who was the next person to own the cap? **The Wicked Witch of the West.**

• What two great things did the Witch order the Monkeys to do before Dorothy came to the Land of Oz? *Idea:* Capture the Winkies and drive Oz from the Land of the West.

• The third thing the Witch had the Monkeys do was the last thing she could make them do. What was that? *Idea:* Attack Dorothy and her friends.

• Where were Dorothy and the others when the King Monkey finished his story? *Idea:* Over the Emerald City.

• How did Dorothy like that ride? *Idea:* She liked it.

Award 4 points or have the students reread to the error limit sign.

Lesson 27   **133**

ANSWER KEY FOR WORKBOOK

Map Skills

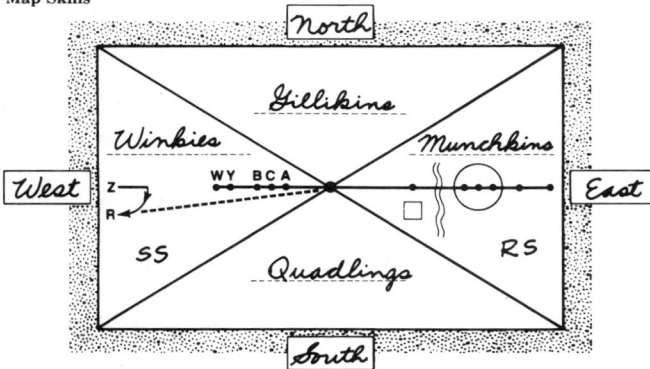

1. Write **North, East, South** and **West** in the boxes around the map.
2. On the map, write the name of the people who live in each land.
3. The **arrows** show where the travelers walked after they left the Witch's castle.
   a. In which direction did they go first?
      East
   b. In which direction did they go next? _West_
4. The letter **R** shows where they were rescued. Who rescued them?
   Winged Monkeys
5. a. Write **RS** on the land that is closest to the **rising** sun.
   b. Write **SS** on the land that is closest to the **setting** sun.
6. The **dotted** line shows how the travelers went to the Emerald City.
   a. How did they get there?
      Circle the correct answer.
      - In a cart
      - (In the air)
      - On a river
      - On a road

   b. Who carried them there?
      Winged Monkeys
7. The **letters** on the map show where the travelers were attacked on the way to the Witch's castle.
   a. Which animals attacked them at A?
      wolves
   b. Which animals attacked them at C?
      crows
   c. Which animals attacked them at B?
      bees
   d. Which people attacked them at Y?
      Winkies
   e. Which animals attacked at W?
      Winged Monkeys

ANSWER KEY FOR SKILLBOOK

PART B

1. a. The Tin Woodman
   b. The Lion
2. a. The Queen of the Field Mice
   b. the Winged Monkeys
   c. The golden cap
   d. *Idea:* Inside the cap
   e. *Idea:* Take them to the Emerald City
3. a. *Idea:* Pulled out his straw and thrown his clothes in a tree
   b. *Idea:* Dropped him over sharp rocks
4. a. North
   b. No
   c. full of mischief
5. a. Quel
   b. *Idea:* Dropped him into the river
   c. *Idea:* They were ruined
6. a. golden cap
   b. three
   c. Quel
7. a. *Idea:* The Witch of the West
   b. *Idea:* Attacked the travelers

PART C

8. a. The Winged Monkeys
   b. The Munchkins
   c. The Winkies
   d. The Winged Monkeys
   e. The Kalidahs
   f. The Winged Monkeys
   g. The Munchkins
9. a. meek
   b. requested
   c. singed
   d. seized
   e. tempt
   f. rage
   g. desperately
   h. cunning
   i. acted very happy

INDEPENDENT WORK

Do all the items in your skillbook and workbook for lesson 27.

WORKCHECK AND AWARDING POINTS

1. *Read the questions and answers for the skillbook and workbook.*
2. *Award points for independent work as follows:*

0 errors	6 points
2 errors	4 points
3, 4, or 5 errors	2 points
5 or more errors	0 points

3. *Award bonus points as follows:*

Correcting missed items or getting all items right	2 points
Doing the writing assignment acceptably	2 points

Lesson 28

Lesson 28

PART A   Word Lists

1	2	3 Vocabulary words	4 Vocabulary words
uneasily	tongue	1. plead	1. tiresome
solemnly	ventriloquism	2. exclaim	2. bald
presently	ache	3. promptly	3. overheard
fortunately	ached		4. humbug
promptly	balloonist		5. ventriloquist
	liquid		6. imitate
	bulge		7. confidence
	bulged		8. consider
			9. gradually
			10. uneasy

WORD PRACTICE AND VOCABULARY

EXERCISE 1   Word family

1. Everybody, find lesson 28, part A in your skillbook. *Wait.* Touch column 1. *Check.* All those words end with the letters **l-y.** Touch under the first word. *Pause.* What word? *Signal.* **Uneasily.**
2. Next word. *Pause.* What word? *Signal.* **Solemnly.**
3. *Repeat step 2 for each remaining word in column 1.*
4. *Repeat the words in column 1 until firm.*

EXERCISE 2   Word practice

1. Everybody, touch under the first word in column 2. *Pause.* What word? *Signal.* **Tongue.**
2. Next word. *Pause.* What word? *Signal.* **Ventriloquism.**
3. *Repeat step 2 for each remaining word in column 2.*
4. *Repeat the words in column 2 until firm.*

EXERCISE 3   Vocabulary review

Task A
1. Everybody, touch column 3. *Check.* First you're going to read the words in column 3. Then we'll talk about what they mean.
2. Touch under the first word. *Pause.* What word? *Signal.* **Plead.**
3. Next word. *Pause.* What word? *Signal.* **Exclaim.**
4. *Repeat step 3 for* ***promptly.***
5. *Repeat the words in column 3 until firm.*

Task B
1. You've learned the meanings for all these words. Word 1 is **plead.** *Call on a student.* What does **plead** mean? *Idea:* Beg.
2. Everybody, what's another way of saying **He begged for another chance?** *Signal.* **He pleaded for another chance.**

Task C
1. Word 2 is **exclaim.** *Call on a student.* What does **exclaim** mean? *Idea:* You say something very forcefully.
2. Everybody, let's hear you **exclaim** this: I don't believe it! *Check for strong, expressive voices.*

Task D
1. Word 3 is **promptly.** *Call on a student.* What does **promptly** mean? *Idea:* On time.
2. Everybody, what's another way of saying **The movie started on time?** *Signal.* **The movie started promptly.**

Lesson 28

PART A Word Lists

1	2	3	4
uneasily	tongue	**Vocabulary words**	**Vocabulary words**
solemnly	ventriloquism	1. plead	1. tiresome
presently	ache	2. exclaim	2. bald
fortunately	ached	3. promptly	3. overheard
promptly	balloonist		4. humbug
	liquid		5. ventriloquist
	bulge		6. imitate
	bulged		7. confidence
			8. consider
			9. gradually
			10. uneasy

EXERCISE 4 Vocabulary development

Task A

1. Everybody, touch column 4. *Check.* First you're going to read the words in column 4. Then we'll talk about what they mean.
2. Touch under the first word. *Pause.* What word? *Signal.* **Tiresome.**
3. Next word. *Pause.* What word? *Signal.* **Bald.**
4. *Repeat step 3 for each remaining word in column 4.*
5. *Repeat the words in column 4 until firm.*

Task B

Now let's talk about what those words mean. Word 1 is **tiresome.** Things that are **tiresome** are very boring. Everybody, what do we call things that are very boring? *Signal.* **Tiresome.**

Task C

Word 2 is **bald.** *Call on a student.* What is different about a person that is **bald?** *Idea:* There isn't any hair on the person's head.

Task D

Word 3 is **overheard.** When you **overhear** something, you hear what other people are saying. If Dorothy heard what the Witch was saying to somebody else, she **overheard** the Witch. Everybody, what did the Scarecrow do when he heard Dorothy talking to somebody else? *Signal.* **He overheard Dorothy talking to somebody else.**

Task E

Word 4 is **humbug.** A **humbug** is a phony person who pretends to be something, but is really not. Everybody, what could we call people who pretend to be something they aren't? *Signal.* **Humbugs.**

Task F

Word 5 is **ventriloquist. Ventriloquists** can talk without moving their lips. They can make it sound like somebody else is actually doing the talking.

Task G

Word 6 is **imitate.** When you **imitate** somebody, you do just what that person does. Let's see you **imitate** this: *Pat your head three times. Wait.* When you patted your head you **imitated** me. Everybody, what did you do? *Signal.* **Imitated you.**

Task H

1. Word 7 is **confidence.** When you have **confidence,** you feel sure that you can do something. Here's another way of saying **You feel sure that you can jump the fence: You have confidence that you can jump the fence.**
   Everybody, what's another way of saying **You feel sure that you can jump the fence?** *Signal.* **You have confidence that you can jump the fence.**
2. Everybody, what's another way of saying **She felt sure that she could jump the creek?** *Signal.* **She had confidence that she could jump the creek.**

Task I

Word 8 is **consider.** When you think over whether you should do something, you **consider** whether you should do it. Here's another way of saying **She thought over whether she should buy the dress: She considered whether she should buy the dress.** Everybody, what's another way of saying **She thought over whether she should buy the dress?** *Signal.* **She considered whether she should buy the dress.**

Task J

1. Word 9 is **gradually. Gradually** is another word for **slowly.**
   Everybody, what's another way of saying **They moved slowly up the mountain?** *Signal.* **They moved gradually up the mountain.**
2. Everybody, what's another way of saying **He slowly became sleepy?** *Signal.* **He gradually became sleepy.**

Task K

Word 10 is **uneasy.** When you don't feel comfortable about doing something, you feel **uneasy** about doing it.
Everybody, what's another way of saying **She felt uncomfortable about giving a speech?** *Signal.* **She felt uneasy about giving a speech.**

Lesson 28

CHAPTER 23
Another Meeting With Oz ⒜

The four travelers walked up to the great gate of the Emerald City and rang the bell. After several rings, the gate was opened by the same Guardian of the Gates they had met before.

"What! Are you back again?" he asked, in surprise. ⒝ The Guardian of the Gates continued, "I thought you had gone to visit the Wicked Witch of the West."

"We did visit her," said the Scarecrow.

"And she let you go again?" asked the man, in wonder.

"She could not help it, for she is melted," explained the Scarecrow.

"Melted! Well, that is good news, indeed," said the man. "Who melted her?" ★2 ERRORS★

"It was Dorothy," said the Lion, solemnly.

"Good gracious!" exclaimed the man, and he bowed very low before her. ⒞

Then he led them into his little room and locked spectacles on their eyes, just as he had done before. Next they passed on through the gate into the Emerald City. When the people heard from the Guardian of the Gates that

Dorothy and the others had melted the Wicked Witch of the West they all gathered around the travelers and followed them in a great crowd to the palace of Oz.

The soldier with the green whiskers was still on guard before the door, but he let them in at once, and they were again met by the beautiful green girl who showed each of them to their old rooms. She told them they could rest there until the great Oz was ready to receive them.

The soldier sent a message to Oz that Dorothy and the other travelers had come back again, after destroying the Wicked Witch. But Oz made no reply. ⒟ Dorothy and the others thought the great Wizard would send for them at once, but he did not. They had no word from him the next day, nor the next, nor the next. The waiting was tiresome and at last they became angry with Oz for treating them so poorly, after they had killed the Witch for him. So the Scarecrow asked the green girl to take another message to Oz, saying that if Oz did not let them in to see him at once they would call the Winged Monkeys to help them. ⒠ When the Wizard was given this message he was so frightened

that he sent word for them to come to the throne room at nine o'clock the next morning. He had once met the Winged Monkeys in the Land of the West, and he did not want to meet them again. ⒡

The travelers spent a sleepless night, each thinking of the gift Oz had promised. Dorothy fell asleep only once, and then she dreamed she was in Kansas, where Aunt Em was telling her how glad she was to have her home again.

Promptly at nine o'clock the next morning the green-whiskered soldier came to them, and four minutes later they all went into the throne room of the great Oz.

Of course each one of them expected to see the Wizard in the shape he had taken before, and all were greatly surprised when they looked around and saw no one at all in the room. They kept close to the door and closer to one another, for the stillness of the empty room was more dreadful than any of the forms they had seen Oz take. ⒢

Presently they heard a voice, that seemed to come from somewhere near the top of the great dome, and it said, solemnly, "I am Oz, the Great and Terrible. Why do you want to see me?"

They looked again in every part of the room, and then, seeing no one, Dorothy asked, "Where are you?"

"I am everywhere," answered the voice, "but to your eyes I am invisible. I will now seat myself upon the throne, so that you may speak with me." The voice seemed to move toward the throne, so

Dorothy and the others walked toward the throne and stood in a row. But Oz was still invisible.

Dorothy said, "We have come to claim our promise, great Oz."

"What promise?" asked Oz.

"You promised to send me back to Kansas when the Wicked Witch was destroyed," said the girl.

"And you promised to give me brains," said the Scarecrow.

"And you promised to give me a heart," said the Tin Woodman.

"And you promised to give me courage," said the cowardly Lion. ⒣ ★11 ERRORS★

"Is the Wicked Witch really destroyed?" asked the voice; and Dorothy noticed that the voice trembled a little.

"Yes," Dorothy answered. "I melted her with a bucket of water."

"Dear me," said the voice. "Well, come to me tomorrow, for I must have time to think it over."

"You've had plenty of time already," said the Tin Woodman, angrily.

"We won't wait a day longer," said the Scarecrow.

"You must keep your promises to us!" exclaimed Dorothy.

The Lion thought he might as well frighten the Wizard, so he gave a large, loud roar, which was so fierce and dreadful that Toto jumped away from him in alarm and tipped over the screen that stood in a corner of the throne

---

STORY READING

EXERCISE 5   Decoding

1. Everybody, turn to page 107 in your textbook. *Wait. Call on a student.* What's the error limit for this chapter? **11 errors.**
2. *Call on individual students to read.*
3. *After the group reads to the 2-error sign without making more than 2 errors, reread the first part aloud and present the comprehension tasks.*
4. *After you have completed the first part, call on individual students to read. Present the comprehension tasks.*

EXERCISE 6   Comprehension tasks

ⓐ Where did we leave Dorothy and the others? *Idea:* In front of the Emerald City.
● How did they get there? *Idea:* The Winged Monkeys carried them.
ⓑ Do you think the Guardian ever expected to see Dorothy and the others again? **No.**
● What do you think he expected to happen to them when they went to the Land of the West? *Idea:* The Wicked Witch would kill them.
ⓒ Why did the Guardian bow low before Dorothy? *Idea:* Because she melted the Wicked Witch.
● Do you think he realizes that she has great power? **Yes.**
ⓓ That's strange. Wouldn't you think that Oz would reply in some way? **Yes.**
● Oz seemed very anxious to get rid of the Witch of the West and now she's destroyed. I would think that he'd be very happy.
ⓔ What kinds of things could they have the Winged Monkeys do? *Ideas:* Bring Oz to them; scare Oz into seeing them.
ⓕ What had happened the last time Oz met the Winged Monkeys? *Idea:* They defeated him.
ⓖ What did they see in the throne room this time? **Nothing.**
● How did they feel? *Ideas:* Surprised; scared.
ⓗ Do you think Oz really forgot about making those promises? **No.**
I wonder what's wrong.
● Read the rest of the chapter to yourselves and be ready to answer some questions.

After all students have finished reading:
● What did Toto do when the Lion roared? *Idea:* Tipped over the screen.

room. They looked at the screen as it fell with a crash, and the next moment all of them were filled with wonder. They saw a little old man with a bald head and a wrinkled face. He was standing in the spot the screen had hidden, and he seemed to be as surprised as they were. The Tin Woodman raised his axe and rushed towards the little man.

The Tin Woodman cried out, "Who are you?"

"I am Oz, the Great and Terrible," said the little man in a trembling voice. "Don't strike me—please don't!—I'll do anything you want me to."

Everybody looked at him in surprise.

"I thought Oz was a great head," said Dorothy.

"And I thought Oz was a lovely lady," said the Scarecrow.

"And I thought Oz was a terrible beast," said the Tin Woodman.

"And I thought Oz was a ball of fire," exclaimed the Lion.

"No; you are all wrong," said the little man, meekly. "I have been making believe."

"Making believe!" cried Dorothy. "Aren't you a great Wizard?"

- Who was behind the screen? *Idea:* A little old man.
- What did the old man do when the Tin Woodman rushed toward him? *Idea:* He said, "Don't strike me, I'll do anything you want me to."
- Was Oz really a great wizard or a humbug? **A humbug.**
- What's a humbug? *Ideas:* A fake; a phony.
- How did he make Dorothy think that he was a head? *Idea:* He made a paper head and hung it.
- What trick did he use to make the Scarecrow think that he was a lovely lady? *Idea:* He dressed up in a dress and a mask.
- How did he make the Tin Woodman think he was a terrible beast? *Idea:* He sewed animal skins together.
- How did he make the Lion think that he was a ball of fire? *Idea:* He hung a ball of cotton from the ceiling and set it on fire.
  So he's not a great wizard after all. In the next chapter, he'll tell how he came to become the Wizard of Oz.

Award 4 points or have the students reread to the error limit sign.

INDEPENDENT WORK

Do all the items in your skillbook and workbook for lesson 28.

"Hush, my dear," he said. "Don't speak so loudly, or you will be overheard—and I will be ruined. I'm supposed to be a great Wizard."

"And aren't you?" Dorothy asked.

"Not a bit, my dear; I'm just a common man."

"You're more than that," said the Scarecrow, in a sad tone. "You're a humbug."

"Exactly so!" declared the little man, rubbing his hands together as if it pleased him. "I am a humbug."

"But this is terrible," said the Tin Woodman. "How will I ever get my heart?"

"Or my courage?" asked the Lion.

"Or my brains?" wailed the Scarecrow.

"But, my dear friends," said Oz, "think of me, and the terrible trouble I'm in at being found out."

"Doesn't anyone else know you're a humbug?" asked Dorothy.

"No one knows it but you—and myself," replied Oz. "I have fooled everyone so long that I thought I would never be found out. It was a great mistake to ever let you into the throne room. Usually I will not even see the people I rule over, and so they believe that I am something terrible."

"But, I don't understand," said Dorothy. "How was it that you appeared to me as a great head?"

"That was one of my tricks," answered Oz. "Step this way, please, and I will tell you all about it."

He led them to a small room in the rear of the throne room, and they all followed him. He pointed to one corner and there was the great head. It was made out of paper, and had a carefully painted face.

"I hung this from the ceiling by a wire," said Oz. "I stood behind the screen and pulled a thread, to make the eyes move and the mouth open."

"But how about the voice?" Dorothy inquired.

"Oh, I am a ventriloquist," said the little man. "I can throw the sound of my voice wherever I want; so that you thought it was coming out of the head. Here are the other things I used to trick you." He showed the Scarecrow the dress and the mask he had worn when he seemed to be the lovely lady. And the Tin Woodman saw that his terrible beast was nothing but a lot of animal skins, sewn together. As for the ball of fire, the false Wizard had also hung that from the ceiling. It was really a ball of cotton, but when oil was poured on it the ball had burned fiercely.

"Really," said the Scarecrow, "you ought to be ashamed of yourself for being such a humbug."

"I am—I certainly am," answered the little man, sorrowfully. "But it was the only thing I could do. Sit down, please—there are plenty of chairs—and I will tell you my story."

ANSWER KEY FOR WORKBOOK

Review Items

1. Write whether each statement about Oz is **true** or **false**.

a. "Oz is a humbug." _true_
b. "Oz wanted the Witch of the West killed." _true_
c. "Oz is a little old man." _true_
d. "Oz is a lovely lady." _false_
e. "Oz was once defeated by the Winged Monkeys." _true_

f. "Oz is a ball of fire." _false_
g. "Dorothy knows what his real form is." _true_

2. Each of the travelers wanted something from Oz.
a. Where did Dorothy want Oz to send her? _Kansas_
b. What did the Scarecrow want from Oz? _brains_
c. What did the Tin Woodman want from Oz? _a heart_

Crossword Puzzle

To work the puzzle, read an item and figure out which word the item describes. Then write the word in the puzzle. Complete the entire puzzle.

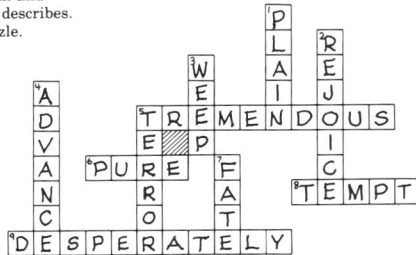

```
              P
              L
        W     A   R
    A   E     I   E
    D  TREMENDOUS J
    V   E   P     I
    A  PURE   F  TEMPT
    N   R   A
    C   O   T
   DESPERATELY
```

Across

5. A very great storm is a _____ storm.
6. If something is not mixed with anything else, it is _____.
8. If you offer someone silver, you _____ them with silver.
9. When you very much want to win, you _____ want to win.

Down

1. A flat place—like a prairie.
2. When you act very happy, you _____.
3. When you cry, you _____.
4. When you move forward, you _____.
5. Another word for **great fear**.
7. The things that happen to you are called your _____.

WORKCHECK AND AWARDING POINTS

1. *Read the questions and answers for the skillbook and workbook.*
2. *Award points for independent work as follows:*

> *0 errors . . . . .6 points*
> *2 errors . . . . .4 points*
> *3, 4, or 5 errors . . . . .2 points*
> *5 or more errors . . . . .0 points*

3. *Award bonus points as follows:*

> *Correcting missed items or getting all items right . . . . .2 points*
> *Doing the writing assignment acceptably . . . . .2 points*

ANSWER KEY FOR SKILLBOOK

PART B

1. a. *Idea:* Surprised
   b. *Idea:* Because she had killed the Witch
2. Call the Winged Monkeys
3. *Idea:* Defeated him
4. a. *Idea:* Nothing
   b. A voice
5. a. *Idea:* A little old man
   b. A humbug
6. a. Paper
   b. *Idea:* Because he was a ventriloquist
   c. *Idea:* A mask and a dress
   d. *Idea:* Skins
   e. *Idea:* Oil and cotton
7. a. The Guardian of the Gates met the travelers
   b. The Scarecrow threatened to call the Winged Monkeys
   c. Toto knocked over a screen

PART C

8. a. Green
   b. Yellow
   c. Blue
9. a. throne room
   b. witch's castle
   c. forest
   d. witch's castle
   e. throne room
10. a. great fear
    b. advanced
    c. admit
    d. desperately
    e. cruelty
    f. tenderly

Lesson 29

PART A Word Lists

1	2	3
experience	imagination	**Vocabulary words**
knowledge	hesitation	1. high spirits
congratulate	explanation	2. knowledge
deceive	imitation	3. experience
imitate		4. congratulate
		5. contents
		6. deceive

WORD PRACTICE AND VOCABULARY

EXERCISE 1 Word practice

1. Everybody, find lesson 29, part A in your skillbook. *Wait.* Touch column 1. *Check.* The words in column 1 are hard words that will be in your reading stories.
2. Touch under the first word. *Check.* The first word is **experience.** What word? *Signal.* **Experience.**
3. Next word. *Pause.* That word is **knowledge.** What word? *Signal.* **Knowledge.**
4. *Repeat step 3 for each remaining word in column 1.*
5. Now let's see if you remember all those words. Touch under the first word in column 1. *Pause.* What word? *Signal.* **Experience.**
6. Next word. *Pause.* What word? *Signal.* **Knowledge.**
7.
8.

EXERCISE 2 Word family

1. Everybody, touch column 2. *Check.* All those words end with the sound **shun.** Touch under the first word. *Pause.* What word? *Signal.* **Imagination.**
2. Next word. *Pause.* What word? *Signal.* **Hesitation.**
3. *Repeat step 2 for each remaining word in column 2.*
4. *Repeat the words in column 2 until firm.*

EXERCISE 3 Vocabulary development

Task A

1. Everybody, touch column 3. *Check.* First you're going to read the words in column 3. Then we'll talk about what they mean.
2. Touch under the first line. *Pause.* What words? *Signal.* **High spirits.**
3. Next word. *Pause.* What word? *Signal.* **Knowledge.**
4. *Repeat step 3 for each remaining word in column 3.*
5. *Repeat the words in column 3 until firm.*

Task B

Now let's talk about what those words mean. The words in line 1 are **high spirits.** When people have **high spirits,** they feel very good.

Task C

Word 2 is **knowledge.** A person's **knowledge** is all the things that person knows. Everybody, what do we call all the things a person knows? *Signal.* **A person's knowledge.**

Task D

1. Word 3 is **experience.** Every time you do something, you have an **experience.** When you go to the store, you have the **experience** of going to the store. Everybody, what do you do when you go to the store? *Signal.* **Have the experience of going to the store.**
2. Everybody, what do you do when you read a book? *Signal.* **Have the experience of reading a book.**

Task E

Word 4 is **congratulate.** When you tell somebody they did a good job, you **congratulate** that person. If you tell John that he did a good job, you **congratulate** John. Everybody, what do you do when you tell Sarah that she did a good job? *Signal.* **You congratulate Sarah.**

Task F

Word 5 is **contents.** The **contents** of something are the things that are inside it. If butterflies are inside a bottle, the **contents** of the bottle are butterflies. Everybody, what are the **contents** of a book if there are poems inside the book? *Signal.* **Poems.**

Task G

Word 6 is **deceive.** When you **deceive** somebody, you trick that person into believing something that is not true. When Oz tricked Dorothy into believing things that were not true, Oz **deceived** Dorothy. Everybody, what did Oz do when he tricked Dorothy into believing things that were not true? *Signal.* **He deceived Dorothy.**

STORY READING

EXERCISE 4 Decoding

1. Everybody, turn to page 111 in your textbook. *Wait. Call on a student.* What's the error limit for this chapter? **12 errors.**
2. *Call on individual students to read.*
3. *After the group reads to the 2-error sign without making more than 2 errors, reread the first part aloud and present the comprehension tasks.*
4. *After you have completed the first part, call on individual students to read. Present the comprehension tasks.*

Lesson 29

CHAPTER 24
The Wizard's Story

PICTURE 1   PICTURE 2

Dorothy and the others sat down and listened while the Wizard told the following tale.Ⓐ

I was born near Kansas. When I grew up I became a ventriloquist, and I was very well-trained at that by a great master.Ⓑ I could imitate any kind of a bird or beast. I could meow like a cat and make it sound so real that birds would be frightened.

After a time I tired of ventriloquism and became a balloonist.Ⓒ

A balloonist works for a circus. He goes up in his balloon on circus day, and calls down to people. Then he gets them to go to the circus. ★2 ERRORS★

Well, one day I went up in a balloon and the ropes got twisted, so that I couldn't come down again. The balloon went way up above the clouds. It went so far up that a current of air struck it and carried it many, many miles away. For a day and a night I traveled through the air, and on the morning of the second day I awoke and found the balloon floating over a strange and beautiful country.

The balloon came down gradually, and I was not hurt a bit. But I found myself among strange people, who, when they saw me come from the clouds, thought I was a great Wizard.Ⓓ Of course, I let them think

I was a Wizard because they were afraid of me, and they promised to doing anything I wanted.

Just to amuse myself, and to keep the people busy, I ordered them to build this city, and my Palace; and they did it all willingly and well. Then I thought, since the country was so green and beautiful, that I would call the city the Emerald City, and to make the name fit better I put green spectacles on all the people, so that everything they saw was green.

The Emerald City is no greener than any other city. But when you wear green spectacles, why of course everything you look green to you.Ⓔ The Emerald City was built a great many years ago, for I was a young man when the balloon brought me here, and I am a very old man now. But my people have worn green glasses on their eyes so long that most of them think it really is an Emerald City. And it certainly is a beautiful place, full of jewels and precious metals, and every good thing that is needed to make people happy. I have been good to the people, and they like me; but ever since this Palace was built I have shut myself up and would not see any of them.Ⓕ

One of my greatest fears was the Witches, for I soon found out that the Witches were really able to do powerful things. There were four of them in this country, and they ruled the people who live in the North and South and East and West. Fortunately, the Witches of the North and South were good, and I knew that would do me no harm. But the Witches of the East and West were terribly wicked and I knew

that if they thought I was not more powerful than they were, they would destroy me. As it was, I lived in deadly fear of them for many years, so you can imagine how pleased I was when I heard your house had fallen on the Wicked Witch of the East.Ⓖ When you came to me I was willing to promise anything if you would only do away with the other Witch.Ⓗ But, now that you have melted her, I am ashamed to say that I cannot keep my promises.

"I think you are a very bad man," said Dorothy.

"Oh, no, my dear. I'm really a very good man; but I'm a very bad Wizard, I must admit."

"Can't you give me brains?" asked the Scarecrow.

"You don't need them. You are learning something every day. A baby has brains, but it doesn't know much. Experience is the only thing that brings knowledge, and the longer you are on earth the more experience you are sure to get," replied Oz.

"That may be all true," said the Scarecrow, "but I shall be very unhappy unless you give me brains."

The false Wizard looked at him carefully.

"Well," he said with a sigh, "I'm not much of a magician, but if you will come to me tomorrow morning, I will stuff your head with brains. I cannot tell you how to use them, however; you must find that out for yourself."Ⓘ
★12 ERRORS★

"Oh, thank you, thank you!" cried

EXERCISE 5 Comprehension tasks

Ⓐ Find the end of the Wizard's story. *Check.* Go back to the beginning.

Ⓑ What does a ventriloquist do? *Idea:* Makes it sound like somebody else is talking.

Ⓒ What did he become? **A balloonist.**

• What does a balloonist do? *Idea:* Flies in a balloon.

• Why didn't Oz become a pilot of an airplane? *Idea:* There were no airplanes invented yet.

• Everybody, look at the pictures. These pictures show things that Oz has done. What is the person in the first picture? *Signal.* **A ventriloquist.**

• What is the person in the second picture? *Signal.* **A balloonist.**

Ⓓ Why did the people think he was a great wizard? *Idea:* Because he came down from the clouds.

Ⓔ Who ordered the people to build something? **Oz.**

• What did he order them to build? **The Emerald City.**

• Did they do it willingly or with a lot of complaints? **Willingly.**

• Is everybody and everything in the Emerald City really green? **No.**

• Why does it look green? *Idea:* Because the people wear green glasses.

Ⓕ How old was Oz when he first shut himself up in the palace? *Idea:* Very young.

• How old is he now? *Idea:* Very old.

• Do most people in the Emerald City think it is really green? **Yes.**

• Why? *Idea:* Because they've worn green glasses for so long.

Ⓖ Which of the Witches was Oz afraid of? *Idea:* Witches of the East and West.

• Who was actually more powerful, those Witches or Oz? **Those Witches.**

• Did the Witches know that? **No.**

• What would have happened if the Witches had known that Oz was not powerful? *Idea:* They would have destroyed him.

Ⓗ Which of the Witches was that? *Idea:* The Wicked Witch of the West.

Ⓘ The Wizard told the Scarecrow that babies have brains, but babies are not smart. Why not? *Idea:* They have no experience.

• What did the Wizard tell the Scarecrow was more important than brains? *Idea:* Experience.

• Read the rest of the chapter to yourselves and be ready to answer some questions.

the Scarecrow. "I'll find a way to use them, never fear!"

"But how about my courage?" asked the Lion, anxiously.

"You have plenty of courage, I am sure," answered Oz. "All you need is confidence in yourself. Every living thing is afraid when it faces danger, but if you have confidence you can face danger even when you are afraid. You have plenty of that kind of courage."

"Perhaps I do, but I'm scared just the same," said the Lion. "I will really be very unhappy unless you give me the sort of courage that will make me forget I am afraid."

"Very well. I will give you that sort of courage tomorrow," replied Oz.

"How about my heart?" asked the Tin Woodman.

"Why, as for that," answered Oz, "I think you are wrong to want a heart. It makes most people unhappy. If you only knew it, you are lucky not to have a heart."

"I don't agree," said the Tin Woodman. "I will bear all the unhappiness without a grumble, if you will give me the heart."

"Very well," answered Oz, meekly. "Come to me tomorrow and I will give you a heart. I have played Wizard for so many years that I may as well continue the part a little longer."

"And now," said Dorothy, "how am I going to get back to Kansas?"

"We will have to think about that," replied the little man. "Give me two or three days to consider the matter and I'll try to find a way to carry you over the desert. In the meantime you will all be treated as my guests, and while you live in the Palace my people will wait upon you and obey your slightest wish. There is only one thing I ask in return for my help—you must keep my secret and tell no one I am a humbug."

They agreed to say nothing of what they had learned, and went back to their rooms in high spirits. Even Dorothy had hope that "The Great and Terrible Humbug," as she called him, would find a way to send her back to Kansas. And if he did, she was willing to forgive him for everything he had done.

The next morning the Scarecrow said to his friends, "Congratulate me. I am going to Oz to get my brains at last. When I return I will be like other men."

"I have always liked you as you were," said Dorothy.

"It is kind of you to like a scarecrow," he replied. "But surely you will think more of me when you hear the splendid thoughts my new brains are going to turn out." Then he said goodbye to them in a cheerful voice and went to the throne room, where he knocked on the door.

"Come in," said Oz.

The Scarecrow went in and found the little man sitting down by the window, thinking hard.

"I have come for my brains," remarked the Scarecrow, a little uneasily.

"Oh yes. Sit down in that chair,

please," replied Oz. "You must excuse me for taking your head off, but I will have to do it in order to put your brains in their proper place."

"That's all right," said the Scarecrow. "You are quite welcome to take my head off, as long as it will be a better one when you put it on again."

So the Wizard unfastened his head and emptied out the straw. Then he entered the back room and got hundreds of pins and needles. After shaking them together thoroughly, he filled the top of the Scarecrow's head with the mixture and stuffed the rest of the space with straw, to hold the pins and needles in place. When he had fastened the Scarecrow's head on his body, he said to him, "I have filled your head with pins and needles. So now you have all the brains you need."

After all students have finished reading:

- The Wizard told the Lion that he needed something other than courage. What did the Lion need? **Confidence.**
- The Wizard told the Tin Woodman that he didn't need a heart because a heart made people feel a certain way. What way is that? *Idea:* Unhappy.
- What did the Wizard tell Dorothy that he would do to solve her problem? *Idea:* Try to find a way to carry her over the desert.
- Oz made Dorothy and the others promise that they would not do something. What was that? *Idea:* Tell people that he was a humbug.
- Who was the first person to visit Oz the next morning? **The Scarecrow.**
- What did Oz put inside the Scarecrow's head? *Idea:* Pins and needles.
- What did the pins and needles prove? *Idea:* That the Scarecrow was very sharp.
- Did the Scarecrow feel smarter with his new brains? **Yes.**
- Who was the next person to visit Oz? **The Tin Woodman.**
- Do you think Oz is going to give him a real heart? *Call on individual students. Responses:* Student preference.

Award 4 points or have the students reread to the error limit sign.

INDEPENDENT WORK

Do all the items in your skillbook and workbook for lesson 29.

"I don't understand," replied the Scarecrow, thoughtfully. "How can I have brains if I have nothing but straw, pins, and needles in my head?"

The Wizard replied, "People who have brains are very sharp. Anybody looking at the pins and needles sticking out of your head will know at once that you are very sharp."

The Wizard patted the Scarecrow on the back and continued, "From now on, you will be a great man, for I have given you new brains."

The Scarecrow was both pleased and proud to have new brains, and after thanking Oz warmly he went back to his friends.

Dorothy looked at him curiously. His head bulged out at the top with brains.

"How do you feel?" she asked.

"I feel wise indeed," he answered earnestly. "When I get used to my brains I will know everything."

"Why are those needles and pins sticking out of your head?" asked the Tin Woodman.

The Scarecrow explained.

The Tin Woodman said, "Well, I must go to Oz and get my heart." So he walked to the throne room and knocked on the door.

"Come in," called Oz, and the Tin Woodman entered.

ANSWER KEY FOR WORKBOOK

Review Items

1. Write whether each statement about Oz is **true** or **false**.
   a. "He lives in the Emerald City."
      true
   b. "He is more powerful than the Witches." *false*
   c. "He is a ventriloquist."
      true
   d. "He worked for a circus."
      true
   e. "He is a large beast."
      false
   f. "He was afraid of the Witches."
      true
   g. "He can fly a balloon."
      true
   h. "He is a good Wizard."
      false
   i. "He is a head without a body."
      false

2. Write which character each statement describes.
   a. This character killed two witches.
      Dorothy
   b. This character ordered some people to build the Emerald City.
      Oz
   c. This character rusts when he cries.
      Tin Woodman
   d. This character has needles and pins in his head.
      Scarecrow
   e. This character is supposed to be the King of Beasts.
      Lion

3. Put the following story events in the right order by numbering them from 1 through 4.
   2 The Monkeys took the travelers to the Emerald City.
   3 Oz told the story of his life.
   1 Oz ordered the travelers to kill the Wicked Witch.
   4 Oz put pins and needles in the Scarecrow's head.

WORKCHECK AND AWARDING POINTS

1. *Read the questions and answers for the skillbook and workbook.*
2. *Award points for independent work as follows:*

0 errors	6 points
2 errors	4 points
3, 4, or 5 errors	2 points
5 or more errors	0 points

3. *Award bonus points as follows:*

Correcting missed items or getting all items right	2 points
Doing the writing assignment acceptably	2 points

ANSWER KEY FOR SKILLBOOK

PART B

1. a. *Idea:* Near Kansas
   b. ventriloquist
   c. balloonist
   d. A balloonist
2. a. *Idea:* The Land of Oz
   b. wizard
   c. The Emerald City
3. a. No
   b. *Idea:* Because they have worn glasses for so long
4. a. No
   b. Yes
   c. *Idea:* Destroyed him
   d. Dorothy
5. confidence
6. unhappy
7. a. needles, pins
   b. sharp

PART C

8. a. huge
   b. advanced
   c. rage
   d. tempt
   e. cunning
   f. large meal
   g. mend
   h. reunited
   i. inlaid
   j. pleaded with
   k. on time

Lesson 30

Lesson 30

PART A   Word Lists

1	2	3
congratulation	**Vocabulary words**	**Vocabulary words**
hesitation	1. imitate	1. shears
imitation	2. confidence	2. sawdust
explanation	3. consider	3. replaced
imagination	4. uneasy	4. tug
	5. contents	
	6. deceive	
	7. gradually	

WORD PRACTICE AND VOCABULARY

EXERCISE 1   Word family

1. Everybody, find lesson 30, part A in your skillbook. *Wait.* Touch column 1. *Check.*
   All those words end with the sound **shun.**
   Touch under the first word. *Pause.*
   What word? *Signal.* **Congratulation.**
2. Next word. *Pause.* What word? *Signal.*
   Hesitation.
3. *Repeat step 2 for each remaining word in column 1.*
4. *Repeat the words in column 1 until firm.*

EXERCISE 2   Vocabulary review

Task A

1. Everybody, touch column 2. *Check.*
   First you're going to read the words in column 2. Then we'll talk about what they mean.
2. Touch under the first word. *Pause.*
   What word? *Signal.* **Imitate.**
3. Next word. *Pause.* What word? *Signal.*
   Confidence.
4. *Repeat step 3 for each remaining word in column 2.*
5. *Repeat the words in column 2 until firm.*

Task B

You've learned the meanings for all these words. Word 1 is **imitate.** Let's see you **imitate** this. *Clap 2 times. Wait.*
When you clapped, you **imitated** me.
Everybody, what did you do? *Signal.*
Imitated you.

Task C

1. Word 2 is **confidence.** *Call on a student.*
   What does **confidence** mean? *Idea:* You feel sure about something.
2. Everybody, what's another way of saying
   She felt sure that she could climb the hill?
   Signal. **She had confidence that she could climb the hill.**
3. Everybody, what's another way of saying
   He felt sure that he could win the race?
   Signal. **He had confidence that he could win the race.**

Task D

1. Word 3 is **consider.** *Call on a student.*
   What does **consider** mean? *Idea:* Think over.
2. Everybody, what's another way of saying
   He thought over whether he should buy the motorcycle? *Signal.* **He considered whether he should buy the motorcycle.**

Task E

1. Word 4 is **uneasy.** *Call on a student.*
   What does **uneasy** mean? *Idea:* Uncomfortable.
2. Everybody, what's another way of saying
   He felt uncomfortable about flying in an airplane? *Signal.* **He felt uneasy about flying in an airplane.**

Task F

1. Word 5 is **contents.** *Call on a student.*
   What are the **contents** of something? *Idea:* What is inside something.
2. Everybody, what are the **contents** of a bottle if there are worms inside the bottle? *Signal.* **Worms.**

Task G

1. Word 6 is **deceive.** *Call on a student.*
   What does **deceive** mean? *Idea:* You trick someone into believing something that is not true.
2. Everybody, what did Oz do when he tricked Dorothy into believing things that were not true? *Signal.* **He deceived Dorothy.**

Task H

1. Word 7 is **gradually.** *Call on a student.*
   What does **gradually** mean? *Idea:* Slowly.
2. Everybody, what's another way of saying
   She slowly became sleepy? *Signal.*
   She gradually became sleepy.

EXERCISE 3   Vocabulary development

Task A

1. Everybody, touch column 3. *Check.* First you're going to read the words in column 3. Then we'll talk about what they mean.
2. Touch under the first word. *Pause.*
   What word? *Signal.* **Shears.**
3. Next word. *Pause.* What word? *Signal.* **Sawdust.**
4. *Repeat step 3 for each remaining word in column 3.*
5. *Repeat the words in column 3 until firm.*

Task B

Now let's talk about what those words mean.
Word 1 is **shears. Shears** are large scissors.
Everybody, what's another name for **large scissors?** *Signal.* **Shears.**

Task C

Word 2 is **sawdust.** *Call on a student.*
What's **sawdust?** *Idea:* Small pieces of wood that fall off during sawing.

Lesson 30

CHAPTER 25
The Balloon

The Tin Woodman stood before Oz and said, "I have come for my heart."

"Very well," answered the little man. "But I will have to cut a hole in your chest, so I can put your heart in the right place. I hope it won't hurt you."

"Oh, no," answered the Tin Woodman. "I won't feel it at all."

So Oz brought a pair of shears and cut a small, square hole in the left side of the Tin Woodman's chest.Ⓐ Then, Oz went to his cupboard and took out a pretty heart that was made entirely of silk and stuffed with sawdust.

★2 ERRORS★

"Isn't it a beauty?" he asked.

"It is, indeed!" replied the Tin Woodman, who was greatly pleased. "But is it a kind heart?"

"Oh very!" answered Oz. He put the heart in the Tin Woodman's chest and then replaced the square of tin.

"There," said Oz. "Now you have a heart that any man would be proud of. I'm sorry I had to put a patch on your chest, but it really couldn't be helped."

"Never mind the patch," exclaimed the happy Tin Woodman. "I am very grateful to you, and will never forget your kindness."

"Don't mention it," replied Oz.

Then the Tin Woodman went back to his friends, who were very happy for him.Ⓑ

The Lion now walked to the throne room and knocked on the door.

"Come in," said Oz.

"I have come for my courage," announced the Lion, entering the room.

"Very well," answered the little man; "I will get it for you."

He went to his cupboard, reaching up to a high shelf and took down a large green bottle. He poured the contents of the bottle into a beautifully carved dish. Then he placed the dish in front of the cowardly Lion, who sniffed at it as if he did not like it.Ⓒ

"What is it?" asked the Lion.

"Courage," replied the Wizard.

"Do I have to drink it?" asked the Lion.

"Of course," said Oz. "You know that courage is something inside of you. If you don't drink it, you will not have courage inside of you."

"But," said the Lion slowly, as he looked at the large dish of liquid. "Do I have to drink all of it?"

Oz replied, "You want to be full of courage, don't you?"

"Yes," said the Lion.

"Then you must drink it all. That is the only way you will be full of courage."

The Lion hesitated no longer, and drank until the dish was empty.

"How do you feel now?" asked Oz.

"Full of courage," replied the Lion, who went joyfully back to his friends to tell them about his good fortune.Ⓓ

When Oz was alone, he smiled at his success in giving the Scarecrow and the Tin Woodman and the Lion exactly what they wanted. He said, "It was easy to make the Scarecrow and the Lion and the Tin Woodman happy, because they imagined I could do anything. But it will take a lot more imagination to carry Dorothy back to Kansas, and I don't know how it can be done."Ⓔ

For three days Dorothy heard nothing from Oz.Ⓕ These were sad days for the girl, although her friends were all quite happy and comfortable. The Scarecrow told them that there were wonderful things in his head, but he would not say what they were because he knew no one could understand them but himself. When the Tin Woodman walked around, he felt his heart rattling in his chest, and he told Dorothy that it was a kinder and more tender heart than the one he had owned when he was made of flesh. The Lion declared he was afraid of nothing on earth, and would gladly face an army of men or a dozen of the fierce Kalidahs.

Task D

1. **Word 3 is replaced.** When you put something back in place, you **replace** that thing. Everybody, what's another way of saying **He put the door back in place?** *Signal.*
   He replaced the door.

2. Everybody, what's another way of saying **He put the book back in place?** *Signal.*
   He replaced the book.

Task E

Word 4 is **tug.** When you **tug** at something, you pull very hard.

STORY READING

EXERCISE 4   Decoding

1. Everybody, turn to page 116 in your textbook. *Wait. Call on a student.* What's the error limit for this chapter? **12 errors.**

2. *Call on individual students to read.*

3. *After the group reads to the 2-error sign without making more than 2 errors, reread the first part aloud and present the comprehension tasks.*

4. *After you have completed the first part, call on individual students to read. Present the comprehension tasks.*

EXERCISE 5   Comprehension tasks

Ⓐ Everybody, touch the place on your chest where the hole would be. *Check.*

● What did Oz use to cut the hole? **Shears.**

● What are shears? *Idea:* Scissors.

Ⓑ What was the heart made of? *Idea:* Silk and sawdust.

● Did the Tin Woodman care that it was a fake heart? **No.**

Ⓒ Everybody, show me how the Lion did that. *Check.*

Ⓓ What was actually in the dish? **Liquid.**

● Was there much of it? **Yes.**

● Why did the Lion have to drink all of it? *Idea:* So he would be full of courage.

Ⓔ Was it easy for the Wizard to think of ways to help the Tin Woodman, the Scarecrow, and the Lion? **Yes.**

● Was Dorothy's problem as easy to solve? **No.**

● Does Oz know how to solve her problem? **No.**

Ⓕ How many days did she wait to hear from Oz? **Three.**

● How do you think Dorothy felt during this time? *Idea:* Sad.

● Why do you think Oz was taking so long to send for Dorothy? *Idea:* He was having a hard time thinking up ways to get her to Kansas.

Thus, each of the friends was satisfied except Dorothy, who wanted more than ever to get back to Kansas.

On the fourth day, Oz sent for Dorothy. Ⓖ When she entered the throne room he said pleasantly, "Sit down, my dear. I think I have found the way to get you out of this country."

"And back to Kansas?" Dorothy asked, eagerly.

"Well, I'm not sure about Kansas," said Oz, "for I haven't the faintest idea where it is. But the first thing to do is to cross the desert, and then it should be easy to find your way home." Ⓗ

"How can I cross the desert?" Dorothy inquired.

"Well, I'll tell you what I think," said the little man. "You see, I came to this country in a balloon. You also came through the air, carried by a cyclone. So I believe the best way to get across the desert will be through the air. Now, it is quite beyond my powers to make a cyclone. But I've been thinking the matter over, and I believe I can make a balloon." Ⓘ ★12 ERRORS★

"How are you going to build a balloon?" asked Dorothy.

"As you know," said Oz, "a balloon is a large bag that floats when it is filled with gas. The balloon I had was made of silk, which was coated with glue to keep the gas from leaking out. I destroyed my old balloon, but I have plenty of silk in the Palace, so it will be no trouble to make a new one. Unfortunately, in this whole country there is no gas to fill the balloon with, to make it float."

"If it won't float," remarked Dorothy, "it will be of no use to me."

"True," answered Oz. "But there is another way to make it float, which is to fill it with hot air. Hot air isn't as good as gas, for if the air were to get cold the balloon would come down in the desert, and we would be lost."

"We!" exclaimed Dorothy. "Are you going with me?"

"Yes, of course," replied Oz. "I am tired of being such a humbug. If I were to go out of this Palace my people would soon discover that I am not a Wizard, and then they would be angry with me for having deceived them. So I have to stay shut up in these rooms all day, and it gets tiresome. I'd much rather go back to Kansas with you and be in a circus again."

"I will be glad to have your company," said Dorothy.

"Thank you," Oz answered. "Now if you will help me sew the silk together, we will begin to work on our balloon."

So Oz got some silk and began to cut it into strips. Dorothy took the strips and sewed them together with needle and thread. First there was a strip of light green silk, then a strip of dark green and then a strip of emerald green; for Oz wanted to make the balloon in different shades of his favorite color. It took three days to sew all the strips together, but when Dorothy was finished they had a big bag of green silk more than twenty feet long.

118   Lesson 30   Textbook

Then Oz painted the inside of the bag with a coat of thin glue, to make it airtight. Then he announced that the balloon was ready.

"But we must have a basket to ride in," Oz said. So he sent the soldier with the green whiskers for a big clothes basket, which he fastened to the bottom of the balloon with many ropes.

When it was all ready, Oz sent word to his people that he was going to make a visit to his great brother Wizard who lived in the clouds. The news spread rapidly throughout the city and everyone came to see him leave.

Oz ordered the balloon carried out in front of the Palace, and the people gazed at it with much curiosity. The Tin Woodman chopped a big pile of wood, and made a fire. Oz held the bottom of the balloon over the fire so that the hot air that rose up from the fire would be caught in the silk bag. Gradually the balloon swelled out and rose into the air, until finally the basket started to leave the ground.

Then Oz got into the basket and said to all the people in a loud voice, "I am now going away to make a visit. While I am gone the Scarecrow will rule over you. I command you to obey him as you would me."

By this time the balloon was tugging hard at the rope that held it to the ground, for the air in the balloon was hot, and this made the inside air so much lighter than the outside air that the balloon started to rise.

"Come, Dorothy!" cried the Wizard. "Hurry up, or the balloon will fly away."

"I can't find Toto anywhere," replied Dorothy, who did not want to leave her little dog behind. Toto had run into the crowd to bark at a kitten, and Dorothy found him at last. She picked him up and ran toward the balloon.

Dorothy was within a few steps of the balloon, and Oz was holding out his hands to help her into the basket, when the ropes suddenly snapped and the balloon rose into the air without her.

"Come back!" Dorothy screamed; "I want to go, too!"

"I can't come back, my dear," called Oz from the basket. "Goodbye!"

"Goodbye!" shouted everyone, and all eyes were turned upwards to where the Wizard was riding in the basket, rising every moment farther and farther into the sky.

And that was the last any of them ever saw of Oz, the wonderful Wizard. He may have reached Kansas safely, and be there now. But the people remembered him lovingly, and said to one another, "Oz was always our friend. When he was here he built this beautiful Emerald City for us, and now that he has gone he has left the wise Scarecrow to rule over us."

But for many days, the people were sad about the loss of the wonderful Wizard.

Lesson 30   Textbook   119

Ⓖ How do you think Dorothy felt now?
Ideas: Excited; happy.
Ⓗ What does Dorothy have to do first?
Cross the desert.
● Where is the desert?
Idea: All around the Land of Oz.
Ⓘ What's Oz going to use to take Dorothy out of the country? **A balloon.**
● Read the rest of the chapter to yourselves and be ready to answer some questions.

After all students have finished reading:

● What did Oz think was the best thing for filling a balloon? **Gas.**
● Did he have any gas? **No.**
● What was he going to use instead of gas? **Hot air.**
● Hot air wasn't as good as gas because something would happen if hot air cooled. What would happen? *Idea:* The balloon would come down.
● What material was he going to make the balloon of? **Silk.**
● Who was going to go in the balloon with Dorothy? **Oz.**
● What did Oz plan to do when he got back to Kansas? *Idea:* Go back to work for the circus.
● The balloon was made of shades of the same color. What color was that? **Green.**
● What did Oz use for a basket at the bottom of the balloon? *Idea:* A clothes basket.
● How did Oz get the air inside the balloon hot? *Idea:* They made a fire under the balloon and the hot air went into the balloon.
● Who made that fire? **The Tin Woodman.**
● Who ruled over the Emerald City when Oz left? **The Scarecrow.**
● Did Oz plan to come back to the Emerald City? **No.**
● Why didn't Dorothy get into the balloon when the Wizard called her? *Idea:* She couldn't find Toto.
● Did Dorothy get into the balloon before it took off? **No.**
● What did Oz say when Dorothy told him to come back? *Idea:* I can't.
● Where is Oz now? *Idea:* No one knows.

Award 4 points or have the students reread to the error limit sign.

INDEPENDENT WORK

Do all the items in your skillbook and workbook for lesson 30.

ANSWER KEY FOR WORKBOOK

Map Skills

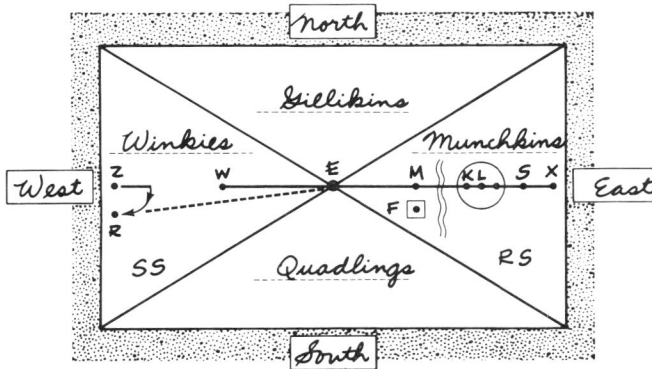

1. Write **North**, **East**, **South** and **West** in the boxes around the map.
2. On the map, write the name of the people who live in each land.
3. **a.** Write **RS** on the land that is closest to the **rising** sun.
   b. Write **SS** on the land that is closest to the **setting** sun.
4. The **dotted line** shows how the travelers went to the Emerald City.
   a. How did they get there?
   Circle the correct answer.

   • In a cart   • On a river
   • (In the air)   • On a road
   • On foot

   b. Who carried them there?

   Winged Monkeys

   c. Write the direction they went.

   East

5. The **dots** on the map tell where things happened.
   a. Write **L** on the dot where Dorothy met the Lion.
   b. Write **X** on the dot where Dorothy and Toto landed.
   c. Write **S** on the dot where Dorothy met the Scarecrow.
   d. Write **K** on the dot where Dorothy met the Kalidahs.
   e. Write **M** on the dot where Dorothy met the mice.
   f. Write **F** on the dot where the Lion was rescued.
   g. Write **E** on the dot that shows the city the travelers visited two times.
   h. Write **W** on the dot where the Winged Monkeys attacked the travelers.
   i. Write **R** on the dot where the Winged Monkeys rescued the travelers.
   j. Write **Z** on the dot where the Wicked Witch melted.

WORKCHECK AND AWARDING POINTS

1. *Read the questions and answers for the skillbook and workbook.*
2. *Award points for independent work as follows:*

0 errors	*.6 points*
2 errors	*.4 points*
3, 4, or 5 errors	*.2 points*
5 or more errors	*.0 points*

3. *Award bonus points as follows:*

Correcting missed items or getting all items right	*.2 points*
Doing the writing assignment acceptably	*.2 points*

ANSWER KEY FOR SKILLBOOK

PART B

1. **a.** *Idea:* Cut a hole in the Tin Woodman's chest
   b. *Idea:* A fake heart
   c. Silk and sawdust
2. **a.** courage
   b. No
   c. *Idea:* So he would be full of courage
3. **a.** Silk
   b. Green
4. **a.** rise
   b. fall
   c. Hot air
5. **a.** A fire
   b. A clothes basket
6. **a.** Ropes
   b. *Idea:* To get Toto
   c. *Idea:* They broke
   d. *Idea:* It went up in the air
7. **a.** No
   b. *Idea:* Sad
8. **a.** Toto
   b. Dorothy
   c. Oz

PART C

9. **a.** timid
   b. tremendous
   c. pack
   d. hit
   e. cunning
   f. swarm
   g. cruelty
   h. flock
   i. fix
   j. begged
   k. mischief
   l. capturing

Lesson 31

<table>
<tr><td colspan="2">

Lesson 31

PART A   Word Lists

1	2
towel	precious
vibrate	ventriloquism
underneath	thorough
collar	through

3
Vocabulary words
1. whisk
2. farewell
3. extend
4. dose
5. utter
6. hush

</td>
<td>

PART B
Reading Checkout Rules

1. If I read the passage in less than one minute, I get points as follows:
   No errors—3 points.
   1 or 2 errors—1 point.
   More than 2 errors—no points.
2. If I take more than one minute to read the passage, I get no points. But I will reread the passage until I can read it in one minute with no more than 2 errors.
3. I will write the number of points I earn in the checkout box for today's lesson.

</td></tr>
</table>

WORD PRACTICE AND VOCABULARY

EXERCISE 1   Word practice

1. Everybody, find lesson 31, part A in your skillbook. *Wait.* Touch under the first word in column 1. *Pause.*
   What word? *Signal.* **Towel.**
2. Next word. *Pause.*
   What word? *Signal.* **Vibrate.**
3. *Repeat step 2 for each remaining word in column 1.*
4. *Repeat the words in column 1 until firm.*
5. *Repeat steps 1–4 for column 2.*

EXERCISE 2   Vocabulary development

Task A

1. Everybody, touch column 3. *Check.*
   First you're going to read the words in column 3. Then we'll talk about what they mean.
2. Touch under the first word. *Pause.*
   What word? *Signal.* **Whisk.**
3. Next word. *Pause.*
   What word? *Signal.* **Farewell.**
4. *Repeat step 3 for each remaining word in column 3.*
5. *Repeat the words in column 3 until firm.*

Task B

1. Now let's talk about what those words mean. Word 1 is **whisk.** When something **whisks,** it moves like a broom that is sweeping.
2. Everybody, what's another way of saying **His tail moved like a broom?** *Signal.* **His tail whisked.**

Task C

Word 2 is **farewell.** Another word for **goodbye** is **farewell.** When you give somebody a **farewell,** you say **goodbye.**
Everybody, what do you give somebody when you say **goodbye?** *Signal.* **A farewell.**

Task D

Word 3 is **extend.** When something is stretched out very far, it is **extended.**
Everybody, show me how you extend your arms to the sides. *Check.*
What did you just do to your arms? *Signal.* **Extended them.**

Task E

Word 4 is **dose.** A **dose** of something is a certain amount of that thing. A certain amount of medicine is a **dose** of medicine. Everybody, what do we call a certain amount of medicine? *Signal.* **A dose of medicine.**

Task F

1. Word 5 is **utter.** Another word for **say** is **utter.** Everybody, what's another way of saying **He said a magic word?** *Signal.* **He uttered a magic word.**
2. Everybody, what's another way of saying **She said her name?** *Signal.* **She uttered her name.**

Task G

Word 6 is **hush.** A word that means **stop talking** is **hush.**
Everybody, what's another way of saying **The crowd suddenly stopped talking?** *Signal.* **The crowd suddenly hushed.**

Lesson 31

CHAPTER 26
The New Plan (A)

Dorothy was sad after the Wizard left without her. She was glad that Oz had a chance to leave the Emerald City, but she missed him. (B)

The Tin Woodman came to her and said, "I feel very sad, for the Wizard was the man who gave me my lovely heart. I would like to cry a little because Oz is gone. Will you kindly wipe away my tears, so that I will not rust?"

"With pleasure," she answered, and brought a towel at once. Then the Tin Woodman wept for several minutes, and she watched the tears and wiped them away with the towel. When he had finished, he thanked her kindly and oiled himself thoroughly, using his jeweled oilcan. (C) ★ 2 ERRORS ★

The Scarecrow was now the ruler of the Emerald City, and although he was not a Wizard the people were proud of him. They said, "There is not another city in all the world that is ruled by a stuffed man." And, so far as they knew, they were quite right.

The morning after the balloon had gone up with Oz, the four travelers met in the throne room and talked matters over. The Scarecrow sat on the big throne and the others stood before him. (D)

"We are not so unlucky," said the new ruler. (E) The Scarecrow continued, "This Palace and the Emerald City belong to us, and we can do whatever we want. Why, just a short time ago I was upon a pole in a farmer's cornfield, and now I am the ruler of this beautiful city, so I am quite satisfied with my life." (F)

The Lion said, "As for me, I am content to know that I am as brave as any beast that ever lived, if not braver."

The Tin Woodman said, "And as for me, I feel that my new heart is the kindest in the land."

"If Dorothy would be content to live in the Emerald City," said the Scarecrow, "we would all be happy together."

"But I don't want to live here," cried Dorothy. "I want to go to Kansas, and live with Aunt Em and Uncle Henry."

"Well, then, what can we do?" inquired the Tin Woodman.

The Scarecrow decided to think, and he thought so hard that the pins and needles in his head began to vibrate. (G)
★ 6 ERRORS ★

The others hushed while the Scarecrow thought. Finally the Scarecrow said, "Let us call in the soldier with the green whiskers and ask his advice."

So the soldier was called to the throne room. He entered timidly, for while Oz was ruler, the soldier had been allowed to come no farther than the door.

The Scarecrow said to the soldier, "This girl wants to cross the desert. How can she do so?"

"I do not know," answered the soldier. "Nobody has ever crossed the desert, other than Oz himself."

"Is there no one who can help me?" asked Dorothy earnestly.

"Glinda might," he suggested.

"Who is Glinda?" inquired the Scarecrow.

"The Witch of the South. She is the most powerful of all the Witches, and rules over the Quadlings. Glinda's castle stands on the edge of the desert, so she may know a way to cross it."

"Glinda is a good Witch, isn't she?" asked Dorothy.

"The Quadlings think she is good," said the soldier, "and she is kind to everyone. I have heard that Glinda is a beautiful woman who knows how to keep young in spite of the many years she has lived."

"How can I get to her castle?" asked Dorothy.

"The road to the south is straight," the soldier answered, "but it is said to be dangerous to travelers. There are wild beasts in the woods, and odd-looking men who can extend their arms and legs. For this reason, none of the Quadlings ever come to the Emerald City." The soldier then left them.

The Scarecrow said, "It seems, in spite of dangers, that the best thing Dorothy can do is to travel to the Land

---

STORY READING

EXERCISE 3 Decoding and comprehension

1. Everybody, turn to page 121 in your textbook. *Wait. Call on a student.* What's the error limit for this chapter? **6 errors.**
2. *Call on individual students to read. Present the tasks specified for each circled letter.*

(A) Where did we leave Dorothy at the end of the last chapter? *Idea:* Watching Oz leave without her.
- Why didn't she go in the balloon with Oz? *Idea:* Because she had to get Toto.
- How do you think she feels? *Idea:* Sad.

(B) Did Dorothy know how to get back to Kansas without the Wizard? **No.**

(C) What did the Tin Woodman use to oil himself with? *Idea:* His oilcan.
- Where did he get that? *Idea:* The Winkies gave it to him.

(D) Why did the Scarecrow sit on the throne? *Idea:* Because he was the ruler now.

(E) Who said that? **The Scarecrow.**

(F) Does the Scarecrow feel that things are bad? **No.**
- Why not? *Ideas:* Because now he is the ruler; because he is no longer on a pole; because he can do whatever he wants.

(G) Do you think the Scarecrow is going to come up with a good idea? **Yes.**
- Read the rest of the chapter to yourselves and be ready to answer some questions.

of the South and ask for Glinda to help her. For, of course, if Dorothy stays here she will never get back to Kansas."

The Tin Woodman remarked to the Scarecrow, "You must have been thinking again."

"I have been," said the Scarecrow.

"I will go with Dorothy," declared the Lion, "for I am tired of your city and long for the woods and the country again. I need a dose of fresh air. Besides, Dorothy will need someone to protect her."

"That is true," agreed the Tin Woodman. "My axe may be of service to her, so I will also go with her to the Land of the South."

"When should we start?" asked the Scarecrow.

"Are you going?" they asked, in surprise.

"Certainly. If it wasn't for Dorothy I would never have had brains. She lifted me from the pole in the cornfield and brought me to the Emerald City. So my good luck is all due to her, and I will never leave her until she starts back to Kansas."

"Thank you," said Dorothy, gratefully. "You are all very kind to me.

But I would like to start as soon as possible."

The Scarecrow said, "Why not call the Winged Monkeys and ask them to carry us to the Land of the South?"

"I never thought of that!" said Dorothy joyfully. "It's just the thing. I'll go at once for the golden cap."

She brought the cap into the throne room and uttered the magic words. Soon the band of Winged Monkeys flew in through the open window and stood beside her.

"This is the second time you have called us," said the King Monkey, bowing before Dorothy. "What do you want?"

"I want you to fly us to the Land of the South."

"It shall be done," said the king, and at once the Winged Monkeys took the four travelers and Toto in their arms and flew away with them. After a long journey, they set the group down in the beautiful country of the Quadlings.

"Farewell, and thank you very much," said Dorothy. And the Monkeys rose into the air and were out of sight in a moment.

Lesson 31   Textbook   **123**

After all students have finished reading:
- Which character might be able to help Dorothy? **Glinda.**
- In which Land does Glinda live? **The Land of the South.**
- Who carried Dorothy to that Land? **The Winged Monkeys.**

Award 4 points or have the students reread to the error limit sign.

EXERCISE 4   Individual reading checkout

1. *For the individual reading checkout, each student will read 100 words. The passage to be read is the shaded area on the reproduced textbook page for lesson 31 in this presentation book.*

2. Today is a reading checkout day. While you're doing your independent work, I'll call on each student to read part of yesterday's chapter.

3. When I call on you, come up to my desk and bring your textbook with you. After you have read, I'll tell you how many points you can write in the checkout box that's at the top of your workbook page.

4. *If the student finishes the passage in one minute or less, award points as follows:*

> 0 errors . . . . .3 points
> 1 or 2 errors . . . . .1 point
> More than 2 errors . . . . .0 points

5. *If a student takes more than one minute to read the passage, the student does not earn any points, but have the student reread the passage until he or she is able to read it in no more than one minute with no more than two errors.*

6. *Have the students read the reading checkout rules on page 44 in their skillbook.*

INDEPENDENT WORK

Do all the items in your skillbook and workbook for lesson 31.

ANSWER KEY FOR WORKBOOK

Map Skills

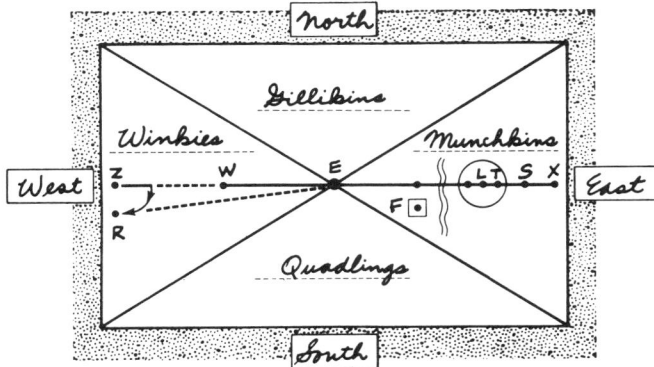

1. Write **North, East, South** and **West** in the boxes around the map.
2. On the map, write the name of the people who live in each land.
3. The map has **dots** to show where different things happened.
   a. Write **E** on the dot where the travelers met Oz.
   b. Write **X** on the dot where Dorothy's house landed.
   c. Write **Z** on the dot where Dorothy melted a witch.
   d. Write **F** on the dot where the Lion almost slept forever.
   e. Write **S** on the dot where Dorothy met the Scarecrow.
   f. Write **T** on the dot where Dorothy met the Tin Woodman.
   g. Write **L** on the dot where Dorothy met the Lion.
   h. Write **W** on the dot where the Monkeys **attacked** the travelers.
   i. Write **R** on the dot where the Monkeys **rescued** the travelers.

4. a. What does the circle show?
   Idea: the forest
   b. What does the wavy line show?
   Idea: the river
5. Some of the lines are **dotted**. How did the travelers move on those lines? **Circle the correct answer.**
   • in the air (circled)   • on the ground
   • by water   • in a cart

ANSWER KEY FOR SKILLBOOK

PART C

1. a. Oz
   b. No
2. a. *Idea:* He would have rusted
   b. Oil
3. a. The Scarecrow
   b. *Idea:* Because he was the new ruler
   c. The Lion, the Scarecrow, the Tin Woodman
   d. Dorothy
   e. *Idea:* Because she wanted to go back to Kansas
4. a. Glinda
   b. The Land of the South
   c. The Winged Monkeys

PART D

5. a. Witch of the West
   b. Witch of the North
   c. Witch of the East
   d. Witch of the West
   e. Witch of the North
   f. Witch of the West
   g. Witch of the East
6. a. preferred
   b. desperately
   c. rejoiced
   d. feast
   e. gently and lovingly
   f. on time
   g. inlaid
   h. together again
   i. spare
   j. bride

WORKCHECK AND AWARDING POINTS

1. *Read the questions and answers for the skillbook and workbook.*

2. *Award points for independent work as follows:*

0 errors	6 points
2 errors	4 points
3, 4, or 5 errors	2 points
5 or more errors	0 points

3. *Award bonus points as follows:*

Correcting missed items or getting all items right	2 points
Doing the writing assignment acceptably	2 points

4. *Remind the students to put the points they earned for their reading checkout, in the box labeled* **CO.**

Lesson 32 ✓

PART A	**Word Lists**	
1	2	3
ease	overheard	Vocabulary words
chorus	singe	1. disgusting
echo	grant	2. chorus
	crackling	
	giant	
	cackling	
	timid	
	timidly	

WORD PRACTICE AND VOCABULARY

EXERCISE 1   Word practice

1. Everybody, find lesson 32, part A in your skillbook. *Wait.* Touch column 1. *Check.*
The words in column 1 are hard words that will be in your reading stories.
2. Touch under the first word. *Check.*
The first word is **ease.**
What word? *Signal.* **Ease.**
3. Next word. *Pause.* That word is **chorus.**
What word? *Signal.* **Chorus.**
4. *Repeat step 3 for* **echo.**
5. Now let's see if you remember all those words. Touch under the first word in column 1. *Pause.*
What word? *Signal.* **Ease.**
6. Next word. *Pause.*
What word? *Signal.* **Chorus.**
7. *Repeat step 6 for* **echo.**
8. *Repeat the words in column 1 until firm.*

EXERCISE 2   Word practice

1. Everybody, touch under the first word in column 2. *Pause.*
What word? *Signal.* **Overhear.**
2. Next word. *Pause.*
What word? *Signal.* **Singe.**
3. *Repeat step 2 for each remaining word in column 2.*
4. *Repeat the words in column 2 until firm.*

EXERCISE 3   Vocabulary development

Task A

1. Everybody, touch column 3. *Check.*
First you're going to read the words in column 3. Then we'll talk about what they mean.
2. Touch under the first word. *Pause.*
What word? *Signal.* **Disgusting.**
3. Next word. *Pause.*
What word? *Signal.* **Chorus.**
4. *Repeat the words in column 3 until firm.*

Task B

1. Now let's talk about what those words mean.
Word 1 is **disgusting.** Something that is really horrible is **disgusting.**
Everybody, what's another way of saying
A really horrible spider? *Signal.*
A disgusting spider.
2. Everybody, what's another way of saying
A really horrible experience? *Signal.*
A disgusting experience.

Task C

Word 2 is **chorus.** A **chorus** of voices is a group of voices that do the same thing.
Everybody, what's another way of saying
A group of voices sang? *Signal.*
A chorus of voices sang.

Lesson 32

CHAPTER 27
The Silver Shoes Ⓐ

The Land of the Quadlings seemed rich and happy. There was field upon field of grain, with well-paved roads running between them. The fences and houses and bridges were all painted bright red, just as they had been painted yellow in the Land of the Winkies and blue in the Land of the Munchkins. Ⓑ The Quadlings were short and good-natured. They were dressed all in red. The red looked bright against the green grass and the yellow grain.

The Monkeys had set Dorothy and the others down near a farmhouse. ★2 ERRORS★ The travelers walked up to it and knocked on the door. It was opened by the farmer's wife, and when Dorothy asked for something to eat the woman gave Dorothy and the Lion a good dinner, with many fruits and nuts, and a bowl of milk for Toto. Ⓒ

"How far is it to Glinda's castle?" asked Dorothy.

"It is not a great way," answered the farmer's wife. "Take the road to the south and you will soon reach it."

They thanked the good woman and started walking by the fields and across the pretty red bridges until they saw a very beautiful red castle in front of them.

Three young girls were in front of the gates, dressed in handsome red uniforms trimmed with gold braid. As Dorothy approached, one of them said to her, "Why have you come to the South Country?"

"To see the good Witch who rules here," she answered. "Will you take me to her?"

"Tell me your name and I will ask Glinda if she will see you," said the girl. Ⓓ

Dorothy and the others told her who they were, and the girl soldier went into the castle. After a few moments she came back to say that Dorothy and the others could see Glinda at once.

Before they went to see Glinda, however, they were taken to a room of the castle, where Dorothy washed her face and combed her hair. The Lion shook the dust out of his mane. The Scarecrow patted himself into his best shape. The Tin Woodman polished his tin and oiled his joints. Ⓔ

Then Dorothy and the others followed the girl soldier into a big room where the Witch Glinda sat upon a throne of rubies. Ⓕ

Glinda looked both beautiful and

124   Lesson 32   Textbook

young to them. Her hair was a rich red and flowed over her shoulders. Ⓖ Her dress was pure white and her eyes were blue. She looked at the girl in a kindly way.

"What can I do for you?" she asked.

Dorothy told the Witch her story. She told how the cyclone had brought her to the Land of Oz and how she had found her companions, and of the wonderful adventures they had had.

"My greatest wish now," she added, "is to get back to Kansas, for Aunt Em will surely think something dreadful has happened to me, and that will make her and my uncle very sad."

Glinda leaned forward and kissed Dorothy.

"Bless your dear heart," Glinda said. "If I tell you of a way to get back to Kansas, will you give me the golden cap?" Ⓗ

"Certainly!" exclaimed Dorothy. "I have it with me now, and when you have it you can command the Winged Monkeys three times."

Glinda smiled and said, "I know just what to do with those three commands."

Dorothy gave the golden cap to the Witch. Then Glinda said to the Scarecrow, "What will you do when Dorothy has left us?"

"I will return to the Emerald City," the Scarecrow replied, "for Oz has made me its ruler, and the people like me. The only thing that worries me is how to return there, for the road to Oz is very dangerous."

"I will command the Winged Monkeys to carry you to the gates of the Emerald City," said Glinda.

Turning to the Tin Woodman, Glinda asked, "What will become of you when Dorothy leaves this country?"

The Tin Woodman leaned on his axe and thought a moment. Then he said, "I became a Tin Woodman because I loved a Munchkin maiden. I would like to go back to the Land of the East and marry her." Ⓘ ★11 ERRORS★

Glinda said to the Tin Woodman, "My second command to the Winged Monkeys will be to carry you safely to the Land of the East so that you may find your maiden."

Then the Witch looked at the big, shaggy Lion and asked, "When Dorothy has returned to her own home, what will become of you?"

The Lion answered, "There is a grand old forest where I used to live and be the king. If I could only get back to that forest, I would be very happy there."

Glinda said, "My third command to the Winged Monkeys will be to carry you to your forest. Then, since I will have used up the powers of the golden cap, I will give it to the King of the Monkeys, so that he and his band may be free at last."

The Scarecrow and the Tin Woodman and the Lion thanked the good Witch Glinda earnestly for her kindness. Dorothy exclaimed, "You are certainly as good as you are beautiful!"

Lesson 32   Textbook   125

EXERCISE 4   Decoding and comprehension

1. Everybody, turn to page 124 in your textbook. *Wait. Call on a student.* What's the error limit for this chapter? 11 errors.

2. *Call on individual students to read. Present the tasks specified for each circled letter.*

Ⓐ This is the last chapter of the novel. We'll find out if Dorothy ever gets back to Kansas.

Ⓑ What color is everything in the Land of the Munchkins? Blue.

● What color is everything in the Land of the Winkies? Yellow.

● What color is everything in the Land of the Quadlings? Red.

● What color is everything in the Emerald City? Green.

Ⓒ What did Dorothy and the Lion have with their dinner? *Idea:* Many fruits and nuts.

Ⓓ Who did Dorothy and the others see outside the gate of the Castle? *Idea:* Three young girls.

● Do you think Glinda will see them? *Response:* Student preference.

Ⓔ Where were they? *Idea:* In a room of the Castle.

● What did Dorothy do to get ready to see Glinda? *Idea:* Washed her face and combed her hair.

● What did the Lion do? *Idea:* Shook the dust out of his mane.

● What did the Scarecrow do? *Idea:* Patted himself into shape.

● What did the Tin Woodman do? *Idea:* Polished his tin and oiled his joints.

Ⓕ What color are rubies? Red.

Ⓖ Everybody, show me how long her hair was.

Ⓗ What is Glinda going to do to get the golden cap? *Idea:* Tell Dorothy of a way to get back to Kansas.

Ⓘ What does the Scarecrow want to do? *Idea:* Return to the Emerald City.

● What does the Tin Woodman want to do? *Idea:* Marry the maiden.

● Read the rest of the chapter to yourselves and be ready to answer some questions.

After all students have finished reading:

● How many times did Glinda plan to use the golden cap to help Dorothy and the others? *Idea:* Three times.

● Then what did she plan to do with the golden cap? *Idea:* Give it back to the Winged Monkeys.

● How would she use the cap to help the Lion? *Idea:* Command the Winged Monkeys to carry the Lion to the forest.

But you have not yet told me how to get back to Kansas."

"Your silver shoes will carry you over the desert," replied Glinda. "If you had known their power you could have gone back to your Aunt Em the very first day you came to this country."

"But then I would not have had my wonderful brains!" cried the Scarecrow. "I might have passed my whole life in the farmer's cornfield."

"And I would not have had my lovely heart," said the Tin Woodman. "I might have stood and rusted in the forest until the end of the world."

"And I would have been a coward forever," declared the Lion. "And no beast in all the forest would have had a good word to say to me."

"This is all true," said Dorothy, "and I am glad I was of use to these good friends. But now that each of them has what he wanted most, I think I would like to go back to Kansas."

"The silver shoes," said the good Witch, "have wonderful powers. And one of the most curious things about them is that they can carry you to any place in the world in the wink of an eye. All you have to do is to knock the heels together three times and command the shoes to carry you wherever you want to go."

"If that is so," said Dorothy, "I will ask them to carry me back to Kansas at once."

She threw her arms around the Lion's neck and kissed him, patting his big head tenderly. Then she kissed the Tin Woodman, who was weeping in a way that was very dangerous to his joints. Then she hugged the soft, stuffed body of the Scarecrow in her arms. Dorothy felt very sad at the thought of leaving her good friends.

Glinda stepped down from her ruby throne and Dorothy thanked her for all the kindness she had shown.

Dorothy picked up Toto and said one last goodbye to her companions. Then she clapped the heels of her shoes together three times, saying, "Take me home to Aunt Em and Uncle Henry!"

Instantly she was whirling through the air, so swiftly that all she could see or feel was the wind whistling past her ears.

Suddenly, Dorothy noticed that she was rolling over on the ground. She sat up and looked around her.

"Oh my!" she cried. She was sitting on the broad Kansas prairie, and just in front of her was the new farmhouse Uncle Henry had built after the cyclone had carried away the old one. Uncle Henry was milking the cows in the barnyard. Toto instantly jumped out of Dorothy's arms and ran toward the barn, whisking his tail from side to side.

Dorothy stood up and found she was in her stocking feet, for the silver shoes had fallen off in her flight through the air, and were lost forever in the desert.

Aunt Em had just come out of the house to water the cabbages when she looked up and saw Dorothy running toward her.

- How did Glinda tell Dorothy to get back to Kansas? *Idea:* To use the power of her silver shoes.
- What did Dorothy have to do to make the shoes work? *Idea:* Knock the heels together three times and tell the shoes to take her back to Kansas.
- What was new in Kansas when Dorothy came back? *Idea:* The house.
- Did she still have the silver shoes? **No.**
- When Dorothy lost her silver shoes, she found she was in her stocking feet. What does that mean: **stocking feet?** *Idea:* She was just wearing her socks.
- How did she feel? *Idea:* Very happy.
- What color had Kansas been before Dorothy left for the Land of Oz? **Gray.**
- *Call on individual students.* How had the colors changed? *Ideas:* The sky was blue; the grass was green; there were yellow flowers; Aunt Em's cheeks were red; the house was white.
- Do you think the colors really changed or that Dorothy had changed? *Response:* Student preference.
  This novel tells us something about what the people wanted and the power they had.
- What did the Scarecrow want? **Brains.**
- But didn't he really have them all the time? **Yes.**
- What did the Tin Woodman want? **A heart.**
- But didn't he have strong feelings before Oz gave him a fake heart? **Yes.**
- What did the Lion want? **Courage.**
- Do you think he had courage in the first place? **Yes.**
- What did Dorothy want? *Idea:* To get back to Kansas.
- And didn't she have the power to get there all the time? **Yes.**
  Here's one thing the novel tells us: You have the power to be whatever you want to be.
  You just have to recognize that power.

Award 4 points or have the students reread to the error limit sign.

"My darling child!" she cried, hugging Dorothy. "Where in the world did you come from?"

"From the Land of Oz," said Dorothy gravely. "And here is Toto, too. And oh, Aunt Em! I'm so glad to be at home again!"

Dorothy told of her story in the Land of Oz, while Aunt Em and Uncle Henry listened, not sure what to make of such a strange tale. But they were indeed glad to have Dorothy back with them once more. After Dorothy finished her story, she looked around and noticed something very strange. No longer was everything gray. The grass seemed almost as green as the Emerald City. And Aunt Em's cheeks seemed to be redder, as if they had been touched with the color from the Land of the Quadlings. The sky was bluer, nearly as blue as the Land of the Munchkins. The sun was as yellow as the Land of the Winkies. And her new house seemed almost as white as Glinda's beautiful dress.

"Oh my," she said to herself with tears in her eyes. "There is no place like home."

THE END

ANSWER KEY FOR WORKBOOK

Review Items

1. Tell which character each sentence describes.
   a. This character was so sad when Oz left that he began to cry.

   Woodman

   b. This character was not hurt when he fell down.

   Scarecrow

   c. This character was the new ruler of the Emerald City.

   Scarecrow

   d. City life did not agree with this character.

   Lion

   e. This character ruled over the Quadlings.

   Glinda

   f. This character lost a shoe over the desert.

   Dorothy

2. Write whether each thing could happen to you in the **field of flowers,** the **river** or the **throne room.**
   a. You see a lovely lady with wings.

   throne room

   b. Your raft gets carried away by the current.

   river

   c. You see a chair made of emeralds.

   throne room

   d. A strong smell puts you to sleep.

   field of flowers

   e. You see hundreds of red flowers.

   field of flowers

   f. You see a little old man in the corner.

   throne room

INDEPENDENT WORK

Do all the items in your skillbook and workbook for lesson 32.

WORKCHECK AND AWARDING POINTS

1. *Read the questions and answers for the skillbook and workbook.*

2. *Award points for independent work as follows:*

0 errors	6 points
2 errors	4 points
3, 4, or 5 errors	2 points
5 or more errors	0 points

3. *Award bonus points as follows:*

Correcting missed items or getting all items right	2 points
Doing the writing assignment acceptably	2 points

ANSWER KEY FOR SKILLBOOK
PART B

1. Red
2. **a.** Rubies
   b. Red
   c. White
3. **a.** The golden cap
   b. To the Emerald City
   c. *Idea:* Rule over the people
   d. To the Land of the East
   e. *Idea:* Marry the Munchkin maiden
   f. To the forest
   g. *Ideas:* Rule over the animals; be the King of Beasts

PART C

4. *Ideas:* Knock the heels together; tell the shoes where to take her
5. **a.** There is no place like home
   b. Green
   c. Blue
   d. Yellow
   e. Red
6. **a.** Munchkins
   b. Winged Monkeys
   c. Winged Monkeys
   d. Winkies
   e. Munchkins
   f. Winkies
7. **a.** desperately
   b. acted very happy
   c. pleaded
   d. mischief
   e. spare
   f. ventriloquist
   g. imitate
   h. confidence
   i. considered
   j. gradual
   k. experience
   l. congratulated
   m. deceived

Lesson 33

Lesson 33

PART A   **Word Lists**

1	2	3
snarling	Vocabulary words	Vocabulary words
worry	1. extend	1. reeds
braid	2. chorus	2. ease
worries	3. hush	3. echo
fierce	4. utter	4. bruise
duckling	5. disgusting	
valley		
blossom		
swan		

PART B   **Hyphens**

Sometimes, words that appear at the end of a printed line are too long to fit on that line. So only the first part of the word appears on the line. That part is followed by a hyphen, which is a mark that looks like this: –Ⓐ

The rest of the word appears at the beginning of the next line.

The next column has a passage with words that run from the end of one line to the beginning of the next line.Ⓑ

That morning Dorothy kissed the pretty green girl goodbye. Then the four travelers walked through the Emerald City toward the gate. When the guard saw them approaching, he knew that they were planning to go on a new adventure. As he unlocked their green spectacles, he congratulated the Scarecrow, who was now the ruler of the city. The guard smiled and gladly shook the Scarecrow's hand.

WORD PRACTICE AND VOCABULARY

EXERCISE 1   Word practice

1. Everybody, find lesson 33, part A in your skillbook. *Wait.* Touch under the first word in column 1. *Pause.*
   What word? *Signal.* **Snarling.**
2. Next word. *Pause.*
   What word? *Signal.* **Worry.**
3. *Repeat step 2 for each remaining word in column 1.*
4. *Repeat the words in column 1 until firm.*

EXERCISE 2   Vocabulary review

Task A

1. Everybody, touch column 2. *Check.*
   First you're going to read the words in column 2. Then we'll talk about what they mean.
2. Touch under the first word. *Pause.*
   What word? *Signal.* **Extend.**
3. Next word. *Pause.*
   What word? *Signal.* **Chorus.**
4. *Repeat step 3 for each remaining word in column 2.*
5. *Repeat the words in column 2 until firm.*

Task B

You've learned the meanings for all these words. Word 1 is **extend.** Everybody, show me how you **extend** your arms to the sides. *Check.* What did you just do to your arms? *Signal.* **Extended them.**

Task C

Word 2 is **chorus.** *Call on a student.*
What is a **chorus?** *Idea:* A group of voices.

Task D

1. Word 3 is **hush.** *Call on a student.*
   What does **hush** mean? *Idea:* To stop talking.
2. Everybody, what's another way of saying **The children suddenly stopped talking?**
   Signal. **The children suddenly hushed.**

Task E

1. Word 4 is **utter.** *Call on a student.*
   What does **utter** mean? *Idea:* Say.
2. Everybody, what's another way of saying He said the alphabet? *Signal.*
   He uttered the alphabet.

Task F

1. Word 5 is **disgusting.** *Call on a student.* What does **disgusting** mean? *Idea:* Really horrible.

2. Everybody, what's another way of saying **A really horrible monster?** *Signal.* **A disgusting monster.**

3. Everybody, what's another way of saying **A really horrible experience?** *Signal.* **A disgusting experience.**

EXERCISE 3 Vocabulary development

Task A

1. Everybody, touch column 3. *Check.* First you're going to read the words in column 3. Then we'll talk about what they mean.

2. Touch under the first word. *Pause.* What word? *Signal.* **Reeds.**

3. Next word. *Pause.* What word? *Signal.* **Ease.**

4. *Repeat step 3 for each remaining word in column 3.*

5. *Repeat the words in column 3 until firm.*

Task B

Now let's talk about what those words mean. Word 1 is **reeds.** Everybody, look at the picture on page 129 of your textbook. *Wait.* The tall grasses growing on the edge of the water are called **reeds.** Everybody, touch the **reeds.** *Check.* What are those grasses called? *Signal.* **Reeds.**

Task C

Word 2 is **ease.** When you do something with **ease,** it's very easy for you to do.

Task D

Word 3 is **echo.** When a sound **echoes,** you can hear it again and again, but it gets softer. Here's an **echo:** "**hello,** hello, hello. . ."

Task E

Word 4 is **bruise.** A **bruise** is a place on your body that is sore. It may be red, or it may be black and blue. Everybody, what do we call a black and blue mark? *Signal.* **A bruise.**

EXERCISE 4 Hyphens

1. Everybody, look at part B. *Call on individual students to read. Present the tasks specified for each circled letter.*

Ⓐ Everybody, what is that mark called? *Signal.* **A hyphen.**

Ⓑ I'll read all the words in each line except the last word. Everybody will read that word together.

● That morning Dorothy kissed the . . . Everybody, figure out the next word and get ready to say it. What word? *Signal.* **Pretty.**

● green girl goodbye. Then the four . . . Everybody, what word? *Signal.* **Travelers.**

● walked through the Emerald City . . . Everybody, what word? *Signal.* **Toward.**

● the gate. When the guard saw them . . . Everybody, what word? *Signal.* **Approaching.**

● he knew that they were . . . Everybody, what word? *Signal.* **Planning.**

● to go on a new adventure. As he . . . Everybody, what word? *Signal.* **Unlocked.**

● their green spectacles, he . . . Everybody, what word? *Signal.* **Congratulated.**

● the Scarecrow, who was now the . . . Everybody, what word? *Signal.* **Ruler.**

● of the city. The guard smiled and . . . Everybody, what word? *Signal.* **Gladly.**

● shook the Scarecrow's hand.

Lesson 33

The Ugly Duckling
by Hans Christian Andersen Ⓐ
PART 1

It was summer, and the valley was beautiful. The wheat was yellow, the oats were green, and the hay was golden. A river flowed through the valley, next to riverbanks that were covered with tall reeds.Ⓑ

It was under those reeds that a duck had built herself a warm nest and was now sitting all day on six eggs. Five of them were white, but the sixth, which was larger than the others, was an ugly gray color. The duck was always puzzled about the egg and wondered why it was so different from the rest. She often wondered if another bird had slipped the egg in while she was swimming in the river. But ducks are neither clever, nor good at counting. So this duck did not worry herself about the egg, but just made sure that it was as warm as the rest.Ⓒ

Because this set of eggs was the first one the duck had ever laid, she was very pleased and proud, even though she was tired of sitting in her nest. However, she knew that if she left her eggs, the ducklings in them might die. So she stayed in her nest, getting off the eggs several times a day only to see if the shells were cracking.Ⓓ

The mother duck had looked at the eggs at least a hundred and fifty times when to her joy she saw tiny cracks on two of them. She hurried back to the nest and drew the eggs closer to each other. Then she sat on them for the rest of the day. The next morning, she noticed cracks in the five white eggs, and by midday two little heads were poking out from the shells. She broke the shells with her bill so that the little ducklings could get out of them. Then she sat steadily for a whole night upon the others. Before the sun arose, the five white eggs were empty, and five pairs of eyes were gazing out upon the green world.Ⓔ

Now the duck had been carefully brought up and did not like dirt, and besides, broken egg shells are not at all comfortable things to sit or walk upon. So the duck pushed the shells out over the side of the nest. She felt delighted to have some other ducks to talk to until the last egg hatched. But day after day went by, and the big egg showed no signs of cracking. The duck grew more and more impatient.

"This egg is a real problem," the duck grumbled to her neighbor one day. "Why, I could have hatched ten eggs in the time that this one has taken."

"Let me look at it," said the neighbor. "Ah, I thought so; it is a turkey's egg. Once, when I was young, I was tricked into sitting on a nest of turkey eggs, and when they were hatched the birds were so stupid that I could not even teach them how to swim."Ⓕ

★8 ERRORS★

"Well, I will give this big egg another chance," sighed the mother duck, "but if it does not come out of its shell in another twenty-four hours, I will just leave it alone and teach the rest of my ducks how to swim properly and how to find their own food. I really can't be expected to do two things at once." And with a fluff of her feathers she pushed the egg into the middle of the nest.

All through the next day she sat on the egg, even giving up her morning bath for fear that a blast of cold air might strike the big egg. In the evening, when she looked at the egg, she thought she saw a tiny crack in the upper part of the shell. She was so filled with hope that she could hardly sleep all night. When the sun arose, she felt something stirring under her. Yes, there it was at last, and as she moved, a big awkward bird tumbled headfirst onto the ground.

The duckling was quite ugly. The mother looked with surprise at the dull brown feathers that covered his back,

---

STORY READING

EXERCISE 5   Decoding and comprehension

1. **Everybody, turn to page 129 in your textbook.** *Wait. Call on a student.* **What's the error limit for this lesson? 8 errors.**

2. *Call on individual students to read. Present the tasks specified for each letter.*

Ⓐ **Hans Christian Andersen was a famous writer from the country of Denmark. He wrote almost two hundred short stories, most of which were fantasies. "The Ugly Duckling" is one of his best known stories.**

Ⓑ **Everybody, close your eyes and get a picture of the valley. Picture the yellow wheat, the green oats, and the golden hay. Picture a river flowing through that valley and picture tall green reeds along the riverbank.**

Ⓒ **Did the mother duck know whether another bird had put a strange egg in the nest? No.**

• **Why not?** *Idea:* Ducks aren't clever or good at counting.

Ⓓ **What does that mean: if the shells were cracking?** *Idea:* The babies were hatching.

• **What would have happened if the mother duck decided not to sit on the eggs all day?** *Ideas:* The eggs wouldn't hatch; the ducklings might die.

Ⓔ **How many eggs did she start out with in her nest? Six.**

• **How many had hatched? Five.**

• **Which egg had not yet hatched?** *Idea:* The big gray egg.

Ⓕ **What kind of eggs had the neighbor duck been tricked into hatching? Turkey eggs.**

• **What kind of trouble did she have with them after they hatched?** *Idea:* She couldn't teach them to swim.

• **Read the rest of the story to yourselves and be ready to answer some questions.**

After all students have finished reading:

• **How long did the mother duck say that she would try to sit on the egg and hatch it? 24 hours more.**

• **Why didn't she want to spend more time than 24 hours more sitting on that egg?** *Idea:* She had to teach her ducklings how to swim and find food.

and at his long clumsy neck. He did not look at all like the little yellow ducklings who were playing in the nest.

The old neighbor came over the next day to look at the new duckling. "No, it is not a young turkey," she said to the mother. "It is skinny and brown, but there is something rather beautiful about it, and it holds its head up well."

"It is very kind of you to say so," answered the mother. "Of course, when you see it by itself it seems all right, but when I compare it with the others, I can see how different it is. However, I cannot expect *all* my children to be beautiful."

Later that day, the mother and her ducklings went down to a clearing by the river. Some full-grown ducks were swimming in the river, and others were waddling around and quacking in chorus. One large duck quacked much louder than the rest, and when he saw the ugly duckling, he said, in a voice that seemed to echo: "I have never seen anything as ugly as that great tall duckling. He is a disgrace. I shall go and chase him away." And he ran up to the brown duckling and bit his neck, making a small bruise.

The brown duckling gave out a loud quack; it was the first time he had felt any pain. His mother turned around quickly.

"Leave him alone," she said fiercely. "What has he done to you?"

"Nothing," answered the loud duck. "But he is so disgusting that I can't stand him."

Although the brown duckling did not understand the meaning of the words that the mean duck had said, he felt he was being blamed for something. He became even more uncomfortable when the mean duck said, "It certainly *is* a great shame that he is so different from the rest of us. Too bad he can't be hatched over again."

The poor little fellow dropped his head, and did not know what to do, but was comforted when his mother answered, "He may not be quite as handsome as the others, but he swims with ease, and he is very strong. I am sure he will make his way in the world as well as anybody."

"I doubt it," said the loud duck, as he waddled off.

Life was very hard for the duckling after that day. He was snapped at by the big ducks when they thought his mother was not looking. Even his brothers and sisters mocked him. Yet, they would not have noticed how different he was if they hadn't heard the loud duck's complaints.

The ugly duckling became sadder and sadder. At last he could bear it no longer and decided to run away. So one night, when the other ducks were asleep, he slipped quietly out of the nest and made his way through the reeds.

Lesson 33 Textbook **131**

- Did the egg hatch in 24 hours? **Yes.**
- What color was the bird inside the egg? **Brown.**
- How else was the bird different from the other ducklings? *Ideas:* It was ugly; it was skinny; it had a long neck.
- Did the mother think that the brown duckling was beautiful? **No.**
- What did the adult duck with the loud voice do when the mother duck brought her ducklings to the river? *Idea:* He called the duckling ugly and bit him.
- After that day, what would the big ducks do when the mother duck wasn't watching? *Idea:* Snapped at the ugly duckling.
- Would the duckling's brothers and sisters have made fun of him if the other ducks hadn't picked on him? **No.**
- What did the brothers and sisters do to make life miserable for the brown duckling? *Idea:* They were mean to him.
- What did the ugly duckling finally decide to do? *Idea:* Run away.
- What were the other ducklings and the mother duck doing when he slipped away? **Sleeping.**

Award 4 points or have the students reread to the error limit sign.

INDEPENDENT WORK

Do all the items in your skillbook and workbook for lesson 33.

ANSWER KEY FOR WORKBOOK

Map Skills

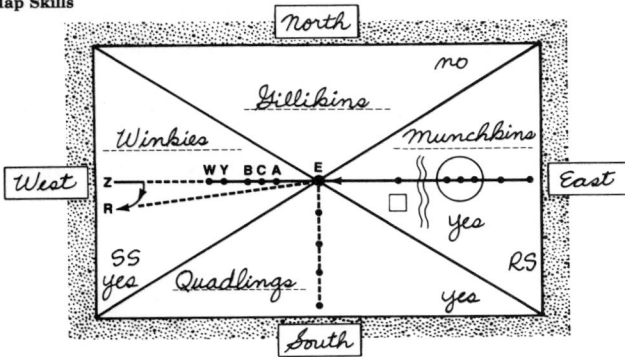

1. Write **North**, **East**, **South** and **West** in the boxes around the map.
2. On the map, write the name of the people who live in each land.
3. a. Write **RS** on the land that is closest to the **rising** sun.
   b. Write **SS** on the land that is closest to the **setting** sun.
4. a. Write **yes** on the lands the travelers visited.
   b. Write **no** on the lands the travelers did not visit.
5. The letters on the map show where things happened.
   a. The **A** shows where the travelers were attacked on the way to the Witch's Castle. Which animals attacked them at **A**?
      wolves
   b. Which animals attacked them at **C**?
      crows
   c. Which animals attacked them at **B**?
      bees
   d. Which people attacked them at **Y**?
      Winkies
   e. Which animals attacked them at **W**?
      Winged Monkeys
   f. Who melted at **Z**? *Idea:*
      Witch of the West
   g. Who rescued them at **R**?
      Winged Monkeys
   h. Who carried them from **R** to **E**?
      Winged Monkeys
7. Write the direction the travelers went to get to Glinda's Castle.
      South

WORKCHECK AND AWARDING POINTS

1. *Read the questions and answers for the skillbook and workbook.*
2. *Award points for independent work as follows:*

0 errors	*6 points*
2 errors	*4 points*
3, 4, or 5 errors	*2 points*
5 or more errors	*0 points*

3. *Award bonus points as follows:*

Correcting missed items or getting all items right	*2 points*
Doing the writing assignment acceptably	*2 points*

ANSWER KEY FOR SKILLBOOK

PART C

1. a. 6
   b. White
   c. Gray
   d. *Ideas:* The eggs wouldn't hatch; the ducklings might die
2. a. *Idea:* Never
   b. *Idea:* To see if the shells were cracking
3. a. The five eggs
   b. *Idea:* Ducklings
   c. A turkey egg
4. a. brown
   b. *Any two:* Ugly; skinny, clumsy
   c. *Idea:* Badly
5. a. *Idea:* Run away
   b. Sleeping
6. a. mother duck
   b. mother duck
   c. ugly duckling
   d. ugly duckling
   e. mean duck
   f. mother duck
   g. ugly duckling
   h. mean duck

PART D

7. a. tenderly
   b. promptly
   c. caught
   d. swarm
   e. ventriloquist
   f. confidence
   g. pack
   h. gradually
   i. trick
   j. flock
   k. replace
   l. bride

Lesson 34

Lesson 34

PART A	Word Lists	PART B	Hyphens

1
blow
scratch
strangle
bowl
stretch
struggle

2
Vocabulary words
1. reflection
2. moss

What is the name for this mark: – ?Ⓐ
   Read the hyphenated words in the passage below.Ⓑ
   The sun was bright as the friends slowly turned toward the Land of the Quadlings. They were all cheerful and chatted happily. Dorothy was now almost certain that she would get home, and the Woodman smiled at her. The brave Lion was wagging his tail back and forth. He was joyful to be outside again. Toto was chasing butterflies, jumping around, and barking merrily all the time.

WORD PRACTICE AND VOCABULARY

EXERCISE 1   Word practice

1. Everybody, find lesson 34, part A in your skillbook. *Wait.* Touch under the first word in column 1. *Pause.* What word? *Signal.* **Blow.**
2. Next word. *Pause.* What word? *Signal.* **Scratch.**
3. *Repeat step 2 for each remaining word in the column.*
4. *Repeat the words in the column until firm.*

EXERCISE 2   Vocabulary development

Task A
1. Everybody, touch column 2. *Check.* First you're going to read the words in column 2. Then we'll talk about what they mean.
2. Touch under the first word. *Pause.* What word? *Signal.* **Reflection.**
3. Next word. *Pause.* What word? *Signal.* **Moss.**

Task B
1. Now let's talk about what those words mean. Word 1 is **reflection.** A **reflection** is the image that you see in a mirror. Everybody, what do we call the image you see in a mirror? *Signal.* **A reflection.**
2. What other kind of surface could you look at and see a **reflection?** *Ideas:* Water; shiny objects; windows.

Task C
Word 2 is **moss. Moss** is made up of tiny green plants that like to grow in the shade. Sometimes moss grows on the shady trunks of trees.

EXERCISE 3   Hyphens

1. Everybody, look at part B.
   Call on individual students to read. Present the tasks specified for each circled letter.
Ⓐ Everybody, what's the answer? *Signal.*
   A hyphen.
Ⓑ I'll read all the words in each line except the last word. Everybody will read that word together.
   • The sun was bright as the friends . . .
     Everybody, what word? *Signal.* **Slowly.**
   • turned toward the Land of the . . .
     Everybody, what word? *Signal.* **Quadlings.**
   • They were all cheerful and . . .
     Everybody, what word? *Signal.* **Chatted.**
   • happily. Dorothy was now almost . . .
     Everybody, what word? *Signal.* **Certain.**
   • that she would get home, and the . . .
     Everybody, what word? *Signal.* **Woodman.**
   • smiled at her. The brave Lion was . . .
     Everybody, what word? *Signal.* **Wagging.**
   • his tail back and forth. He was . . .
     Everybody, what word? *Signal.* **Joyful.**
   • to be outside again. Toto was . . .
     Everybody, what word? *Signal.* **Chasing.**
   • butterflies, jumping around, and . . .
     Everybody, what word? *Signal.* **Barking.**
   • merrily all the time.

The Ugly Duckling

PART 2

The ugly duckling walked for a long time that night. At last he reached a wide plain, full of soft, mossy places where the reeds grew. Here he rested, but he was too tired and too frightened to fall asleep. The reeds began to move when the sun rose, and the duckling saw that he had accidentally ventured into a group of wild geese. Ⓐ

"You *are* ugly," said the wild geese when they had looked him over. "But it does not matter to us, so you are welcome to stay here."

So for two whole days the duckling lay quietly among the reeds, eating what food he could find, and drinking the marsh water until he felt strong again. He wanted to stay where he was forever, for he was so comfortable and happy, away from the other ducks, with nobody to bite him and tell him how ugly he was. Ⓑ

He was thinking about how contented he was, when two young geese saw him. They were having their evening splash among the reeds, looking for their supper.

"We are tired of this place," they said. "So tomorrow we will fly to another place, where the lakes are larger and the food is better. Will you come with us?"

"Is it nicer than this place?" asked the duckling doubtfully. The words were hardly out of his mouth when two shots rang out and the two geese were stretched dead before him. Ⓒ

At the sound of the gun the rest of the wild geese flew into the air. For a few minutes the firing continued. While the shooting was going on, the ugly duckling, who could not fly, waddled along through the shallow water. He had gone just a few feet when he noticed a dog standing on the bank gazing at him, with a long red tongue hanging out of its mouth. The duckling grew cold with terror and tried to hide his head beneath his little wings. But the dog sniffed at him and trotted away. Now the duckling was able to hide himself in some tall reeds.

"I am so ugly that dogs won't eat me," he said to himself. Ⓓ The duckling curled up in the soft grass until the shots died away in the distance. ★6 ERRORS★

He stayed in the reeds for several months. For a while he was quite happy and content; but winter was approaching.

Snow began to fall, and everything became wet and uncomfortable.

One day in late fall the sun was setting like a great scarlet globe, and the river, to the duckling's amazement, was getting hard and slippery. The duckling heard a sound of whirring wings. High up in the air a flock of swans flew by. They were as white as the snow that had fallen during the night, and their long necks with yellow bills were stretched toward the south. They were going to a land that was warm in the winter. Oh, if he only could have gone with them! But that was not possible, of course. Besides, what sort of companion would an ugly duckling like him be to those beautiful swans?

Every morning grew colder and colder, and the duckling had to work hard to keep himself warm. Soon, he was never warm.

After one bitterly cold night, he discovered that he could not move his legs, and that his feathers were frozen to his body. The duckling's life might have ended that day; however, a man walked through the reeds and saw what had happened. He picked up the duckling and tucked him under his sheepskin coat, where the duckling's frozen feathers began to thaw a little.

Instead of going on to his work, the man turned back and took the bird to his children, who gave the bird something to eat. Then they put him in a box by the fire before they went to school. When the children returned from school, the duckling was much more comfortable than he had been in a long time. They were kind children, and wanted to play with him, but the duckling had never played in his life. He thought that the children were trying to tease him, and he ran straight out the door, and hid himself in the snow among the bushes at the back of the house.

He never could remember exactly how he spent the rest of the winter. He knew only that he was very cold and that he never had enough to eat. But eventually things grew better. The earth became softer, and the sun felt hotter. The birds sang, and the flowers once more appeared in the grass. When the duckling stood up, he felt different than he had ever felt before. His body seemed larger, and his wings stronger. Something pink looked at him from the side of a hill. He thought he would fly toward it and see what it was. He spread his wings and in a moment he was flying.

Oh, how glorious it felt to be rushing through the air, wheeling first one way and then the other! He had never thought that flying could be like that! The duckling was almost sorry when he drew near the pink thing and found that it was only a small apple tree covered with pink blossoms. The apple tree was beside a cottage. Behind the cottage, a garden ran down to the banks of a river.

The duckling fluttered slowly to the

EXERCISE 4   Decoding and comprehension

1. Everybody, turn to page 132 in your textbook. *Wait. Call on a student.* What's the error limit for this lesson? **6 errors.**
2. *Call on individual students to read. Present the task specified for each circled letter.*

Ⓐ Why had the duckling left his own nest? *Idea:* Because all the other ducks were mean to him.

● What time of day was it when he had left? **Nighttime.**

● What had he accidentally ventured into? *Idea:* A group of wild geese.

● How do you think those geese will treat him? *Response:* Student preference.

Ⓑ How long had he been with the geese? **Two days.**

● How did he feel with them? *Idea:* Comfortable and happy.

Ⓒ What happened? *Idea:* A hunter shot the geese.

Ⓓ Why did he think that the dog wouldn't eat him? *Idea:* He was too ugly.

● Read the rest of the story to yourselves and be ready to answer some questions.

After all students have finished reading:

● How did the weather change after the duck had left the geese? *Idea:* It got colder. The story says that the river became hard and slippery.

● What was happening to the river? *Idea:* It was freezing.

● What did the duckling see in the sky overhead just before the winter set in? **Swans.**

● What color were the swans? **White.**

● In which direction were the swans going? **South.**

● Why? *Idea:* Because they wanted to go where it was warm.

● What happened to the duckling one bitterly cold night? *Idea:* His feathers froze to his body.

● Who saved him? **A man.**

● What did the duckling think was happening when the children were trying to play with him? *Idea:* He thought they were teasing him.

● So, what did he do? *Idea:* Ran outside.

ground and paused for a few minutes near the river. As he was gazing around, a group of swans walked slowly by. The duckling remembered the swans he had seen so many months ago. He watched them with great interest. One by one, they stepped into the river and floated quietly upon the water as if they were a part of it.

"I will follow them," said the duckling to himself. "As ugly as I am, I would rather be killed by the swans than suffer all I have suffered from the cold, and from the ducks who have treated me so poorly." And he flew quickly down to the water and swam after them as fast as he could.

It did not take him long to reach them, for they had stopped to rest in a green pool shaded by a tree. And as soon as they saw him coming, some of the younger swans swam out to meet him with cries of welcome. The duckling hardly understood these cries. He approached the swans gladly, yet he was trembling.

The duckling turned to one of the older birds and said, "If I am to die, I would rather have you kill me. I don't know why I was ever hatched, for I am too ugly to live." And as he spoke, he bowed his head and looked down into the water.

Reflected in the still pool he saw

many white shapes, with long necks and golden bills. He looked for his dull brown body and his awkward skinny neck. But no such body was there. Instead, he saw a beautiful white swan beneath him. With great amazement, he spread his wings and looked at his reflection in the water. At that moment, the mother duck that had hatched him was swimming by with three of her children, who were now full-grown

ducks. The beautiful young swan heard the mother duck say to her children, "Look over there at that splendid swan with his wings spread. It must be the most beautiful creature in the world."

And when the duckling had seen his true self at last, he felt that all his suffering had been worth it. Otherwise, he would never have known what it was like to be really happy.

- At which time of year did things become better for the duckling? *Idea:* In the spring.
- That spring, something caught his attention. What was it? *Ideas:* Something pink; an apple tree.
- How did the duckling get over to the apple tree? **He flew.**
- Had he ever done that before? **No.**
- What kind of birds did the duckling see near the riverbank? **Swans.**
- What did the duckling do when the swans went into the river? *Idea:* He followed them.
- How did the younger swans respond when he approached them? *Idea:* They welcomed him.
- When he looked into the water, he saw a reflection. What was the color of the bodies that he saw? **White.**
- Who was passing by as the ugly duckling was looking at his reflection in the water? *Idea:* The mother duck and three of her children.
- What kind of bird had the ugly duckling become? **A swan.**
- What did the mother say about how he looked? *Idea:* He was beautiful.
- Do you think she knew that the swan was the ugly duckling? **No.**

Award 4 points or have the students reread to the error limit sign.

INDEPENDENT WORK

Do all the items in your skillbook and workbook for lesson 34.

ANSWER KEY FOR WORKBOOK

Review Items

1. Write which character could have said each sentence.
   a. "I want to marry a Munchkin maiden." *Woodman*
   b. "I want to rule over the Emerald City." *Scarecrow*
   c. "I want to be the King of Beasts." *Lion*
   d. "There is no place like home." *Dorothy*
   e. "It's so nice to see Uncle Henry smile." *Dorothy*
   f. "I do not know where this balloon will carry me." *Oz*
   g. "The Winged Monkeys will take me to the middle of the country." *Scarecrow*
   h. "The Winged Monkeys will take me to the forest." *Lion*
   i. "The Winged Monkeys will take me to the Land of the East." *Woodman*
   j. "The silver shoes carried me to Kansas." *Dorothy*
   k. "I hope to work for a circus again." *Oz*

2. If Dorothy had used the power of the silver shoes, some things would be different.
   a. The Scarecrow would not have *brains*
   b. The Lion would not have *courage*
   c. The Tin Woodman would not have *a heart*

3. When Dorothy came back to Kansas, it seemed to her that many things had a new color.
   a. What color had those things been before? *gray*
   Write the color that each thing seemed to have:
   b. the sky *blue*
   c. the grass *green*
   d. the sun *yellow*
   e. Aunt Em's cheeks *red*
   f. the house *white*

4. Dorothy learned something about these colors: blue, white, red, green, and yellow. Write the color that reminded Dorothy of these things in Oz:
   a. Quadlings *red*
   b. Munchkins *blue*
   c. Winkies *yellow*
   d. Emerald City *green*
   e. Glinda *white*

WORKCHECK AND AWARDING POINTS

1. *Read the questions and answers for the skillbook and workbook.*
2. *Award points for independent work as follows:*

> 0 errors . . . . .6 points
> 2 errors . . . . .4 points
> 3, 4, or 5 errors . . . . .2 points
> 5 or more errors . . . . .0 points

3. *Award bonus points as follows:*

> *Correcting missed items
> or getting all items right . . . . .2 points
> Doing the writing
> assignment acceptably . . . . .2 points*

ANSWER KEY FOR SKILLBOOK

PART C

1. a. geese
   b. No
   c. *Idea:* They were kind to him
2. a. *Idea:* They were shot
   b. *Idea:* He couldn't fly
3. *Idea:* Because he was too ugly
4. a. White
   b. South
   c. *Idea:* To be warm
   d. Yes
   e. *Idea:* He was too ugly
5. a. A man
   b. The children
6. a. Spring
   b. *Idea:* He flew
   c. No
   d. An apple tree
7. a. *Idea:* They greeted him
   b. *Idea:* By looking in the water
   c. *Idea:* A swan
   d. *Idea:* The mother duck
   e. *Idea:* That he was beautiful

PART D

8. a. mischief
   b. confidence
   c. congratulated
   d. experience
   e. tricking
   f. replacing
   g. goodbye
   h. extended

Lesson 35

Lesson 35

PART A   Hyphens

What is the name for this mark? –Ⓐ
Read the hyphenated words in the passage below.Ⓑ

In the morning they tra-
veled until they reached a forest. There was no way of going around it. It seemed to extend to the right and left farther than they could see. However, the Woodman and the Scarecrow left the group and soon discovered a way to enter the forest.

Lesson 35

Open Range
by Kathryn and Byron Jackson

Prairie goes to the mountain,
    Mountain goes to the sky.
The sky sweeps across to the distant hills
And here, in the middle,
    Am I.

Hills crowd down to the river,
    River runs by the tree.
Tree throws its shadow on sunburnt grass
And here, in the shadow,
    Is me.

Shadows creep up the mountain,
    Mountain goes black on the sky,
The sky bursts out with a million stars
And here, by the campfire,
    Am I.

136   Lesson 35   Textbook

EXERCISE 1   Hyphens

1. Everybody, find lesson 35, part A in your skillbook. *Wait. Call on individual students to read. Present the tasks specified for each circled letter.*
Ⓐ Everybody, what's the answer? *Signal.* **A hyphen.**
Ⓑ I'll read all the words in each line except the last word. Everybody will read that word together.
   - In the morning they . . .
   Everybody, what word? *Signal.* **Traveled.**
   - until they reached a . . .
   Everybody, what word? *Signal.* **Forest.**
   - There was no way of . . .
   Everybody, what word? *Signal.* **Going.**
   - around it. It seemed to . . .
   Everybody, what word? *Signal.* **Extend.**
   - to the right and left . . .
   Everybody, what word? *Signal.* **Farther.**
   - than they could see . . .
   Everybody, what word? *Signal.* **However.**
   - the Woodman and the . . .
   Everybody, what word? *Signal.* **Scarecrow.**
   - left the group and soon . . .
   Everybody, what word? *Signal.* **Discovered.**
   - a way to enter the . . .
   Everybody, what word? *Signal.* **Forest.**

EXERCISE 2   Poem

1. Everybody, turn to page 136 in your textbook. *Wait.* Today we're going to read a poem. I'll read the poem first. Follow along and get a picture of the scene that the poem describes. *Read the entire poem.*
2. The poem tells about a place at different times of day. Listen to the first stanza again and get a picture of the prairie, the mountain, the sky, and the hills. *Read the first stanza.*
   - Where is the person standing? *Ideas:* On the prairie; between the mountain and the hills; under the sky.
   - What is in the distance? *Ideas:* The mountain; the hills.
3. Listen to the second stanza and get a picture of the river, the tree, and the shadow. *Read the second stanza.*
   - What runs by the tree? **The river.**
   - Where is the person? *Idea:* In the shadow of the tree.
   - What does sunburnt grass look like? *Ideas:* Brown, gray.
   - What time of day do you think it is? *Idea:* Noon.
4. Listen to the third stanza and get a picture of how the mountain and the sky change. *Read the third stanza.*
   - The poem says that, "Shadows creep up the mountain." Why is that happening? *Idea:* The sun is going down. That's why the mountain goes black on the sky.
   - The poem says that, "The sky bursts out with a million stars." What time of day is it now? *Idea:* Night.
   - Where is the person at the end of the poem? *Ideas:* By the campfire; under the stars.
5. Your turn to read the poem. *Call on different students to read one stanza each.*

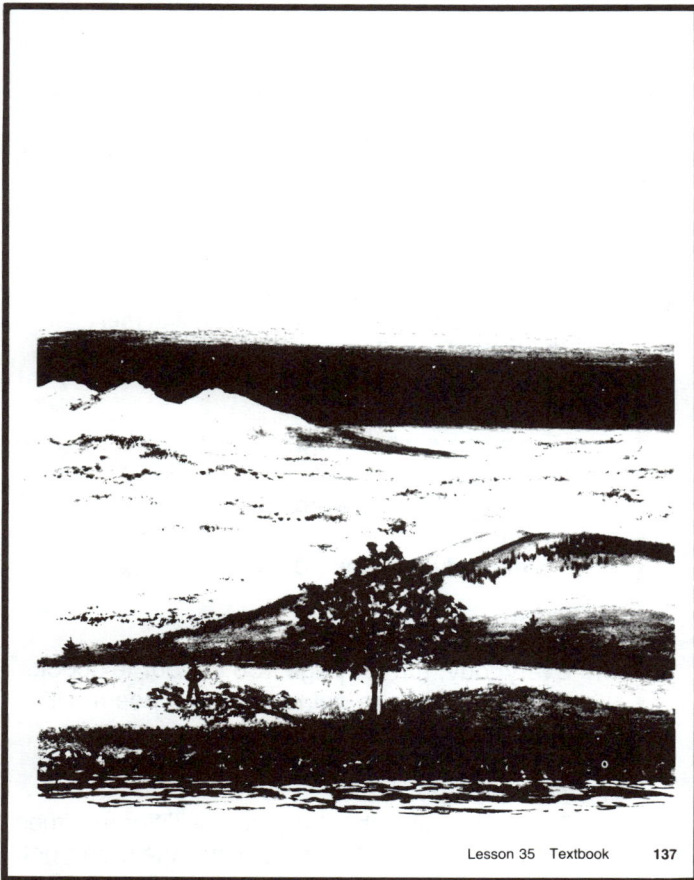

EXERCISE 3   Special projects

1. Everybody, turn to page 41 in your workbook and read it silently. *Wait.*
2. Every student should work on at least one project. I'll name the projects, and you raise your hand if the project I name is the one you want to work on.
   List students who volunteer for each project.
3. *Allow students extra time to complete their projects.*

INDEPENDENT WORK

Do all the items in your skillbook and workbook for lesson 35.

WORKCHECK AND AWARDING POINTS

1. *Read the questions and answers for the skillbook and workbook.*
2. *Award points for independent work as follows:*

> *0 errors* . . . .*6 points*
> *2 errors* . . . .*4 points*
> *3, 4, or 5 errors* . . . .*2 points*
> *5 or more errors* . . . .*0 points*

3. *Award bonus points as follows:*

> *Correcting missed items*
> *or getting all items right* . . . .*2 points*
> *Doing the writing*
> *assignment acceptably* . . . .*2 points*

ANSWER KEY FOR SKILLBOOK

PART B

1. **a.** capture
   b. considered
   c. contents
   d. experience
   e. congratulated
   f. mischief
   g. disgusting
   h. utter
   i. tiny green plants
   j. reflection

ANSWER KEY FOR WORKBOOK

Special Projects

1. If you have seen the movies *The Wizard of Oz* or *The Wiz,* you know that the book and the movies are not the same in all details.

   Compare one of the movies with the book. Make up a list of the ways that the movie is different from the book. Your list should show what is different about the characters, the setting, and the story.

   When your list is complete, read it to the class. Other students may add items to the list. Then take a vote on each item. Ask the other students, "Was this item better in the book or in the movie?" Write down the number of students who liked the item best in the book and the number who liked it best in the movie.

   When you finish, you will have the class's opinion on how the book compares to the movie.

2. Put on a play that shows how Dorothy and the others discovered that Oz was a humbug.

   First reread lesson 28. Then figure out what each character will say. You don't have to use the exact words that appear in the book. Finally, figure out who will play each part.

   When you put on the play, you can use some simple scenery to show where the play takes place. If the play goes well, you might want to put it on for another classroom.

3. Make a large wall map that shows all the places that Dorothy visited in the Land of Oz.

   Color the parts of the map with the right colors. Make small drawings on the map to show the Emerald City, the Witch's Castle, and the other places.

   Finally, draw a line to show the route that Dorothy took. Your line should connect all the places that she visited.

Lesson 36 ✓

Lesson 36

PART A **Word Lists**

1	2	3
England	sway	**Vocabulary words**
London	disbelief	1. barbed wire
Derick	inexpensive	2. alert
ridiculous	swayed	3. nag
		4. pasture
		5. strand
		6. develops
		7. plod
		8. thoroughbred
		9. nudge

WORD PRACTICE AND VOCABULARY

EXERCISE 1   Word practice

1. Everybody, find lesson 36, part A in your skillbook. *Wait.* Touch under each word in column 1 as I read it.
2. The first word is **England.**
3. Next word. **London.**
4. *Repeat step 3 for each remaining word in column 1.*
5. Your turn. Read the first word. *Signal.* **England.**
6. Next word. *Signal.* **London.**
7. *Repeat step 6 for each remaining word in column 1.*
8. *Repeat the words in column 1 until firm.*

EXERCISE 2   Word practice

1. Everybody, touch under the first word in column 2. *Pause.*
   What word? *Signal.* **Sway.**
2. Next word. *Pause.*
   What word? *Signal.* **Disbelief.**
3. *Repeat step 2 for each remaining word in column 2.*
4. *Repeat the words in column 2 until firm.*

EXERCISE 3   Vocabulary development

Task A

1. Everybody, touch column 3. *Check.*
   First you're going to read the words in column 3. Then we'll talk about what they mean.
2. Touch under the first line. *Pause.*
   What words? *Signal.* **Barbed wire.**
3. Next word. *Pause.*
   What word? *Signal.* **Alert.**
4. *Repeat step 3 for each remaining word in column 3.*
5. *Repeat the words in column 3 until firm.*

Task B

Now let's talk about what those words mean.
The words in line 1 are **barbed wire.**
Barbed wire is **wire** with very sharp, steel thorns or **barbs** attached to it.

Task C

Word 2 is **alert.** Something that is **alert** is full of attention.
Everybody, what's another way of saying **Her expression was full of attention?**
Signal. **Her expression was alert.**
Everybody, what's another way of saying **The horse looked full of attention.** *Signal.*
The horse looked alert.

Task D

Word 3 is **nag.** An old broken-down horse is called a **nag.** Everybody, what's an old broken-down horse called? *Signal.* **A nag.**

Task E

Word 4 is **pasture.** A **pasture** is a field for farm animals.

Task F

Word 5 is **strand.** A **strand** is a single strip of something. **A single hair** is **a strand of hair.**
Everybody, what's **a single wire** called? *Signal.*
A strand of wire.

Task G

1. Word 6 is **develops.** When something **develops,** it grows. Everybody, what's another way of saying **Her skills grew?** *Signal.*
   Her skills developed.
2. Everybody, what's another way of saying **A bad habit grew?** *Signal.*
   A bad habit developed.

Task H

Word 7 is **plod.** When you **plod,** you move at a very slow, tired pace. Everybody, what are you doing when you move at a very slow, tired pace? *Signal.* **Plodding.**

Task I

Word 8 is **thoroughbred.** A **thoroughbred** is a special breed of horse that is used for racing. Everybody, what do we call a special breed of horse that is used for racing? *Signal.*
A thoroughbred.

Task J

Word 9 is **nudge.** A **nudge** is a gentle push. Everybody, what do we call a gentle push? *Signal.* **A nudge.**
What's another way of saying **She gave the gate a gentle push?** *Signal.*
She gave the gate a nudge.

A Horse to Remember
by Luisa Miller
PART 1

Nobody knows exactly how Nellie developed her bad habit, but she developed it. And nothing that Mr. Briggs or Tara did seemed to break her of the habit.(A) The Briggs family lived in England, on a small farm about 50 miles from London.(B)

ENGLAND

London

Briggs' Farm

138   Lesson 36   Textbook

The farm was too small to keep Mr. Briggs and his family busy all the time, so Mr. Briggs had a full time job on the railroad. He and his wife Betsy worked the small farm during their spare time. Tara, their daughter, also helped them.

Because the farm was so small, the Briggs family didn't own a tractor. They used horses to plow the fields in the spring. That's why they had Nellie.(C) They got Nellie when she was three years old. She wasn't a very good-looking horse. She was a large, gray horse with tiny black spots. Her legs were heavy and her back was swayed.(D)

When she was only three, she already looked like a ten-year-old horse. But the Briggs thought that the horse would be well-suited to their needs. Nellie was gentle. She loved to have somebody ride her. She was a good worker, and in most situations, she obeyed very well.(E) During the planting season, Mr. Briggs or Tara would harness her to the plow with another horse, Derick, a large brown horse that looked handsome when he stood alone in the fields or in the small barn next to the house. Derick looked at least twice as handsome when he was hitched to the plow, next to Nellie. Derick looked so straight and tall and alert. Nellie looked like an old swaybacked nag.

Lesson 36   Textbook   **139**

STORY READING

EXERCISE 4   Decoding and comprehension

1. Everybody, turn to page 138 in your textbook. *Wait. Call on a student.*
   What's the error limit for this lesson?
   13 errors.
2. *Call on individual students to read. Present the tasks specified for each circled letter.*
3. From now on, there is no two-error sign. So see if you can read the first part the way I would read it.

(A) Who had the bad habit? **Nellie.**
- Who tried to break her of that habit? *Idea:* Mr. Briggs and Tara.
- Did their attempts to break the habit work? **No.**

(B) London is the largest city in England. The map shows London and the Brigg's farm. Everybody, touch London. *Check.*
- Touch the Briggs' farm. *Check.*
- In which direction would you go to travel from the Briggs' farm to downtown London? **East.**
- About how far would you have to go? **50 miles.**

(C) We know two things about Nellie. What is Nellie? **A horse.**
- What's the problem with Nellie? *Idea:* She has a bad habit.

(D) The picture shows Nellie in a small pasture on the Briggs' farm.
   Everybody, touch her back. *Check.*
   When a horse's back arches down like that, the horse is called swaybacked. Good horses aren't swaybacked. But Nellie is.

(E) Did she obey very well in all situations? **No.**

Although Nellie behaved very well in most situations, she had her bad habit. That habit was jumping fences. (F) The first time the Briggs found out about this habit was during a thunderstorm that occurred one summer night. Nellie was four years old at the time. Tara was looking out the kitchen window at the bending trees and the driving rain. From time to time, a brilliant flash of lightning would streak through the sky and make things appear to be as bright as day. Following each flash would come a terrible crash of thunder. It was during one of these flashes that Tara noticed Nellie, standing right outside the kitchen door, eating flowers from the flower garden next to the kitchen door. Tara called to her mother. "Nellie got out of the pasture." (G)

"You must have left the gate open," her mother replied.

Tara put on her raincoat, went outside, and led Nellie back to the small pasture that surrounded the barn. But when she approached the gate, she noticed that it was firmly bolted. (H) She led Nellie through the pasture, then walked around the entire pasture, checking the fence to make sure that it had not blown down. The fence was in perfect condition. It was over four feet high, with four strands of barbed wire. When Tara went back inside, she reported to her mother the condition of the gate and the fence. Then she added, "I don't know how she got out, Mom. The only possible way would be to jump over the fence, but . . ." Her voice trailed off. The idea of Nellie jumping a four-foot

fence was ridiculous. (I)

Mr. and Mrs. Briggs didn't think that Nellie could jump that high either, until a few minutes later, when they saw Nellie once more nibbling on flowers in the garden next to the kitchen door.

Tara's father asked, "Are you sure you checked the entire fence, Tara?"

"Every part of it," Tara replied.

Mr. Briggs shook his head gravely. His expression was one of disbelief. "Perhaps I'd better have a look at it myself," he said, and reached for his raincoat. (J) Mrs. Briggs was curious about Nellie's strange escapes, so she went outside with Mr. Briggs and Tara. Mr. Briggs led Nellie back through the pasture, bolted the gate carefully, and walked around the entire pasture, shining a flashlight on every part of the fence. It was in perfect condition.

Mr. Briggs then shook his head and said, "If this isn't the strangest thing . . ." Before he could finish his statement, a brilliant bolt of lightning made the sky bright. The bolt was followed by another and another. To the wonder of the Briggs family, they saw how Nellie had escaped from the pasture. There she was, in a moment of dazzling bright light, looking as if she was frozen in midair, clearing the top wire of the fence easily.

"I don't believe it!" Mr. Briggs exclaimed. Tara said nothing. She was still staring into the darkness at the spot where Nellie had been caught in the light. Two things amazed Tara. The first was that Nellie—plodding, swaybacked Nellie— would jump like that. Tara had never seen

any horse jump so high, not even the mayor's horse, which was a handsome thoroughbred that looked shimmering red-brown when he stood in the sunlight.

The other thing that amazed Tara was that when she saw Nellie frozen in the air, she didn't look like an old plow horse. She looked very graceful, with her front legs tucked up under her head and her back legs extended. She looked beautiful. (K)

★ 13 ERRORS ★

Mr. Briggs didn't seem to appreciate Nellie's beauty. He said, "We've got a serious problem, I'm afraid." He called Nellie, led her back through the pasture, then into the barn, where he put her in a stall and attached a rope to her so that she couldn't get out. He explained, "I think that the thunder frightens her. So whenever it looks like rain, we're going to have to tie her up in the barn."

The plan worked for a while, until Nellie figured out how to bite through the rope. The side door of the barn didn't close well. So a few moments after biting through the rope, Nellie nudged the door open, trotted into the pasture, jumped the fence, and went straight to the flower garden.

At first, Nellie jumped the fence only during thunderstorms. But within two

months after her first escape, she began jumping fences whenever she was alone for more than a few minutes. One time she jumped the pasture fence and the fence next to the road. She then jumped four fences on the neighboring farm, three fences on the next farm, and stopped to eat in Mr. Fanning's vegetable garden.

After Tara rode Nellie back, put her in the barn, and tied her up, her father said sternly, "Tara, I know you like Nellie. So do I, and so does your mother. But she is becoming far too much of a problem. Unless we can figure out some inexpensive way of keeping her inside, we're going to have to get rid of her."

"Couldn't we make the fence higher?" Tara asked.

"It would be very expensive," her father explained. "The top wire on the fence is attached to the fence posts. But the posts don't go up more than a few inches beyond the top wire. So we'd have to put in new posts all the way around the pasture. I can't afford to do that."

Tara came up with other suggestions, but her father didn't approve of them. Then Mr. Briggs concluded, "Well, I hope we can come up with some solution. If we can't, Nellie must go."

(F) Now we know what her bad habit was. What was it? *Idea:* Jumping fences.

(G) Where was Nellie supposed to be? *Idea:* In the pasture.

● What's a pasture? *Idea:* A field for farm animals.

(H) Was the gate open? **No.**

(I) Everybody, show me how high a fence that is four feet would be. *Check.*

● Would you think that a swaybacked horse like Nellie could jump higher than that? **No.**

(J) What is Mr. Briggs thinking? *Idea:* Tara didn't check the fence carefully enough.

● What's he going to do? *Idea:* Check the fence himself.

(K) Two things about Nellie amazed Tara. What was the first thing? *Idea:* That she could jump so high.

● What was the other thing? *Idea:* She looked beautiful when she jumped.

● Read the rest of the story to yourselves and be ready to answer some questions.

After all students have finished reading:

● At first Nellie jumped the fence on only some occasions. What occasions were those? *Idea:* During thunderstorms.

● Why didn't the plan of tying her up in the barn work well? *Idea:* She bit through the rope and got out of the barn.

● One time, she really did a lot of fence jumping. Where did Tara find her? *Idea:* In somebody's vegetable garden.

● After that incident, Tara suggested a plan for keeping her in the pasture. What was the plan? *Idea:* Make the fence higher.

● Why would this plan cost too much money? *Idea:* They'd have to put in new posts.

● Her father wanted an inexpensive plan. What does that mean **an inexpensive plan?** *Idea:* A plan that doesn't cost very much.

● What was going to happen to Nellie if they couldn't come up with an inexpensive plan? *Idea:* They'd have to sell Nellie.

Award 4 points or have the students reread to the error limit sign.

INDEPENDENT WORK

Do all the items in your skillbook and workbook for lesson 36.

ANSWER KEY FOR WORKBOOK

Story Items

Horse 1

Nellie

Horse 2

Horse 3

Horse 4

1. One of the animals above is Nellie.
   a. Write the name Nellie over that horse.
   b. Horse 1 is not Nellie. Why not?

   It does not have spots.

   c. Horse 3 is not Nellie. Why not?

   It is not swaybacked.

2. What was Nellie's bad habit?

   jumping fences

3. a. In which country does this story take place? *England*
   b. Near what city does the story take place? *London*

Map Skills

4. Below is a map of England.

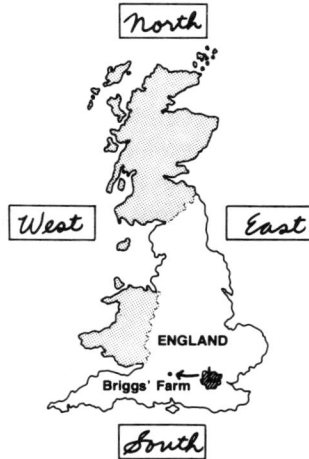

a. Write **North, South, East,** and **West** in the boxes around the map.
b. Write **L** in the center of London.
c. Draw an **arrow** from London to the Briggs' farm.
d. In which direction do you go from London to reach the Brigg's farm?

   West

e. How many miles do you travel when you go from London to the Brigg's farm? *50*

Crossword Puzzle

To work the puzzle, read an item and figure out which word the item describes. Then write the word in the puzzle. Complete the entire puzzle.

Across

3. When you say something very forcefully, you _____.
6. A person who can talk without moving his lips is a _____.
7. If you hold something gently, you hold it _____.
8. The material on the inside of a coat is the _____ of the coat.
9. All the things that a person knows.
10. When something is _____, it is put together again.

Down

1. When you talk in a grumpy way, you _____.
2. A very great storm is a _____ storm.
4. If you feel that you can do something, you have _____.
5. Naughty behavior.

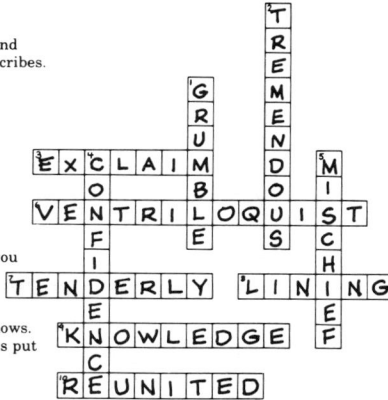

170   Lesson 36

WORKCHECK AND AWARDING POINTS

1. *Read the questions and answers for the skillbook and workbook.*
2. *Award points for independent work as follows:*

   > 0 errors . . . . .6 points
   > 2 errors . . . . .4 points
   > 3, 4, or 5 errors . . . . .2 points
   > 5 or more errors . . . . .0 points

3. *Award bonus points as follows:*

   > *Correcting missed items*
   > *or getting all items right* . . . . .2 points
   > *Doing the writing*
   > *assignment acceptably* . . . . .2 points

ANSWER KEY FOR SKILLBOOK

PART B

1. a. *Idea:* Night
   b. Lightning
2. a. *Ideas:* Beautiful; graceful
   b. *Idea:* Jump so well
3. vegetable garden
4. a. *Idea:* Making the fence higher
   b. *Idea:* It would cost too much
5. *Idea:* She chewed through the rope

PART C

6. a. False
   b. True
   c. True
   d. True
   e. True
   f. True
   g. False
   h. False
   i. True
   j. False
7. a. confidence
   b. slowly
   c. things that were inside
   d. caught
   e. replaced
   f. extended
   g. disgusting
   h. dose
   i. echo
   j. bruised

Lesson 37

WORD PRACTICE AND VOCABULARY

EXERCISE 1   Word practice

1. Everybody, find lesson 37, part A in your skillbook. *Wait.* Touch under each word in column 1 as I read it.
2. The first word is **encyclopedia.**
3. Next word. **Steeplechase.**
4. *Repeat step 3 for each remaining word in column 1.*
5. Your turn. Read the first word. *Signal.* **Encyclopedia.**
6. Next word. *Signal.* **Steeplechase.**
7. *Repeat step 6 for each remaining word in column 1.*
8. *Repeat the words in column 1 until firm.*

EXERCISE 2   Word family

1. Everybody, touch column 2. *Check.* All those words have the sound **ou** in them. Touch under the first word. *Pause.* What word? *Signal.* **Mound.**
2. Next word. *Pause.* What word? *Signal.* **Loudly.**
3. *Repeat step 2 for each remaining word in column 2.*
4. *Repeat the words in column 2 until firm.*

EXERCISE 3   Vocabulary review

Task A

1. Everybody, touch column 3. *Check.* First you're going to read the words in column 3. Then we'll talk about what they mean.
2. Touch under the first word. *Pause.* What word? *Signal.* **Nudge.**
3. Next word. *Pause.* What word? *Signal.* **Alert.**
4. *Repeat step 3 for develop.*
5. *Repeat the words in column 3 until firm.*

Task B

1. You've learned the meanings for all these words. Word 1 is **nudge.** *Call on a student.* What is a **nudge?** *Idea:* A gentle push.
2. Everybody, what's another way of saying **She gave the gate a gentle push?** *Signal.* **She gave the gate a nudge.**
3. Everybody, what's another way of saying **He gave his brother a gentle push?** *Signal.* **He gave his brother a nudge.**

Task C

1. Word 2 is **alert.** *Call on a student.* What does **alert** mean? *Idea:* Full of attention.
2. Everybody, what's another way of saying **The dog looked full of attention.** *Signal.* **The dog looked alert.**

Task D

1. Word 3 is **develop.** *Call on a student.* What does **develop** mean? *Idea:* Grow.
2. Everybody, what's another way of saying **His skills grew?** *Signal.* **His skills developed.**

EXERCISE 4   Vocabulary development

Task A

1. Everybody, touch column 4. *Check.* First you're going to read the words in column 4. Then we'll talk about what they mean.
2. Touch under the first line. *Pause.* What words? *Signal.* **Resist the impulse.**
3. Next line. *Pause.* What words? *Signal.* **Barrier and obstacle.**
4. *Repeat step 3 for cock your head and blurt out.*
5. Next word. *Pause.* What word? *Signal.* **Stall.**
6. *Repeat step 5 for each remaining word in column 4.*
7. *Repeat the words in column 4 until firm.*

Task B

1. Now let's talk about what those words mean. The words in line 1 are **resist the impulse.** When you **resist the impulse** to do something, you don't do something that you really want to do. If you don't buy toys you really want, you **resist the impulse** to buy toys.
2. Everybody, what do you do if you don't buy toys you really want? *Signal.* **You resist the impulse to buy toys.**
3. What do you do if you don't tramp through a puddle when you really want to? *Signal.* **You resist the impulse to tramp through a puddle.**

Task C

The words in line 2 are **barrier and obstacle.** A **barrier** or an **obstacle** is something that blocks your way. A tree that is in the road is an **obstacle** in the road.

Lesson 37

PART A   **Word Lists**

1	2	3	4
encyclopedia	mound	**Vocabulary words**	**Vocabulary words**
steeplechase	loudly	1. nudge	1. resist the impulse
obstacles	ground	2. alert	2. barrier and obstacle
exhaustion	mounted	3. develop	3. cock your head
endurance	sound		4. blurt out
	grouch		5. stall
			6. stray
			7. exhausted
			8. endurance

Task D

The words in line 3 are **cock your head.**
When you **cock your head,** you tilt it to one side. Everybody, show me how you cock your head. *Check.*

Task E

The words in line 4 are **blurt out.**
When you say something very suddenly, you **blurt it out.** Everybody, what do you do when you say something very suddenly? *Signal.*
You blurt it out.

Task F

Word 5 is **stall.** One meaning of **stall** is a small room with walls that don't go to the ceiling. Farmers keep horses in stalls that are inside barns.

Task G

Word 6 is **stray.** A **stray** animal is one that is far from its home. A dog that is far from its home is a stray dog. Everybody, what's a sheep that is far from its home? *Signal.*
A stray sheep.

Task H

Word 7 is **exhausted.** When you're very, very tired, you're **exhausted.**
Everybody, what's another way of saying **She was very, very tired?** *Signal.*
She was exhausted.

Task I

1. Word 8 is **endurance.** Somebody who has a lot of **endurance** can keep on going. A horse that can keep on going has a lot of endurance.
2. A runner who can keep on going has a lot of something. What is that something? *Signal.*
Endurance.

STORY READING

EXERCISE 5   Decoding and comprehension

1. Everybody, turn to page 142 in your textbook. *Wait. Call on a student.*
   What's the error limit for this lesson?
   10 errors.
2. *Call on individual students to read. Present the tasks specified for each circled letter.*
3. Remember, from now on, there is no 2-error sign. So see if you can read the first part the way I would read it.

Lesson 37

A Horse to Remember
PART 2

Tara's father had told her that the Briggs family might have to get rid of Nellie. As Tara prepared for bed that night, she felt very discouraged. Her mind kept turning over possible ideas about how she could keep Nellie inside the pasture, but all the ideas cost money. Nellie couldn't stay tied up in her stall all day, but if Nellie was left alone in the pasture . . .Ⓐ

Tara got into bed and tried to sleep, but Nellie kept popping into her mind. And every time she thought about Nellie, she remembered the instant she first saw Nellie leaping the fence.

Tara punched her pillow, rolled over angrily, and told herself that she had to come up with a solution to the problem. Suddenly, she sat upright in bed with a smile. An idea came to her with such force that she wondered why she hadn't thought of it before. "No horse can jump like that," she said aloud. "She's probably the greatest jumping horse in the world."Ⓑ

Tara had to resist the impulse to jump out of bed and tell her parents of the plan that was forming in her mind. But she controlled herself. "I'll get all the facts first," she said to herself. "Then I'll tell them about it."Ⓒ

142   Lesson 37   Textbook

Most farmers get up very early because there are many chores that they must do before breakfast—milk cows, gather eggs, feed the animals, and take care of any problems with the animals. Sometimes animals are sick. Sometimes stray dogs bother the animals.Ⓓ During the last part of the growing season, crops must be checked.

The morning after Tara got her marvelous idea, she got up very early, when the sky was still dark, with just a hint of light along the horizon to the east.Ⓔ

Tara went through the books on the living room shelves to see if she could find out more about jumping horses. After searching through three books on horses, she tried the ancient encyclopedia that was on the bottom shelf. She first looked in the index, and then turned to the book that told about steeplechases.Ⓕ A steeplechase is a horse race, but it's different from the kind of race that is most popular in the United States. Horses in a steeplechase do not simply run around a mile long track. They run farther and they do more than just run. They jump barriers and obstacles. Some barriers are wide ditches filled with water. Other barriers include fences, hedges, and shelves. The shelves are the

most dangerous. A horse must leap from a mound and land on ground that is three or four feet lower than the mound.Ⓖ

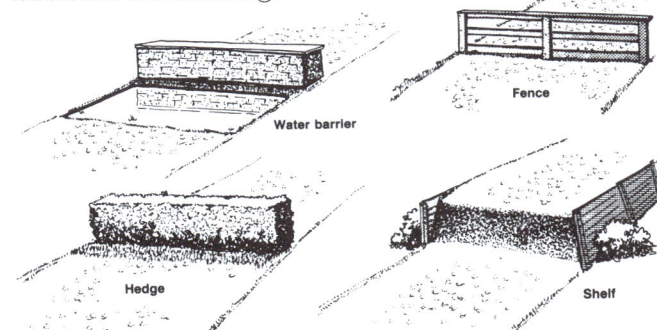

Water barrier

Fence

Hedge

Shelf

The encyclopedia informed Tara that younger horses are not permitted to compete in steeplechases because the bones in their legs are still growing. They may suffer broken bones from the jumps, and Tara knew what that meant. A horse with a bad broken leg is usually killed.

As Tara read more about steeplechases, she began to have serious doubts about whether her idea was as good as she thought it was. Part of the description in the encyclopedia told about the Grand National Steeplechase Championship that was held each year. The description said that sometimes as many as fifty horses enter the competition, but usually no more than a handful of them are able to finish. Some horses fall from exhaustion. Some fail to

make one of the thirty jumps in the four-and-a-half mile course. Some throw their riders and continue the race without them.Ⓗ

The description provided Tara with some good news. The horses entered in steeplechases do not have to be thoroughbreds.Ⓘ Usually, the only requirement for the horses that are entered is that they are at least four years old.Ⓙ According to the encyclopedia description, "The horses that win this event are usually large horses with tremendous endurance." The encyclopedia also pointed out that thoroughbreds are sometimes entered in steeplechases but that the most successful horses are only part thoroughbred. The other part may be Arabian.Ⓚ ★10 ERRORS★

Lesson 37   Textbook   **143**

Ⓐ What would happen? *Idea:* She'd jump the fence.

Ⓑ If she's the greatest jumping horse in the world, what do you think Tara's idea is? *Idea:* Make her into a jumping horse.

Ⓒ If her plan is to make Nellie into a jumping horse, what kind of facts would she need? *Call on individual students. Ideas:* Where to jump her; how to train her; how to ride her.

● Where would you go to find out facts about training jumping horses and facts about the kinds of things that jumping horses must do? *Call on individual students. Ideas:* Stables; racetracks; libraries; encyclopedias; trainers.

Ⓓ What are some chores that farmers must do before breakfast? *Call on individual students. Ideas:* Milk cows; gather eggs; feed animals; take care of any problems with the animals.

Ⓔ Was the sky light when Tara got up? **No.**

● Where was the only light part of the sky? *Idea:* The horizon to the east.

● How much light was there on the eastern horizon? *Idea:* Just a little.

Ⓕ Was the encyclopedia new? **No.**

● First she looked in the index. What is the index? *Idea:* A place that tells you where to look to find what you want.

● Then she looked up something in one of the books. What did she look up? **Steeplechases.**

Ⓖ Everybody, look at the picture. It shows some of the jumps that a horse must take in a steeplechase.

● What kind of jump is the most dangerous? **Shelf.**

● Touch the fence. *Check.*

● Touch the hedge. *Check.*

● Touch the water barrier. *Check.*

● Touch the shelf. *Check.*

Ⓗ How long is the course for the Grand National Steeplechase Championship? **Four and a half miles.**

● How many horses may start the race? **Fifty.**

● How many usually finish? *Idea:* A few.

● Tell me some things that may happen to horses in this steeplechase. *Call on individual students. Ideas:* Fall from exhaustion; miss jumps; throw their rider; hurt themselves.

Ⓘ What is that good news she read about? *Idea:* Steeplechase horses don't have to be thoroughbreds.

● Why is that good news to Tara? *Idea:* Because Nellie is not a thoroughbred.

Ⓙ What's usually the only requirement for a horse? *Idea:* They're at least four years old.

Ⓚ What kind of horses usually win the steeplechase? *Idea:* Large horses with great endurance.

● The story says that horses have a great deal of endurance. What does that mean? *Ideas:* They can run and jump for long periods of time.

Lesson 37   **173**

Tara looked out the window in thought after reading the description. The eastern sky was now quite bright and the roosters in the barn were beginning to crow loudly. Tara was just about ready to forget about the idea of training Nellie to be a jumping horse, when Mrs. Briggs padded down the stairs in her bare feet. She said, "What are you reading about so early in the morning?"

Tara explained. Her mother smiled and cocked her head. "I've never seen a horse that could jump like Nellie, but I'm sure there are lots of them. Some very rich people do nothing but raise horses for steeplechases. It wouldn't surprise me if a lot of them could outjump our old Nellie."

"She's not that old," Tara objected. "She's only four years old."

"I know," her mother said thoughtfully. Then she snapped her fingers and said, "Why don't you talk to the blacksmith, Mr. Jones? He used to make shoes for steeplechase horses when he lived in Liverpool. I'm sure that he could tell you a lot about the chances that our Nellie might have as a jumping horse."

• • •

When a blacksmith makes horseshoes, you can hear the ringing of his hammer on red-hot metal many blocks away. Tara had never talked much with Mr. Jones because he seemed to be a grouchy person who always complained about things. But after Tara had finished with her chores, she rode Nellie down the road to the village, following the ringing

144 Lesson 37 Textbook

sounds. While she was still on Nellie's back, she looked down at Mr. Jones and waited for the old man to look up. Then Tara blurted out, "I want to know what I'd have to do to make Nellie a jumping horse and if she's good enough to compete in steeplechases."

Mr. Jones had been hammering on a horseshoe that he held with a long pair of tongs. He dipped the shoe into a bucket of water and waited until the sizzling sound stopped. Then he took an old rag from his pocket and wiped the sweat from his face. He studied Nellie for a few moments, then smiled. "Why would you want to make her a jumping horse?" he asked at last.

Before Tara could answer, Mr. Jones continued. "She's a plow horse, not the kind of noble beast that is used in steeplechases."

"But she can jump like no horse I've ever seen," Tara said.

"Oh, can she now?" Mr. Jones asked in a doubting tone. He wiped his blackened hands on the filthy rag and said, "I'll tell you what I'll do. If you can show me that she can jump, I'll help you train her. But I'm not going to be responsible for any injury that she might have when she falls."

Mr. Jones began looking around for a pole that he could use as a jumping barrier. He talked to himself as he searched through his workshop. "I'll have to make it about four feet high."

Tara said, "Your fence out back is about that high. Why don't we just have Nellie jump that fence?"

"No," Mr. Jones replied firmly. "I'm having no part of that poor old nag getting torn up on a barbed wire."

"Here," Tara said, getting down from Nellie's back. "She won't get hurt. Let me show you." Before Mr. Jones could object, Tara slid through the strands of barbed wire and ran into the field beyond the fence. Then she turned and called, "Come on, Nellie."

The horse looked up quickly, trotted toward the fence, and just as Mr. Jones started to say, "But she can't . . ." Nellie cleared the fence with a foot to spare.

Tara smiled and patted Nellie on the nose. But Mr. Jones didn't smile. He stood there with his mouth hanging open, his dirty rag in his hand, and his eyes were wide. "I don't believe it," he said.

Lesson 37 Textbook 145

- Are the successful steeplechase horses usually thoroughbreds or part thoroughbred? *Idea:* Part thoroughbred.
- Read the rest of the story to yourselves and be ready to answer some questions.

After all students have finished reading:

- Who came downstairs as Tara was reading? **Her mother.**
- She told Tara that she should talk to somebody about jumping horses. Who was that? **Mr. Jones.**
- What kind of work did Mr. Jones do? *Idea:* He was a blacksmith.
- Why did he know about steeplechase horses? *Idea:* He used to work with them.
- Why hadn't Tara talked to him very much in the past? *Idea:* He seemed too grouchy.
- What did Mr. Jones say he would do if Tara showed that the horse could really jump well? *Idea:* Help train Nellie to jump.
- How did Mr. Jones want to test the horse's jumping ability? *Idea:* Put up a pole to make a jumping barrier.
- What did Tara suggest for a test? *Idea:* Have Nellie jump the fence.
- How did Mr. Jones respond to Tara's idea? *Idea:* He didn't like the idea.
- Why didn't he want Nellie to try jumping the fence? *Idea:* He thought Nellie might hurt herself.
- What did Tara do before Mr. Jones could object? *Idea:* Ran into the field behind the fence.
- About how high was the fence? **Four feet.**
- Did Nellie have any trouble jumping the fence? **No.**
- How did Mr. Jones respond when he saw Nellie do that? *Idea:* He was amazed.
- Everybody, look at the picture of Mr. Jones and Tara. *Check.*
  Touch the horseshoe that Mr. Jones is making. *Check.*
  Touch the tongs that he is holding. *Check.*
- Why doesn't he just hold that horseshoe with his hand? *Idea:* Because the horseshoe is very hot.

Award 4 points or have the students reread to the error limit sign.

ANSWER KEY FOR WORKBOOK

Story Items

1. Tara looked in the *index* of the encyclopedia to find out more about training Nellie.
2. Name **three** chores that most farmers do before breakfast. *Ideas:*
   a. *milk cows*
   b. *gather eggs*
   c. *feed animals, take care of animals*

3. Below is a part of the index page in the encyclopedia:

	Book	Page
Steel Yard	7	211
Steeple–bush	9	593
Steeplechase	9	601
Steer	9	624
Steering wheel	8	119
Stegosaurus	4	283

   a. Circle the item that Tara was interested in.
   b. Which book of the encyclopedia would she read to find out about that item? *9*
   c. Write the page number for that item? *601*

4. Tara read about the jumps a horse must take in a steeplechase. She read about the **fence**, the **hedge**, the **shelf**, and the **water barrier**. Write the name of the correct jump underneath each picture.

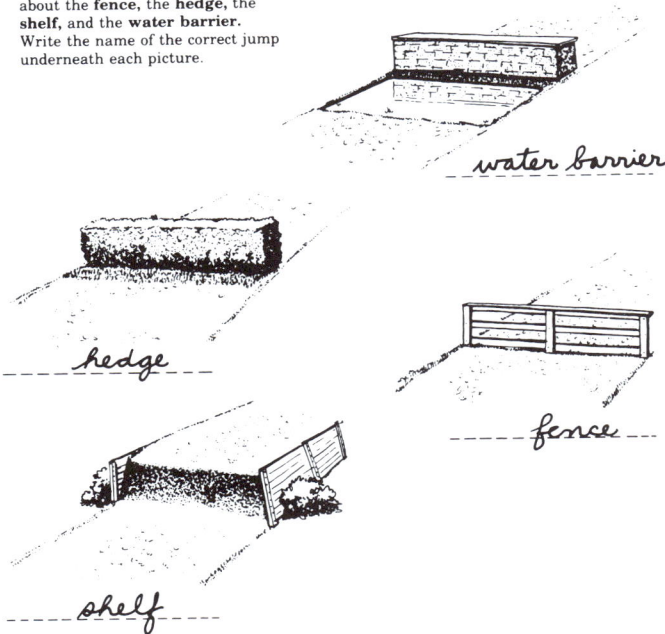

water barrier

hedge

fence

shelf

5. a. How long is the course for the Grand National Steeplechase Championship? *4½ miles*
   b. How many horses may start the race? *50*
   c. How many horses usually finish? **Circle the correct answer.**
   • all of the horses
   • (only a few horses)
   • almost all of the horses

6. Name **two** bad things that can happen to horses in the steeplechase. *Ideas:*
   a. *Fall from exhaustion; Throw their riders*
   b. *Fail to make a jump*

7. **Circle** the word that describes Mr. Jones.
   (•grouchy) • pleasant • young

INDEPENDENT WORK

Do all the items in your skillbook and workbook for lesson 37.

WORKCHECK AND AWARDING POINTS

1. *Read the questions and answers for the skillbook and workbook.*
2. *Award points for independent work as follows:*

0 errors	6 points
2 errors	4 points
3, 4, or 5 errors	2 points
5 or more errors	0 points

3. *Award bonus points as follows:*

Correcting missed items or getting all items right	2 points
Doing the writing assignment acceptably	2 points

ANSWER KEY FOR SKILLBOOK

PART B

1. *Idea:* She jumped over fences
2. *Idea:* Make Nellie into a jumping horse
3. a. *Idea:* Read books about horses
   b. *Idea:* In an encyclopedia
4. a. *Ideas:* They run farther; they jump barriers
   b. *Any three:* ditches; fences; hedges; shelves
   c. Shelf
   d. *Idea:* They are at least four years old
5. a. sunrise
   b. *Ideas:* Mrs. Briggs; her mother
   c. Mr. Jones
6. Ringing sounds
7. a. *Idea:* A blacksmith shop
   b. *Idea:* Help train her
   c. *Idea:* Jumped over the fence

PART C

8. a. Ruby
   b. Diamond
   c. Emerald
   d. A cyclone
9. a. considered
   b. congratulated
   c. contents
   d. said
   e. echo
   f. bruise

Lesson 38

Lesson 38

PART A   Word Lists

1	2	3	4
anvil	demonstrate	**Vocabulary words**	**Vocabulary words**
Arabian	select	1. blurt out	1. brace yourself
abruptly	encyclopedia	2. resist the impulse	2. abruptly
Ealing	customer	3. barrier and obstacle	3. gallop
dilapidated	mayor	4. endurance	4. dilapidated
	competition	5. exhausted	5. marvel
	thirty		6. spectators
			7. mock

WORD PRACTICE AND VOCABULARY

EXERCISE 1   Word practice

1. Everybody, find lesson 38, part A in your skillbook. *Wait.* Touch under each word in column 1 as I read it.
2. The first word is **anvil.**
3. Next word. **Arabian.**
4. *Repeat step 3 for each remaining word in column 1.*
5. Your turn. Read the first word. *Signal.* **Anvil.**
6. Next word. *Signal.* **Arabian.**
7. *Repeat step 6 for each remaining word in column 1.*
8. *Repeat the words in column 1 until firm.*

EXERCISE 2   Word practice

1. Everybody, touch under the first word in column 2. *Pause.*
   What word? *Signal.* **Demonstrate.**
2. Next word. *Pause.*
   What word? *Signal.* **Select.**
3. *Repeat step 2 for each remaining word in column 2.*
4. *Repeat the words in column 2 until firm.*

EXERCISE 3   Vocabulary review

Task A

1. Everybody, touch column 3. *Check.*
   First you're going to read the words in column 3. Then we'll talk about what they mean.
2. Touch under the first line. *Pause.*
   What words? *Signal.* **Blurt out.**
3. Next line. *Pause.*
   What words? *Signal.* **Resist the impulse.**
4. *Repeat step 3 for barrier and obstacle.*
5. Next word. *Pause.*
   What word? *Signal.* **Endurance.**
6. *Repeat step 5 for exhausted.*
7. *Repeat the words in column 3 until firm.*

Task B

You've learned the meanings for all these words. The words in line 1 are **blurt out.**
Call on a student. What does **blurt out** mean?
Idea: To say something very suddenly.
Everybody, what do you do when you say something very suddenly? *Signal.*
You blurt it out.

Task C

1. The words in line 2 are **resist the impulse.** *Call on a student.* What does **resist the impulse** mean? *Idea:* You don't do something you really want to do.
2. Everybody, what do you do if you don't buy toys you really want? *Signal.*
You resist the impulse to buy toys.
3. Everybody, what do you do if you don't swim in the river when you really want to? *Signal.*
You resist the impulse to swim in the river.

Task D

The words in line 3 are **barrier and obstacle.** *Call on a student.* What are **barriers** and **obstacles?** *Idea:* Things that get in your way.

Task E

1. Word 4 is **endurance.** *Call on a student.* What is **endurance?** *Idea:* The ability to keep on going.
2. *Call on a student.* What do we know about a horse that can keep on going? *Idea:* It has endurance.

Task F

1. Word 5 is **exhausted.** *Call on a student.* What does **exhausted** mean? *Idea:* Very, very tired.
2. Everybody, what's another way of saying **He was very, very tired?** *Signal.*
He was exhausted.

EXERCISE 4 Vocabulary development

Task A

1. Everybody, touch column 4. *Check.*
First you're going to read the words in column 4. Then we'll talk about what they mean.
2. Touch under the first line. *Pause.*
What words? *Signal.* **Brace yourself.**
3. Next word. *Pause.*
What word? *Signal.* **Abruptly.**
4. *Repeat step 3 for each remaining word in column 4.*
5. *Repeat the words in column 4 until firm.*

Task B

Now let's talk about what those words mean.
The words in line 1 are **brace yourself.**
When you **brace yourself,** you tighten up your muscles and get ready for a great jolt. If you're falling off your bike and getting ready to hit the ground, you're bracing yourself.

Task C

1. Word 2 is **abruptly.** Another word for **suddenly** is **abruptly.** Everybody, what's another way of saying **She stopped suddenly?** *Signal.*
She stopped abruptly.
2. Everybody, what's another way of saying **They turned around suddenly?** *Signal.*
They turned around abruptly.

Task D

Word 3 is **gallop.** When horses **gallop,** they run almost as fast as they can. Everybody, what are horses doing when they run almost as fast as they can? *Signal.* **Galloping.**

Task E

Word 4 is **dilapidated.** Something that is really broken-down and in bad shape is **dilapidated.** Everybody, what do we call something that is really broken-down and in bad shape? *Signal.* **Dilapidated.**

Task F

Word 5 is **marvel.** When you **marvel** over something, you think that thing is marvelous.

Task G

Word 6 is **spectators. Spectators** are people who watch an event, such as a horse race. Everybody, what do we call people who watch an event? *Signal.* **Spectators.**

Task H

Word 7 is **mock.** Praise that is **not sincere** is **mock** praise. Everybody, what is encouragement that is not sincere? *Signal.*
Mock encouragement.

Lesson 38

A Horse to Remember

PART 3

"A deal is a deal," Mr. Jones said after Tara demonstrated two more times that Nellie could clear the fence with ease. "I told you I would help you train her if she could jump. And train her I will."(A)

"You don't really have to," Tara said. "I . . ."

Mr. Jones interrupted. "I'll also have to train a rider, you know. And I suppose that rider will be you."

"I'd love to be her rider," Tara said. "But you don't have to . . ."

"It's not a chore, Tara," the old man said with a cold expression. "When I worked with steeplechase horses, I always dreamed of having one of my own. I never did, of course. But I dreamed. And now I have a chance to do something more interesting than standing over an anvil hammering out horseshoes and fixing wheels."(B)

"If you could train Nellie and me, I'd be very grateful," Tara said.

Mr. Jones grunted and then pointed at the horse. "You know, that horse is not what she seems to be when you first look at her. Her swayback makes you think that she's a broken-down nag. But when you take a good look, she's as strong as an ox. Her legs are good. Maybe a little heavy, but good. And her color. I think she may be part Arabian."(C)

Later that day, Tara told her parents that Mr. Jones would help her. She also told them that they would work hard with Nellie each day and that Nellie would be tied up in the pasture or in the barn the rest of the time.

During the weeks that followed, Tara spent a lot of time with Mr. Jones. Tara discovered that although Mr. Jones talked like a grouch, he was a very fine person. He laid out a little course in the pasture behind his shop. He made four jumps. Each one was a little less than three feet high. He explained to Tara, "When you can stay on her jumping over these jumps, we'll make them higher."

The jumps stayed at the same height for three weeks. During those three weeks, Tara fell off Nellie more than twenty times.(D) At first, she lost her balance when Nellie took off. Nellie seemed to fly upward very suddenly. To stay on her, Tara had to lean very far forward, with her head right against Nellie's neck.(E) Tara found out about leaning forward the hard way. Four times, she didn't lean forward far enough, and when Nellie took off, she fell backwards.(F)

After Tara learned about leaning forward for Nellie's takeoff, she learned about bracing herself for the landing.(G) The first

146   Lesson 38   Textbook

time she didn't fall off on the takeoff, she fell on the landing. She flew right over Nellie's head when she landed and Nellie almost stepped on her.(H) By the third day of practice, Tara was able to make most of the jumps without falling, but just about the time that she thought she had mastered the art of jumping, Nellie would fool her by jumping a little higher than she had expected or by coming down a little more abruptly.(I)

Several times, Tara had the wind knocked out of her. One time she hurt so badly that she couldn't keep the tears from

forming in her eyes. As she lay there on her back, looking up at the spots in front of her eyes, she wondered whether she really wanted to become the rider of a jumping horse.(J)

Before the first month of training had gone by, the poles on the barriers were raised half a foot.(K) Two weeks later, they went up another half foot. Then the training moved from the pasture to a stream south of the village.

The banks of the stream were very steep. In most places, the stream that flowed between the banks was three or four

Lesson 38   Textbook   147

EXERCISE 5   Decoding and comprehension

1. Everybody, turn to page 146 in your textbook. *Wait. Call on a student.* What's the error limit for this lesson? **12 errors.**

2. *Call on individual students to read. Present the tasks specified for each circled letter.*

(A) Where are Tara and Mr. Jones? *Idea:* At Mr. Jones' shop.

● What had Nellie just done? *Idea:* Jumped a four-foot fence.

● What had Mr. Jones said he would do if Nellie could jump well? *Idea:* Train Nellie to be a jumping horse.

(B) The anvil is the iron stand that the blacksmith hammers on. There's an anvil in the picture on page 145. Look at the anvil in that picture. *Check.*
Now turn back to page 146.

(C) What color is Nellie? *Ideas:* Gray; gray with black spots.
That's the same color that some Arabian horses are. Maybe Nellie is part Arabian.

(D) When did Mr. Jones say that he would make the jumps higher? *Idea:* When Tara could stay on Nellie while she jumped.

● How high were the jumps at first? *Idea:* A little less than three feet.

● How long did the jumps stay at the same height? **Three weeks.**

● How well could Tara stay on Nellie as she cleared the jumps? *Idea:* Not well.

● How long did it take her to improve? **Three weeks.**

(E) When Nellie took off, what did Tara have to do to stay on her? *Idea:* Lean far forward.

● What would happen if she didn't lean very far forward? *Ideas:* She would lose her balance; she would fall off.

(F) Which way did Tara fall off the horse when Nellie took off? **Backwards.**
Remember that.

(G) What did she have to learn about the landing? *Idea:* How to brace herself.

(H) When did she fall this time? *Idea:* On the landing.

● Did she fall forward or backward? **Forward.**
Remember that.

● Why did she fall forward? *Idea:* Because she didn't brace herself.

(I) If Nellie took off faster than Tara had expected, would Tara fall forward or backward? **Backward.**

● Which way would she fall if Nellie came down more abruptly than she expected? **Forward.**

(J) When Tara was laying on her back, what was she looking up at? **Spots in front of her eyes.**

● Were those spots really in the air? **No.**

feet lower than the banks. Mr. Jones selected a place where there was a wide, flat area below the banks. The streambed was nearly thirty feet wide. The stream ran slowly next to one of the banks. The other bank was perfect for jumping. The sand below the perfect bank was soft, but not so soft that the horse would sink into it when she landed. (L)

First, Nellie jumped off the bank without a rider. Then Tara mounted her and got ready for jumping her first shelf. "Remember," Mr. Jones told her, "you'll have to lean way, way back when you land, or you'll go flying right over her head." (M)

★12 ERRORS★

Tara's heart was beating so loudly that she could hear it in her ears. "Come on, Nellie," she said, and nudged her heels into Nellie's belly. Nellie broke into a gentle run, took off at the edge of the bank, and sailed gracefully to the sand below. Tara stayed on. She shouted, "Good horse," and she felt very proud. When Nellie jumped, Tara felt like part of her. Tara seemed to know exactly where she would land and how it would feel.

Mr. Jones was smiling. Then his expression quickly became stern. "Now try it with a fast run," he said. Tara led Nellie back up the bank. She got on Nellie's back and rode her about a hundred feet from the bank. Then she bent forward, gave Nellie a sharp nudge with her heels, and shouted, "Go, Nellie, go!"

Within two steps, Nellie was at a full gallop, going much faster than Tara had intended. Before Tara realized that Nellie was going so fast that she could seriously injure herself, she was already approaching the bank. Tara leaned forward, grabbed a handful of Nellie's mane with her right hand, and hung on. With a tremendous bound, Nellie took one great leap from the bank, sailed over the entire streambed, and landed on the other bank.

Somehow, Tara managed to stay on until Nellie abruptly stopped after landing.

148   Lesson 38   Textbook

She stopped right in front of a row of thick bushes, and Tara went sailing into those bushes.

Tara walked from the bushes, brushing herself off. Mr. Jones was coming toward her in a waddling run. "Tara, are you all right?"

Tara nodded her head. In an angry tone, Mr. Jones shook his finger at Nellie and hollered, "You! You are the most amazing horse I have ever seen in my life. You are the greatest jumping horse that ever lived!" Then Mr. Jones' face broke into a broad, wrinkled smile. "Amazing!" he shouted. "Amazing!"

When Nellie, Tara and Mr. Jones returned to the blacksmith shop, an angry customer met them. It was the mayor. Mr. Jones had promised to have the mayor's tractor wheel repaired by today. "I'm sorry," Mr. Jones said flatly. "But I won't get it done until next week. I'm very busy training Nellie here to be a steeplechase champion."

The mayor laughed and said, "You've been working around hot fires too much, Elmer, if you think you'll ever make anything out of that nag."

"Is that so?" Mr. Jones said, as he approached the mayor. "Well, I've just about decided to have Tara enter Nellie in the jumping contest at Ealing next month."

"Are you quite serious?" the mayor demanded. "There will be some fine horses in that contest. In fact, I'm entering one of my own. You couldn't possibly think that poor old Nellie could stand a chance in that competition."

"Tell you what I'll do," Mr. Jones said. "I'll fix your tractor wheel for free if Nellie does not win."

The mayor laughed and shook his head. "If you're fool enough to repair the wheel for nothing, I'm not going to argue with you."

Mr. Jones turned to Tara and stared at her with cold eyes. Suddenly, he winked.

Lesson 38   Textbook   **149**

- Have you ever seen spots in front of your eyes following a bad fall or blow? *Response:* Student preference.
  Then you know how Tara must have felt.
- (K) What does that tell you about Tara? *Idea:* She was learning how to jump Nellie.
- (L) Everybody, look at the picture. Touch the stream next to the bank. *Check.*
- Touch the streambed. *Check.*
- Touch the bank that was perfect for jumping. *Check.*
- Is that bank like a shelf? **Yes.**
- How wide was the flat area below the banks? **Nearly 30 feet.**
- What is that area called? **A streambed.**
- Is the sand in the streambed hard or soft? **Soft.**
- (M) Which part of jumping from a shelf is the hardest for the rider, the takeoff or the landing? **The landing.**
- What happens on the landing if you're not careful? *Idea:* You fall over the horse's head.
- Would you fall forward or backward? **Forward.**
- Read the rest of the story to yourselves and be ready to answer some questions.

After all students have finished reading:

- The first time Nellie jumped from the bank, where did she land? *Idea:* On the sand.
- Did Tara stay on Nellie? **Yes.**
- The story says that Tara felt like part of Nellie during the jump. What does that mean? *Idea:* She and Nellie moved at the same time.
- Before the second jump, Mr. Jones wanted Nellie to run differently. How did he want her to run? *Idea:* Faster before she jumped.
- Did she go very fast? **Yes.**
- What did she do on that jump? *Idea:* She landed on the other bank.
- When did Tara fall off? *Idea:* When Nellie stopped after landing.
- What did Tara fall into? **Bushes.**
- What did Mr. Jones say about Nellie after she had jumped the streambed? *Ideas:* You are the most amazing horse that I have ever seen; you are the greatest jumping horse that ever lived; amazing.
- When they returned to the blacksmith shop, who was waiting for them? **The mayor.**
- Why was he angry? *Idea:* Because Mr. Jones was supposed to have fixed his wheel.
- Why didn't Mr. Jones have the wheel ready? *Idea:* Because he'd been training Nellie and Tara.
- What did the mayor think about Nellie as a jumping horse? *Idea:* He didn't think Nellie could jump.

Award 4 points or have the students reread to the error limit sign.

ANSWER KEY FOR WORKBOOK

Story Items

PICTURE 1

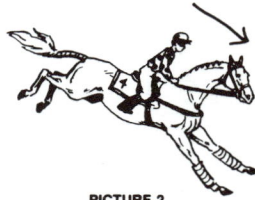

PICTURE 2

1. a. Picture 1 shows a horse taking off for a jump. Draw an **arrow** from the rider to show the direction the rider would fall if the rider is not braced.

   b. Picture 2 shows a horse landing abruptly. Draw an **arrow** from the rider to show the direction the rider would fall if the rider is not braced.

2. Look at the picture below.

3. The **arrows** in the picture below show Nellie's jumps with Tara.

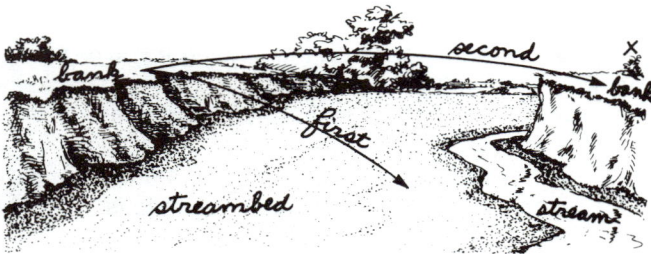

a. Label the streambed.
b. Label the stream.
c. Label the banks.

a. Write **first** on the arrow that shows her first jump with Tara.
b. Write **second** on the arrow that shows her second jump with Tara.
c. Write **X** to show where Tara landed when Nellie stopped.

Crossword Puzzle

To work the puzzle, read an item and figure out which word the item describes. Then write the word in the puzzle. Complete the entire puzzle.

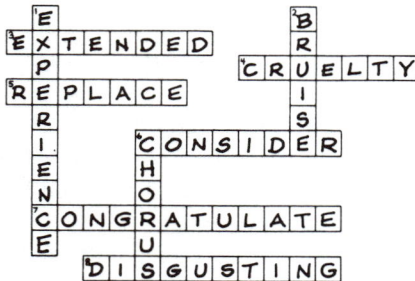

Across

3. When something is stretched out very far, it is _____.
4. When someone is cruel, that person acts with _____.
5. When you put a new thing in place of an old thing, you _____ the thing.
6. When you think over something, you _____ that thing.
7. When you tell Betty she did a good job, you _____ Betty.
8. Something that is really horrible is _____.

Down

1. Every time you do something, you have an _____.
2. A place on your body that is sore is a _____.
6. A group of voices that do the same thing.

INDEPENDENT WORK

Do all the items in your skillbook and workbook for lesson 38.

WORKCHECK AND AWARDING POINTS

1. *Read the questions and answers for the skillbook and workbook.*
2. *Award points for independent work as follows:*

> 0 errors . . . . .6 points
> 2 errors . . . . .4 points
> 3, 4, or 5 errors . . . . .2 points
> 5 or more errors . . . . .0 points

3. *Award bonus points as follows:*

> *Correcting missed items
> or getting all items right . . . . .2 points
> Doing the writing
> assignment acceptably . . . . .2 points*

ANSWER KEY FOR SKILLBOOK

PART B

1. a. *Idea:* Help train her
   b. *Idea:* She jumped over the fence
2. a. *Idea:* Behind his shop
   b. Four
   c. *Idea:* About three feet
3. a. *Idea:* When Tara could stay on Nellie
   b. Three weeks
4. a. taking off
   b. landing
   c. backwards
   d. forwards
5. *Idea:* About thirty feet
6. a. The mayor
   b. *Idea:* Fixed his tractor wheel
   c. *Idea:* Fix the wheel for free

PART C

7. a. Green
   b. Blue
   c. Yellow
   d. Red
8. a. gradually   **g.** grew
   b. deceived   **h.** alert
   c. experiences   **i.** pasture
   d. knowledge   **j.** plodding
   e. extended   **k.** endurance
   f. uttered   **l.** resisted the impulse

Lesson 39

> ## Lesson 39
>
> ### PART A   Word Lists
>
> | 1 | 2 | 3 | 4 |
> |---|---|---|---|
> | official | decorate | **Vocabulary words** | **Vocabulary words** |
> | circular | Arabian | 1. brace yourself | 1. mount a horse |
> | triangular | fiftieth | 2. mock | 2. officials |
> | Rudy | hooves | 3. abruptly | 3. shabby |
> | reins | | 4. gallop | 4. numb |
> | numb | | 5. dilapidated | |
> | | | 6. marvel | |
> | | | 7. spectators | |

WORD PRACTICE AND VOCABULARY

EXERCISE 1   Word practice

1. Everybody, find lesson 39, part A in your skillbook. *Wait.* Touch under each word in column 1 as I read it.
2. The first word is **official.**
3. Next word. **Circular.**
4. *Repeat step 3 for each remaining word in column 1.*
5. Your turn. Read the first word. *Signal.* **Official.**
6. Next word. *Signal.* **Circular.**
7. *Repeat step 6 for each remaining word in column 1.*
8. *Repeat the words in column 1 until firm.*

EXERCISE 2   Word practice

1. Everybody, touch under the first word in column 2. *Pause.*
   What word? *Signal.* **Decorate.**
2. Next word. *Pause.*
   What word? *Signal.* **Arabian.**
3. *Repeat step 2 for each remaining word in column 2.*
4. *Repeat the words in column 2 until firm.*

EXERCISE 3   Vocabulary review

Task A

1. Everybody, touch column 3. *Check.*
   First you're going to read the words in column 3. Then we'll talk about what they mean.
2. Touch under the first line. *Pause.*
   What words? *Signal.* **Brace yourself.**
3. Next word. *Pause.*
   What word? *Signal.* **Mock.**
4. *Repeat step 2 for each remaining word in column 3.*
5. *Repeat the words in column 3 until firm.*

Task B

1. You've learned the meanings for all these words. The words in line 1 are **brace yourself.** *Call on a student.* What does **brace yourself** mean? *Idea:* When you tighten your muscles and get ready for a great jolt.
2. Everybody, if you're falling off your bike and getting ready to hit the ground, what do you do? *Signal.* **Brace yourself.**

Task C

Word 2 is **mock.** *Call on a student.*
What is **mock** encouragement? *Idea:* Encouragement that is not sincere.

Task D

1. Word 3 is **abruptly.** *Call on a student.*
   What does **abruptly** mean? *Idea:* Suddenly.
2. Everybody, what's another way of saying **We turned around suddenly?** *Signal.* **We turned around abruptly.**

Task E

Word 4 is **gallop.** *Call on a student.*
What is a **gallop?** *Idea:* When a horse runs almost as fast as it can.

Task F

Word 5 is **dilapidated.** *Call on a student.*
What does **dilapidated** mean? *Idea:* Broken-down and in bad shape.

Task G

Word 6 is **marvel.** *Call on a student.*
When you **marvel** over something, what do you think about the thing? *Idea:* You think that thing is marvelous.

Task H

Word 7 is **spectators.** *Call on a student.*
What are **spectators?** *Idea:* People who watch an event.

EXERCISE 4   Vocabulary development

Task A

1. Everybody, touch column 4. *Check.*
   First you're going to read the words in column 4. Then we'll talk about what they mean.
2. Touch under the first line. *Pause.*
   What words? *Signal.* **Mount a horse.**
3. Next word. *Pause.*
   What word? *Signal.* **Officials.**
4. *Repeat step 3 for each remaining word in column 4.*
5. *Repeat the words in column 4 until firm.*

Task B

Now let's talk about what those words mean. The words in line 1 are **mount a horse.** When you **mount a horse,** you get on the horse. Everybody, what are you doing when you get on a horse? *Signal.* **Mounting a horse.**

Task C

Word 2 is **officials. Officials** are people who see to it that the rules are followed. The **officials** at a race are the people who see to it that the horses and riders follow all the rules.

PART A   **Word Lists**

1	2	3	4
official	decorate	Vocabulary words	Vocabulary words
circular	Arabian	1. brace yourself	1. mount a horse
triangular	fiftieth	2. mock	2. officials
Rudy	hooves	3. abruptly	3. shabby
reins		4. gallop	4. numb
numb		5. dilapidated	
		6. marvel	
		7. spectators	

Lesson 39

A Horse to Remember
PART 4

The jumping contest at Ealing was a colorful affair. Ealing was about forty miles from the Briggs' farm. Ⓐ

ENGLAND

London

Briggs' Farm

Ealing

150   Lesson 39   Textbook

Mr. Jones put Nellie in the back of his dilapidated truck. Ⓑ Mr. Jones drove as Tara sat next to him. Tara's mother and father followed in their car. Two boys from Tara's school rode with them. A third vehicle followed the Briggs' car. It was packed with seven neighbors. All of them had seen Nellie jump, and had marveled over her ability. Just before the vehicles had left Mr. Jones' shop, one of the neighbors had shouted, "You'll hear some cheers for old Nellie even if she doesn't win."

Mr. Jones responded coldly, "She'll win."

Just before the contest was to begin, Tara became so nervous that she didn't think she'd be able to ride. Things were so confusing that her mind seemed to go numb. Officials for the race examined the horse, asked Tara questions, and had Mr. Jones and Tara's father fill out some forms. Then one official said, "Well, she's a strong horse. She might even finish the race." Ⓒ

Tara didn't answer the official. She smiled politely, feeling very embarrassed. She was wearing a shiny green shirt that her mother had made for her and riding boots that were too big for her. She wore a helmet and motorcycle goggles that she had found in Mr. Jones' shop. Her outfit looked very shabby compared to the ones

Task D

Word 3 is **shabby.** Something that looks very cheap and in poor condition is **shabby.** Everybody, what do we call something that looks very cheap and in poor condition? *Signal.* **Shabby.**

Task E

Word 4 is **numb.** When you have no feeling in part of your body, that part is **numb.** When a dentist gives you a shot, the shot makes your teeth and mouth numb.

STORY READING

EXERCISE 5   Decoding and comprehension

1. Everybody, turn to page 150 in your textbook. *Wait. Call on a student.* What's the error limit for this lesson? **10 errors.**
2. *Call on individual students to read. Present the tasks specified for each circled letter.*

Ⓐ In which country does the story of Nellie take place? **England.**
- Near which large city does the Briggs family live? **London.**
- Which direction would you have to go from the Briggs farm to reach London? **East.**
- How far would you go? *Idea:* About 50 miles.
- What's the name of a town that you would go through just before reaching London? **Ealing.**
- What event is happening at that place? **A jumping contest.**
- Everybody, look at the map. *Check.* The map shows Ealing and the route that Tara and the others would take from the Briggs' farm. Everybody, touch the farm. *Check.*
- Now follow the route to Ealing. *Check.*
- Which direction do you go to from the farm to reach Ealing? **East.**
- Where would you go if you continued in that direction? **London.**

Ⓑ Where was Nellie? *Idea:* In the back of Mr. Jones' truck.
- Was that truck in good shape? **No.**

Ⓒ Name some things that happened before the race began. *Call on individual students. Ideas:* Officials examined Nellie; asked Tara questions; had Mr. Jones and Mr. Briggs fill out forms.
- When the official said that Nellie might even finish the race, did he think that she could win? **No.**

the other riders wore. And Nellie looked even shabbier compared to the other horses. Some of them were so beautiful that they gave Tara chills as she looked at them. One great horse was as white as snow. Another was as black as night. That horse was probably the most beautiful. When it moved, it glistened and every muscle in its fine body seemed to ripple and announce that this horse had great power.

Tara tried to keep Nellie away from the other horses that were exercising and prancing about. Ⓓ From time to time, one of the riders would look over at Nellie and smile. Before leaving the farm, Tara had decorated her neck with ribbons of green silk. When she had put the ribbons on Nellie, she had thought that Nellie looked pretty. But now, she thought Nellie looked silly. "We'll show them," she said softly to her, but she knew that Nellie and her rider must have looked pretty strange in the company of these other horses.

There were about a thousand spectators, most of them gathered near the finish line. Ⓔ As handlers led the horses to the starting line, an announcement came over the loudspeakers. Ⓕ The spectators turned toward the loudspeakers as the announcement began. "Ladies and gentlemen, welcome to the fiftieth running at Ealing. As you know, this is a one-mile circular course with five jumps. The horses go around the course three times." Ⓖ

The announcer continued, "For a horse to finish, it must be successful in clearing all fifteen jumps and must still have a rider on it at the end of the course. A rider who falls may mount his horse and continue running the course. The hardest parts of the course are the two fence jumps. Both fences are slightly more than five feet high and they are spaced close together. So the horse must clear the first and within a few strides get ready for the second. In a few moments, the race will begin." Ⓗ

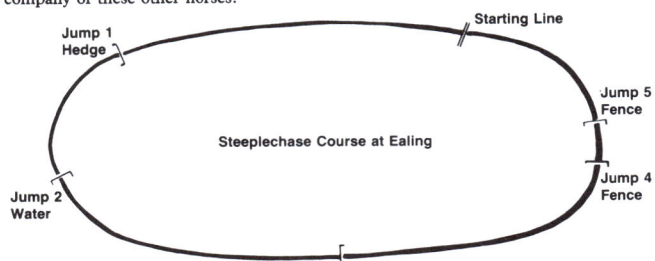

Jump 1 Hedge — **Starting Line**

Steeplechase Course at Ealing

Jump 5 Fence

Jump 4 Fence

Jump 2 Water

Jump 3 Shelf

A handler led Nellie to the starting line and stood next to the horse. Tara judged that there were more than twenty-five horses in this race. She put on her motorcycle goggles and looked at the other horses. She could see the mayor's horse, with the mayor's oldest son on him. The mayor's son shouted to Tara, "You'll need those goggles. Rudy here is going to throw a lot of mud in your face." He patted Rudy on the neck. Ⓘ

Tara was still trying to organize her thoughts when a terribly loud gun sounded. Ⓙ ★10 ERRORS★

Nellie jumped and threw Tara. The other horses pounded across the soft ground, throwing chunks of grass and dirt into the air.

Fortunately, Tara managed to hold on to the reins when she fell. Nellie wanted to run. "Stop," she shouted. "Stop."

Nellie pulled Tara along the ground for a few steps, then she stopped calmly, waiting for Tara to mount her. The spectators shouted mock encouragement to Tara. "You can still win," one of them shouted, and the spectators broke into laughter.

By the time Tara told Nellie, "Go Nellie! Run fast!" the other horses were so far ahead that Tara could no longer hear the pounding of their hooves. She bent forward and let Nellie run, but not as fast as Nellie wanted to run. She remembered what Mr. Jones had told her. "It's a long, tiring race. And a good horse will run until it drops dead. So you hold her in. Don't let

Ⓓ Why do you think she didn't want Nellie to be next to these horses? *Idea:* She wouldn't look very good.

Ⓔ How many spectators were there? *Idea:* About a thousand.

• What are spectators? *Idea:* People who watch events.

Ⓕ Who led the horses to the starting line? **Handlers.**

Handlers are people who lead the horses around before and after the race.

Ⓖ Everybody, look at the picture. *Check.*

• Touch the starting line. *Check.*

• How long is the course? **One mile.**

• How many jumps are in the course? **Five.**

• How many times do the horses go around the course? **Three times.**

• If the horses go around the course three times, how many miles will the horses run? **Three miles.**

• And how many jumps will the horses have to make? **Fifteen.**

Ⓗ Can a rider mount a horse again if the rider falls? **Yes.**

• What's the hardest part of the course? *Idea:* The two fence jumps.

• How high are those fences? *Idea:* About five feet high.

• What else makes this part of the course hard? *Idea:* The fences are spaced close together, which makes it hard for the horse to jump the second fence.

Ⓘ What is the name of the mayor's horse? **Rudy.**

• Why did the mayor's son think that Tara would need goggles? *Idea:* He thought that Rudy would throw mud in Tara's face.

• Everybody, look at the picture. *Check.* You can see the horses lined up at the starting line. Everybody, see if you can touch Nellie in that picture. *Check.*

• Touch Tara's goggles. *Check.*

• The reins are the straps the rider holds to direct the horse. Touch the reins that Tara is holding. *Check.*

Ⓙ What did the gun signal? *Idea:* The race had started.

• Read the rest of the story to yourselves and be ready to answer some questions.

After all students have finished reading:

• When Tara fell, did Nellie **run away** without a rider? **No.**

• Why not? *Idea:* Tara kept hold of the reins.

• When Tara got on Nellie's back, where were the other horses? *Idea:* Far ahead of them.

• Did Tara tell Nellie to run as fast as she wanted to? **No.**

• What could happen to Nellie if she ran as fast as she wanted? *Idea:* She might get hurt.

her go at full speed."

Tara followed Mr. Jones' directions, but it seemed hopeless. The first jump was the hedge jump. One horse had already fallen trying to go over the first jump and the rider was walking slowly toward the starting line with his back covered with grass stains. The other horses were already approaching the third jump when Nellie was clearing the first jump. For an instant, Tara's attention was drawn to the crowd near the first jump. Almost in one voice they said, "Ooooo," as Nellie cleared it. Now Tara could hear the people near the first jump applauding Nellie's performance.

Now the second jump and more applause. Two more horses out of the race— one of them standing next to the jump, holding one of its front hooves off the ground. "I hope he's all right," Tara said to herself.

Then she heard part of an announcement over the loudspeakers. She couldn't hear it very well above the sound of squeaking leather, pounding hooves, and heavy breathing. From what she could hear, she gathered that the announcer was talking about Nellie. Here's what Tara heard: ". . . call your attention to . . . She's worth watching . . . a long way behind, but possibly the best jumper in . . ."

The two fence jumps were at the end of the circle, jumps four and five. The crowd cheered wildly as Nellie cleared these jumps. Three other horses hadn't cleared them. Tara's mind was starting to

clear now and she was becoming more confident. She started around the course the second time. She figured that there were only about ten horses left in the race. She was already catching up to some of them. One of them was the mayor's horse. The other was the brilliant white horse. But far ahead of these horses was the black horse. It was at least three jumps ahead of Nellie. She hadn't gained on that horse at all.

During the second round of the course, Nellie caught up to the mayor's horse at the second jump. Tara could see that the mayor's horse was tiring and straining. Nellie was still running easily. The second jump was a water jump about ten feet across. Nellie and the mayor's horse took off for the jump at exactly the same time. Nellie cleared the jump with at least five feet to spare. The mayor's horse got off a poor jump, landed with its front hooves in the water, stumbled, and fell forward, tossing the mayor's son from the saddle. Tara looked back. The mayor's son was sitting in the water. The horse was standing up.

Tara heard the loudspeakers. "Her name is Nellie," the announcer was saying. "And she jumps as if she had rockets in her feet."

Loud shouts of "Come on, Nellie!" came from the crowd.

Tara finished the second round of the course and started the third round. Nellie was starting to breathe very hard now, and Tara could feel her tug a little with each stride. She was tiring. But still the black horse was three jumps ahead of her.

- On the first time around the circular course, Tara heard part of an announcement. What was the announcer saying about Nellie? *Idea:* She's worth watching; she's possibly the best jumper.
- When Nellie started around the course the second time, how many horses were still in the competition? *Idea:* About ten.
- How many were in the competition when the race began? *Idea:* More than twenty-five.
- So, how many horses had already dropped out of the steeplechase? *Idea:* About fifteen.
- What kind of jump did Nellie and the mayor's horse approach at the same time? *Idea:* A water jump.
- Describe what the two horses did on that jump. *Idea:* Nellie cleared it easily, but the mayor's horse stumbled and threw its rider.
- When Tara had rounded the course for the second time and started around for the third time, which horse was still far ahead? **The black horse.**
- How far ahead? *Idea:* Three jumps ahead.
- Had Nellie gained on that horse at all? **No.**

Award 4 points or have the students reread to the error limit sign.

INDEPENDENT WORK

Do all the items in your skillbook and workbook for lesson 39.

WORKCHECK AND AWARDING POINTS

1. *Read the questions and answers for the skillbook and workbook.*
2. *Award points for independent work as follows:*

> 0 errors . . . . .6 points
> 2 errors . . . . .4 points
> 3, 4, or 5 errors . . . . .2 points
> 5 or more errors . . . . .0 points

3. *Award bonus points as follows:*

> Correcting missed items
> or getting all items right . . . . .2 points
> Doing the writing
> assignment acceptably . . . . .2 points

ANSWER KEY FOR WORKBOOK

Map Skills

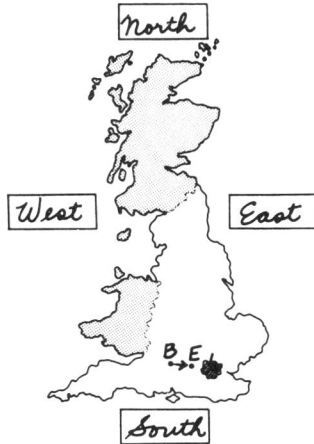

1. **a.** Write **North, West, South,** and **East** in the boxes around the map.
   b. Write the name of the country the map shows.
   England
   c. Write **L** on the city of London.
   d. Write **E** on the city of Ealing.
   e. Write **B** on the Briggs' farm.
   f. Draw an **arrow** from the Briggs' farm to Ealing.
2. **a.** In which direction did the Briggs family go to reach Ealing?
   East
   b. How many miles did they travel to get to Ealing? _40_
   c. How many miles is it from Ealing to London? _10_

3. Look at the picture of the course at Ealing.

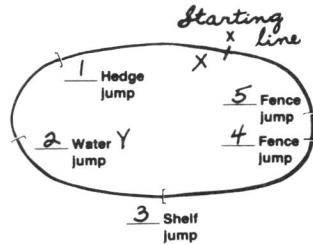

   a. Label the starting line.
   b. Number the jumps from **1** through **5.**
   c. Write **X** to show where Nellie threw Tara.
   d. Write **Y** to show where the mayor's son was tossed from the saddle.

Story Items

4. **a.** How long is the course at Ealing?
   1 mile
   b. How many times do the horses go around the course? _3_
   c. So, how many miles will the horses run to finish the entire race?
   _3_
5. **a.** How many jumps are in the course? _5_
   b. So, how many jumps will the horses have to make to finish the race? _15_

6. **Circle the correct answers.**
   a. What shape was the jumping course at Ealing?
   - triangular   • (circular)
   - rectangular
   b. How did the crowd respond to Nellie at the beginning of the race?
   - with sadness
   - with real encouragement
   - (with mock encouragement)
   c. How did the crowd respond to Nellie later in the race?
   - with sadness
   - (with real encouragement)
   - with mock encouragement

ANSWER KEY FOR SKILLBOOK

PART B

1. 1000
2. **a.** _Idea:_ The fence jumps
   b. _Idea:_ Because they were so close together
3. **a.** _Idea:_ She fell off Nellie
   b. The reins
4. No
5. _Idea:_ At the third jump
6. **a.** No
   b. _Idea:_ Because it was a long race
7. **a.** Black
   b. Gray
8. **a.** _Idea:_ The water jump
   b. _Idea:_ Cleared it
   c. _Idea:_ Fell in the water
9. **a.** The black horse
   b. _Idea:_ None
   c. Three

PART C

10. **a.** extended
    b. grew
    c. single strip
    d. moved at a very slow, tired pace
    e. nudged
    f. resisted the impulse
    g. stray
    h. obstacle
    i. endurance
    j. blurted out
    k. dilapidated

Lesson 40

Lesson 40

PART A Word Lists

1	2	3
concentrate	familiar	**Vocabulary words**
photographer	camera	1. push a horse too hard
idiot	statue	2. let a horse out
Kelvin	Nighthawk	3. hold a horse in
caution		4. caution
Liverpool		5. magnificent
		6. turf

WORD PRACTICE AND VOCABULARY

EXERCISE 1 Word practice

1. Everybody, find lesson 40, part A in your skillbook. *Wait.* Touch under each word in column 1 as I read it.
2. The first word is **concentrate.**
3. Next word. **Photographer.**
4. *Repeat step 3 for each remaining word in column 1.*
5. Your turn. Read the first word. *Signal.* **Concentrate.**
6. Next word. *Signal.* **Photographer.**
7. *Repeat step 6 for each remaining word in column 1.*
8. *Repeat the words in column 1 until firm.*

EXERCISE 2 Word practice

1. Everybody, touch under the first word in column 2. *Pause.*
   What word? *Signal.* **Familiar.**
2. Next word. *Pause.*
   What word? *Signal.* **Camera.**
3. *Repeat step 2 for each remaining word in column 2.*
4. *Repeat the words in column 2 until firm.*

EXERCISE 3 Vocabulary development

Task A

1. Everybody, touch column 3. *Check.*
   First you're going to read the words in column 3. Then we'll talk about what they mean.
2. Touch under the first line. *Pause.*
   What words? *Signal.* **Push a horse too hard.**
3. Next line. *Pause.*
   What words? *Signal.* **Let a horse out.**
4. *Repeat step 3 for **hold a horse in.***
5. Next word. *Pause.*
   What word? *Signal.* **Caution.**
6. *Repeat step 5 for each remaining word in column 3.*
7. *Repeat the words in column 3 until firm.*

Task B

Now let's talk about what those words mean. The words in the **first three lines** are expressions that people use when they talk about how to ride horses. The words in line 1 are **push a horse too hard.** When you **push a horse too hard,** you try to make the horse go too fast. Everybody, what are you doing when you try to make the horse go too fast? *Signal.* **Pushing a horse too hard.**

Task C

The words in line 2 are **let a horse out.** When you **let a horse out,** you let it run faster when it wants to run faster.
Everybody, what are you doing when you let a horse run faster when it wants to run faster? *Signal.* **Letting a horse out.**

Task D

The words in line 3 are **hold a horse in.** When you **hold a horse in,** you don't let it run faster even though it wants to run faster. Everybody, what are you doing when you don't let a horse run faster even though it wants to run faster? *Signal.* **Holding a horse in.**

Task E

1. Word 4 is **caution.** When you **caution** somebody, you **warn** that person about something. Here's another way of saying **He warned his brother about using the car: He cautioned his brother about using the car.**
2. Everybody, what's another way of saying **He warned his brother about using the car?** *Signal.* **He cautioned his brother about using the car.**
3. Everybody, what's another way of saying **She warned her father about the loose wire?** *Signal.* **She cautioned her father about the loose wire.**

Task F

1. Word 5 is **magnificent.** Another word for **wonderful** or **marvelous** is **magnificent.** Everybody, what's another way of saying **It was a marvelous race?** *Signal.* **It was a magnificent race.**
2. Everybody, what's another way of saying **They went to a wonderful party?** *Signal.* **They went to a magnificent party.**

Task G

Word 6 is **turf.** Another word for **ground covered with grass** is **turf.** Everybody, what's another word for ground covered with grass? *Signal.* **Turf.**

Lesson 40

A Horse to Remember
PART 5

Tara didn't want to push Nellie too hard, but she wanted her to win. Oh, how she wanted her to win. As Tara cleared the first jump on the third round, she heard a familiar voice above the cheering crowd. "Let her out Tara! Let her out!" It was Mr. Jones' voice.Ⓐ

"Okay," Tara said to herself, and bent forward. "A little faster, Nellie." She nudged Nellie with her heels and Nellie responded by running a little faster.

Tara cleared the second jump and then looked ahead. She had now passed all the horses except one, the black horse, which was now less than two jumps ahead and approaching the fourth jump.Ⓑ Nellie was gaining on the black horse, but all the black horse had to do to finish the race was to clear jumps four and five and then run to the finish line. Nellie could not make up the distance.Ⓒ

But Tara decided to try. She put her head right against Nellie's neck, out of the wind. She was concentrating on the third jump when she heard a loud roar from the crowd. After completing the jump, she looked toward the finish line. The black horse was approaching the finish line, but without a rider.Ⓓ The rider had fallen off at the fifth jump and the brave horse had

154   Lesson 40   Textbook

continued alone to the finish line.Ⓔ

Now the crowd was cheering wildly. Tara looked behind to see if any horses were gaining on Nellie. None were even near. So she held Nellie in a little bit and Nellie cleared the last two jumps with two easy bounds. The crowd roared with delight as Nellie—swaybacked Nellie—ran easily across the finish line.Ⓕ

Photographers pointed cameras at Tara and Nellie. Flash bulbs went off. Hundreds of people crowded around the tired horse. A wrinkled, smiling face pushed through the crowd.Ⓖ "I knew she could do it," Mr. Jones hollered, giving Nellie a big hug. Then he grabbed the reins, shouted at the crowd to move back, and began to walk the horse.Ⓗ

Tara jumped down, gave Nellie a big hug, and started walking next to Mr. Jones. Tara couldn't stop smiling. No matter how hard she tried, and how many times she told herself that she must look like a grinning idiot, she smiled, and smiled, and smiled.

Tara smiled all the way home. In her lap, she held the large first prize trophy. It was all gold, topped with a statue of a handsome horse leaping over a jump. Tara thought that the horse on the trophy

looked much more handsome than Nellie, but that didn't matter. Nellie was the greatest horse in the world.

Tara stopped smiling when Mr. Jones' truck pulled up in front of the blacksmith shop. A long, black expensive-looking car was parked in front of the shop, and a tall man in a dark suit was standing next to the car. As Tara and Mr. Jones got out of the truck, the man approached them. "I'm Kelvin Longly," he said in a pleasant voice. "I own Night-

hawk, the black horse that would have beaten Nellie if it hadn't thrown his rider."

"That's a beautiful horse," Tara said. "I'm sorry for you that he didn't win."

Mr. Longly said, "I'll come right to the point. If you hadn't fallen at the starting line, you might have beaten Nighthawk. And I don't like that kind of doubt. I bought Nighthawk because he was a winner. That's what I want, a winner. And because your horse may be the real winner,

Lesson 40   Textbook   155

STORY READING

EXERCISE 4   Decoding and comprehension

1. Everybody, turn to page 154 in your textbook. *Wait. Call on a student.* What's the error limit for this lesson? **10 errors.**
2. *Call on individual students to read. Present the tasks specified for each circled letter.*

Ⓐ What did Mr. Jones say? **Let her out!**
● Where was Nellie when Tara heard Mr. Jones say that? *Idea:* Clearing the first jump on the third round.
● How many times had Nellie already gone around the course? **Two times.**
● What does that mean: **Let her out?** *Idea:* Let Nellie go as fast as she can.
Ⓑ Which jump had Tara just cleared? **The second jump.**
● Which jump was the black horse approaching? **The fourth jump.**
● How many jumps ahead was the black horse now? **Two.**
● Was Nellie gaining on that horse? **Yes.**
Ⓒ Could Nellie catch the black horse before he finished? **No.**
Ⓓ What made the crowd roar? *Idea:* The black horse was approaching the finish line.
● Which horse will be the first to cross the finish line? **The black horse.**
● Will that horse be the winner? **No.**
● Why not? *Idea:* The black horse doesn't have a rider.
Ⓔ Can the black horse win the race? **No.**
● Why not? *Idea:* The rider has to be on the horse when it passes the finish line.
● What happened to the rider? *Idea:* He fell off at the fifth jump.
Ⓕ Who won? **Nellie.**
● How do you think the mayor feels? *Ideas:* Surprised; angry; disappointed.
● The story says that Tara held Nellie in a little bit when she saw that no horse was close behind. What does that mean: **held her in?** *Idea:* Tara didn't let her go as fast as she wanted to.
Ⓖ Whose face is that? **Mr. Jones'.**
Ⓗ A horse has to walk around after a long race or the horse may become very sick.

Lesson 40   **187**

I want to buy her." ①

"I'm sorry," Tara said. "We couldn't sell her."

By now, the cars that followed Mr. Jones' truck from Ealing were parked and everybody who had been riding in them was standing behind Tara and Mr. Jones. Tara's father said, "How much are you prepared to pay for Nellie?"

Tara was shocked and she looked at her father. "But Dad . . ." she started to say.

"Tara," her father interrupted. "Let's hear what Mr. Longly has to say." ① ★10 ERRORS★

Mr. Longly looked at Tara's father and said, "I paid twenty-five thousand pounds for Nighthawk, and I'm willing to pay the same amount for Nellie."

A pound is worth over two dollars. Tara's father earned less than six thousand pounds a year, working for the railroad. The farm brought in another thousand pounds a year, but no more. So you can understand why Mrs. Briggs gasped when Mr. Longly made his offer for Nellie. She said, "Twenty-five thousand pounds is more money than we'll earn in . . ."

Mr. Briggs interrupted. "Well," he said. Then he faced Mr. Longly, and Tara noticed that her father's hand was trembling. "Well," Mr. Briggs repeated. "I think we have to talk this over with Tara. Would it be all right if I gave you a call in a day or two?"

"Certainly," Mr. Longly said. He handed Tara's father a card with his phone number on it. "Call me any time," he said

pleasantly. Then he said, "farewell," and got in the back seat of his car. Tara heard him tell the driver to drive to Longly's place in London.

Tara was no longer smiling. She was stunned. As soon as the black car pulled away, she turned to her father and said, "But Dad, you can't sell Nellie. She's the best . . ."

Mr. Briggs interrupted quietly. "Tara," he said, "we'll talk about it at home."

Mr. Jones pointed his finger at the truck and said, "I think Tara's right. That horse may be the best jumping horse that has ever lived."

"I respect your opinion," Mr. Briggs said. "But I'm not sure that we should try to keep anything as valuable as Nellie. If she's worth twenty-five thousand pounds, she should have an owner who can afford horses that are worth that much. I'm just a poor farmer."

"Oh Dad, you can't . . ."

"Tara we'll talk about it at home."

The thought of losing Nellie hurt so much that it almost tore Tara's heart out. She ached with far more pain than she had experienced when she had fallen from Nellie's back. And she couldn't believe that her father would even think of getting rid of Nellie.

Tara drove to the farm with Mr. Jones, who was silent during the trip. Tara just stared straight ahead, as the old truck bounced down the road. Once Tara said, "He can't do that. It's not fair."

Without taking his eyes from the

road, Mr. Jones said, "He's your father. You listen to what he says and you obey him."

"I'll try." Tara said, almost choking. "I'll try."

When Mr. Jones pulled up in back of the house, he said, "You take care of Nellie. I'm going to say a few things to your father."

Tara led Nellie from the truck, unbolted the gate, and then stopped. She could hear Mr. Jones speaking very loudly inside the house. "If you knew anything about horses, you would know that your Nellie is worth much more than twenty-five thousand pounds. People pay that much for a steeplechase horse that has a chance of winning. Nellie has a lot more

than a chance. She will win. I've seen horses sell for fifty thousand pounds that couldn't stay within three jumps of Nellie. If you want to sell her, give her a chance to show what she can do. Then you can name your own price."

Tara could hear other voices, but she couldn't hear what they were saying. Slowly, she led Nellie into her stall. She gave Nellie a big hug and said, "You're the most beautiful horse in the world."

When she looked up, her father and Mr. Jones were standing at the barn door, smiling. Tara's father said, "Well, I guess we're going to have to keep old Nellie for a while."

Tara started smiling again.

---

① What's the name of the man who is talking about buying Nellie? **Mr. Longly.**

- Do you think Mr. Longley is very rich? **Yes.**

- Why? *Ideas:* Because he is offering money for Nellie; because he drives an expensive car.

- What's the name of Mr. Longley's horse? **Nighthawk.**

- Why did he buy that horse? *Idea:* Because he thought it was a winner.

- Why does he want to buy Nellie? *Ideas:* Because he thinks Nellie can beat Nighthawk; because he thinks Nellie is a winner.

① Does it sound as if Mr. Briggs might be interested in selling Nellie? **Yes.**

- Do you think Tara would ever sell the horse if the choice was hers? **No.**

- Read the rest of the story to yourselves and be ready to answer some questions.

After all students have finished reading:

- How much had Mr. Longly paid for Nighthawk? *Idea:* 25 thousand pounds.

- How much is a pound worth? *Idea:* Over two dollars.
  So 25 thousand pounds is worth more than 50 thousand dollars.

- Did Tara's father earn as much as 25 thousand pounds a year? **No.**

- He made only about 6 thousand pounds a year. So how many years would it take the Briggs family to make 25 thousand pounds? *Idea:* About four years.

- Why did Tara's mother gasp when she heard the offer that Mr. Longly made? *Idea:* She was shocked by the large amount of money.

- When Tara and Mr. Jones arrived at the Briggs' farm, what did Tara do? *Idea:* Took care of Nellie.

- What did Mr. Jones do? *Idea:* Went inside to talk to Mr. Briggs.

- What was Mr. Jones saying inside the house? *Idea:* Nellie is valuable.

- Mr. Jones said that Mr. Briggs could name his own price after Nellie proved how good she was. What does that mean: **name your own price?** *Idea:* Ask for as much money as you want.

- Was the offer that Mr. Longly made such a good one after all? **No.**

- When Tara put Nellie in her stall, what did she tell Nellie? *Idea:* That she was the most beautiful horse in the world.

- How did Tara feel? *Idea:* Sad.

- What made her feel a lot better? *Idea:* Her father told her that he was going to keep Nellie.

Award 4 points or have the students reread to the error limit sign.

ANSWER KEY FOR WORKBOOK

Review Items

1. Write the name of the correct jump underneath each picture.

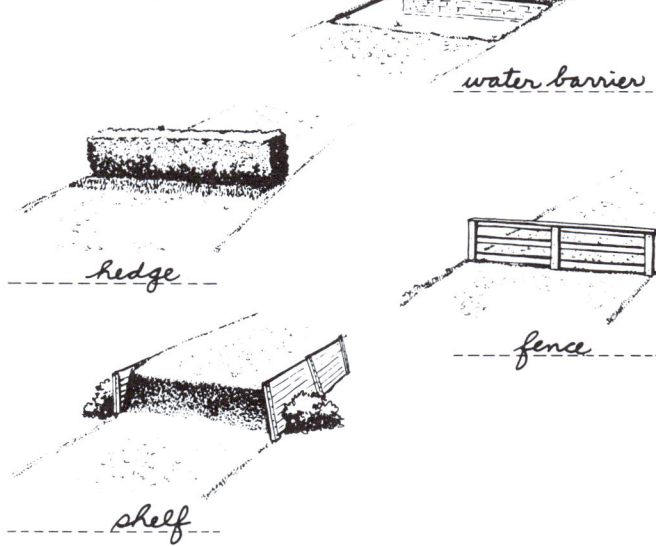

water barrier

hedge

fence

shelf

Map Skills

2. Look at the picture below of the course at Ealing.

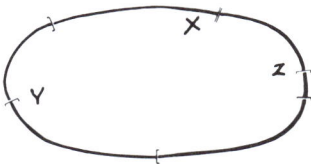

X

Y

Z

a. Write **X** to show where Nellie threw Tara.
b. Write **Y** to show where Nellie caught up with the mayor's horse.
c. Write **Z** to show where the black horse threw off its rider.

Story Items

3. a. How long is the course at Ealing?

1 mile

b. How many times will the horses go around the course?

3

c. So, how many miles will the horses run to finish the entire race?

3

4. a. How many jumps are in the course? _5_

b. So, how many jumps will the horses have to make to finish the race? _15_

5. **Use the words in the box to fill in the blanks.**

| forward | backward |

a. Tara fell _backward_ when Nellie heard the starting gun.
b. Tara fell _forward_ when Nellie landed on the bank next to the stream.

INDEPENDENT WORK

Do all the items in your skillbook and workbook for lesson 40.

WORKCHECK AND AWARDING POINTS

1. *Read the questions and answers for the skillbook and workbook.*
2. *Award points for independent work as follows:*

0 errors	*.6 points*
2 errors	*.4 points*
3, 4, or 5 errors	*.2 points*
5 or more errors	*.0 points*

3. *Award bonus points as follows:*

Correcting missed items or getting all items right	*.2 points*
Doing the writing assignment acceptably	*.2 points*

ANSWER KEY FOR SKILLBOOK

PART B

1. a. Mr. Jones
   b. *Idea:* Let her out!
2. a. The black horse
   b. *Idea:* Because it lost its rider
   c. *Idea:* He had fallen off
3. *Idea:* Because she was so far ahead
4. a. *Idea:* Mr. Longly
   b. Nellie
   c. 25,000 pounds
   d. *Idea:* About four
5. a. Mr. Briggs
   b. Tara
6. a. Mr. Jones
   b. 25,000
7. a. *Idea:* Mr. Briggs and Mr. Jones
   b. *Idea:* He would keep Nellie

PART C

8. a. Kansas
   b. Land of the East
   c. The Emerald City
   d. Kansas
   e. *Idea:* Work with tin
   f. *Idea:* Work with gold
9. a. very fine
   b. tough
   c. soft
   d. type of cotton

Lesson 41

Lesson 41

PART A   Word Lists

1	2	3	4 Vocabulary words	5 Vocabulary words
hedge	incredible	urge	1. turf	1. lagging behind
sledge	photographer	eighteenth	2. caution	2. prance
nudge	concentrate	twenty	3. magnificent	3. dangling
ledge	microphone	twentieth		4. straining
	photograph			5. frantically

WORD PRACTICE AND VOCABULARY

EXERCISE 1   Word family

1. Everybody, find lesson 41, part A in your skillbook. *Wait.* Touch column 1. *Check.* All those words end with the letters **d-g-e.** Touch under the first word. *Pause.* What word? *Signal.* **Hedge.**
2. Next word. *Pause.* What word? *Signal.* **Sledge.**
3. *Repeat step 2 for each remaining word in column 1.*
4. *Repeat the words in column 1 until firm.*

EXERCISE 2   Word practice

1. Everybody, touch under the first word in column 2. *Pause.* What word? *Signal.* **Incredible.**
2. Next word. *Pause.* What word? *Signal.* **Photographer.**
3. *Repeat step 2 for each remaining word in column 2.*
4. *Repeat the words in column 2 until firm.*
5. *Repeat steps 1–4 for column 3.*

EXERCISE 3   Vocabulary review

Task A
1. Everybody, touch column 4. *Check.* First you're going to read the words in column 4. Then we'll talk about what they mean.
2. Touch under the first word. *Pause.* What word? *Signal.* **Turf.**
3. Next word. *Pause.* What word? *Signal.* **Caution.**
4. *Repeat step 3 for* **magnificent.**

Task B
You've learned the meaning for all these words. Word 1 is **turf.** *Call on a student.* What is **turf?** *Idea:* Ground covered with grass.

Task C
1. Word 2 is **caution.** *Call on a student.* What does **caution** mean? *Idea:* Warn.
2. Everybody, what's another way of saying **She warned her brother about the slippery street?** *Signal.* **She cautioned her brother about the slippery street.**

Task D
1. Word 3 is **magnificent.** *Call on a student.* What does **magnificent** mean? *Ideas:* Marvelous; wonderful.

2. Everybody, what's another way of saying **They saw a marvelous sunset?** *Signal.* **They saw a magnificent sunset.**
3. Everybody, what's another way of saying **I won a wonderful prize?** *Signal.* **I won a magnificent prize.**

EXERCISE 4   Vocabulary development

Task A
1. Everybody, touch column 5. *Check.* First you're going to read the words in column 5. Then we'll talk about what they mean.
2. Touch under the first line. *Pause.* What words? *Signal.* **Lagging behind.**
3. Next word. *Pause.* What word? *Signal.* **Prance.**
4. *Repeat step 3 for each remaining word in column 5.*
5. *Repeat the words in column 5 until firm.*

Task B
1. Now let's talk about what those words mean. The words in line 1 are **lagging behind.** Another way of saying **dropping back** is **lagging behind.** Everybody, what's another way of saying **dropping back?** *Signal.* **Lagging behind.**
2. Everybody, what's another way of saying **The white horse was dropping back?** *Signal.* **The white horse was lagging behind.**

Task C
Word 2 is **prance.** When a horse **prances,** it steps around as if it wants to start running. Everybody, what is the horse doing when it steps around as if it wants to start running? *Signal.* **Prancing.**

Task D
1. Word 3 is **dangling.** When something is hanging loosely it is **dangling.** Everybody, what's another way of saying **The string was hanging loosely?** *Signal.* **The string was dangling.**
2. Everybody, what's another way of saying **Her foot was hanging loosely in the water?** *Signal.* **Her foot was dangling in the water.**

Task E
Word 4 is **straining.** When you make your body work as hard as it can work, you're **straining** your body. Everybody, what are you doing when you make your body work as hard as it can work? *Signal.* **You're straining your body.**

Task F
1. Word 5 is **frantically.** When people act very wild and nervous, they are acting **frantically.** Everybody, what are they doing when they act very wild and nervous? *Signal.* **Acting frantically.**

Lesson 41

A Horse to Remember
PART 6

The Grand National Steeplechase Championship is run on one of the most demanding steeplechase courses in the world.Ⓐ The course is shaped like a triangle. It has sixteen jumps. The distance around the triangular course is a little over two miles, and the horses must go around the course twice. On the first time around, the horses must go over all sixteen jumps. On the second time around, the horses go over only fourteen jumps. Altogether, the horses must run about four and a half miles and take thirty jumps.Ⓑ

Only those horses with incredible endurance can finish this demanding event. But a lot of horses try each year. They come from all over the world—from the

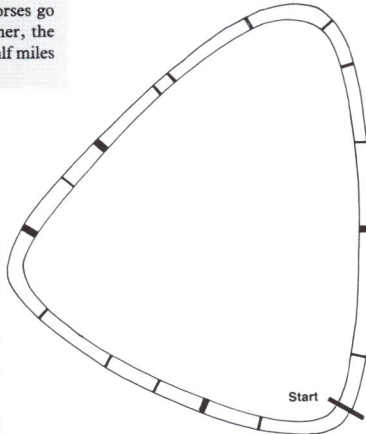

158   Lesson 41   Textbook

United States, France, Australia, and Japan. Many horses that enter the competition are worth a lot of money. These horses are big and strong and have a great deal of endurance.

The Grand National Steeplechase Championship takes place near the large city of Liverpool, which is about two hundred miles north of London.Ⓒ By the time Nellie, Tara, Mr. Jones, and more than twenty people from Tara's village made the long trip to Liverpool, people were no longer laughing at Nellie.Ⓓ Nel-

lie had entered two steeplechases after winning the jumping contest at Ealing. She won first prize in one of those contests and she didn't win the other contest even though she was the first horse to cross the finish line. She had thrown Tara on a hedge jump. Tara had tumbled to the ground without holding onto the reins, and Nellie had continued to the finish line without her. But when she had thrown Tara, Nellie was ahead of the other horses and she was clearly the best jumping horse in the field.Ⓔ

Shortly before the trip to Liverpool, Mr. Longly had visited the Briggs and had made another offer for Nellie. This time, he had offered thirty-five thousand pounds, and he had cautioned Tara, "You may be making a great mistake. Nellie is very good on these shorter courses. But Nighthawk has tremendous endurance. The rider was holding him in near the end of the race at Ealing when you were gaining on him. And I know that Nighthawk can run the four and a half miles at Liverpool. I honestly don't think that your Nellie will be able to stay with him."Ⓕ
★6 ERRORS★

The words that Longly had said kept popping into Tara's mind as she rode to Liverpool in the cab of the truck. Tara had already practiced running a four mile course with Nellie, and she had done very well, but the course used for the practice was not as difficult as the one at Liverpool. Some of the jumps at Liverpool were over five feet high, and there were many jumps.

Lesson 41   Textbook   159

---

2. Everybody, what's another way of saying **The crowd yelled wildly?** *Signal.*
   The crowd yelled frantically.
3. Everybody, what's another way of saying **He ran around nervously?** *Signal.*
   He ran around frantically.

STORY READING

EXERCISE 5   Decoding and comprehension

1. Everybody, turn to page 158 in your textbook. *Wait. Call on a student.* What's the error limit for this lesson? **6 errors.**
2. *Call on individual students to read. Present the tasks specified for each circled letter.*

Ⓐ What does that mean: **one of the most demanding courses?** *Idea:* One of the hardest.

Ⓑ Look at the picture. What shape is the course? **Triangular.**
- How far does a horse run to go around it one time? *Idea:* A little over two miles.
- How many jumps does the horse have to make going around the course the first time? **Sixteen.**
- How many times does a horse have to go around the entire course? **Two.**
- So how far does the horse have to run? *Idea:* About four and a half miles.
- How many jumps does the horse have to make altogether? **Thirty.**

Ⓒ Everybody, touch London on the map. *Check.* Now move north and west until you come to Liverpool. *Check.* Touch the Brigg's farm. *Check.*
- If you went to Liverpool from the Briggs' farm, what is the main direction you would travel? **North.**

Ⓓ Why do you think they stopped laughing? *Idea:* Because Nellie was a great jumping horse.

Ⓔ Think back. How many races had Nellie entered before going to Liverpool? **Three.**
- How many did she win? **Two.**
- Why didn't she win that third race? *Idea:* Because she threw Tara.

Ⓕ Listen to that part again. *Read from* Ⓔ *to* Ⓕ.
- Mr. Longly gives Tara an argument about why it would be a good idea for her to sell Nellie. Why does he think that Nellie might not win at Liverpool? *Idea:* Because Nellie may not have the endurance.
- Mr. Longly explained Nellie was gaining on Nighthawk at the end of the race at Ealing. Was Nighthawk going as fast as he could? **No.**
- Read the rest of the story to yourselves and be ready to answer some questions.

• • •

This time, Tara was ready for the starting gun. Tara wore a smart green jacket and riding boots that fit. Nellie wore handsome green ribbons and the number "31." At the starting line more than fifty horses lined up side by side. On one side of Nellie was a handsome Arabian horse that was almost white, with just a hint of gray spots on its legs. On the other side was Nighthawk. Even in this field of magnificent horses, Nighthawk was still the most beautiful. He pranced and kicked at the turf with his front hooves as he shook his head and snorted.

Tara lowered the goggles that were attached to her new helmet, patted Nellie on the neck and listened to the announcements. The announcer introduced each horse, told where it was from, and gave some information about it. When the announcer said, "And number thirty-one . . ." a tremendous roar went up from the crowd. The announcer told about Nellie's record in jumping contests and then said, "Nellie is one of the horses that you should keep your eye on during this competition." The announcer then continued, "Another great horse that you should watch is Nighthawk."

At last the announcer stopped, the thousands of people who had gathered to watch the competition became silent, the riders got ready and . . . the race began.

160   Lesson 41   Textbook

After all students have finished reading:

- How far had Tara practiced running with Nellie? **Four miles.**
- Was the course she practiced on as difficult as the one at Liverpool? **No.**
- Name some reasons why the steeplechase at Liverpool was so demanding. *Call on several students. Responses:* It was a longer course; it had higher jumps; it had more jumps.
- Was Tara wearing the same outfit at Liverpool that she had worn at Ealing? **No.**
- Tell me some things about her Liverpool outfit that was different. *Call on several students. Responses:* She wore a green jacket; her riding boots fit.
- Describe the horses that were on both sides of Nellie. *Idea:* Nighthawk; a white Arabian horse.
- Part of the story said that Nighthawk snorted. Show me how a horse makes a snorting sound.
- What number was Nellie? **Thirty-one.**
- How did the crowd respond when she was announced? *Idea:* They roared.
- Which was the most beautiful horse in the field? **Nighthawk.**
- If you were Tara would you be worried about Nighthawk? *Call on several students. Responses:* Student preference.

Award 4 points or have the students reread to the error limit sign.

EXERCISE 6   Individual reading checkout

1. *For the individual reading checkout, each student will read 125 words. The passage to be read is the shaded area on the reproduced textbook page for lesson 41 in this presentation book.*
2. Today is a reading checkout day. While you're doing your independent work, I'll call on each student to read part of yesterday's chapter.
3. When I call on you, come up to my desk and bring your textbook with you. After you have read, I'll tell you how many points you can write in the checkout box that's at the top of your workbook page.
4. *If the student finishes the passage in one minute or less, award points as follows:*

0 errors	3 points
1 or 2 errors	1 point
More than 2 errors	0 points

5. *If a student takes more than one minute to read the passage, the student does not earn any points, but have the student reread the passage until he or she is able to read it in no more than one minute with no more than two errors.*

INDEPENDENT WORK

Do all the items in your skillbook and workbook for lesson 41.

ANSWER KEY FOR WORKBOOK

Map Skills

Review Items

2. Look at the riders.

PICTURE 1

PICTURE 2

If the riders are not braced, they will fall.

a. Will the rider in picture 1 fall forward or backward?

backward

b. Will the rider in picture 2 fall forward or backward?

forward

1. Look at the map.
   a. Write **North, West, South** and **East** in the boxes around the map.
   b. What is the name of the country the map shows? *England*
   c. Write **L** on the city of London.
   d. Write **E** on the city of Ealing.
   e. Write **P** on the city of Liverpool.
   f. Write **B** on the Briggs' farm.
   g. Draw an arrow from the Briggs' farm to Liverpool.
   h. What is the main direction you would travel to get from Liverpool to the Brigg's farm? *South*

WORKCHECK AND AWARDING POINTS

1. *Read the questions and answers for the skillbook and workbook.*

2. *Award points for independent work as follows:*

   > 0 errors . . . . .6 points
   > 2 errors . . . . .4 points
   > 3, 4, or 5 errors . . . . .2 points
   > 5 or more errors . . . . .0 points

3. *Award bonus points as follows:*

   > Correcting missed items
   > or getting all items right . . . . .2 points
   > Doing the writing
   > assignment acceptably . . . . .2 points

4. *Remind the students to put the points they earned for their reading checkout, in the box labeled **CO**.*

ANSWER KEY FOR SKILLBOOK

PART B

1. **a.** *Idea:* Over 2 miles
   b. Two times
   c. *Idea:* About four and a half miles
   d. 16
   e. 30
2. **a.** 21
   b. 9
3. **a.** triangular
   b. circular
4. **a.** endurance
   b. Nighthawk
5. holding Nighthawk in
6. **a.** 2
   b. 1
7. **a.** 50
   b. 31
8. Nighthawk
9. *Any two:* New jacket, new riding boots, new helmet
10. *Any two:* It was long; there were many jumps; the jumps were high

PART C

11. **a.** false
    b. true
    c. true
    d. true
    e. true
    f. true
    g. false
    h. false
    i. true
    j. false
12. **a.** shabby
    b. endurance
    c. dilapidated
    d. spectators
    e. numb
    f. officials
    g. developed
    h. braced himself
    i. gently pushing

Lesson 42

Lesson 42

PART A   Word Lists

1	2	3	4
advantage	continued	American Indians	couple
domestic	developed	garbage	civilized
relatives	returned	garage	uncivilized
examining	domesticated	alligators	receives
cooperation	required	humans	possible
unprotected			possibly

5
Vocabulary words
1. lagging behind
2. frantically
3. straining
4. dangling

6
Vocabulary words
1. domestic animals
2. relatives
3. jawbone
4. cooperate
5. venture
6. unprotected

WORD PRACTICE AND VOCABULARY

EXERCISE 1   Word practice

1. Everybody, find lesson 42, part A in your skillbook. *Wait.* Touch under each word in column 1 as I read it.
2. The first word is **advantage.**
3. Next word. **Domestic.**
4. *Repeat step 3 for each remaining word in column 1.*
5. Your turn. Read the first word. *Signal.* **Advantage.**
6. Next word. *Signal.* **Domestic.**
7. *Repeat step 6 for each remaining word in column 1.*
8. *Repeat the words in column 1 until firm.*

EXERCISE 2   Word family

1. Everybody, touch column 2. *Check.* All those words end with the letters **e-d.** But be careful, because **e-d** makes different sounds in the words. Touch under the first word. *Pause.* What word? *Signal.* **Continued.**
2. Next word. *Pause.* What word? *Signal.* **Developed.**
3. *Repeat step 2 for each remaining word in column 2.*
4. *Repeat the words in column 2 until firm.*

EXERCISE 3   Word practice

1. Everybody, touch under the first line in column 3. *Pause.* What words? *Signal.* **American Indian.**
2. Next word. *Pause.* What word? *Signal.* **Garbage.**
3. *Repeat step 2 for each remaining word in column 3.*
4. *Repeat the words in column 3 until firm.*
5. Touch under the first word in column 4. *Pause.* What word? *Signal.* **Couple.**
6. *Repeat steps 2–4 for column 4.*

EXERCISE 4   Vocabulary review

Task A

1. Everybody, touch column 5. *Check.* First you're going to read the words in column 5. Then we'll talk about what they mean.
2. Touch under the first line. *Pause.* What words? *Signal.* **Lagging behind.**
3. Next word. *Pause.* What word? *Signal.* **Frantically.**
4. *Repeat step 3 for each remaining word in column 5.*
5. *Repeat the words in column 5 until firm.*

Task B

You've learned the meanings for all these words. *Call on a student.* What does **lagging behind** mean? *Idea:* Dropping back.
Everybody, what's another way of saying **Nellie was not dropping back?** *Signal.*
Nellie was not lagging behind.

Task C

1. Word 2 is **frantically.** *Call on a student.* What does **frantically** mean? *Ideas:* Nervously; wildly.
2. Everybody, what's another way of saying **The boy ran around nervously?** *Signal.*
The boy ran around frantically.
3. Everybody, what's another way of saying **The spectators yelled wildly?** *Signal.*
The spectators yelled frantically.

Task D

Word 3 is **straining.** *Call on a student.* What does **straining** your body mean? *Idea:* Making your body work as hard as it can.

Task E

1. Word 4 is **dangling.** *Call on a student.* What does **dangling** mean? *Idea:* Hanging loosely.
2. Everybody, what's another way of saying **Her foot was hanging loosely over the side of the boat?** *Signal.* **Her foot was dangling over the side of the boat.**
3. Everybody, what's another way of saying **The rope was hanging loosely?** *Signal.*
The rope was dangling.

EXERCISE 5   Vocabulary development

Task A

1. Everybody, touch column 6. *Check.*
First you're going to read the words in column 6. Then we'll talk about what those words mean.
2. Touch under the first line. *Pause.*
What words? *Signal.* **Domestic animals.**
3. Next word. *Pause.* What word? *Signal.*
Relatives.
4. *Repeat step 3 for each remaining word in column 6.*
5. *Repeat the words in column 6 until firm.*

Task B

1. Now let's talk about what those words mean. The words in the first line are **domestic animals. Domestic animals** are animals that live with people.
2. Everybody, what do we call animals that live with people? *Signal.* **Domestic animals.**

Task C

1. Word 2 is **relatives.** Your **relatives** are the people in your family. Animals have relatives, too. Those relatives are animals from the same family. Cats, tigers, lions, and leopards are relatives. They are members of the cat family.
2. Everybody, what do we call members of the same family? *Signal.* **Relatives.**

Task D

1. Word 3 is **jawbone.** The **jawbone** is the bone that is attached near the bottom of your ear. That bone moves when you open your mouth.
2. Everybody, move your **jawbone.** *Check.*

Task E

1. Word 4 is **cooperate.** When you **cooperate,** you work together or play together with somebody else.
2. Everybody, what are you doing when you work together with somebody else? *Signal.*
Cooperating.

Task F

1. Word 5 is **venture.** When you **venture,** you do something that is like an adventure.
2. Everybody, what are you doing when you do something that is like an adventure? *Signal.*
Venturing.

Task G

1. Word 6 is **unprotected.** Something that is **not protected** is **unprotected.**
2. Everybody, what word means **not protected?** *Signal.* **Unprotected.**

Lesson 42

A Horse to Remember

PART 7

As the horses started the race, they snorted and grunted. Some of the riders shouted and urged their horses to go fast. In the distance was a deafening roar from the crowd. Tara was aware of all these things, but her mind was concentrating on Nellie. She put Nellie into a very slow, easy run and noticed the way she was moving. Tara checked to make sure that she was sitting forward in the saddle and moving easily with Nellie.

Some of the other horses shot away from the starting line very fast. When Tara looked at them pulling far ahead of Nellie, she felt anxious, but she remembered what Mr. Jones had told her. "The idea is not to be the winner when you reach the first jump or even the fifth jump. The idea is to be the winner at the finish line. Hold Nellie in until there are only three or four jumps left in the race. Then let her out if you have to." Ⓐ

Tara looked around to see which horses were near Nellie. About three-fourths of the horses were ahead of her. A few were lagging behind. But right next to Nellie was the magnificent Nighthawk, matching Nellie stride for stride. Ⓑ The two horses were running almost as if they were one horse. They approached the first jump together, in step. They both cleared the jump at the same instant, traveling almost the same height and landing almost together. "This is incredible," Tara said to herself, as a thunderous roar went up from the crowd.

Now the second jump, a great hedge that was at least five feet high. Five riders failed to make this jump. The crowd gasped loudly as one of the horses directly in front of Nellie charged up to the hedge and then stopped abruptly, tossing its rider over the hedge. For a moment Nellie got off stride with Nighthawk. She had to turn a little to the right to avoid the horse standing in front of the hedge. But Nellie and Nighthawk once more pleased the crowd by jumping over the hedge together and landing at almost the same instant. ". . . Two incredible horses," the announcer said. "If they continue this way, we'll have two winners. . ."

Now came a high fence jump followed by a difficult shelf. One horse was on its side snorting and trying to stand up, but the horse was unsuccessful. Ⓒ

Nighthawk and Nellie cleared the fence and the shelf together. But Tara wasn't prepared for the jolt of the landing from the shelf jump. She fell forward and grabbed onto Nellie's neck. She was out of the saddle, with one leg dangling near Nellie's front shoulder. Somehow, she managed to get back into the saddle. As she scolded herself for being careless, she heard a large cheer from the crowd. Ⓓ

By the time Nellie and Nighthawk had gone around the course one time, only about a dozen horses were left in the race. Horses and riders had been scattered on the ground near every jump. Some horses had been seriously injured. Tara tried not to think about Nellie getting injured. She told herself, "Nellie will win if I can stay on her." But as Nighthawk and Nellie started on their second time around the course, Tara thought about what Mr. Longly had said. Ⓔ Tara glanced over at Nighthawk. Nighthawk's mouth was open and he tossed his head from time to time. But he was running with ease. Only three horses were ahead of Tara now, the white Arabian and two brown horses. They seemed to be straining. Nighthawk and Nellie, still running stride for stride, caught the Arabian horse at the eighteenth jump. They passed the other two horses before the twentieth jump. "There are only ten more jumps to go," Tara said to herself. But a moment after having that thought, Tara noticed that Nighthawk was moving ahead. Tara's first impulse was to stay with him. But then she remembered what Mr. Jones had told her. Ⓕ Tara held Nellie at an easy run and watched nervously as Nighthawk pulled away, by ten feet, by twenty feet, now by thirty feet.

When Nellie had cleared the twenty-sixth jump, Nighthawk was at least fifty feet ahead. Ⓖ ★11 ERRORS★ "Go Nellie," Tara shouted and nudged her. "Go!" Nellie bounded forward with such speed that Tara was amazed. Nellie was covered with sweat and breathing hard. But she ran with the kind of power you would expect from a horse that was just starting a race.

The crowd was screaming and cheering, and the announcer was shouting, "She's not out of this race yet. Look at her go."

Nellie caught up to Nighthawk two steps before the twenty-seventh jump. The

STORY READING

EXERCISE 6   Decoding and comprehension

1. Everybody, turn to page 161 in your textbook. *Wait. Call on a student.* What's the error limit for this lesson? **11 errors.**

2. *Call on individual students to read. Present the tasks specified for each circled letter.*

Ⓐ Mr. Jones explained the **wrong idea** and the **right idea** about the race.

• What was the wrong idea about the race? *Idea:* To be the winner when you reach the first jump.

• What was the right idea? *Idea:* To be the winner at the finish line.

• So how fast did Tara start the race? *Idea:* Slow and easy.

• What did some of the other horses do? *Idea:* Started very fast.

• How long is Tara supposed to hold Nellie in? *Idea:* Until there are only three or four jumps left.

• Then what should she do? *Idea:* Let Nellie out.

Ⓑ What does that mean: **Matching Nellie stride for stride?** *Idea:* She was moving right along with Nellie.

• Get a picture of that in your mind, Nellie and Nighthawk running stride for stride together at an easy run.

Ⓒ What do you think is wrong with that horse? *Idea:* It might have a broken leg. That horse is probably seriously injured.

Ⓓ Why was the crowd cheering? *Idea:* Because Tara stayed in the saddle.

Ⓔ What had Mr. Longly said? *Idea:* Nighthawk could beat Nellie.

Ⓕ What had Mr. Jones told Tara? *Idea:* To hold Nellie in until the last three or four jumps.

• How do you think Tara feels to see Nighthawk moving ahead? *Idea:* She doesn't like it.

Ⓖ How many more jumps were left in the race after the 26th jump? **Four.**

• So could Tara let Nellie out yet? **Yes.**

• About how far ahead was Nighthawk? **50 feet.** That's a lot of distance to make up.

• Read the rest of the story to yourselves and be ready to answer some questions.

After all students have finished reading:

• What did Nellie do when Tara told her to run fast? *Idea:* She ran very fast.

• At which jump did she catch Nighthawk? **The twenty-seventh.**

horses jumped together again. But this time they didn't land together. Nellie landed at least five feet ahead of Nighthawk, and that was as close as Nighthawk ever came to Nellie for the rest of the race. Nellie moved away from Nighthawk so fast that Tara could hardly believe what was happening. Nellie cleared the rest of the jumps with ease and ran to the finish line at least three hundred feet ahead of Nighthawk.

Above the frantic crowd and the thunderous applause, Tara could hear the announcer ". . . A new track record . . . the greatest steeplechase horse that has ever run on this course. . ."

There were pictures and questions from reporters and prizes for winning the race. Tara made a brief victory speech. As a reporter held a microphone in front of her face and people with television cameras crowded close, she said, "I knew she could do it if I could stay on her. She's incredible."

The trip home was a very pleasant one. Imagine winning the Grand National Steeplechase Championship with a horse that everybody called an old nag. Tara polished the first-prize trophy with the sleeve of her jacket as she rode in the cab of the truck.

After arriving at the farm, Tara took care of Nellie and gave her a special dinner and an extra special brushing. Then Tara, Mr. Jones, Tara's parents, and all the neighbors gathered at the Briggs' farmhouse for a dinner and celebration. During dinner the phone kept ringing. Reporters wanted to talk to Tara. Mr. Longly made a new offer over the phone. This time, he offered one hundred thousand pounds for Nellie. People called to congratulate Tara and Nellie. After the seventh call, Mr. Briggs took the phone off the hook so that callers wouldn't disturb the celebration.

After dinner, Mr. Briggs made an announcement. "I was worried about having enough money to keep Nellie, but with the prizes Nellie has won, we have enough money to keep her forever."

Mr. Jones shook his finger and said, "You have enough money to keep ten horses forever." Everybody laughed.

The most important part of Tara's story ends here, but Nellie's story went on. She ran the Grand National Steeplechase Championship course two more times and won each time she entered. She became the most photographed, most talked about steeplechase horse that ever lived. When she was nine years old, she gave birth to a magnificent male colt. The colt's father was a very famous black horse, and the colt looked more like his father than his mother. After Nellie was ten years old, she retired from racing, but she had two more colts after she retired. Nellie lived until Tara was a grown woman with a family of her own. The day Nellie died was a very sad day, but Tara had fond memories of her and something else to remind her of Nellie—one of Nellie's colts. This gray horse has also won the Grand National Steeplechase Championship at Liverpool.

- What happened after that jump? *Idea:* Nighthawk never caught up with Nellie.
- About how far ahead was Nellie at the end of the race? **300 feet.**
- What news did the announcer give after Nellie had finished? *Idea:* That Nellie had set a new track record.
- After dinner Mr. Briggs said that there was no problem keeping Nellie? Why? *Idea:* Nellie has won so many prizes.
- How many horses did Mr. Jones say the Briggs family could afford to keep? **Ten.**
- How many more times did Nellie win the Grand National Steeplechase Championship? **Two.**
- The story gives some hints about who the father of Nellie's first colt was. Who was the father? **Nighthawk.**
- How old was Nellie when she retired from racing? **Ten years old.**
- Did she have any more colts after that time? **Yes.**

Award 4 points or have the students reread the story to the error limit sign.

INDEPENDENT WORK

Do all the items in your skillbook and workbook for lesson 42.

ANSWER KEY FOR WORKBOOK

Map Skills

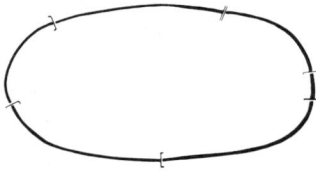

1. Look at the picture of the course at Ealing.

a. How long is the course at Ealing?

1 mile

b. How many times do the horses go around the course?

3

c. So, how many miles do the horses run to finish the entire race?

3

d. How many jumps are in the course?

5

e. So, how many jumps do the horses have to make to finish the race?

15

2. Look at the picture of the course at Liverpool.

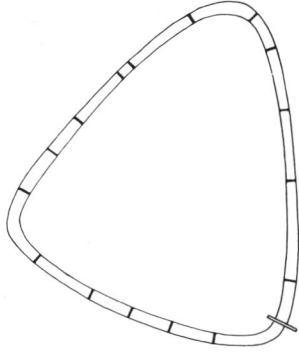

a. How long is the course at Liverpool? *Idea: over 2 miles*

b. How many times do the horses go around the course?

twice

c. So, how many miles do the horses run to finish the race?

Idea: 4½

d. How many jumps are in the course the first time around?

16

e. So, how many jumps do the horses make to finish the race?

30

Crossword Puzzle

To work the puzzle, read an item and figure out which word the item describes. Then write the word in the puzzle.
Complete the entire puzzle.

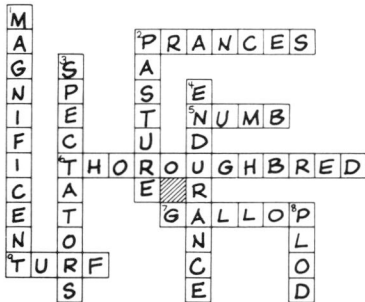

Across

2. When a horse steps around as if it wants to start running, it _____.

5. When you have no feeling in a part of your body, that part is _____.

6. A special breed of horse that is used for racing.

7. When horses run very quickly, they _____.

9. Ground with grass on it.

Down

1. Another word for **wonderful** or **marvelous.**

2. A field for farm animals.

3. People who watch an event are _____.

4. A horse that can keep on going and going has a lot of _____.

8. When you move at a very slow, tired pace, you _____.

WORKCHECK AND AWARDING POINTS

1. *Read the questions and answers for the skillbook and workbook.*

2. *Award points for independent work as follows:*

> 0 errors . . . . .6 points
> 2 errors . . . . .4 points
> 3, 4, or 5 errors . . . . .2 points
> 5 or more errors . . . . .0 points

3. *Award bonus points as follows:*

> *Correcting missed items
> or getting all items right . . . . .2 points
> Doing the writing
> assignment acceptably . . . . .2 points*

ANSWER KEY FOR SKILLBOOK

PART B

1. three / four
2. Nighthawk
3. held Nellie at an easy run
4. let Nellie out
5. **a.** Nighthawk
   b. 50 feet
   c. *Idea:* Sped up
6. **a.** The 27th
   b. Nellie
   c. Nellie
7. set a new track record
8. **a.** 10 years old
   b. three times
9. **a.** *Idea:* Nellie's colt
   b. *Idea:* The Steeplechase Championship

PART C

10. **a.** Dorothy
    b. Scarecrow, Tin Woodman, Lion, Oz
11. **a.** Emerald
    b. Ruby
    c. Diamond
12. **a.** Gray
    b. *Idea:* Land of the Munchkins
    c. *Idea:* Land of the Winkies
    d. *Idea:* The Emerald City
    e. *Idea:* Land of the Quadlings
13. **a.** barriers
    b. stray
    c. mock
    d. numb
    e. cautioned
    f. marvelous
    g. suddenly

Lesson 43

Lesson 43

PART A   Word Lists

1	2	3	4	5
successful	China	domestic	house cat	**Vocabulary words**
rodents	Africa	domesticate	half	1. advantages
prey	Asia	pieces	respect	2. rodents
guaranteed	Egypt	warmth	jerky	3. prey
generation	India	domesticated	keen	4. guarantee
		jawbone	eyesight	5. generation
		wolves		6. sleek
				7. keen

WORD PRACTICE AND VOCABULARY

EXERCISE 1   Word practice

1. Everybody, find lesson 43, part A in your skillbook. *Wait.* Touch under each word in column 1 as I read it.
2. The first word is **successful.**
3. Next word. **Rodents.**
4. *Repeat step 3 for each remaining word in column 1.*
5. Your turn. Read the first word. *Signal.* **Successful.**
6. Next word. *Signal.* **Rodents.**
7. *Repeat step 6 for each remaining word in column 1.*
8. *Repeat the words in column 1 until firm.*

EXERCISE 2   Word family

1. Everybody, touch column 2. *Check.*
   All those words are the names of places.
   Touch under the first word. *Pause.*
   What word? *Signal.* **China.**
2. Next word. *Pause.* What word? *Signal.* **Africa.**
3. *Repeat step 2 for each remaining word in column 2.*
4. *Repeat the words in column 2 until firm.*

EXERCISE 3   Word practice

1. Everybody, touch under the first word in column 3. *Pause.* What word? *Signal.* **Domestic.**
2. Next word. *Pause.* What word? *Signal.* **Domesticate.**
3. *Repeat step 2 for each remaining word in column 3.*
4. *Repeat the words in column 3 until firm.*
5. Touch under the first line in column 4. *Pause.* What words? *Signal.* **House cat.**
6. *Repeat steps 2–4 for each remaining word in column 4.*

EXERCISE 4   Vocabulary development

Task A

1. Everybody, touch column 5. *Check.*
   First you're going to read the words in column 5. Then we'll talk about what they mean.
2. Touch under the first word. *Pause.* What word? *Signal.* **Advantages.**
3. Next word. *Pause.* What word? *Signal.* **Rodents.**
4. *Repeat step 3 for each remaining word in column 5.*
5. *Repeat the words in column 5 until firm.*

Task B

1. Now let's talk about what those words mean. Word 1 is **advantages.** The **advantages** of a plan are the ways that plan is better than another plan.
2. *Call on a student.* Why is the plan of riding a bike to school better than walking to school? *Ideas:* It doesn't take as long; it's more fun; etc. You told me some **advantages** of riding a bike to school. What did you tell me? *Idea:* Advantages of riding a bike to school.

Task C

1. Word 2 is **rodents. Rodents** are a family of animals that includes rats, mice, squirrels, and beavers.
2. Everybody, what kind of animals are rats, mice, squirrels, and beavers? *Signal.* **Rodents.**

Task D

1. Word 3 is **prey.** The animal that you are hunting is your **prey.** Here's another way of saying **The lion hunted deer: The lion's prey was deer.**
2. Your turn. What's another way of saying **The lion hunted deer?** *Signal.* **The lion's prey was deer.**

Task E

1. Word 4 is **guarantee.** If you **make sure** that something will happen, you **guarantee** that the thing will happen. If a girl **makes sure** that she will win the race, she **guarantees** that she will win the race.
2. Your turn. What is she doing if she makes sure that she will win the race? *Signal.* **Guaranteeing that she will win the race.**
3. What is she doing if she makes sure that she will finish her homework? *Signal.* **Guaranteeing that she will finish her homework.**

Task F

1. Word 5 is **generation.** A **generation** is a group of children who grow up together.
2. Your grandparents are from one generation. *Call on a student.* Who were the children of your grandparents? *Idea:* My parents.
   So, your grandparents are from **one** generation. Your parents are from the **next** generation.
3. *Call on a student.* Name somebody from the generation that followed your parent's generation. *The student should name somebody from his or her generation.*
   When you grow up, your children will be from the **next** generation.

Task G

1. Word 6 is **sleek.** Something that is **sleek** is **very smooth.**
2. Everybody, what's another word for **very smooth?** *Signal.* **Sleek.**

Lesson 43

PART A Word Lists

1	2	3	4	5
successful	China	domestic	house cat	Vocabulary words
rodents	Africa	domesticate	half	1. advantages
prey	Asia	pieces	respect	2. rodents
guaranteed	Egypt	warmth	jerky	3. prey
generation	India	domesticated	keen	4. guarantee
		jawbone	eyesight	5. generation
		wolves		6. sleek
				7. keen

Task H

1. Word 7 is **keen**. If your **hearing** is **very good**, you have **keen hearing**.
2. Everybody, what kind of **eyesight** do you have if your **eyesight** is **very good?** *Signal.*
   Keen eyesight.
   What kind of **understanding** do you have if your **understanding** is **very good?** *Signal.*
   Keen understanding.

STORY READING

EXERCISE 5 Decoding and comprehension

1. Everybody, turn to page 165 in your textbook. *Wait. Call on a student.* What's the error limit for this passage? **10 errors.**
2. *Call on individual students to read. Present the tasks specified for each circled letter.*

Lesson 43

The Domestication of Animals Ⓐ
PART 1

Wild Animals and Domestic Animals

All animals can be divided into just two groups: wild animals and domestic animals. Ⓑ

Wild animals do not live with people. Ⓒ Wild animals live in forests, jungles, rivers, and oceans. Bears, tigers, snakes, eagles, alligators, and sharks are wild animals. Ⓓ

Domestic animals live with people. Ⓔ They live in people's houses or on people's farms. Dogs, horses, cows, chickens, and goats are domestic animals. Ⓕ

Thousands and thousands of years ago, all animals were wild. But some animals were relatives of animals that are now domesticated. There were wild dogs that looked like wolves. There were wild goats that climbed mountains, wild horses that ran across the prairies, even wild chickens and wild sheep. Ⓖ

The first animal to become domesticated was the dog. Ⓗ The dog became domesticated thousands of years ago when people still lived in caves. Ⓘ The cave people had to hunt to stay alive. But they were not very good hunters, because they could not run as fast as the wild animals, and they were not as strong as many of these animals. Ⓙ

We don't know exactly how the cave people trained the first dogs to hunt with them. But we do know some facts about the way the people lived and some facts about the early dogs. We know that people did not use dogs until after people had discovered how to use fire. Ⓚ

Garbage Piles

How do we know that the people had fire before they had dogs? By examining the garbage piles that these people left behind in caves.

There's a simple rule about garbage piles: **Things closer to the bottom of the pile went into the pile earlier. Things closer to the top of the pile went into the pile later.** Ⓛ

The next page shows the kind of garbage pile that has been found in caves.

Ⓐ There are headings in this passage that tell about what you will read. The first thing you are going to read about is wild animals and domestic animals. Touch the first heading. *Check.*
- Read that heading.
  Wild Animals and Domestic Animals.
- Find the next heading. Everybody, touch that heading. *Check.*
- Read that heading. **Garbage Piles.**
  What are you going to read about in that part? *Idea:* Garbage piles.
- Find the next heading. Everybody, touch that heading. *Check.*
- Read that heading. **The Domestication of Dogs.**
  What are you going to read about in that part? *Idea:* The domestication of dogs.
- Find the last heading. Everybody, touch that heading. *Check.*
- Read that heading. **Plans for getting food.**
  What are you going to read about in that part? *Idea:* Plans for getting food.
- Everybody, go back to the first heading. What are you going to read about in that part? *Idea:* Wild animals and domestic animals.

Ⓑ What are the two groups of animals?
Wild animals and domestic animals.

Ⓒ What's the rule about wild animals? *Idea:* Wild animals do not live with people.

Ⓓ Name some other wild animals. *Ideas:* Lions, elephants, giraffes, etc.

Ⓔ What do you know about domestic animals?
Domestic animals live with people.

Ⓕ Where do you find domestic animals? *Idea:* In people's houses; on people's farms.
- Name some other domestic animals. *Ideas:* Cats, sheep, turkeys, etc.

Ⓖ Were there any domestic animals thousands and thousands of years ago? **No.**
- Were there relatives of animals that are now domesticated? **Yes.**
- What kind of relative was there for the dog? *Idea:* Wild dogs.
- What kind of relative was there for the goat? *Idea:* Wild goats.

Ⓗ Which animal was the first to be domesticated? **The dog.**

Ⓘ Did that happen a few hundred years ago or thousands of years ago?
Thousands of years ago.

Ⓙ Name two reasons that the cave people were not very good hunters. *Ideas:* They weren't as fast as wild animals; they weren't as strong.

Ⓚ Did people have domestic dogs before or after they had fire? **After.**
Remember, fire came before domestic dogs.

Ⓛ Listen to that rule again: Things closer to the **bottom** of the pile went into the pile earlier. Things closer to the **top** of the pile went into the pile later.
- *Have several students repeat the rule.*

GARBAGE PILE

bones chewed by dogs and burnt pieces of wood

bones and burnt pieces of wood

bones

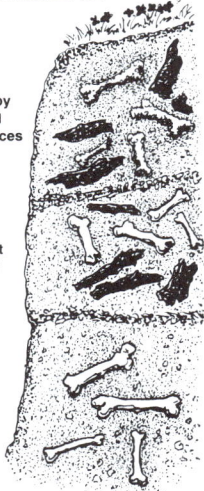

Which is closer to the bottom of the pile, burnt pieces of wood or bones? Ⓜ So which went into the pile earlier, bones or burnt pieces of wood? Ⓝ

Which is closer to the bottom of the pile, burnt pieces of wood or bones chewed by dogs? Ⓞ So which went into the pile earlier, burnt pieces of wood or bones chewed by dogs? Ⓟ

The garbage piles tell us that at first people did not have fire, later they had fire, and still later they had dogs. We also know

some facts about early wild dogs. We know that these dogs were not as good at hunting as the wolves that lived at the same time. The big difference between the wild dog and the wolf was in the jawbone. The wolf had a tremendously powerful jawbone. The wild dog had a smaller and far less powerful jawbone. Ⓠ

The Domestication of Dogs

There were some good reasons for cooperation between the wild dogs and people. The wild dogs could do some things that people could not do very well. People had some things that would make life easier for the wild dogs. Ⓡ

Possibly, the wild dogs came near the cave during the cold winter days. They might have smelled the food cooking inside. They might have felt the warmth of the fire. They might have been very hungry because they had not been very successful at hunting. Possibly, one of the puppies ventured inside the cave to try to pick up a scrap of meat. Possibly, the people inside the cave tried to get rid of the wild dogs by throwing something at them, like a heavy bone. The dogs might fight over the bone and then would return to the mouth of the cave, howling and waiting for another bone. Ⓢ

Puppies may have been the first wild dogs to come inside the caves and live with people. They were wild, but a young wild animal is easier to tame than an older one. If a puppy receives food and warmth, the puppy will become very happy living with people and will learn to love people, just as

---

a puppy learns to love the dogs that it lives with in a pack. Ⓣ ★10 ERRORS★

The cave people may have learned to hunt with their tame dogs by accident. Possibly, a couple of puppies lived with them in the cave. The puppies may have been very happy and may have followed the people as they went hunting. As the puppies grew older, the people may have discovered that their dogs could do things that they couldn't do. The dogs could track other animals by following the scent of those animals. The dogs could warn the cave people of danger that the people could not see and could not hear. If a dangerous animal was near, the dog's fur would stand up, and the dog would growl and become very excited.

When the tame dogs grew up, they had puppies. These tame puppies lived with the cave people. The tame puppies responded to the cave people in the same way that wild puppies respond to the leaders of a pack of wild dogs. Wild puppies learn to obey the leader dogs. Tame puppies learn to obey people. The tame puppies don't know that the people are not part of their pack, and they respond to people the same way they respond to leader dogs.

When the dogs were tamed by the cave people, we say that the cave people domesticated the dogs.

Plans for Getting Food

For thousands of years, cave people hunted with their dogs. This plan worked

well, but it had some problems. The main problem was that the people had to follow the wild animals they hunted. When the deer and the other wild animals moved from one place to another, the people had to follow them or starve. The wild animals moved around a lot, which meant that the people were on the move all the time, going from one place to another.

After thousands of years, people started to work out better plans. Some people domesticated animals other than dogs. They caught wild goats and wild sheep. The people took these animals with them as they hunted. If hunting was not good, they would kill one of these animals and eat it.

Some people developed another plan. Instead of following wild animals from place to place, they stayed in one place and raised domestic animals. These people were the first farmers. Farming had a big advantage over hunting. When a hunter kills a wild goat, the only food the hunter gets is the meat of the goat. But when a farmer raises goats, the farmer gets goat milk for many years. When the goat is old, the farmer can still kill the goat for its meat.

When people became farmers, they did not move from place to place. Instead, they brought plants and animals to the place where they lived. This plan made it possible for larger numbers of people to live in one place, because it was possible for the people to keep more food in one place.

Ⓜ What's the answer? **Bones.**
Remember, bones were closer to the bottom of the pile.

Ⓝ What's the answer? **Bones.**

● How do you know that bones went into the pile earlier? *Idea:* Because they're closer to the bottom of the pile.

Ⓞ What's the answer? **Burnt pieces of wood.**

Ⓟ What's the answer? **Burnt pieces of wood.**

Ⓠ In the wild dog and the wolf, what part was different? **The jawbone.**

● How was the wolf's jawbone different from that of the wild dog? *Idea:* The wolf's jawbone was bigger and more powerful.

● Which animal would be the best hunter? **The wolf.**

● Why? *Idea:* Because it had a more powerful jawbone.

Ⓡ Listen to that part again. *Read from* Ⓠ *to* Ⓡ.

● In hunting with people, which animal might be more useful? **The wild dog.**

● Figure out some ways the people could help the wild dogs. *Call on several students. Ideas:* Give them food; give them a warm place to stay.

Ⓢ This passage names some things that may have happened. Do we know which of the things actually did happen? **No.**

Ⓣ Which are easier to tame, puppies or older dogs? **Puppies.**

● If a puppy receives food and warmth from people, how will that puppy feel about living with people? *Idea:* Happy.

● Read the rest of the passage to yourselves and be ready to answer some questions.

After all students have finished reading:

● When does a puppy treat a person like a leader dog? *Idea:* When the puppy grows up with that person.

● The cave people had to move from place to place a lot. Why? *Idea:* To follow the wild animals they hunted.

● What would happen if the people did not follow the deer and other animals? *Idea:* They'd starve.

● One plan that early people worked out was to domesticate other animals. Which other animals? **Goats and sheep.**

● What would people do with goats and sheep when they couldn't find wild animals? *Idea:* Kill and eat them.

● What was another plan that people developed? **Farming.**

● Did farmers move from place to place? **No.**

● What is one of the advantages of keeping a goat for many years instead of killing it right away? *Idea:* You can get milk from the goat.

Award 4 points or have the students reread to the error limit sign.

ANSWER KEY FOR WORKBOOK

Study Skills

1. Below is part of an encyclopedia index.

Subject	Book	Page
dolphins	4	362
domes	12	23
domestic animals	4	476
domestic science	11	231
Dominic, Saint	9	502
Dominican Republic	4	745

  a. Which subject would tell you about animals that live with people?

    domestic animals

  b. Which book would you read to find out about that subject? ___4___

  c. Which page of that book would you look for? ___476___

Review Items

2. Put the following story events in the right order by numbering them from 1 through 5.

  _4_ Nellie won the race at Liverpool.

  _1_ Tara found out about Nellie's bad habit.

  _3_ Nellie won the race at Ealing.

  _2_ Mr. Jones agreed to train Nellie.

  _5_ Nellie had a colt.

INDEPENDENT WORK

Do all the items in your skillbook and workbook for lesson 43.

WORKCHECK AND AWARDING POINTS

1. *Read the questions and answers for the skillbook and workbook.*

2. *Award points for independent work as follows:*

> 0 errors . . . . .6 points
> 2 errors . . . . .4 points
> 3, 4, or 5 errors . . . . .2 points
> 5 or more errors . . . . .0 points

3. *Award bonus points as follows:*

> *Correcting missed items
> or getting all items right* . . . . .2 points
> *Doing the writing
> assignment acceptably* . . . . .2 points

ANSWER KEY FOR SKILLBOOK

PART B

1. **a.** Wild
   b. Domestic
2. **a.** wild
   b. domestic
   c. domestic
   d. wild
   e. domestic
   f. domestic
   g. wild
   h. wild
   i. domestic
   j. domestic
3. **a.** Dog
   b. thousands of years ago
4. A wild puppy
5. **a.** *Ideas:* They could get food; they could stay warm
   b. Hunt
6. **a.** Bones
   b. Bones
   c. Burnt pieces of wood
   d. The use of fire
7. find animals to hunt
8. **a.** *Ideas:* Goat; sheep
   b. No
   c. Farmers
   d. *Ideas:* Milk, cheese

PART C

9. **a.** Ealing
   b. Liverpool
   c. Ealing
   d. Briggs' Farm
   e. Liverpool
10. **a.** endurance
    b. mock
    c. officials
    d. magnificent
    e. ground covered with grass
    f. lag behind
    g. straining
    h. warned

Lesson 44

Lesson 44

PART A   **Word Lists**

1	2	3	4
popular	falcon	camel	generation
talons	hawk	mongoose	domestication
various	dove	cheetah	Egyptian
	turkey	donkey	position
		weasel	cooperation
		llama	
		mule	
		cobra	

5	6
Vocabulary words	**Vocabulary words**
1. advantages	1. generation
2. unprotected	2. guarantee
3. venture	3. prey
4. cooperate	4. rodents
5. relatives	

WORD PRACTICE AND VOCABULARY

EXERCISE 1   Word practice

1. Everybody, find lesson 44, part A in your skillbook. *Wait.* Touch under each word in column 1 as I read it.
2. The first word is **popular.**
3. Next word. **Talons.**
4. *Repeat step 3 for* **various.**
5. Your turn. Read the first word. *Signal.* **Popular.**
6. Next word. **Talons.**
7. *Repeat step 6 for* **various.**
8. *Repeat the words in column 1 until firm.*

EXERCISE 2   Word family

1. Everybody, touch column 2. *Check.*
   All those words are the names of birds.
   Touch under the first word. *Pause.* What word? *Signal.* **Falcon.**
2. Next word. *Pause.* What word? *Signal.* **Hawk.**
3. *Repeat step 2 for each remaining word in column 2.*
4. *Repeat the words in column 2 until firm.*

EXERCISE 3   Word family

1. Everybody, touch column 3. *Check.*
   All those words are the names of animals.
   Touch under the first word. *Pause.* What word? *Signal.* **Camel.**
2. Next word. *Pause.* What word? *Signal.* **Mongoose.**
3. *Repeat step 2 for each remaining word in column 3.*
4. *Repeat the words in column 3 until firm.*

EXERCISE 4   Word family

1. Everybody, touch column 4. *Check.*
   All those words end with the sound **shun.**
   Touch under the first word. *Pause.* What word? *Signal.* **Generation.**
2. Next word. *Pause.* What word? *Signal.* **Domestication.**
3. *Repeat step 2 for each remaining word in column 4.*
4. *Repeat the words in column 4 until firm.*

EXERCISE 5   Vocabulary review

Task A
1. Everybody, touch column 5. *Check.*
   First you're going to read the words in columns 5 and 6. Then we'll talk about what they mean.
2. Touch under the first word in column 5. *Pause.* What word? *Signal.* **Advantages.**
3. Next word. *Pause.* What word? *Signal.* **Unprotected.**
4. *Repeat step 3 for each remaining word in column 5.*
5. *Repeat the words in column 5 until firm.*
6. *Repeat steps 2–5 for column 6.*

Task B
Word 1 is **advantages.** *Call on a student.* Name some **advantages** of riding in a car instead of riding on a motorcycle. *Ideas:* Riding in a car is more comfortable; you don't have to wear a helmet; you can't get wet.

Task C
Word 2 is **unprotected.** *Call on a student.* What does **unprotected** mean? *Idea:* Not protected.

Task D
Word 3 is **venture.** *Call on a student.* What does **venture** mean? *Idea:* You do something that is like an adventure.

Task E
Word 4 is **cooperate.** *Call on a student.* What does **cooperate** mean? *Idea:* You work together with somebody else.

Task F
Word 5 is **relatives.** *Call on a student.* What are **relatives?** *Idea:* Members of the same family.

Task G
Word 1 in column 6 is **generation.** *Call on a student.* What is a **generation.** *Idea:* A group of children who grow up together.

Task H
1. Word 2 is **guarantee.** *Call on a student.* What does **guarantee** mean? *Idea:* Making sure of something.
2. Everybody, what is a boy doing if he makes sure that he will do the dishes? *Signal.* **Guaranteeing that he will do the dishes.**
3. Everybody, what is a girl doing if she makes sure that she will feed the dog? *Signal.* **Guaranteeing that she will feed the dog.**

Task I
Word 3 is **prey.** *Call on a student.* What is an animal's **prey?** *Idea:* Something an animal hunts.

Task J
Word 4 is **rodents.** *Call on a student.* Name some **rodents.** *Ideas:* Rats, mice, squirrels, and beavers.

Lesson 44

The Domestication of Animals
PART 2

The Uses of Domestic Animals

When people started to farm, they did not stop using animals to help them hunt. Instead, people continued to use hunting animals. And these people started to domesticate other animals for a greater number of uses. The three main uses for domestic animals were:

1. To help people hunt
2. To provide, meat, milk, and eggs
3. To carry things Ⓐ

Animals that Help People Hunt

The house cat was first domesticated as a hunting animal. The domestication of the cat took place in Egypt about three thousand years ago. Ⓑ Three thousand years ago, people had been using dogs as hunting animals for a long time. But the Egyptians had a hunting problem that dogs could not help solve.

The Egyptians raised grain and they stored this grain in large buildings. Mice would get into the storage buildings and feast on the grain. These rodents would sometimes eat half the grain that was being stored. Ⓒ Dogs couldn't help the Egyptians very much, because the dogs were not very good at catching the mice and rats. The dogs would chase after these rodents, but often they would fail to catch their prey.

Cats solved that problem, because they had no trouble catching mice. A few cats in a storage building guaranteed that mice would not eat the grain. The Egyptians were so grateful to the cats that they made large statues of cats, and they treated cats with great respect. Ⓓ

Some people trained larger members of the cat family, such as cheetahs. Cheetahs are as big as large dogs, but they can run extremely fast—up to sixty miles per hour. They became very popular with hunters in India. Ⓔ

People have trained other hunting animals, such as the ferret and the mongoose. A ferret is half the size of a cat, but it can catch rats and rabbits. A ferret can move some parts of its body so quickly that it is

168 Lesson 44 Textbook

STORY READING

EXERCISE 6 Decoding and comprehension

1. **Everybody, turn to page 168 in your textbook.** *Wait. Call on a student.* **What's the error limit for this passage? 10 errors.**
2. *Call on individual students to read. Present the tasks specified for each circled letter.*

Ⓐ **Tell me the first use of domestic animals. To help people hunt.**

- **Tell me the second use of domestic animals. To provide meat, milk, and eggs.**
- **Tell me the third use of domestic animals. To carry things.**
- **The next three sections of this passage tell about those three uses. There are headings in the passage that tell about each use. The first use was to help people hunt.**
- **Everybody, touch the heading that tells about that use.** *Check.*
- **Read that heading. Animals that help people hunt.**
- **The next use is to provide meat, milk, and eggs. Everybody, touch the heading that tells about that use.** *Check.*
- **Read that heading. Animals that provide meat, milk, and eggs.**
- **The next use is to carry things. Everybody, touch the heading that tells about that use.** *Check.*

- **Read that heading. Animals that carry things.**
- **Everybody, go back to the heading: Animals that Help People Hunt.** *Check.*
- **What are you going to learn about in that section?** *Idea:* Animals that help people hunt.

Ⓑ **About how long ago was the house cat domesticated? Three thousand years ago.**
- **What was it domesticated for? Hunting.**
- **Where did that happen? In Egypt.**

Ⓒ **What would those rodents sometimes do?** *Idea:* Eat the grain.
- **Name the rodents that would do this. Mice.**
- **How do you think the Egyptian people felt about the mice eating half the grain they stored?** *Idea:* They didn't like it.

Ⓓ **Which animal solved the problem of the rodent in the grain? Cats.**
- **Why didn't dogs solve the problem?** *Idea:* Dogs weren't good at catching mice.
- **What did the cats do to gain great respect?** *Idea:* Killed the mice.
- **What did the Egyptians do to show they were grateful to the cats?** *Ideas:* Made statues of cats; treated them with respect.

Ⓔ **What members of the cat family did people use in India? Cheetahs.**
- **How big is a cheetah?** *Idea:* As big as a big dog.
- **What great advantage does a cheetah have over a dog or any other animal?** *Idea:* It can run very fast.
- **How fast can it run?** *Idea:* Up to 60 miles per hour.

Ⓕ **How fast can a ferret move? Quickly.**
- **How would that speed help it hunt other animals?** *Idea:* It's faster than the other animals.

Ⓖ **What's the name of the special hunting animal used in India? Mongoose.**
- **Which animal does the mongoose kill? Cobras.**
- **Why are people afraid of cobras?** *Idea:* Cobras can kill you.
- **The passage says that one bite from the cobra means death. What does that mean?** *Idea:* You'll die if the cobra bites you.

Ⓗ **Look at the picture below. It shows a mongoose ready to attack a cobra. Everybody, touch the spot of the cobra the mongoose will attack.** *Check.*

Ⓘ **Picture A shows a hawk on the ground. What are the claws of the hawk called? Talons.**
- **Touch the talons.** *Check.*
- **Picture B shows the hawk in the air. What is that hawk doing?** *Idea:* Attacking another bird.
- **Hawks have keen eyesight. What does that mean?** *Idea:* They can see things that are a long way off.

204 Lesson 44

impossible to see the movement. If a ferret has its head turned in one direction and then turns it to look in another direction, you don't see the movement. You simply see the head looking one way. An instant later, you see the head looking the other way. Ⓕ

The mongoose is an animal that was domesticated in India for a special hunting use. Mongooses kill large poisonous snakes called cobras that live in India. People are extremely afraid of cobras because one bite from the cobra means death. Ⓖ

The mongoose is about the size of a cat. The mongoose is extremely powerful and its fast, jerky movements permit it to kill cobras with ease. When a mongoose fights a cobra, the cobra rears up and leans back. When the cobra is in that position, the mongoose moves over the cobra's head, quickly grabs the cobra by the back of the neck and kills it. Ⓗ

cobra

mongoose

Hunters all over the world have used falcons, hawks, and other birds of prey to hunt with. These birds have extremely strong claws, called talons. They have keen eyesight and good speed. They can catch birds in the air, or rabbits on the ground. Ⓘ

hawk attacking bird
PICTURE B

hawk

PICTURE A

Animals that Provide Meat, Milk, and Eggs Ⓙ

Animals such as goats, cattle and chickens, are very important to people, because they give meat and other food. Goats and cows give milk; chickens give eggs; they all give meat. But people use these food-giving animals for many things besides meat, milk and eggs. The thick skin from cows and pigs is used to make leather. Sheep fur is used to make wool. Feathers from the birds are sometimes used to fill jackets and blankets.

Cattle, goats, sheep and pigs were domesticated first. Later, birds such as geese, ducks, turkeys and chickens were domesticated. Ⓚ

Animals that Carry Things Ⓛ
★10 ERRORS★

Many different animals have been used to carry things. The camel was one of the first carrying-animals to be domesticated. People all over Africa and Asia loved the camel because it could be trained to carry large loads for a long distance. Donkeys, mules and horses were also trained to carry things.

In South America, the llama was widely used to carry things. The llama is very good at climbing mountains and walking in places without roads. In Africa and India, some people were able to domesticate elephants. The elephant can carry tremendous loads. It can easily push a truck over or carry a tree that weighs more than a ton.

Since the invention of the train, the car and the airplane, carrying animals have become less important to people.

How Animals Changed by Being Domesticated

When animals are domesticated, they change over time. The reason they change is that some animals are better domestic animals than others. Let's say that a group of cave people who hunted with dogs had several dogs. Let's say that one male dog was much better than any other male at hunting because it had a keen sense of smell. Let's say that one female dog was also much better than the other females at

hunting. If these two dogs had puppies, some of their puppies would be better hunters than any of the other dogs in the pack. If the cave people kept only the best hunting dogs, the dogs would slowly change from one generation to the next generation. After several hundred years, the dogs would be much better at hunting than the dogs cave people had at first.

Chickens, horses, and goats changed in the same way dogs changed. If the early farmers kept the chickens that laid the biggest eggs, the eggs would grow larger and larger from generation to generation. At first, the chicken eggs might be no bigger than a ping-pong ball. But if the early farmers kept only the chickens that laid the biggest eggs, the eggs would get much bigger.

The same thing would happen with horses. If the farmers kept only those horses that were the biggest and most powerful, horses would change from generation to generation. After hundreds of years, there would be very big horses, much bigger than the horses the earlier farmers had.

Look at all the various kinds of dogs. Remember, at one time there were no guard dogs or dogs that could track animals as well as a hound dog of today. All these dogs developed because people kept only the dogs that were best at tracking, or the best guards, or the smartest.

Ⓙ What's this section going to tell about? *Idea:* Animals that provide meat, milk, and eggs.

● What did the section you just read tell about? *Idea:* Animals that help people hunt.

Ⓚ Which was domesticated first, the cow or the chicken? **The cow.**

● What comes from the skin of cows and pigs? **Leather.**

● What material is made from sheep fur? **Wool.**

● What is wool? *Idea:* A warm, heavy material.

Ⓛ What is this section going to tell about? *Idea:* Animals that carry things.

● What did the last section tell about? *Idea:* Animals that provide meat, milk, and eggs.

● What did the section before that tell about? *Idea:* Animals that help people hunt.

● You're going to read the rest of the passage to yourselves. Notice that there is one more heading that tells about how animals changed by being domesticated. Try to remember the facts about how animals changed. Be ready to answer some questions.

After all students have finished reading:

● What was one of the first carrying animals to be domesticated? **The camel.**

● What advantages did a camel have over other animals? *Idea:* It could carry large loads for a long distance.

● Name some other animals that were domesticated to carry things. *Responses:* Horses, elephants, mules, donkeys, llamas.

● Which is the strongest carrying animal? **The elephant.**

● The passage told about some things that an elephant can do. Name one of those things. *Ideas:* Push a truck over; carry a tree that weighs more than a ton.

● Which inventions have made the carrying animals less important to people in recent years? *Ideas:* The train, the car, and the airplane.

● If you had several hunting dogs, how could you start to change the dogs so that after many generations you would have better hunting dogs? *Idea:* Keep the best hunting dogs.

● If you started with chickens that laid eggs no bigger than ping-pong balls, how could you change the chickens so that after many generations they would lay big eggs? *Idea:* Keep the chickens that laid the biggest eggs.

● If you started with several horses, how could you change the horses so that after many generations they would be much smarter? *Idea:* Keep the smartest horses.

Award 4 points or have the students reread to the error limit sign.

ANSWER KEY FOR WORKBOOK

Story Items

1. Name three domesticated animals that are used for hunting. *Ideas*:
   a. _dogs, falcons, hawks_
   b. _cats, cheetahs_
   c. _ferrets, mongooses_

2. Name three domesticated animals that are used for food. *Ideas*:
   a. _goats, sheep_
   b. _cattle, pigs, ducks_
   c. _chickens, turkeys, geese_

3. Name three domesticated animals that are used for carrying things. *Ideas*:
   a. _camels, llamas_
   b. _donkeys, mules_
   c. _horses, elephants_

INDEPENDENT WORK

Do all the items in your skillbook and workbook for lesson 44.

WORKCHECK AND AWARDING POINTS

1. *Read the questions and answers for the skillbook and workbook.*

2. *Award points for independent work as follows:*

   ```
   0 errors . . . . . . . . . . . . . . . . . . .6 points
   2 errors . . . . . . . . . . . . . . . . . . .4 points
   3, 4, or 5 errors . . . . . . . . . . . . . .2 points
   5 or more errors . . . . . . . . . . . . . .0 points
   ```

3. *Award bonus points as follows:*

   ```
   Correcting missed items
   or getting all items right . . . . . . . . .2 points
   Doing the writing
   assignment acceptably . . . . . . . . . . .2 points
   ```

ANSWER KEY FOR SKILLBOOK

PART B

1. a. The dog
   b. *Idea:* Hunting
2. a. hunting
   b. carrying
   c. hunting
   d. carrying
   e. food
   f. carrying
   g. food
   h. hunting
3. a. Egypt
   b. *Ideas:* Mice; rodents
   c. *Idea:* They caught the rodents
   d. *Ideas:* They made statues of the cats; they treated the cats with respect
4. a. Cobra
   b. *Idea:* Kill that person
5. talons
6. a. leather
   b. eggs
   c. wool
7. a. Llama
   b. An elephant
   c. *Ideas:* Trains, cars, airplanes
8. a. biggest
   b. bigger

PART C

9. a. domestic
   b. wild
   c. domestic
   d. domestic
   e. wild
   f. wild
   g. domestic
   h. domestic
10. a. obstacle
    b. suddenly said
    c. develop
    d. spectators
    e. shabby
    f. magnificent
    g. dangled
    h. frantically

Lesson 45 ✓

Lesson 45

PART A   Word Lists

1	2	3	4
gnawed	fiction	flavor	**Vocabulary words**
fantasy	champion	comb	1. gnaw
bargain	selection	flavored	2. bargain
	nation	combed	3. shall
	domestication		4. pounce
	imagination		5. accept

WORD PRACTICE AND VOCABULARY

EXERCISE 1   Word practice

1. Everybody, find lesson 45, part A in your skillbook. *Wait.* Touch under each word in column 1 as I read it.
2. The first word is **gnawed.**
3. Next word. **Fantasy.**
4. *Repeat step 3 for* **bargain.**
5. Your turn. Read the first word. *Signal.* **Gnawed.**
6. Next word. *Signal.* **Fantasy.**
7. *Repeat step 6 for* **bargain.**
8. *Repeat the words in column 1 until firm.*

EXERCISE 2   Word family

1. Everybody, touch column 2. *Check.*
   All those words end with the sound **shun.**
   Touch under the first word. *Pause.* What word?
   Signal. **Fiction.**
2. Next word. *Pause.* What word? *Signal.*
   Champion.
3. *Repeat step 2 for each remaining word in column 2.*
4. *Repeat the words in column 2 until firm.*

EXERCISE 3   Word practice

1. Everybody, touch under the first word in column 3. *Pause.* What word? *Signal.* **Flavor.**
2. Next word. *Pause.* What word? *Signal.* **Comb.**
3. *Repeat step 2 for each remaining word in column 3.*
4. *Repeat the words in column 3 until firm.*

EXERCISE 4   Vocabulary development

Task A

1. Everybody, touch column 4. *Check.*
   First you're going to read the words in column 4. Then we'll talk about what they mean.
2. Touch under the first word. *Pause.* What word? *Signal.* **Gnaw.**
3. Next word. *Pause.* What word? *Signal.* **Bargain.**
4. *Repeat step 3 for each remaining word in column 4.*
5. *Repeat the words in column 4 until firm.*

Task B

1. Now let's talk about what those words mean. Word 1 is **gnaw.** When you chew on something that is very hard, you **gnaw** on that thing. Everybody, what's another way of saying **The beaver chewed a hole in the tree?** *Signal.* **The beaver gnawed a hole in the tree.**
2. Everybody, what's another way of saying **The dog chewed on the bone?** *Signal.* **The dog gnawed on the bone.**

Task C

Word 2 is **bargain.** When you make a deal with someone, you make a **bargain** with that person. Everybody, what are you doing when you make a deal with someone? *Signal.* **Making a bargain with that person.**

Task D

Word 3 is **shall.** In some cases, the word **shall** means the same thing as the word **will.** Everybody, what's another way of saying **I will give it to you?** *Signal.* **I shall give it to you.**

Task E

Word 4 is **pounce.** When you jump on something, you **pounce** on that thing. Everybody, what's another way of saying **The tiger jumped on the rabbit?** *Signal.* **The tiger pounced on the rabbit.**

Task F

1. Word 5 is **accept.** When you take a gift that is offered, you **accept** that gift. Everybody, what do you do if you take a gift that is offered? *Signal.* **You accept that gift.**
2. What do you do if you agree to a bargain that is offered? *Signal.* **You accept that bargain.**

Fact and Fiction

There are two main types of things that you read. One type of reading material is **fact material.** Ⓐ Fact material is true. It tells about things the way they really are. The passsages that you read in the last two lessons are fact material. These passages presented facts about the domestication of animals. Ⓑ

The second type of reading material is **fiction.** Ⓒ Fiction is something that never happened. *The Wizard of Oz* is fiction. Many things described in the novel could not happen. For example, lions don't talk and people do not have magical powers. Ⓓ

Not all fiction material is the same. The story about Nellie is a fictional story, but the things that happened in the story are things that actually could happen. Farm horses like Nellie have won steeplechases. The Grand National Steeplechase

does take place near Liverpool. The problems that Tara had when she was learning to jump are real problems that anybody could have when learning to jump. So, although the story about Nellie is fiction, it is close to fact. Ⓔ

Some fiction is very far from fact. Stories of animals talking and thinking the way people think are very far from fact. Fictional stories that are far from fact are called fantasy. Ⓕ

The story that you will start today is a fantasy. Ⓖ It tells about the domestication of animals. The story is titled, "The Cat that Walked by Himself." You already know facts about the domestication of cats and other animals. Ⓗ When you read about the cat that walked by himself, compare the things that happen in the story with the facts that you know about the domestication of animals.

The Cat that Walked by Himself Ⓐ
by Rudyard Kipling
PART 1

Once upon a time, all animals were wild. The dog was wild, and the cow was wild, and the horse was wild, and the sheep was wild—as wild as wild could be—and they walked in the wild woods. But the wildest of all the wild animals was the cat. He walked by himself, no matter where he went. Ⓑ

Of course, the man was wild too. He was very wild. He didn't even begin to be tame until he married the woman, and she told him that she did not like his wild ways.

She picked out a nice dry cave to live in, and she lit a nice fire at the back of the cave, and she spread clean sand on the floor, and she said, "Wipe your feet dear when you come in, so we can keep our house neat and clean." Ⓒ

That night, the man and the woman ate wild sheep which had been roasted on the fire and flavored with wild onion and wild pepper. The man was very happy and he went to sleep in front of the fire, but the woman sat up and looked at the fire.

EXERCISE 5   Comprehension passage

1. Everybody, turn to page 171 in your textbook. *Wait.*
2. *Call on individual students to read. Present the tasks specified for each circled letter.*

Ⓐ What's one type of reading material? **Fact material.**

Ⓑ Is fact material true or false? **True.**

• What kind of material was in the selections on the domestication of animals? **Fact material.**

Ⓒ What's the second type of reading material? **Fiction.**

Ⓓ Is The Wizard of Oz fact or fiction? **Fiction.**

• Name three things in that story that could not possibly happen. *Ideas:* Lions don't talk; people don't have magical powers; scarecrows don't come to life.

Ⓔ Is the Nellie story **close to fact** or **far from fact?** **Close to fact.**

• Is The Wizard of Oz **close to fact** or **far from fact?** **Far from** fact.

• Does anything happen in The Wizard of Oz that could not actually happen? **Yes.**

Ⓕ What do we call fictional stories that are very far from fact? **Fantasy.**

• Is The Wizard of Oz very far from fact? **Yes.** A Horse to Remember is fiction, but it is not very far from fact, so it is not fantasy.

Ⓖ So is it close to fact or far from fact? **Far from fact.**

Ⓗ Why were cats domesticated? *Idea:* Because they got rid of mice.

EXERCISE 6   Decoding and comprehension

1. Everybody, turn to page 172 in your textbook. *Wait. Call a student.* What's the error limit for this lesson? **6 errors.**
2. *Call on individual students to read. Present the tasks specified for each circled letter.*

Ⓐ Who is the author of this story? **Rudyard Kipling.**

Rudyard Kipling was a famous writer who wrote many stories about animals.

Ⓑ When this story begins, how many domesticated animals were there? **None.**

• Which was the wildest of all animals? **The cat.**

Ⓒ Do you think this part about the woman tells things that are facts? **No.**

Out in the wild woods all the wild animals gathered together where they could see the light of the fire a long way off, and they wondered what it meant.

Then the Wild Horse stamped with his wild foot and said, "Oh my friends and enemies, why have the man and the woman made that great light in that great cave, and what harm will it do us?"

The Wild Dog lifted up his wild nose and smelled the smell of roast sheep, and said, "I will go to the cave and see, for I think something smells good. Cat, come with me."

"No," said the Cat. "I am the Cat who walks by himself, no matter where I go. So I will not go with you."

"Then we can never be friends," said the Wild Dog, and he trotted off to the cave. But when the Wild Dog had gone a little way, the Cat said to himself, "It doesn't matter where I go, so I will go and see what happens." Ⓓ The cat followed the Wild Dog softly, very softly, and hid himself where he could hear everything.

When the Wild Dog reached the mouth of the cave, he lifted up his nose and sniffed the beautiful smell of the roast sheep. The woman heard him and said, "Wild Dog, what do you want?"

The Wild Dog said, "What smells so good?"

Then the woman picked up a roasted sheep bone, threw it to the Wild Dog, and said, "Wild Dog, taste and try."

The Wild Dog gnawed the bone, and it was more delicious than anything he had ever tasted. When he was finished he said,

"Give me another." Ⓔ ★6 ERRORS★

The woman said, "Wild Dog, if you help my man to hunt during the day and guard this cave at night, I will give you as many roast bones as you need."

"Ah," said the Cat, listening. "This is a very wise woman, but she is not as wise as I am."

The Wild Dog crawled into the cave and laid his head on the woman's lap and said, "Good friend, I will help your man to hunt during the day, and at night I will guard your cave."

"Ah," said the Cat, listening. "That is a very foolish dog." And the Cat went back through the wild woods, walking by himself and waving his wild tail. But he never told anybody what he had seen and heard.

When the man woke up he said, "What is that Wild Dog doing here?" And the woman said, "His name is not Wild Dog anymore. His new name is First Friend, because he will be our friend forever. Take him with you when you go hunting."

That day, the woman cut great, green armfuls of fresh grass from a meadow in the wild woods. She dried the grass by the fire.

Out in the wild woods, all the wild animals wondered what had happened to the Wild Dog, and at last the Wild Cow stamped her foot and said, "I will go and see why the Wild Dog has not returned. Cat, come with me."

"No!" said the Cat. "I am the Cat who walks by himself, no matter where I go. So

---

I will not go with you." But secretly, he followed the Wild Cow, very softly, and hid himself where he could hear everything.

When the Wild Cow reached the mouth of the cave, she lifted up her nose and sniffed the beautiful smell of the dried grass. The woman heard the Cow and said, "Wild Cow, what do you want?"

The Wild Cow said, "Where is the Wild Dog?" But the Cow kept staring at the dried grass.

The woman laughed and said, "Wild Cow, I think you are more interested in grass than you are in the Wild Dog."

The Wild Cow said, "That is true. Give me the grass to eat."

The woman said, "Wild Cow, if you will give me your milk, I will let you eat the wonderful grass three times a day."

"Ah," said the Cat as he listened from his hiding place. "This is a clever woman, but she is not as clever as I am."

Ⓓ This story is fantasy. But it tells things about the Cat that may remind you of real cats. Did you ever notice how cats like to be by themselves? They like to do things their own way.

Ⓔ What does that mean: **he gnawed the bone?** *Idea:* He chewed the bone.

● Read the rest of the story to yourselves and be ready to answer some questions. When you read the rest of the story, remember which animal was domesticated first, which was domesticated next, and so forth. Also remember the new names that the woman gives the animals when they become domesticated.

After all students have finished reading:

● One animal saw the domestication of the other animals. Which animal was that? **The Cat.**

● How many animals did the cat tell about what he saw and heard? **None.**

● When the dog did not return, which animal went to the cave to find out what happened? **The Wild Cow.**

● What was inside the cave that interested the Cow? **The grass.**

● What deal did the woman make with the Cow? *Idea:* If the cow would give milk, the woman would feed the grass to the cow.

The Wild Cow said, "I will give you my milk if you give me the wonderful grass."

"Ah," said the Cat. "That is a very foolish Cow." And the Cat went back through the wild woods, walking by himself and waving his wild tail. But he never told anybody about what he had seen and heard.

When the man and the dog came back from hunting, the man said, "What is the Wild Cow doing here?"

And the woman said, "Her name is not Wild Cow anymore, but the Giver of Good Food. She will give us warm, white milk forever, and I will take care of her while you and the First Friend go hunting."

On the next day, the woman gathered grass again. Then she sat in front of the cave and made a collar from old animal skins.

That night, the wild animals got together again to talk about the Wild Dog and the Wild Cow. At last, the Wild Horse said, "I will go and see why they have not returned. Cat, come with me."

"No," said the Cat, "I will not come." But he secretly followed the Wild Horse, very softly, and hid himself where he could hear everything.

When the Wild Horse reached the cave, he smelled the dried grass. The woman heard him and said, "Wild Horse, what do you want?"

The Wild Horse said, "Where are the Wild Dog and the Wild Cow?" But the horse kept staring at the grass.

The woman laughed and said, "I think you are more interested in grass than in the Wild Dog or the Wild Cow."

The Wild Horse said, "That is true. Give me the grass to eat."

The woman said, "If you will wear this collar, and be our servant, I will let you eat the grass three times a day."

"Ah," said the Cat, as he listened from his hiding place. "This is a very clever woman, but she is not as clever as I am."

The Wild Horse said, "I will wear the collar and be your servant if you give me the wonderful grass."

"Ah," said the Cat, listening. "That is a very foolish horse." And he went back through the wild woods, walking by himself and waving his wild tail. But he never told anybody what he had seen and heard.

When the man and the dog came back from hunting, the man said, "What is the Wild Horse doing here?"

And the woman explained, "His name is no longer Wild Horse, but the First Servant. He will carry us from place to place forever. You can ride on his back when you go hunting, and he will pull the animals you kill."

That night, the wild animals had another meeting. The Wild Sheep said, "I'm not going to that cave. No animal that has gone to that place has come back."

The Wild Chicken, the Wild Goose, and all the other animals agreed. So, no animal went to the cave that night. Instead, they all went back to their homes.

Lesson 45   Textbook   **175**

- What new name did the Cow get? **Giver of Good Food.**
- When the Cow did not return, which animal went to the cave to find out what happened? **The Wild Horse.**
- That animal asked another animal to go along. Which animal was asked? **The Cat.**
- And what did the Cat say? *Idea:* No, I will not come.
- What was inside the cave that interested the Horse? *Idea:* The grass.
- What did the Horse agree to do for the dried grass? *Idea:* Wear the collar and be a servant.
- What did the Horse have to wear? **A collar.**
- On the night after the Horse was domesticated, the animals had another meeting. How many animals wanted to go to the cave to find out what happened? **None.**
- So where did all the animals go that night? **Home.**

Award 4 points or have the students reread to the error limit sign.

INDEPENDENT WORK

Do all the items in your skillbook and workbook for lesson 45.

ANSWER KEY FOR WORKBOOK

Review Items

1. Write the three main uses that people have for domesticated animals. *Idea*:
   a. *hunting*
   b. *food*
   c. *carrying*
2. Write the use people had for each animal.
   a. dog *hunting*
   b. cow *food*
   c. horse *carrying*

3. Write which character each statement describes. Choose from **Tara, Mr. Briggs,** or **Mr. Jones.**
   a. This character owned a farm. *Mr. Briggs*
   b. This character was a blacksmith. *Mr. Jones*
   c. This character rode Nellie. *Tara*
   d. This character had trained horses before. *Mr. Jones*
   e. This character almost sold Nellie. *Mr. Briggs*
   f. This character was the youngest. *Tara*

WORKCHECK AND AWARDING POINTS

1. *Read the questions and answers for the skillbook and workbook.*

2. *Award points for independent work as follows:*

0 errors	6 points
2 errors	4 points
3, 4, or 5 errors	2 points
5 or more errors	0 points

3. Award bonus points as follows:

Correcting missed items or getting all items right	2 points
Doing the writing assignment acceptably	2 points

ANSWER KEY FOR SKILLBOOK

PART B

1. a. A cave
  b. Fire
2. a. *Idea:* Roast sheep
  b. *Idea:* A bone
  c. *Idea:* Hunt
  d. *Idea:* Guard the cave
  e. First Friend
3. a. *Idea:* To dry it
  b. The Wild Horse and the Wild Cow
  c. The Wild Cow
  d. Milk
  e. Giver of Good Food
  f. A collar
  g. First Servant
4. a. woman
  b. cat
  c. horse
  d. woman
  e. cat
  f. woman
  g. cow
  h. dog

5. a. fact
  b. fiction
  c. fact
  d. fact
  e. fiction
  f. fiction

PART C

6. a. turf
  b. prance
  c. generation
  d. prey
  e. cooperating
  f. ventured
  g. relative
  h. guarantee

Lesson 46

Lesson 46
PART A   **Word Lists**
fantasy
flavored
accept
bargain

WORD PRACTICE AND VOCABULARY

EXERCISE 1   Word practice

1. Everybody, find lesson 46, part A in your skillbook. *Wait.* Touch under the first word in the column. *Pause.* What word? *Signal.* **Fantasy.**
2. Next word. *Pause.* What word? *Signal.* **Flavored.**
3. *Repeat step 2 for each remaining word in the column.*
4. *Repeat the words in the column until firm.*

EXERCISE 2   Neither–Nor Sentences

1. Everybody, find part B. I'll show you how to change sentences using the words **neither** and **nor.** Everybody, which words? *Signal.*
   Neither and nor.
   - I'll read sentence 1.
     The man was not happy and was not sad.
   - Now I'll read how the sentence is changed by using **neither** and **nor. The man was neither happy nor sad.**
   - Everybody, say that sentence. *Signal.*
     The man was neither happy nor sad.
     Repeat until firm.
2. I'll read sentence 2.
   She would not play and would not sleep.
   - Now I'll change the sentence using **neither** and **nor.**
     She would neither play nor sleep.
   - Everybody, say that sentence. *Signal.*
     She would neither play nor sleep.
     Repeat until firm.
3. I'll read sentence 3.
   The boy would not smile and would not talk.
   - Everybody, say it another way using **neither** and **nor.** *Pause. Signal.*
     The boy would neither smile nor talk.
     Repeat until firm.
4. I'll read sentence 4.
   The dog could not fight and could not hunt.
   Everybody, say it another way using **neither** and **nor.** *Pause. Signal.*
   The dog could neither fight nor hunt.
   Repeat until firm.
5. Later, you'll rewrite the sentences for all the items in part B.

STORY READING

EXERCISE 3   Decoding and comprehension

1. Everybody, turn to page 176 in your textbook. *Wait. Call on a student.* What's the error limit for this lesson? **7 errors.**
2. *Call on individual students to read. Present the tasks specified for each circled letter.*

Lesson 46

The Cat that Walked by Himself

PART 2

The man and woman were now living with three animals. Ⓐ On the day after the wild animals decided not to send any more animals to the cave, the Cat waited to see what the wild animals would do. No animal moved from the wild woods. So the Cat walked to the cave by himself. He saw the woman milking the Cow, and he saw the light of the fire in the cave, and he smelled the warm, white milk. Ⓑ

The Cat went up to the woman and said, "Where are the Wild Dog, the Wild Cow, and the Wild Horse?"

The woman laughed and said, "Wild Cat, go back to the wild woods again, for we have all the friends and servants we need." Ⓒ

The Cat said, "I am not a friend, and I am not a servant. I am the Cat who walks by himself, and I want to go into your cave." Ⓓ

The woman said, "I saw you hiding near the cave when First Friend came here. If you wanted to come inside, why didn't you come in with First Friend on that first night?"

The Cat grew very angry and said, "I want to go inside."

The woman laughed and said, "You are the Cat who walks by himself, no matter where you go. You are neither a friend nor a servant. You have said it yourself. So go away and walk by yourself." Ⓔ

Then the Cat pretended to be sorry and said, "Can't I ever come into the cave? Can't I ever sit by the warm fire? Can't I ever drink the warm, white milk?" Ⓕ Then the Cat smiled and continued before the woman could answer. "You are very wise and very beautiful. You should not be cruel, even to a cat."

The woman smiled and said, "I knew I was wise, but I did not know I was beautiful." She gazed at the Cat for a few moments. Then she said, "I think you are very cunning, and you are trying to trick me. But I will make a bargain with you. If I ever praise you, you may sit near the mouth of the cave forever." Ⓖ

"And if you praise me twice?" said the Cat.

"I never shall," said the woman, "but if I praise you twice, you may sit in the back of the cave by the fire." Ⓗ

"And if you praise me three times?" said the Cat.

"I never shall," said the woman, "but if I praise you three times, you may drink the warm, white milk anytime you wish." Ⓘ ★7 ERRORS★

176   Lesson 46 Textbook

Then the Cat arched his back and said, "I accept your bargain." And he went away through the wild woods, walking by himself and waving his wild tail.

That night when the man and the horse and the dog came home from hunting, the woman did not tell them about the bargain she had made with the Cat because she was afraid that they might not like it.

The Cat went far away and hid himself in the wild woods. After many days passed, the woman forgot all about him, and the bargain she had made. A Bat that hung inside the cave knew where the Cat was hiding, and every evening the Bat would fly to the Cat with news of what was happening in the cave.

One evening the Bat said, "There is a baby in the cave. He is new and fat, and the woman is very fond of him."

"Ah," said the Cat, listening. "And what is the baby fond of?"

"Let's see," the Bat said thoughtfully. "He is fond of things that are soft, and he is fond of warm things he can hold in his arms when he goes to sleep. And he is very fond of being played with."

"Ah," said the Cat, with a cunning smile. "The time has come for me to move into the cave."

The next morning, the Cat walked through the wild woods and hid very near the cave until the man and the dog and the horse went hunting. The woman was busy trying to cook that morning, and the baby's crying bothered her. So she carried the baby outside the cave and gave him a handful of pebbles to play with. But still the baby cried.

The Cat approached the baby, put out his paw, and patted the baby softly on the cheek. The baby cooed and smiled. The Cat rubbed against the baby's knees and tickled the baby under his fat chin with his tail. The baby laughed, and the woman heard the baby laugh.

The Bat said, "Woman, that baby is happy because a wild animal is entertaining him."

Without going outside of the cave, the woman responded. "That wonderful animal is a marvel. That animal has done a great service for me."

Suddenly, the woman noticed that the Cat was sitting quite comfortably inside the cave, near the mouth of the cave. "Woman," said the Cat, "you have praised me and now I can sit in the cave forever. But remember, I am the Cat who walks by himself, no matter where I go."

The woman was very angry. She shut her lips tightly, picked up a ball of thread, and began to sew.

Suddenly, the baby cried because the Cat was no longer entertaining him. The woman went outside, but she could not hush the baby. The baby struggled and kicked and cried.

"Woman," said the Cat, "give me a ball of thread, and I will show you how to make your baby laugh as loudly as he is now crying."

"I will do so," said the woman, "but I will not praise you if you do it."

She gave the Cat a ball of thread, and the Cat ran after it. He patted it with his

Lesson 46 Textbook   177

Ⓐ **Name them.** *Ideas:* The Wild Dog, the Wild Cow, the Wild Horse.

Ⓑ **Why do you think the Cat has come to the cave?** *Idea:* To find out what happened to the animals.

Ⓒ **Who is their friend?** *Idea:* The Wild Dog.

● **Who are their servants?** *Idea:* The Wild Cow and the Wild Horse.

Ⓓ **Does the Cat want to do some work if they let him stay in the cave?** **No.**

Ⓔ **Why did the woman think that the Cat should go away?** *Idea:* He is neither a friend nor a servant.

Ⓕ **Listen to that part again. You can almost hear the cat meowing.** *Read from* Ⓔ *to* Ⓕ.

Ⓖ **What's going to happen if the woman praises the Cat one time?** *Idea:* He can sit near the mouth of the cave forever.

Ⓗ **What's going to happen if the woman praises the Cat twice?** *Idea:* He can sit in the back of the cave by the fire.

Ⓘ **What's going to happen if the woman praises the Cat a third time?** *Idea:* He can drink the milk anytime he wants.

● **Let's go over those again. What happens if the woman praises the Cat one time?** *Idea:* He can sit near the mouth of the cave forever.

● **What happens if the woman praises the Cat a second time?** *Idea:* He can sit in the back of the cave near the fire.

● **What happens if the woman praises the cat a third time?** *Idea:* He can drink milk anytime he wants.

● **Read the rest of the story to yourselves and be ready to answer some questions. Find out when the Cat decides to try to trick the woman and how the Cat tries to trick her.**

After all students have finished reading:

● **Who brought the cat news of what was going on in the cave?** **The Bat.**

● **One day, the Bat told the Cat that something was new in the cave. What was that?** *Idea:* A baby.

● **What was the woman doing when the baby was outside the cave crying?** *Idea:* Cooking.

● **What did the Cat do to make the baby happy?** *Idea:* Rubbed against the baby's knees and tickled the baby with his tail.

● **Did the woman praise the animal that entertained the baby?** **Yes.**

● **Did she know which animal was entertaining him?** **No.**

● **What did the Cat do as soon as the woman praised him?** *Idea:* Sat inside the cave.

paws and rolled head over heels, and tossed the thread backward over his shoulder and chased it between his legs and pretended to lose it, and pounced down upon it again. The baby started to laugh loudly and scramble after the Cat all around the cave. Then the baby grew tired. He put his arms around the soft Cat and held it.

"Now," said the Cat, "I will sing the baby a song that will put him to sleep for an hour." The Cat began to purr, loud and low, until the baby fell fast asleep. The woman smiled as she looked down upon the two of them and said, "That was wonderful. You are a very clever Cat."

Suddenly, the Cat was sitting quite comfortably at the back of the cave, close to the fire.

"Woman," said the Cat, "you have praised me twice, and now I can sit by the warm fire at the back of the cave forever. But remember, I am the Cat who walks by himself, no matter where I go."

Now the woman was very, very angry. She resolved not to praise the Cat again.

Hours later, the cave grew so still that a little mouse crept out of a corner and ran across the floor.

"Woman," said the Cat, smiling. "I see that a little mouse lives in your cave."

"Oh, no," said the woman.

"Ah," said the Cat. "Then you should do something to get rid of it."

The woman said, "Oh please get rid of it, and I will always be grateful to you."

The Cat made one jump and caught the mouse. The woman said, "A hundred thanks. Even the First Friend is not quick enough to catch little mice. You are a very skillful animal."

The Cat walked over to a bowl and began lapping up the warm, white milk. The cat paused and licked his chops. "Woman," he said. "You have praised me three times, and now I can drink the warm, white milk any time I wish. But remember—I am still the Cat who walks by himself, no matter where I go."

Then the woman laughed and said, "Cat, you are as clever as I am, and I will be glad to keep my bargain with you."

That evening, when the man and the dog came into the cave, the woman told all of them the story of the bargain.

And the Cat just sat by the fire and smiled.

- How did the Cat make the baby laugh after the woman could not hush the baby? *Idea:* Played with the thread.
- After the Cat made the baby laugh, the Cat said that he would put the baby to sleep. How did he do that? *Idea:* He let the baby hold him, and purred.
- Did the woman praise the cat? **Yes.**
- What did the Cat do? *Idea:* Sat at the back of the cave, near the fire.
- What did the Cat do to make the woman praise him a third time? *Idea:* Caught a mouse.
- Was the woman still angry with the Cat? **No.**
- What did the Cat have to do to stay in the cave near the fire and drink the white milk? *Idea:* Nothing.
- Part of the story said that the baby was cooing. Show me how a baby coos. *Check.*
- After the Cat drank the milk, he licked his chops. Show me how a cat does that. *Check.*

Award 4 points or have the students reread to the error limit sign.

FACT GAME

FACT GAME SCORECARD

1	2	3	4	5	6	7	8	9	10
11	12	13	14	15	16	17	18	19	20
21	22	23	24	25	26	27	28	29	30

2. **a.** What is the name of the horse race that includes barriers and obstacles?
   b. In which city and country does the National Championship of that race take place?
3. **a.** What is the class name for animals that do not live with people?
   b. Animals that live with people are called _____ animals.
4. Look at the picture of the garbage pile.

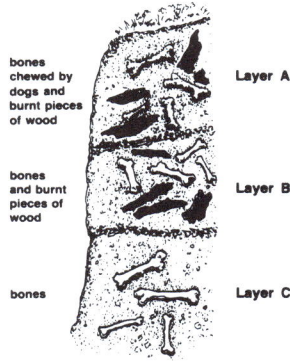

bones chewed by dogs and burnt pieces of wood — **Layer A**

bones and burnt pieces of wood — **Layer B**

bones — **Layer C**

   a. Which layer shows when people started to have dogs?
   b. Which layer shows when people started to have fire?
   c. Which of those two layers came first?
5. **a.** Which was the first animal to be domesticated?
   b. What activity did that animal help people with?
6. Tell whether each animal was used for **hunting,** for **food** or for **carrying things.**
   a. The horse
   b. The cow
   c. The goat
   d. The cheetah
7. Tell whether each thing is **fact** or **fiction.**
   a. An article about horses from an encyclopedia.
   b. A story about talking animals.
   c. The story about Nellie.
8. Tell which animal was given each name.
   a. The Giver of Good Food
   b. The First Friend
   c. The First Servant
9. Tell which character wanted each thing from Oz.
   a. Brains
   b. A heart
   c. A trip back to Kansas
   d. Courage

10. **a.** Tell the name of place X.
    b. Tell the name of city Y.
    c. Which direction do you go to get from Y to X?
11. Tell which Land each group of people lived in.
    a. Gillikins
    b. Munchkins
    c. Winkies
    d. Quadlings
12. Tell which direction each arrow points. Start with arrow A.

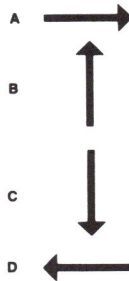

A →
B ↑
C ↓
D ←

EXERCISE 4   Fact game

1. Everybody, find lesson 46 in your workbook. *Wait.* You're going to play a game that uses the facts you have learned. Here are the rules: The player rolls the dice, figures out the number of the question, reads that question out loud, and answers it. The monitor tells the player if the answer is right or wrong. If it's wrong, the monitor tells the right answer. If it's right, the monitor gives the player one point. Don't argue with the monitor. The dice goes to the left and the next player has a turn.

2. If the game goes smoothly, all players in that game will earn 5 bonus points. I'll tell the groups whether they earn the bonus points. Each player who gets more than 13 points will earn another 5 bonus points. You'll play the game for 20 minutes.

3. *Divide students into groups of four or five. Assign monitors. Tell monitors the answers are on workbook page 122. Circulate as students play the game. Comment on groups that are playing well.*

4. At the end of 20 minutes, have all students who earned more than ***13 points*** stand up. *Award 5 bonus points to those players. Award points to monitors. Monitors receive the number of points earned by the highest performer in the group.*

● *Tell the monitor of each game that ran smoothly:* Your group did a good job. Give yourself and each of your players 5 bonus points.

● Everybody, write your game points in box FG on your point chart. Write your bonus points in the **bonus** box.

INDEPENDENT WORK

Do all the items in your skillbook for lesson 46.

WORKCHECK AND AWARDING POINTS

1. *Read the questions and answers for the skillbook and workbook.*

2. *Award points for independent work as follows:*

0 errors	*. . . . . 6 points*
2 errors	*. . . . . 4 points*
3, 4, or 5 errors	*. . . . . 2 points*
5 or more errors	*. . . . . 0 points*

3. *Award bonus points as follows:*

Correcting missed items or getting all items right	*. . . . . 2 points*
Doing the writing assignment acceptably	*. . . . . 2 points*

ANSWER KEY FOR FACT GAME

2. **a.** Steeplechase
    b. Liverpool, England
3. **a.** Wild animals
    b. domestic
4. **a.** A
    b. B
    c. B
5. **a.** The dog
    b. Hunting
6. **a.** Carrying things
    b. Food
    c. Food
    d. Hunting
7. **a.** Fact
    b. Fiction
    c. Fiction
8. **a.** The Wild Cow
    b. The Wild Dog
    c. The Wild Horse
9. **a.** The Scarecrow
    b. The Tin Woodman
    c. Dorothy
    d. The Lion
10. **a.** Brigg's farm
    b. Liverpool
    c. South
11. **a.** Land of the North
    b. Land of the East
    c. Land of the West
    d. Land of the South
12. A—East
    B—North
    C—South
    D—West

ANSWER KEY FOR SKILLBOOK

PART B

1. The man was neither happy nor sad.
2. She would neither play nor sleep.
3. The boy would neither smile nor talk.
4. The dog could neither fight nor hunt.

PART C

5. **a.** *Ideas:* Hunt; guard the cave
    b. *Ideas:* Be a servant; carry things
    c. *Idea:* Give milk
6. **a.** friends / servants
    b. The woman
    c. beautiful
7. **a.** *Idea:* The cat could sit near the mouth of the cave.
    b. *Idea:* The Cat could sit in the back of the cave.
    c. *Idea:* The Cat could drink milk
8. *Idea:* A baby
9. **a.** *Idea:* Laugh
    b. Yes
    c. *Idea:* Sat near the mouth of the cave
10. **a.** *Idea:* Played with a ball of thread.
    b. Yes
    c. *Idea:* Sat near the back of the cave
11. **a.** A mouse
    b. Yes
    c. *Idea:* Drank milk
12. **a.** No
    b. Yes
13. **a.** cat
    b. woman
    c. woman
    d. cat
    e. woman
    f. cat
    g. woman

PART D

14. **a.** strained
    b. made sure
    c. cooperate
    d. sleek
    e. keen

Lesson 47

Lesson 47

PART A   **Word Lists**

1	2	3
Warren	merchant	**Vocabulary words**
Alice	voyage	1. toss and turn
Whittington	observe	2. stroll
	threaten	3. stammer
	unbearable	4. fetch
		5. transport
		6. coach

WORD PRACTICE AND VOCABULARY

EXERCISE 1   Word practice

1. Everybody, find lesson 47, part A in your skillbook. *Wait.* Touch under each word in column 1 as I read it.
2. The first word is **Warren.**
3. Next word. **Alice.**
4. *Repeat step 3 for* **Whittington.**
5. Your turn. Read the first word. *Signal.* **Warren.**
6. Next word. *Signal.* **Alice.**
7. *Repeat step 6 for* **Whittington.**
8. *Repeat the words in column 1 until firm.*

EXERCISE 2   Word practice

1. Everybody, touch under the first word in column 2. *Pause.* What word? *Signal.* **Merchant.**
2. Next word. *Pause.* What word? *Signal.* **Voyage.**
3. *Repeat step 2 for each remaining word in column 2.*
4. *Repeat the words in column 2 until firm.*

EXERCISE 3   Vocabulary development

Task A
1. Everybody, touch column 3. *Check.* First you're going to read the words in column 3. Then we'll talk about what they mean.
2. Touch under the first line. *Pause.* What words? *Signal.* **Toss and turn.**
3. Next word. *Pause.* What word? *Signal.* **Stroll.**
4. *Repeat step 3 for each remaining word in column 3.*
5. *Repeat the words in column 3 until firm.*

Task B
Now let's talk about what those words mean. The words in line 1 are **toss and turn.** When you can't go to sleep and you keep changing position, you **toss and turn.**

Task C
Word 2 is **stroll.** When you **stroll,** you walk slowly. Everybody, what are you doing when you are walking slowly? *Signal.* **Strolling.**

Task D
Word 3 is **stammer.** When you have trouble saying something, you **stammer.**
What are you doing when you have trouble saying something? *Signal.* **Stammering.**

Task E
Word 4 is **fetch.** When you get something and bring it back, you **fetch** that thing. When a dog goes after a ball and brings it back to you, the dog **fetches** that ball. Everybody, what does the dog do? *Signal.* **Fetches that ball.**

Task F
1. Word 5 is **transport.** When you **transport** something, you take it from one place to another. Here's another way of saying **He took a box from his house to the store: He transported a box from his house to the store.**
   Everybody, what's another way of saying **He took a box from his house to the store?** *Signal.* **He transported a box from his house to the store.**
2. Everybody, what's another way of saying **They took the furniture from the hallway to their office?** *Signal.*
   They transported the furniture from the hallway to their office.

Task G
Word 6 is **coach.** One meaning of **coach** is a vehicle that you can sit inside. In the old days there used to be **coaches** that were pulled by horses. Today, there are railroad **coaches.**

EXERCISE 4   Neither–Nor Sentences

1. Everybody, find part B. I'll show you how to change sentences using the words **neither** and **nor. Everybody, which words?** *Signal.*
   Neither and nor.
   ● I'll read sentence 1.
   He could not swim and he could not dive.
   ● Now I'll change the sentence using **neither** and **nor. He could neither swim nor dive.**
   ● Everybody, say that sentence. *Signal.*
   He could neither swim nor dive.
   Repeat until firm.
2. I'll read sentence 2.
   She was not happy and she was not sad.
   ● Your turn. Change the sentence using **neither** and **nor.** *Pause. Signal.*
   She was neither happy nor sad.
   Repeat until firm.
3. Later, you'll rewrite the sentences for all the items in part B.

Lesson 47

London

The story in today's lesson takes place around the year 1360. That's over six hundred years ago. The story takes place in London, England. At that time, London was already a large city, and many people lived there. Many streets were made of dirt, and they were lined with houses that looked a little bit like the houses we have today. But those houses had no electricity, no gas, and no running water.(A)

However, those houses did have one thing that we still have today—mice. There were mice in every house, and they created quite a few problems. The solution to the mice problem involved an animal that you know.(B) Many houses had cats, and the people loved them.

The main characters in the story you will read are Dick Whittington and a cat.(C) Another character in the story is named Mister Warren. Mister Warren was a trading merchant. Trading merchants were like traveling salespersons. They would buy goods, such as cloth, shoes, and dishes, in one country, and sell them in other countries.(D) Because England is an island, the merchants had to transport the goods they bought in England by ships.(E) They had to take long voyages in these ships to get to the other countries.

180 Lesson 47 Textbook

Dick Whittington
by Andrew Lang
PART 1

Dick Whittington was born in a small town far away from London. He was a very young boy when his father and mother died. He was so young that he never knew them. No one took care of him, so he dressed in rags and strolled around the country.

One day, this orphan met a strange man who was going to London. The man said that the streets of London were paved with gold. The idea of gold streets pleased young Dick very much, and he decided to go with the man. But when they got to London, Dick saw that the streets were covered with dirt instead of gold. He also observed that the man who had brought him to London had quickly disappeared.(A)

So Dick found himself in a strange place, without a friend, without food, and without money. The poor boy was so cold and so hungry that he began to beg.(B) He was not successful.(C) At last a rich trading merchant stopped and said, "Why don't you work for a living, instead of begging?"

"I would love to work," said Dick, as he fell to his knees to plead with the merchant. "I will work for you if you will let me. I am just a poor country boy, and I do not know anyone in London."

Then Dick tried to get up, but he was so weak that he fell down. The merchant felt so sorry for Dick that he carried him to his house. Then the merchant, whose name was Mister Warren, ordered his servants to give Dick some meat and drink.(D) When Dick had finished his meal, Mister Warren ordered the cook to let Dick help her around the kitchen.

Dick should have been very happy in the Warren's house. He had enough to eat, and he made friends with some of the people who lived there. Mister Warren's daughter, Miss Alice, was very kind to Dick. The cook, however, was a mean

Lesson 47 Textbook **181**

EXERCISE 5   Comprehension passage

1. Everybody, turn to page 180 in your textbook. *Wait.*
2. *Call on individual students to read. Present the tasks specified for each circled letter.*

(A) In which city does the story take place? **London.**
- In which country does it take place? **England.**
- About how many years ago does the story take place? **Six hundred.**
- How were the streets in London different back then? *Idea:* They were made of dirt.
- How were the houses different? *Idea:* They had no electricity, no gas, and no running water.
- If a house didn't have running water, how would you get water inside the house? *Idea:* You'd have to carry it in buckets.
- Which story that you have read took place near London? *Idea:* The story about Nellie.

(B) Name that animal. **Cat.**
(C) Who are the main characters? **Dick Whittington and a cat.**
(D) What did trading merchants do? *Idea:* They bought goods in one country and sold them in another.
(E) How did they have to transport goods from England? **By ship.**

EXERCISE 6   Decoding and comprehension

1. Everybody, look at page 181 in your textbook. *Wait. Call on a student.* What's the error limit for this lesson? **7 errors.**
2. *Call on individual students to read. Present the tasks specified for each letter.*

(A) Was Dick born in London? **No.**
- What had happened to Dick's parents? *Idea:* They died when he was young.
- Who brought him to London? *Idea:* A strange man.
- What had the man told him about London? *Idea:* The streets were paved with gold.
- What that true? **No.**
- What happened to the man shortly after Dick arrived in London? *Idea:* He disappeared.

(B) What does a person do when the person begs? *Idea:* The person asks for money or food.
(C) Did he get money from begging? **No.**
(D) Listen to that last sentence again. Then the merchant, whose name was Mister Warren, ordered his servants to give Dick some meat and drink. What was the merchant's name? **Mister Warren.**
- What does the sentence tell you that lets you know the merchant was quite rich? *Ideas:* He had servants; he gave Dick food.

woman, and she made life difficult for Dick. She made him work from dawn to darkness, without a moment's rest. Ⓔ If Dick stopped working for even a second, she would threaten to hit him with her rolling pin. So Dick did as she said, without complaining. Ⓕ

But the cook was not Dick's only problem. He had to sleep in the attic, where there were many mice. Ⓖ The mice ran all over the room at night, and Dick could not get very much sleep. Soon he became tired. He was tired of work and tired of mice, and he began to long for the country again. Ⓗ ★7 ERRORS★

One morning, the cook sent Dick to the market to buy some food. On his way to the market, Dick saw a penny lying on the ground, and he put it in his pocket. He bought the food for the cook, and he was about to leave the market when he saw a woman with a cat under her arm. He ran up to her and asked her if she would sell him the cat. When Dick explained to her that he had only one penny in all the world, she felt sorry for him and let him have the cat for a penny.

Dick hid the cat in the attic, for fear that the cook would make him give it away. The cat went right to work, and frightened away all the mice. That night, Dick slept soundly for the first time in weeks.

The very next day, Mister Warren called all his servants together and said, "I am sailing to Spain to do some trading. I would like each one of you to give me something that I can try to sell. I will give you whatever money I get in return."

The servants were excited by this announcement. They had heard that traders could make a lot of money by selling ordinary things like cloth and shoes. All the servants ran to their rooms to get something for Mister Warren. The cook brought her rolling pin. Dick was glad to see the rolling pin go, but he was also sad, for he had nothing to give Mister Warren.

Miss Alice, who was sitting next to her father, said, "Why Dick, aren't you going to give something to my father?"

Dick blushed and began to stammer. "I—I have nothing to give," he said. "I am wearing everything I own."

But Alice continued, "don't you have anything else? Come now, you must have something that you can give."

Dick hesitated a moment, then said, "Well, I do have a cat that I bought yesterday for a penny."

"Fetch your cat, then, Whittington," said Mister Warren. "I will take it with me."

So Dick went to the attic, got his cat, and delivered it to Mister Warren, with tears in his eyes. He knew that the mice would come back again, but he said nothing. The servants laughed at Dick, and the cook laughed the loudest of all. She exclaimed, "That boy has tears in his eyes over a silly cat."

Mister Warren left with the cat later that day. Dick went sadly back to work and tried not to pay attention to the cook, who continued to make fun of him and his cat. He did not sleep well that night, for the mice soon found out that the cat was gone, and they began to run all over the attic again. Dick tossed and turned and finally resolved to leave the Warren's house the next day. He did not ever expect to see his cat again, and another day with the cook would be too much to take.

Ⓔ **What time of day is dawn?** *Idea:* Early morning.

● **If you work from dawn to darkness, at which time of day do you stop working?** *Idea:* Nighttime.

Ⓕ **Look at the picture. What is the cook holding? A rolling pin.**
You use a rolling pin to roll out dough for pie crusts.

● **What do you think she's saying to Dick?** *Response:* Student preference.

Ⓖ **Where is the attic of a house?** *Idea:* At the top of the house.

Ⓗ **What does that mean: long for the country again?** *Idea:* He missed the country and wanted to be there again.

● **Read the rest of the story to yourselves and be ready to answer some questions.**

After all students have finished reading:

● **What did Dick find on the way to the market? A penny.**

● **What did he use that penny for?** *Idea:* To buy a cat.

● **What did he do with the cat when he brought it back from the market?** *Idea:* Hid it in his room.

● **What did the cat do that night?** *Idea:* Frightened away the mice.

● **How did Dick sleep that night? Soundly.**

● **The next day, Mr. Warren said that he was sailing to another country. Which country? Spain.**

● **What was Mr. Warren going to do with the things that the servants gave him?** *Idea:* Sell them.

● **What did the cook give him? Her rolling pin.**

● **What did Dick give Mr. Warren? The cat.**

● **How were things different in the attic that night?** *Idea:* The mice came out again.

● **So what did Dick resolve to do the next day?** *Idea:* Leave Mr. Warren's house.

Very early the next morning, Dick slipped out of the back door and set off through the streets of London. After he left the city, he sat down on a rock to try to figure out where he should go. Just then, the church bells began to ring, and the strangest thing happened. Dick thought he heard the bells say: "Come back, come back, Whittington. Three times Mayor of London."

"Mayor of London!" he said to himself. "I would do anything to be the Mayor of London and ride around in a fine coach.

Perhaps I should go back. The cook is not unbearable, and I may be able to get another cat. Besides, there is nothing for me in the country."

So Dick ran back to London and slipped into the Warren's back door just as the cook was coming to work. No one knew that he had left, and everything was the same as it had been before. The cook still made his life difficult, and the mice still kept him up at night. However, Dick kept on working, for he believed the promise of the bells.

- When Dick left London, he heard something that made him return. What did he hear? **Bells.**
- What did he think the bells told him to do? *Idea:* Come back to London.
- Dick thought the bells were promising him something. How many times would he be Mayor of London? **Three.**
- So what did Dick do after he heard the bells? *Idea:* Went back to the Warren's house.
- Who knew that he had slipped out earlier that morning? *Idea:* Nobody.

Award 4 points or have students reread to the error limit sign.

INDEPENDENT WORK

Do all the items in your skillbook and workbook for lesson 47.

WORKCHECK AND AWARDING POINTS

1. *Read the questions and answers for the skillbook and workbook.*
2. *Award points for independent work as follows:*

0 errors	6 points
2 errors	4 points
3, 4, or 5 errors	2 points
5 or more errors	0 points

3. *Award bonus points as follows:*

Correcting missed items or getting all items right	........2 points
Doing the writing assignment acceptably	..........2 points

ANSWER KEY FOR WORKBOOK

Review Items

1. Name three hunting animals. *Ideas:*
   a. *dogs, falcons, hawks*
   b. *cats, cheetahs*
   c. *ferrets, mongooses*

2. Name three food-giving animals. *Ideas:*
   a. *goats, sheep*
   b. *cattle, pigs, ducks*
   c. *chickens, turkeys, geese*

3. Name three carrying animals. *Ideas:*
   a. *camels, llamas*
   b. *donkeys, mules*
   c. *horses, elephants*

ANSWER KEY FOR SKILLBOOK

PART B

1. He could neither swim nor dive.
2. She was neither happy nor sad.
3. They could neither walk nor run.
4. The women could neither sew nor cook.

PART C

5. a. 600
   b. *Idea:* In other countries
6. a. London
   b. England
   c. *Idea:* A strange man
   d. *Idea:* Streets paved with gold
   e. *Idea:* He disappeared
   f. *Idea:* He was hungry
   g. Mr. Warren
7. a. The cook
   b. *Idea:* Because of the mice
8. a. A penny
   b. A cat
   c. *Idea:* Put it in the attic

9. a. *Idea:* Sell them
   b. *Idea:* Give it to the servants
   c. A rolling pin
   d. A cat
10. *Idea:* Run away
11. a. Bells
   b. *Idea:* He would be mayor
   c. *Idea:* Mr. Warren's house

PART D

12. a. fact
   b. fiction
   c. fact
   d. fiction
   e. fact
   f. fact
   g. fiction
13. a. marvelous
   b. very smooth
   c. wildly
   d. dangled
   e. relatives

Lesson 48 ✓

Lesson 48

PART A Word Lists

1	2	3	4
miserable	imagination	purchase	**Vocabulary words**
whirring	fiction	voyage	1. stammer
Yukon	domestication	palace	2. pounce
Juneau	champion	merchant	3. stroll
glacier	selection		4. gnaw
	solution		5. accept

5	6
Vocabulary words	**Vocabulary words**
1. give credit	1. midday
2. elect	2. bill
3. college	3. hatch
4. brass	4. modest
5. impatient	

WORD PRACTICE AND VOCABULARY

EXERCISE 1 Word practice

1. Everybody, find lesson 48, part A in your skillbook. *Wait.* Touch under each word in column 1 as I read it.
2. The first word is **miserable.**
3. Next word. **Whirring.**
4. *Repeat step 3 for each remaining word in column 1.*
5. Your turn. Read the first word. *Signal.* **Miserable.**
6. Next word. *Signal.* **Whirring.**
7. *Repeat step 6 for each remaining word in column 1.*
8. *Repeat the words in column 1 until firm.*

EXERCISE 2 Word family

1. Everybody, touch column 2. *Check.* All those words end with the sound **un.** Touch under the first word. *Pause.* What word? *Signal.* **Imagination.**
2. Next word. *Pause.* What word? *Signal.* **Fiction.**
3. *Repeat step 2 for each remaining word in column 2.*
4. *Repeat the words in column 2 until firm.*

EXERCISE 3 Word practice

1. Everybody, touch under the first word in column 3. *Pause.* What word? *Signal.* **Purchase.**
2. Next word. *Pause.* What word? *Signal.* **Voyage.**
3. *Repeat step 2 for each remaining word in column 3.*
4. *Repeat the words in column 3 until firm.*

EXERCISE 4 Vocabulary review

Task A

1. Everybody, touch column 4. *Check.* First you're going to read the words in column 4. Then we'll talk about what they mean.
2. Touch under the first word. *Pause.* What word? *Signal.* **Stammer.**
3. Next word. *Pause.* What word? *Signal.* **Pounce.**
4. *Repeat step 3 for each remaining word in column 4.*
5. *Repeat the words in column 4 until firm.*

Task B

You've learned the meanings for all these words. Word 1 is **stammer.** *Call on a student.* What does **stammer** mean? *Idea:* You have trouble saying something.

Task C

1. Word 2 is **pounce.** *Call on a student.*
What does **pounce** mean? *Idea:* You jump on something.
2. Everybody, what's another way of saying **The mongoose jumped on the cobra?** *Signal.*
The mongoose pounced on the cobra.

Task D

Word 3 is **stroll.** *Call on a student.*
What does **stroll** mean? *Idea:* Walk slowly.

Task E

1. Word 4 is **gnaw.** *Call on a student.*
What does **gnaw** mean? *Idea:* Chew on something that is very hard.
2. Everybody, what's another way of saying **The dog chewed on the bone?** *Signal.*
The dog gnawed on the bone.

Task F

Word 5 is **accept.** *Call on a student.*
What does **accept** mean? *Idea:* You take something that is offered.

EXERCISE 5 Vocabulary development

Task A

1. Everybody, touch column 5. *Check.*
First you're going to read the words in columns 5 and 6. Then we'll talk about what they mean.
2. Touch under the first line in column 5. *Pause.* What words? *Signal.* **Give credit.**
3. Next word. *Pause.* What word? *Signal.* **Elect.**
4. *Repeat step 3 for each remaining word in column 5.*
5. *Repeat the words in column 5 until firm.*
6. Touch under the first word in column 6. *Pause.* What word? *Signal.* **Midday.**
7. *Repeat steps 3–5 for column 6.*

Task B

The words in line 1 of column 5 are **give credit.** When you **give credit** to somebody, you praise that person. If you praise somebody for having a good idea, you **give the person credit** for having that idea. Everybody, what do you do when you praise somebody for having a good idea? *Signal.* **Give the person credit for having that idea.**

Task C

Word 2 is **elect.** When people **elect** somebody to be a mayor, the people give more votes for that person than for anybody else. Everybody, what do they do for the person when they give that person the most votes? *Signal.*
They elect that person.

Task D

Word 3 is **college.** A **college** is a school that is more difficult than high school. After you finish high school, you may choose to go to college.

Task E

Word 4 is **brass.** Pennies are made of copper. If you melt copper and mix it with tin, you end up with a shiny metal that looks almost gold in color. That metal is **brass.**

Task F

Word 5 is **impatient.** When you are **impatient,** you are so eager for something to happen that you have trouble waiting. Everybody, how do you feel when you are so eager for something to happen that you have trouble waiting? *Signal.* **Impatient.**

Task G

Word 1 is **midday. Midday** is around noon. Everybody, what time is it at **midday?** *Signal.* **Around noon.**

Task H

Word 2 is **bill.** A bird's beak is sometimes called a **bill.**

Task I

Word 3 is **hatch.** When eggs crack open and little birds come out of them, we say the eggs **hatch.** Everybody, what do we say happens when the eggs crack open? *Signal.*
The eggs hatch.

Task J

Word 4 is **modest.** The opposite of a person who brags a lot is a person who is **modest.** The **modest** person does good things but doesn't brag about them. Everybody, what kind of person does good things but doesn't brag about them? *Signal.* **A modest person.**

Dick Whittington

PART 2

While Dick was having his problems at the Warren house, his cat was having a terrible time on the sailing ship. The ship ran into a storm on its very first night out, and the wind tossed the ship about like a leaf. At one time it seemed as if the ship would certainly sink, but Mister Warren helped the captain with the sails, and the rest of the crew worked frantically. Somehow they managed to keep the ship floating until the storm died down.

But the storm had blown the ship far off course. The captain did not know where they were, and nothing seemed familiar to him.Ⓐ There was nothing he could do now, for the ship was caught in a strong current, and it would just have to go where the current took it.Ⓑ

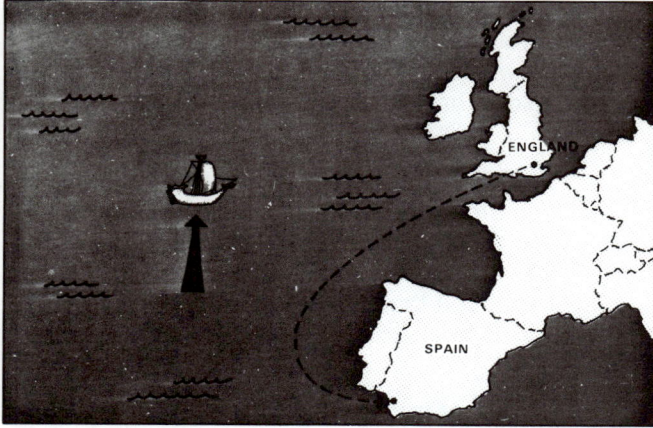

At last, the ship came to an island. Some people from the island came out in a small boat to meet the ship. When Mister Warren showed them the things he had to sell, they invited him to come to the island with them to meet their queen.

So Mister Warren put as many goods as he could into the small boat. However, he had to leave the cat on the ship, for there was no more room on the boat. When he left for the island, he promised the captain that he would come back the next day.

Mister Warren was stunned when he saw the queen's palace. It was made out of marble, and the doors were solid brass. Rich carpets covered the floors, and the chairs seemed to be made of gold. The queen was happy to see Mister Warren. She looked at the things that he had brought, and agreed to buy all of them for a very good price.Ⓒ

Then the queen invited Mister Warren to have dinner with her. They went into a huge dining room, where many people were already waiting. Servants brought in hundreds of dishes, and put all of them on the table. However, the instant the dishes were put down, an amazing number of mice came out of the walls and climbed on to the table. They began feasting on the food.

Mister Warren, in amazement, turned to the queen and asked her if this happened every night. "Oh, yes," answered the queen. "There is nothing we can do. I would give a lot of money to be freed of these disgusting animals, for they not only destroy our dinner, but also keep us awake at night as they gnaw through our walls."Ⓓ ★7 ERRORS★

Mister Warren jumped for joy. He remembered poor Whittington and his cat, and he told the queen that he had a creature on board his ship that would frighten all the mice away immediately.

"Bring this creature to me," said the queen. "If it does what you say I will load your ship with gold and jewels. But go quickly. I am impatient to see this creature."

So Mister Warren hurried back to the ship, grabbed the cat, and returned to the palace. Meanwhile, the queen had ordered another dinner. When Mister Warren came back with the cat, the servants brought out the dishes as they had done before, and set the dishes down on the table. Once again the mice immediately came out of the walls. But instantly the cat ran along the table and frightened them all away. The queen was delighted by this sight, and praised the cat highly.

After the cat had chased away all the mice, it jumped on the queen's lap and began to purr. The queen turned to Mister Warren and exclaimed, "You have given us something truly wonderful. I will order my servants to fill your ship with gold and jewels at once."

It took a whole day to load the ship, and the captain could not believe how well Mister Warren traded. The captain did not know that all the gold was for a cat that had been purchased for a penny.

The ship sailed back to England without any problems. When it arrived, Mister

---

EXERCISE 6   Decoding and comprehension

1. Everybody, turn to page 185 in your textbook. *Wait. Call on a student.* What's the error limit for this lesson? **7 errors.**
2. *Call on individual students to read. Present the tasks specified for each circled letter.*

Ⓐ What had the storm done? *Idea:* Blown the ship off course. Look at the picture. It shows a map with a sailing ship on it. The dotted arrow shows the course the captain had intended to take.
- What country does that course lead to? **Spain.**
  The map shows where the ship actually is. You can see it is far off course.
- In which direction would the ship have to go to get back on course? **East.**
- So in which direction had the wind blown the ship? **West.**

Ⓑ The map shows the current that the ship was caught in.
- In which direction is the current taking the ship? **North.**

Ⓒ Did Mr. Warren expect to see a rich palace on the island? **No.**
- What did the queen agree to buy? *Idea:* Everything Mr. Warren had brought.

Ⓓ How would you like to live in that palace? *Response:* Student preference.
- What does that mean: **The mice gnawed through the walls?** *Idea:* They ate through the walls.
- Read the rest of the story to yourselves and be ready to answer some questions.

After all students have finished reading:
- What did Mr. Warren say he had that would solve the problem with the mice? **The cat.**
- What did the queen say she would do if the cat could get rid of the mice? *Idea:* Load up the ship with gold and jewels.
- What happened when the queen again served dinner? *Idea:* The cat frightened the mice and rats away.

Warren loaded all the gold into six carts. He then hooked the carts together and found four strong horses to pull them. He rode proudly through the streets of London until he came to his house.

"Whittington," he shouted. "Come and see what I got for trading your cat."

Dick, who was working in the kitchen, heard Mister Warren, but he did not want to greet him, for he was afraid that Mister Warren wanted to make fun of him. But Miss Alice came to the kitchen door and said, "Hurry, Dick, you really must see this."

So Dick ran to the front door and could scarcely believe his eyes and ears when Mister Warren showed him the gold and told him what had happened.

"Your cat has given you more money than I am worth in all the world," said Mister Warren. "May you long enjoy these riches and be happy."

Dick did not know what to do. He tried to give the gold back to Mister Warren, but Mister Warren refused to take it. So Dick gave him part of the gold, and then Dick gave a little gold to each of the servants. He even gave some gold to the cook, although she hardly deserved it.

Later that day Dick went out to buy some clothes. When he returned, his face was washed, his hair was curly, and he was dressed in a splendid suit. Miss Alice, who had always liked Dick, fell in love with him. A few years later they were married.

They lived very happily, and when Dick became older, he was made Mayor of London three times. He was a very good mayor, for he fed the poor people, and built colleges and hospitals. And when people would see him in the street, they would point to him and say, "He owes it all to his cat."

The Real Dick Whittington

Although the story you have just read is fiction, some parts of it really happened. There really was a man named Dick Whittington, and he really became Mayor of London three times. He lived from about 1350 to 1420. There really was a Mister Warren, and Dick really married his daughter, Alice Warren. Dick was always very kind to poor children and did many things for them when he was Mayor of London. And, as far as we know, he loved cats.

But some parts of the story did not happen. Mister Warren did not really get blown away to a strange island, and nobody gave him a ship full of gold for just one cat.

The first person to tell this story was probably Dick Whittington himself. People would ask him how he got to be so rich and famous, and he was too modest to say that he had done it all by himself. So he gave all the credit to his cat, and to the bells that he heard as he was running away from London.

- How many carts did it take to hold all the gold and jewels that the queen gave for the cat? **Six.**
- Dick gave away part of the gold to different people. Name some of them. *Ideas:* Mr. Warren; the servants; the cook.
- Who did Dick marry? **Miss Alice.**
- What job did he later have? **Mayor of London.**
- How many times was he Mayor of London? **Three.**
- Is this a factual story or a fictional story? **Fictional.**
- Name some things in the story that actually did happen. *Call on individual students. Responses:* Dick was really Mayor of London three times; there really was a Mr. Warren; Dick really married Alice Warren; he really lived around 1350.
- Name some things in the story that were fictional. *Call on individual students. Responses:* Mister Warren did not get blown away to a strange island; nobody gave him a ship full of gold for the cat.

Award 4 points or have the students reread to the error limit sign.

INDEPENDENT WORK

Do all the items in your skillbook and workbook for lesson 48.

ANSWER KEY FOR WORKBOOK

Map Skills

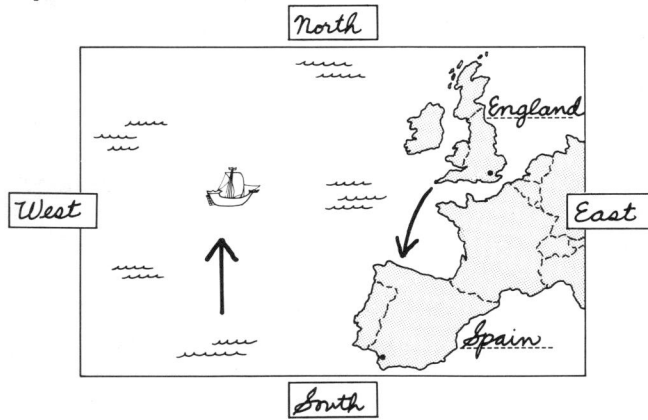

1. Write **North, East, South** and **West** in the boxes.
2. On the map, write each name in the correct blank.
   a. England
   b. Spain
3. a. Draw an **arrow** from England to the land that Mister Warren wanted to go to.
   b. Draw an **arrow** on the ocean to show the direction the currents moved Mr. Warren's ship.

Review Items

4. Write **The Cat that Walked** after each statement that tells about the cat in "The Cat that Walked by Himself." Write **Whittington** after each statement that tells about the cat in "Dick Whittington."
   a. This cat talked with the woman.
   The Cat that Walked
   b. This cat chased mice in the attic.
   Whittington
   c. This cat went on a ship.
   Whittington
   d. This cat played with a baby.
   The Cat that Walked
   e. This cat cost one penny.
   Whittington
   f. This cat was wise enough to trick a woman.
   The Cat that Walked
   g. This cat was traded for a lot of gold.
   Whittington
   h. This cat made a bargain.
   The Cat that Walked
   i. This cat chased a mouse in a cave.
   The Cat that Walked

WORKCHECK AND AWARDING POINTS

1. *Read the questions and answers for the skillbook and workbook.*
2. *Award points for independent work as follows:*

0 errors	6 points
2 errors	4 points
3, 4, or 5 errors	2 points
5 or more errors	0 points

3. *Award bonus points as follows:*

Correcting missed items or getting all items right	2 points
Doing the writing assignment acceptably	2 points

ANSWER KEY FOR SKILLBOOK

PART B

1. a. *Idea:* A storm
   b. *Idea:* The current
   c. *Idea:* An island
2. *Idea:* There was no room in the boat
3. a. *Idea:* Mice
   b. *Idea:* Ate it
   c. *Ideas:* Gold; jewels
   d. The cat
4. a. Six
   b. *Idea:* Give them back to Mr. Warren
   c. *Any two:* Mr. Warren, Alice, the cook; the servants
5. a. *Any two:* Face washed, hair curly, new suit
   b. Miss Alice
   c. mayor
6. a. fact   d. fact
   b. fiction   e. fiction
   c. fact   f. fact

PART C

7. a. Mister Warren
   b. cook
   c. Dick
   d. Alice
   e. queen
8. a. Nellie
   b. Tara
   c. Mr. Jones
   d. Liverpool
9. a. frantically
   b. guarantee
   c. venture
   d. prey
   e. keen

226   Lesson 48

Lesson 49

Lesson 49

PART A   Word Lists

1	2	3	4	5
eventually	scramble	Dawson	**Vocabulary words**	**Vocabulary words**
rustle	grumble	Skagway	1. give credit	1. eventually
descend	middle		2. elect	2. scrambled
boulder	comfortable		3. brass	3. disgraceful
treacherous	tumble		4. impatient	4. lean
	waddle		5. modest	5. vivid
	mantel			6. descended
				7. treacherous

WORD PRACTICE AND VOCABULARY

EXERCISE 1   Word practice

1. Everybody, find lesson 49, part A in your skillbook. *Wait.* Touch under each word in column 1 as I read it.
2. The first word is **eventually.**
3. Next word. **Rustle.**
4. *Repeat step 3 for each remaining word in column 1.*
5. Your turn. Read the first word. *Signal.* **Eventually.**
6. Next word. *Signal.* **Rustle.**
7. *Repeat step 6 for each remaining word in column 1.*
8. *Repeat the words in column 1 until firm.*

EXERCISE 2   Word family

1. Everybody, touch column 2. *Check.* All those words end with the sound **lll.** Touch under the first word. *Pause.* What word? *Signal.* **Scramble.**
2. Next word. *Pause.* What word? *Signal.* **Grumble.**
3. *Repeat step 2 for each remaining word in column 2.*
4. *Repeat the words in column 2 until firm.*

EXERCISE 3   Word practice

1. Everybody, touch under the first word in column 3. *Pause.* What word? *Signal.* **Dawson.**
2. Next word. *Pause.* What word? *Signal.* **Skagway.**
3. *Repeat the words in column 3 until firm.*

EXERCISE 4   Vocabulary review

Task A

1. Everybody, touch column 4. *Check.* First you're going to read the words in column 4. Then we'll talk about what they mean.
2. Touch under the first line. *Pause.* What words? *Signal.* **Give credit.**
3. Next word. *Pause.* What word? *Signal.* **Elect.**
4. *Repeat step 3 for each remaining word in column 4.*
5. *Repeat the words in column 4 until firm.*

Task B

1. You've learned the meanings for all these words.
2. The words in line 1 are **give credit.** *Call on a student.* What does **give credit** mean? *Idea:* You praise somebody for having a good idea.

Task C

Word 2 is **elect.** *Call on a student.* What does it mean when people **elect** somebody? *Idea:* People give more votes for that person than for anybody else.

Task D

Word 3 is **brass.** *Call on a student.* What is **brass**? *Idea:* A metal that is a mixture of copper and tin.

Task E

Word 4 is **impatient.** *Call on a student.* What does **impatient** mean? *Idea:* You are so eager for something to happen that you have trouble waiting.

Task F

Word 5 is **modest.** *Call on a student.* What does **modest** mean? *Idea:* You do good things, but don't brag about them.

EXERCISE 5   Vocabulary development

Task A

1. Everybody, touch column 5. *Check.* First you're going to read the words in column 5. Then we'll talk about what they mean.
2. Touch under the first word. *Pause.* What word? *Signal.* **Eventually.**
3. Next word. *Pause.* What word? *Signal.* **Scrambled.**
4. *Repeat step 3 for each remaining word in column 5.*
5. *Repeat the words in column 5 until firm.*

Task B

1. Now let's talk about what those words mean. Word 1 is **eventually.** Another word for **at last** is **eventually.** Everybody, what's another way of saying **She came home at last?** *Signal.* **She came home eventually.**
2. Everybody, what's another way of saying **At last, he grew up?** *Signal.* **Eventually, he grew up.**

Task C

Word 2 is **scrambled.** When you **scramble,** you move as fast as you can.

Lesson 49

PART A Word Lists

1	2	3	4	5
eventually	scramble	Dawson	**Vocabulary words**	**Vocabulary words**
rustle	grumble	Skagway	1. give credit	1. eventually
descend	middle		2. elect	2. scrambled
boulder	comfortable		3. brass	3. disgraceful
treacherous	tumble		4. impatient	4. lean
	waddle		5. modest	5. vivid
	mantel			6. descended
				7. treacherous

Task D

Word 3 is **disgraceful.** When you do something that is terrible, you do something that is **disgraceful.** Everybody, what's another word for something that is terrible? *Signal.* **Disgraceful.**

Task E

Word 4 is **lean.** People who are **lean** have no fat on their bodies. Everybody, what's the word that describes somebody with no fat? *Signal.* **Lean.**

Task F

1. Word 5 is **vivid.** Something that is very clear and easy to see is **vivid.** Here's another way of saying **The mountains were very easy to see: The mountains were vivid.** Everybody, what's another way of saying **The mountains were very easy to see?** *Signal.* **The mountains were vivid.**
2. Everybody, what's another way of saying **The blue color was easy to see?** *Signal.* **The blue color was vivid.**

Task G

1. Word 6 is **descended.** Listen to this sentence and see if you can figure out what the word **descended** means. Everybody, what word? *Signal.* **Descended.**
2. Listen. First the bird flew up high, then the bird slowly **descended** to the trees below.
3. *Call on a student.* What could **descended** mean? *Idea:* Came down.

Task H

1. Word 7 is **treacherous.** Another word for **very dangerous** is **treacherous.** Everybody, what's another way of saying **The trail was very dangerous?** *Signal.* **The trail was treacherous.**
2. Everybody, what's another way of saying **The mountain was very dangerous?** *Signal.* **The mountain was treacherous.**

Lesson 49

Trees
by Harry Behn

Trees are the kindest things I know,
They do no harm, they simply grow

And spread a shade for sleepy cows,
And gather birds among their boughs.

They give us fruit in leaves above,
And wood to make our houses of,

And leaves to burn on Hallowe'en,
And in the Spring new buds of green.

They are the first when day's begun
To touch the beams of morning sun,

They are the last to hold the light
When evening changes into night,

And when a moon floats on the sky
They hum a drowsy lullaby,

Of sleepy children long ago . . .
Trees are the kindest things I know.

190   Lesson 49   Textbook

Lesson 49   Textbook   191

POEM READING

Exercise 6   First poem

1. Everybody, turn to page 190 in your textbook. *Wait.*
2. Today, we're going to read two poems. The first is about trees; the second is about rain.
3. I'll read the first poem. Follow along and get a picture of the things the poem describes. *Read the poem "Trees."*
4. The poem uses some words that you may not know.
- The first word is **shade. Shade** is a shadow.
- The next word is **boughs. Boughs** are branches.
- The next word is **beams.** A **beam** of light is a ray of light. The picture on page 191 shows some beams of light passing through the tree.
- The last word is **lullaby.** A **lullaby** is a song that adults sing to put children to sleep.
5. Now let's talk about some of the parts of the poem.
- One part says that trees spread a shade for sleepy cows. Why do you think cows like that shade? *Idea:* It's cool.
- Another part says that trees gather birds among their boughs. Why do the boughs gather birds? *Idea:* Birds like to perch there.
- Another part says that trees are the first to touch the beams of morning sun. Why do trees touch the beams first? *Idea:* They're higher than other things.
- Another part says that trees are the last to hold the light when evening changes into night. Why are they the last to hold the light? *Idea:* They're higher.
- Another part says that when the moon floats on the sky, trees hum a drowsy lullaby. What time of day is it when this happens? *Idea:* Night. What would make the trees hum? *Idea:* The wind.
6. Your turn to read the poem. *Call on different students to read the poem.*

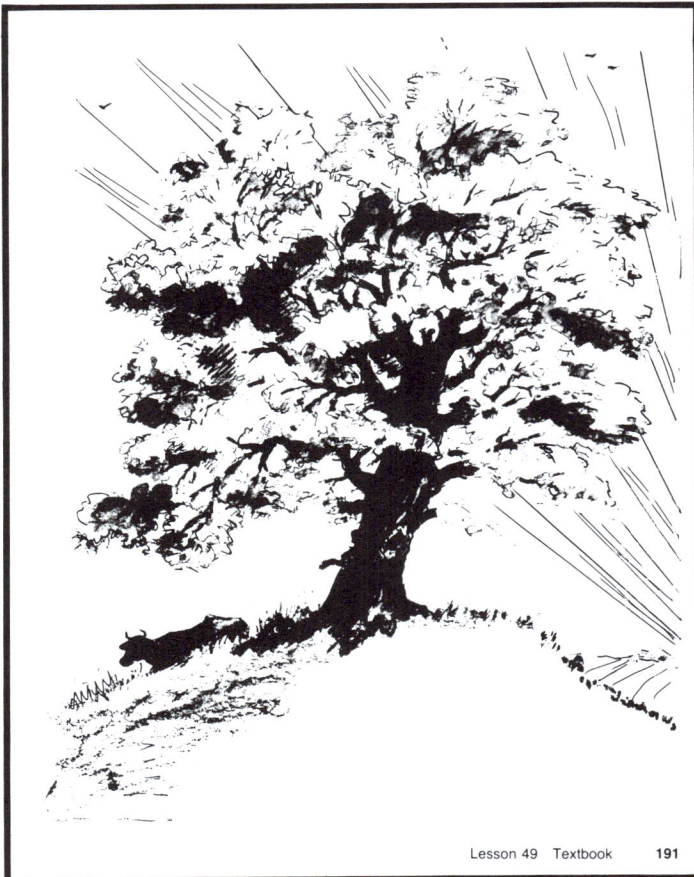

In Time of Silver Rain
by Langston Hughes

In time of silver rain
The earth
Puts forth new life again,
Green grasses grow
And flowers lift their heads,
And over all the plain
The wonder spreads
    Of life,
    Of life,
    Of life!

In time of silver rain
The butterflies
Lift silken wings
To catch a rainbow cry,
And trees put forth
New leaves to sing
In joy beneath the sky
As down the roadway
Passing boys and girls
Go singing, too,
In time of silver rain
    When spring
    And life
    Are new.

EXERCISE 7   Second poem

1. Everybody, turn to page 192. Follow along as I read this poem.
   Read the poem "In Time of Silver Rain."
2. The poem tells about a season of the year. What season? **Spring.**
   That's when the grasses grow and the flowers lift their heads.
- Name some of the things that are coming to life. *Ideas:* Grass, flowers, trees, bushes.
- The poem says that butterflies lift silken wings to catch a rainbow cry. The rainbow cry might be the colors of the rainbow.
- How would you know if a butterfly had caught a rainbow cry? *Idea:* It would have colors.
- The poem says that trees put forth new leaves to sing in joy beneath the sky. You sing in joy when you're happy. The tree sings in joy by putting out new leaves.
- Why would the tree want to sing in joy? *Idea:* It's happy to be growing again.
3. Your turn to read the poem. *Call on different students to read the poem.*

ANSWER KEY FOR WORKBOOK

Map Skills

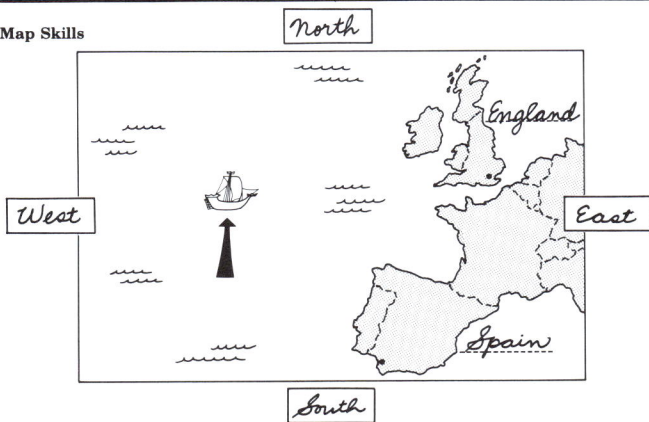

1. Write **North, West, East,** and **South** in the boxes.

2. On the map, write each name in the correct blank.
   a. England
   b. Spain

Crossword Puzzle

To work the puzzle, read an item and figure out which word the item describes. Then write the word in the puzzle. Complete the entire puzzle.

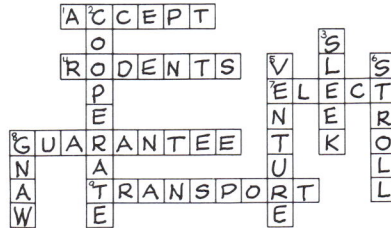

Across

1. When you take a gift that is offered, you _____ the gift.
4. A family of animals that includes rats, mice, squirrels and beavers.
7. When people vote for mayor, they _____ the mayor.
8. If you make sure that something will happen, you _____ that the thing will happen.
9. When you _____ something, you take it from one place to another.

Down

2. When you work together with somebody else, you _____ with that person.
3. Something that is very smooth and graceful is _____.
5. Something that is like an adventure is a _____.
6. When you walk slowly, you _____.
8. When you chew on something hard, you _____ on that thing.

INDEPENDENT WORK

Do all the items in your skillbook and workbook for lesson 49.

WORKCHECK AND AWARDING POINTS

1. *Read the questions and answers for the skillbook and workbook.*
2. *Award points for independent work as follows:*

> 0 errors . . . . .6 points
> 2 errors . . . . .4 points
> 3, 4, or 5 errors . . . . .2 points
> 5 or more errors . . . . .0 points

3. *Award bonus points as follows:*

> *Correcting missed items*
> *or getting all items right* . . . . .2 points
> *Doing the writing*
> *assignment acceptably* . . . . .2 points

ANSWER KEY FOR SKILLBOOK

PART B

1. a. She is neither short nor lean.
   b. He was neither cunning nor smart.
2. a. straining
   b. cooperate
   c. keen
   d. transport
   e. fetch

Lesson 50

Lesson 50

PART A   **Word Lists**

1	2	3	4
		Vocabulary words	**Vocabulary words**
ugly	volcano	1. scramble	1. rustling
quietly	volcanic	2. lean	2. flounder
doubtfully	glacier	3. eventually	3. miserable
hardly	Juneau	4. disgraceful	4. crest
bitterly	Yukon	5. treacherous	5. boulder
exactly		6. descend	6. rapids
		7. vivid	

WORD PRACTICE AND VOCABULARY

EXERCISE 1   Word family

1. Everybody, find lesson 50, part A in your skillbook. *Wait.* Touch column 1. *Check.*
   All those words end with the letters **l-y.**
   Touch under the first word. *Pause.*
   What word? *Signal.* **Ugly.**
2. Next word. *Pause.* What word? *Signal.* **Quietly.**
3. *Repeat step 2 for each remaining word in column 1.*
4. *Repeat the words in column 1 until firm.*

EXERCISE 2   Word practice

1. Everybody, touch under the first word in column 2. *Pause.* What word? *Signal.* **Volcano.**
2. Next word. *Pause.* What word? *Signal.* **Volcanic.**
3. *Repeat step 2 for each remaining word in column 2.*
4. *Repeat the words in column 2 until firm.*

EXERCISE 3   Vocabulary review

Task A

1. Everybody, touch column 3. *Check.*
   First you're going to read the words in column 3. Then we'll talk about what they mean.
2. Touch under the first word. *Pause.*
   What word? *Signal.* **Scramble.**
3. Next word. *Pause.* What word? *Signal.* **Lean.**
4. *Repeat step 3 for each remaining word in column 3.*
5. *Repeat the words in column 3 until firm.*

Task B

You've learned the meanings for all these words. Word 1 is **scramble.** *Call on a student.*
What do you do when you **scramble?** *Idea:* You move as fast as you can.

Task C

Word 2 is **lean.** *Call on a student.*
If somebody is lean, how would you describe that person? *Idea:* That person has no fat.

Task D

1. Word 3 is **eventually.** *Call on a student.*
   What does **eventually** mean? *Idea:* At last.
2. Everybody, what's another way of saying **She came home at last?** *Signal.*
   She came home eventually.
3. Everybody, what's another way of saying **At last, he grew up.** *Signal.*
   Eventually, he grew up.

Task E

Word 4 is **disgraceful.** *Call on a student.*
What does **disgraceful** mean? *Idea:* Terrible.

Task F

1. Word 5 is **treacherous.** *Call on a student.*
   What does **treacherous** mean? *Idea:* Very
   dangerous.
2. Everybody, what's another way of saying
   The trail was very dangerous? *Signal.* **The
   trail was treacherous.**
3. Everybody, what's another way of saying
   The mountain was very dangerous? *Signal.*
   The mountain was treacherous.

Task G

Word 6 is **descend.** *Call on a student.*
What does **descend** mean? *Idea:* Come down.

Task H

1. Word 7 is **vivid.** *Call on a student.*
   What does **vivid** mean? *Ideas:* Clear; easy to see.
2. Everybody, what's another way of saying
   The mountains were clear and easy to see?
   Signal. **The mountains were vivid.**
3. Everybody, what's another way of saying
   The blue color was easy to see? *Signal.*
   The blue color was vivid.

EXERCISE 4 Vocabulary development

Task A

1. Everybody, touch column 4. *Check.*
   First you're going to read the words in
   column 4. Then we'll talk about what they
   mean.
2. Touch under the first word. *Pause.* What word?
   Signal. **Rustling.**
3. Next word. *Pause.* What word? *Signal.*
   Flounder.
4. *Repeat step 3 for each remaining word in column 4.*
5. *Repeat the words in column 4 until firm.*

Task B

Now let's talk about what those words mean.
Word 1 is **rustling.** A **rustling** sound is the
sound that is made when something moves
through grass or bushes. Everybody, what kind
of sound is made when something moves
through grass or bushes? *Signal.*
A rustling sound.

Task C

Word 2 is **flounder.** When you **flounder,** you
move around awkwardly without any direction.
Everybody, what are you doing when you're
moving around awkwardly without any
direction? *Signal.* **Floundering.**

Task D

1. Word 3 is **miserable.** When you feel very, very
   bad, you feel **miserable.**
   Everybody, what's another way of saying
   She felt bad because of the cold? *Signal.*
   She felt miserable because of the cold.
2. Everybody, what's another way of saying
   She was sick and felt very bad? *Signal.*
   She was sick and felt miserable.

Task E

Word 4 is **crest.** The top of a hill is the **crest** of
the hill. Everybody, what's the top of a hill
called? *Signal.* **The crest of the hill.**

Task F

Word 5 is **boulder.** A **boulder** is a very large
rock. Everybody, what's another name for a
very large rock? *Signal.* **Boulder.**

Task G

Word 6 is **rapids. Rapids** are places where
rivers flow downhill very rapidly. The water in
steep rapids sprays up and makes very large
waves.

Lesson 50

Journey to Dawson
PART 1

Beginning in lesson 52, you will read an exciting story that takes place in the gold fields of Northern Canada.

Before you begin that story, you will learn some facts about the gold fields and the trip that people took to reach those fields. Pretend that you are a person going to the gold fields. And pretend that you are living in the year 1896.

In 1896, gold was discovered in Northern Canada near a town called Dawson. You decide to go to Dawson and find your fortune in gold.Ⓐ

All the routes to the gold fields are dangerous. You decide to take a boat down the Yukon River, but before you can go down the Yukon River, you must get to it, which is a difficult and dangerous job. The Yukon River begins in lakes that are high in the mountains. You must climb high into the mountains before you reach those lakes.

The map shows the route that you will take to reach Dawson. The route is marked with a blue line.Ⓑ The line on the map starts in Juneau, Alaska.Ⓒ Then the line goes north into the mountains until it reaches Skagway.Ⓓ Then the line goes still farther north, over the mountains, until it comes to one of the magnificent lakes that flows into the Yukon.Ⓔ From this lake you travel on the Yukon until you eventually reach the tiny town of Dawson.

The journey from Juneau to Dawson is very long and very dangerous. But you also experience a dangerous journey trying to reach Juneau. You approach Juneau from the sea. This approach is treacherous because of the tides.Ⓕ

Each day the sea rises a little and descends a little. This change in the level of the sea is called the tides. Twice each day, the tides go out and make the beaches larger. Then the tides come back in and make the beaches smaller.Ⓖ

The tides near Juneau are so powerful that, when the water level rises, the water rushes inland with the speed of a race horse. It sweeps everything in its path along at that speed. In less than an hour, it moves over twenty miles inland, flooding areas that are dry when the tides are out. A boat caught in this tide would probably be tumbled about and smashed to bits.Ⓗ

194   Lesson 50   Textbook

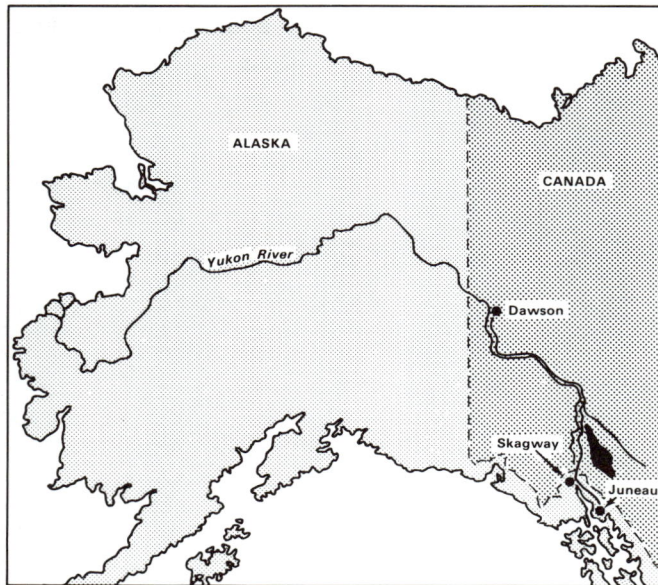

Lesson 50   Textbook   195

STORY READING

EXERCISE 5   Factual article

1. Everybody, turn to page 194 in your textbook. *Wait.*
2. *Call on individual students to read. Present the tasks specified for each circled letter.*

Ⓐ In what year are you living? **1896.**
- Where are you going? **To the gold fields.**
- Why? *Idea:* To find gold.

Ⓑ Everybody, look at the map. It shows the route that you will take down the Yukon River. The map shows Alaska and part of Northern Canada. Start at the beginning of the blue line and follow the line until you come to the lake. *Check.*

- You will have to go through great mountains to reach that lake. Now follow the line through the lake and along the Yukon River all the way to Dawson. *Check.*

Ⓒ Touch the town of Juneau on the map. *Check.*

Ⓓ Follow the route from Juneau to Skagway. *Check.* Skagway is high in the mountains.

Ⓔ Follow the route from Skagway until you reach the lake. *Check.* Before you can reach the lake, you'll have to climb far up into the mountains. After you pass through the lake, you'll go north and west. Follow the line through the lake and on the Yukon River, all the way to Dawson. *Check.*

Ⓕ Why is the voyage dangerous? *Idea:* Because of the tides.

Ⓖ If the tide is high, will the beach be bigger or smaller? **Smaller.**

- If the tide is low, will the beach be bigger or smaller? **Bigger.**
  Remember, when the tides are higher, the ocean rises and the water covers part of the beach.

Ⓗ Imagine a tide with that much power, moving inland over 20 miles and filling dry places with water.

You take a small boat from the ship and reach the shore safely. When you arrive at Juneau, you may get the impression that you are in a wonderland. Rows and rows of great mountains stand like giant castles. And between some of these mountains are great ice floes called glaciers, which flow down to lakes. The glaciers actually move, as millions of tons of ice and snow in the mountains push down on them. You see one great glacier near Juneau. It moves slowly into a lake, and looks like a huge tongue with its tip cut off. Ⓘ

As you stand on the rocky shore of this lake and listen, you can hear the glacier moving. It creaks and groans. Then, from time to time, huge chunks of ice fall off the end of the glacier and tumble into the icy lake, making a sound like distant thunder. When the end of this glacial tongue breaks off, you observe something that is almost unbelievable. The jagged end of the glacier is blue—as blue as the sky. The blue is most vivid just after the end of the glacier falls off. Then the blue begins to fade and become lighter. Ⓙ

You leave Juneau and continue north on your way to the gold fields. Your next stop will be a little place called Skagway, which is very close to the Canadian border.

Walking along a path, you leave Juneau and climb into the mountains. On your right, for nearly a hundred miles, is an incredible glacier that has hundreds of ice tongues that extend down into the pass. From time to time, you notice smoke drifting from a huge volcanic mountain on your left. Ⓚ

Skagway is a little village, and prices here are disgraceful. Everything that reaches Skagway must be brought in over the difficult trail that you have just taken. So things like a glass of milk might cost as much as twenty dollars. In Skagway, you make arrangements to take a boat the rest of the way up to the gold fields. Ⓛ Other people seeking gold will go on this boat with you, and each person will have to pay a small fortune for the guide who takes you on the treacherous journey. Ⓜ

Now the guide leads you and the others as you tramp overland from Skagway through amazing mountain passes. In the middle of this overland route, you cross the border of Alaska and enter Canada. At last you reach the lake. You are ready to start on your boat trip.

It is early morning, and you can see your breath, although it is still summertime. The lake, which is nearly a hundred miles long, is surrounded by mountains with their peaks hidden in the clouds. The only sounds are those of occasional fish splashing in the lake and early morning birds. Some chirp, some cry, and some seem to scream. Ⓝ

Ⓘ **What makes the glaciers move?** *Idea:* Tons of ice and snow pushing down on them.
Ⓙ **What keeps happening to the end of the glacier?** *Idea:* It keeps falling off.
● **What color is the tip of the glacier just after the end falls off?** **Blue.**
Ⓚ **How long is the glacier?** *Idea:* Almost 100 miles long.
● **What is on your left as you travel north along the glacier?** *Idea:* A volcano.
● **What do you see coming from the volcano?** **Smoke.**
Ⓛ **The gold fields are near the town you are going to. What's the name of that town?** **Dawson.**
Ⓜ **What does that mean: a small fortune?** *Idea:* It costs a lot of money.
Ⓝ **Everybody, get a picture of that lake.**
● **What time is it?** *Idea:* Early morning.
● **How long is the lake?** *Idea:* Nearly 100 miles long.
● **What sounds do you hear?** *Ideas:* Fish splashing; birds chirping.

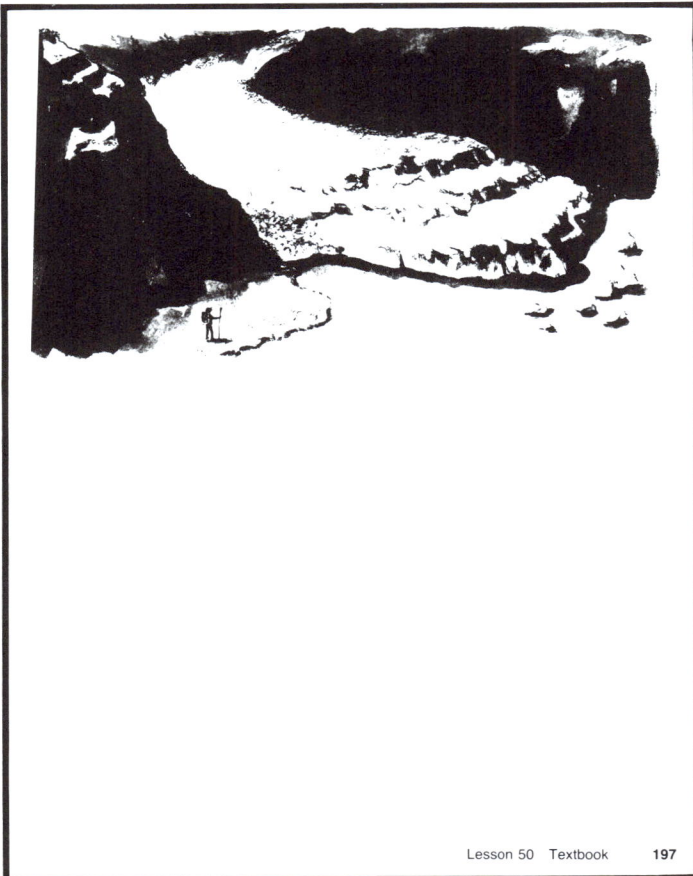

ANSWER KEY FOR WORKBOOK

Review Items

1. Write the use for each animal. Choose from **hunting, food,** or **carrying.**

   a. donkey *carrying*

   b. cow *food*

   c. cat *hunting*

   d. camel *carrying*

   e. mongoose *hunting*

Study Skills

2. Below is part of an encyclopedia index.

Subject	Book	Page
Youngstown	5	211
Yucatan	11	16
yucca	12	95
Yugoslavia	15	181
Yukon	18	331
yule	20	529

   a. Which subject would tell you about a river in Northern Canada?

   Yukon

   b. Which book would you read to find out about that subject? *18*

   c. Which page of that book would you look for? *331*

INDEPENDENT WORK

Do all the items in your skillbook and workbook for lesson 50.

WORKCHECK AND AWARDING POINTS

1. *Read the questions and answers for the skillbook and workbook.*

2. *Award points for independent work as follows:*

> 0 errors . . . . .6 points
> 2 errors . . . . .4 points
> 3, 4, or 5 errors . . . . .2 points
> 5 or more errors . . . . .0 points

3. *Award bonus points as follows:*

> Correcting missed items
> or getting all items right . . . . .2 points
> Doing the writing
> assignment acceptably . . . . .2 points

ANSWER KEY FOR SKILLBOOK

PART B

1. **a.** 1896
   b. Dawson
2. Juneau
3. Blue
4. **a.** Skagway
   b. Alaska
   c. *Idea:* They cost too much
   d. lake

PART C

5. **a.** fact
   b. fiction
   c. fact
   d. fact
   e. fact
   f. fiction
6. **a.** cooperate
   b. transport
   c. strolled
   d. coaches
   e. impatient

Lesson 51

Lesson 51

PART A   Word Lists

Vocabulary words
1. murmur
2. whittling
3. sneer
4. coil
5. exchanged
6. flickered
7. hurl
8. limp

WORD PRACTICE AND VOCABULARY

EXERCISE 1   Vocabulary from context

Task A
1. Everybody, find lesson 51, part A in your skillbook. *Wait.* Touch the column. *Check.* First you're going to read the words in the column. Then we'll talk about what they mean.
2. Touch under the first word. *Pause.* What word? *Signal.* **Murmur.**
3. Next word. *Pause.* What word? *Signal.* **Whittling.**
4. *Repeat step 3 for each remaining word in the column.*
5. *Repeat the words in the column until firm.*

Task B
1. I'll say sentences that contain some words that you'll read in a story. Each sentence has a part that you may be able to figure out by listening to the rest of the sentence.
2. Listen to the first sentence and see if you can figure out what the word **murmur** means. Everybody, what word? *Signal.* **Murmur.**
3. Listen. When the wind did not blow, you could hear the **murmur** of insects and other living things.
4. *Call on a student.* What could **murmur** mean? *Idea:* A low sound.

Task C
1. Listen to the second sentence and see if you can figure out what the word **whittling** means. Everybody, what word? *Signal.* **Whittling.**
2. Listen. With his knife, John Thornton was **whittling** on a branch and shaping it into an ax handle.
3. *Call on a student.* What could **whittling** mean? *Ideas:* Carving; cutting.

Task D
1. Listen to the third sentence and see if you can figure out what the word **sneer** means. Everybody, what word? *Signal.* **Sneer.**
2. Listen. His smile turned into a mocking **sneer,** with his lips curled in disgust.
3. *Call on a student.* Show me what that **sneering** expression looks like. *Check.*

Task E
1. Listen to the fourth sentence and see if you can figure out what the word **coil** means. Everybody, what word? *Signal.* **Coil.**
2. Listen. He wound his whip around his hand until the whip was in a neat **coil.**
3. *Call on a student.* What could **coil** mean? *Ideas:* Circle; ring; spiral.

Task F
1. Listen to the fifth sentence and see if you can figure out what the word **exchanged** means. Everybody, what word? *Signal.* **Exchanged.**
2. Listen. He did not like using the whip, so he **exchanged** the whip for a club.
3. *Call on a student.* How would he do that? *Idea:* Put down the whip and pick up the club.

Task G
1. Listen to the sixth sentence and see if you can figure out what the word **flickered** means. Everybody, what word? *Signal.* **Flickered.**
2. Listen. The fire first burned brightly, then **flickered**, then finally went out.
3. *Call on a student.* What was it doing when it was **flickering**? *Idea:* Burning unsteadily.

Task H
1. Listen to the seventh sentence and see if you can figure out what the word **hurl** means. Everybody, what word? *Signal.* **Hurl.**
2. Listen. When he threw the rock, he wasn't sure how far he could **hurl** it.
3. *Call on a student.* What could **hurl** mean? *Idea:* Throw.

Task I
1. Listen to the eighth sentence and see if you can figure out what the word **limp** means. Everybody, what word? *Signal.* **Limp.**
2. Listen. At first he struggled with every muscle, but then his body grew **limp** as a wet towel.
3. *Call on a student.* What could **limp** mean? *Idea:* Flimsy.

Lesson 51

Journey to Dawson
PART 2 ⓐ

ALASKA

CANADA

Yukon River

Dawson

Skagway

Juneau

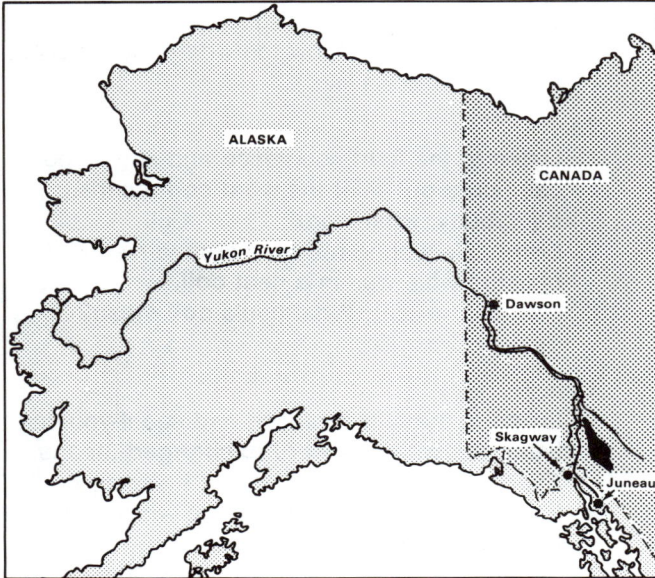

198   Lesson 50   Textbook

As you and the others seat yourselves in the small riverboat, ripples move out from the boat across the mirror surface of the water. You will never forget this moment. You are the only people for a hundred miles in any direction. You and the others are alone among the tall pines and spruces. ⓑ Some of the trees along the shore of the lake are so huge that ten people, standing side-by-side, could hide behind one of them. They reach up so far that, if you stand directly under one and look up, you become dizzy. Everything around you is so grand, so magnificent, that your mind is dazzled.

You and the others row the riverboat across the glassy lake. All day and all the next day and all the next day, you row. By now your hands are raw from pulling on the oars. ⓒ And your nights are now miserable because swarms of mosquitos and biting insects attack you and your party as soon as the sun sets.

At last, you come to the north end of the lake. Here the river starts and, for the moment, you're delighted. Your delight quickly changes into fright when you start down the river. ⓓ The lake that you have been on is very high in the mountains. But the gold fields are far below in a place called the Yukon Valley. The river that flows north and west to the gold fields is named the Yukon River. As the river flows from the lake down into the valley, it roars through steep passes that snake between great mountains. In places, the Yukon tumbles and thunders in clouds of spray

Lesson 51   Textbook   199

STORY READING

EXERCISE 2   Decoding and comprehension

1. Everybody, turn to page 198 in your textbook. *Wait. Call on a student.* What's the error limit for this lesson? **6 errors.**
2. *Call on individual students to read. Present the tasks specified for each circled letter.*

ⓐ Where did we leave you on your trip to Dawson? *Ideas:* In a boat; on a lake.
- How long is that lake? *Idea:* Nearly 100 miles long.
- Name some things that you see and hear. *Ideas:* Fish; birds; mountains; clouds.
- Everybody, touch the lake on the map. *Check.*
- Show the route that you will follow from the lake to the gold fields. *Check.*
That river comes down out of the mountains. It must be a very dangerous journey.

ⓑ Everybody, look at the picture. *Check.* Pines and spruces are large trees that stay green all year long. You can see some of them along the shore in the picture. Everybody, touch a pine or a spruce. *Check.*

ⓒ What does that mean: **Your hands are raw?** *Idea:* Your hands hurt.
- What would your hands look like if they were raw? *Ideas:* Red; bloody; cut up.
- What would they feel like? *Idea:* Sore.

ⓓ Why are you delighted? *Idea:* You've made it across the lake.
- Will you have to row as hard when you go down the river? **No.**
- Why not? *Idea:* The river goes down the mountains.

ⓔ Picture that water. The river is calm. You stand up in the boat and look down.
- Why do you feel a little dizzy? *Idea:* You feel like you are up very high.
That water must be very clear.
- Read the rest of the story to yourselves and be ready to answer some questions.

After all students have finished reading:
- What river do you go down after leaving the large lake? **The Yukon River.**
- Are all parts of this river the same? **No.**
- Which parts of the river are frightening? *Idea:* The rapids.
- Can your boat go through all the rapids? **No.**
- Why not? *Idea:* It's too dangerous.

and dazzling white water. In other places it becomes wide and shallow. Here you can see the bottom of the river so clearly that there doesn't seem to be any water between the boat and the bottom of the river. Even in places where the water is ten feet deep, the water is so invisible that if you stand up in the boat and look down, you feel as if you are standing ten feet in the air. (E)

★6 ERRORS★

When you come to these still places in the river, you observe the things around you. You see fish—thousands of them—in the river. Some are three or four feet long. And they move in great schools. You look at the trees and incredible jagged rocks that line the banks of the river.

But when you come to places where the river roars down through a narrow pass, you don't think of anything except scrambling through the pass. Above the roaring water you hear the guide shouting directions, "Pull right, pull right." But his voice is nearly drowned in the thunderous sound of the great river as it hammers and bounces the tiny boat through the snarling, icy water. When the river again slows down, your hands are numb from the cold and your feet ache from being in the freezing water that flounders around in the bottom of the boat.

Some passes are so steep that the boat would become nothing but splinters if it tried to go through them. On a still day, you can hear the thundering sound of the rapids more than two miles away. From this distance, the sound is like a far off

wind rustling through the trees. As you get closer, you hear the roar, louder and louder. If you don't row to the bank and get your boat out of the river at this point, the current will move so fast that you won't be able to stop the boat. You'll get close to the steep banks, but the boat will be moving so fast that it will nudge the bank a few times and then continue helplessly. It will slide over the glassy crest of the top of the rapids, dive into great waves that are topped with spray, and scoot down the rapids until it hits a boulder.

When you approach one of these terrible rapids, your guide directs you to row to the bank. Everybody gets out, unloads the supplies from the boat, pulls the boat on shore, and turns it over to drain out all the water. Then the difficult part starts; you must carry the boat and all the supplies along a rock ledge next to the river. Sometimes, transporting the boat and supplies for a mile takes all day. It takes so long because you must first haul the boat up hundreds of feet to a ledge above the river. Then you must carry the boat through dense forests and over very rough paths made by deer and other animals. Sometimes, you carry the boat on the edge of cliffs that are directly above the river. One wrong step, and you could tumble hundreds of feet into the swirling rapids below.

At last the river reaches the Yukon Valley. Now the river moves more steadily, north and west. You must travel only about two hundred miles farther to reach

200   Lesson 51   Textbook

Dawson. The days move by slowly and the nights become longer and colder. No longer do the mosquitos bother you as much at night. The days go by slowly, as the boat floats down the Yukon. You see wild animals—wolves, deer, moose, and millions of birds. On all sides are fantastic mountains, topped with a dazzling white mantle that reaches down to the broad, green valley on either side of the river. The valley is dotted with wild flowers and birds, and with an occasional bear standing on its hind legs looking at the strange sight of a boat on the river.

When you reach the tiny town of

Dawson, your hands are lean and hard. And you feel as if you've left everything you know far, far behind. Even your memories of cities and people are dull. As you stand on the outskirts of this strange little town, you feel as if you are a part of the northern country. At the same time, you feel like a lonely stranger who doesn't belong in this land. The cold air, the crystal waters, and the green meadows do not belong to people, but to the wild things that grow here. The great mountains stand like gigantic guards, keeping people out. But you are here because hidden in those mountains are great riches.

Lesson 51   Textbook   201

- So what do you do when you come to one of those terrible rapids? *Idea:* Take the boat around the rapids.
- How long does it sometimes take to carry the boat and supplies one mile? **All day.**
- After you leave the worst rapids, you come to a valley. What is the name of the valley? **The Yukon Valley.**
- Name some things that you see along the Yukon Valley. *Ideas:* Wild animals; birds; mountains; wild flowers.
- At last you come to your destination. What's the name of that town? **Dawson.**
- Why do you feel like a stranger in that part of the world? *Idea:* The land belongs to the wild things that grow there.
- What riches are hidden in the mountains? **Gold.**

Award 4 points or have the students reread to the error limit sign.

EXERCISE 3   Individual reading checkout

1. *For the individual reading checkout, each student will read 125 words. The passage to be read is the shaded area on the reproduced textbook page for lesson 51 in this presentation book.*

2. Today is a reading checkout day. While you're doing your independent work, I'll call on each student to read part of yesterday's chapter.

3. When I call on you, come up to my desk and bring your textbook with you. After you have read, I'll tell you how many points you can write in the checkout box that's at the top of your workbook page.

4. *If the student finishes the passage in one minute or less, award points as follows:*

0 errors . . . . .3 points
1 or 2 errors . . . . .1 point
More than 2 errors . . . . .0 points

5. *If a student takes more than one minute to read the passage, the student does not earn any points, but have the student reread the passage until he or she is able to read it in no more than one minute with no more than two errors.*

INDEPENDENT WORK

Do all the items in your skillbook and workbook for lesson 51.

ANSWER KEY FOR WORKBOOK

Map Skills

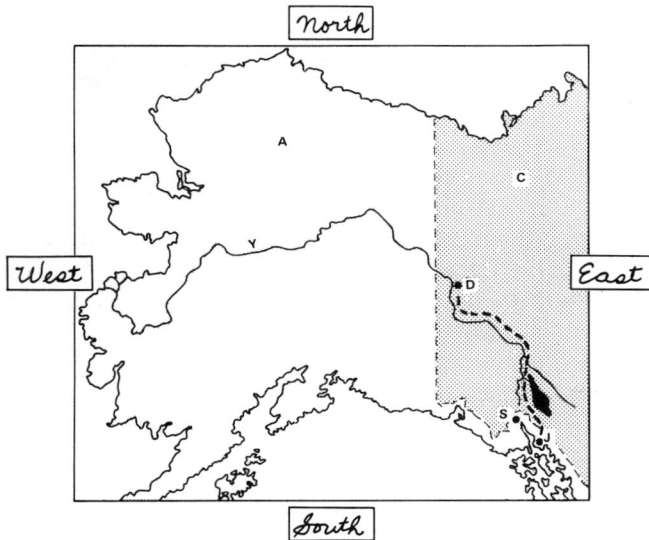

1. Write **North, South, East,** and **West** in the boxes around the map.
2. **a.** What's the name of city **J**?
   Juneau
   b. What's the name of town **S**?
   Skagway
   c. What's the name of river **Y**?
   Yukon
   d. What's the name of town **D**?
   Dawson
   e. What's the name of state **A**?
   Alaska
   f. What's the name of country **C**?
   Canada
3. On the map, draw a **dotted** line to show the trip you would take to look for gold.

WORKCHECK AND AWARDING POINTS

1. *Read the questions and answers for the skillbook and workbook.*
2. *Award points for independent work as follows:*

0 errors	6 points
2 errors	4 points
3, 4, or 5 errors	2 points
5 or more errors	0 points

3. *Award bonus points as follows:*

Correcting missed items or getting all items right	2 points
Doing the writing assignment acceptably	2 points

4. *Remind the students to put the points they earned for their reading checkout, in the box labeled* **CO.**

ANSWER KEY FOR SKILLBOOK

PART B

1. **a.** 1896
   b. Dawson
2. Blue
3. **a.** Yukon River
   b. *Idea:* Rapids
   c. No
   d. *Idea:* One day
4. Yukon Valley
5. *Any five:* Mosquitos, wolves, deer, moose, birds, bear, fish

PART C

6. **a.** I would neither run nor jump.
   b. They are neither laughing nor singing.
7. **a.** The Cat that Walked by Himself
   b. The Cat that Walked by Himself
   c. Dick Whittington
   d. Dick Whittington
   e. The Ugly Duckling
   f. The Ugly Duckling
   g. The Cat that Walked by Himself
   h. Dick Whittington
   i. The Ugly Duckling
8. **a.** Green
   b. White
   c. Red
   d. Blue
   e. Yellow
   f. White
   g. Blue
   h. Black
9. **a.** fetch
   b. college
   c. coach
   d. give credit
   e. terrible
   f. hurried

Lesson 52

Lesson 52

PART A	Word Lists		
1	**2**	**3**	**4**
overhead	mine	**Vocabulary words**	**Vocabulary words**
hillslope	miner	1. flicker	1. lingered on
waterfall	baggage	2. sneer	2. buds
motionless	cricket	3. murmur	3. staggered
downstream	Thornton	4. hurl	4. sap
	exchanged	5. coil	5. runners
		6. miserable	
		7. reflection	

WORD PRACTICE AND VOCABULARY

EXERCISE 1 Word family

1. Everybody, find lesson 52, part A in your skillbook. *Wait.* Touch column 1. *Check.* All those words are made up of two shorter words. Touch under the first word. *Pause.* What word? *Signal.* **Overhead.**
2. Next word. *Pause.* What word? *Signal.* **Hillslope.**
3. *Repeat step 2 for each remaining word in column 1.*
4. *Repeat the words in column 1 until firm.*

EXERCISE 2 Word practice

1. Everybody, touch under the first word in column 2. *Pause.* What word? *Signal.* **Mine.**
2. Next word. *Pause.* What word? *Signal.* **Miner.**
3. *Repeat step 2 for each remaining word in column 2.*
4. *Repeat the words in column 2 until firm.*

EXERCISE 3 Vocabulary review

Task A

1. Everybody, touch column 3. *Check.* First you're going to read the words in column 3. Then we'll talk about what they mean.
2. Touch under the first word. *Pause.* What word? *Signal.* **Flicker.**
3. Next word. *Pause.* What word? *Signal.* **Sneer.**
4. *Repeat step 3 for each remaining word in column 3.*
5. *Repeat the words in column 3 until firm.*

Task B

Word 1 is **flicker.** *Call on a student.* What does **flicker** mean? *Idea:* Shine unsteadily.

Task C

Word 2 is **sneer.** *Call on a student.* Show me what a **sneer** looks like. *Check.*

Task D

Word 3 is **murmur.** *Call on a student.* What is a **murmur.** *Idea:* A sound.

Task E

Word 4 is **hurl.** *Call on a student.* What does **hurl** mean? *Idea:* Throw.

Task F

Word 5 is **coil.** *Call on a student.* If something is in a **coil**, what shape does that thing have? *Ideas:* Round; circular; spiral.

Task G

Word 6 is **miserable.** *Call on a student.* How do you feel when you feel **miserable?** *Idea:* Very, very bad.

Task H

Word 7 is **reflection.** *Call on a student.* What is a **reflection**? *Idea:* The image that you see in a mirror or on shiny surfaces.

EXERCISE 4 Vocabulary from context

Task A

1. Everybody, touch column 4. *Check.* First you're going to read the words in column 4. Then we'll talk about what they mean.
2. Touch under the first line. *Pause.* What words? *Signal.* **Lingered on.**
3. Next word. *Pause.* What word? *Signal.* **Buds.**
4. *Repeat step 3 for each remaining word in column 4.*
5. *Repeat the words in column 4 until firm.*

Task B

1. I'll say sentences that contain some words that you'll read in today's story. Each sentence has a part that you may be able to figure out by listening to the rest of the sentence.
2. Listen to the first sentence and see if you can figure out what the words **lingered on** mean. Everybody, what words? *Signal.* **Lingered on.**
3. Listen. In Alaska it was dawn by three in the morning, and twilight **lingered on** till nine at night.
4. *Call on a student.* What could **lingered on** mean? *Idea:* Keep on lasting or keep on going.

Task C

1. Listen to the second sentence and see if you can figure out what the word **buds** means. Everybody, what word? *Signal.* **Buds.**
2. Listen. The trees were bursting into young **buds** that would soon become full-grown leaves.
3. *Call on a student.* What could **buds** mean? *Idea:* Leaves that are forming.

Task D

1. Listen to the third sentence and see if you can figure out what the word **staggered** means. Everybody, what word? *Signal.* **Staggered.**
2. Listen. The man was so tired and cold that when he tried to walk, he **staggered** and almost fell.
3. *Call on a student.* What could **staggered** mean? *Ideas:* Walked unsteadily; stumbled.

Lesson 52

PART A   Word Lists

1	2	3 Vocabulary words	4 Vocabulary words
overhead	mine	1. flicker	1. lingered on
hillslope	miner	2. sneer	2. buds
waterfall	baggage	3. murmur	3. staggered
motionless	cricket	4. hurl	4. sap
downstream	Thornton	5. coil	5. runners
	exchanged	6. miserable	
		7. reflection	

Lesson 52

The Yukon Valley

The story that you will read today takes place near Dawson, in the Yukon Valley. Ⓐ The story begins in early spring, just as the ice is melting. The rivers are frozen during the winter, so that miners who venture to the gold fields are able to follow the Yukon on foot. The miners use dog sleds and use the Yukon River as their winter trail. Ⓑ

A dog sled is built to carry heavy loads. It has runners along the bottom that slide over snow and ice. Its sides are high enough to hold baggage. Ⓒ

The sled is pulled by a team of five to thirteen dogs. The best dog, called the "lead dog," is at the front of the team. Ⓓ Sled dogs are big and strong.

The dogs learn how to work together, and they learn the different commands that the driver gives. When the driver wants them to turn right, he says, "Gee!" When he wants them to turn left, he says, "Haw!" When he wants them to start running, he says, "Mush on!" Ⓔ

202   Lesson 52   Textbook

Task E

Now let's talk about what the last two words mean. Word 4 is **sap. Sap** is a sticky liquid that is just underneath the bark of trees. If the bark is cut during the winter, no sap comes out. If the bark is cut during the spring, a lot of sap oozes out.

Task F

Word 5 is **runners.** The **runners** of a sled are two strips that slide along the snow. The runners are the only part that comes in contact with the snow.

STORY READING

EXERCISE 5   Comprehension passage

1. Everybody, turn to page 202 in your textbook. *Wait. Call on individual students to read.*
2. *Present the tasks specified for each circled letter.*

Ⓐ Which country is Dawson in —Canada or the United States? **Canada.**

Ⓑ What did the miners use for their winter trail? **The Yukon River.**

● Why don't they fall in the river? *Idea:* The river is frozen.

Ⓒ Everybody, look at the picture of the dog sled. Touch the runners that slide over the ice and snow. *Check.*

Ⓓ What do they call the best dog? **The lead dog.**

● Where is that dog? *Idea:* In front of the others.

● Why do you think they put the best dog at the front of the team? *Idea:* So the others will follow.

Ⓔ Remember, gee means right, haw means left, and mush on means to start running. Turn your head in the direction I say. Gee . . . Haw . . . Again. Gee . . . Haw.

● What would I say to make you start running? **Mush on.**
Remember those commands, because they'll come up in a later part of this lesson.

Buck
by Jack London Ⓐ
PART 1

It was beautiful spring weather along the Yukon. Each day the sun rose earlier and set later. Ⓑ It was dawn by three in the morning, and twilight lingered on till nine at night. The whole long day was a blaze of sunshine. Ⓒ The ghostly winter silence had given way to the great spring murmur of awakening life.

This murmur arose from all the land, and filled it with the joy of living. The murmur came from the things that lived and moved again, things that had been almost dead and that had not moved during the long months of winter. The sap was rising in the pines. The trees were bursting out in young buds, as shrubs and vines were putting on fresh green leaves. Crickets sang in the nights, and in the days all kinds of creeping, crawling things came out into the sun. Squirrels were chattering, birds were singing, and overhead the wild geese flew up from the south in V's that split the air. Ⓓ

From every hillslope came the trickle of running water, the music of unseen waterfalls. Everything was thawing, bending, snapping. The Yukon was straining to break loose from the ice that held it motionless. The river flowed under sheets of ice and ate away at the ice from below; the sun ate from above. Cracks formed in the ice on the river's surface, and thin sheets of ice fell into the river.

John Thornton stepped out of his small tent and looked down the Yukon. Ⓔ He could hear the ice cracking, and wondered how long it would be before the water flowed freely again. Ⓕ Thornton looked to the north and saw the spot where the White River joined the Yukon. He looked to the south and saw a dog sled coming slowly up the frozen river. He looked at the dog sled for a long time, and he did not like what he saw.

A full hour went by before the dogs and their two drivers staggered into John Thornton's camp. Ⓖ When they arrived, the dogs dropped down as though they had all been struck dead. One of the drivers sat down on a log to rest. He sat down very slowly and carefully. He looked very stiff. The other man stood next to the sled and did the talking.

John Thornton was whittling the last

Lesson 52   Textbook   **203**

touches on an ax handle he had made from a stout branch. He whittled and listened, gave brief replies, and good advice. He knew the kind of driver he was talking to, and as he gave advice, he was certain that they would not follow it. Ⓗ

★7 ERRORS★

The man sneered and said, "They told us down at Skagway that the trail on the frozen river wasn't safe and that we shouldn't try to take the sled to Dawson. They told us we couldn't make it this far, but here we are."

"And they told you true," John Thornton answered. "The bottom's likely to drop out of the trail at any moment. Only fools, with the blind luck of fools, could have made it. I tell you straight, I wouldn't risk my body on that ice for all the gold in Dawson."

"That's because you're not a fool, I suppose," said the man. "All the same, we'll go on to Dawson." He uncoiled his whip, and yelled to the lead dog, "Get up there, Buck! Get up there! Mush on!"

Thornton went on whittling. It was a bad idea to get between a fool and his foolish ideas; the world would not change with the loss of those two fools.

But the dog team did not get up at the command. The team had passed into the stage where whipping was required to get it moving. The whip flashed out. John Thornton bit his lip. An old husky was the first to crawl to its feet. A brown dog followed. A white mutt came next, yelping with pain. A fourth dog made painful efforts. Twice he fell over, but on the third attempt he was able to rise. Buck made no effort to get up. He lay quietly where he had fallen. He neither whined nor struggled. Several times Thornton started to speak, but changed his mind. Tears came into his eyes. At last he stood up and walked away.

This was the first time Buck had failed, and his failure drove the foolish man into a rage. He exchanged the whip for a club. Buck still refused to move. Like his mates, he was barely able to get up, but unlike them, he made up his mind not to get up. He had a feeling of disaster, because he had felt the thin ice under his feet all day. He sensed disaster, out there ahead on the ice where his master was trying to drive him. He refused to stir.

Buck had suffered so greatly that the spark of life within him flickered and went down. It was nearly out. He felt strangely numb. Then, the last feeling of pain left him. He no longer felt anything.

And then, suddenly, without warning, John Thornton uttered a cry that was like the cry of an animal. He sprang upon the man who held the club, and hurled him backward. The man fell as if struck by a falling tree. The other man looked on, but was too stiff and cold to get up.

John Thornton stood over Buck, struggling to control himself. He was too angry to speak.

"If you strike that dog again, I'll lay into you," he at last managed to say in a choking voice.

"It's my dog," the man replied. "Get out of my way, or I'll fix you. I'm going to

204   Lesson 52   Textbook

EXERCISE 6   Decoding and comprehension

1. Everybody, look at page 203 in your textbook. *Wait. Call on a student.* What's the error limit for this lesson? **7 errors.**
2. *Call on individual students to read. Present the tasks specified for each circled letter.*

Ⓐ Jack London was an American writer who went on the Gold Rush and wrote about what he saw there. This story is taken from his most famous book, The Call of the Wild.

Ⓑ Were the days getting longer or shorter? **Longer.**

Ⓒ Imagine a day that long. The sun rises at three in the morning and doesn't set until nine at night.

• Does anyone know why the days are so long on the Yukon? *Idea:* Because it's so far north.

Ⓓ Everybody, get a picture of that place as I read the description again. *Read from C to D.*

Ⓔ What's the name of the first character in this story? **John Thornton.**

Ⓕ Was the river completely free of ice yet? **No.** Most of the river was still under a sheet of ice.

Ⓖ How many men were coming up the river? **Two.**

Ⓗ Did Thornton like these men? **No.**

• Was Thornton giving them good advice? **Yes.**

• Did he think they would follow it? **No.**

• Read the rest of the story to yourselves and be ready to answer some questions.

After all students have finished reading:

• What place were the foolish men trying to reach? **Dawson.**

• What did one man do to try to make the dog team get going? *Idea:* Whipped them.

• Which dog did not stir? **Buck.**

• This dog sensed disaster. Why? *Idea:* He knew how thin the ice on the river was.

• As Buck lay quietly where he had fallen, what did Thornton do at first? *Ideas:* Got tears in his eyes; stood up and walked away.

• What did Thornton do to the man who was holding the club? *Idea:* Knocked him backward.

Dawson."

Thornton stood between him and Buck. The man pulled out a hunting knife. But Thornton quickly rapped the man's knuckles with the ax handle, knocking the knife to the ground. He rapped his knuckles again as the man tried to pick up the knife. Then Thornton stooped, picked up the knife himself, and cut Buck's harness with two strokes.

The man had no fight left in him. Besides, Buck was too near death to be of further use in hauling the sled. A few minutes later the two men started the sled down the river. Buck heard them go and raised his head to watch. The dogs were limping and staggering. One man guided the sled from the side, and the other stumbled along in the rear.

As Buck watched them, Thornton knelt beside him and with rough, kindly hands searched for broken bones. He found nothing more than many bruises and a state of terrible hunger. Dog and man watched the sled crawling along over the ice. Suddenly, they saw its back end drop down. A scream came to their ears as one man fell through the ice. They saw the other man turn and make one step to run back.

Just then, a whole section of ice gave way and the dogs and the man disappeared. A yawning hole was all that was to be seen. The bottom had dropped out of the trail.

John Thornton and Buck looked at each other.

"You poor beast," said John Thornton, and Buck licked his hand.

Lesson 52   Textbook   **205**

- Who had a knife? *Idea:* The man who Thornton knocked backward.
- What did Thornton use the knife for? *Idea:* To cut Buck's harness.
- Where was Buck as the sled continued along the frozen river? *Idea:* With Thornton.
- What happened to the men as they continued along the river trail? *Idea:* They fell into the river.
- How hurt was Buck? *Idea:* Badly.

Award 4 points or have the students reread to the error limit sign.

INDEPENDENT WORK

Do all the items in your skillbook and workbook for lesson 52.

WORKCHECK AND AWARDING POINTS

1. *Read the questions and answers for the skillbook and workbook.*
2. *Award points for independent work as follows:*

0 errors . . . . *6 points*
2 errors . . . . *4 points*
3, 4, or 5 errors . . . . *2 points*
5 or more errors . . . . *0 points*

3. *Award bonus points as follows:*

Correcting missed items or getting all items right . . . . *2 points*
Doing the writing assignment acceptably . . . . *2 points*

ANSWER KEY FOR WORKBOOK

Review Items

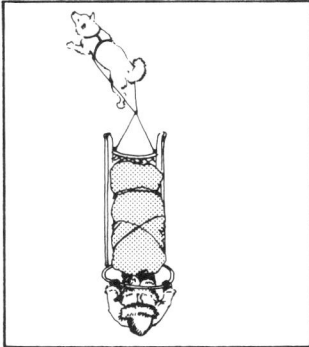

1. **a.** Which direction is the dog turning?

   left

   b. Which command is the driver giving?

   Haw!

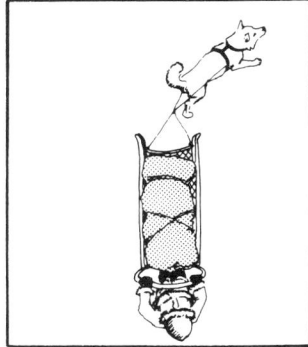

2. **a.** Which direction is the dog turning?

   right

   b. Which command is the driver giving?

   Gee!

Map Skills

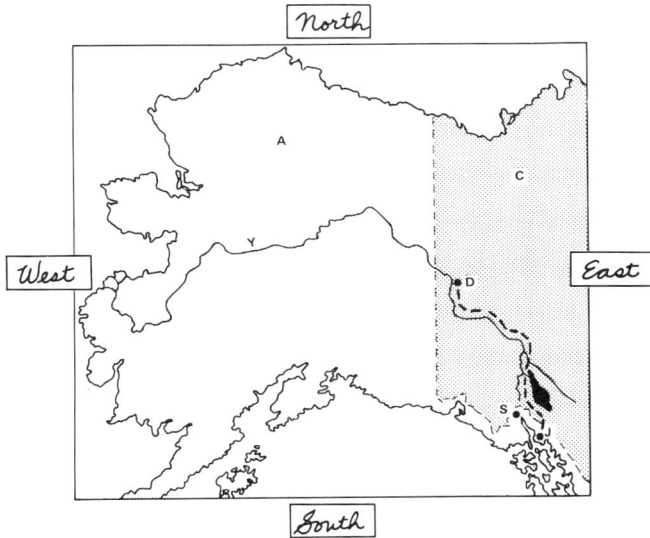

3. **a.** Write **North, South, East,** and **West** in the boxes around the map.

   b. What's the name of city **J**?

   Juneau

   c. What's the name of town **S**?

   Skagway

   d. What's the name of river **Y**?

   Yukon

   e. What's the name of town **D**?

   Dawson

   f. On the map, draw a **dotted** line to show the trip you would take to look for gold.

ANSWER KEY FOR SKILLBOOK

PART B

1. **a.** Yukon River
   b. Early spring
   c. *Ideas:* Three in the morning; early morning
   d. *Ideas:* Nine at night; late at night
2. the ice was thawing
3. **a.** Two
   b. Dawson
   c. *Ideas:* Very tired; bad
   d. *Idea:* The thin ice
   e. No
4. **a.** Mush on
   b. Buck
   c. *Idea:* Whipped them
   d. Buck
5. *Idea:* He had felt the thin ice under his feet
6. **a.** John Thornton
   b. *Idea:* He didn't want Buck beaten any more
   c. A knife
   d. *Idea:* The harness
7. *Idea:* It fell into the river
8. **a.** Driver
   b. Driver
   c. Driver
   d. Thornton
   e. Thornton
   f. Thornton
   g. Driver

PART C

9. **a.** walked slowly
   b. modest
   c. elected
   d. terrible
   e. eventually
   f. hatch
   g. lean
   h. rustling

Lesson 53

Lesson 53 ✓

Lesson 53

PART A   Word Lists

1	2	3	4
Hans	tumble	**Vocabulary words**	**Vocabulary words**
tolerate	grumble	1. lingered on	1. recover
haunt	muscle	2. stagger	2. embrace
naked	scramble		3. ideal
	comfortable		4. affection
			5. haunt
			6. tolerated
			7. naked
			8. grapple

PART B   Main Idea Sentences

Mary   Tom   Maria

1   2   3

WORD PRACTICE AND VOCABULARY

EXERCISE 1   Word practice

1. Everybody, find lesson 53, part A in your skillbook. *Wait.* Touch under each word in column 1 as I read it.
2. The first word is **Hans.**
3. Next word. **Tolerate.**
4. *Repeat step 3 for each remaining word in column 1.*
5. Your turn. Read the first word. *Signal.* **Hans.**
6. Next word. *Signal.* **Tolerate.**
7. *Repeat step 6 for each remaining word in column 1.*
8. *Repeat the words in column 1 until firm.*

EXERCISE 2   Word family

1. Everybody, touch column 2. *Check.* All those words end with the letters **l-e.** Touch under the first word. *Pause.* What word? *Signal.* **Tumble.**
2. Next word. *Pause.* What word? *Signal.* **Grumble.**
3. *Repeat step 2 for each remaining word in column 2.*
4. *Repeat the words in column 2 until firm.*

EXERCISE 3   Vocabulary review

Task A

1. Everybody, touch column 3. *Check.* First you're going to read the words in column 3. Then we'll talk about what they mean.
2. Touch under the first line. *Pause.* What words? *Signal.* **Lingered on.**
3. Next word. *Pause.* What word? *Signal.* **Stagger.**

Task B

You've learned the meanings for these words. The words in line 1 are **lingered on.** *Call on a student.* What does **lingered on** mean? *Idea:* Kept on going.

Task C

Word 2 is **stagger.** *Call on a student.* Show me how you **stagger.** *Check for an unsteady walk.*

EXERCISE 4   Vocabulary from context

Task A

1. Everybody, touch column 4. *Check.* First you're going to read the words in column 4. Then we'll talk about what they mean.
2. Touch under the first word. *Pause.* What word? *Signal.* **Recover.**
3. Next word. *Pause.* What word? *Signal.* **Embrace.**
4. *Repeat step 3 for each remaining word in column 4.*
5. *Repeat the words in column 4 until firm.*

Task B

1. I'll say sentences that contain some words that you'll read in today's story. Each sentence has a part that you may be able to figure out by listening to the rest of the sentence.
2. Listen to the first sentence and see if you can figure out what the word **recover** means. Everybody, what word? *Signal.* **Recover.**
3. Listen. He was very sick for two weeks, but after that time, he began to **recover** from his sickness.
4. *Call on a student.* What could **recover** mean? *Idea:* Get back your strength.

Task C

1. Listen to the second sentence and see if you can figure out what the word **embrace** means. Everybody, what word? *Signal.* **Embrace.**
2. Listen. He threw his arms around his mother and gave her a warm **embrace.**
3. *Call on a student.* What could **embrace** mean? *Idea:* Hug.

Task D

1. Listen to the third sentence and see if you can figure out what the word **ideal** means. Everybody, what word? *Signal.* **Ideal.**
2. Listen. She was so good in all her school work that she was an **ideal** student.
3. *Call on a student.* What could **ideal** mean? *Idea:* Excellent.

Task E

1. Listen to the fourth sentence and see if you can figure out what the word **affection** means. Everybody, what word? *Signal.* **Affection.**
2. Listen. She loved her dog and she showed her **affection** by letting him stay in her room.
3. *Call on a student.* What could **affection** mean? *Idea:* Fondness.

Task F

1. Listen to the fifth sentence and see if you can figure out what the word **haunt** means. Everybody, what word? *Signal.* **Haunt.**
2. Listen. At first he was just bothered by the dream, but later, the dream began to **haunt** him.
3. *Call on a student.* What could **haunt** mean? *Ideas:* Really worry; disturb.

Task G

1. Listen to the sixth sentence and see if you can figure out what the word **tolerated** means. Everybody, what word? *Signal.* **Tolerated.**
2. Listen. The dog didn't like Hans, but the dog **tolerated** Hans.
3. *Call on a student.* What could **tolerated** mean? *Idea:* Put up with.

Task H

1. Listen to the seventh sentence and see if you can figure out what the word **naked** means. Everybody, what word? *Signal.* **Naked.**
2. Listen. Some rocks were covered with moss, but other rocks were **naked.**
3. *Call on a student.* What could **naked** mean? *Idea:* Without covering.

Task I

1. Listen to the eighth sentence and see if you can figure out what the word **grapple** means. Everybody, what word? *Signal.* **Grapple.**
2. Listen. He didn't want to wrestle, but the ape grabbed him and began to **grapple** with him.
3. *Call on a student.* What could **grapple** mean? *Ideas:* Wrestle; fight.

EXERCISE 5   Main idea sentences

1. Everybody, find part B in your skillbook. *Wait.* Look at picture 1. You're going to **tell** the main idea of picture 1. Here's how you do that. First you tell who is doing the action. Then you tell the main thing that person is doing.
   - Everybody, who is doing the action? *Signal.* **Mary.**
   - *Call on a student.* Tell the main thing that Mary is doing. *Idea:* Drinking from a glass.
   - Here's one way to say the whole main-idea sentence. **Mary is drinking from a glass.**
   - Everybody, say that main-idea sentence. Get ready. *Signal.* **Mary is drinking from a glass.**
2. Everybody, look at picture 2. You're going to **tell** the main idea of that picture. Here's how you do that. First you tell who is doing the action. Then you tell the main thing that person is doing.
   - Everybody, who is doing the action? *Signal.* **Tom.**
   - *Call on a student.* Tell the main thing that Tom is doing. *Idea:* Riding a bike.
   - Everybody, say the whole main-idea sentence. Get ready. *Signal.* **Tom is riding a bike.**
3. Use your lined paper to **write** main-idea sentences for all the pictures in part B. At the beginning of the first line, write **1.** Then write the main-idea sentence for picture 1.
   - Everybody, what number are you going to write at the beginning of the next line? *Signal.* **2.**
   - Everybody, what number are you going to write at the beginning of the next line? *Signal.* **3.**
4. Write your sentences now. *Check.*
5. *Call on a student.* Read all three of your main-idea sentences.

Buck

PART 2

John Thornton had been staying in the tent for two months. He had come down the Yukon with two other men, Pete and Hans. But John Thornton had frozen his feet, and his partners had left him there to recover while they went up the river to get logs for a raft. (A) John Thornton, Hans, and Pete planned to take the raft to Dawson later that spring. John was still limping slightly at the time he rescued Buck, but with the continued warm weather the limp went away.

Buck slowly got his strength back. He would lie by the riverbank during the long spring days, watch the running water, and listen to the songs of birds and the hum of nature. Buck's wounds healed, his muscles swelled out, and the flesh came back to cover his bones. Buck now weighed as much as a full-grown man.

John Thornton was an ideal master. Other men took care of their dogs in a businesslike way. But John Thornton treated Buck as if he were his own child. He always had a kindly greeting and a cheering word. He would sit down for long talks with Buck. At these times, he would take Buck's head between his hands, and rest his own head upon Buck's. Then he would shake Buck back and forth, and talk softly

to him. Buck knew no greater joy than John Thornton's embrace and the sound of his voice. (B)

Buck had a strange way of showing his love for Thornton. He would often seize Thornton's hand in his mouth and hold it so tightly that teeth marks would show for some time afterward. For the most part, however, Buck kept his love to himself. He went wild with happiness when Thornton touched him or spoke to him, but he did not beg for the man's affection. (C)

Buck would lie for hours at Thornton's feet and look up into his face. He would study the face and follow each expression with keen interest. Sometimes, he would lie farther away and watch the outlines of the man and the movements of his body. The strength of Buck's gaze would often make John Thornton turn his head around. The man would return the gaze, without speaking. Thornton's love shone out of his eyes, just as Buck's did.

For a long time after his rescue, Buck did not like Thornton to get out of his sight. From the moment Thornton left the tent to when he entered it again, Buck would follow at his heels. The dog remembered that all of his former masters had left him. He was afraid that Thornton would

STORY READING

EXERCISE 6   Decoding and comprehension

1. Everybody, turn to page 206 in your textbook. *Wait. Call on a student.* What's the error limit for this lesson? **8 errors.**

2. *Call on individual students to read. Present the tasks specified for each circled letter.*

(A) How long had Thornton been in the tent? **Two months.**

● Who had he come to the Yukon with? *Idea:* Pete and Hans.

● Where were those men now? *Idea:* Up the river.

● Why hadn't Thornton gone with them? *Idea:* Because he had frozen his feet.

(B) Was John Thornton businesslike when he took care of Buck? **No.**

● How did Thornton treat Buck? *Idea:* Like a child.

● How did Buck change when he recovered from his bruises and hunger? *Idea:* He became strong.

(C) Did Buck love Thornton? **Yes.**

● Did Buck beg for affection? **No.**

● What would a dog do to beg for affection? *Call on individual students. Ideas:* Whine; paw his master's knee; push his head into his master's lap.

pass out of his life just as all the other masters had. (D) ★8 ERRORS★

Even in Buck's dreams, he was haunted by the fear of Thornton leaving. At such times he would shake off sleep and creep through the chill to the flap of the tent, where he would stand and listen to the sound of his master's breathing.

Buck responded with joy to only one person—Thornton. Other gold rushers might praise or pet Buck, but he was cold toward them, and he would often get up and walk away. When Hans and Pete finally arrived on the raft, Buck refused to notice them until he learned that they were Thornton's friends. After that he tolerated them. They were very much like Thornton, living close to the earth, thinking simply and seeing clearly. They soon understood Buck and his ways.

Buck's love for Thornton seemed to grow and grow. Nothing was too great for Buck to do, when Thornton commanded. One day, the men and Buck were sitting on the edge of a cliff that fell away, straight down, to naked rock three hundred feet below. John Thornton was sitting near the edge, with Buck at his shoulder. Hans and Pete were nearby. "Get ready to grab Buck," Thornton said to Hans and Pete. Then Thornton commanded, "Jump, Buck!" and pointed over the cliff. Buck sprang forward. An instant later the three men grappled with Buck on the edge of the cliff, then they dragged him back to safety.

"I don't want to be the man that lays hands on you while that dog is around," Pete said, nodding his head toward Buck.

The very next day, Buck and the men got on the raft, and headed down the Yukon to Dawson. Several days later, all four of them were walking around the muddy streets of the town, when they came upon two men having a fight. Thornton stepped in between the two men to try to stop them from fighting. Buck lay down in the street, put his head on his paws, and watched his master's every move.

Suddenly, one man struck out, straight from the shoulder. He hit Thornton and sent him spinning. Thornton fell down.

Those who were looking on heard what was neither bark nor yelp, but something more like a roar. They saw Buck's body rise up in the air as he left the ground for the man. The man threw out his arm, and was hurled backward to the street, with Buck on top of him.

The crowd quickly descended upon Buck, and pulled him off the man. He growled furiously and attempted to rush back in. Hans and Pete had to struggle to hold him back. A "miner's meeting" was called on the spot. The miners who saw what had happened decided that the dog was only protecting his master, so Buck was set free. But he was now famous, and from that day his name spread through every mining camp along the Yukon.

(D) Had Buck had many other masters? **Yes.**
- What had happened to them? *Idea:* They had left him.
- What did Buck do to show that he was afraid that Thornton would leave him? *Idea:* He followed him around all the time.
- Read the rest of the story to yourselves and be ready to answer some questions.

After all students have finished reading:
- How did Buck respond to other miners that petted him? *Ideas:* He was cold; he would walk away.
- One day Thornton tested Buck in a very silly way. Where were Thornton, Hans, and Pete when this happened? *Idea:* On a cliff.
- What did Thornton do? *Idea:* Told Buck to jump off the cliff.
- What did Buck do? *Idea:* Jumped.
- Why didn't Buck go sailing over the edge of the cliff? *Idea:* Because the men held him back.
- Pete said, "I don't want to be the man that lays hands on you while that dog is around." What did Pete mean by that? *Idea:* Buck would defend Thornton.
- Where did Buck and the others go on the following day? **To Dawson.**
- They came upon two men in the street. What were those men doing? **Fighting.**
- What did Thornton try to do? *Idea:* Stop them from fighting.
- What happened to Thornton? *Idea:* One of the men hit him.
- Then what happened? *Idea:* Buck attacked the man.
- The miners had a meeting about what Buck did. What did the miners decide? *Idea:* Buck could go free.
- Who became famous after that incident? **Buck.**

Award 4 points or have the students reread to the error limit sign.

INDEPENDENT WORK

Do all the items in your skillbook and workbook for lesson 53.

ANSWER KEY FOR WORKBOOK

Crossword Puzzle

To work the puzzle, read an item and
figure out which word the item describes.
Then write the word in the puzzle.
Complete the entire puzzle.

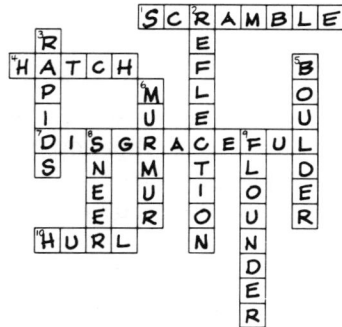

```
            S C R A M B L E
            E
        R   F
   H A T C H L         B
   P     M U E         O
   I     U  T          U
   D I S G R A C E F U L
   S   N M   T   L     D
       E U   I   O     E
       E R   O   U     R
   H U R L   N   N
               D
               E
               R
```

Across

1. When you _____, you move as fast as you can.
4. When eggs crack open and birds come out, the eggs _____.
7. When you do something that is terrible, you do something _____.
10. When you throw a rock, you _____ the rock.

Down

2. The image that you see in a mirror is a _____.
3. Places where rivers flow downhill rapidly.
5. A very large rock.
6. When the wind died down, the girl could hear the _____ of insects.
8. His smile turned into a mocking _____.
9. When you move around awkwardly without any direction, you _____.

WORKCHECK AND AWARDING POINTS

1. *Read the questions and answers for the skillbook and workbook.*

2. *Award points for independent work as follows:*

0 errors	6 points
2 errors	4 points
3, 4, or 5 errors	2 points
5 or more errors	0 points

3. *Award bonus points as follows:*

Correcting missed items or getting all items right	2 points
Doing the writing assignment acceptably	2 points

ANSWER KEY FOR SKILLBOOK

PART B

1. *Idea:* Mary is drinking from a glass.
2. *Idea:* Tom is riding a bike.
3. *Idea:* Maria is tying her shoes.

PART C

4. a. Pete and Hans
    b. *Idea:* To get well
    c. A raft
    d. *Idea:* To go to Dawson
5. a. *Ideas:* Very well; like his own child
    b. *Idea:* Biting his hand
    c. *Idea:* Because his old masters had
    d. *Idea:* Cold
6. a. *Idea:* On a cliff
    b. Jump
    c. *Idea:* Jump
    d. *Idea:* The men
7. a. Yukon
    b. A raft
    c. Dawson
8. a. *Idea:* To stop the fight
    b. *Idea:* Hit him
    c. *Idea:* Jumped on him
    d. *Idea:* To protect Thornton
    e. *Idea:* Because he was only protecting his master
    f. *Idea:* Because of what he had done
9. a. Thornton
    b. Thornton
    c. Buck
    d. Buck
    e. Buck
    f. Hans
    g. Hans

PART D

10. a. gave credit
    b. scrambled
    c. modest
    d. treacherous
    e. elect
    f. miserable
    g. floundered
    h. vivid

Lesson 54

Lesson 54

PART A   Word Lists

1	2	3	4	5
guilty	particularly	**Vocabulary words**	**Vocabulary words**	**Vocabulary words**
Eldorado	instantly	1. affection	1. mountain pass	1. jutted out
jutted	desperately	2. grapple	2. strangle	2. reared up
pistol	apparently	3. tolerate	3. flushed	3. stretch
ashore		4. recover	4. guilty	4. clutched
rouse		5. embrace		
lunge		6. haunt		
		7. ideal		

WORD PRACTICE AND VOCABULARY

EXERCISE 1   Word practice

1. Everybody, find lesson 54, part A in your skillbook. *Wait.* Touch under each word in column 1 as I read it.
2. The first word is **guilty.**
3. Next word. **Eldorado.**
4. *Repeat step 3 for each remaining word in column 1.*
5. Your turn. Read the first word. *Signal.* **Guilty.**
6. Next word. *Signal.* **Eldorado.**
7. *Repeat step 6 for each remaining word in column 1.*
8. *Repeat the words in column 1 until firm.*

EXERCISE 2   Word family

1. Everybody, touch column 2. *Check.* All those words end with the letters **l-y.** Touch under the first word. *Pause.* What word? *Signal.* **Particularly.**
2. Next word. *Pause.* What word? *Signal.* **Instantly.**
3. *Repeat step 2 for each remaining word in column 2.*
4. *Repeat the words in column 2 until firm.*

EXERCISE 3   Vocabulary review

Task A

1. Everybody, touch column 3. *Check.* First you're going to read the words in column 3. Then we'll talk about what they mean.
2. Touch under the first word. *Pause.* What word? *Signal.* **Affection.**
3. Next word. *Pause.* What word? *Signal.* **Grapple.**
4. *Repeat step 3 for each remaining word in column 3.*
5. *Repeat the words in column 3 until firm.*

Task B

You've learned the meanings for all these words. Word 1 is **affection.** *Call on a student.* What does **affection** mean? *Idea:* Fondness.

Task C

Word 2 is **grapple.** *Call on a student.* What do you do when you **grapple** with someone? *Idea:* You wrestle that person.

Task D

Word 3 is **tolerate.** *Call on a student.* What does **tolerate**   *Idea:* Put up with.

Task E

Word 4 is **recover.** *Call on a student.* What does **recover** mean? *Idea:* Get back your strength.

Task F

Word 5 is **embrace.** *Call on a student.* What is an **embrace?** *Idea:* A hug.

Task G

Word 6 is **haunt.** *Call on a student.* What does it mean when something **haunts** you? *Idea:* It really worries you.

Task H

Word 7 is **ideal.** *Call on a student.* What does **ideal** mean? *Idea:* Excellent.

EXERCISE 4   Vocabulary development

Task A

1. Everybody, touch column 4. *Check.* First you're going to read the words in column 4. Then we'll talk about what they mean.
2. Touch under the first line. *Pause.* What words? *Signal.* **Mountain pass.**
3. Next word. *Pause.* What word? *Signal.* **Strangle.**
4. *Repeat step 3 for each remaining word in column 4.*
5. *Repeat the words in column 4 until firm.*

Task B

Now let's talk about what those words mean. The words in line 1 are **mountain pass.** A **mountain pass** is a passageway between mountains. Everybody, what do we call a passageway between mountains? *Signal.* **A mountain pass.**

Task C

Word 2 is **strangle.** Here's another way of saying **He choked the wolf: He strangled the wolf.** Everybody, what's another way of saying **He choked the wolf?** *Signal.* **He strangled the wolf.**

Task D

Word 3 is **flushed.** When you blush, your face is **flushed.** Everybody, what happens when you blush? *Signal.* **Your face is flushed.**

Task E

1. Word 4 is **guilty.** A person who commits a crime is **guilty** of the crime. A person who makes a mistake is guilty of the mistake. Everybody, a person who commits a crime is *Pause. Signal.* **Guilty of the crime.**
2. A person who makes a mistake is *Pause. Signal.* **Guilty of the mistake.**

Lesson 54

PART A   Word Lists

PART B   Main Idea Sentences

Write the main idea sentence for each row of pictures below.

EXERCISE 5   Vocabulary from context

Task A

1. Everybody, touch column 5. *Check.* First you're going to read the words in column 5. Then we'll talk about what they mean.
2. Touch under the first line. *Pause.* What words? *Signal.* **Jutted out.**
3. Next line. *Pause.* What words? *Signal.* **Reared up.**
4. Next word. *Pause.* What word? *Signal.* **Stretch.**
5. *Repeat step 4 for* **clutched.**
6. *Repeat the words in column 5 until firm.*

Task B

1. I'll say sentences that contain some words that you'll read in today's story. Each sentence has a part that you may be able to figure out by listening to the rest of the sentence.
2. Listen to the first sentence and see if you can figure out what the words **jutted out** mean. Everybody, what words?. *Signal.* **Jutted out.**
3. Listen. The rocks **jutted out** so far into the river that the boat could hardly get around them.
4. *Call on a student.* What could **jutted out** mean? *Idea:* Stuck out.

Task C

1. Listen to the second sentence and see if you can figure out what the words **reared up** mean. Everybody, what words? *Signal.* **Reared up.**
2. Listen. The horse **reared up** on its hind legs and threw the rider off.
3. *Call on a student.* What could **reared up** mean? *Idea:* Stood up quickly.

Task D

1. Listen to the third sentence and see if you can figure out what the word **stretch** means. Everybody, what word? *Signal.* **Stretch.**
2. Listen. They were going through a bad **stretch** of rapids.
3. *Call on a student.* What could **stretch** mean? *Ideas:* Part; area.

Task E

1. Listen to the fourth sentence and see if you can figure out what the word **clutched** means. Everybody, what word? *Signal.* **Clutched.**
2. Listen. He reached out and **clutched** the slippery rocks with both hands.
3. *Call on a student.* What could **clutched** mean? *Idea:* Held tightly.

EXERCISE 6   Main idea sentences

1. Everybody, find part B in your skillbook. *Wait.* The three pictures in each row show something that happened. You're going to **tell** the main idea that is shown in these pictures. Remember, first tell who is doing the action. Then tell the main thing that person is doing.
   - Look at the pictures in row 1. Everybody, who is doing the action? *Signal.* **Albert.**
   - *Call on a student.* Tell the main thing that Albert is doing. *Idea:* Cooking a meal.
   - Everybody, say the whole main-idea sentence. Get ready. *Signal.* **Albert is cooking a meal.**
2. Look at the pictures in row 2. You're going to **tell** the main idea that is shown in the pictures. Remember, first tell who is doing the action. Then tell the main thing that person is doing.
   - Everybody, who is doing the action? *Signal.* **Patty.**
   - *Call on a student.* Tell the main thing that Patty is doing. *Idea:* Building a house.
   - Everybody, say the whole main-idea sentence. Get ready. *Signal.* **Patty is building a house.**
3. Later, you'll write the main-idea sentences for each row of pictures in part B.

Lesson 54

Buck
PART 3

In the fall of that year, Buck saved John Thornton's life.Ⓐ The three partners were moving a long and narrow boat down a bad stretch of rapids on the Forty Mile Creek. Hans and Pete moved along the bank and guided the boat with a rope. Thornton remained in the boat and pushed it along with a pole. From time to time, Thornton shouted directions to his partners on the bank. Buck ran along the bank. He was worried and anxious, and he never took his eyes off his master.Ⓑ

They came to a particularly bad spot, where a ledge of rocks jutted out into the river. The boat started to fly downstream in a swift current. Hans and Pete tried to stop the boat by yanking on the rope. But the boat hit the rocks and flipped over. Thornton was flung out of the boat. He floated downstream toward the worst part of the rapids—a stretch of wild water in which no swimmer could live.

Buck sprang into the water instantly.Ⓒ At the end of three hundred

yards, in the middle of a mad swirl of water, he caught up to Thornton. When he felt the man grasp his tail, Buck headed for the bank. He swam with all his splendid strength. But the progress to the bank was slow while the man and dog traveled downstream with amazing speed.Ⓓ
★6 ERRORS★

The man and the dog could hear the loud roaring of rapids below them. They could see the rocks that thrust through the water like the teeth of an enormous comb. They could feel the current becoming more swift. Thornton knew that it would be impossible to reach the shore. Suddenly, he was hurled into a rock with crushing force. He let go of Buck and clutched the rock's slippery top with both hands. Then he shouted, "Go, Buck! Go!"

Buck could not hold his own, and he was swept farther downstream, struggling desperately, but unable to swim back to Thornton. When he heard Thornton's command repeated, he reared up in the water, threw his head high, then turned toward the shore. He swam powerfully, and was dragged ashore by Pete and Hans.

They knew that Thornton could cling to the slippery rock for only a few minutes. They ran as fast as they could up the bank to a point far above where Thornton was hanging on. They attached the rope to Buck's neck and shoulders, and threw him into the stream. He struck out boldly, but not far enough into the stream. He came within six feet of Thornton, but then the current carried him past the struggling man.

Hans promptly pulled with the rope, as if Buck were a boat. Buck was jerked under the surface, and he remained under the surface until his body struck against the shore and he was hauled out. He was half drowned, and Hans and Pete threw themselves upon him, pounding the breath into him and the water out of him. He staggered to his feet and fell down. The faint sound of Thornton's voice came to them, and although they could not make out the words, they knew that he could not hold on any longer. His master's voice acted on Buck as if it were an electric shock. He sprang to his feet and ran up the bank ahead of the men to the point he had jumped from before.

Again the rope was attached, and again Buck was thrown into the raging stream. But this time he swam far out into the stream. He had made a mistake once, but he would not be guilty of it a second time. Buck swam on until he was directly upstream from Thornton. Then he turned, and with the speed of an express train, he headed down toward his master. Thornton saw him coming. Buck struck him with the whole force of the current behind him. Thornton reached up and grabbed Buck's shaggy neck with both hands. Hans tied the rope around a tree, and Buck and Thornton were jerked under the water. The man and dog were strangling, choking, sometimes one on top, and sometimes the other, dragging over the jagged bottom, and smashing against rocks. At last, they came toward the bank.

EXERCISE 7   Decoding and comprehension

1. Everybody, turn to page 209 in your textbook. *Wait Call on a student.* What's the error limit for this lesson? **6 errors.**
2. *Call on individual students to read. Present the tasks specified for each circled letter.*
Ⓐ What time of year was it when Thornton rescued Buck? **Spring.**
● What time of year is it now in the story? **Fall.**
Ⓑ Everybody, look at the picture. Who is on the shore with the ropes? **Hans and Pete.**
● Who is in the boat? **Thornton.**
● Where is Buck? *Idea:* On the bank.
● That river looks very rough.
Ⓒ What happened to the boat? *Idea:* It turned over.
● What happened to Thornton when the boat flipped? *Ideas:* He fell into the water; he floated downstream.
Ⓓ What did Buck do? *Idea:* He jumped in to save Thornton.
● What was making Thornton and Buck travel downstream? *Idea:* The swift current.
● Were they trying to go downstream? **No.**
● Where were they trying to go? *Idea:* To the riverbank.
● Was their progress toward the bank fast or slow? **Slow.**
● Everybody, turn back to page 209 and look at the picture again. Run your finger in the direction the water is moving. *Check.*
So if you tried to swim toward the bank, you'd be moving toward the shore slowly. At the same time, the current would still be moving you downstream very quickly.
● Read the rest of the story to yourselves and be ready to answer some questions.
After all students have finished reading:
● When Thornton and Buck were speeding downstream, what stopped them? *Idea:* Thornton hit a rock.
● What did Thornton tell Buck to do? *Idea:* Go.
● When Buck reached the shore, what did Hans and Pete attach to him? *Idea:* A rope.
● What did they do next? *Idea:* Threw him into the stream.
● Did Buck reach Thornton on the first try? **No.**
● Why not? *Idea:* The current carried him past Thornton.
● Did Buck reach Thornton on the second try? **Yes.**
● What did Hans and Pete do as soon as Buck reached Thornton? *Idea:* Tied the rope around the tree.

As soon as they reached the shore, both man and dog passed out. When Thornton came to, he looked for Buck. Hans and Pete were standing over Buck's limp and apparently lifeless body. Thornton was bruised and battered, yet he got up and went carefully over to Buck's body. He found that the dog was alive, but he had broken ribs.

"That settles it," he announced. "We camp right here." They camped until Buck's ribs mended and he was able to travel again.

That winter, at Dawson, Buck did something that made him even more famous than he already was. The incident started with a conversation in the Eldorado Hotel. Some men were bragging about their favorite dogs. These men were arguing that Buck was not the best dog. Thornton spoke loudly in Buck's favor. One man stated that his dog could start a sled with five hundred pounds on it and walk off with it. A second man bragged six hundred, and a third seven hundred.

"That's nothing," said John Thornton. "My dog, Buck, can start a thousand pounds."

A rich miner named Matthewson demanded, "Are you saying he can walk off with it for a hundred yards?"

"Yes, walk off with it for a hundred yards," John Thornton said cooly.

"Well," Matthewson said, slowly, so that all could hear, "I would offer a prize of one thousand dollars to any dog who could pull such a load. But I don't believe that any dog alive could do it." So saying, he slammed down a sack of gold dust the size of a rolling pin.

Nobody spoke. Thornton could feel a flush of warm blood creeping up his face. His tongue had tricked him. He did not know whether Buck could start a sled with a thousand pounds on it. Half a ton! He had great faith in Buck's strength and often thought that he was capable of starting such a load. But he had never tested it. The eyes of a dozen men fixed upon him, silent and waiting.

Lesson 54   Textbook   **211**

- What did Buck and Thornton both do when they reached the shore? *Idea:* Passed out.
- Why? *Idea:* They were exhausted.
- That winter in Dawson, Thornton had a strange conversation with some other men. What were those men arguing about? *Idea:* Who was the best dog.
- How much weight did Thornton say that Buck could pull on a sled? **1,000 pounds**.
- Name the man who said that Buck couldn't do it. **Matthewson.**
- What prize did that man offer? **$1,000.**
- Did Thornton know whether Buck could start such a load? **No.**
- The story says that Thornton's tongue had tricked him. What does that mean? *Idea:* He had talked too much.

Award 4 points or have the students reread to the error limit sign.

INDEPENDENT WORK

Do all the items in your skillbook and workbook for lesson 54.

WORKCHECK AND AWARDING POINTS

1. *Read the questions and answers for the skillbook and workbook.*
2. *Award points for independent work as follows:*

0 errors	6 points
2 errors	4 points
3, 4, or 5 errors	2 points
5 or more errors	0 points

3. *Award bonus points as follows:*

Correcting missed items or getting all items right.	2 points
Doing the writing assignment acceptably	2 points

ANSWER KEY FOR WORKBOOK

Story Items

1. The map shows the river where Thornton almost lost his life.

a. Which arrow shows the direction of the current? **A**

b. Which letter shows the object that Thornton was hanging onto? **C**

c. Which letter shows where Buck was thrown into the river? **D**

d. Which letter shows where Buck and Thornton were pulled out of the river? **E**

Review Items

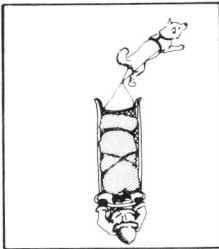

2. a. Which direction is the dog turning? *right*

b. Which command is the driver giving? *Gee !*

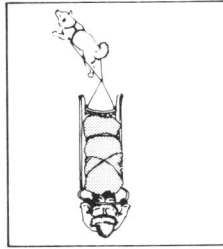

3. a. Which direction is the dog turning? *left*

b. Which command is the driver giving? *Haw !*

ANSWER KEY FOR SKILLBOOK

PART B

1. *Idea:* Albert is cooking a meal.
2. *Idea:* Patty is building a house.
3. *Idea:* Don is doing exercises.

PART C

4. **a.** Thornton
   b. Hans, Pete, and Buck
   c. A rope
5. **a.** *Idea:* Rocks
   b. *Idea:* He was thrown into the water
   c. *Idea:* Jumped into the water
   d. His tail
   e. Their progress downstream
   f. rock
6. **a.** Pete and Hans
   b. A rope
   c. *Idea:* Threw Buck into the water
   d. No
   e. Hans
   f. *Idea:* Poor
7. **a.** Yes
   b. Thornton
   c. *Idea:* Hans and Pete hauled them back in
   d. His ribs
8. **a.** *Idea:* Their dogs
   b. 1000
   c. Matthewson
   d. $1,000
   e. No

PART D

9. **a.** impatiently
   b. eventually
   c. miserable
   d. rustled
   e. reflection
   f. rapids
   g. crest
   h. very large rock
   i. staggered
   j. sound

Lesson 55

Lesson 55

PART A   Word Lists

1
admiration
condition
conversation
affection

2
Vocabulary words
1. quiver
2. grate

3
Vocabulary words
1. rouse
2. witnessed
3. lunged
4. outskirts

PART B
Vocabulary Sentences

1. He was sleeping soundly and even when his mother shook him, he would not <u>rouse</u>.
2. Most of the people who <u>witnessed</u> the race saw Tina fall down.
3. The lion gathered all its strength and suddenly <u>lunged</u> forward.
4. He wanted to live very near the city, so he bought a place on the <u>outskirts</u> of the city.

PART C   Main Idea Sentences

Write the main idea sentences for pictures **1, 2** and **3.** Then write the main idea sentence for the row of pictures in item **4.**

WORD PRACTICE AND VOCABULARY

EXERCISE 1   Word family

1. Everybody find lesson 55, part A in your skillbook. *Wait.* Touch column 1. *Check.* All those words end with the sound **shun.** Touch under the first word. *Pause.* What word? *Signal.* **Admiration.**
2. Next word. *Pause.* What word? *Signal.* **Condition.**
3. *Repeat step 2 for each remaining word in column 1.*
4. *Repeat the words in column 1 until firm.*

EXERCISE 2   Vocabulary development

Task A

1. Everybody, touch column 2. *Check.* First you're going to reach the words in column 2. Then we'll talk about what they mean.
2. Touch under the first word. *Pause.* What word? *Signal.* **Quiver.**
3. Next word. *Pause.* What word? *Signal.* **Grate.**
4. *Repeat the words in column 2 until firm.*

Task B

Now let's talk about what those words mean. Word 1 is **quiver.** Another word for **tremble** or **vibrate** is **quiver.**
Everybody, what's another way of saying **The feather vibrated?** *Signal.*
The feather quivered.

Task C

1. Word 2 is **grate.** When something **grates,** It grinds against a hard surface.
Everybody, what's another way of saying **The rock ground against the sidewalk?** *Signal.* **The rock grated against the sidewalk.**
2. What's another way of saying **The shovel ground against the ice?** *Signal.*
The shovel grated against the ice.

EXERCISE 3   Vocabulary from context

Task A

1. Everybody, touch column 3. *Check.* First you're going to read the words in column 3. Then we'll talk about what they mean.
2. Touch under the first word. *Pause.* What word? *Signal.* **Rouse.**
3. Next word. *Pause.* What word? *Signal.* **Witnessed.**
4. *Repeat step 3 for each remaining word in column 3.*

Task B

1. Everybody, find part B in your skillbook. *Check.* I'll read those sentences. You figure out what the underlined part in each sentence means.
2. Sentence one: He was sleeping soundly and even when his mother shook him, he would not rouse. *Call on a student.* What could **rouse** mean? *Ideas:* Move; wake up.
3. *Repeat step 2 for each remaining sentence.*
   Answer Key: Sentence 2. Idea: Saw.
              Sentence 3. Idea: Charged.
              Sentence 4. Idea: Near the edge.

EXERCISE 4 Main idea sentences

1. Everybody, find part C in your skillbook. You're going to **tell** the main idea for these pictures. But you're going to use one class name to tell who is doing the action.
● The names in picture 1 are Jerry, Henry, and Bill. Look at the picture and figure out a class name for Jerry, Henry, and Bill.
● Everybody, what are Jerry, Henry, and Bill? *Signal.* **Boys.**
● Now tell the main thing that the boys are doing? *Call on a student. Idea:* Eating a meal.
● Everybody, say the whole main-idea sentence. Get ready. *Signal.* **The boys are eating a meal.**

Lesson 55

Buck

PART 4ⓐ

Matthewson looked at Thornton coldly and said, "I've got a sled standing outside now, with twenty, fifty-pound sacks of flour on it. That's a thousand pounds."

Thornton did not reply. He did not know what to say. He glanced from face to face like a man who has lost the power of thought. The face of Jim O'Brien, an old-time comrade, caught his eyes.

Jim O'Brien shook his head solemnly and said, "I don't have much faith that the beast can pull such a load."Ⓑ

The men poured out of the Eldorado into the street to see the test. The tables were deserted. Soon, several hundred men, in heavy fur coats, stood around the sled.Ⓒ

The sled, loaded with a thousand pounds of flour, had been standing for a couple of hours in the intense cold. It was sixty below zero, and the runners had frozen fast to the hard-packed snow. O'Brien and Matthewson argued about starting the sled. O'Brien suggested that Thornton could knock the runners loose from the ice

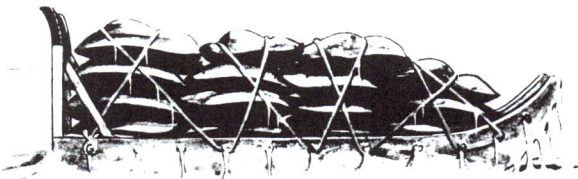

---

2. You're going to **tell** the main idea for picture 2. But you're going to use one class name to tell who is doing the action. The names in the picture are Mrs. Jones, Mrs. Arthur, and Mrs. Yerby.
● Look at the pictures and figure out a class name for Mrs. Jones, Mrs. Arthur, and Mrs. Yerby.
● *Call on a student.* What are Mrs. Jones, Mrs. Arthur, and Mrs. Yerby? *Idea:* Women.
● Now tell the main thing that the women are doing. *Call on a student. Idea:* Building a house.
● Everybody, say the whole main-idea sentence. Get ready. *Signal.* **The women are building a house.**
3. Later you'll write main-idea sentences for all the pictures in part C.

STORY READING

EXERCISE 5 Decoding and comprehension

1. Everybody, turn to page 212 in your textbook. *Wait. Call on a student.* What's the error limit for this lesson? **6 errors.**
2. *Call on individual students to read. Present the tasks specified for each circled letter.*
Ⓐ What did Matthewson offer for a prize? **One thousand dollars.**
● What would Buck have to do to win that prize? *Idea:* Start a sled weighing 1000 pounds.
● Who had said that Buck could do that? **Thornton.**
● Was Thornton sure that Buck could do it? **No.**
● Why do you think some of those men have so much money? *Idea:* Because they've been mining for gold.
Ⓑ Does O'Brien think that Buck will be able to start a thousand-pound load and pull it? **No.**
● How far will Buck have to pull it once he starts it? **100 yards.**
Ⓒ What season is it? **Winter.**
● How cold do you think it is outside? *Idea:* Very cold.
Get a picture of all those miners standing around the sled, ready to see a dog try to pull a 1000 pound load.

before Buck began pulling. Matthewson insisted that Buck would have to pull the sled with the runners as they were—in the frozen grip of the snow. Most of the men who had witnessed the contest decided in Matthewson's favor. Ⓓ

Not one man beside Thornton thought that Buck would succeed. Now that Thornton looked at the sled, he was heavy with doubt.

"Three thousand," Matthewson suddenly shouted. "Thornton, I'll pay you three thousand dollars if your dog can pull that load!" Ⓔ

Thornton's face showed his doubt, but his fighting spirit was up. That spirit failed to recognize the impossible. The regular team of ten dogs was curled up in the snow in front of the sled. The team was unhitched, and Buck, with his own harness, was put in front of the sled. He sensed the excitement, and he felt that in some way he must do a great thing for John Thornton. Ⓕ ★6 ERRORS★

The crowd began to murmur with admiration at Buck's splendid appearance. He was in perfect condition, without an ounce of extra flesh. He weighed one hundred and fifty pounds. His furry coat shone like silk. His muscles showed in tight rolls underneath his skin. The men felt these muscles and said they were as hard as iron.

Suddenly, a tall man said, "Gad, sir! Gad, sir! I offer you eight hundred dollars for him, sir, before the test, sir; eight hundred for that dog just as he stands."

Thornton shook his head no and stepped to Buck's side.

The crowd fell silent. Everybody knew that Buck was a magnificent animal; but the twenty, fifty-pound sacks of flour were more than any dog could pull.

Thornton knelt down by Buck's side. He took his head in his two hands and rested his cheek on Buck's cheek. He did not playfully shake him, or murmur softly. But he whispered something in the dog's ear. Buck whined eagerly.

The crowd was watching curiously. The affair was growing mysterious. It seemed like a magic trick. As Thornton got to his feet, Buck seized Thornton's hand between his jaws, pressing in with his teeth and releasing slowly. It was Buck's answer.

Thornton stepped back. "Now, Buck," he said.

Buck pulled his harness tight, then let it slacken a bit.

"Gee!" Thornton's voice rang out, sharp in the tense silence.

Buck followed the command. He swung to the right, ending the movement in a lunge that jerked the harness and stopped his one hundred and fifty pounds. The load quivered, and a crisp crackling rose from under the runners.

"Haw!" Thornton commanded.

Buck made the same move, this time to the left. The crackling turned into a snapping. The sled turned slightly and the runners slipped and grated several inches to the side. The sled was broken out. Men were holding their breath.

"Now, MUSH ON!"

Lesson 55   Textbook   **213**

Thornton's command cracked out like a shot. Buck threw himself forward, tightening the harness with a jarring lunge. His whole body was gathered together in the tremendous effort. His muscles knotted under his silky fur. His great chest was low to the ground, his head forward and down, while his feet were flying and his claws scarred the hard-packed snow. The sled swayed, trembled, and started forward. One of Buck's feet slipped, and one man groaned aloud. Then the sled slowly moved ahead.

Men gasped and began to breathe again, unaware that for a moment they had stopped breathing. Thornton was running behind, encouraging Buck with short, cheery words. The distance had been measured off, and as he neared the pile of firewood which marked the end of the hundred yards, the men began to cheer loudly. The cheer burst into a roar as Buck passed the firewood and halted at command. Every man was clapping wildly, even Matthewson. Hats and mittens flying in the air. Men were shaking hands, and they did not care whose hand they shook.

But Thornton fell on his knees beside Buck. Head against head, and Thornton was shaking him back and forth. Those who gathered close heard him talking to Buck and he talked softly and lovingly.

"Gad, sir! Gad, sir!" sputtered the tall man. "I'll give you a thousand for him, sir, a thousand, sir—twelve hundred, sir."

Thornton rose to his feet. His eyes were wet. The tears were streaming down his cheeks. "No, sir," he said to the tall man, "no, sir. You can't buy this dog for any amount of money."

Buck seized Thornton's hand in his teeth. Thornton shook him back and forth.

The men drew back a ways, and none dared to disturb the man and his dog.

Ⓓ **What did O'Brien suggest that Thornton should be able to do before Buck started pulling?** *Idea:* Knock the runners loose from the ice.

● **What did Matthewson say?** *Idea:* Buck had to pull the sled out of the ice.

● **Would it be harder to move the sled if the runners are frozen in place or if they are free to move?** **Frozen in place.**

● **Most of the men decided in favor of Matthewson. What does that mean?** *Idea:* They want to do it Matthewson's way.

Ⓔ **Suddenly Matthewson changed the prize. How much did he offer?** **Three thousand dollars.**

Ⓕ **How many dogs normally pulled Matthewson's sled?** **Ten.**

● **Read the rest of the story to yourselves and be ready to answer some questions. Pay particular attention to the strategy that Thornton uses to break the runners free from the snow. He does something very clever.**

After all students have finished reading:

● **To break the runners lose, Thornton gave Buck a series of commands. What was the first command?** **Gee.**

● **In which direction did Buck lunge?** **Right.**

● **Then what command did Thornton give?** **Haw.**

● **In which direction did Buck lunge?** **Left.**

● **What happened to the runners when Buck lunged to the right and then to the left?** *Idea:* They broke free of the ice.

● **What command did Thornton give next?** **Mush on.**

● **Did Buck pull the load for 100 yards?** **Yes.**

● **How did the men who were watching respond?** *Idea:* They cheered.

● **What about Matthewson?** *Idea:* He cheered too.

● **After Buck had pulled the load, how much money did the tall man offer for Buck?** **1200 dollars.**

● **What did Thornton tell the tall man?** *Idea:* That he couldn't buy Buck.

● **What did the crowd do at the end of the story as Thornton talked to Buck?** *Idea:* They left them alone.

Award 4 points or have the students reread to the error limit sign.

INDEPENDENT WORK

Do all the items in your skillbook and workbook for lesson 55.

Review Items

1. Put the following events in the right order by numbering them from **1 through 4.**

<u>3</u> Buck saved John Thornton from drowning.

<u>2</u> John Thornton ordered Buck to jump off a cliff.

<u>4</u> Buck pulled a thousand-pound sled.

<u>1</u> John Thornton saved Buck's life.

2. Write which character each statement describes. Choose from **Matthewson, Buck,** or **Thornton.**

a. His skin looked like silk.

Buck

b. His hand was bitten.

Thornton

c. He lost a lot of money one day.

Matthewson

d. He weighed one hundred and fifty pounds. *Buck*

e. He would do anything for his master.

Buck

WORKCHECK AND AWARDING POINTS

1. *Read the questions and answers for the skillbook and workbook.*

2. *Award points for independent work as follows:*

> *0 errors . . . . .6 points*
> *2 errors . . . . .4 points*
> *3, 4, or 5 errors . . . . .2 points*
> *5 or more errors . . . . .0 points*

3. *Award bonus points as follows:*

> *Correcting missed items*
> *or getting all items right . . . . .2 points*
> *Doing the writing*
> *assignment acceptably . . . . .2 points*

ANSWER KEY FOR SKILLBOOK

PART C

1. The boys are eating a meal.
2. The women are building a house.
3. The dogs are pulling a sled.
4. Phil is planting a tree.

PART D

5. **a.** Winter
   b. *Idea:* 60 below zero
   c. *Idea:* They had frozen to the snow
   d. ten
   e. *Idea:* Sacks of flour
6. **a.** *Idea:* Perfect condition
   b. No
   c. 150
   d. *Idea:* Buck was a great dog
7. **a.** *Idea:* Bit it and let go
   b. Gee
   c. To the right
   d. *Idea:* A crackling noise
   e. Haw
   f. To the left
   g. *Idea:* They came unstuck
8. **a.** Mush on
   b. *Ideas:* Forward; straight
   c. 100 yards
   d. *Idea:* The finish line
   e. *Idea:* They were excited
   f. *Idea:* Because Buck won

PART E

9. **a.** terrible
   b. hatch
   c. floundered
   d. vivid
   e. rapids
   f. murmuring
   g. sneer
   h. exchanged
   i. recover
   j. hugged

Lesson 56

Lesson 56

PART A	Word Lists		PART B
			Vocabulary Sentences

1
Mount Whitney
Los Angeles
scenery
Pennsylvania
barren

2
Mount Shasta
Glen Ellen
groove
grove
combine
combined

3
Vocabulary words
1. guilty
2. grate
3. lunged
4. rouse
5. outskirts
6. witness

4
Vocabulary words
1. scenery
2. barren
3. splinters
4. topple
5. shredded

PART B
Vocabulary Sentences

1. He stood outside the cabin and looked at the beautiful <u>scenery</u> that surrounded it.
2. The hills were <u>barren</u> with no trees and no bushes.
3. He hit the wooden block with an ax and the block became a pile of <u>splinters</u>.
4. They sawed through the great tree and slowly it began to <u>topple</u>.
5. The lion clawed the scarecrow's coat until the coat was completely <u>shredded</u>.

WORD PRACTICE AND VOCABULARY

EXERCISE 1   Word practice

1. Everybody, find lesson 56, part A in your skillbook. *Wait.* Touch under the words in column 1 as I read them.
2. The words in the first line are **Mount Whitney.**
3. Next line. **Los Angeles.**
4. Next word. **Scenery.**
5. *Repeat step 4 for each remaining word in column 1.*
6. Your turn. Read the first line. *Signal.* **Mount Whitney.**
7. Next line. *Signal.* **Los Angeles.**
8. Next word. *Signal.* **Scenery.**
9. *Repeat step 8 for each remaining word in column 1.*
10. *Repeat the words in column 1 until firm.*

EXERCISE 2   Word practice

1. Everybody, touch under the first line in column 2. *Pause.* What words? *Signal.* **Mount Shasta.**
2. Next line. *Pause.* What words? *Signal.* **Glen Ellen.**
3. Next word. *Pause.* What word? *Signal.* **Groove.**
4. *Repeat step 3 for each remaining word in column 2.*
5. *Repeat the words in column 2 until firm.*

EXERCISE 3   Vocabulary review

Task A

1. Everybody, touch column 3. *Check.* First you're going to read the words in column 3. Then we'll talk about what they mean.
2. Touch under the first word. *Pause.* What word? *Signal.* **Guilty.**
3. Next word. *Pause.* What word? *Signal.* **Grate.**
4. *Repeat step 3 for each remaining word in column 3.*
5. *Repeat the words in column 3 until firm.*

Task B

You've learned the meanings for all these words. Word 1 is **guilty.** *Call on a student.* What does it mean when a person is **guilty** of something? *Idea:* The person did something.

Task C

Word 2 is **grate.** *Call on a student.* What does it mean when something **grates** against another thing? *Idea:* It grinds against it.

Task D

Word 3 is **lunged.** *Call on a student.* What does **lunged** mean? *Idea:* Charged.

Task E

Word 4 is **rouse.** *Call on a student.* What does **rouse** mean? *Ideas:* Move; wake up.

Task F

Word 5 is **outskirts.** *Call on a student.* What does it mean when something is near the **outskirts** of a town? *Idea:* It is near the edge of the town.

Task G

Word 6 is **witness.** *Call on a student.* What do you do when you **witness** an event? *Idea:* You see the event.

EXERCISE 4   Vocabulary from context

Task A

1. Everybody, touch column 4. *Check.* First you're going to read the words in column 4. Then we'll talk about what they mean.
2. Touch under the first word. *Pause.* What word? *Signal.* **Scenery.**
3. Next word. *Pause.* What word? *Signal.* **Barren.**
4. *Repeat step 3 for each remaining word in column 4.*
5. *Repeat the words in column 4 until firm.*

Task B

1. Everybody, find part B in your skillbook. *Check.* I'll read those sentences. You figure out what the underlined part in each sentence means.
2. Sentence one: He stood outside the cabin and looked at the beautiful <u>scenery</u> that surrounded it. *Call on a student.* What could **scenery** mean? *Idea:* Surroundings.
3. *Repeat step 2 for each remaining sentence.*
   Answer Key: Sentence 2. Ideas: Bare; naked.
   Sentence 3. Idea: Little pieces of wood.
   Sentence 4. Idea: Fall down.
   Sentence 5. Idea: Tore up.

STORY READING

EXERCISE 5   Decoding and comprehension

1. Everybody, turn to page 215 in your textbook. *Wait. Call on a student.* What's the error limit for this lesson? **6 errors.**

Lesson 56

California

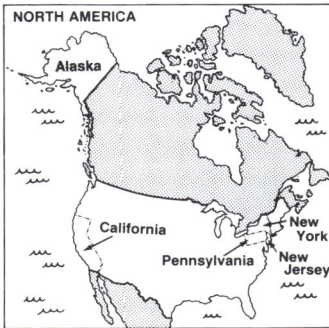

The next story you will read takes place in California. You will learn some facts about California in this passage. Ⓐ

The Size of California

The northern border of California is about eight hundred miles from the southern border. The length of California, from north to south, is as great as the distance from Chicago to New York. Alaska is the largest state in the United States, but California is also very large. Ⓑ If we combined the states of New York, Pennsylvania, and New Jersey, these combined states would not be as large as California. Ⓒ

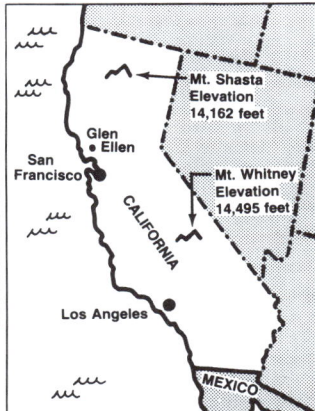

Weather in California

Because California is so large, the weather is different in different parts of the state. The weather in the northern part of California is mild and pleasant. The weather in the southern part of California is very dry and very hot. In the early 1900's the movie makers moved to southern California because the weather was so dry and sunny. It was easy to make movies outdoors. Ⓓ

Mountains in California

California is not only large, it has some of the most impressive scenery in the world. A chain of mountains runs from north to south through the state, and although these mountains are not as impressive as the ones that you would see in Alaska or Northern Canada, they are very large compared to other mountains in the main part of the United States. Ⓔ The largest mountain in the main part of the United States is in this chain of mountains. It is Mount Whitney and it rises 14,495 feet above sea level. The top of that mountain is almost three miles above sea level. Ⓕ Another high mountain in California is Mount Shasta, which is a volcano that is 14,162 feet above sea level. California has many other mountains that are over two miles above sea level.

When you climb one of these huge mountains, it is just like going north. The higher you go, the colder the air becomes. Ⓖ And as you go higher, the plants change. At the bottom of the mountain are large trees. As you go up past five thousand feet, the trees begin to change. They are not as large, because they have trouble growing.

At the bottom of the mountain, the weather is warm and the trees can grow quickly. But when you go up about five thousand feet, the weather is colder, and the trees cannot grow as quickly. Heavy snow falls during the winter, and this snow bends tree branches down and breaks them. Ⓗ ★6 ERRORS★

As you go up to ten thousand feet, the weather is even colder than it was at five thousand feet. Up here, great amounts of snow fall during the winter. Sometimes, twenty or thirty feet of snow may fall. Imagine the trouble that a young tree has growing up here. During the winter, the tree may be buried under many feet of snow. The tree can't even begin growing until the snow melts away and the leaves of the tree can reach the sunlight. In early summer, the tree finally starts to grow, but the growing season is very short. In early fall, the snows begin again, once more burying the young tree. It is no wonder that the trees have a hard time growing up here.

When you go up to around twelve thousand feet, the trees disappear. The ground is too cold for them to grow. Now there are just barren slopes, and the plants that grow are a lot like the plants that grow in Alaska and Northern Canada. Even in the middle of the summer, there are patches of wet snow up here. And as you go higher, the patches become larger. The peaks of some mountains, such as Shasta and Whitney, are covered with snow all year round. The weather at the top of these mountains is a lot like the weather at the North Pole.

Remember, when you climb up a mountain, the weather and the plants change. They change the same way they would change if you went toward the North Pole.

2. *Call on individual students to read. Present the tasks specified for each circled letter.*

Ⓐ There are headings in this passage that tell about what you will read.
- Find the first heading. *Check.*
  Read that heading. **The Size of California.**
  What are you going to read about in that part? *Idea:* The size of California.
- Find the next heading. *Check.*
  Read that heading. **Weather in California.**
  What are you going to read about in that part? *Idea:* Weather in California.
- Find the next heading. *Check.*
  Read that heading. **Mountains in California.**
  What are you going to read about in that part? *Idea:* Mountains in California.
- Find the next heading. *Check.*
  Read that heading. **Trees in California.**
  What are you going to read about in that part? *Idea:* Trees in California.
- Find the last heading. *Check.*
  Read that heading. **Glen Ellen.**
  What are you going to read about in that part? *Idea:* Glen Ellen.
  Everybody, go back to the first heading.
Ⓑ About how far is it from the northern border of California to the southern border? *Idea:* 800 miles.
- Which state is the largest? **Alaska.**
Ⓒ Everybody, look at the map of North America. The map shows Alaska, California, and three states on the east coast.
- What's the largest state? **Alaska.**
- Which is bigger, California or the three states on the east coast? **California.**
Ⓓ Everybody, look at the map of California. Touch the southern border of California.
- What country touches the southern border? **Mexico.**
- Everybody, touch the city of Los Angeles. Los Angeles is near the southern border of California.
Ⓔ Everybody, run your finger down the chain of mountains that goes north to south in California. *Check.*
Ⓕ Everybody, touch Mount Whitney on the map. *Check.*
- How high above sea level is the top of that mountain? **14,495 feet.**
  That's almost three miles high.
Ⓖ Listen to that statement: "The higher you go, the colder the air becomes."
- Say that statement: *Call on several students.*
- Where would the air be the hottest, at the bottom, at the middle, or at the top? **At the bottom.**
- Where would the air be the coldest? **At the top.**
  So going up any mountain is just like going north.

Mountains in California

California is not only large, it has some of the most impressive scenery in the world. A chain of mountains runs from north to south through the state, and although these mountains are not as impressive as the ones that you would see in Alaska or Northern Canada, they are very large compared to other mountains in the main part of the United States.(E) The largest mountain in the main part of the United States is in this chain of mountains. It is Mount Whitney and it rises 14,495 feet above sea level. The top of that mountain is almost three miles above sea level.(F) Another high mountain in California is Mount Shasta, which is a volcano that is 14,162 feet above sea level. California has many other mountains that are over two miles above sea level.

When you climb one of these huge mountains, it is just like going north. The higher you go, the colder the air becomes.(G) And as you go higher, the plants change. At the bottom of the mountain are large trees. As you go up past five thousand feet, the trees begin to change. They are not as large, because they have trouble growing.

At the bottom of the mountain, the weather is warm and the trees can grow quickly. But when you go up about five thousand feet, the weather is colder, and the trees cannot grow as quickly. Heavy snow falls during the winter, and this snow bends tree branches down and breaks them.(H) ★6 ERRORS★

216   Lesson 56   Textbook

As you go up to ten thousand feet, the weather is even colder than it was at five thousand feet. Up here, great amounts of snow fall during the winter. Sometimes, twenty or thirty feet of snow may fall. Imagine the trouble that a young tree has growing up here. During the winter, the tree may be buried under many feet of snow. The tree can't even begin growing until the snow melts away and the leaves of the tree can reach the sunlight. In early summer, the tree finally starts to grow, but the growing season is very short. In early fall, the snows begin again, once more burying the young tree. It is no wonder that the trees have a hard time growing up here.

When you go up to around twelve thousand feet, the trees disappear. The ground is too cold for them to grow. Now there are just barren slopes, and the plants that grow are a lot like the plants that grow in Alaska and Northern Canada. Even in the middle of the summer, there are patches of wet snow up here. And as you go higher, the patches become larger. The peaks of some mountains, such as Shasta and Whitney, are covered with snow all year round. The weather at the top of these mountains is a lot like the weather at the North Pole.

Remember, when you climb up a mountain, the weather and the plants change. They change the same way they would change if you went toward the North Pole.

Trees in California

California has impressive mountains. The trees in California are also impressive—particularly the redwood trees. California used to have incredible redwood forests that ran along the coast from Oregon through northern California and all the way down into the central part of California.

Imagine, a tree that is over 350 feet tall. That's as tall as a thirty-five story building. Imagine how people felt when they crossed the mountain range from the east and approached the coast. As they followed trails toward the coast, they saw their first redwoods. These people had probably never seen a tree that was more than four or five feet through the middle. A tree that size is huge. But it would be a very small redwood. Some redwoods are eighteen feet through the middle. That's as wide as a large bedroom. There is more lumber in one redwood tree than in twenty normal-sized trees.

About 150 years ago, people began to cut the redwood trees down. When one of these enormous trees toppled, it made a sound like thunder. Hundreds of tons of force would strike the forest floor.

People who lived in houses under one of these enormous trees were afraid of what might happen during a windstorm. If the wind ever tore the top from the tree and if that top fell on the house, it would crush the house as easily as you could crush a matchbox.

Millions of people moved to California because they liked the idea of living in a place with warm winters. And as they moved in, the redwoods were cut down, by the hundreds of thousands. At one time, a great forest of redwoods extended from the city of San Francisco down along the coast. Now there is hardly a redwood left in this area.

Glen Ellen

The story that you will read in the next lesson takes place about forty miles north of San Francisco, in a place called Glen Ellen. The country around Glen Ellen is beautiful. There are rolling hills that are covered with grooves of trees. Some of these oak trees keep their green leaves all year round. These trees are called live oaks. The branches of live oaks spread very wide. Some live oaks spread more than one hundred feet.

In the winter and spring, the hills around Glen Ellen are bright green. In the distance are a few redwoods. A great deal of rain falls during the winter and spring, and flowers bloom everywhere as early as March. But as the season changes from spring into summer, the rains stop and the days become clear. Now the hills will receive very little rain until late fall. By midsummer, the rolling hills are golden because the grass dries up and turns golden. The country is still beautiful, with the green groves of live oaks sprinkled around the golden hills.

Lesson 56   Textbook   217

- Is the weather colder at the bottom of the mountain or at the top of the mountain? **At the top.**
(H) Tell why the trees grow more slowly above five thousand feet? *Idea:* The weather is colder.
- So where would it snow more during the winter? *Idea:* At the top.
- Read the rest of the story to yourselves. Find out how the plants on the mountain change at ten thousand feet and twelve thousand feet. Also, find out where the next story will take place, and find that place on the map.

After all students have finished reading:

- How big are the trees at the bottom of the mountain? *Idea:* Very big.
- How do they change above five thousand feet? *Idea:* They aren't as big.
- How do they change at ten thousand feet? *Ideas:* They are very small.
- How do they change when you get around twelve thousand feet? *Idea:* They disappear.
- Around twelve thousand feet, the plants are a lot like the plants you would see in a different part of the world. Where would you see those plants? **Alaska and Northern Canada.**
- When you go to the very top of a large mountain like Mount Whitney, is the weather warmer or colder than it is at twelve thousand feet? **Colder.**
- Where would you find weather that is like the weather at the top of a very high mountain? **The North Pole.**
So think of that. When you go farther and farther up a mountain, it is just like going closer and closer to the North Pole.
- The passage told about the very large trees that grow in California.
- What's the name of the tree that sometimes grows 350 feet tall? **Redwood.**
- A tree that tall is as large as a building that is how many stories tall? *Idea:* Thirty-five.
- What's the name of the place you will read about in the next story? **Glen Ellen.**
- That place is about forty miles north of a large city in California. Which city? **San Francisco.**
- Everybody, look at the map on page 215. Touch San Francisco. *Check.*
- In which direction do you go from San Francisco to get to Glen Ellen? **North.**
- Describe the country near Glen Ellen. *Ideas:* It is beautiful; it has rolling hills; it has live oak trees; it has a few redwood trees.
- What is the weather like in the winter? **Rainy.**
- Name the season in which there is almost no rain. **Summer.**
- How does the color of the hills change in summer? **They turn golden.**

Award 4 points or have the students reread to the error limit sign.

EXERCISE 6   Special projects

1. Everybody, turn to lesson 56 in your workbook. We're going to do these projects.
2. Read that section to yourself. Read it carefully so that you have the information you need to decide what you want to do. After you have read the section, we'll discuss it.
3. *After students have finished reading:*
   Every student should work on at least one project. I'll name the projects, and you raise your hand if the project I name is the one you want to work on.
   - Project 1. Make a scale model of a dog sled. Who wants to work on that project?
     List students who volunteer.
   - Project 2. Draw a large picture of a dog sled. Who wants to work on that project?
     List students who volunteer.
   - Project 3. Draw a map of the journey from Juneau to Dawson. Who wants to work on that project?
     List students who volunteer.
4. *Allow students extra time to carry out their projects.*

INDEPENDENT WORK

Do all the items in your skillbook and workbook for lesson 56.

ANSWER KEY FOR WORKBOOK

Special Project

1. Dog sleds were an important part of the story about Buck. They were also important in real life. Without dog sleds, it would have been very difficult for people to live in the far north.

   One of the great advantages of a dog sled is that it is so easy to build. It only requires a few long pieces of wood and some kind of covering for the bottom and the back. It is much simpler to build than other vehicles, such as cars or bicycles.

   Find out all you can about how dog sleds were built. Look at the pictures in your textbook, then look up dog sleds in an encyclopedia or in other reference books.

   Build a model of a dog sled. You can glue pieces of wood together and use cloth for the bottom and the back. You can even use pencils or heavy cardboard. If you want, you can hook up some toy dogs to the front of the sled. Try to make your model look as realistic as possible.

2. If you don't have materials to make a model, draw a picture of the dog sled. Include as many parts as you can. Show the dogs and show the kind of scenery that might be around the dog sled.

3. Look at the maps in your textbook and in an atlas. Then draw a large map of the area you would cover going from Juneau to Dawson. Draw in the ocean and the shorelines. Show where the mountains, lakes, and rivers are. Show where the different cities and countries are.

   After you have finished the map, draw a line to show the path you would take from Juneau to Dawson. Put numbers along that line to show the different points on your journey. If you want, you can write a description of the things you would see at each point. You can take your descriptions from the story or from other books.

WORKCHECK AND AWARDING POINTS

1. *Read the questions and answers for the skillbook and workbook.*
2. *Award points for independent work as follows:*

   ```
   0 errors . . . . . . . . . . . . . . . . . . . . .6 points
   2 errors . . . . . . . . . . . . . . . . . . . . .4 points
   3, 4, or 5 errors . . . . . . . . . . . . . .2 points
   5 or more errors . . . . . . . . . . . . . .0 points
   ```

3. *Award bonus points as follows:*

   ```
   Correcting missed items
   or getting all items right . . . . . . . . .2 points
   Doing the writing
   assignment acceptably . . . . . . . . . . .2 points
   ```

ANSWER KEY FOR SKILLBOOK

PART C

1. *Idea:* Meg hit a home run.
2. *Idea:* The girls are putting on a play.
3. *Idea:* The men are playing basketball.

PART D

4. 800 miles
5. north
6. **a.** 12,000
   b. 1,000
7. Mount Whitney
8. *Idea:* About 12,000 feet
9. The top
10. *Idea:* Because it's colder at 10,000 feet
11. **a.** Redwoods
    b. About 350 feet
    c. 35
12. **a.** Glen Ellen
    b. Redwoods and live oaks
    c. San Francisco

PART E

13. **a.** eventually
    b. lean
    c. reflections
    d. very dangerous
    e. boulder
    f. threw
    g. excellent
    h. affection
    i. tolerated

Lesson 57

Lesson 57

PART A	Word Lists	PART B

Vocabulary Sentences

1	2
Madge Irvine	effortless
Oregon	blackberry
bristle	outskirts
squirm	meadowlark
miracle	

1. After he rolled on the wet grass and dirt, his pants were <u>soiled</u>.
2. The <u>meadowlark</u> spread its wings, raised its head, and began to sing.
3. A dog has two hind legs and two <u>forelegs</u>.
4. <u>He</u> ordered his dog to stop and the dog <u>halted</u> immediately.
5. <u>He</u> experienced many <u>hardships</u>— hunger, pain, and long <u>hours</u> of hard work.

3	4
Walt	**Vocabulary words**
starve	1. splinters
starvation	2. topple
brow	3. scenery
	4. shredded
	5. barren

5	6
Vocabulary words	**Vocabulary words**
1. effortlessly	1. soiled
2. spring	2. meadowlark
3. fangs	3. forelegs
4. miracle	4. halt
	5. hardships

WORD PRACTICE AND VOCABULARY

EXERCISE 1 Word practice

1. Everybody, find lesson 57, part A in your skillbook. *Wait.* Touch under the words in column 1 as I read them.
2. The words in the first line are **Madge Irvine.**
3. Next word. **Oregon.**
4. *Repeat step 3 for each remaining word in column 1.*
5. Your turn. Read the first line. *Signal.* **Madge Irvine.**
6. Next word. **Oregon.**
7. *Repeat step 6 for each remaining word in column 1.*
8. *Repeat the words in column 1 until firm.*

EXERCISE 2 Word family

1. Everybody, touch column 2. *Check.* All those words are made up of two shorter words. Touch under the first word. *Pause.* What word? *Signal.* **Effortless.**
2. Next word *Pause.* What word? *Signal.* **Blackberry.**
3. *Repeat step 2 for each remaining word in column 2.*
4. *Repeat the words in column 2 until firm.*

EXERCISE 3 Word practice

1. Everybody, touch under the first word in column 3. *Pause.* What word? *Signal.* **Walt.**
2. Next word. *Pause.* What word? *Signal.* **Starve.**
3. *Repeat step 2 for each remaining word in column 3.*
4. *Repeat the words in column 3 until firm.*

EXERCISE 4 Vocabulary review

Task A

1. Everybody, touch column 4. *Check.* First you're going to read the words in column 4. Then we'll talk about what they mean.
2. Touch under the first word. *Pause.* What word? *Signal.* **Splinters.**
3. Next word. *Pause.* What word? *Signal.* **Topple.**
4. *Repeat step 3 for each remaining word in column 4.*
5. *Repeat the words in column 4 until firm.*

Task B

You've learned the meanings for all these words. Word 1 is **splinters.** *Call on a student.* What are **splinters?** *Idea:* Little pieces of wood.

Task C

Word 2 is **topple.** *Call on a student.*
What does **topple** mean? *Idea:* Fall down.

Task D

Word 3 is **scenery.** *Call on a student.*
What is **scenery?** *Idea:* Surroundings.

Task E

Word 4 is **shredded.** *Call on a student.*
What does **shredded** mean? *Idea:* Torn up.

Task F

Word 5 is **barren.** *Call on a student.*
What does **barren** mean? *Ideas:* Bare; naked.

EXERCISE 5   Vocabulary development

Task A

1. Everybody, touch column 5. *Check.*
   First you're going to read the words in column 5. Then we'll talk about what they mean.
2. Touch under the first word. *Pause.*
   What word? *Signal.* **Effortlessly.**
3. Next word. *Pause.* What word? *Signal.* **Spring.**
4. *Repeat step 3 for each remaining word in column 5.*
5. *Repeat the words in column 5 until firm.*

Task B

Now let's talk about what those words mean.
Word 1 is **effortlessly.** When you do something **effortlessly,** you do it in a way that looks like you use no effort at all.
Everybody, what is a boy doing who looks as if he skates with no **effort?** *Signal.*
Skating effortlessly.

Task C

Word 2 is **spring.** One meaning of **spring** is a place where fresh water bubbles out of the ground. Everybody, what's the name of a place where fresh water bubbles out of the ground? *Signal.* **A spring.**

Task D

Word 3 is **fangs. Fangs** are the four long, pointed teeth that dogs and cats have. You have tiny **fangs.** Touch them. *Check.*

Task E

Word 4 is **miracle.** A very strange event that cannot be explained is a **miracle.** Everybody, what do we call a very strange event that cannot be explained? *Signal.* **A miracle.**

EXERCISE 6   Vocabulary from context

Task A

1. Everybody, touch column 6. *Check.*
   First you're going to read the words in column 6. Then we'll talk about what they mean.
2. Touch under the first word. *Pause.*
   What word? *Signal.* **Soiled.**
3. Next word. *Pause.* What word? *Signal.*
   Meadowlark.
4. *Repeat step 3 for each remaining word in column 6.*
5. *Repeat the words in column 6 until firm.*

Task B

1. Everybody, find part B in your skillbook. *Check.*
   I'll read those sentences. You figure out what the underlined part in each sentence means.
2. Sentence one: After he rolled on the wet grass and dirt, his pants were <u>soiled</u>.
   Call on a student. What could **soiled** mean? *Idea:* Dirty.
3. *Repeat step 2 for each remaining sentence.*
   Answer Key: Sentence 2. Idea: Bird.
   Sentence 3. Idea: Front legs.
   Sentence 4. Idea: Stopped.
   Sentence 5. Idea: Severe difficulties.

Lesson 57

Brown Wolf
by Jack London Ⓐ
PART 1

Madge Irvine put on her walking shoes and walked to the front door of the small mountain cottage. Her husband Walt was waiting for her outside, enjoying the warm California sun. Ⓑ Madge looked at the forest that surrounded the cottage, then turned to her husband.

"Where's Wolf?" she asked.

"He was here a moment ago," said Walt. "He was chasing a rabbit the last I saw of him."

"Wolf! Wolf! Here, Wolf!" she called, as they left the cottage and took the trail that led down through the forest to the county road.

Walt put the little finger of each hand between his lips and began to whistle loudly. Ⓒ Madge and Walt heard a crashing in the bushes and then, forty feet above them, on the edge of a cliff, a large animal appeared.

218   Lesson 57   Textbook

His body and coat and tail were like a huge timber wolf's, but his color showed that he was really a dog. No wolf was ever colored like him. He was brown, deep brown, red-brown, brown in every way. His back and shoulders were a warm brown, and his belly was a brownish yellow. His throat and paws were light brown, and his eyes were golden. Ⓓ

Wolf's front legs knocked a pebble loose, and he watched the fall of the pebble with pointed ears and sharp eyes until it struck at the Irvine's feet. Then he looked right at them and seemed to laugh.

"Come here, Wolf," Walt called out to him.

His ears flattened back and down at the sound as if an invisible hand was patting him on the head. They watched him scramble into the forest. Then they proceeded on their way. He joined them several minutes later, but he did not stay for long. A pat and a rub around the ears from the man, and a longer hug from the woman, and he was far down the trail in front of them, gliding effortlessly over the ground like a true wolf. Ⓔ

The man and woman loved the dog very much, but it had been hard for them to win his love. He had drifted in about three years ago. Tired and hungry, he had killed a rabbit right next to their cottage, and then crawled away and slept by the spring at the foot of the blackberry bushes. He had snarled at Walt the next morning, and he had snarled at Madge when she gave him a large pan of bread and milk. Ⓕ

Wolf continued to be an unfriendly dog, and refused to let them lay hands on him. Every time they came near, he would show his fangs and his hair would bristle. Ⓖ But he remained by the blackberry bushes, sleeping and resting, and eating the food they gave him. He remained because he was weak, and several days later, when he felt better, he disappeared.

And that should have been the end of him. But, the very next day, Walt had to take a business trip north, to Oregon. Riding along on the train, near the California-Oregon border, he happened to look out of the window and saw his unfriendly guest moving along the road, tired, dust-covered, and soiled from two hundred miles of travel. Ⓗ

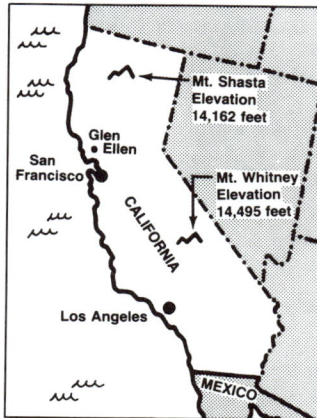

Mt. Shasta
Elevation
14,162 feet

Glen
Ellen

San
Francisco

Mt. Whitney
Elevation
14,495 feet

CALIFORNIA

Los Angeles

MEXICO

Lesson 57   Textbook   219

EXERCISE 7   Decoding and Comprehension

1. Everybody, turn to page 218 in your textbook. *Wait. Call on a student. What's the error limit for this lesson?* **10 errors.**

2. *Call on individual students to read. Present the tasks specified for each circled letter.*

Ⓐ Today's story is written by the same man who wrote the story about Buck—Jack London. This story is about another dog. The story takes place in a part of the world that is far from the country that Buck lived in.

• What's the title of this story? **Brown Wolf.**
• Who is the author of Brown Wolf? **Jack London.**
• What other story did he write? **Buck.**

Ⓑ What are the names of two characters that have been introduced in this story? **Madge and Walt Irvine.**

• What kind of house do Madge and Walt live in? *Idea:* A cottage.
• In what state does this story take place? **California.**

Ⓒ Did you ever know anyone who could whistle that way? *Response:* Student preference.

Ⓓ What kind of animal was Wolf? **A dog.**

• Listen to that part again and get a picture of Wolf. *Read the paragraph that ends with* Ⓓ.
• What was it about Wolf that told you he wasn't a true wolf? *Idea:* His color.
• Describe his color. *Ideas:* Brown; golden eyes; brownish yellow belly.

Ⓔ Why do you think Wolf didn't want to stay with Madge and Walt? *Ideas:* He liked to walk ahead of them; he wanted to run around.

Ⓕ Was Wolf friendly when they first met him? **No.**

• How long had they known Wolf? **About three years.**

Ⓖ What does that mean? **His hair would bristle?** *Idea:* It would stand on end.

Ⓗ Where was Walt when he saw Wolf again? *Ideas:* On a train; near the Oregon border.

• How far from the cottage was Walt? *Idea:* Two hundred miles.
• Everybody, look at the map. *Check.* What's the name of the state that Walt is going to? **Oregon.**
• Everybody, touch the border between California and Oregon. *Check.*
• Everybody, touch the place where Walt was when he saw Wolf. *Check.*
• In which direction was Wolf going? **North.** Wolf seems to want to go north for some reason.

Walt got off the train at the next station, bought a piece of meat, and captured the dog on the outskirts of the town. Walt transported Wolf back to Glen Ellen in the baggage car, and took him back to the mountain cottage. Wolf was tied up for a week, and the Irvines tried everything to make him happy. But he only snarled at their soft-spoken love words.

They soon discovered that he never barked. In all the time they had him, he never barked. ① ★10 ERRORS★

To win Wolf's affection became a problem. Walt liked problems. He had a metal tag made, on which was stamped: "Return to Walt Irvine, Glen Ellen, California." This tag was put on a collar and strapped around the dog's neck. Then Wolf was let loose, and he promptly disappeared. A day later, a telegram came from a county over one hundred miles north. In twenty hours, the dog had gone over a hundred miles and was still going north when he was captured.

Wolf was sent back by train. The Irvines tied him up for three days, and he was let loose once again. This time he got all the way north to Oregon when he was caught and returned. Always, as soon as he received his freedom, he fled—and always he fled north.

Another time, the dog crossed all of Oregon, and most of Washington, before he was picked up and returned. The speed with which he traveled was remarkable. On the first day's run he was known to cover as much as a hundred and fifty miles, and after that he would go a hundred miles

a day until caught. He always arrived back lean and hungry and mean, and always left fresh and lively, making his way northward for some reason that no one could understand.

But at last, after a year of running away, he accepted the Irvines and decided to remain at the cottage where he had killed the rabbit and slept by the spring. After he decided to stay, a long time went by before he allowed the man and woman to pet him. He only liked the Irvines and no guest at the cottage could ever make friends with him. A low growl greeted every approach. If anyone was foolish enough to come nearer, the naked fangs appeared, and the growl became a snarl.

The Irvines could only guess at his past life. They figured that he must have come up from the south when he first came to their cottage. Mrs. Johnson, their nearest neighbor, thought he was a Yukon dog. She said that her brother, who was looking for gold up there, had told her about dogs like Wolf.

The Irvines agreed with Mrs. Johnson. The tips of Wolf's ears had obviously been so severely frozen at some time that they would never quite heal again. Besides, he looked like the photographs of the Yukon dogs they saw in magazines and newspapers. They often wondered about his past, and tried to imagine what his Yukon life had been like. They knew that the north still drew him, for at night they sometimes heard him crying softly; and when the north wind blew and the bite of frost was in the air, he would let out a sad

cry like a long wolf howl. Yet he never barked; nothing could make him bark.

• • •

Wolf paused by Madge and Walt for a quick pat on the head. Then he glided quickly ahead of them. Both Madge and Walt seemed to be thinking about Wolf as they followed him down the path. It was a long way to the county road, and when they came to a clearing, they sat down on a log.

A tiny stream flowed out of the forest, dropped over a slippery stone, and ran across the path at their feet. From the valley arose the song of meadowlarks, while around them great yellow butterflies fluttered in and out, through sunshine and shadow.

They heard a sound from the path. It was a crunching of heavy feet. As Walt and Madge looked at each other, a man came into view around the turn of the trail. He

was sweaty. With a handkerchief in one hand he mopped his face, while in the other hand he carried a new hat. He was a well-built man, and his muscles seemed on the point of bursting out of the new black clothes he wore.

"Warm day," said Walt.

The man paused and nodded. "I guess I ain't much used to the warmth," he said. "I'm used to cold weather."

"You don't find any of that in this country," Walt laughed.

"Should say not," the man answered. "And I ain't lookin' for it either. I'm trying to find my sister. Maybe you know where she lives. Her name's Johnson, Mrs. William Johnson."

"You must be her Yukon brother!" Madge cried, her eyes bright with interest. "We've heard so much about you."

"Yes ma'am, that's me," he answered. "My name's Miller, Skiff Miller. I just thought I'd surprise her."

- Read the rest of the story to yourselves and be ready to answer some questions.

After all students have finished reading:

- In which direction did Wolf always go when he was set free? **North.**
- How far could he travel on the first day's run? *Idea:* As much as 150 miles.
- How far would he travel each day after the first day? *Idea:* A hundred miles.
- One time he went all the way to Oregon. Was that the farthest he ever went? **No.**
- At another time, which state did he reach? **Washington.**
- In which direction is Washington from California? **North.**
- When Wolf was returned from these trips, would he be friendly? **No.**
- The Irvines figured out that Wolf must have been coming from south of Glen Ellen when he first came to their cottage. What had made them think that he had come from the south? *Idea:* Because he always went north.
- A neighbor of the Irvine's had an idea about Wolf. Where did she think he had come from? *Idea:* The Yukon.
- As Madge and Walt went down the path, they stopped to rest. Who did they meet? *Idea:* Skiff Miller.
- Was Skiff Miller used to hot weather? **No.**
- Where had he just come from? *Idea:* The Yukon.
- Who was he looking for? *Ideas:* His sister; Mrs. Johnson.

Award 4 points or have the students reread to the error limit sign.

INDEPENDENT WORK

Do all the items in your skillbook and workbook for lesson 57.

ANSWER KEY FOR WORKBOOK

Review Items

1. Write **fact** or **fiction** for each item.

   a. Wolves do not bark. *fact*
   b. California has a long chain of mountains running through it. *fact*

   c. Animals talk to their masters. *fiction*
   d. Some dogs can travel one hundred miles in one day. *fact*
   e. All dogs travel north when they run away. *fiction*

2. Write **true** or **false** for each item.

   a. Redwood trees are usually short. *false*
   b. California is one of the smallest states in the United States. *false*

   c. Los Angeles is a city in southern California. *true*
   e. When you go up a mountain, the plants change. *true*

WORKCHECK AND AWARDING POINTS

1. *Read the questions and answers for the skillbook and workbook.*

2. *Award points for independent work as follows:*

0 errors	6 points
2 errors	4 points
3, 4, or 5 errors	2 points
5 or more errors	0 points

3. *Award bonus points as follows:*

Correcting missed items or getting all items right	2 points
Doing the writing assignment acceptably	2 points

ANSWER KEY FOR SKILLBOOK

PART C

1. *Idea:* Fred went shopping.
2. *Idea:* Donna rescued the cat.
3. *Idea:* The girls went sailing.
4. *Idea:* The people worked in the yard.

PART D

5. California
6. a. *Idea:* By his coloring
   b. Poor shape
   c. *Idea:* Not friendly
   d. *Idea:* Disappeared
   e. North
7. a. North
   b. Wolf
8. a. A collar
   b. where to send Wolf
9. a. Washington
   b. 150
   c. 100
10. a. *Ideas:* A Yukon dog; a sled dog
    b. *Idea:* A sad cry
11. a. south
    b. *Idea:* He always went north
12. a. Skiff Miller
    b. Black
    c. Strong
    d. *Ideas:* The Yukon; Canada
    e. *Ideas:* His sister; Mrs. Johnson
13. Bark

PART E

14. a. Rover would neither bark nor bite.
    b. The baby is neither crawling nor crying.
15. a. impatient
    b. disgraceful
    c. treacherous
    d. top
    e. sneer
    f. naked
    g. wrestled
    h. descended
    i. guilty

Lesson 58

Lesson 58

PART A   Word Lists

1	2	3	4	5
potato	forelegs	droopy	**Vocabulary words**	**Vocabulary words**
erect	footpads	cripple	1. miracle	1. erect
decisive	hardship	tense	2. spring	2. reappear
misery	heartbreaking	intense	3. fangs	3. decisive
		owl	4. effortlessly	4. misery
		crippled	5. halt	5. tussle
			6. forelegs	6. intense
			7. hardships	

PART B   Main Idea Passages

Write the main idea sentence for each of these passages.

1. Roses grow in the summer.
   Pansies grow in the summer.
   Buttercups grow in the summer.

2. Flowers produce oxygen.
   Trees produce oxygen.
   Grass produces oxygen.

3. Trucks need gasoline.
   Cars need gasoline.
   Motorcycles need gasoline.

WORD PRACTICE AND VOCABULARY

EXERCISE 1   Word practice

1. Everybody, find lesson 58, part A in your skillbook. *Wait*. Touch under each word in column 1 as I read it.
2. The first word is **potato.**
3. Next word. **Erect.**
4. *Repeat step 3 for each remaining word in column 1.*
5. Your turn. Read the first word. *Signal*. **Potato.**
6. Next word. *Signal*. **Erect.**
7. *Repeat step 6 for each remaining word in column 1.*
8. *Repeat the words in column 1 until firm.*

EXERCISE 2   Word family

1. Everybody, touch column 2. *Check*.
   All those words are made up of two shorter words. Touch under the first word. *Pause*. What word? *Signal*. **Forelegs.**
2. Next word. *Pause*. What word? *Signal*. **Footpads.**
3. *Repeat step 2 for each remaining word in column 2.*
4. *Repeat the words in column 2 until firm.*

EXERCISE 3   Word practice

1. Everybody, touch under the first word in column 3. *Pause*. What word? *Signal*. **Droopy.**
2. Next word. *Pause*. What word? *Signal*. **Cripple.**
3. *Repeat step 2 for each remaining word in column 3.*
4. *Repeat the words in column 3 until firm.*

EXERCISE 4   Vocabulary review

Task A
1. Everybody, touch column 4. *Check*.
   First you're going to read the words in column 4. Then we'll talk about what they mean.
2. Touch under the first word. *Pause*. What word? *Signal*. **Miracle.**
3. Next word. *Pause*. What word? *Signal*. **Spring.**
4. *Repeat step 3 for each remaining word in column 4.*
5. *Repeat the words in column 4 until firm.*

Task B
You've learned the meanings for all these words. Word 1 is **miracle.** *Call on a student.* What is a **miracle?** *Idea:* A very strange event that cannot be explained.

Task C
Word 2 is **spring.** *Call on a student.* What is a **spring?** *Idea:* A place where fresh water bubbles out of the ground.

Task D
Word 3 is **fangs.** *Call on a student.* What are **fangs?** *Idea:* Long, pointed teeth.

Task E
Word 4 is **effortlessly.** *Call on a student.* When you do something **effortlessly,** how do you do it? *Idea:* So that it looks like you use no effort.

Task F
Word 5 is **halt.** *Call on a student.* What does **halt** mean? *Idea:* Stop.

Task G
Word 6 is **forelegs.** *Call on a student.* What are **forelegs.** *Idea:* Front legs.

Task H
Word 7 is **hardships.** *Call on a student.* What are **hardships?** *Idea:* Severe difficulties.

EXERCISE 5   Vocabulary development

Task A
1. Everybody, touch column 5. *Check*.
   First you're going to read the words in column 5. Then we'll talk about what they mean.
2. Touch under the first word. *Pause*. What word? *Signal*. **Erect.**
3. Next word. *Pause*. What word? *Signal*. **Reappear.**
4. *Repeat step 3 for each remaining word in column 5.*
5. *Repeat the words in column 5 until firm.*

Task B
1. Now let's talk about what those words mean. Word 1 is **erect.** When something is **erect,** it stands up straight. Here's another way of saying **The dog's ears stood up straight: The dog's ears were erect.** Everybody, what's another way of saying **The dog's ears stood up straight?** *Signal*. **The dog's ears were erect.**
2. Everybody, what's another way of saying **She held her head up straight?** *Signal*. **She held her head erect.**

Lesson 58

PART A   Word Lists

1	2	3	4	5
potato	forelegs	droopy	**Vocabulary words**	**Vocabulary words**
erect	footpads	cripple	1. miracle	1. erect
decisive	hardship	tense	2. spring	2. reappear
misery	heartbreaking	intense	3. fangs	3. decisive
		owl	4. effortlessly	4. misery
		crippled	5. halt	5. tussle
			6. forelegs	6. intense
			7. hardships	

PART B   Main Idea Passages

Write the main idea sentence for each of these passages.

1. Roses grow in the summer.
   Pansies grow in the summer.
   Buttercups grow in the summer.

2. Flowers produce oxygen.
   Trees produce oxygen.
   Grass produces oxygen.

3. Trucks need gasoline.
   Cars need gasoline.
   Motorcycles need gasoline.

Task C

1. Word 2 is **reappear.** When something **reappears,** it comes back into sight. Here's another way of saying **She came back into sight: She reappeared.**
   Everybody, what's another way of saying **She came back into sight?** *Signal.*
   She reappeared.

2. Listen. **The car went around the corner and then came back into sight.**
   Everybody, what's another way of saying **The car went around the corner and then came back into sight?** *Signal.*
   The car went around the corner and then reappeared.

Task D

1. Word 3 is **decisive.** If your actions look as if you've made up your mind, your actions are **decisive.** Everybody, what do we call actions that look as if you've made up your mind? *Signal.* **Decisive actions.**

2. Running that looks as if you've made up your mind is decisive running. Everybody, what do we call running that looks as if you've made up your mind? *Signal.* **Decisive running.**

Task E

Word 4 is **misery.** When you feel **miserable,** you are in **misery.** Everybody, what are you in when you feel miserable? *Signal.* **Misery.**

Task F

Word 5 is **tussle.** When you **tussle** with somebody, you **wrestle** with that person. Everybody, what are you doing when you wrestle with a friend? *Signal.*
Tussling with a friend.

Task G

1. Word 6 is **intense.** When something is **intense,** it is very strong.
   Everybody, what's another way of saying **Her concentration was very strong?** *Signal.*
   Her concentration was intense.

2. Everybody, what's another way of saying **The scent was very strong.** *Signal.*
   The scent was intense.

3. Everybody, what's another way of saying **Her desire to win was very strong?** *Signal.*
   Her desire to win was intense.

EXERCISE 6   Main idea passages

1. Everybody, find part B in your skillbook. *Wait.* Look at passage 1.
   - You're going to figure out the main idea of that passage. To figure out the main idea, you do the same thing you do with pictures. First you tell what is doing the action. Then you tell the main thing the group of things does.
   - I'll read the passage.
     Roses grow in the summer. Pansies grow in the summer. Buttercups grow in the summer.
   - The passage names three different things that do something.
     What are the three things that are named?
     Roses, pansies and buttercups.
   - What's a class name for roses, pansies and buttercups? **Flowers.**
   - Now tell me what the flowers do.
     They grow in the summer.
     Yes, they grow in the summer.
   - Say the whole main-idea sentence.
     Flowers grow in the summer.

2. Everybody, look at passage 2.
   - You're going to figure out the main idea of that passage. Remember, first you tell what is doing the action. Then you tell what that group of things does.
   - *Call on a student to read passage 2.*
     Flowers produce oxygen. Trees produce oxygen. Grass produces oxygen.
   - The passage names three different things that do something.
     What are the three things that are named?
     Flowers, trees, and grass.
   - What's a class name for flowers, trees, and grass? **Plants.**
   - Now tell me what the plants do.
     They produce oxygen.
   - Say the whole main-idea sentence.
     Plants produce oxygen.

3. Later you will write main-idea sentences for all the passages in part B.

Lesson 58

Brown Wolf

PART 2

Madge stood up to show Skiff Miller the way to his sister's house. Ⓐ "Do you see that redwood?" she said, pointing up the canyon. "Take the litte trail that turns off to the right. It's the shortcut to her house. You can't miss it."

"Yes,'m, thank you, ma'am," he said.

"We'd like to hear you tell about the Yukon," Madge said. "Could we come over one day while you are at your sister's? Or, better yet, won't you come over and have dinner with us?"

"Yes'm, thank you, ma'am," he mumbled. Then he continued, "I ain't stopping long. I have to be pulling north again. I go out on tonight's train."

Madge was about to say that it was too bad, when Wolf trotted into the clearing.

Skiff Miller froze. He had eyes only for the dog, and a great wonder came into his face. "Well, I'll be hanged," he said, slowly and solemnly.

He sat down on the log, leaving Madge standing. At the sound of his voice, Wolf's ears had flattened down, then his mouth had opened in a laugh. He trotted slowly up to the stranger and first smelled his hands, then licked them. Ⓑ

Skiff Miller patted the dog's head and slowly and solemnly repeated, "Well, I'll be hanged."

"Excuse me, ma'am," he said the next moment. "I was just surprised, that's all."

"We're surprised, too," she answered slowly. "We never saw Wolf act friendly toward a stranger."

"Is that what you call him—Wolf?" Miller asked.

Madge nodded. "But I can't understand his friendliness toward you—unless it's because you're from the Yukon. He's a Yukon dog, you know."

"Yes'm," Miller said, working away. He lifted one of Wolf's forelegs and examined the footpads, pressing them and denting them with his thumb. "Kind of soft," he remarked. "He ain't been on a trail for a long time." Ⓒ

"I say," Walt broke in, "it's remarkable the way he lets you handle him."

Skiff Miller got up and asked, sharply, "How long have you had him?"

But just then the dog, squirming and rubbing against the newcomer's legs, opened his mouth and barked. It was a loud bark, brief and joyous, but a bark.

222   Lesson 58   Textbook

EXERCISE 7   Decoding and comprehension

1. Everybody, turn to page 222 in your textbook. *Wait. Call on a student.* What's the error limit for this lesson?
2. *Call on individual students to read. Present the tasks specified for each circled letter.*

Ⓐ Where were they? *Ideas:* In a clearing; near a stream.

Ⓑ Is this the way that Wolf greets strangers? **No.**

• Why do you think Wolf is behaving this way? *Idea:* He knows something about Skiff Miller.

Ⓒ How does Skiff know that Wolf hasn't been on a trail for a long time? *Idea:* The pads of his paws are soft.

• What happens to the pads of a dog's paw when he's on a trail? *Idea:* They get tough.

Lesson 58   Textbook   **223**

Lesson 58   **271**

Walt and Madge stared at each other. The miracle had happened. Wolf had barked.

"It's the first time he ever barked," Madge said.

"First time I ever heard him, too," Miller replied.

Madge smiled at Miller. "Of course," she said, "since you have only seen him for five minutes."

Skiff Miller looked at her. "I thought you understood," he said slowly. "I thought you'd figured it out from the way he acted. He's my dog. His name ain't Wolf. It's Brown." Ⓓ ★6 ERRORS★

"Oh, Walt!" Madge cried to her husband.

Walt demanded, "How do you know he's your dog?"

"Because he is," was the reply.

"That's no proof," Walt said sharply.

In his slow way, Skiff Miller looked at the dog, then said, "The dog's mine. I raised him and I guess I ought to know. Look here. I'll prove it to you."

Skiff Miller turned to the dog. "Brown!" His voice rang out sharply, and at the sound the dog's ears flattened down. "Gee!" The dog made a swinging turn to the right. "Now mush on!" Abruptly the dog stopped turning and started straight ahead, halting obediently at command.

"I can do it with whistles," Skiff Miller said proudly. "He was my lead dog. Somebody stole him from me three years ago, and I've been looking for him ever since."

224   Lesson 58   Textbook

Madge's voice trembled as she asked, "But—but are you going to take him away with you?"

The man nodded.

Madge asked, "Back into that awful Yukon?"

He nodded and added, "Oh, it ain't so bad as all that. Look at me. Pretty healthy man—ain't I?"

"But the dogs! The terrible hardship, the heartbreaking work, the starvation, the frost! Oh, I've read about it and I know."

Miller said nothing.

Madge paused a moment, then said, "Why not leave him here? He is happy. He'll never suffer from hunger—you know that. He'll never suffer from cold and hardship. Everything is soft and gentle here. He will never feel a whip again. And as for the weather—why, it never snows here."

"Yes, it's hot here," Skiff Miller said and laughed.

"But answer me," Madge continued. "What do you have to offer him in that Yukon life?"

"Food, when I've got it, and that's most of the time," came the answer.

"And the rest of the time?"

"No food."

"And the work?"

"Yes, plenty of work," Miller blurted out impatiently. "Work without end, and hunger, and frost, and all the rest of the hardships—that's what he'll get when he comes with me. But he likes it. He's used to it. He knows that life. He was born to it and brought up in it. And you don't know

anything about it—you don't know what you're talking about. That's where the dog belongs, and that's where he'll be happiest."

"The dog doesn't go," Walt announced. "So there is no need for any more talk."

"What's that?" Skiff Miller demanded. His brows lowered and his face became flushed.

"I said, the dog doesn't go, and that settles it," Walt said. "I don't believe he's your dog. You may have seen him sometime. You may have sometimes driven him for his owner. But his obeying the ordinary driving commands of the trail doesn't prove that he is yours. Any dog in the Yukon would obey you as he obeyed. Besides, he is probably a valuable dog, and that might explain why you want to have him."

Skiff Miller's huge muscles bulged under the black cloth of his black coat as he carefully looked Walt up and down. His face hardened, then he said, "I reckon there's nothing in sight to prevent me from taking the dog right here and now."

Walt's face flushed, and the striking muscles of his arms and shoulders seemed to stiffen and grow tense. Madge quickly stepped between the two men.

"Maybe Mr. Miller is right," she said. "I am afraid that he is. Wolf does seem to know him, and certainly he answers to the name of 'Brown.' He made friends with him instantly, and you know that's something he never did with anybody before. Besides, look at the way he barked. He was just bursting with joy."

"Joy over what?" asked Walt.

"Finding Mr. Miller, I think," answered Madge.

Walt's striking muscles relaxed, and his shoulders seemed to droop with hopelessness. "I guess you're right, Madge," he said. "Wolf isn't Wolf, but Brown. He must belong to Mr. Miller."

Lesson 58   Textbook   225

Ⓓ Why is Wolf friendly toward Miller? *Idea:* He knows Miller.

• What's Wolf's real name? **Brown.**

• How do you think Madge and Walt feel? *Ideas:* Sad; scared; worried.

• Read the rest of the story to yourselves and be ready to answer some questions.

After all students have finished reading:

• What did Miller do to prove that the dog was his dog? *Idea:* Gave him trail commands.

• How long ago had the dog been stolen from Miller? **Three years.**

• What did Miller want to do with Wolf? *Idea:* Take Wolf with him.

• What did Madge want Miller to do with Wolf? *Idea:* Leave him with her.

• Which life would be more pleasant for Wolf, life in California or life in the Yukon? **Life in California.**

• Would Wolf get fed regularly in the Yukon? **No.**

• Why did Miller think that the dog would be happiest in the Yukon? *Ideas:* Because he was born there; he's used to it.

• At first, Walt argued with Miller about the dog. Why did Walt think that Miller didn't prove anything by showing that the dog would obey his commands like **Gee** and **Mush on?** *Idea:* Wolf could have learned those commands from someone else.

• Who said that the dog probably did belong to Miller? **Madge.**

• What reasons did she give for drawing that conclusion? *Ideas:* Wolf knew Miller; Wolf answered to the name of 'Brown'; he made friends with Miller; he barked.

• So what do you think is going to happen to the dog? *Response:* Student preference.

• How do you think that makes the Irvines feel? *Idea:* Sad.

•. Show me how you look when your shoulder's droop. *Check.*

Award 4 points or have the students reread to the error limit sign.

INDEPENDENT WORK

Do all the items in your skillbook and workbook for lesson 58.

ANSWER KEY FOR WORKBOOK

Story Items

1. Write whether each thing could happen to Wolf in the **Yukon** or in **California**.
   a. He would be hungry.
      Yukon
   b. He would be warm.
      California
   c. He would never feel a whip.
      California
   d. He would work all day.
      Yukon
   e. He would be cold.
      Yukon
   f. He would be well fed.
      California

Crossword Puzzle

To work the puzzle, read an item and figure out which word the item describes. Then write the word in the puzzle. Complete the entire puzzle.

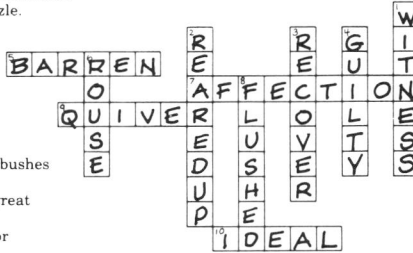

BARREN / AFFECTION / QUIVER / IDEAL
(crossword grid answers: BARREN, AFFECTION, QUIVER, IDEAL, ROUSE, REFED, RELUCTANT, GULITY, WITNESS, REUP, HE)

Across

5. A hill with no trees and no bushes is a _____ hill.
7. She loved her cat and had great _____ for it.
9. Another word for **tremble** or **vibrate**.
10. She was so good in school that she was an _____ student.

Down

1. When you see a race, you _____ that race.
2. The horse _____ _____ on its hind legs and threw its rider off. (2 words)
3. At last, he began to _____ from his sickness.
4. A person who commits a crime is _____ of that crime.
6. He was sleeping soundly and no one could _____ him.
8. When you blush, your face is _____.

WORKCHECK AND AWARDING POINTS

1. *Read the questions and answers for the skillbook and workbook.*
2. *Award points for independent work as follows:*

0 errors	6 points
2 errors	4 points
3, 4, or 5 errors	2 points
5 or more errors	0 points

3. *Award bonus points as follows:*

Correcting missed items or getting all items right	2 points
Doing the writing assignment acceptably	2 points

ANSWER KEY FOR SKILLBOOK

PART B

1. *Idea:* Flowers grow in the summer.
2. *Idea:* Plants produce oxygen.
3. *Idea:* Vehicles need gasoline.

PART C

4. *Idea:* The people are waiting for a bus.
5. *Idea:* Rhonda fixed a flat tire.

PART D

6. a. Skiff Miller
   b. Bark
   c. *Idea:* Because they had never heard Wolf bark
7. a. Skiff Miller
   b. Brown
   c. *Idea:* By showing that Wolf followed his commands
   d. Gee; Mush on
8. a. *Idea:* Back to the Yukon
   b. In California
   c. *Idea:* In the Yukon
   d. *Idea:* Because he used to live there
9. *Any two:* Wolf would never be hungry; never be cold; never suffer hardships; never feel a whip.
10. a. No
    b. *Idea:* Because they were the commands that most dogs in the Yukon could follow
    c. *Idea:* To prevent them from fighting
11. a. Yes
    b. *Any two:* Wolf seemed to know Miller; Wolf answers to the name of Brown; Wolf made friends with Miller right away; Wolf barked when he saw Miller
    c. Yes

PART E

12. a. miserable
    b. clear and easy to see
    c. trade
    d. hurled
    e. got its strength back
    f. ideal
    g. put up with
    h. clutched

Lesson 59

WORD PRACTICE AND VOCABULARY

EXERCISE 1   Word practice

1. Everybody, find lesson 59, part A in your skillbook. *Wait.* Touch under each word in column 1 as I read it.
2. The first word is **reluctant.**
3. Next word. **Determination.**
4. *Repeat step 3 for each remaining word in column 1.*
5. Your turn. Read the first word. *Signal.* **Reluctant.**
6. Next word. *Signal.* **Determination.**
7. *Repeat step 6 for each remaining word in column 1.*
8. *Repeat the words in column 1 until firm.*

EXERCISE 2   Word family

1. Everybody, touch column 2. *Check.* All of those words have the sound **ur** in them. Touch under the first word. *Pause.* What word? *Signal.* **Curled.**
2. Next word. *Pause.* What word? *Signal.* **Gurgled.**
3. *Repeat step 2 for each remaining word in column 2.*
4. *Repeat the words in column 2 until firm.*

EXERCISE 3   Word practice

1. Everybody, touch under the first word in column 3. *Pause.* What word? *Signal.* **Picnic.**
2. Next word. *Pause.* What word? *Signal.* **Runt.**
3. *Repeat step 2 for each remaining word in column 3.*
4. *Repeat the words in column 3 until firm.*

EXERCISE 4   Vocabulary review

TASK A

1. Everybody, touch column 4. *Check.* First you're going to read the words in column 4. Then we'll talk about what they mean.
2. Touch under the first word. *Pause.* What word? *Signal.* **Reappear.**
3. Next word. *Pause.* What word? *Signal.* **Decisive.**
4. *Repeat step 3 for each remaining word in column 4.*
5. *Repeat the words in column 4 until firm.*

Task B

1. You've learned the meaning for all these words. Word 1 is **reappear.** *Call on a student.* What does **reappear** mean? *Idea:* Come back into sight.
2. Everybody, what's another way of saying **The car went around the corner and then came back into sight?** *Signal.* **The car went around the corner and then reappeared.**

Task C

Word 2 is **decisive.** *Call on a student.* What does **decisive** mean? *Idea:* You make up your mind about something.

Task D

Word 3 is **misery.** *Call on a student.* When you are in **misery,** how do you feel? *Idea:* Miserable.

Task E

1. Word 4 is **intense.** *Call on a student.* What does **intense** mean? *Idea:* Very strong.
2. Everybody, what's another way of saying **Her concentration was very strong?** *Signal.* **Her concentration was intense.**

Task F

Word 5 is **tussle.** *Call on a student.* What does **tussle** mean? *Idea:* Wrestle.

Task G

1. Word 6 is **erect.** *Call on a student.* What does **erect** mean? *Idea:* Standing up straight.
2. Everybody, what's another way of saying **His ears stood up straight?** *Signal.* **His ears were erect.**

EXERCISE 5 Vocabulary development

Task A

1. Everybody, touch column 5. *Check.*
   First you're going to read the words in column 5. Then we'll talk about what they mean.
2. Touch under the first word. *Pause.*
   What word? *Signal.* **Litter.**
3. Next word. *Pause.* What word? *Signal.* **Reluctant.**
4. *Repeat step 3 for each remaining word in column 5.*
5. *Repeat the words in column 5 until firm.*

Task B

Now let's talk about what those words mean. Word 1 is **litter.** A **litter** is a group of puppies that are born at the same time. Sometimes a mother dog has a **litter** of more than ten puppies. We call a group of eleven puppies born at the same time a **litter** of eleven puppies. Everybody, what do we call a group of twelve puppies born at the same time? *Signal.*
A litter of twelve puppies.

Task C

1. Word 2 is **reluctant.** When you are **reluctant** to do something, you don't want to do it very much. Here's another way of saying **He really didn't want to go to the party: He was reluctant to go to the party.**
   Everybody, what's another way of saying **He really didn't want to go to the party?**
   Signal. **He was reluctant to go to the party.**
2. Everybody, what's another way of saying **She really didn't want to eat spinach?**
   Signal. **She was reluctant to eat spinach.**

Task D

Word 3 is **limp.** When you walk with a **limp,** you have trouble moving one of your legs.

Task E

Word 4 is **crippled.** When people are **crippled,** something is wrong with their legs or their back so they have trouble walking. Some crippled people can't walk at all. Other crippled people can walk, but they walk with a limp.

Task F

Word 5 is **sensitive.** Something is **sensitive** if it can react to things that are very faint. A **sensitive** nose can react to smells that are very faint. Everybody, what would we call eyes that can react to images that are very faint?
Signal. **Sensitive eyes.**

Task G

Word 6 is **determination.** When you do something with great **determination,** you do it as if nothing will stop you. If you run as if nothing will stop you, you run with great determination. Everybody, what are you doing when you work as if nothing will stop you?
Signal. **Working with great determination.**

EXERCISE 6 Vocabulary from context

Task A

1. Everybody, touch column 6. *Check.*
   First you're going to read the words in column 6. Then we'll talk about what they mean.
2. Touch under the first word. *Pause.*
   What word? *Signal.* **Loafed.**
3. Next word. *Pause.* What word? *Signal.* **Afford.**
4. *Repeat step 3 for* **operated.**
5. *Repeat the words in column 6 until firm.*

Task B

1. Everybody, find part B in your skillbook. *Check.*
   I'll read those sentences. You figure out what the underlined part in each sentence means.
2. Sentence one: He was so lazy that he always loafed when he was supposed to be working.
   Call on a student. What could **loafed** mean?
   Idea: Didn't work.
3. *Repeat step 2 for each remaining sentence.*
   Answer Key: Sentence 2. Idea: Have enough money for.
   Sentence 3. Idea: Worked on.

EXERCISE 7 Main idea passages

1. Everybody, find part C in your skillbook. *Wait.*
   Look at passage 1.
● You're going to figure out the main idea of that passage. To figure out the main idea, you do the same thing you do with pictures. First you tell what is doing the action. Then you tell the main thing the group of things does.
● I'll read the passage.
   Wild deer live in the jungle. Wild tigers live in the jungle. Wild apes live in the jungle.
● The passage names three different things that do something.
● What are the three things that are named?
   Wild deer, wild tigers and wild apes.
● What's a class name for wild deer, wild tigers and wild apes? **Wild animals.**
● Now tell me what the wild animals do?
   They live in the jungle.
   Yes, they live in the jungle.
● Say the whole main-idea sentence.
   Wild animals live in the jungle.
2. *Call on a student to read passage 2.*
   Vanessa dug a hole. Then Vanessa picked up a tree. Vanessa put the tree in the hole.
● Who does the action in that passage? **Vanessa.**
● Vanessa did a lot of different things. But she did only one main thing. What was that? *Idea:* She planted a tree.
   Yes, she planted a tree.
● Say the whole main-idea sentence.
   Vanessa planted a tree.
3. Later you will write main-idea sentences for all the passages in part C.

Lesson 59

Brown Wolf

PART 3

The three people were silent for a moment, then Madge brightened up and said, "Perhaps Mr. Miller will sell us the dog. We can buy him." Ⓐ

Skiff Miller shook his head. "I had five dogs," he said. "Wolf was the leader. Somebody once offered me twelve hundred dollars for him. I didn't sell him then, and I ain't selling him now. Besides, I think a mighty lot of that dog. I've been looking for him for three years. I couldn't believe my eyes when I saw him just now. I thought I was dreaming. It was too good to be true."

"But the dog," Madge said quickly. "You haven't considered the dog."

Skiff Miller looked puzzled.

"Have you thought about him?" she asked.

"I don't know what you're driving at," Miller said.

"Maybe the dog has some choice in the matter," Madge went on. "Maybe he has his likes and dislikes. You haven't considered him. You give him no choice. It hasn't even entered your mind that he might prefer California to Alaska. You consider only what you like. You treat him like a sack of potatoes." Ⓑ

This was a new way of looking at it, and Miller's face hardened as he started to think to himself.

"If you really love him," Madge continued, "you would want him to be happy, no matter where he is."

Miller asked, "Do you think he'd sooner stay in California?"

Madge nodded her head. "I'm sure of it."

Skiff Miller started thinking out loud. "He was a good worker. He's done a lot of work for me. He never loafed on me, and he was great at getting a new team into shape. He's got a head on him. He can do everything but talk. He knows we're talking about him."

The dog was lying at Skiff Miller's feet, his head down close to his paws, his ears erect and listening. His eyes were quick and eager to follow the sounds of one person and then the other.

Miller went on. "There's a lot of work in him yet. He'll be good for years to come."

Skiff Miller opened his mouth and closed it again without speaking. Finally he said, "I'll tell you what I'll do. Your remarks, ma'am, make sense. He has

worked hard, and maybe he's earned a soft place and has got a right to choose. Anyway, we'll leave it up to him. Whatever he says, goes. You people stay right here sitting down. I'll say goodbye, and I'll walk off. If he wants to stay, he can stay. If he wants to come with me, let him come. I won't call him to come and don't you call him to come back." Ⓒ ★7 ERRORS★

Miller paused a moment, then added, "Only, you must play fair. Don't call him after my back is turned."

"We'll play fair," Madge said. "I don't know how to thank you."

"I don't see that you've got any reason to thank me," he replied. "Brown ain't decided yet. Now you won't mind if I go

away slow? It's only fair, since I'll be out of sight in a hundred yards."

Madge agreed, and added, "and I promise you that we won't do anything to try to change his mind."

"Well, then, I might as well be getting along," Skiff Miller said. And he got ready to leave.

Wolf lifted his head quickly, and still more quickly got to his feet when Miller shook hands with Madge. Wolf sprang up on his hind legs, resting his forepaws on Madge's hip and at the same time, licking Skiff Miller's hand. When Miller shook hands with Walt, Wolf repeated his act, resting his weight on Walt and licking both men's hands.

STORY READING

EXERCISE 8   Decoding and comprehension

1. Everybody, turn to page 226 in your textbook. *Wait. Call on a student.* What's the error limit for this story? **7 errors.**

2. *Call on individual students to read. Present the tasks specified for each circled letter.*

Ⓐ Who are the three people? *Idea:* Skiff Miller, Madge and Walt.

● Had the people agreed about which person Wolf really belonged to? **Yes.**

● Which person? **Skiff Miller.**

● What suggestion is Madge making now? *Idea:* Maybe Skiff will sell Wolf to the Irvines.

Ⓑ Madge is arguing that the dog should have a choice. Tell me what you would do to give the dog a choice about where he wanted to stay or who he wanted to be with. *Call on several students. Responses:* Student preference.

Ⓒ What's Miller going to do? *Idea:* Walk away and let Wolf decide whether to stay or follow.

● What are Madge and Walt going to do? *Idea:* Sit still and not say anything to Wolf.

● How will they know what choice Wolf makes? *Idea:* He will either stay with Madge and Walt or follow Miller.

● Read the rest of the story to yourselves and be ready to answer some questions.

After all students have finished reading:

● What did Madge and Walt agree to do when Miller walked away? *Idea:* Not speak to Wolf, or make any movement toward him.

"It ain't no picnic, I can tell you that," Miller said. These were his last words, as he turned and went slowly up the trail.

Wolf watched him go about twenty feet, as though waiting for the man to turn and come back. Then, with a quick, low whine, Wolf sprang after him, caught up to him, gently grabbed Miller's hand between his teeth, and tried gently to make him stop.

But Miller did not stop. Wolf raced back to where Walt Irvine sat, catching his coat sleeve in his teeth and trying to drag him toward Miller.

Wolf wanted to be in two places at the same time, with the old master and the new, but the distance between them was increasing. He sprang about excitedly, making short nervous leaps and twists, now toward one person, now toward the other, not knowing his own mind, wanting both and unable to choose, uttering quick, sharp whines and beginning to pant.

He sat down, thrust his nose upward, and opened his mouth wide. He was ready to howl.

But just as the howl was about to burst from his throat, he closed his mouth and looked long and steadily at Miller's back. Suddenly Wolf turned his head, and looked just as steadily at Walt. The dog received no sign, no suggestion and no clue as to what he should do.

As Wolf glanced ahead to where the old master was nearing the curve of the trail, Wolf became excited again. He sprang to his feet with a whine, and then, struck by a new idea, turned toward Madge. He had ignored her up to now, but now, he went over to her and snuggled his head in her lap, nudging her arm with his nose—an old trick of his when begging for favors. He backed away from her and began to twist playfully. All his body, from his twinkling eyes and flattened ears to the wagging tail, begged her to tell him what to do. But Madge did not move.

The dog stopped playing. He was saddened by the coldness of these people who had never been cold before.

He turned and gently gazed after the old master. Skiff Miller was rounding the curve. In a moment he would be gone from view. Yet he never turned his head, plodding straight onward, as though he had no interest in what was occurring behind his back.

And then he went out of view. Wolf waited for him to reappear. He waited a long minute, silently, without movement, as though turned to stone. He barked once, and waited. Then he turned and trotted back to Walt Irvine. He sniffed his hand and dropped down heavily at his feet, watching the trail where it curved from view.

The tiny stream that slipped down the stone seemed to gurgle more loudly than before. Except for the meadowlarks, there was no other sound. The great yellow butterflies drifted silently through the sunshine and lost themselves in the sleepy shadows. Madge smiled at her husband.

A few minutes later Wolf got on his feet. His movements were decisive. He did

not glance at the man and woman. His eyes were fixed on the trail. He had made up his mind. They knew it. And they knew that they had lost.

Wolf started to trot away, and Madge had to force herself not to call him back. She remembered the promise she had made to Skiff Miller. Walt's solemn look showed that he also remembered the promise.

Wolf's trot broke into a run. He made leaps that were longer and longer. Not once did he turn his head. He cut sharply across the curve of the trail and was gone.

- **In the story, when Miller walked off, he said, "It ain't no picnic." What did he mean?** *Idea:* It was a very hard thing for him to do.
- **Did Madge and Walt keep their promise? Yes.**
- **As Miller started to walk away, Wolf ran to him and then did something to Miller. What did he do?** *Idea:* Took Miller's hand in his mouth and tried to make him stop.
- **Why?** *Idea:* Because he didn't want Miller to go.
- **Then Wolf ran to Walt. What did Wolf try to do to Walt?** *Idea:* Drag him after Miller.
- **Why?** *Idea:* Because he wanted Miller and Walt to stay together.
- **Then Wolf became excited. What was going through Wolf's head?** *Idea:* He didn't know whether to follow Miller or stay with the Irvines.
- **Wolf went to Madge. What did he do?** *Idea:* He nudged her arm with his nose.
- **What did Madge do?** *Idea:* Nothing.
- **Was Miller still in sight when Wolf finally made up his mind about what he should do? No.**
- **What did Wolf finally do.** *Idea:* Followed Miller.
- **How do you think the Irvines felt?** *Idea:* Sad.

Award 4 points or have the students reread to the error limit sign.

INDEPENDENT WORK

Do all the items in your skillbook and workbook for lesson 59.

ANSWER KEY FOR WORKBOOK

Review Items

1. Write which character each statement describes. Choose from **Madge, Skiff** or **Wolf.**
   a. This character wore black clothes.
      Skiff
   b. This character stepped between two people who were arguing.
      Madge
   c. This character was different shades of brown. *Wolf*
   d. This character wanted to be in two places at once. *Wolf*
   e. This character could command a dog sled. *Skiff*

Map Skills

2. Look at the map.

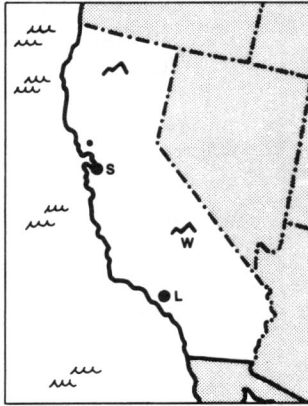

   a. Which state does the map show?
      California
   b. What's the name of city L?
      Los Angeles
   c. What's the name of city S?
      San Francisco
   d. What's the name of mountain W?
      Mt. Whitney

WORKCHECK AND AWARDING POINTS

1. *Read the questions and answers for the skillbook and workbook.*
2. *Award points for independent work as follows:*

0 errors	6 points
2 errors	4 points
3, 4, or 5 errors	2 points
5 or more errors	0 points

3. *Award bonus points as follows:*

Correcting missed items or getting all items right	2 points
Doing the story writing assignment acceptably	2 points

ANSWER KEY FOR SKILLBOOK

PART C

1. *Idea:* Wild animals live in the jungle.
2. *Idea:* Vanessa planted a tree.
3. *Idea:* The children go to Jefferson School everyday.
4. *Idea:* The plants in the fields come up to your waist.

PART D

5. *Idea:* Carlos won the race.
6. *Idea:* The cats are playing with string.

PART E

7. a. Madge
   b. *Idea:* Happy
   c. California
8. a. Skiff Miller
   b. *Idea:* Stay where they were
   c. *Idea:* Walk away
   d. *Idea:* No one
   e. *Idea:* The Irvines
   f. Skiff Miller
9. a. *Idea:* To make him stop or stay
   b. *Idea:* To keep the men together
   c. No
10. a. Madge
    b. *Idea:* She thought Wolf was going to stay
11. a. *Idea:* That Wolf was going with Miller
    b. *Idea:* Because she'd promised not to
    c. *Ideas:* With Miller; back to the Yukon

PART F

12. a. The table is neither tall nor made of wood.
    b. Her dress was neither long nor pretty.
13. a. eventually
    b. miserable
    c. embraced
    d. affection
    e. guilty
    f. saw
    g. lunged
    h. scenery
    i. barren
    j. miracle

Lesson 60

Lesson 60

PART A   Word Lists

1	2	3
North Carolina	cripple	**Vocabulary words**
coax	incredible	1. sensitive
Yodeler	snuggle	2. reluctant
	tickle	3. limp
	tussle	4. determination
	tumble	5. litter
		6. crippled
		7. loafed
		8. afford

PART B   Main Idea Passages

Write the main idea sentence for each of these passages.

1. Maria looked through a lens.
   Then Maria said, "Smile."
   Then Maria pushed a button on her camera.

2. The dog dug a hole.
   The dog put a bone in the hole.
   The dog filled the hole with dirt.

3. Tina put the pencil into the sharpener.
   Then Tina turned the handle.
   Tina pulled the pencil out of the sharpener.

4. Some hammers are made of steel.
   Some saws are made of steel.
   Some screwdrivers are made of steel.

5. All robins have feathers.
   All pigeons have feathers.
   All penguins have feathers.

WORD PRACTICE AND VOCABULARY

EXERCISE 1   Word practice

1. Everybody, find lesson 60, part A in your skillbook. *Wait.* Touch under the words in column 1 as I read them.
2. The words in the first line are **North Carolina.**
3. Next word. **Coax.**
4. *Repeat step 3 for* **Yodeler.**
5. Your turn. Read the first line. *Signal.* **North Carolina.**
6. Next word. *Signal.* **Coax.**
7. *Repeat step 6 for* **Yodeler.**
8. *Repeat the words in column 1 until firm.*

EXERCISE 2   Word family

1. Everybody, touch column 2. *Check.* All those words end with the sound **lll.** Touch under the first word. *Pause.* What word? *Signal.* **Cripple.**
2. Next word. *Pause.* What word? *Signal.* **Incredible.**
3. *Repeat step 2 for each remaining word in column 2.*
4. *Repeat the words in column 2 until firm.*

EXERCISE 3   Vocabulary review

Task A

1. Everybody, touch column 3. *Check.* First you're going to read the words in column 3. Then we'll talk about what they mean.
2. Touch under the first word. *Pause.* What word? *Signal.* **Sensitive.**
3. Next word. *Pause.* What word? *Signal.* **Reluctant.**
4. *Repeat step 3 for each remaining word in column 3.*
5. *Repeat the words in column 3 until firm.*

Task B

1. You've learned the meanings for all those words. Word 1 is **sensitive.** *Call on a student.* What does it mean when a person has a sensitive nose? *Idea:* The nose reacts to things that are very faint.
2. Everybody, what would we call eyes that can react to images that are very faint? *Signal.* **Sensitive eyes.**

Lesson 60

PART A Word Lists

1	2	3
North Carolina	cripple	**Vocabulary words**
coax	incredible	1. sensitive
Yodeler	snuggle	2. reluctant
	tickle	3. limp
	tussle	4. determination
	tumble	5. litter
		6. crippled
		7. loafed
		8. afford

PART B Main Idea Passages

Write the main idea sentence for each of these passages.

1. Maria looked through a lens.
   Then Maria said, "Smile."
   Then Maria pushed a button on her camera.

2. The dog dug a hole.
   The dog put a bone in the hole.
   The dog filled the hole with dirt.

3. Tina put the pencil into the sharpener.
   Then Tina turned the handle.
   Tina pulled the pencil out of the sharpener.

4. Some hammers are made of steel.
   Some saws are made of steel.
   Some screwdrivers are made of steel.

5. All robins have feathers.
   All pigeons have feathers.
   All penguins have feathers.

Task C

1. Word 2 is **reluctant.** *Call on a student.* What does **reluctant** mean? *Idea:* You don't want to do something very much.
2. Everybody, what's another way of saying **He really didn't want to go to the party?** *Signal.* He was reluctant to go to the party.
3. Everybody, what's another way of saying **She really didn't want to eat spinach?** *Signal.* **She was reluctant to eat spinach.**

Task D

Word 3 is **limp.** *Call on a student.*
What does it mean when somebody walks with a **limp**? *Idea:* That person has trouble moving one leg.

Task E

Word 4 is **determination.** *Call on a student.*
What does **determination** mean? *Idea:* You do something as if nothing will stop you.

Task F

Word 5 is **litter.** *Call on a student.*
What is a **litter?** *Idea:* A group of puppies born at the same time.

Task G

Word 6 is **crippled.** *Call on a student.*
What does it mean when somebody is **crippled?** *Idea:* That person has trouble walking.

Task H

Word 7 is **loafed.** *Call on a student.*
What does **loafed** mean? *Idea:* Spent time doing nothing.

Task I

Word 8 is **afford.** *Call on a student.*
What does **afford** mean? *Idea:* Have enough money for.

EXERCISE 4   Main idea passages

1. Everybody, find part B in your skillbook. *Wait.* Look at passage 1.
   ● I'll read passage 1.
   Maria looked through a lens. Then Maria said, "Smile." Then Maria pushed a button on her camera.
   ● Everybody, who does the action in this passage? *Signal.* **Maria.**
   ● Maria did a lot of different things. But she did only one main thing. *Call on a student.* What was that? *Idea:* She took a picture. Yes, she took a picture.
   ● Everybody, say the whole main-idea sentence. Get ready. *Signal.* **Maria took a picture.**
   Repeat until firm.
2. Later you will write the main-idea sentences for each of the passages in part B.

Lesson 60

Adventure on the Rocky Ridge
by Donna Clearwater
PART 1

Little Martha never knew that she was almost given away when she was still a tiny puppy. She didn't know she was a runt, the smallest puppy in a litter of twelve puppies. And she didn't know that her mother was a prize hunting dog and that the people who owned her mother raised the best hunting dogs in North Carolina. Little Martha didn't understand that the owners kept only the best puppies from each litter. Those were the biggest, and the strongest. The rest were given away.Ⓐ

Little Martha's first memories were ones of great happiness and terrible sadness. Her eyes were still closed when she was born and they remained closed for two weeks.Ⓑ During the time when her eyes were closed, Martha experienced great joy when she snuggled next to her warm mother. She also felt great despair because one of the large puppies in the litter would push her away, and Martha would lie there, shivering and cold.Ⓒ Martha would squeal little sounds of misery as she lay there, but her mother couldn't do much to help her. There were just too many puppies in the litter and the mother could not take care of all of them. So during her first days of life, Martha spent a lot of time aching from hunger and shivering from cold.

Julie Owl saved Martha. Julie was the twelve-year-old daughter of the people who owned Martha. Julie pleaded with her father not to give the little runt away. "I'll take care of her, daddy," she said. "Really, I will. I'll feed her and you'll see. She'll be a fine dog."

Mr. Owl was reluctant to keep the runt.Ⓓ "Julie," he explained, "why don't you take one of the other puppies? I'll give you any other puppy in the litter. But that runt won't be as healthy as the others. It will always be . . ." He stopped short in the middle of his explanation as he looked at Julie's pleading eyes. Julie was crippled. She could walk, but with a limp. Her father realized why she wanted that puppy. She saw herself in that puppy. So her father smiled and said, "Maybe you're right. Maybe that puppy will grow up to be a fine dog."Ⓔ

Julie's face brightened. She threw her arms around her father's neck. "Oh, thank you, Daddy!" she said in a choked voice. "I'll take very good care of her. And I'll name her Martha."

230   Lesson 60   Textbook

That was a very strange name for a hound dog. Outside in the kennel were dogs with the names of Boomer, Flash, Duke, and Queenie. There was Prince and Princess, Dodger, and Digger. But no dog with a name like Martha.

Julie mothered Martha. She got a little bottle and fed Martha six times a day. Julie made a warm bed for Martha next to her own bed. She held Martha and petted her and talked to her, and kissed her. She loved Martha the way a mother loves her baby.Ⓕ

All the dogs that Mr. Owl raised had an incredible sense of smell. Although Mr. Owl didn't know it at the time, Martha's nose was more sensitive than the nose of any other dog he had ever raised. In fact, it was better than the nose of any other dog in North Carolina, and possibly better than any other nose in the world.Ⓖ

★9 ERRORS★

Even when Martha's eyes were still closed, she recognized Julie's smell. At first, however, Martha wasn't wild about this smell. Whenever Julie's smell came near, it meant that Martha would be removed from the wonderful smells of Martha's mother, and the smells of her brothers and sisters. But after a while, Martha began to love Julie's smell. She learned that the smell meant warm milk, and soft petting, and a nice blanket to keep her warm.

Shortly after the puppies' eyes opened, Mr. Owl tested them to see which

Lesson 60   Textbook   231

STORY READING

EXERCISE 5   Decoding and comprehension

1. Everybody, turn to page 230 in your textbook. *Wait. Call on a student.* What's the error limit for this lesson? **9 errors.**

2. *Call on individual students to read. Present the tasks specified for each circled letter.*

Ⓐ What kind of dog is Martha's mother? *Idea:* A hunting dog.

● Why did Martha come close to being given away when she was still a tiny puppy? *Idea:* Because she was a runt.

● What is a runt? *Idea:* The smallest puppy in the litter.

● How many puppies were in the litter? **Twelve.**

● Where did the people who owned Martha live? **North Carolina.**

Ⓑ Are puppies born with their eyes open? **No.**

● How long does it take before they open their eyes? *Idea:* Two weeks.

Ⓒ When would Martha feel great joy? *Idea:* When she was close to her mother.

● When did she feel great despair? *Idea:* When another puppy pushed her away.

Ⓓ What does that mean: **He was reluctant to keep the runt?** *Idea:* He didn't want to raise Martha.

● Why was he reluctant? *Idea:* He didn't think the puppy was worth raising as a hunting dog.

Ⓔ What did Julie see in the puppy? *Idea:* Herself.

● Why? *Idea:* Both she and the dog were handicapped.

● What was wrong with the puppy? *Idea:* She was a runt.

● What was wrong with Julie? *Idea:* She was crippled.

Ⓕ Who named Martha? **Julie.**

● What were the names of the other dogs? *Ideas:* Boomer, Flash, Duke, Queenie, Prince, Princess, Dodger, Digger.

● How often did Julie have to feed Martha? *Idea:* Six times.

● What did Julie feed Martha? *Idea:* Milk.

● Where did Martha sleep? *Idea:* Next to Julie's bed.

Ⓖ What is surprising about little Martha? *Idea:* She has an incredible sense of smell.

● Does Julie's father know about Martha's nose? **No.** I wonder if he'll find out about it.

● Read the rest of the story to yourselves and be ready to answer some questions.

After all students have finished reading:

● Why did Martha learn to love Julie's smell? *Idea:* Because Julie's smell meant warm milk and warm blankets.

ones would be the best hunting dogs. The test was simple. He placed all the puppies in a shallow box. He put a screen over the top of the box, so that if a puppy tried to climb out of the box or jump out, the puppy would bang its head on the screen. Then he put the mother dog just outside the box and waited. The best puppies were the ones that would bang, and bang, and bang, until they had little raw spots on the top of their heads. Any puppy that would do that would not give up. That meant that the puppy would grow into a dog with great determination. It would hunt and hunt, no matter how rough the country was and no matter how tired it was.

Julie put Martha in the box with the other puppies. Some of the big puppies banged and banged against the screen. They whined and cried, but they kept banging against the screen. Martha whined and cried too, but she didn't jump up, not once. Julie knew that her father would think that Martha was no good, so she tried to coax Martha to jump. But still Martha sat there, without jumping, as the other puppies pushed her around. At last, Julie removed her from the box. She held Martha and said, "It's all right. You're still going to be the best dog in the world."

Martha was like all the other puppies. After the puppies learn to run and jump, they begin to play. Sometimes Martha's brothers and sisters would get too rough for her, but she still loved it. She was happy just to be with them, particularly when they were getting ready to play. One of them would usually start playing by grabbing another's droopy ear and taking a nip out of it. Then the tussling would begin. The two puppies would growl and tumble over each other. Soon the others would join in. When the wrestling became too rough, one of them would run from the group, waiting for the others to follow. Soon there would be more growling and tumbling and fun.

It seems the only experience that is more exciting to a young hound than playing is the scent of an animal like a rabbit or a deer. It's difficult to describe the feeling to a person because people don't have the sense of smell that dogs have. But when a hound catches the scent of another animal, it's something like the feeling you experience when you look at an incredible fireworks display at night. Just as you feel a sense of delight over the explosion of colors in the night sky, the hound feels an explosion of delight. At the same time that the experience is delightful, it is like a terrible hunger. The dog wants more, and more, and more. The dog wants to keep following that scent forever. For the hound dog, it's the greatest experience in the world.

Martha first discovered this marvelous experience when she was watching her brothers and sisters tussle in the meadow behind Julie's house. The puppies were now three months old. Martha had been wrestling with the others, but they were too rough for her. One of her brothers had knocked her down so hard that she had let out a yelp and lost all interest in playing. As she watched them tussling, she suddenly felt something that was more inter-

esting than anything else she had ever experienced. The wind carried it. She held her nose high in the air and tried to catch more of it. Then she let out a little howl and wanted to get closer to the smell. She left the others and put her nose near the ground. She began sniffing very fast. "Yes, yes," her nose told her. "Get closer. Follow it." She did. She was no bigger than a half-grown cat. Her ears were so long that when she tried to run with her nose to the ground, she kept stepping on her ears with her front paws.

Just as the smell was becoming so intense that Martha could hardly stand it, she caught another scent—Julie's. Julie picked her up and said, "You can't go hunting yet. You have to stay with the others." Martha cried and squirmed and tried to get away. But Julie held onto her and limped slowly back to the place where the other puppies were playing.

- Shortly after the puppies' eyes opened, Julie's father tested them to see which would be the best hunters. Describe the way he tested them. *Idea:* He put them in a box with a lid on it. He put their mother next to the box. He watched to see which ones didn't give up trying to get out of the box.
- What would you know about a puppy that would keep banging and banging against the screen? *Idea:* That puppy would hunt with great determination.
- How well did Martha do on this test? *Idea:* Poorly.
- What kind of games do puppies like to play? *Ideas:* Tumble; wrestle.
- Did Martha like those games? **Yes.**
- What's the only experience for a young hound that is more exciting than playing? *Idea:* The scent of an animal.
- Why don't people understand how a hound feels when it catches the scent of an animal? *Idea:* They don't have the sensitive nose that hounds have.
- The story told that the way the hound feels is something like you might feel if you see fireworks. The story also said that the feeling the dog has is like a great hunger. Why is it like a great hunger? *Idea:* The hound wants more and more of it.
- When Martha was three months old, she discovered the marvelous feeling of following the scent of an animal. Where was Martha at the time? *Idea:* In the meadow.
- What had she been doing? *Idea:* Playing with her brothers and sisters.
- What did she do when she caught the smell? *Idea:* Began to follow it.
- Why didn't she keep on following the scent? *Idea:* Julie picked her up.

Award 4 points or have the students reread to the error limit sign.

INDEPENDENT WORK

Do all the items in your skillbook and workbook for lesson 60.

ANSWER KEY FOR WORKBOOK

Review Items

1. Write **fact** or **fiction** for each item.
   a. Some dogs can travel one hundred miles in one day. _fact_
   b. Wolves howl, but do not bark. _fact_
   c. California has a long chain of mountains running through it. _fact_
   d. All dogs travel north when they run away. _fiction_
   e. Animals talk to their masters. _fiction_

Map Skills

2. Look at the map.

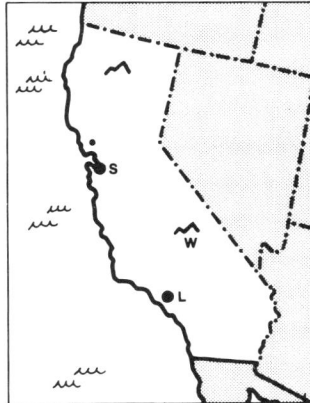

a. Which state does the map show? _California_
b. What's the name of city S? _San Francisco_
c. What's the name of city L? _Los Angeles_
d. What's the name of mountain W? _Mt. Whitney_

WORKCHECK AND AWARDING POINTS

1. *Read the questions and answers for the skillbook and workbook.*
2. *Award points for independent work as follows:*

   0 errors . . . . .6 points
   2 errors . . . . .4 points
   3, 4, or 5 errors . . . . .2 points
   5 or more errors . . . . .0 points

3. *Award bonus points as follows:*

   Correcting missed items or getting all items right . . . . .2 points
   Doing the writing assignment acceptably . . . . .2 points

ANSWER KEY FOR SKILLBOOK

PART B

1. *Idea:* Maria took a picture.
2. *Idea:* The dog buried a bone.
3. *Idea:* Tina sharpened a pencil.
4. *Idea:* Some tools are made of steel.
5. *Idea:* All birds have feathers.

PART C

6. a. *Idea:* Smaller
   b. *Idea:* Give her away
   c. runt
   d. *Idea:* biggest and strongest
   e. Julie
   f. Yes
7. a. In her bedroom
   b. *Idea:* A bottle
   c. 6 times a day
8. 2 weeks
9. a. *Idea:* Sense of smell
   b. No
10. The smells of the other dogs
11. a. box
    b. A screen
    c. Martha's mother
    d. *Ideas:* Banging their heads; keep on trying
    e. *Idea:* Whined but didn't jump
12. a. Three months old
    b. *Idea:* Playing
    c. *Idea:* Smelling an animal

PART D

13. a. soiled
    b. vivid
    c. clutched
    d. lunged
    e. scenery
    f. fell down
    g. shredded
    h. spring
    i. halt